FIRST DAY OF THE SOMME

FIRST DAY OF THE SOMME

ANDREW MACDONALD

HarperCollins*Publishers*

For my darling wife, Lara Schönberger

HarperCollins*Publishers*

First published in 2016
by HarperCollins*Publishers* (New Zealand) Limited
Unit D1, 63 Apollo Drive, Rosedale, Auckland 0632, New Zealand
harpercollins.co.nz

HarperCollins*Publishers*
Unit D1, 63 Apollo Drive, Rosedale, Auckland 0632, New Zealand
Level 13, 201 Elizabeth Street, Sydney NSW 2000
A 53, Sector 57, Noida, UP, India
1 London Bridge Street, London, SE1 9GF, United Kingdom
2 Bloor Street East, 20th floor, Toronto, Ontario M4W 1A8, Canada
195 Broadway, New York NY 10007, USA

National Library of New Zealand cataloguing-in-publication data:

Macdonald, Andrew, 1973-
First day of the Somme : the complete account of Britain's worst
-ever military disaster / Andrew Macdonald.
ISBN 978-1-77554-040-3 (print)
ISBN 978-1-77549-077-7 (online)
1. Somme, 1st Battle of the, France, 1916. 2. World War, 1914–1918
—Campaigns—France—Somme. 3. World War, 1914–1918—
Battlefields—France. I. Title.
940.4272—dc 23

Front cover image: A wounded British soldier with his German captor
(author's collection)
Back cover image: A high-explosive shell strikes a road near Miraumont,
June 1916 (author's collection)
Cover design by HarperCollins Design Studio
Typeset in Minion Pro by Kirby Jones
Printed and bound in Australia by Griffin Press
The papers used by HarperCollins in the manufacture of this book are
a natural, recyclable products made from wood grown in sustainable
plantation forests. The fibre source and manufacturing processes meet
recognised international environmental standards, and carry certification.

Contents

Preface

This book began on a paddock just outside Ovillers in northern France, one of the killing fields of the Battle of the Somme. On 1 July 1916, the first day of the battle, this was a place of death and destruction; nowadays it is once more a sleepy hamlet surrounded by peaceful farmland. In 2008, my wife and I were on the trail of her long-deceased great uncle, *Reservist* Friedrich Bauer, of Infantry Regiment 180, who survived the carnage of 1 July only to perish a few days later. He has no known grave. (In 1918, Friedrich's younger brother and brother-in-law-to-be also lost their lives on the Western Front, along with two of my own great-great-uncles in the New Zealand Division. Three of these four have known graves.)

As we wandered across the British and German battle lines of 1916, I mused on the immensity of the losses on that single day and its enduring significance in military history. Britain's official casualty roll for 1 July came in at 57,470. Of these, 19,240 were dead, a further 35,493 were wounded and 2737 others were recorded as either missing or prisoners of war. It was the British army's greatest one-day loss, so too for Newfoundland whose regiment of civilian soldiers was also destroyed amid the tornado of machine-gun and artillery fire. Casualties in the opposing *XIV Reserve Korps* were about 12,000 on 1 July, including roughly 3000 dead.

These appalling losses resulted from an Allied plan to end the stalemate that had endured since soon after the beginning of the war. The Allies on one side and the Germans on the other had dug a chain of increasingly heavily defended trench lines running from coastal Belgium south through northern France to Switzerland. Months of skirmishes and thrust and counterthrust had resulted in little movement of the lines and an increasingly troglodytic and brutalised existence for troops. Clearly, the eviction of the German army from occupied territories was going to require a major Allied offensive in 1916, attempts in 1914–15 having proved fruitless.

In collaboration with his French counterpart Joseph Joffre, British commander-in-chief General Sir Douglas Haig devised such an offensive in the Picardy department of northern France for mid-1916. Haig's plan was for Fourth Army, commanded by Lieutenant-General Sir Henry Rawlinson, to bust into the German lines astride the Roman road between Albert and Bapaume, with the yet-to-be formed Reserve Army, commanded by General Sir Hubert Gough, following on to restart mobile warfare and, hopefully, over time and with more resources, drive the German army out of France, then Belgium and ultimately back to its home-country borders. Further north, part of Lieutenant-General Sir Edmund Allenby's Third Army would undertake a small diversionary operation. To the south, coalition partner France would attack in co-operation, astride the slow-moving River Somme. In addition it was hoped the Somme offensive would relieve some of the pressure on the French forces at Verdun.

The first day of the offensive, launched at 7.30 a.m. on 1 July, proved disastrous for the British army, with many of its casualties occurring within the first hour and most by midday. Moreover, the minor gains in ground at the southern end of Haig's battlefield merely provided a jumping-off line for what became the four-and-a-half-month attritional slog that we now know as the Battle of the Somme. It would chew through hundreds of thousands of Allied and German soldiers before petering out in the November rain and the onset of the European winter. Campaigning on the Western Front resumed in 1917.

Villages, woods and other locations swamped by the 1916 fighting, many of them figuring in the disaster of 1 July, became equally well known in Britain, the Commonwealth and Germany. In the 1920s and 1930s these otherwise anonymous places were spoken of in hushed tones in veterans' homes and clubs, and at reunions. Nowadays many of them have returned to obscurity, overshadowed by legions of other foreign-sounding names from more recent conflicts. The Somme and its first day, though, linger 100 years later as international bywords for horror and degradation and ineptitude and death.

In military terms, however, the Somme was a key element in converting Haig's army of largely civilian soldiers into one of skilled professionals. The subsequent rise of the platoon as an essential tactical building block, the fine-tuning of command and control, and the use of technology and combined-arms operations, among many other elements, can all be traced back to the Somme, including its first day. Many of these lessons were on show at the successful Battle of Messines, on 7 June 1917, with its effective planning and preparation, closer co-operation between infantry, artillery, engineering and air assets, and use of massive underground mines. Yet, Third Ypres, in the latter half of 1917, showed there was still much to be learned and, in reality, it would be 1918 before Haig and his generals put together a war-winning formula that resulted in the Armistice on 11 November of that year.

Pondering all of this as I returned again and again to the battlefields, I began to consider the possibility of writing a new history of that calamitous first day of the Somme. There are plenty of books on the subject, ranging from the British two-volume official history *Military Operations, France and Belgium 1916*, soldier memoirs and various accumulations of eyewitness accounts, studies about specific battalions, coffee-table glossies, paperback self-guided tours, a few books touching on the German experience, and pocket-sized easy reads on war poets. I spied one yawning omission, however. Nobody, in recent times, it seemed, had attempted to write a meaningful both-sides-of-the-hill account of the first day of the Somme, nor indeed for any other battle of the First World War. In terms of the Somme, the only book that came close was Martin Middlebrook's soldier-centric *The First Day on the Somme*, which included a limited German element from the trenches. Written in 1971, it was already 20 years old when I read it at high school. History, it seemed, had almost entirely been written by the victor.

My objective, then, was to write a detailed and balanced Anglo-German history of the fighting on 1 July, focusing on the disaster that unfolded in the British sector of the battlefield, to identify what went so horribly wrong and occasionally right, as well as how and why. I desired to give voices to the participants of this industrial-scale tragedy, and, somewhat unusually, allow them direct comment as part of the analysis. Subject management alone meant that this was best achieved by examining the battle according to the geographic sectors allocated to each of the six British army corps involved. That in turn made it easier to marshal the experiences, opinions and decision-making of British and German commanders, along with those of the legion of men in their respective formations.

Since the arrival of Middlebrook's classic, relatively little dealing with the tragedy of 1 July has appeared in a single-volume format. Perhaps this was with good reason: the first day of the Somme was a massive engagement with lots of moving parts, more than a few shades of grey and, by now, plenty of 100-year-old conundrums that needed deciphering. Several people queried why I was bothering at all with my project, claiming the bones were well picked over. This proved incorrect. Time and again I had to resolve many questions that had not previously been addressed satisfactorily or even answered at all. Haig's whereabouts on 1 July and his interactions with Rawlinson that day were prominent among them. This was true also of the actions, reactions and rationales of various other Allied commanders, along with strategic and tactical thinking in the opposing armies. In short, while the pool of Somme literature appeared to be brimming to the point of overflow, it was neither complete nor exhaustive and specifically so in relation to the first day.

On several occasions during my research it became clear that I was reading official documents, diaries, memoirs and books that had seldom been viewed previously, if at all. This applied particularly to the journals of British and German senior commanders, on many occasions to those of private soldiers, and also to the myriad official documentation housed at various archives. As a result this book is populated with frequently unpublished British and German voices. All up close to 600 soldiers and officers are named or quoted, and almost one in four of these are German. (That ratio seems about right given the differing strengths of the opposing armies.) This rich collection of eyewitness accounts was not without method: I wanted to capture not only the soldiers' impressions of 1 July and the build-up to it, but also their sensory perceptions, their mood and spirit, and their thinking. Some soldiers wrote plenty and others not so much; together their words capture the essence of their ordeal.

A good deal of other fresh ground is broken, too, particularly when it comes to the collaborative decision-making by Haig and Rawlinson. Their performances are weighed — for the first time ever — against those of senior German commanders. *General-der-Infanterie* Erich von Falkenhayn, the German Chief of General Staff, along with subordinate *General-der-Infanterie* Fritz von Below and *Generalleutnant* Hermann von Stein, respectively the commanders of Second Army and XIV Reserve Corps, feature prominently. These commanders and their five principal divisional commanders played critical roles in the 1 July fighting that are frequently either marginalised or airbrushed more or less completely from British accounts. Fresh, unbiased research has allowed me to right that long-standing wrong.

I have opted to discuss the engagement along traditional lines. I begin by looking at background and agreed strategies for the offensive, cover the build-up in detail, on both sides, and then provide a sector-by-sector account of the day's events, again including perspectives from both sides. Detailed maps throughout will assist readers in following the flow of events. The conclusion examines all of this and critically evaluates senior British, German and French commanders at a strategic level, but also looks at the tactical implications of the day's outcome. Overall, my goal — one I hope I have achieved — was to compile the most complete and detailed picture of the first day of the Somme yet written.

Andrew Macdonald
April 2016

Author's Note

To fully appreciate the strategies and movements of the opposing forces along the Somme on 1 July 1916, it helps to understand the structure of and chains of command in the opposing armies.

Military formations at the Somme

British

Fourth Army was responsible for launching the lion's share of the first day of the Somme attack, with Third Army undertaking also only a small diversionary operation. Fourth Army was much larger than Third Army given the scope of its planned operations and the influx of manpower and resources.

On the morning of 1 July, Fourth Army had a total strength of 511,676 officers and men, mostly in infantry, artillery and cavalry units, as well as army and corps headquarters troops. There were, additionally, fewer than 8000 French and Indian personnel. Fourth Army had a total of six corps on its ration roll. One of these, II Corps, was in General Headquarters' reserve. The others — III, VIII, X, XIII and XV Corps — participated in the attack. Third Army's VII Corps was also engaged.

British army corps generally each had three divisions attached, but sometimes, as in the case of VIII Corps, that number could rise to four. The total strength of each division was an average of 21,600 of all ranks spread primarily across various infantry, artillery, engineer, pioneer, machine-gun, trench-mortar, medical and workshop units.

Each division comprised three infantry brigades, each of these with four battalions. There were four infantry companies to a battalion. The average attack strength of a battalion on 1 July was 761 soldiers of all ranks, which was below nominal strength after the deduction of non-fighting personnel and a percentage of fighting troops left out of battle.

Although every division had its own field artillery, these were, along with heavy artillery, controlled by corps headquarters. A number of Royal Flying Corps squadrons were included in the order of battle, with some attached to GHQ, as well as army and corps headquarters.

German

Second Army comprised XIV Reserve Corps and XVII Corps, the former engaged against the British Third and Fourth Armies on the first day of the Somme. In addition it had the three divisions of VI Reserve Corps in army reserve. Fourteenth Reserve Corps numbered about 95,000 soldiers of all ranks. It comprised six divisions, each with several permanent regiments of infantry and artillery organised within one or more brigades respectively.

Twenty-six Reserve and 2nd Guards Reserve Divisions consisted of four regiments each, whereas the 12th Infantry, 28th Reserve, 52nd Infantry and 10th Bavarian Infantry Divisions comprised three. The latter division was split up across XIV Reserve Corps' sector to be used in the front line or as reserves by other divisions. An infantry regiment usually numbered 2750–3000 officers and men and had at least one machine-gun company attached, if not two. Regiments usually comprised three battalions, sometimes four. Each battalion had four companies of about 250 soldiers of all ranks.

Divisions had their own field and heavy artillery, whether permanently on strength or attached for a period of time from either corps headquarters or divisions in reserve. Observation balloons were deployed by divisions, while three squadrons of aircraft were attached to corps headquarters. Miscellaneous divisional troops included construction, medical, trench-mortar, pioneer, engineer and communications units, among others.

German ranks

German ranks mentioned in this book are listed below, along with their British equivalents. Note, however, this is not an exhaustive list of German ranks and appointments for the First World War.

German rank	British equivalent
Military personnel	
Kanonier	Gunner
Fahrer	Driver
Infanterist, Landsturmann, Musketier, Reservist, Ersatz-Reservist, Schütze, Soldat, Grenadier	Private
Gefreiter	Lance-Corporal
Unteroffizier	Corporal
Vizefeldwebel	Staff-Sergeant
Feldwebel	Sergeant-Major
Offizierstellvertreter	Officer deputy (an appointment, not a rank)
Leutnant, Leutnant-der-Reserve, Leutnant-der-Landwehr	Second-Lieutenant
Oberleutnant, Oberleutnant-der-Reserve	Lieutenant
Hauptmann, Hauptmann-der-Reserve	Captain
Major	Major
Oberstleutnant	Lieutenant-Colonel
Oberst	Colonel
Generalmajor	Major-General
Generalleutnant	Lieutenant-General
General-der-Infanterie	General (of infantry)
Generalfeldmarschall	Field-Marshal
Medical personnel	
Oberstabsarzt	Major (or higher)
Stabsarzt	Captain
Other	
Fliegertruppoffizier	Flying troop officer

Casualty figures

Chapters 5–10 (pages 140–356) include footnotes detailing the formal names of battalions involved in the fighting. In each case the number of casualties suffered on 1 July is stated, along with the source document. Casualties for longer periods are given where more precise information is not available. The type of casualty is abbreviated as follows: d (for dead), which includes soldiers who were killed or died of wounds; w (wounded); m (missing in action); and p (prisoner of war). In some cases casualty figures for even a single battalion can vary between different sources, but only one has been cited. These figures should generally be regarded as preliminary estimates of casualties. For each of these battalions a separate and comparative figure for the number of fatalities on 1 July is quoted from Soldiers Died in the Great War (SDGW), published by His Majesty's Stationery Office in 1921. These SDGW data will help readers appreciate the fate of many of those soldiers who were initially reported to be missing, wounded or a prisoner of war on 1 July.

Maps

Throughout this book maps provide a useful reference point for following the course of battle on 1 July, and the units involved. The maps are based on those included in the British official history, *Military Operations, France and Belgium 1916*. Further detail has been sourced from a variety of other texts, among them the German volume *Somme-Nord, I Teil*. All maps include a distance gauge with imperial and metric conversions. Contour lines are shown with grey-scale gradients and the elevation above sea level is expressed in metres, as was the case with British maps in 1916.

Dramatis Personae

The following are the major characters in this book. They are arranged with the most senior commanders first, followed by subordinates in alphabetical order.

British Commanders

General Sir Douglas Haig: Commander of the British army on the Western Front. His Fourth and Third Armies were together responsible for launching the first day of the Somme attack on 1 July 1916.

Lieutenant-General Sir Henry Rawlinson: Commander of the Fourth Army, which undertook the main British attempt to break into and then through the German positions using its III, VIII, X, XV and XIII Corps between Serre and Montauban.

Lieutenant-General Sir Edmund Allenby: Commanded the Third Army, which played a small diversionary role at Gommecourt on 1 July, using its VII Corps to assist the northern flank of Fourth Army.

General Sir Hubert Gough: Was at the helm of the then yet-to-be-formed Reserve Army, which would come together on Fourth Army busting into the German lines. It was to subsequently be responsible for exploiting Fourth Army's gains and, it was hoped, bring a return to mobile warfare.

Lieutenant-General Sir Launcelot Kiggell: Haig's chief of staff.

Brigadier-General John Charteris: Haig's chief of intelligence.

Lieutenant-General Sir Walter Congreve, VC: Commander of XIII Corps and its successful attack either side of Montauban.

Lieutenant-General Sir Henry Horne: Led XV Corps' partially successful operations around Fricourt and Mametz.

Lieutenant-General Sir Aylmer Hunter-Weston: Commanded VIII Corps' bungled attacks between Serre, Beaumont Hamel and the River Ancre.

Lieutenant-General Sir Thomas Morland: In charge of X Corps' ultimately failed operations between the River Ancre, Schwaben Redoubt, Thiepval and Leipzig Redoubt.

Lieutenant-General Sir William Pulteney: Oversaw the failed attack of III Corps between Leipzig Redoubt, Ovillers and La Boisselle.

Lieutenant-General Sir Thomas Snow: Led VII Corps' fruitless diversionary operation at Gommecourt, which was intended to draw German attention away from nearby VIII Corps at the northern end of Fourth Army's battle sector.

German Commanders

General-der-Infanterie **Erich von Falkenhayn:** Chief of General Staff, Supreme Army Command. Falkenhayn was de facto supreme commander of the German army.

General-der-Infanterie **Fritz von Below:** Commander of the Second Army, whose XIV Reserve and XVII Corps, respectively north and south of the River Somme, opposed the Anglo-French operation on 1 July with varying degrees of success and failure.

Generalleutnant **Hermann von Stein:** Headed XIV Reserve Corps and was responsible for defending Second Army's positions north of the River Somme, against the British Third and Fourth Armies and the French XX Corps.

Oberst **Fritz von Lossberg:** A defensive expert brought in as Second Army's replacement chief of staff following the outcome of 1 July (his predecessor having been sacked). He would influence future German defensive practices on the Somme.

Generalleutnant **Karl von Borries:** In charge of 52nd Infantry Division between Gommecourt salient and Serre, portions of whose line were attacked unsuccessfully by elements of VII and VIII Corps.

Generalleutnant **Martin Châles de Beaulieu:** Oversaw 12th Infantry Division between Montauban and the River Somme, this ground almost entirely overrun by XIII Corps and the French XX Corps on 1 July.

Generalleutnant **Ferdinand von Hahn:** Led 28th Reserve Division between La Boisselle, Fricourt and Mametz. It faced about half of III Corps, which it defeated, but was itself largely overwhelmed by XV Corps around Fricourt and Mametz.

Generalleutnant **Franz *Freiherr* von Soden:** Commanded 26th Reserve Division between Serre, Beaumont Hamel, the River Ancre, Thiepval, Leipzig Redoubt and Ovillers. His division defended its line against most of VIII Corps, all of X Corps and the remainder of III Corps, and successfully blocked Fourth Army's planned main axis of advance.

Generalleutnant **Richard *Freiherr* von Süsskind-Schwendi:** Oversaw 2nd Guards Reserve Division, which successfully defended Gommecourt salient opposite VII Corps.

Generalmajor **Hermann *Ritter* von Burkhardt:** In command of 10th Bavarian Division, which was split up across XIV Reserve Corps' sector.

French Commanders

General Joseph Joffre: Commander-in-Chief of the French Army. His Sixth Army would attack on 1 July as part of the British-French offensive with, at least in part, a view to reducing the pressure on the French Second Army at Verdun.

General Marie-Emile Fayolle: At the helm of the French Sixth Army, which attacked either side of the River Somme on 1 July in co-operation with Rawlinson's Fourth Army. In contrast to the British force, Fayolle's army turned in a very successful performance.

General Ferdinand Foch: Commanded the French *Groupe des Armées du Nord*, comprising the French Sixth and Tenth Armies, which were respectively astride the River Somme and further north near Arras.

General Philippe Pétain: Led the French Second Army at the Battle of Verdun.

CHAPTER 1

A Mother Named 'Attrition'

General Sir Douglas Haig's grand plan for 1 July 1916

'As the day of battle approaches so is one worried by alterations and modifications.'[1]

— General Sir Henry Rawlinson, commander of Fourth Army

NOBODY KNOWS EXACTLY what General Sir Douglas Haig thought as he stood before Napoleon Bonaparte I's tomb in Paris. Outside it was a silver-skied March 1916 afternoon, but Haig, the Commander-in-Chief (C-in-C) of the British army and one of the architects of the soon-to-be-launched Somme offensive, was indoors treading the magnificent halls of Les Invalides with his chief of intelligence, Brigadier-General John Charteris. Haig was taciturn, and his thoughts probably harked back to his time at Staff College, Camberley, when he had studied the long-dead French general. Perhaps Haig was paying homage to Napoleon; perhaps he was seeking inspiration for his own operational planning ahead of the Somme. Charteris, for his part, pondered how the bold Frenchman might have tackled the first day of the Somme: 'If Napoleon's spirit was near his tomb, did he wish to pull D.H.'s ear and wish him luck, and tell him the secret of victory? Would he have had any magic of strategy in these days of trenched positions, without any flank, and guns that range 10 miles?'[2]

The Somme was almost certainly on Haig's mind as he surveyed the stone paean to the Corsican's victories, such as that at Jena-Auerstedt in 1806, when his infantry broke through a Prussian defensive line and cavalry routed the disarrayed enemy. The broad themes of this Napoleonic victory would become central to Haig's Somme thinking.

Biographers have penned Haig as a dour, asthmatic, career-focused, lowland Scot rich in ambiguities. A committed Presbyterian, he was said to possess Spartan self-discipline and self-sacrifice in pursuit of military efficiency.[3] Such dedication led to pillories that Haig was ambitious, self-absorbed, aloof, socially awkward, cold, formal and intense. The epithets continued: unpopular, abrupt, abrasive, dim-witted, limited to military literature, inarticulacy, without close friends and indifferent to women. Yet these criticisms go more to his uncompromising work ethic than the man. The anecdote-driven lens also reveals a more likeable side to Haig: loyal, educated and intelligent, organised, determined, reticent, a married family man and well-read. All had a basis in reality: Haig was a complex, driven professional, whose reserved character was laced with situational contradictions.

War correspondent Philip Gibbs went with opinion when he described Haig as a good-looking chap who lacked a 'magic touch' with people:[4] 'He was constitutionally unable to make a dramatic gesture before a multitude, or to say easy, stirring things to officers and men whom he reviewed. His shyness and reserve prevented him also from knowing as much as he ought to have known about the opinions of officers and men.'[5]

Paring Haig's character back to its essence remains akin to grasping at shadows. Just one expert psychological assessment of the man exists, albeit long due an overhaul. 'The evidence suggests that Haig's burning ambition to succeed overlay a pronounced fear of failure, itself a product of childhood.'[6] More specifically, this stemmed from a deep-rooted desire to prove his worth and ability to his mother, which dated back to childhood and unfavourable comparison with his siblings.[7] The product in adulthood was an authoritarian character full of controlled aggression and tendencies towards obsessive, orderly, obstinate behaviour, along with a penchant for detail and fastidious appearance.[8] His psychological makeup was unemotional, lacking in compassion, heavily critical of others and demanding of absolute loyalty.[9] Haig was also overly sensitive to criticisms and questions, and generally mistrustful of others.[10] All of this was set against the austere Victorian tenets of 'heroic masculinity,' namely physical health, self-restraint and devotion to duty,[11] whether military or religious. Haig's authoritarianism had as much to do with his feelings of inadequacy as his habitual optimism and determination to do ever better, which were linked to his achievement-driven character.

These traits were apparent as Haig built his military career over the three decades leading to 1914. Born in Edinburgh on 19 June 1861 to a middle-class family, Haig was educated at Clifton College and then Brasenose College, Oxford (1880–3). He left university without a degree to enter the Royal Military Academy, Sandhurst, in 1884. The colour-blind cadet was commissioned into the 7th (Queen's Own) Hussars as a lieutenant in 1885, thereafter serving in India (1886–92), then attending Staff College, Camberley (1896–7). Service and limited action with then Major-General Sir Horatio Kitchener's staff in the Sudan followed (1898). Afterwards Haig was brigade-major to 1st Cavalry Brigade at Aldershot. During the South African or Second Boer War (1899–1902) he served first as then General Sir John French's chief of staff and next at the helm of a column chasing various Boer guerilla leaders and enforcing a scorched-earth policy. Haig finished that war as lieutenant-colonel commanding 17th Lancers, an appointment he held until 1903. Back in England, he served as aide-de-camp to King Edward VII (1902–3), then, becoming the youngest major-general in the British army, as Inspector-General of Cavalry, India (1903–6). In 1905 he became engaged to one of Queen Alexandra's maids of honour, the Honourable Dorothy Maud Vivian. The couple, who married in the private chapel of Buckingham Palace, had produced four children by 1919.

Subsequent military posts for Haig included several at the War Office, London (1906–9), which showed that he was seen as a trusted pair of hands. First he was Director of Military Training and then Director of Staff Duties. In these roles, Haig — perceived as a forward-thinking and professionally minded general by the then Secretary of State for War, Richard Haldane — ushered in a series of essential but not always welcome reforms that pulled Militia, Yeomanry and Volunteers into a single Territorial Force. At this time Haig also oversaw the writing of *Field Service Regulations*, 1909, which became the core doctrine for 'the training for war, and the organisation in war, of the whole British Army.'[12]

This work, which provided the framework for deploying the British Expeditionary Force (BEF) in 1914, revealed Haig possessed a 'cool head and proved that his reputation as a shrewd practical soldier in peace held good in war. On the veldt, in India or at home he mastered problems consistently. ... Douglas Haig earned not only the praise of Edward VII and his heir [George V] but the esteem of a wide circle amongst the officer corps. Talented, self-effacing, handsome, orthodox, he was the very model of a British Major General.'[13]

Knighthood and promotion to Chief of Staff, India (1909–12), followed. Then, following his return to England, came advancement to the post of General Officer Commanding Aldershot Command (1912–14). Haig, by now a lieutenant-general, was still in this job when pan-European war broke out.

The First World War's origins date from the 19th century, when Prussia shifted the balance of European power with its battlefield defeats of Austria in 1866 and France in 1870–1. 'Iron Chancellor' Otto von Bismarck then united the various German states into a Prussian-led German empire. It was the most powerful state in Europe and an ally of Austria-Hungary, as per their treaty of 1879. By mid-1888, the German throne belonged to Kaiser Wilhelm II, a grandson of Queen Victoria and cousin to both King George V and Russia's tsar, Nicholas II. He was an aggressive, vain man with expansionist political policies and an unwelcome programme of naval re-armament. He desired a *Mitteleuropa*, German-speak for a Berlin-dominated economic zone in the centre of Europe. Kaiser Wilhelm II's 'bellicose and clumsy' overtures along these lines saw France and Russia form an uneasy alliance in 1894 founded on shared strategic worries about Kaiser Wilhelm II's ambitions.[14] Britain was concerned by the threat Germany posed to the *status quo* of power in Europe and the security of its home islands.[15] It placed store in the Treaty of London (1839), which guaranteed Belgium's neutrality and had been signed by Britain, Austria-Hungary, France, Prussia, Russia, the Netherlands and Belgium. Britain had reached a point of diplomatic accommodation with France and Russia, reaching agreements with these nations in 1904 and 1907 respectively, but was not part of the alliance agreed between those two countries. In early 1914, pan-European politics was charged with tension. Britain, France and Russia were suspicious of a Germany that had cast itself into a diplomatic corner; all the situation lacked was a tinderbox to set the continent ablaze.

Two shots rang out in central Sarajevo, capital of the Austro-Hungarian province of Bosnia and Herzegovina. It was 28 June 1914 and Archduke Franz Ferdinand of Austria and his wife Sophie, Duchess of Hohenberg, were dead. Nineteen-year-old Serbian insurgent Gavrilo Princip was triggerman, protesting against Bosnia's inclusion in the Austro-Hungarian Empire. A month of increasingly aggressive diplomatic posturing and unrealistic demands now known as the July Crisis followed. Kaiser Wilhelm II played the faux aggrieved innocent when he said 'there can no longer be any doubts, England, France and Russia have conspired themselves together to fight an annihilation war against us.'[16] He then ranted about his cousins: 'To think that George [V] and Nicky [II] should have played me false! If my grandmother [Queen Victoria] had been alive, she would never have allowed it.'[17] This was akin to schoolyard whingeing, except that European stability was at stake. With an air of grim inevitability, Austria-Hungary declared war on Serbia on 28 July, with Germany following suit against Russia (1 August), France (3 August) and Belgium (4 August).

Britain had long realised that a successful German conquest of Western Europe — specifically the coastal strips of Belgium and France — would undermine its strategic and economic position, and demanded Belgium's neutrality as per the Treaty of London. Britain had fought for centuries to keep these two territories out of hostile hands, and nothing had changed by 1914. Germany's response was unsatisfactory, and Britain declared war at 11 p.m. on 4 August. German Chancellor Theobald von Bethmann-Hollweg claimed it was unbelievable that war had been declared over a 'mere scrap of paper,' meaning the Treaty of London, but everything else suggested he and Kaiser Wilhelm II knew full well what the German Empire's brinkmanship would bring.[18]

As one historian has written, 'Seeking to break out of self-created diplomatic encirclement, and achieve hegemony in Europe, the German leadership risked war in 1914 and embraced it when it occurred. In doing so, Germany took Europe on the first step towards the Somme.'[19]

German military commanders had foreseen the dangers of fighting a two-front war of attrition against the French in the west and Russians in the east, and set down the means to avoid this in their so-called Schlieffen Plan. The strategy adopted — there were actually several to choose from within the overall plan — was to push several German armies through northern Belgium and into France, forcing a quick surrender. With the west shored up, the German army would then turn its might against Russia.

The fighting began when the Kaiser's troops swept into Luxembourg, France and Belgium in August 1914 on what would become the Western Front, while two Russian armies attacked Germany on the future Eastern Front. In early August the first 100,000 men of the BEF landed in France and began fighting alongside the 62-division French army to stem the German juggernaut. What followed were the 1914 battles of Mons, Le Cateau, the Marne and the Aisne: in sum, a retreat to the outskirts of Paris followed by an Anglo-French fightback that retook some of the lost ground. A so-called 'race' to the North Sea ensued as each side tried to out-manoeuvre the other, but this faded into a stalemate. All that remained of the war in the west that was supposed to have been over by Christmas was hundreds of miles of opposing trenches and no end in sight. The parallel trenches ran across the continent from the North Sea to Switzerland. One side was occupied by Germany and the other by Britain, France and Belgium. Germany's Schlieffen Plan had failed to produce a six-week victory over France, and the fighting on the Eastern Front demanded ever more men and materiel. Within months any hopes of a short conflict were dead, succeeded by increasingly industrialised killing and economic mobilisation, whose reign of horror would last until late 1918.

Fighting in Western Europe in 1915 altered neither diplomatic nor tactical impasses. Casualties were heavy and the German army remained ensconced in Belgium and France. Britain remained the junior Allied partner, and France wanted it to make a greater contribution of manpower, take over more of the line to free up French troops for use elsewhere, and launch attacks in its own right. On the Italian Front, which along with France and Belgium comprised the Western European operational theatre, the fighting between the Austro-Hungarian and Italian armies had devolved into a stalemate in 1915. On the Eastern Front, Russia, which was also an operational theatre, had ceded more ground to the German army and wanted some of the pressure it faced relieved by an offensive in the west. Operations in the Balkans, Egypt, Africa, Asia and Australasia were never going to alter the fact that Western Europe was the main theatre of war. British attacks at Neuve Chapelle (10–13 March), Aubers (9 May), Festubert (15–25 May), Givenchy (15–16 June) and Loos (25 September–14 October) produced negligible results and lengthy casualty lists. French army attacks in 1915 were similarly non-productive. If the German army enjoyed a qualitative advantage in the east, the same was not true in the west, where the opposing armies were broadly matched in terms of firepower and technology, even if the well-dug-in defender enjoyed a tactical advantage over its attackers, who had to advance exposed across no-man's-land to reach the enemy's front line. Germany had no plans to quit France, Belgium or Russia, which, along with Britain, still wanted the enemy out. The absence of a negotiated peace or battlefield resolution on the Western Front in 1915 guaranteed the Allied armies would have to find a military solution to the deadlock in 1916.

The Battle of Loos in September–October 1915 was among the earliest on the Western Front to feature divisions of Britain's so-called New Army of civilian volunteers. The creation of the New Army was driven by the Secretary of State for War, Field Marshal Lord Kitchener, who rightly believed the First World War would be a lengthy conflict, requiring a field army comprising millions of men. He resolved not to enlarge the Territorial Force, which was itself rapidly expanding following the outbreak of war, but to recruit from the civilian population of military-aged males. His New Army, also known as Kitchener's Army, would be based on and administered by the existing regimental system. Printing presses churned out thousands upon thousands of recruiting posters featuring slogans such as 'Your King and Country Need You'. The rallying call from the hero of the Sudan appealed to the masses. It played to communities' patriotism and willingness to fight the enemy for King and Country, but also promised an escape from the mundane, a chance of adventure, of work and all the other myriad attractions the army held for young men of that time. Volunteers flooded in; the existing regimental structures could not cope. Civilian committees were set up to promote and manage the manpower drive. So were created the Service or Pals battalions, the latter referring to those raised from a single locality,

The War in Europe, 1916

NORWAY

SWEDEN

North Sea

DENMARK

Balt

UNITED KINGDOM

○ Hamburg

Berlin ○

GERMAN EMPIRE

Liverpool ○
Birmingham ○
○ London
Bristol ○

NETHERLANDS

BELGIUM
○ Brussels
LX.

○ Frankfurt

Calais ○

○ Paris

Rhine

Vie

Bud

English Channel

Atlantic Ocean

Bern ○
SWITZERLAND

○

FRANCE

Bay of Biscay

○ Bordeaux

Marseille ○

ITALY

Adriatic

CORSICA

○ Rome

Madrid ○

SARDINIA

PORTUGAL SPAIN

SICILY

Lisbon ○

Tangier ○ ○ Gibraltar

Algiers ○

Tunis ○

Mediterr

MOROCCO

ALGERIA

TUNISIA

Tripoli ○

LIBYA

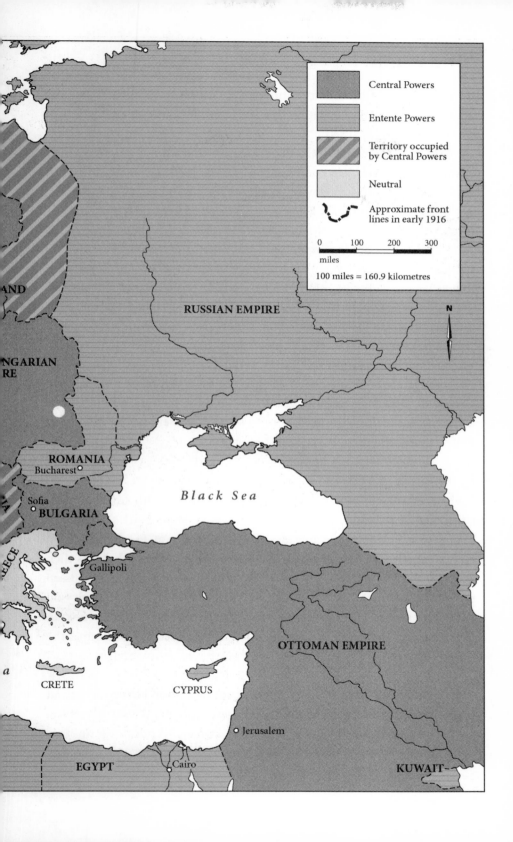

		Central Powers
		Entente Powers
		Territory occupied by Central Powers
		Neutral
		Approximate front lines in early 1916

0   100   200   300

miles

100 miles = 160.9 kilometres

N

RUSSIAN EMPIRE

AND

NGARIAN
RE

ROMANIA
Bucharest

Sofia
BULGARIA

Black Sea

ECE

Gallipoli

a

CRETE   CYPRUS

OTTOMAN EMPIRE

Jerusalem

EGYPT   Cairo   KUWAIT-

community or stratum of society. These Pals battalions of the New Army were the pride of their communities; the dangers of concentrating any community's best and brightest in a single military unit during a time of war had yet to be realised.

Against this backcloth of escalation towards total war, Haig advanced his career. He commanded I Corps throughout the battles of 1914. Promotion to full general came on 20 November 1914, at the end of the First Battle of Ypres. On Christmas Day he became commander of First Army during the reorganisation of the BEF by its then commander, Field Marshal French. What followed was command through the abortive battles of 1915, from which Haig managed to emerge with his reputation intact; he was subsequently feted by a string of politicians.[20] Haig had a long-standing personal affinity for French, who had served with distinction in the Second Boer War but retained a difficult relationship with Kitchener. Haig's affinity for French proved to be no barrier to his placing increasingly less store in the C-in-C's professional ability. So began a cautious campaign of intrigue by envelope and whisper to George V, Kitchener and others. It was founded on Haig's professional concerns, his ambition and, of course, his ever-present underlying belief that he could and indeed would do better.

Haig probably knew he was French's most likely successor as C-in-C by the spring of 1915, and his subsequent criticism of French to several key powerbrokers back in London strongly suggests he aimed to take advantage of the situation. The poor results of 1915's battles, the heavy casualties and finally the fine detail of the failure at Loos crystallised Haig's belief that French had no handle on the nature of what was then modern warfare and that he had to go. French — realising he had been politically out-manoeuvred by his underling and that he had run dry on Whitehall favour — resigned as C-in-C. Fifty-five-year-old Haig took up the reins as commander of the BEF on 19 December 1915, writing at the time: 'I had only one idea, namely to do my utmost to win the war.'[21]

THE ALLIED STRATEGY for 1916 was hammered out during the second Inter-Allied Conference, held at Chantilly, France, on 6–8 December 1915. General Joseph Joffre, C-in-C of the French armies, presided over military representatives from Britain (Field Marshal French, who was just about to be supplanted by Haig), France (Major-General Maurice Pellé, Joffre's chief of staff), Russia, Italy and Serbia. Joffre set the agenda and on the third day a string of prosaically worded resolutions were signed off. It was agreed that a decisive outcome to the war could only be achieved in its principal theatres, namely the Anglo-French, Russian and Italian fronts.[22] This was to be achieved by powerful, co-ordinated offensives on each, launched simultaneously or in quick succession. The resolutions continued:

> The general action should be launched as soon as possible.
> The Allied Armies will therefore endeavour to hasten the
> augmentation of their resources in men and material [sic] so that
> they can make their maximum effort as soon as possible. It is very
> desirable that their maximum effort should materialise at a date as
> soon as possible after the end of March.[23]

The offensive could take place before the end of March if circumstances warranted it. Moreover, each of the separate powers should be prepared to stop a German offensive on their respective fronts, and assist the others in this situation to 'the fullest possible extent.'[24] The wearing down of the enemy by means of local and partial offensives would begin immediately. It was on these resolutions that the Anglo-French armies began lumbering towards a mid-1916 offensive in Picardy, northern France.

Britain's Cabinet sanctioned these Chantilly resolutions following recommendations by its War Committee, which met in London on 23 and 28 December. Memos supporting the conference's outcome were lodged by the British army's Chief of Imperial General Staff, General Sir Archibald Murray, and then General Sir William Robertson, who replaced Murray from 23 December. The War Committee agreed on 28 December that France and Flanders would remain the main theatre of war, with resources being concentrated there rather than at other theatres. Every effort would be made to carry out offensive operations on the Western Front in the spring, in close co-operation with Britiain's Allies and in the greatest possible strength.[25] The actual plan of attack for spring, as recommended by Murray, would be 'left to the commanders in the field.'[26]

That job fell to Haig. Kitchener told Haig, in a job-description letter dated 28 December, that defeat of the enemy on the Western Front by combined and co-operating Allied armies was his primary objective. Haig's command was essentially an independent one, Kitchener stated, meaning that Haig was not subordinate to 64-year-old 'Papa' Joffre.[27] 'I pointed out,' wrote Haig of a conversation with another French general about the Allied offensive, 'that I am not under General Joffre's orders, but that would make no difference, as my intention was to do my utmost to carry out General Joffre's wishes on strategical [sic] matters, as if they were orders.'[28] It was very much a case of all care and no responsibility.

As it turned out, the War Committee would wrangle over the Chantilly resolutions for another three months. Convened on 13 January, two weeks after the initial meetings, it added a crucial caveat to its December decision, stating 'it must not be assumed that such offensive operations are finally decided on.'[29] Haig's mandate to begin preparing for an attack was thus heavily qualified. The principal dissenters — First Lord of the Admiralty Arthur Balfour and Minister of Munitions David Lloyd George — were opposed to a premature Western Front offensive, launched before sufficient men and materiel had been accumulated. It was not so much a question of whether, but of when. Delaying beyond spring seemed sensible.[30] Come March–April, the committee's concerns had shifted to French and Russian strategy for 1916, and what operations the latter might have in the pipeline that Britain was not immediately aware of. Lloyd George was concerned that the Allies were in danger of backsliding towards a repeat of the abortive battles of 1915, and the massive pressure on the French army at Verdun lingered in the background. The committee, along with Kitchener and Robertson, remained in favour of a concerted and considered Allied offensive. Kitchener was adamant that beginning the offensive in spring would give it sufficient time to be carried through to fulfilment,[31] and that Haig would not be drawn into a purely British operation.[32] The committee concluded the only effective way to support Russia's fragile position was to launch a large Anglo-French offensive, and that satisfying Haig's demand for weapons was a priority. Finally, on 7 April, the committee issued a firm statement in favour of a spring offensive and told Haig he now had 'the authority for which he asks.'[33]

Sharp-minded and grand-bellied Joffre knew in late-December 1915 that Haig had Cabinet's mandate for a major collaborative operation. He wrote to French-speaking Haig on 30 December, the pair having met twice in the preceding week, and set out his New Year's shopping list. Joffre had already told his 64-year-old subordinate General Ferdinand Foch — the live-wire commander of Groupe des Armées du Nord, comprising the French Sixth and Tenth Armies — to examine the possibilities for a 'powerful offensive' south of the River Somme. This would be conducted among a palette of other attacks at various points along the French-held portions of the Western Front, some to be part of the general offensive agreed at Chantilly and others to 'hold the enemy in uncertainty.'[34] Stout, gentle Joffre, the son of a cooper, continued:

> The French offensive would be greatly aided by a simultaneous offensive of the British forces between the [River] Somme and Arras. Besides the interest which this last area presents on account of its close proximity to that where the effort of the French Armies will be made, I think that it will be a considerable advantage to attack the enemy on a front where for long months the reciprocal activity of the troops opposed to each other has been less than elsewhere.[35]

Three weeks later, before Haig had replied, Joffre was rapping at the door of his headquarters in St Omer with a new line of action, apparently at the behest of a French government concerned about the rising number of casualties. Before the main Allied attack on the Somme, Joffre now wanted a pair of April–May preliminaries to wear out the German army and exhaust enemy reserves. He wanted Haig to sanction a British attack north of the Somme on about 20 April and on a frontage of at least 20,000 yards (11.4 miles). Joffre, writing to Haig on 23 January, saw such attacks as critical to the French cause, and said they should comprise 15– 18 British divisions and be followed by another operation elsewhere. Haig favoured a combined operation but was opposed to Joffre's proposals, which would exhaust the British army, run up casualties and ultimately be regarded as failures because they failed to produce decisive results.

Haig and Joffre squared these differences at a mid-February conference. 'I am glad to say,' crowed Haig in a letter to George V, 'that on both points [the second being for the British army to take over the French Tenth Army's front near Arras, as raised by Joffre in December 1915] they gave way and agreed to my arguments.'[36] Joffre quit his plans for April–May preliminary enterprises and Haig agreed that an Anglo-French offensive should be carried on astride the Somme on or about 1 July, preceded a few weeks earlier by a partial attack at the La Bassée–Ypres area of southern Belgium. Haig also agreed that if a German offensive was launched in Russia then the Anglo-French attack would begin as soon as possible. So it was that the origins of the first day of the Somme were seeded amid the tangle of Anglo-French relations with the bald strategy of attrition.

There was, as one historian has written, a trinity of military perspectives to attrition:

> For the allies, strategic attrition meant overstretching and
> grinding down Germany's powers of resistance to such a point that
> she would break; operational attrition meant using up the army's
> manpower reserves to break the Western Front stalemate, restore
> mobile warfare and force the German army back to the Rhine;
> and tactical attrition meant killing Germans on the Somme, with
> inevitable loss to the attackers at the same time.[37]

These were the Anglo-French views of attrition, but the German high command had no intention of being forced back to its home-country borders. It was already planning to open the Battle of Verdun on the banks of the River Meuse, about 150 miles east of Paris.

Even by the morally bankrupt standards of trench fighting on the Western Front, Verdun marked the start of an altogether more horrifying style of machine-age warfare. *General-der-Infanterie* Erich von Falkenhayn, the German Chief of General Staff, Supreme Army Command, planned the offensive to run up French casualties and force a compromised peace.[38] It began on 21 February 1916 when 1220 German artillery guns belched a dawn-till-dusk tempest of steel over the French positions, raging destruction and death and flinging men and debris about. Then German infantry went in. So the formula was repeated for three days. On 25 February, Fort Douamont, one of several key elements of the French defences, fell. French reserves were thrown into battle and gradually stabilised the tottering line. The fighting spluttered along in fits and starts of shellfire that pulverised villages, churned their ruins into the clay and left a sea of overlapping craters that reeked of stagnant water and death. The onslaught continued until 18 December, claiming more than 330,000 German casualties and 377,000 French.[39] This was industrialised warfare on a scale far beyond that seen in 1915; but, as always, whichever army and nation endured the longest, had the greater resources and suffered the least casualties would win the grotesque attritional contest. The strategy was not lost on Allied leaders who resolved to answer Falkenhayn's tough question at Verdun with a Somme rejoinder; the two offensives were umbilically linked spectres born of a mother named 'Attrition.'

Haig's interest in a Belgium offensive lingered, even as the Somme moved centre stage and the vicious Verdun fighting rumbled along. He had, as early as 14 January — the day after the War Committee imposed its caveat — told General Sir Herbert Plumer, commander of Second Army, to consider schemes in Belgium against the Messines–Wytschaete ridge, Lille and the forest of Houthulst.[40] Three months later, having just received the War Committee's go-ahead, Haig told Plumer to begin preparations for the capture of the ridge, using 20 large mines rammed with explosives to obliterate German defences.[41] The successful Battle of Messines eventually took place in mid-1917 as a precursor to the Third Ypres offensive. Meantime, at the end of May, Haig told Plumer to accelerate his preparations, as the northern offensive might be launched ahead of the Somme, and by 5 June he was considering switching the main British effort to Plumer's sector if Fourth Army met stubborn resistance.[42] At General Headquarters (GHQ) in St Omer, Haig's staff were also exploring the possibility of a semi-amphibious attack along the French coast from Nieuport towards Ostende, but this did not eventuate. Throughout early 1916 Haig saw an offensive in southern Belgium as either an alternative or a complement to the Somme, and only put these plans on hold once the fighting in Picardy had begun to put a squeeze on all available resources.[43]

GENERAL SIR HENRY Rawlinson's rise to the command of Fourth Army followed a career of service in India, Burma, Sudan and South Africa. He was born in London in 1864 to a well-off family. His father was a well-connected British East India Company army officer, politician and keen scholar of all things Mesopotamian. Rawlinson was educated at Eton, and graduated from the Royal Military Academy, Sandhurst, aged 19 in 1884 as an infantry lieutenant. Service in King's Royal Rifle Corps and Coldstream Guards followed, as did stints in India as Lieutenant-General Sir Frederick (later Lord and Field Marshal) Roberts' aide-de-camp (1884–6), and in Burma (1886–7). The tall, lanky Rawlinson campaigned against the Dervishes of Sudan as part of Kitchener's staff in the dusty advance on Omdurman (1898), and commanded a field column with distinction in South Africa (1899–1902). Back in England, he became commandant of the Staff College (1903–6). Promotions followed, first to brigadier-general commanding 2nd Infantry Brigade at Aldershot (1907–9), and then Major-General commanding 3rd Division on Salisbury Plain (1910). Shortly after war broke out in 1914, 'Rawly' took command of 4th Division in France. Then followed command of IV Corps (1914–15) as lieutenant-general, and of Fourth Army from January 1916. Rawlinson was always regarded as a 'star man' within the officer corps and his rise to the helm of Fourth Army was linked to the breadth of his service, the patronage of Roberts and Kitchener,[44] and the necessary wartime expansion of the British army.

Rawlinson was a complex character. Casual acquaintances found him a cheery, affable soul with a good sense of humour. This was army cinematographer Lieutenant Geoffrey Malins' experience: 'While waiting [to film], the General came over to me and began chatting about my work.'[45] Lieutenant-General Sir Alexander Godley, a pallbearer at Rawlinson's 1925 funeral, wrote in his 1939 autobiography that the balding army commander was ambitious, clever and charming.[46] War correspondent Philip Gibbs thought the general 'genial' with a 'roguish eye,' and said he possessed 'initiative and courage of decision and a quick intelligence.'[47] But he suspected there was more to the moustachioed 'Cad' — as Rawlinson was sometimes known — than his avuncular veneer implied:

> Before the battles of the Somme I had a talk with him among his
> maps, and found that I had been to many places in his line which
> he did not seem to know. He could not find them very quickly
> on his large-sized maps, or pretended not to, though I concluded

that this was 'camouflage,' in case I might tell 'old Fritz' that such places existed.[48]

Others were mistrustful. Charteris thought Rawlinson professionally capable, but suspected him of wanting to supplant Haig.[49] The C-in-C described him as an intelligent and experienced commander but believed him to be fundamentally insincere.[50] Major-General Francis Davies, whom Rawlinson had attempted to scapegoat for his own piecemeal use of reserves at Neuve Chapelle, was altogether more damning. An embittered Davies said he and his staff had lost confidence in Rawlinson because they believed that if his 'personal interests required it, he [Rawlinson] would throw over his subordinate Commanders and that he would not hold to any [verbal] order which he had given.'[51] Rawlinson was likeable when it suited, evasive when convenient and a ruthless, devious careerist who had no qualms when it came to advancing his own interests at the expense of others.[52]

None of this stopped Haig from placing Rawlinson at the helm of Fourth Army in early 1916. Both had studied military history, possessed enquiring minds and had collaborated together as army and subordinate corps commander throughout 1915, as well as earlier in their careers. Haig saw Rawlinson as the best man to command Fourth Army:[53] he was an experienced campaigner with proven staff skills and, particularly after Haig saved him from being sent home following the Davies incident, appeared to be compliant and controllable. It was at Haig's behest that Rawlinson began planning Fourth Army's attack on the Somme.

Rawlinson had long seen artillery as central to securing battlefield victory for his infantry. This was the case ahead of Neuve Chapelle, for instance, when Rawlinson wrote: 'An undertaking such as that which is under consideration depends for its success almost entirely on the correct and efficient employment of the artillery. It is primarily an artillery operation and if the artillery cannot crush and demoralise the enemy's infantry by their fire effect the enterprise will not succeed.'[54] But Haig had intervened with much more ambitious goals for Neuve Chapelle and then later on Loos. While both battles were failures, they very much confirmed to Rawlinson that the correct path forward was applying 'bite-and-hold' tactics to seize and defend limited portions of enemy territory.[55] This exercise would then be repeated time and again, slowly grinding the enemy back and forcing him into costly counterattacks. 'If we had not tried to do too much [at Neuve Chapelle] our losses would have been one quarter what they were and we should have gained just as much ground[,] but the idea of pushing through the Cav[alry] ... was the origin of our heavy losses.'[56] Rawlinson saw these repeated bite-and-hold battles as the solution to the Western Front conundrum, ahead of Haig's preponderance for operations with much wider objectives, and realised this type of fighting required scientific gunnery, ample ammunition and meticulous planning, and even then was unlikely to bring about an end to the trench deadlock swiftly.[57]

Rawlinson was far from alone in this thinking. His views were shared by General Marie-Emile Fayolle, commander of the French Sixth Army, who had arrived at the following conclusion:

> We have understood that we cannot run around like madmen in the successive enemy positions. Doctrine is taking shape. If there are so many defensive positions, there will need to be as many battles, succeeding each other as rapidly as possible. Each one needs to be organised anew, with a new artillery preparation. If one goes too quickly, one risks a check. If one goes too slowly, the enemy has time to construct successive defensive lines. That is the problem, and it is extremely difficult.[58]

As it turned out, though, Rawlinson's operational thinking going into 1916 differed strikingly from Haig's, despite it being based on the same battles.

Haig had taken a very different set of lessons from the bigger British battles of 1915, Neuve Chapelle and Loos, which together had run up about 70,000 British casualties against total German losses of at least 36,000. In both cases Haig had favoured more ambitious objectives than Rawlinson. Ahead of Neuve Chapelle, for instance, Haig commented in his diary that the battle was a 'serious offensive movement with the object of breaking the German line and consequently our advance is to be pushed vigorously. Very likely an operation of considerable magnitude may result.'[59] Around the village of Neuve Chapelle, in March 1915, four divisions of Rawlinson's

IV Corps, in Haig's First Army, broke into the German defensive line, and came within an ace of breaking through it.[60] Loos, six months later, was the British army's first truly large-scale offensive operation. It comprised six British divisions of Haig's I and IV Corps. Once again, the initial British break into the German positions went undeveloped. At both battles the initial progress was slowed by casualty-heavy, localised fighting as the enemy's defensive line stiffened, which eventually led to the calling off of the attacks. At Loos, for example, Haig believed that but for the mishandling of reserves by Field Marshal French — they had been too far back to exploit the initial success and used in a piecemeal fashion — it would have been possible to break through the German positions and into the open ground beyond. Instead, the enemy was allowed time to reinforce and strengthen his defensive lines.[61] Going into 1916, he concluded Rawlinson-style bite-and-hold battles would not produce an end to the Western Front stalemate in and of themselves. Haig firmly believed the German front defensive line could be pierced, given appropriate planning and artillery, and that thereafter speed of advance and commitment of reserves to exploit initial successes were the keys to defeating the enemy.[62]

On this latter point, Haig envisaged that battle would develop through four successive stages. It would begin with manoeuvring for position, followed by wearing out the enemy and drawing in his reserves, then delivering a decisive blow to break the enemy's resistance and finally winning victory.[63] Whereas Rawlinson held the opinion that fighting on the Western Front was still at the wearing-out stage, Haig very much believed that the time for decisive action was at hand.

RAWLINSON MOVED INTO his new headquarters — a chateau at Querrieu, about five miles east of the city of Amiens — as a veil of snow descended on the village's white-walled cottages and surrounding fields. He immediately began work on his Somme attack plan. Even before arriving, Rawlinson and his retinue of staff officers had been out and about, assessing Fourth Army's positions on the Somme and, from afar, those held by the German army opposite. He wrote in his diary:

We do not want to waste our strength in minor and premature operations, but to save up all the troops and ammunition for a really big effort in the summer, when all the Allies can strike simultaneously, and with their full power. Our new front consists of fine rolling country, rather like Salisbury Plain. It has great possibilities, and is a very pleasant change from the mud flats of Flanders.[64]

Rawlinson was initially upbeat about the ground north of the River Somme and its suitability for a large-scale attack in mid-1916. Artillery observation was 'excellent' and there was 'an unlimited number of artillery positons well covered from view — within 2000 yards of our present line & the facilities for assembling the assaulting infantry columns behind the trench line are the best I have seen anywhere.'[65] The barbed-wire coils protecting the German front-line position were of good quality, though those fronting positions further back were weaker.[66] There was also great potential for artillery enfilade into the German lines.[67]

The British army's positions north of the Somme crisscrossed about 15 miles of gentle spurs and valleys. Lieutenant-General Sir Edmund Allenby's Third Army looked across at the sharp Gommecourt salient. To the south, a die-straight road running from Albert northeast to Bapaume passed obliquely through the sector held by Rawlinson's Fourth Army, crossing its front line at roughly the halfway mark, between the villages of Ovillers and La Boisselle. To the north, past the willow-lined banks of the marshy River Ancre valley and long before Gommecourt, the red-brick villages of Serre and Beaumont Hamel were hemmed in by the German lines, with gently rising land beyond. South of the slow-moving Ancre, the terrain climbed sharply into the Thiepval–Morval ridge, in places 500 feet above sea level, which ran northwest–southeast for over eight miles. This ridge was entirely in German hands and was crowned by Pozières village on the old Roman road linking Albert and Bapaume, which was trod by Julius Caesar's legions in 54 BC. Fourth Army's front-line trench followed a slightly oblique line to the ridge as it progressed southeast from around Thiepval, the gap between it and the ridge steadily widening with each successive yard. Rawlinson's southern-most positions were almost entirely on or facing the ridge's lower foothills, and overlooked by the enemy's front line, which ran over the Thiepval, Ovillers, La Boisselle, Fricourt and Mametz Spurs, at the western end of the Mametz–Montauban ridge, and into the valleys between, and incorporated the fortified farming hamlets after which they were named. Any British attack on the Somme was guaranteed to be uphill, against German positions that overlooked all approaches.

Haig later reflected on the German defences facing his armies:

The first and second [trench] systems each consisted of several lines of deep trenches, well provided with bomb-proof shelters and with numerous communication trenches connecting them. The front of the trenches in each system was protected by wire entanglements, many of them in two belts forty yards broad, built of iron stakes interlaced with barbed wire, [with the core] often almost as thick as a man's finger.

The numerous woods and villages in and between these systems of defence had been turned into veritable fortresses. … The salients in the enemy's line, from which he could bring enfilade fire across his front, were made into self-contained forts, and often protected by mine fields; while strong redoubts [defensive fortifications equipped with numerous machine guns] and concrete machine-gun emplacements had been constructed in positions from which he could sweep his own trenches should these be taken. The ground lent itself to good artillery observation on the enemy's part, and he had skilfully arranged for crossfire by his guns.

These various systems of defence, with the fortified localities and other supporting points between them, were cunningly sited to afford each other mutual assistance and to admit of the utmost possible development of enfilade and flanking fire by machine guns and artillery. They formed, in short, not merely a series of successive lines, but one composite system of enormous depth and strength. Behind his second system of trenches, in addition to woods, villages and other strong points prepared for defence, the enemy had several other lines already completed; and we had learnt from aeroplane reconnaissance that he was hard at work improving and strengthening these and digging fresh ones between them, and still further back.[68]

These were impressive, carefully sited defences with formidable firepower that required considerable thought, preparation, materiel and men even to be broken into, let alone broken through.

Rawlinson's initial optimism about a Somme offensive was now tempered by a gloomy Kitchener, who was suspicious of shifting French intentions in light of Verdun. They met in Paris at the end of March, Rawlinson having just recovered from a bout of influenza. The French refusal to wind down operations in Salonika had annoyed Kitchener, who was convinced the French wanted to palm off the main burden of Western Front fighting on the British.[69] Kitchener — who would meet a watery North Sea death in June when the Russia-bound HMS *Hampshire* struck a mine off the Orkney Islands — was opposed to a big attack on the Somme and preferred limited offensives that would run up German casualties. He doubted the war would be over in 1916, and said it would be unwise for Haig's armies to launch a large-scale offensive alone and incur heavy casualties in the process.[70] 'There is a good deal in what he says,' noted Rawlinson later, adding that Kitchener would have to 'talk strongly' to Haig, who had already 'set his mind on a large offensive here north of the Somme.'[71] The next day, 31 March, Rawlinson returned to Querrieu and found that his chief of staff, Major-General Archibald Montgomery, had drafted a plan for a bite-and-hold offensive, which was sent to Haig on 3 April. Rawlinson explained his thinking:

> All my Corps Commanders are opposed to the unlimited
> [objective style of attack favoured by Haig]. After what K[itchener]
> said yesterday I am inclined to think that we should be wiser to
> adopt the limited [objective] one and to look to winning the war
> in 1917, not in 1916. If K[itchener] cannot replace our losses we
> should be foolish to incur them without a certainty of success
> which I cannot guarantee.[72]

Rawlinson's preference for bite-and-hold operations always influenced his Somme thinking, and was reinforced by Kitchener's caution, a growing appreciation of the German defences opposite his army and valid concerns over the potential costs involved without any certainty of securing success.

Rawlinson's proposal was for an advance on a frontage of about 20,000 yards (11.4 miles) to a depth of 2000–5000 yards.[73] These figures were determined by the 200 heavy artillery howitzers available, according to a ratio of one barrel for every 100 yards.[74] Rawlinson selected the undulating ground between Serre and Maricourt — essentially the entire frontage of his army — as suitable, also taking into account observation over the German front defensive position, the number of troops and reserves available and required, flank protection and the extent of the enemy's defences.[75] As the plan stated: 'The high ground about Pozières is most important, as it gives the enemy a marked advantage in command and observation and covers from view a considerable part of his second line of defences.'[76] Rawlinson noted the string of fortified villages built into the German first defensive position, along with the wire entanglements fronting it, and that these were not so well developed before the second defensive position. 'The latter is at a distance varying from 2000 to 5000 yards behind the front system. Parts of it, though not actually out of range of our guns, will be difficult to deal with, as they are only observable from the air.'[77]

Rawlinson's plan was based on his earlier assessment of the potential battlefield, the pitfalls he likely saw at that time and the lessons he had taken forward from 1915.[78] At the heart of his pitch were the questions of attack structure and artillery preparation. The first considered whether to rush the enemy's defences in a single attack, as at Loos, or deliver a two-phase operation. The second was whether to precede the attack with an intense bombardment of 5–6 hours, or a longer one of 48–72 hours.[79] After 'careful' consideration, and after weighing up the relative merits and weaknesses of either proposition, Rawlinson opted for a two-phase attack prefaced with a 50–60-hour bombardment.[80] He saw a rush-style attack as risky and akin to a gamble.[81] He then, in his proposal to Haig, paraphrased Kitchener's argument for a wearing-out battle:

Our object rather seems to be to kill as many Germans as possible with the least loss to ourselves, and the best way to do this appears to me to be to seize points of tactical importance which will provide us with good observation and which we may feel quite certain the Germans will counter-attack. These points to be, not only one of special tactical importance with a view to a further advance, but to be such that the Germans will be compelled to counter-attack them under disadvantages likely to conduce to heavy losses, which we can only ensure if these tactical points are not too far distant from our gun positions.[82]

Rawlinson was unsurprisingly espousing a bite-and-hold operation, a plan attuned to the operational thinking of cigar-chomping Foch.

Although favouring an attack north of Arras, Foch had got on with planning an operation south of the Somme involving 35-plus divisions, as instructed by Joffre.[83] The silver-headed general, who like Joffre hailed from the Pyrenees, had learned much from the Artois and Champagne battles of 1915. Reversing his pre-war love affair with the power of the offensive, he now believed the limitations of offensive technology meant that breaking through the German lines — as opposed to breaking into them — was not immediately possible.[84] Foch, like Rawlinson and Generals Fayolle and Philippe Pétain (the latter the commander of the French Second Army at Verdun), further believed offensives of attrition needed to be progressed in methodical, limited-objective steps.[85] All four had concluded that robust artillery support was essential to the infantry's success, from deciding the breadth of the attack, to the depth of objectives and the batteries' roles in either destroying or suppressing German gunners before and during battle.[86] Foch insisted artillery be applied according to tactical tasks and where it was needed most, rather than being spread thinly across a wide area to a somewhat crude ratio of yards per barrel, as Fourth Army did.[87] Foch and Rawlinson saw more value in repeated break-in battles than in those that chased a breakthrough from the outset, but differed when it came to the best method of deploying artillery to support an attack.[88]

As it turned out, Rawlinson's plan did not survive first contact with Haig, who wrote:

I think we can do better than this by aiming at getting as large a combined force of French and British across the Somme and fighting the Enemy in the open! With this end, a manoeuvre on the part of Fourth Army is necessary. Roughly, the plan should be:

establish our left on the ridge about Serre, and operate eastwards to capture Pozières–Combles Ridges. ... If we are lucky in surprising and capturing Serre fairly rapidly, then mounted troops and machine-guns should at once be sent to occupy Miraumont and Grandcourt, and operate so as to take the enemy's defences towards Thiepval in reverse.[89]

Haig thought Rawlinson and Montgomery's plan showed no thought of reasoned distribution of troops, strategy or surprise.[90] He was really saying that in his eyes they lacked imagination and their idea was not ambitious enough. A more optimistic Haig — inspired by Joffre, who, contrary to his own generals, believed the German front and second positions could be pierced in a first assault — contemplated a breakthrough, followed by a wheel and sweep (clean-up) behind the German front.[91] By contrast, Rawlinson was pushing for an operation comprising deliberate stages and resembling the slow and sure nature of siege warfare.[92] Haig further thought the proposed long bombardment would signpost an attack to the enemy, and preferred the surprise and morale-busting qualities of a much shorter one. This divergence in thinking between Haig and Rawlinson was nothing less than fundamental, but the C-in-C was calling the shots and immediately demanded a rewrite from his Fourth Army commander.

HAIG AND JOFFRE spent much of March and April thrashing out the strategic details of the offensive, and how their armies might best co-operate. Joffre favoured a combined attack in both time and place, which threw the importance of the British capture of the Mametz–Montauban–La Briqueterie ridgeline into relief for its value as flank protection for Fourth Army at the southern end of its sector, and in facilitating the French advance between there and the River Somme. Subsequent attacks would push the line towards the Bapaume–Péronne road, about five miles behind the German front line and also beyond the Thiepval–Morval Ridge.

Joffre thought the key to exploiting the first assault was getting French troops beyond the Somme south of Péronne, where it ran behind and broadly parallel to the German front line. He believed this would be more easily achieved if the natural barrier imposed by the slow-moving waterway was outflanked north of its acute southward bend at Péronne.[93] As Joffre saw it, the ultimate goal of the Anglo-French joint venture was to establish Rawlinson's and Fayolle's armies in open country on the arc of Bapaume–Rancourt–Péronne–Ham. In Joffre's eyes the weak point in the scheme lay north of the river, and that had a lot to do with lingering suspicions over whether the British would pull their weight given Haig's ongoing interest in a Flanders attack.[94] It was for this reason that Joffre cancelled any preliminary operations, hoping to focus Haig's mind on the Somme, and began espousing a concentrated offensive progressing in successive stages determined by artillery coverage.[95]

Haig now spelled out the operation he wanted Rawlinson to put on paper. It would be part of a wider Anglo-French attack, with operations also to be undertaken by the Russians and Italians elsewhere. In the first phase, Fourth Army would establish a defensive flank on the Serre–Grandcourt Spur at the northern end of its sector and also capture the high ground about Pozières in the centre, along with the spurs tapering off towards Beaucourt, Grandcourt and Fricourt. A simultaneous attack between Fricourt and Maricourt would quickly seize the Mametz–Montauban–La Briqueterie ridgeline — broadly, the southern lip of Caterpillar Valley. Thereafter, in the second phase, the Ginchy–Bazentin-le-Grand Ridge — effectively the German second defensive line in this part of the battlefield and part of Caterpillar Valley's northern lip — was to be captured, with assistance to be given to the French around Combles. 'Operations subsequent to those [phases] … must depend on the degree of success gained and on developments which cannot be foreseen.'[96] Haig continued: 'The object will continue to be to prevent the enemy from re-establishing his line of defence and to exploit to the full all opportunities opened up for defeating his forces within reach, always, however, with due regard to the need to assist the French Army to effect passage of the River Somme.'[97]

Haig further expected the attack to be pushed forward as rapidly as possible, and stressed that opportunities to use cavalry supported by artillery, machine guns and infantry should be actively sought.[98] He warned that it was inadvisable to push isolated and disorganised troops beyond the reach of possible support if the enemy was still capable of launching successful counterattacks. He was more sanguine when it came to having strong, organised groups press forward. The risks to infantry if it advanced beyond the effective artillery support could be foreseen, and 'to a great extent guarded against by careful previous arrangement for providing artillery support, for throwing in reinforcements as required to fill gaps in the line and to cover flanks that may become exposed ... and generally, for providing the means of holding what may be gained.'[99] Haig was already considering mobile warfare after breaking into and then through the German second defensive position.

Rawlinson said he would defer to Haig's specifications, then chewed through several pages justifying his now redundant proposal.[100] 'On it may possibly depend the tactics of one of the greatest battles the British Army have ever fought and I fully recognise the responsibility.'[101] He agreed to factor the neighbouring French attack into his plans, and said that while the prospect of capturing the high ground north of Pozières was alluring, he was concerned about cutting the more distant enemy barbed wire, the potential for disorganisation of his own forces and the possible inability of artillery to support his most advanced infantry from existing battery positions.[102] He was further annoyed by the extension of his southern flank around Montauban, which required an additional division but no extra artillery,[103] and said his army had insufficient resources to include the Gommecourt salient in its operation.[104] He still believed a 50–60-hour bombardment was needed to cut the German wire, and, misinterpreting Haig's instruction, planned to use massed cavalry south of Grandcourt to help protect the attack's north flank if enemy forces were reduced to a serious state of demoralisation.[105] Rawlinson disagreed with much of Haig's rationale, and specifically with the length of the bombardment and vulnerability of any troops attacking more distant German positions.

Rawlinson also knew he did not have to agree with orders to follow them, as he explained in a carefully worded missive to GHQ: 'I, however, fully realise that it may be necessary to incur these risks in view of the importance of the object to be attained. This will, no doubt, be decided by the commander-in-chief, and definite instructions sent to me in due course.'[106] Rawlinson was very obviously providing a paper-trail defence that transferred blame to Haig if the more ambitious attack went wrong.

Haig saw this guileless turn for what it was and his 16 May response provided the basis for what was to become Britain's first day of the Somme. The Serre–Grandcourt Spur, Pozières, Contalmaison and Montauban were the objectives to be attained on the first day of fighting. The capture of Montauban was subject to co-operation with the French army and assistance from their artillery. 'It is understood,' wrote Haig, deftly paring Rawlinson's paper-trail defence away, 'that you concur in this view and that your plan of attack will be designed accordingly.'[107] This was a wily move: Haig was challenging Rawlinson either to directly oppose his scheme, or to give it his tacit approval. Haig had, however, conceded a number of points, which implied he was listening to his subordinate. The Gommecourt diversion was now Third Army's job and the bombardment would be a methodical one, 'until the officers commanding the attacking units are satisfied that the obstacles to their advance have been adequately destroyed.'[108] One all-arms cavalry division would be at Rawlinson's disposal during the operations. Haig had insisted his broader scope of operations for the first day of the Somme be retained, and placed the burden of tactical responsibility squarely back on Rawlinson's shoulders.

Lieutenant-General Sir Launcelot Kiggell, Haig's chief of staff, explained after the war, in a letter to the British official historian, the difference in Haig's and Rawlinson's thinking at this juncture:

> Sir D.H.'s original plan was to aim at pushing the attack originally right through to the German guns. He found such decided unwillingness to attempt too much, supported by Rawlinson too, that he decided it would be unwise to demand more than those responsible for execution [of the operation] felt within their power. Their view was that each day's advance should be limited to a line which could be effectively covered by our artillery without its having to move forward. This, I gathered, was due to previous experience of counter-attacks against [infantry] advances pushed beyond effective artillery support and to the heavy losses of bodies [of infantry] dashing forward without adequate support or flank protection.[109]

It appeared the bones of Fourth Army's first day of the Somme were almost decided. Eleven divisions would attack on a frontage of about

25,000 yards (14.2 miles), to a depth of 3000–4000 yards in the north and 2000–3000 yards in the south. Defensive flanks would be formed around Serre in the north and around Montauban in the south, the latter adjacent to the French Sixth Army. The German second defensive line between Serre and Pozières on the Albert–Bapaume road would be captured, including the village of Ovillers. Thereafter south — and all shy of the enemy's second positions — the villages of La Boisselle, Contalmaison, Fricourt, Mametz and Montauban would be seized, too.

Artillery support was increased to 220 heavy howitzers, which would provide a five-day bombardment before the infantry went in. Villages not assailed directly would be doused with gas shells, and infantry advancing nearby screened by smoke. All-arms cavalry formations would be used to protect the flanks and, in the case of soldiers on horseback, help the infantry capture its objectives. Further progress depended on how the battle unfolded. Additionally, Third Army's diversion at Gommecourt would stop enemy reserves from being moved south, this area having been selected over alternative options at Vimy Ridge and Monchy-au-Bois, southwest of Arras, for its potential value in assisting the hoped-for drive towards Bapaume. This was almost entirely Haig's plan, with several key concessions that showed some flexibility on his part and quietened Rawlinson.

Firm as this plan looked, it was about to undergo more change as Verdun chewed through French lives. In mid-April, 39 French divisions were supposed to attack alongside Fourth Army on the Somme, but, by early June, Joffre was no longer talking in specific numbers and was anticipating a prolonged operation.[110] The initial objective, Joffre said, should be the German first defensive position, and he now thought it premature to fix any objective beyond the enemy's third defensive position, which was under construction.[111] He had scaled back excitable Foch's plans to an extent that just 12 infantry divisions of Sixth Army were left to complement Rawlinson's attack.[112] What had begun as a French-led joint offensive had been watered down by Joffre to one in which the French army played a minor role,[113] which was just as Kitchener had predicted in his conversations with Rawlinson.

Haig expanded Fourth Army's operational scope to compensate for the fast-eroding French element. The strategic goals were to kill

The Somme: Haig's Plan for 1 July 1916

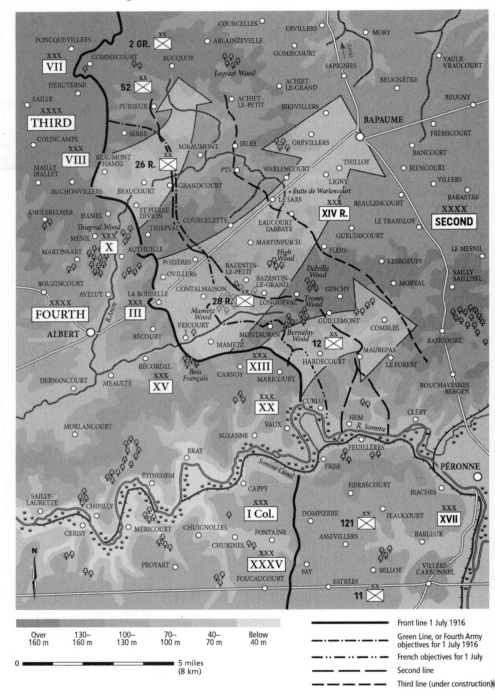

Over 160 m	130–160 m	100–130 m	70–100 m	40–70 m	Below 40 m

0 ⎯⎯⎯⎯⎯⎯ 5 miles (8 km)

——————— Front line 1 July 1916

—·—·—·— Green Line, or Fourth Army objectives for 1 July 1916

—··—··— French objectives for 1 July

— — — — Second line

▬ ▬ ▬ ▬ Third line (under construction)

Germans and relieve the pressure on Verdun.[114] The first objective, the so-called Green Line, remained the German second defensive position, Serre–Pozières–Contalmaison, with a strong defensive flank formed on the Serre–Grandcourt Spur.[115] The second phase, or Brown Line, would see the defensive flank extended to Martinpuich, allowing Fourth Army simultaneously to 'advance our line eastward to the line Montauban–Martinpuich.'[116] A third objective, the ridge running from Martinpuich via High Wood to Ginchy,[117] was also added. All of this meant that Fourth Army's operation was now focused east, rather than southeast towards the French, and its objectives from a single day's fighting were effectively doubled. It did not stop there. Three all-arms cavalry divisions would be amassed to strike out towards Bapaume, about nine miles behind the German front line. Fourth Army's rejigged operation order stated that the attack's aim was to break the enemy's defensive system and fully exploit 'all opportunities opened up for defeating his forces within reach.'[118]

Rawlinson formed an opinion on precisely when the cavalry would be committed to battle as part of General Sir Hubert Gough's yet-to-be-formed Reserve Army, but only after lengthy talks with Haig, Kiggell and Major-General Sir Noel 'Curly' Birch, Artillery Advisor at GHQ. Rawlinson wrote after their meeting on 18 June:

> Goughy [sic] is to be under me and I am to decide when he is to
> go forward with the Cavry [sic]. If he does I shall reinforce him
> with the nearest fresh Divisions that are available. … If we are not
> successful in gaining the Green Line with comparative ease the
> Cavry [sic] will not be pushed through and it is doubtful even if
> we shall attack the Brown Line for it may be advisable to send the
> GHQ reserve up north as soon as we have drawn all the German
> reserves down here. However, this will be decided as soon as we
> know what happens in the first day of the operations.[119]

Next day, Rawlinson worked through the detail with Montgomery.

> He [Montgomery] thinks we shall not be able to get the Cavry
> [sic] through until we are in possession of the Brown Line which
> are the objectives for the second phase of the operations. I shall

have to go into this matter in further detail when Goughy [sic] has worked out his lines of getting them [the Cavalry] through and I am not prepared yet to say which the moment will be. It is highly important and is just one of those chances which if it did come off might result in our smashing up the hostile lines of defence on a really wide front.[120]

Rawlinson obviously saw potential if cavalry was committed at just the right moment, but, equally, he was already tending towards a very conservative set of conditions for committing those all-arms units to battle.

While Fourth Army's orders were increasing in scope, those of the French army were, as mentioned, being pared back. Foch's short-lived initial plans were devised around the German defences and the course of the River Somme. South of its bend at Péronne, the river and the numerous fortified villages and woods posed tactical headaches for the infantry to overcome. Foch's plan issued on 14 April had envisaged a three-army attack: in the south Tenth Army was to establish a defensive flank; in the centre another yet-to-be-designated army was to push up to and across the river; and to the north Sixth Army, whose jumping-off line crossed the waterway at Curlu, was to support this breakthrough, co-operate with the British and press towards the Bapaume–Péronne road. But Verdun had intervened, and within six weeks the proposed three-army strike was cut to the three corps of Fayolle's Sixth Army. By the end of May, Fayolle's brief was little more than to support Rawlinson.[121] The proposed breakout south of Péronne and beyond the river was dumped, and the attack to the north of the river became the main axis of French advance.[122] One army corps would attack north of the river, supporting the British flank in addition to taking its own objectives, and two south of it. Quick-minded Foch and Fayolle envisaged a brisk conquest of the German first position followed by an immediate advance on the second, with the infantry supported from start to finish by artillery.

TWO DAYS AFTER Fourth Army's operational orders were inked on 14 June, Haig received an intelligence report outlining the enemy's Somme strength and reserves. The report's content only served to entrench his belief that great things were achievable by his Fourth and Reserve Armies. It revealed there were 'only' 32 German battalions facing the main British attack, and 'only' 65 more to be rushed forward as reinforcements within the first week of battle.[123] 'We shall therefore have considerable numerical superiority,' wrote Haig, 'and prompt action taken to develop a success gained in the assault on the first objective may give great results.'[124] Haig clearly interpreted this intelligence report in the most charitable possible light; once the breakthrough was effected, he believed there was at least a five-day window for his cavalry to roam over enemy territory beyond Pozières Ridge towards Bapaume, Arras and Monchy-le-Preux, a village just east of Arras, and potentially further afield. Nowhere did he mention that his most ambitious plans required nothing less than a collapse of the German army opposite Rawlinson's Fourth Army.

This intelligence report only consolidated Haig's intention, stated in early June, of using his cavalry along 'the lines of 1806,' a direct reference to Napoleon's victory at Jena–Auerstedt.[125] 'Thus,' wrote two historians of the Somme, 'machine-guns, quick-firing artillery, barbed wire, and trenches, none of which had been present at Jena, were wished away by the commander-in-chief as he sought to return to simpler times and decisive victories.'[126] As potential epics went, this one could not have been scripted better: cavalryman Haig was planning a 40-mile advance and in the process figuratively riding to rescue the French at Verdun.

It was never quite that simple. Haig's looking to Napoleon for inspiration was no bad thing, so long as he realised the Corsican's victories belonged to a different era, had taken place on different ground, had faced different defences and had been defined by altogether different technology. Neuve Chapelle and Loos had shown Haig that breaking into thin-line German positions was possible, and therefore — so the theory ran in his mind — punching into the open ground beyond was not merely wishful thinking. Equally, however, he did not want to see a repeat of those battles' second-day failures.[127] Moreover, he recognised that applying all of this to the vastly more sophisticated German positions on the Somme was a materially different proposition. On 16 June, he said the push towards Bapaume and then Monchy-le-Preux was conditional on achieving a break-in, namely the fall of Pozières Ridge.[128] If a further advance eastwards turned out not to be advisable, the 'most profitable course' would probably be to transfer 'our main efforts' quickly to another portion of the British front, namely that held by Second Army in Belgium.[129] Haig reinforced this five days later: 'If the first attack goes well every effort must be made to develop the success to the utmost by firstly opening a way for our cavalry and then as quickly as possible pushing the cavalry through to seize Bapaume.'[130] In brief, Haig was advocating a breakthrough battle as his preferred outcome and saw the break-in as a prerequisite of achieving that, rather than necessarily being an immediate end in itself.

Haig's conclusion was founded on a misinterpretation of Joffre's correspondence, along with Joffre's perceptions of Verdun, of Russia's just-launched Brusilov Offensive and of the wider war on the Western and Eastern Fronts. He had interpreted Joffre's early June reference to 'knocking out the German army on the Western Front, or at least an important part of their forces' too favourably. He believed Joffre was suggesting that decisive results were possible — whereas the Frenchman's clumsily communicated intent was nothing more than to secure a strong British commitment to a sustained offensive.[131] Moreover, Joffre had hinted that the Verdun fighting had ground down the German army and soaked up its reserves, which was a conclusion Haig's own intelligence officials had reached independently. Haig — his four-stage-battle thinking coming to the fore — saw the 1914 battles as the manoeuvre element, and the subsequent fighting in 1915 and early 1916, including that at Verdun, as the wearing-out phase.[132] Haig met with Prime Minister Herbert Henry Asquith in the second week of June in London, and told him the 1916 offensive would be sustained and attritional. But — as we have seen — his thoughts were very definitely tending elsewhere.[133] Haig actually saw the Somme as a logical extension of 1914–15 fighting and a potentially decisive blow to break enemy resistance, followed by exploitation, but in his mind it was always better to promise too little and then deliver much.

Kiggell set out to justify his boss's thinking, again. Writing 20 years after the fact, he said it had never been his understanding that Haig wanted a breakthrough battle.[134] 'Our hope at the time as I understood it was to force the enemy from his entrenched positions, [and] follow up success with cavalry so far as might prove possible and judicious.'[135] Kiggell was arguing semantics and on thin ice. GHQ's correspondence with Rawlinson may not have actually stated the word 'breakthrough' but as a sum of parts — particularly the missives of 16 and 21 June — it was abundantly clear that this was Haig's favoured goal. This was the case as early as February, when Kitchener complained to intelligence chief Charteris that someone from GHQ had been talking about a breakthrough.[136] In his post-war memoir, Charteris said he had no difficulty in believing it was Haig: 'I fancy he himself has been using the term break-through to some of the visitors [to GHQ], and it has reached K's [Kitchener's] ears!'[137] Kiggell was always a Haig supporter and it was tiringly predictable to find him later attempting to portray his old boss in a positive light.

Rawlinson now revealed Haig's grand plan to his six corps commanders, which must have been difficult given he had never really believed in its most optimistic goals. At a conference with these officers on 22 June Rawlinson explained that the British attack was now the main operation on the Somme, and also outlined Haig's increased objectives for the initial infantry attack. He told them an opportunity might occur to push cavalry through to confirm success, and then relayed Haig's orders verbatim. Before he did, Rawlinson said it might not be possible to break the German line and push cavalry through towards more distant objectives in the first rush.[138] It would not be possible at all if the first German position was not captured until the afternoon:[139]

> A situation may supervene later when the attack on the Brown
> Line takes place for pushing the cavalry through; but until we can
> see what is the [state] of the battle, it is impossible to predict what
> moment we shall be able to undertake this, and the decision will
> rest in my hands to say when it can be carried out.[140]

From these words alone it was apparent that Rawlinson still had nil appetite for the most ambitious elements of Haig's plan. His lack of enthusiasm, which could have been perceived as borderline subversive, cannot have gone unnoticed by his corps commanders, who had to implement it at the tactical level and produce results on the ground.

Haig likely suspected Rawlinson was damning his plans with faint praise. He visited Rawlinson on 27 June and was horrified by what he heard. 'He has ordered his troops to halt for an hour and consolidate on the enemy's last line! Covered by an artillery barrage!'[141] This order ran almost contrary to Haig's and hinged on whether the enemy had reserves on the spot for a counterattack on the day of battle.[142] It vaguely suggested Rawlinson had misunderstood GHQ's speculative operational objectives, but a more probable explanation was that he had knowingly interpreted and communicated them to corps commanders through his bite-and-hold lens.

Haig wasted no time in putting Rawlinson back on track, directing him to prepare for a rapid-advance attack. He stressed the importance of having corps commanders use their cavalry and mounted troops should the opportunity arise. 'In my opinion,' reiterated Haig, 'it is better to prepare to advance beyond the Enemy's last line of trenches, because we are then in a position to take advantage of any breakdown in the Enemy's defence. Whereas if there is a stubborn resistance put up, the matter settles itself. On the other hand if no preparations for an advance are made till next morning, we might lose a golden opportunity.'[143]

So it was that Gough's Reserve Army infantry and cavalry were expected to push on towards Bapaume, then roll up the enemy's positions towards Monchy-le-Preux, near Arras, if German resistance broke. Neat as this sounded, the detail was only hammered out late on 27 June after lengthy talks between Haig, Kiggell, Rawlinson and Gough.[144] The latter was to have his headquarters at Albert as soon as Pozières Ridge fell, with his command comprising a pair of Fourth Army's divisions presently in corps reserve, namely III Corps' 19th (Western) and X Corps' 49th (West Riding) Divisions.[145] Infantry of 19th and 49th would be pushed forward ahead of the cavalry towards Pys, Irles and Le Sars so that 'no time may be lost' in exploiting a breakdown in German resistance.[146] As Reserve Army advanced, 17th (Northern) Division, which was XV Corps' reserve, would strike out towards Bazentin-le-Petit and High Wood and protect III Corps' southern flank, while VIII Corps would cover X Corps' northern wing.[147] One squadron of cavalry would be attached to each of 19th, 49th and 17th Divisions and the order for their advance would be given by Reserve Army. It was only after these divisions crossed the German second defensive line that they would come under Gough's command; until then they and their committal to battle belonged entirely to Rawlinson. As Haig put it, 'I agreed to this arrangement.'[148]

Rawlinson apparently agreed with all of this, too, except that he did not really. Next day he issued a memo outlining how reserve infantry divisions were to open the way for cavalry if enemy resistance broke down.[149]

> I issued orders for the advance of the 49, 19 and 17 Divisions which
> are the reserves of these [III, X and XV] Corps as soon as the
> Green Line is taken always provided that we get the Green Line
> easily and without too heavy fighting. I think they all understand
> and Goughy [sic] will take command of these divisions as soon as
> they cross the Green Line.[150]

That was the theory, but Rawlinson, according to his diary of 30 June, doubted he would ever have to enact it. 'I am full of hope we may succeed but we shant [sic] get the Green Line without a good hard fight.'[151] In effect Rawlinson was saying his single stated condition for committing his reserve divisions on 1 July — the Green Line being 'easily' captured — was unlikely to be met. It was a troubling epitaph that revealed the extent of the chasm between Haig's and Rawlinson's operational thinking, and their differing expectations on the eve of battle.

The date of the Anglo-French operation was penned down for 29 June after a good deal of vacillation, with scope for it to be postponed due to bad weather. At a conference on 26 May at Montreuil, Haig had promised Joffre that Fourth Army would be ready to attack on 20 June, but that the best date — as far as numbers of British troops and materiel accumulated went, and he needed at least 12 days' notice — would be 15 August.[152] Joffre said the British would not be called upon to attack until about 1 July, and Haig said he would raise no objection so long as there was no postponement once a specific date had been set.[153] It was a wishful request given the backcloth of change, more so given the prospect already existed that Haig's army might have to undertake the offensive alone.[154] An escalation in the fighting at Verdun and a political crisis in Paris saw 25 June mooted as a start date, but this passed quickly, and 29 June and 1 July were then suggested by the French as alternatives. Haig was concerned that the British concentration of troops would be rumbled by the enemy, who might attack at a weaker point elsewhere along the line. Eventually Haig, Joffre and their respective headquarters settled on 29 June. The bombardment was to open early on 24 June and last for five days. Rain on 28 June and again on the night of 29–30 June saw the infantry attack postponed to 1 July, with the bombardment extended, too.

By this time the War Committee had established a firm handle on Germany's strategic direction for 1916, and recognised that Verdun had eroded France's ability to provide a major contribution to the Somme offensive.[155] Moreover, wrote a pair of historians, 'France was developing a jaundiced attitude towards its Entente partners. The idea was developing in France … that the British were accumulating military resources for some future project entirely to their own benefit, and were disregarding France's imminent needs.'[156] Haig, who had travelled to London to meet with the committee in early June, confirmed all of this, and said the French army was being progressively worn threadbare. In light of this he had already agreed to a start date that was earlier than his ideal of 15 August.[157] Robertson, the Chief of Imperial General Staff, now confirmed 26 British and 14 French divisions would begin the attack, that artillery and other preparations were proceeding satisfactorily, and that he 'thought we could get on all right.'[158] Few seemed bothered that he did not know how many artillery guns the German army had on the Somme, only that they were probably superior to the British accumulation.[159] Perhaps that was because a day earlier gifted conversationalist and public speaker Lloyd George had given the committee well-received assurances and data showing improved British artillery and ammunition production.[160] Whatever the case, Whitehall had committed to the Somme out of coalition necessity and political pragmatism and — in conflict with its earlier reservations — was allowing the British army to shoulder the main burden of the Anglo-French offensive.

In short, the British army's final attack orders were the laboured sum of the shifting sands of coalition warfare. Haig had followed the edicts of a dithering War Committee, negotiated a sensitive relationship with Joffre, and dealt with a borderline-subversive Rawlinson along the way. Although first conceived to evict the German army by a powerful, co-ordinated Allied offensive of strategic attrition, the Somme was quickly bent into something else as charnel-house Verdun unfolded, French commitment waned and the Russian army went on the attack in Ukraine.

Rawlinson, Foch and Fayolle were bite-and-hold realists who envisaged a lengthy campaign of tactical attrition, which began with killing lots of Germans and would eventually produce victory. Joffre thought in terms of what could be, but his initial ambitions were heavily influenced by uncertainty about British commitment to the joint offensive, and were both warped and suppressed by Verdun. Haig thought in terms of operational attrition, which meant busting the stalemate with a break-in battle, followed by a Napoleon-inspired breakthrough and a return to mobile operations. His optimistic outlook and Britain's part in the offensive only became more speculative as the start date of 29 June, and then 1 July, neared. If the orders for Britain's first day of the Somme were inked amid confusion out of coalition necessity in the shadow of Verdun, they were also a foolscap encapsulation of Haig's flawed character and its influence on his operational thinking.

CHAPTER 2

'I Learned to Hate the Place'

British trench life, training and preparations,
August 1915 to 23 June 1916

*'There is something painfully sad about war. I do not speak
from the soldier's point of view. This is not really so bad. He
merely takes a risk, his eyes open. If he is hit, he has lost the
throw [of the dice] and there the matter ends.'*[1]

— Captain Charlie May, 22nd Manchesters

LIFE WAS CHEAP within the muddy British trenches on the Somme
in the year before the offensive began. 'One felt a good deal of inward
apprehension & realised one's future might be pretty brief,' wrote a
fatalistic Lieutenant Derick Capper, 8th Royal Sussex.[2] 'I thought,' noted a
despairing Private George Pollard, 11th East Lancashires, 'there is no way
out of it.'[3] Most everybody feared injury over death: a life lived with loss
of limb, disfigured face, blindness or lingering mental trauma horrified.
'The prospect of pain naturally appals me somewhat,' said soon-to-be-
dead Lieutenant Ernest Polack, 4th Gloucesters, 'and I am taking morphia
in with me to battle.' 'Death,' continued Polack, who was killed in mid-
July 1916, held 'no terrors for me in itself.'[4] Memories of happier times
became phantasms that might never have been, might never be again. 'If
I get killed,' pondered an existentially minded Captain John Upcott, 9th
Devons, 'what next?'[5]

Suppression of fear was an ongoing struggle. Private Frank Moakler, Newfoundland Regiment, prayed to God — 'I did not know of anyone else who could help me' — and lived to die an old man.[6] Sergeant Alex Fisher, 10th King's Own Yorkshire Light Infantry, placed himself into a 'sort of' mental cocoon, but retained 'all my faculties and my abilities and also my awareness.'[7] And, yet, the mental struggle to still his quivering hands continued.[8] Private Ernest Grindley, 19th Manchesters, saw one man terrified by shellfire run 'screaming towards the rear.'[9] Most did not run, but many thought twice for fear of letting their pals down, stigmatising their families or ending up in a lonely spot before a firing squad.[10] Lieutenant Capper spoke for many when he said, 'I was no hero and as scared (or "windy" as we called it then) as the next man, but most scared of all of showing it.'[11] So lived thousands under the shadow of death, each unsure whether that day or the next would be their last. 'This,' thought Pollard, 'is going to be my future.'[12]

GENERAL SIR DOUGLAS Haig brought 19 divisions together in his six army corps opening the Somme offensive. Thirteen were to be directly involved, with a further six in reserve. Eleven were Kitchener divisions, plus four each of first-line Territorial Force and Regular Army divisions that also included numerous new recruits. Fourteen of the 19 divisions had seen at least five months' service in the trenches since 1915, and 12 would be participating in their first major offensive. Six had fought at Loos, Neuve Chapelle and Aubers Ridge in 1915, and one at Gallipoli.

The first British troops arrived on the Somme in August 1915 when Third Army took over a large portion of previously French-held land north of the River Somme. Come early March 1916, General Sir Henry Rawlinson's just-formed Fourth Army acquired the southern 20 miles of Third Army's positions, which would eventually comprise the rump of the 1 July battlefield, and the latter army's VIII, X and XIII Corps. By the end of April, III and XV Corps were spliced into Rawlinson's order of battle. Eight of his divisions were previously Third Army, and 11 more arrived in March–June 1916. The inescapable conclusion was that most of the soldiers in Haig's Somme strike force were new to the Picardy area of northern France, and novices when it came to fighting large-scale offensives of the type he was planning, which meant there was plenty of work to be done to prepare them for the upcoming battle.

It was this Haig referred to when assessing the various divisions comprising the British army in March 1916. 'I am strengthening the long line which I have recently taken over, and training the troops. I have not got an Army in France really, but a collection of divisions untrained for the field. The actual field Army will be evolved from them.'[13]

This Darwinian process began with a salutary introduction to the trenches crisscrossing more than 20 miles of downs from Gommecourt salient to just north of the Somme. Each of the six army corps was allocated a set area 3500–5000 yards wide, as the crow flew, although the yardage of actual front-line trenches within each was much longer.[14] Third Army's VII Corps surrounded Gommecourt salient. In Fourth Army's area, VIII Corps held the line facing Serre–Beaumont Hamel, X Corps was in the trenches across the River Ancre and facing Thiepval–Leipzig Redoubt, III Corps was opposite Ovillers and La Boisselle, XV Corps faced Fricourt–Hill 110–Mametz, and XIII Corps looked over at Montauban. Each division was responsible for the front-line system in its own area, as well as the fretwork of trenches behind. Headquarters and accommodation dugouts, along with machine-gun, signalling and observation posts, were studded throughout. As a rule, each division deployed two brigades in depth in their front-line system, on a two-battalion frontage, with a third in reserve. Fourth Army's anodyne order of battle belied its role as a defensive scheme.

Soldiers saw little of this wider tactical organisation beyond the parallelogram of trenches that was temporarily home to their platoon, company or battalion. Events beyond the several crenellated traverses bounding each twelve-man section's little portion of the line were more often heard than seen; a barrage or firefight a hundred yards or so away might warrant a terse diary mention, but that was about it. Snatching a nosey glance over the parapet to find out what was going on was to court a bullet. For individual soldiers and sections all that mattered was surviving their own four- to eight-day trench tour, getting sufficient food and sleep, and finishing enough labouring work, sentry duty and other tasks to please the boss, not what had happened to some unknown bloke further along the line.

Some sense of life within these earthen parentheses can be had today from the viewing area on the Caribou Memorial at Newfoundland

Memorial Park near Beaumont Hamel. Look out towards the old two-storey cottage off to the right and you can see the front-line system's dog-legged rows of fire, support and reserve ditches, and the intersecting communication trenches for those trudging into or out of the line. You can see the traverses that once marked the worldly boundaries for innumerable small groups of soldiers for days at a time; in summer they are grass-clad, sprinkled with daisies and beguiling. Back then they were all about dirt and sandbags, and the wafting stench of corpses mixed with the aroma of Haig's unwashed legion.

This troglodytic life was mostly about routine. 'We did 2 hours' sentry, 2 hours' work & 2 hours' rest on the fire step,' said Sergeant Thomas Bennett, 2nd Bedfords, of his daytime rota, which included a period at dusk and dawn when every man would 'stand to' in case of an enemy attack in the half-light. 'My regiment were never allowed in dugouts in the front line and always we had to look about for salvage such as old iron & used cartridge cases.'[15] Sergeant George Osborn, 2nd South Wales Borderers, was 'up all night working and doing sentry. No sleep again last night. Standing to this morning, working all day.'[16] Lance-Corporal John Cousins, 7th Bedfords, complained the 'only rest one had was to lay on a ground sheet when off sentry duty.'[17] Then there was the nervous tension of after-dark lookout work, he said, recalling the 'panic firing at night when a rat ran across the [observation] slit of the trench parapet.'[18] Private Pollard was another sleep-deprived sentry:

Once, looking towards the barbed-wire, I started to think I saw
posts taking shape and beginning to move. 'Jack! Jack!' I said to
Pilky, my sergeant, 'They're coming over!' 'Come down,' he said,
'there's now't there.' Just then, they came round with the rum
ration — it was a big thing was the rum ration — I thought 'Am I
going to refuse?' I was a teetotaller, but … I took it.[19]

The drudgery of trench life brought with it physical and mental exhaustion, which in the wee small hours could play cruel tricks on the mind.

Autumn of 1915 and winter of 1915–16 were despised for their knee- and thigh-deep mud. Private Squire Brookes, 16th Manchesters, said late-

September 1915 marked the beginning of a 'month or two of sheer misery. This was much the most horrible period of my war.'[20] One officer likened clawing through trench gloop to 'the sensations of flies in treacle.'[21] Lieutenant Aubrey Moore, 1/5th Leicesters, hoped the 'Germans were in the same state.'[22] Makeshift sumps dug into trench floors sometimes worked, other times not. Duckboards floated with the rising water levels. Buckets were used to slop water and mud out, and hand-cranked pumps carried water over parapets. 'Of course,' wrote 36th (Ulster) Division's historian, 'it presently filtered back into the trench bottom.'[23] Wet, mud-caked uniforms and greatcoats meant being chilled through for prolonged periods of time. 'For warmth we had charcoal braziers in dugouts: charcoal was burned as it gave off no smoke,' said Private Clarrie Jarman, 7th Queen's Royal West Surreys.[24] Hobnailed boots offered little protection from trench foot, which was an affliction that disgusted Lance-Corporal Cousins: 'We all suffered from trench feet a condition brought on by the feet being wet for days on end. The skin seemed to swell and leave the flesh. Large blisters appeared and the stench was appalling. Body filthy, no washing, no water to wash, waterlogged shell holes were urine contaminated even reserve trenches were little better.'[25] Gumboots, dry socks and tubs of water-resistant whale oil to be rubbed liberally on to the feet were the solutions to trench foot, but from mud there was no escape, as Captain Upcott explained: 'Mud will kill anything, it gets into your soul, just as it oozes into your boots and hair and under your clothes. One becomes just a sticky machine, which carries on because it has got to.'[26] Trench life through the autumn of 1915 and the winter of 1915–16 was miserable and sickness rates skipped higher. 'I don't know how the men stand it,' wrote soon-to-be-dead Lieutenant Billy Goodwin, 8th York & Lancasters.[27]

Corpse-fed rats scampered over sleeping soldiers, gnawed into food stores and spread whatever filth and bacteria they had picked up along the way. They nested in discarded kits, in earthy burrows and in the chest cavities of no-man's-land's dead. They urinated or defecated wherever they pleased. They were in every dugout and every trench traverse. 'In one dugout called "Vermin Villa" if a match was struck the rats would scatter,' wrote Corporal Henry Allen, 12th Middlesex.[28] Lieutenant Eric Kirkland-Laman, 2nd South Wales Borderers, said 'one impudent beggar actually sat on my chest during the night.'[29] Some slashed at the pink-tailed rodents with spades, stabbed at them furiously with bayonets, or hurled anything to hand at them. Shooting at them was forbidden. Out of the lines, soldiers and rats alike moved into billets and tents. 'They came in droves to the villages,' said Private Jarman.[30] Rifleman Cecil Tennant, 1/9th Londons (Queen Victoria's Rifles), recalled a barn near Bray where 'they crawled over us in search of food and anything edible disappeared.'[31] Controlling the rat plague was impossible: the vermin multiplied faster than they could be killed.

Body lice were equally reviled. Soldiers were 'lousy' within weeks of arriving at the front, whether from sleeping on old, infested straw in some dugout or barn, or from inheriting poorly cleaned clothing from the stores.[32] 'Our clothing after being in the line was pretty lousy. In fact we were hardly ever free from lice,' wrote Private Jarman.[33] Lice bites could cause trench fever, its symptoms — high temperatures, headaches, rashes and leg pains — requiring hospital treatment.[34] Itchy soldiers scoured their clothing for these parasites and their eggs. In the trenches there was no chance of washing, but behind the lines there were tepid showers, delousing baths and ineffective uniform-fumigation services. Rifleman Henry Barber, 1/5th Londons (London Rifle Brigade), explained:

At about three week intervals our shirts and underwear were sent
for fumigation but the process failed to kill the eggs which were
laid in the seams of our clothing. We received a clean shirt &
before putting it on a match was lit & run up & down the seams.
The eggs exploded like a miniature Chinese Cracker.[35]

Whether in the trenches or in the billets and barns far behind, there was no escape from the chronic irritation of body lice. 'I learned to hate the place,' said Gunner Victor Parker, Royal Field Artillery (RFA), frustrated by the vermin plague.[36]

Shellfire was the main cause of casualties among the pruritic British soldiers on the Somme. Few forgot their baptism; few expected to live much longer. The initial elation of Rifleman Noel Lockhart, London Rifle Brigade, 'did not last long as one saw men, one's friends, drop one after another.'[37] Dreaded *Minenwerfer* drums, or 'sausages,' somersaulted 'over & over as they catapulted towards you,' said Private Walter Aust, 10th East Yorkshires. It was, he said, 'very unnerving'[38] to see their parabola marked at night by a sparking fuse. Private Arthur England, 8th Norfolks, explained the early warning system: 'Sentries gave warning by shouting "Sausage right" or "Sausage left." ... It was easy to avoid them [*Minenwerfer* drums] by moving into the next [trench] traverse. In the air they looked like jam tins. Actually they were more the size of oildrums.'[39] Meantime, 'Whizz-Bangs' were invisible to the eye and gave only the briefest of screams before pitching quickly to earth and exploding.[40] Bigger projectiles — 'Jack Johnsons' or 'Coal Boxes' — could be heard whistling down long before they struck. Private Pollard likened these to a train roaring towards him, but one that was 'coming through the air and blowing up around me.'[41] He was 'never so scared in my life. I wee'd four times in the first five minutes.'[42] Gunner James Brew, RFA, witnessed several infantrymen crying and praying under shellfire.[43] Rifleman Lockhart saw one man shouting, 'For Christ's sake, stop it only for a few minutes!'[44] Gas shells flopped to earth and burst with a distinctive pop. Goodwin said these lachrymatory shells gave off a 'Spring smell' and made 'your eyes smart like blazes.'[45] Private Jarman was one of many who learned to live on his wits, mastering the art of when 'to take cover and when not to,'[46] or when to don a gas mask in quick order. The audio-visual warning system for detecting where enemy shells would land was crude and fraught with danger, but it was all there was.

Captain Richard Archer-Houblon, Royal Horse Artillery, was impressed by the staccato lights and thumping guns of nightly artillery activity:

> One could watch the flashes darting and spitting in the darkness, while hundreds and hundreds of Verey lights and coloured rockets soared up and hung flickering and spluttering in the air; the glowing parabolas of trench mortar bombs, each ending in the most appalling and shattering crash, would cut the sky; and over all roared the dull booming and thunder of batteries and batteries of guns.[47]

Soldiers' bodies were broken, eviscerated, vaporised by shell blasts, or by shrapnel that zipped about. Private Colin Coom, 16th Middlesex, never forgot stepping over a 'torn, dead & mangled body.'[48] Lieutenant Kirkland-Laman was horrified to report the fate of one soldier as 'believed to be blown to bits' and another as decapitated.[49] Sergeant Roland Richardson, 1/5th Londons (London Rifle Brigade), recalled one length of trench that contained 11 corpses: 'One [of the dead was] naked above the waist. A nose pushed through the floor of the trench and a scalped Tommy lay with exposed brain. A hand protruded from the earthy trench wall and some callous humourist had placed an Army biscuit in the dead fingers.'[50] Other soldiers were killed by enemy marksmen and machine-gunners. Private Moakler suffered from survivor's guilt when a friend was shot on the spot where he had been sitting moments before. 'He was hit in the throat and died instantly. I always felt that I had set up that sniper.'[51] Cynicism and noir humour were used to avoid thinking about dead friends, or to postpone grief. Tenth East Yorkshires' first Somme casualty was its football team goalkeeper. 'He has stopped one at last,' someone joked to Private Aust.[52] Corpses of trench dead were carried out on stretchers, or their gore in horse-hair sacks; their remains were buried in cemeteries further back. The dead of no-man's-land were harder to fetch in and, as Rifleman Lockhart said, were 'left where they were if convenient.'[53] At every turn the Somme trenches were sated with death and traumatic injury.

Fourth Army's casualty figures for the period from the start of March to 23 June 1916, for instance, give a sobering glimpse of death and its many causes prior to the Somme offensive. The army recorded about 10,000 total casualties, of which 1678 were killed, 7955 were wounded and 260 were missing.[54] This equated to about 10 battalions, almost the entire infantry component of a single division, even before the preparatory bombardment for the first day of the Somme began. Other data showed that of the army's 5742 casualties in April and May, 3428 (59.7%) were due to shellfire, 1090 (19%) were caused by grenades, 963 (16.8%) were the result of rifle fire, while a further 191 (3.3%) men went missing and 70 (1.2%) casualties were attributed to enemy mines.[55] This data excluded VII Corps' casualties, and was devoid of the human element. Bombardier Ben Bloye, Royal Garrison Artillery (RGA), lost his friend, Corporal Thomas Flavel, RGA, to a fatal wound. He died on 11 April 1916 and is buried at Wimereux Communal Cemetery. 'He was a great chap, always cool, calm and collected, debonair and a great favourite with the girls, and he had lots of fun, but he did not grow old — like me.'[56]

Death in the skies was less frequent. Thirty-two Royal Flying Corps (RFC) aircrew died on operations for Fourth and Third Armies in the period between 1 August 1915 and 23 June 1916. Six were killed by Saxon ace *Leutnant* Max Immelmann, a man with unfathomable eyes and a cleft chin who was a holder of the famed *Pour-le-Merite* medal. He was killed aged 25 in mid-June 1916. Immelmann, Field Flying Detachment 62, was lionised by the German press and soldiers at the front faithfully followed his tally of aerial victories. 'I thought you would like to know that Immelmann has shot down his eleventh airplane near here,' wrote an impressed *Gefreiter* Leo Graü, Reserve Field Artillery Regiment 26.[57]

In all, the RFC amassed 185 aircraft across 11 squadrons on the Somme. These were deployed at GHQ (21st, 27th and 60th Squadrons and part of 70th), Fourth Army headquarters (22nd and 24th Squadrons) or army corps headquarters (3rd, 4th, 8th, 9th and 15th Squadrons). These 18-aircraft squadrons — variously equipped with BE2c, FE2b, RE7, Morane-Saulnier N, Martinsyde Elephant, Sopwith 1½ strutters and DH2 planes — had mostly arrived in France in late 1915 and the first half of 1916. They were quickly put to work locating enemy artillery guns for counter-battery shoots, photographing German defensive positions, bombing more-distant targets and various other missions that included destroying hostile observation balloons.[58] In May and June the RFC extensively photographed the German XIV Reserve Corps' positions north of the River Somme and the images were pored over by intelligence officers for any snippet of information — perhaps a new trench here, a dugout or a thickening of barbed-wire entanglements there. There were two Kite Balloon Sections (1st and 5th), whose observers kept a vigil on the German lines day and night, while aircraft of other squadrons assisted on long-range bombing missions. The aircrews' job was dangerous — they risked mechanical failure, pilot error, roving enemy fighters and anti-aircraft batteries — but it was essential to both building up a detailed picture of and harassing the German defences.

Lieutenant Alfred Evans, 3rd Squadron, RFC, soon tired of helping III and XV Corps' gunners register their fall of shot behind La Boisselle, Fricourt and Mametz as anti-aircraft shells spluttered around his Morane monoplane. He reckoned that only an expert observer could spot German light-gauge railway lines, infantry badger trails and water pipes from several thousand feet aloft:

> The shading which crept and thickened along the German reserve
> trenches showed that the German working parties were active
> at night if invisible in the day time. For the shading spelt barbed
> wire. Only about half a dozen times during those three months
> did I have the luck to catch a German battery firing. When that
> happened one ceased the ranging work and called up something
> really heavy, for preference a nine-inch howitzer battery, which
> pulverised the Hun.[59]

IN THE ARTILLERY lines the accumulation of field and heavy batteries accelerated throughout March–June 1916, alongside planning for the upcoming offensive. Haig amassed 1769 guns to support the attacking corps of Fourth and Third Armies. Of these, 1537 belonged to Rawlinson's army and a further 232 were behind VII Corps, part of Third Army, at Gommecourt. Most of the field artillery brigades had arrived with the divisions to which they were attached, while the heavy batteries turned up separately, some towards late-June. Work immediately began to prepare the gun positions, which included digging camouflaged pits to house the weapons, constructing stable platforms to ensure accurate firing, laying telephone lines between batteries and various headquarters, and sinking dugouts for the crew and ammunition storage, among myriad other tasks. To even the most casual of observers, great confidence was derived from what appeared to be an overwhelming number of guns and with what seemed an endless supply of ammunition stored up for the offensive.[60]

For the gun crews the eight weeks to 23 June, the eve of the preparatory bombardment, were busy with the labour of readying their fire positions. Captain Cecil Brownlow, RFA, said the soft chalkstone allowed elaborate emplacements for his 18-pounders: 'Pit props and steel rails formed the frame work carrying four to six feet of cover which was sodded over. Intricate systems of cable connected guns to OP [Observation Posts], to infantry battalion and to brigade headquarters.'[61]

Bombardier Leonard Ounsworth, RGA, reckoned it took a week to dig a firing position near Bray for his 60-pounder heavy gun 'with pick and shovel.'[62] Second-Lieutenant Archibald Laporte, RFA, expanded on the type of work involved:

> Nightly we imported large quantities of sandbags, pit props, concrete bursters [to detonate enemy shells before they penetrated the gun pits], cupola iron, revetting material, iron girders, rations, water and what-not, for we had to construct gun-pits with overhead cover, dig dug-outs for Officers, Sergeants, gun detachments and signallers and for the storage of ammunition, and to lay down a system of telephonic communication. All this material had to be obtained from the dumps by ceaseless importunity and carted by night from distant wagon lines.[63]

Each of the field and heavy guns had to be ranged, which meant landing shot at specific points with a certain margin of error. Artillerymen were put through refresher courses on ranging their weapons according to fuse and cartridge settings, wind direction and speed, temperature, muzzle velocity and shell type. Ammunition was stored by each battery (for example: 18-pounders, 354 rounds per gun; 6-inch howitzers, 200; 8-inch howitzers, 90) and there were dumps near each (18-pounders, 1000 per gun; 6-inch howitzers, 650; 8-inch howitzers, 500), plus thousands more shells held at depots. When all that was done the gunners made up numbers on fatigue parties, which meant more digging and hauling work under cover of darkness.[64]

The work of fatigue parties included lugging rations up to the trenches. The fare was the Maconochie's brand of tinned meat and vegetable stew, along with canned bully beef, rissoles, bread, cheese and the infamously tough army biscuits.[65] 'Tins of hard biscuits were placed in the front line for us to eat as we liked: they were like dog biscuits,' wrote Private Jarman.[66] The ideal was to eat the meat rations hot, but they could also be consumed cold. All this was washed down with hot char (tea) and topped off with a Ruby Queen cigarette. '"Rations up!" was a welcome cry down the trenches,' said an unconvincing Private Coom.[67] His preferred 'feast' was rissoles, which were carried up to the line in sacks and tasted 'delicious when most of the canvas fibres were removed.'[68] Food often lacked hygiene. 'Meat brought up to us in the front line was ALIVE, frequently,' wrote a disgusted Rifleman Lockhart.[69] Private William Senescall, 11th Suffolks, saw a ration party serve up some stew not long after a gas-shell bombardment, and fumes were still in the air: 'As they bent over to dish out their eyes were streaming tears into the stew. It tasted no worse anyway.'[70] Food parcels from home were keenly anticipated. Sweets were popular, as were OXO cubes, Bovril sachets and packets of raisins to tart up the army menu.[71] 'I had sent to me a 4lb box of chocolates which miraculously reached me intact,' wrote Private Cyril Mawbey, 7th Loyal North Lancashires. 'I was the most popular man in the platoon for days.'[72] If the army fare did not taste all that pleasant, it was at least plentiful, and with patience, a pinch of imagination and supplements sent over from Blighty could be made at least palatable.[73]

By night the trenches were alive with soldiers toiling to complete lengthy lists of tasks before first light and a well-aimed bullet. That meant plenty of spade labour to clear old trenches and cut new ones, complete with firing steps, dugouts and observation posts. Just as much time was spent installing timber revetments to support trench walls, burying cables and doing numerous other jobs such as repairing or laying barbed-wire entanglements. It was this work that Lieutenant Edgar Willmer, 17th King's, described when he said his nightly routine was one of 'trying to make the trenches fit for occupation by human beings. ... One waited till nightfall and then walked over the top to the front line.'[74] Private Brookes added that 'Wiring parties, pumping [water] in addition to sentry duty kept us busy most of the day & night. We were just as well doing those things as there was no way we could rest.'[75] The exhausting, relentless work of maintaining a defensible and liveable trench system continued on through late 1915 and through the first half of 1916.

Navvying in no-man's-land was much more dangerous. Stray fusillades of machine-gun fire and roving enemy patrols posed deadly dangers. Silence and secrecy were essential. Rattling equipment, jangling coils of wire, the dull thuds of mallets, and the crisp ring of spade and pick striking metal or stone were dead giveaways.[76] Men spoke in whispers. They stifled coughs and never sparked up a tab (cigarette) lest they invite a bullet. Private England set the scene: 'Either side might open up with machine-gun fire. Patrols of three or four men would go out to locate enemy posts or to get a prisoner, or to mend wire. Verey lights [also known as flares] would go up and you needed to Freeze — still.'[77] Private Coom remembered enemy bullets 'hissed past in the dark like bees.'[78] Captain Upcott recalled an incident where 'after getting all my working parties in, I let off my Lewis guns on the German parties; to judge by the squealing, we hit something out in No Man's Land.'[79] Digging assembly trenches for the attack and posts for listening to or observing enemy activity were tasks often spread over several nights, and came with increased risk of being rumbled by the enemy, as Rifleman Barber remembered:

> Never have I dug so quickly or so quietly. Within an hour we were down three or four feet. … The next night we went back to build a fire step & fill sandbags for a parapet. This was as nerve wracking as the first night. There was a fear that the enemy might have occupied our new trench & were preparing a welcome. However, all was well.[80]

And then, said Private Brookes, losing track of time could be equally fatal:

> We had left the going out [to an observation post in no-man's-land] rather late & in quickly increasing daylight a Jerry machinegun opened up making us do even time over the last 100 yards. As I slid into the trench some (not much) of the rum [he was carrying] was spilled and, although I thought I had done rather well not to lose the lot, it was a few hours before my 'bloody clumsiness' was forgiven & forgotten.[81]

Such working parties were screened by infantrymen lying doggo (in hiding) at intervals in long, rank grass, to thwart German patrols bent on disrupting progress and inflicting casualties. Private Aust lay 100 yards from the enemy parapet: 'At first [I] thought about all the horrible possibilities. Amazingly, after a few minutes lying there I found myself nodding to sleep and when I felt the N.C.O.'s hand press on my back (the signal to withdraw) I nearly jumped out of my skin.'[82] Few of the soldiers in no-man's-land by night had ever felt so thrillingly alive as when they lay there, exposed and within an ace of death.

It was a sensation those on no-quarter raiding parties stealing across no-man's-land knew well. Some of these parties were supported by artillery fire, which pared away wire and isolated specific sections of German trench to facilitate the raiders' entry. Others were not, and relied on stealth, wire cutters and Bangalore torpedo explosives to get through. In the period 1 April–23 June there were at least 18 night-time raids noted by Fourth Army, these endeavours by 7th, 8th, 19th (Western), 29th, 31st, 32nd, 34th, 36th (Ulster) and 48th (South Midland) divisions taking place up and down the line and usually around the midnight hour. The objectives of the after-dark cutthroats who took part in these raids were capturing or killing German soldiers, gathering intelligence, destroying hostile defences, tossing bombs down the entrances of dugouts and generally causing disruption to enemy garrisons. Most raids involved about 50 soldiers, but the number depended on the task at hand. It was a brutal business. Clubs, hatchets, pistols, grenades and knuckledusters were the weapons in vogue, along with the ubiquitous rifle and bayonet. Fists did the trick too, as Sergeant Richardson recalled after nabbing one prisoner who came too close to be bayonetted: 'I closed with my foe, seized his throat after throwing him, and with knee on his chest, began to throttle him. It is hard to kill an enemy when he is already vanquished, so I stood over him.'[83] This man and other prisoners were raced back across no-man's-land and interrogated; others resisted and were shot dead. From these raids and innumerable smaller patrols, a detailed assessment of XIV Reserve Corps' composition, command structures, fighting worth and morale was worked up by Fourth Army intelligence and circulated but, alarmingly, very little reference was made in this document to the numerous dugouts and wire entanglements that most raiders mentioned in their debriefing reports.[84]

Opposing trench lines were usually 250–500 yards apart, but this depended on the lay of the land. At La Boisselle, on a corner of ground still scarred today from shell and mine blasts, known then and since as the Glory Hole, the trenches were a few yards apart. Now it is a fenced-off grass paddock filled with gorse bushes and the occasional stray cat stalking field mice; back then it was all about chaos, corpses and snipers. It smelled of sour earth, fly-blown flesh and cordite. The trenches at the Glory Hole, a most hated and feared part of the line, were close enough for the enemy to be heard coughing, chatting and stomping along duckboards. Private England was there, part of a three-man team holding an isolated post:

Dead silence. Every time one's ground sheet rustled it sounded like thunder. I was having an uncomfortable doze huddled up in the corner by the grenades when Bill Daniels who was on watch woke me with an urgent hoarse whisper,
    'England give me one of those ruddy bombs.'
    'What for?' sleepily.
    'There's a bloody Hun in the front fork [of a nearby enemy trench].'
    So I passed him one, and he threw it.[85]

It turned out the 'bloody Hun' was Captain Bernard Ayre, 8th Norfolks, on a one-man epic into the German line. Ayre escaped with a peppering of shrapnel. Later, England and Daniels bumped into him and were greeted 'with the broadest of grins and a "Good morning."'[86] Twenty-four-year-old Ayre, along with three others from his family in the Newfoundland Regiment, was killed on 1 July. He is buried at Carnoy Military Cemetery. Daniels fell two years later, the 34-year-old's body lost. England died aged 103 in Yarmouth, with the memory of his long-dead friends lingering until the end.

Attitudes towards German soldiers were complex. Few encountered living enemy personnel; the Germans were shadowy figures across no-man's-land devoid of names, faces and personalities. 'My feeling towards the Germans was that they were just fighting for the Fatherland as I was for England,' said Driver Charles Garrand, RFA, expressing a common opinion.[87] Most realised their fragile, hardship-laden existence was shared by the enemy, which led to transient periods of empathy.[88] Referring to the rescue of a wounded soldier from no-man's-land during which no shot was fired, Lieutenant Kirkland-Laman said that 'chivalry is not altogether dead.'[89] That did not stop some from shouting abuse at the German trenches to provoke a reaction and gain targets for British snipers.[90] 'Come over comrade, we want to make peace,' yelled one British soldier in good German across no-man's-land.[91] It was an unlikely invitation. Fear of the enemy remained constant, particularly for those in no-man's-land. 'With such an experience I became scared stiff,' wrote Private William Corbett, 15th Royal Scots, of narrowly dodging a German soldier out between the lines one night.[92] Outright hatred was rare unless sparked by some personal grievance, usually the killing of a close friend or family member. One who demonstrated such animosity was future Victoria Cross (VC) winner Captain Wilfrith Elstob, 16th Manchesters, who grieved for several dead friends and 'had more than normal aversion to "The Bosche."'[93] Opinions could shift quickly. At one stage Private Aust said it was 'difficult to hate' the enemy, but he later confessed to screaming 'Bastards, Bastards, Bastards' when he saw British soldiers killed.[94] 'The Boche', 'Hun' or 'Jerry' was generally regarded as just doing his job, but the individual British soldier's attitude very much depended on his morale, personality and experience.

Morale and the shifting sands of its two interrelated components, mood and spirit, were affected by all manner of factors. Mood was transitory and was influenced by weather, food and the physical condition of troops. Spirit related to the willingness of soldiers to continue fighting, which had a lot to do with their mood, outlook on life, motivations for fighting, belief in the purpose of being at war and their view of both junior and senior commanders. Falls in mood and spirit could be charted by a rise in the underlying number of disciplinary cases formally dealt with by military law.

There were, for example, 30,295 field-general courts martial convened by the British army between October 1915 and September 1916. These produced 26,581 convictions. Most were for drunkenness, absence without leave, miscellaneous military offences, disobedience and insubordination.[95] Forty-eight British soldiers were executed on the Western Front between August 1915 and June 1916.[96] Revealingly, however, the number of soldiers sent to military prison in February–June 1916 was range-bound at 0.9–1.1 per 1000, and in May–June dropped from close to 1.1 per 1000 to about 1.0.[97] Concurrently, the total number of soldiers in the British army in France markedly increased. That the underlying number of soldiers locked up in the five months to 1 July barely fluctuated suggests morale was broadly stable and arguably even improved ahead of the Somme.

Minor disciplinary matters were dealt with on the spot by the soldier's non-commissioned officers (NCOs) and subalterns. These so-called 'crimes' could include failing to shave, being dressed untidily, losing equipment and so forth. Chronic offenders were disciplined by company and battalion commanders, as were those whose offence was more serious but not enough to warrant a court martial. Maybe they had given some lip to an officer or been boozed in billets. Usually such actions resulted in a reprimand, confinement to barracks, being docked 28 days' pay or fined up to 10 shillings, extra guard and fatigues duty, or field punishment. Private John Allsop, 15th West Yorkshires, got two weeks' Field Punishment No. 1 for objecting to extra fatigue work. 'Every other day I was chained to a gun carriage or tree for one hour bound hands behind me & padlock & chains to my feet.'[98] Sergeant Osborn later recalled how 2nd South Wales Borderers' NCOs dealt summarily with stragglers on the march to the Somme: 'Those that hung back the slightest were punched, pushed and kicked to make them keep up. … If it had been on Gallipoli there would have been a few fatal accidents that night.'[99] The brutality of Osborn's experience was unusual, and his sentiment rarer still. The business of keeping an army together required strict discipline that was mostly enforced at unit level.

Mood, as noted earlier, was seasonal. In the drier months of August–September 1915 and April–June 1916 the general mood improved and 'life in the trenches became bearable,' said Private Brookes.[100] This was at least partially inspired by the advent of spring in 1916, wrote Captain Archer-Houblon:

> All the spring the Somme country was beautiful. Gorgeous
> patches of colour lay on every slope, for the derelict land, running
> wild with weeds, seeded and reseeded, and grew again the same
> self-sown crops in wanton profusion, and great blazes of scarlet
> poppies, yellow mustard, blue cornflowers and rich crimson clover
> ran riot everywhere in the open sun-bathed fields.[101]

Private William Slater, 18th West Yorkshires, said fine weather helped him to decide his lot was not 'going to be so terrible after all.'[102] But the warmer weather also brought with it more fatigue work. 'The result,' wrote Lieutenant Claude Good, 1/7th Sherwood Foresters, 'was a tired and weary battalion.'[103] Banter and wit helped pass the time,[104] and mutual support was found within platoons and sections, which were in effect surrogate families. Alert junior commanders quietly monitored their men and kept their minds occupied with one task or another; where they failed, discipline could become problematic. As Corporal George Coppard, Machine Gun Corps, wrote, 'They [the men] were wholly loyal to their own [platoon] officers, and that was as far as their confidence went.'[105] The ebb and flow of mood was part and parcel of active service and prior to the Somme it was robust enough to underpin a keen fighting spirit.

It was a point that senior commanders seized upon. Haig observed the 'men are in splendid spirits.'[106] Rawlinson said his 511,676-strong army, which on 26 June included about 239,991 British infantry in 235 battalions, was up to strength and that the 'spirit of all ranks is excellent.'[107] Brigadier-General John Charteris, Haig's chief of intelligence, said ahead of the Somme offensive that the 'spirits of our own men are at their best.'[108] These assertions were borne out by the accounts of the men themselves. In early 1916, Lieutenant Capper, for instance, thought there was a 'general feeling of urgent & purposeful preparation for "The Push" everywhere.'[109] He continued: 'Everybody was optimistic.'[110] Private Thomas Frank, 2nd Yorkshires, said morale in his battalion was 'as high as it was possible to get.'[111] Lieutenant Geoffrey Malins, a British army cinematographer, wrote that ahead of the 'great day' there was 'a mysterious something which affected every one' at General Headquarters, adding that a colonel had told him that 'my chance to make history was coming.'[112] Soldiers' willingness to continue fighting grew more resolute as the weather warmed and signs of a looming offensive increased.

These tell-tale signs of the offensive were evident to all infantry units revolved out of the line in the period March–June 1916. In the 16 days to 26 June, an additional 58,721 infantrymen in 54 battalions joined Fourth Army.[113] It was no surprise that men like Rifleman Barber 'slowly but surely learned that a big offensive was to be mounted & that we would be engaged.'[114] Huge dumps holding all kinds of war materiel sprang up overnight, along with prisoner-of-war cages, medical dressing stations and any number of other posts. Capper said the area was 'becoming somewhat crowded with infantry being moved into the support area,'[115] while Private Thomas Easton, 21st Northumberland Fusiliers, noted Bécourt Wood was 'a seething mass of life. Artillery transport, every conceivable kind of store was housed within the wood.'[116] Lieutenant Moore recorded that 'guns galore' and ammunition were brought up nightly.[117] Captain David Kelly, Leicestershire Regiment, said the 'air was now full of rumours of the coming Somme offensive.'[118] Lieutenant Malins said initially speculation was rife as to exactly where the attack would take place. 'Some thought on the northern part of our line, others the centre; others, again, the south. ... The one topic of conversation was — the coming Great offensive.'[119] As preparations continued apace and resources were accumulated, wagging tongues across the ranks soon realised where the offensive would be launched — it was becoming glaringly obvious — but had to guess at when it would begin.

As Capper wrote in late June:

> There was definitely a feeling of exhilaration that great events
> were impending, which might at last break the trench deadlock
> & even bring the end of the war within sight. I never came across
> any foreboding of the appalling losses and endless weary [Somme]
> struggle that finally petered out in the late autumn mud that was
> to come. I thank God we had no inkling of it. At least our morale
> was high. We were all set to prove that the 'New Armies' could do
> as well and possibly better than the 'Old Contemptibles' [of the
> British Expeditionary Force in 1914].[120]

OUT OF THE trenches soldiers were put up in barns holding anything from 10 to 150 men, and in other makeshift accommodation.[121] Of the latter, enough tents and wooden-framed huts with tarpaulin coverings to shelter the roughly 15,000 infantrymen of each division were the norm, and were spread across six or seven villages and woods.[122] Such huts contained 'close billets,' a euphemism for 'pigeon-hole' bunks that gave each soldier six feet by two feet to doss down on a sheaf of straw. In some cases the shelter was merely a canvas sheet draped over stacked-up ammunition boxes, and somewhat less frequently sties, which were not always suitable for human habitation. Officers and senior NCOs usually enjoyed billets with beds or camp stretchers in farm houses, living alongside the houses' French owners. Each soldier settlement had its own piped water supply and permanent staff. These camps were like gold-rush towns, minus the lawlessness, and provided basic shelter, food and hygiene, but not much else.

Food behind the lines was trench fare, supplemented with whatever could be bought, scrounged or stolen. Produce such as potatoes, apples and cabbage was available for a price, or to the opportunist. Private Mawbey spied an unharvested potato field: 'Entrenching tools were never put to a better use. Cadged a Dixie lid plus some dripping and I was in business.'[123] Tenth Essex was on manoeuvres when a skittish hare bolted. 'One shout sufficed to raise every spade from the attitude of industry to that of destruction,' recorded the regimental history.[124] 'Very few hares escaped. Of course, it was close season, but — well, there was a war on, and we'd had such a lot of bully and stew; that must be our excuse.' It was a good deal more difficult to come by whole sheep, pigs, cattle or fowl, which were often squirrelled away by their owners. 'The [French] inhabitants were convinced that we would clear the place of every kind of animal, and that therefore all live stock was being conveyed to cellars,' wrote Brigadier-General Henry Croft, 68th Brigade.[125] Private Coom sourced extra food from estaminets (small bars), cafés and farm cottages:

> We would ask for 'der oof,' 'pom de ter fritz,' 'du pang' & 'café sivuplay.' Two eggs fried with a load of chips, a third of French twist loaf & a mug of home ground coffee. All for a franc. ... There would often be an estaminet & we would have lots of fun & banter with the licensee & his family, supported by 'vin blanc' & 'vin rouge'. That's what the deadly stuff was called & some of us soon called it 'plonk'.[126]

Captain Archer-Houblon remembered that many houses were converted to shops with signage advertising their wares: 'From eggs and boot-polish, the list of wares for sale would range to "socks, bibles, beer and rosaries", and the best one was in Albert: "Blood Oranges And Funeral Wreaths."'[127] The whereabouts of brothels was passed by word of mouth: 'The women cannot keep pace with demand, with the result that large venereal hospitals are established for officers and men in France and England,' wrote Lieutenant-Colonel Frank Crozier, 9th Royal Irish Rifles. 'In the towns when the boys are more on their own, going and coming, lounging in clubs, hotels, and estaminets, the danger of excessive drinking must be added to the toll, as drink excites the sexual organs and makes men careless.'[128] In no time there was a roaring trade between Haig's hungry legion and French locals profiting from soldiers who had more than a few different appetites.

Predictably, the selection of rich, fresh food available behind the lines had consequences for stomachs no longer used to it. Veterans later politely told of suffering from diarrhoea as a result, but at the time they had — in the coarse language of farms and factories — a dose of the 'squirts,' 'shits,' or 'trots.'[129] That placed a demand on latrines, which were banks of long-drops without doors for privacy, or, as an unimpressed Rifleman Lockhart experienced, 'simply a deep trench with a pole across.'[130] When full, said latrines were topped with earth and new ones dug.

As well as the behind-the-lines bunkum of parades and inspections of various types — including the occasional 'dangle' parade for detecting venereal disease — there was weapons and fitness training, route marches and frequent trips to the musketry range. Then there were fatigues, the bane of every soldier, more so given a manpower shortage meant infantrymen were co-opted as labourers. Thirty-second Division, for instance, dug new assembly and communication trenches and more than 50 emplacements for trench mortars, and also piped a water supply system up to the front line. Its soldiers dug about 19.6 miles of trenches for burying communication cables, and laid about 160 miles of wiring. It also erected 28 bridges across trench systems for artillery guns, built some 72 emplacements for gas cylinders and then lugged 671 of these cylinders up to the front. The division's men also constructed numerous shell-proof shelters and dugouts for soldiers and storing ammunition.[131] Fatigues meant being put to work on any one of a thousand often back-breaking jobs.

While fatigues were part and parcel of active service, they were also disliked for their around-the-clock nature and the physical strain they placed on already exhausted bodies and minds.[132] Private England whiled away hours making fascines to bolster trench walls: 'Supplied with a coil of wire, some pliers and a quantity of brushwood, you tied the latter into bundles — like peasticks. Given a fine day this was considered "cushy". Sometimes the job would be the more hum-drum one of peeling potatoes — "spud bashing."'[133] For Corporal Arthur Durrant, 18th Durham Light Infantry, it was repairing or digging trenches,[134] while for Private Brookes it was guard duties and night-time carrying parties.[135] Lieutenant Capper's platoon was sent to the Chipilly sawmills, which, despite the demanding work of felling trees with cross-cut saws and axes, 'cheered me very much as it meant an interesting job & comfortable quarters.'[136] Brigade-Major Alexander Johnston, 7th Brigade, was one of several staff officers who noted the knock-on problems this work caused. 'High Command appear unable to understand that troops in the front line get practically no rest during their tour of four to six days there, and that they must have a little rest on coming out if they are to be physically and mentally fit for the intense strain of battles.'[137] It was a valid concern, but with the offensive near and deadlines wafer-thin, it was always destined to fall on deaf ears.

Providing labour for mining was another drain on already tired soldiers. Mining had long been a staple of trench warfare on the Western Front. The Somme was no exception. The mine corridors, often deep underground and hundreds of feet long, were the domain of specialist tunnelling companies comprising men recruited from the pits back home. Their work involved burrowing listening galleries to gather intelligence, digging tunnels to locate and blow up rival German passages; carving dozens of shallow trenches known as 'Russian Saps' under no-man's-land (which would be opened on 1 July for use as trenches, communication lanes or emplacements for machine guns and mortars); and engineering lengthy galleries whose heads were packed with massive explosive charges to obliterate above-ground German defences. Eight of these galleries — two at Mametz, three at Fricourt, two at La Boisselle and one at Beaumont Hamel — were packed with enough ammonal explosive to gouge out craters of such breadth and depth that sightseers to the two surviving Somme voids are still left in awe. Eleven smaller mines were also sunk, nine around Mametz and two at La Boisselle.[138] All of this subterranean work represented an important element of Fourth Army's attack plans, with the explosive-packed mines designed to help infantry cross no-man's-land at key points.

Fourth Army had five tunnelling companies attached. The 252nd operated between Hébuterne and Beaumont Hamel, the 179th from just south of the latter village to La Boisselle, the 178th before Fricourt, the 174th opposite Mametz and the 183rd in the Carnoy–Maricourt sector.[139] Each numbered 344–570 officers and men,[140] and, by the time infantrymen-cum-labourers were added, could total more than 2000 soldiers, or roughly two battalions.[141]

Tunnelling work was high-stress and claustrophobic, and was completed in pitch darkness or the flickering glow of air-starved candles. All engaged in this work risked gas poisoning, tunnel collapse or oblivion if enemy miners detonated a camouflet, a small underground blast. At the tunnel leading to Lochnagar mine near La Boisselle, Private England fretted about 'whether the whole [show] would suddenly go up with a bang.'[142] Rifleman Frederick Williams, 1/9th Londons (Queen Victoria's Rifles), was in the narrow mines — the corridors were just 24 inches square — inherited from the French on Hill 110, near Fricourt. Hand-drawn bellows pumped air down the shaft, he said, but 'even so the air was not good, the temperature was very warm, [and] the light from the candles was reduced to a mere glimmer.'[143] Lieutenant Norman Dixon, attached to 178th Tunnelling Company, was in the shafts that later formed the multiple Tambour explosions near Fricourt. He listened for sounds of German mining activity oscillating through the chalkstone: 'If they were making an explosive chamber to put the charge in, you could hear a much more hollow sound and then, following that, you would hear the sinister sliding of bags of explosives into the chamber, and following that, you got out … if you could … otherwise there would have been no following that.'[144] All knew that silence was essential to secrecy and longevity. That meant no wild swinging of pick or spade. The clay, chalkstone and flint tunnel had to be wetted, sliced out with a spade or bayonet and passed back in sacks for disposal. By the end of June the tunnellers had finished their work and laid the charges. Only repair gangs remained to keep the sap and mine entrances open.

Back above ground, the railway lines feeding Fourth Army's mining and other units with supplies of materiel, ammunition and guns were barely sufficient.[145] Just two track lines approached the battle front between the River Somme and Arras. These spurs converged on

Albert and were offshoots of the Amiens–Doullens–St Pol–Bethune and Amiens–Abbeville–Calais lines. The chief difficulty was that these lines catered to competing demands. Rawlinson inspected portions of the railway system in early April 1916: 'I also went to the station to look at the junction and rail head. It is cramped and wants attention.'[146] About 50 trains a day plied these tracks with cargoes of coal for the railways, munitions factories and the city of Paris.[147] In addition, Fourth Army required 31 trains daily — 11 full of miscellaneous supplies, 14 bearing ammunition, and six carrying reinforcements, remounts and engineering stores.[148] Third Army needed about 28 trains daily. 'These numbers,' wrote the official historian, 'might be expected to rise in times of stress, when there were many wounded, to 70 [for Fourth Army] and 58 [for Third Army] trains respectively.'[149] The only way to achieve this capacity was to cut trains carrying stone to improve roads.[150] Additional track lines were laid at Rawlinson's demand, including a line to a large ammunition dump at Contay, west of Albert. Other improvements included extra railheads — there were 13 in total[151] — and sidings. These railheads were all less than 10 miles from the front, which meant motor- and horse-drawn vehicles were able to transport the freight to more advanced supply dumps.[152] There can be little doubt that the railway network was overburdened, and only just able to provide Fourth and Third Armies with the resources they needed daily and to stockpile for the offensive.[153]

Roads from the railheads into the forward area were too few and of poor quality. Those leading to the pre-war rural service centres just behind the front line — Foncquevillers, Hébuterne, Auchonvillers, Martinsart, Authuille, Aveluy, Albert, Bécourt, Meaulte, Bray, Carnoy, Suzanne and Maricourt, along with others further back — had to suffice. None was designed for either heavy or intensive traffic. Their surfaces were three inches of gravel on a soft chalkstone base and lacked camber for drainage. Brigadier-General Acton Schreiber, Chief Royal Engineer (CRE), III Corps, said this surface disintegrated when penetrated by water and became a gooey slick,[154] causing many a vehicle to slip-slide crazily along. Dirt side roads failed faster. In summer the surfaces held, but in the waterlogged months there was no hope. The laying of hefty planks to form a stable corduroy-like tarmac occurred in places, but mostly not, and there was a distinct lack of shingle, trucks and rollers for the carriageways, which needed widening and turning bays in places. Then there were the rival tasks of supply columns and maintenance gangs. They learned to work around one another.[155] Schreiber said it was 'impossible to exaggerate' the difficulties of maintaining the roads across his and other corps, adding that 'the situation was nothing but a continuous state of insufficient material, transport and men.'[156] Rawlinson left much unsaid when he noted the 'roads and approaches have been carefully prepared.'[157] Everything else suggests the state of the road network was a source of anxiety for Rawlinson before battle, but traffic control and repair prioritisation avoided a breakdown.

Traffic censuses for the Somme reveal the burden on the road network. At Chateau Gate, in the 24 hours to 7 p.m. on 27 June, the traffic included eight infantry battalions, 486 motor cars, 501 lorries, 399 motorcycles, 64 ambulances, 8 water-tank lorries and wagons, 230 men on horseback, 162 general service wagons, 178 bicycles and 11 limbers and wagons belonging to Royal Engineers.[158] Another census was taken at Fricourt cemetery in the 24 hours to 9 a.m. on 22 July. It included 26,536 soldiers, 63 artillery guns, 13 gun carriages, 898 light motor cars and ambulances, 95 buses and light tenders, 617 motorcycles, 813 motor lorries, 3756 horse-drawn wagons, 5404 horses, 1043 bicycles, 10 bulldozers and 8 machine guns.[159] Not all of this traffic was headed in the same direction or at the same speed, which made controlling the flow much more difficult for those tasked with the job.

Traffic-control policy to avoid gridlocked lanes was comprehensive. Supply dumps, refilling points and roads were sign-boarded. Maps showed the respective routes vehicles heading to and from the forward area had to use. Control posts were set up at the entrances and exits of villages and towns, along with crossroads, to regulate traffic flow. The 'duties thrown on the traffic control staff were far heavier than those in a great city,' more so as the offensive neared.[160] Traction engines towing large artillery guns, lorries and horse-drawn wagons laden with ammunition and materiel, and long columns of infantry all converged on the logistics network bound for some destination or another on some kind of essential work. 'Although there were often blocks owing to breakdowns, and delays due to the bad state of the roads,' wrote the official historian, 'the general circulation was never seriously impeded;

but it was sometimes slowed down, and transport was long hours on the road.'[161] The system and rules were enforced by military police, which allowed the logistics network to remain open and the flow of resources forward — although frequently touch-and-go where foot and wheel traffic converged — continued.

Staff Captain Geoffrey Codrington, 63rd Brigade headquarters, explained traffic control on the single-lane road to Bécourt Valley. Nightly in June this road in XV Corps' area was plied by at least 60 three-ton lorries. It was 'controlled on the Railway block system and only a certain number of lorries were admitted to each section at a time. This system was rigidly enforced by a control post on the road. ... The ordinary nightly supply work — rations and R.E. stores — was worked in with the lorries delivering stores for the offensive, on a regular time table, and all lorries had to be clear by daylight.'[162]

These stores and ammunition were accumulated at camouflaged and concealed dumps throughout each divisional sector. Main divisional dumps were about two miles behind the front line and supplied brigade-controlled advanced dumps about three-quarters of a mile from the trenches. RE supply dumps were about 500 yards behind the line. These dumps held all manner of materiel, from timber to corrugated iron, barbed wire to telephone cable, hand grenades to small-arms ammunition (SAA) and flares, screw pickets to sandbags, and tools to food. Ammunition dumps followed a similar format, but due to their explosive potential these were constructed some distance from railheads and roads, and reached by dedicated corduroy carriageways of sturdy timber planks. SAA, grenades and artillery ammunition were stored in boxes or sheds and camouflaged to avoid the prying eyes of enemy bombers. These payloads were then transported forward by lorries and horse-drawn wagons. By 20 June the allocation of ammunition to the guns was all but complete. Thereafter projectiles were stored at the railhead dumps. The dumps were laden with materiel and ammunition by late June, but only time and the outcome of the offensive's initial stages would reveal whether or not they held sufficient.

The perennial difficulty was how to get materials from the forward supply dumps into the front line.[163] Roads and tracks close to and leading into the trenches were often open to direct enemy observation by day and searching artillery fire by night. Transports foolish enough to use them would be shelled and probably destroyed. The solution was, as mentioned earlier, to use resting infantry as night-time carrying parties, but that was not without problems, noted Captain George Fenton, 151st Field Company, RE: 'Working parties and carrying parties were provided to assist, but the materials, especially the barbed wire, rapidly dwindled in transit up, as the bearers floundered in the mire, and then tipped the troublesome load into the nearest shell-hole rather than carry it further.'[164] Private Charles Binstead, 1st Hampshires, knew carrying duty well:

> Sometimes it was food in sandbags, water in petrol tins or ammunition, wire and post for wiring. ... It was hard work as the ground was thick with mud and the communication trenches a quarter filled with water and where the duckboards have floated away from over the sump holes it would be about 4 ft deep, many a night we would walk on the top [out of the trench] and take a chance on what the Germans threw over.[165]

While there was undoubtedly some loss of materiel lugged forward, the vast majority of soldiers knew first-hand the importance of their work and toiled hard to keep the front line supplied.

Providing water for men, mules and horses was a high priority. As more divisions arrived on the Somme so the demand for drinking, washing, bathing and laundry water rose. Water supplies were organised by Fourth Army and implemented by each of its army corps. Responsibility for the network of pumps, filtration units, storage tanks, bore holes and a complex network of 4- and 6-inch pipes leading close to the front line belonged to corps engineers. Each corps possessed 80 water carts with 200-gallon tanks, while Fourth Army retained a fleet of 303 water lorries, with tanks that each held up to 550 gallons. Water points near the trenches consisted of 2000-gallon waterproof canvas tanks on the ground with refilling hoses and taps for supply. Looking ahead, Brigadier-General George Cartwright, CRE, VIII Corps, noted 'arrangements for pushing forward water supplies in the event of an advance was deemed to be of vital importance as in this chalk country the wells were slow filling and gave but a limited supply.'[166] For the moment there was enough water to slake demand, and specifically to quench the thirst of thousands of soldiers exhausted by endless training for the Somme.

FOURTH ARMY'S assault divisions underwent battle training well behind the lines in May–June 1916. Each battalion completed about two weeks of manoeuvres, which were based on best-practice, or doctrinal, pamphlets issued to officers by GHQ. *SS109: Training of Divisions for Offensive Action*, for instance, was designed to ensure uniform standards of tactical proficiency across battalions and corps. It was expanded on by *Fourth Army Tactical Notes*. 'Mid-June, 1916,' wrote Lieutenant-Colonel Crozier, 'sees us back near Forceville, polishing the book of words of the "Acid Test."'[167] These pamphlets gave guidance on all manner of subjects, from trench-to-trench attacks, the setting of and consolidation of captured objectives, use of Stokes mortars and Lewis guns, communication with other units, headquarters and aeroplanes, and importantly the actual formation of attack. Both emphasised the infantry's role over that of the artillery.[168] 'Troops once launched to the attack,' stated *SS109*, 'must push on at all costs till the final objective is reached.'[169] Of course there would be heavy casualties, it said, but 'the magnitude of the interests at stake necessitate the greatest self-sacrifice from one and all.'[170]

The advance into and beyond the enemy front line was to be achieved by old-school linear attacks, or wave after wave of infantry pressing forward. This linear-wave structure was widely adopted — albeit, as will be seen in later chapters, with some variance between battalions, brigades and divisions. Objectives for each wave were to be clearly defined, with each adding fresh impetus to the advance of the one preceding it.[171] 'The attack must aim at continuity and must be driven home without intermission, so that the attack gradually works forward till the endurance of the enemy is broken.'[172] Units were to practise dealing with localised hold-ups on the battlefield, but these were portrayed as little more than temporary impasses and certainly nothing akin to the outright failure of an attack.[173] Four-wave attacks were considered ideal and most likely to produce results, three-wave attacks less so, with two- and one-line enterprises thought likely to fail.[174] Each battalion was to be proficient in leap-frogging others in order to achieve its own more distant set of objectives.[175] Captured ground was to be quickly consolidated and flanks protected against counterattack. In brief, the attack structure was that of an irrepressible, multi-layered infantry juggernaut, but nowhere, if all went wrong, was the potential for multiple battalions to be concertinaed in no-man's-land and shot to pieces considered.

So it was that tactical-level units and formations rehearsed their schemes of attack. Each division trained on land selected because of its resemblance to their part of the battlefield. Opinions on the merits of the training varied: 10th Essex alleged its routine was 'never once monotonous,'[176] but 2nd Essex captured the mood when it described the schedule as one of 'monotonous repetition.'[177] British and German trenches, along with known machine-gun strongpoints and dugouts that had been identified by the RFC's photographs were marked by shallow scrapes of earth, marker flags or strips of calico tape.[178] Eighth Division's historian summed it up when he said the ground had been specially prepared to represent, as far as possible, the features and defences of the sector to be attacked.[179] One of the benefits, said 18th (Eastern) Division's somewhat upbeat historian, among others, was that on the day of battle 'each man knew the exact spot he was to make for, and what to do when he got there.'[180]

This was an advantage that soldiers recognised. Lieutenant Moore said his men 'probably knew the outline of the German trench system better than they [the enemy] did. Every corner, every trench junction was engraved in our minds.'[181] Corporal Norman Menzies, 2nd Royal Scots Fusiliers, added that every man had 'his job explained to him, and each battalion had its objective, and so everything was prepared for a real advance. Also every platoon officer and platoon sergeant had a map of the German territory, which we had all seen.'[182] Private Leslie Bell, 10th Royal Inniskilling Fusiliers, believed his battalion could have attacked 'eyes shut [as] we had practised it so much.'[183] Rifleman Tennant was overwhelmed by 'thorough instructions as to where to make for.'[184] Captain Wilfred 'Billie' Nevill, 8th East Surreys — who went on to find lasting fame and death on 1 July — felt that 'altogether everything is going on quite smoothly. ... The Company is going on A1 and doing awfully well.'[185] The repetition was boring, but soldiers well knew its purpose was to give them every opportunity to produce results on the battlefield.

Nineteenth (Western) Division's 14-day training schedule was typical. Platoons practised getting into and out of deep trenches, bayonet fighting, fire discipline and rapid reloading, movement in extended order, reconnaissance and unit intercommunication, and a variety of other exercises.[186] Lewis gunners and Stokes mortar teams were given instructions specific to their weapons, usually on deploying them as mobile firepower and laying either destructive or suppressing fire on a specific point of resistance. Specialist signalling, machine-gun, engineer, pioneer and medical units rehearsed their roles alongside the infantry and also separately.[187] These exercises were repeated at platoon, company, battalion and brigade levels for greater co-ordination and celerity of execution. This also ensured that on the training ground multiple units could, as part of a larger formation, seamlessly deploy and move forward under mock shellfire and distant small-arms fire represented by marker flags and umpires with whistles, and then defend just-captured ground.[188] The idea was to bring all units up to a homogenous level of tactical skill, but no matter how well intended, the training obviously lacked the realism of battle.

Platoon commander Lieutenant William Colyer, 2nd Royal Dublin Fusiliers, set the scene with more than a hint of scepticism:

> The whole of the division was assembled and grouped for the attack. After the usual explanations and pow-wows, beginning from the brass-hats and commanding officers and finishing with the platoon officers and section leaders, we moved across country against imaginary Bosche trenches. As we went along the various bodies of men unfolded themselves into smaller groups, and eventually into extended order, as per programme, according to the amount of opposition which we were supposed to be encountering. After some time, having advanced a great distance and captured an immense tract of country (with such surprising ease that we all felt it was a pity we hadn't thought of doing it this way before) a halt would be called.[189]

Complainants inevitably targeted staff officers, or so-called brass-hats. Private Senescall said these officers explained the purpose of the training in over-simplified terms: 'All we had to do was to advance for three quarters of a mile. ... That was what we were told and with the discipline and belief that Brass Hats were demi-gods we believed it.'[190] Private Stanley Henderson, 16th Northumberland Fusiliers, thought the rehearsals 'seemed just as simple as walking through a park with no opposition.'[191] Pollard was more cynical: 'We rehearsed taking Serre three times a day; it was a joke. ... It was outlined that we would take the first line in so many minutes, on to the second line in so many minutes, and so on. Well, it didn't seem very practical to me.'[192] A somewhat highly strung Captain Upcott had a particular aversion to bayonet training: 'Mentally it destroys my temper for several hours. My views on physical training can hardly be put on paper. I have always disliked being made an ape of.'[193] Soldiers and to a lesser extent junior commanders were inveterate grumblers, although, with the benefit of hindsight, their complaints about over-simplifying the hoped-for flow of battle were not entirely without merit.

Further up the military hierarchy there were also several who questioned aspects of the training. Brigadier-General James Jardine, 97th Brigade, was concerned that the infantry was being drilled to advance too far behind mock barrages, and that on battle day ran the risk of being caught in no-man's-land by alert German machine-gunners when the supporting British shellfire moved on. He told Rawlinson that the infantry should be within 30–40 yards of the German trenches when the shellfire lifted, and that a small number of casualties due to friendly fire was also to be expected: 'I could see he did not like what I said for he replied, "Oh, 30 to 40 yards!!" "Well, Sir," I said, "that's what the Japanese did [in the Russo-Japanese war of 1904–5]." And his reply was, "Oh, the Japanese," in a rather sneering way.'[194] Another, Brigade-Major Johnston, the staff officer at 7th Brigade headquarters, queried the value of intensive training:

These very detailed Training Programmes seem to regimental officers as little more than eyewash to alleviate the suspicions of Superior Authority that without them troops will perform no training, or the wrong kind of training. The programmes are, however, generally cut down to meet day-to-day conditions, experienced commanding officers using some discretion in the matter.[195]

Overall these varied complaints were given little consideration by division, corps and army headquarters staffs that were almost entirely focused on installing a basic level of tactical know-how rather than addressing more qualitative questions about the purpose and value of training.

Criticisms designed to improve the training and standard attained by the various units were dealt out by officer observers. At the boots-on-the-ground level it was platoon and company commanders who provided critique. As Private Pollard recalled, all the 'mistakes of the day were later gone over.'[196] First Essex said great care was taken to 'remedy defects, and particular attention was paid to efficient mopping up and consolidation of strongpoints.'[197] Some platoons and companies learned their work quickly. Lieutenant Douglas Branson, 1/4th York & Lancasters, said his platoon was 'praised for our attack practices while others get the reverse.'[198] More pointed suggestions came from battalion, brigade and divisional commanders inspecting formation manoeuvres.[199] Corporal Coppard explained how this worked: 'Staff officers, red-tabbed and beribboned, dashed all over the place with immense bravado, giving their orders and comments in crackling military style. I certainly admired them for their immaculate appearance. Most Tommies looked such a scruffy lot by comparison.'[200] Two officers of 10th Essex commented dryly that 'We soon got the hang of our [divisional] commander's instructions.'[201] Lieutenant Colyer remembered pauses to allow staff officers to 'ride up again and there would be criticisms, more explanations and pow-wows.'[202] Schooling an entire army in the template of attack to be used on the first day of the Somme was not without its challenges, and the onus of responsibility fell largely on the tactical-level officers accompanying their men into battle.

Part of that work involved discussing the battlefield and objectives with fellow officers and their men. Captain Duncan Martin, 9th Devons, famously made a plasticine model of the land and reckoned his battalion would be raked by fire from a specific strongpoint near Mametz.[203] He was not alone; Private Wilfred Crook, 1st Somerset Light Infantry, and his platoon also 'carefully studied models and the layout of the network of trenches.'[204] Some platoons supplemented their first-hand knowledge of the battlefield with maps showing objective lines and enemy defences. Others, such as one Liverpool Pals platoon going over the top at

Montauban, were shown through 'the trench periscope the ground over which we had to advance.'[205] The commander of 9th Royal Irish Rifles, Crozier, explained how his company commanders prepared for attacking Schwaben Redoubt: 'I lecture the whole battalion in a big barn, aided by a cloth map twenty feet square. ... I hear each company commander lecture his company in the same way. We are word-perfect. Will our acting be as good? Shall we play our parts well?'[206] Come late June, Haig was pleased with the results. 'Several have said that they have never before been so instructed and informed of the nature of the operation before them.'[207] He clearly wanted to believe that pre-Somme training had started the process of converting his 'collection' of divisions into a well-trained army. But he was wrong to place store in assessments obviously tailored to please his ear. Besides, it was far too early to determine whether the training was even suitable for the type of attack Haig envisaged.

For the six corps commanders, the weeks leading to 1 July were jammed with administrative work, inspections, conferences, meetings, reconnoitring of the ground, and assessment of divisional training. To these ends, Rawlinson thought his corps commanders were the 'best we have got,' 'know their job' and 'the great majority are proved fighters.'[208] However, 'VIII Corps is the weak one.'[209] Lieutenant-General Sir Henry Horne, XV Corps, found it 'very hot walking about the trenches' opposite Fricourt, and said he had yet to familiarise himself with the divisions under his command.[210] Lieutenant-General Sir Walter Congreve, VC, commanding XIII Corps, spent much of May–June meeting with other commanders, inspecting training and assessing preparations, whether ammunition stores, artillery or roads.[211] Lieutenant-General Sir Thomas Morland, X Corps, was similarly occupied,[212] as was Lieutenant-General Sir Aylmer Hunter-Weston, VIII Corps. Hunter-Weston was 'entirely content' that all possible had been done to ensure success on 1 July, which included his critiquing the tactical training organised by divisional commanders.[213] He wanted VIII Corps' attack to retain its structure for as long as possible, and for reserve troops to be intelligently committed to battle. 'This has been a very pronounced fault in most of the training exercises that I have seen,' he wrote.[214] These commanders all told Haig and Rawlinson that their preparations and training were thorough and proceeding to plan. 'Work of all kinds is being pushed forward as rapidly as possible,' wrote Rawlinson in a summary of corps-level preparations.[215] It was scarcely surprising that on the eve of battle Haig assessed his subordinates, whose busy schedules and upbeat feedback he was well aware of, as 'full of confidence.'[216]

By midnight on 23 June, Haig had all but run out of time to prepare for battle. Artillery, infantry and aircraft were all forward, ammunition stockpiled and distributed, jumping-off lines prepared and the troops trained according to the latest tactical doctrine. The logistics network feeding resources onto the Somme front was groaning under the strain of peak capacity, but was nonetheless managing to fulfil its role. Overworked infantry, pioneer and engineering units revealed a shortage of manpower, but morale remained firm. Against this backcloth, the pace of work was more frenetic than efficient. Soldiers wrote of relentless, mostly one-dimensional training, yet their superiors told Haig and Rawlinson all was going well. The template training in linear-wave tactics was useful but over-simplified exercises, was predomininatly infantry focused, marginalised the role of the enemy, lacked realism and assumed the battle would unfold almost exactly as planned. Everything, then, hinged on whether the artillery could smash a path forward for and support the infantry on battle day, both jobs requiring huge supplies of guns and ammunition. At the time, few were asking tough questions about whether this plan would succeed, or if it was well enough resourced, and certainly not Haig, Rawlinson or their corps commanders. Optimists outnumbered realists and the belief shared by Haig and Rawlinson the day before battle was that everything possible had been done to ensure success on 1 July. So began the final countdown to a day that would be remembered as Britain's worst-ever military tragedy.

CHAPTER 3

'Artillery is Decisive'

German Second Army and XIV Reserve Corps prepare for battle, January 1915 to 23 June 1916

*'In April 1916 the English positions before us stirred into
life, where before they had been quiet.'*[1]
— *Unteroffizier* Peter Collet, Infantry Regiment 66

MUD-SPATTERED GERMAN soldiers cocked their weary eyes
skyward from beneath pork-pie caps, spiked leather *Pickelhauben* or the
occasional coalscuttle helmet when any aircraft zipped overhead.[2] By the
spring of 1916 they reckoned most aircraft were British and these, wrote
Vizefeldwebel Georg Frisch, Reserve Infantry Regiment 109 (RIR109),
snooped deep behind the German lines or swooped low and peppered
trenches and artillery emplacements with machine-gun fire.[3] Soon enough
the gripes began. 'Actually, where are our planes?' pondered *Oberst* Robert
Mack, commander of Bavarian Field Artillery Regiment 19 (BFAR19).[4] It
was a fair question, and hardly surprising given the numerical superiority
enjoyed by the Royal Flying Corps (RFC) in early 1916.[5] As *Leutnant* Paul
Fiedel, Infantry Regiment 23 (IR23), said of aerial dogfights, 'All too often
the German trench garrison gave an anxious glance skyward as the more
numerous enemy aircraft fell like hawks onto a dove.'[6]

The dangerous work of German aerial observation continued.
Fliegertruppoffizier Arthur Koch, Artillery Air Detachment 221, arrived

on the Somme with his squadron in March 1916 and by June most of its flights produced aerial skirmishes.[7] The squadron was occasionally put to work photographing British positions astride the Albert–Bapaume highway, but was more often used by *Generalleutnant* Hermann von Stein's XIV Reserve Corps for target-spotting and for observing the fall of shellfire for 26th Reserve and 28th Reserve Divisions' gunners. Dogfights, flying accidents and casualties meant the four-aeroplane squadron of LVG biplanes was frequently at three-quarter strength. 'Our artillery is glad when we can at least keep the British airmen from their neck,' said Koch.[8] By early June the build-up of British artillery, aircraft and troops opposite XIV Reserve Corps left him in no doubt as to exactly what was afoot: 'An attack is to be expected.'[9]

Such news was no surprise to the senior German commanders. *General-der-Infanterie* Erich von Falkenhayn, Chief of General Staff, Supreme Army Command, later referred to the Anglo-French attack as 'long-expected and hoped-for.'[10] Falkenhayn's subordinate, *General-der-Infanterie* Fritz von Below, commanding Second Army on the Somme, had anticipated a British attack north of the waterway from as early as February 1916.[11] As the year progressed, the Danzig-born general — who had an impressive moustache and unkempt eyebrows that made him appear wild-eyed — had grown increasingly alarmed at the accumulation of enemy forces and materiel. In March, 62-year-old Below had proposed a bold thrust to 'pre-empt the British and throw their plans into confusion.'[12] In theory it was a grand idea; in practice there was not enough time or resources.[13] Below restated his concerns in late May, once again championing a multi-phase operation on a 12.4-mile front to a depth of 15.5 miles, with a mid-June start:[14] 'The attack cannot begin soon enough. The British have been reinforced so strongly north of the Somme that there can hardly be any remaining doubt concerning their plans for an offensive.'[15] It was unclear, he said, exactly what part of XIV Reserve Corps' lines would be targeted and how, and whether the British would launch their attack within days, or were 'waiting for further reinforcements, or an improvement in the training of their troops.'[16] Below was back in touch with Supreme Army Command on 2 June, this time with plans for a limited pre-emptive strike between St Pierre Division and Ovillers,[17] effectively conceding that a larger operation was unviable, but signalling that this otherwise anonymous tract of land needed to be held as a priority.

Two days later the Russian army began its Brusilov Offensive in Galicia — nowadays western Ukraine — which proved to be the end of Below's proposed plans to disrupt the British accumulation of men and materiel. General Aleksei Brusilov's four armies buckled the Austro-Hungarian defensive line in Galicia after a short, sharp preparatory bombardment on 4 June. Within the month the Austro-Hungarian army, unable to concentrate its reserves to stem the wide-fronted breakthough, had lost 350,000 prisoners and 400 artillery guns. Tireless, quick-thinking Falkenhayn later agreed to fling all available reserves into the threatened area, lest 'we should have seen a complete collapse of the whole front in Galicia.'[18] He continued: 'There is no doubt that even so limited a withdrawal of reserves made the position on the Western Front much less favourable. The intention of nipping in the bud, by means of a heavy counter-attack, the offensive then being prepared by the English had to be dropped.'[19]

So it was that Below's requests for reinforcements in June were met by Falkenhayn only as far as events elsewhere allowed.[20] By 1 July, XIV Reserve Corps had five divisions — 2nd Guards Reserve, 52nd Infantry, 26th Reserve, 28th Reserve and 12th Infantry — in the line between Monchy-au-Bois and the River Somme. Another, 10th Bavarian Infantry, was in immediate support, about one-third in the line and two-thirds just behind. In army reserve were the three divisions of VI Reserve Corps: 185th Infantry around Bapaume, 12th Reserve near Rancourt and 11th Reserve much further back around Marcoing. Many of VI Reserve Corps' artillery batteries had been attached to Stein's XIV Reserve Corps.[21] South of the river, Below had seven more divisions. With these resources in mind, Falkenhayn rejected a proposed tactical withdrawal from the Somme that would have seen 'excellent positions' exchanged for 'others less good.'[22] He also believed the French were too weakened by Verdun to play a major role in any Somme offensive, placed little store in the fighting capabilities of the British New Armies,[23] and reckoned Second Army could weather the looming storm.[24] In effect, Verdun- and Galicia-focused Falkenhayn was betting that Below and Stein had the resources and defensive positions to defeat the looming Allied attack.[25]

German commanders refined their views on the extent and focus of the Allied offensive throughout June.[26] Falkenhayn initially expected Alsace-Lorraine would be the focal point and then, when the Picardy–Artois area appeared more likely, that *Kronprinz* (Prince) Rupprecht of Bavaria's Sixth Army at Arras would be targeted.[27] He considered a pre-emptive attack there, but Sixth Army did not have the men or guns.[28] Prince Rupprecht had noted the shift of British and French divisions south and, along with prisoner interrogations and artillery activity on Second Army's front, concluded that an offensive in that area was 'imminent.'[29] Stein agreed, and by 23 June was telling Supreme Army Command that 'I expect the enemy will attack the whole [XIV Reserve Corps] front. He possesses the forces to do so.'[30] In early June, Below forecast British attacks on the Gommecourt and Fricourt salients, accompanied by an attempt to hold the intervening ground with shellfire or a minor attack.[31] His opinion evolved with Prince Rupprecht's and Stein's. 'The supposed frontage of the enemy's offensive was fairly clearly established [by late June] as extending from the neighbourhood of Gommecourt, on the north, to the neighbourhood of the Roman road about 8 kilometres [5 miles] south of the Somme [River].'[32]

Uncompromising Falkenhayn had already prescribed how such a defensive battle should be waged. Not an inch of territory should be ceded, he said, even if it would result in better-placed defensive positions.[33] In 1915 he had issued guidance on constructing defensive positions,[34] which was mostly confined to the roles of infantry and machine guns.[35] The content had been derived from battlefield experience; it recognised that enemy artillery firepower was critical, and also that the infantry had an increasing arsenal of defensive mechanisms, such as machine guns, available. Falkenhayn — who was said to be a man of 'excellent disposition' — insisted that the 'thin' defensive systems of 1914–15 should be expanded, with second- and possibly third-trench systems constructed behind the first.[36] Each position would be independently defensible and consist of two trenches. The first position would be the main defensive line, while the second needed to be sufficiently far back that it could not be hit by concentrated hostile shellfire and required a fresh deployment of enemy artillery and infantry to be attacked.[37] This front-loaded defensive scheme was implemented through XIV Reserve Corps and Second Army in 1915, and with time evolved into the formidable defence-in-depth schemes in place throughout late 1916 and into 1917.

Stein's XIV Reserve Corps numbered about 95,000 men, most serving in the regiments of its regionally recruited infantry divisions. North to south,[38] 2nd Guards Reserve Division (*Generalleutnant* Richard *Freiherr* von Süsskind-Schwendi) and 52nd Infantry Division (*Generalleutnant* Karl von Borries) held the ground around Gommecourt and Serre, while 26th Reserve Division (*Generalleutnant* Franz *Freiherr* von Soden) was in the line from just south of Serre, via Beaumont Hamel and Thiepval, to Ovillers. Twenty-eighth Reserve Division (*Generalleutnant* Ferdinand von Hahn) was ensconced around La Boisselle, Fricourt and Mametz, while 12th Infantry Division (*Generalleutnant* Martin Châles de Beaulieu) was around Montauban and south to the River Somme. Tenth Bavarian Infantry Division (*Generalmajor* Hermann *Ritter* von Burkhardt) was in corps reserve. These divisions were drawn mostly from Württemberg and Baden. Other units present had been recruited from the Hanseatic towns or were populated by Mecklenburgers, Westphalians, Thuringians, Saxons, Bavarians and Rhinelanders.[39] It was these men who, in the 18 months to 1 July, turned XIV Reserve Corps' positions into formidable defensive strongholds.

Stein's corps held 28 miles of dog-legged trenches and rolling downs astride the River Ancre. A pilot flying high enough might have likened the front line here to a wonky human head in profile. Gommecourt salient took the appearance of a bushy eyebrow, while the terrain around Beaumont Hamel more or less marked the tip of the nose, with the Ancre crossing the trench line at roughly the location of the nostrils. Thiepval was the philtrum, Leipzig Redoubt and La Boisselle marked the upper and lower lips, while the marked curve of the line around the Fricourt–Mametz salient was the chin. Stein's corps had held this land since 1914, first against the French, and from August 1915 opposite the British.

Below and Stein had long regarded the ridge between Pozières on the Albert–Bapaume highway and St Pierre Divion in the River Ancre valley as the cornerstone of their defences north of the River Somme.[40] The importance of this ground was first recognised as early as 1914, and Soden's 26th Reserve Division had spent months installing successive parallelograms of trenches supported by powerful redoubts studded with fortified villages and brimming with carefully sited machine guns. If the British were to hold this high ground they could observe large portions of the German defensive network crisscrossing its eastern slopes as they tapered off towards Bapaume, and could therefore tellingly direct artillery fire. It was this ridgeline — around the notorious Schwaben Redoubt, on the lofty heights above Thiepval, then across gentle slopes leading up from Ovillers and La Boisselle to Pozières at its highest point — that Below and Stein identified as a lynchpin of their positions. *Leutnant-der-Reserve* Matthaus Gerster, Reserve Infantry Regiment 119 (RIR119), explained the danger posed by the loss of Schwaben Redoubt:

> They [the British] would be sitting on the highest part of the
> Thiepval Plateau [on the Pozières Ridge], able to observe far into
> the rear areas and to overlook all the approach routes and battery
> positions, especially those north of the Ancre. Thiepval itself
> would have been threatened from the rear, [and to the north]
> St Pierre Divion would have fallen and Beaumont Hamel would
> have become untenable, because it would have been overlooked
> from three sides.[41]

So, too, Pozières, Ovillers and La Boisselle would undoubtedly have been lost. German commanders were blunt about the importance of the ridge and Schwaben Redoubt: 'If the enemy gets established there, he is to be ejected at once.'[42] It was for this reason that Below and Stein spared no effort in turning the approaches to Pozières Ridge into a defensive fortress.

This thinking was underpinned by concerns about what might happen if the expected Allied offensive punched through the German lines south of the River Ancre, more so if these gains were exploited in a northeasterly direction and driven forcefully towards the Arras area.[43] In effect this would unravel Second Army's northern battle sector, catch Prince Rupprecht's Sixth Army on its exposed southern flank and potentially complement any eastwards drive by French forces in that vicinity. If this happened, German commanders recognised that, at least hypothetically, there would be far-reaching strategic consequences for Second Army's tenure on the Somme.

Further north, XIV Reserve Corps' sector was equally sensitive to a British advance. Here the Redan Ridge–Beaucourt and Serre–Grandcourt Spurs, both terminating in the Ancre valley, would potentially see Stein's, Soden's and Borries' positions north of that waterway unravelled,[44] followed by those immediately to the south. These spurs, wrote *Stabsarzt* Dr Richard Schwartz, Reserve Infantry Regiment 121 (RIR121), yielded extensive views 'of the Ancre valley and beyond to the heights of Thiepval and Pozières.'[45] If the Serre–Grandcourt Spur, also known as Serre Heights, fell, 'Beaumont [Hamel] and Thiepval would have automatically fallen,' added *Hauptmann* Georg *Freiherr* von Holtz, RIR121.[46] Soden's gun lines north of the Ancre would become untenable, denuding Thiepval and Pozières of northern flank support. If this happened, the 26th's positions south of the river would be jeopardised. 'Had Serre heights fallen into the possession of the enemy the whole [divisional] front could have been shaken. The danger was therefore enormous,' wrote Soden in his post-war memoir.[47] It was with good reason that Stein's estate north of the Ancre was also said to be 'impregnable' to enemy attack.[48]

Not so XIV Reserve Corps' defences south of Fricourt, namely at Mametz and Montauban. Here the trench systems held by 28th Reserve and 12th Infantry Divisions zigzagged over a tangle of shallow valleys and waterways 2.5–4 miles in advance of the main ridgeline, which continued between Pozières and Longueval. Most of these positions were open to at least some observation from the British or French lines. Both divisions regarded Hill 110 as must-hold ground because it overlooked their defences immediately around Fricourt and Mametz.[49] However, German records are silent on the tactical and strategic value of the gentle Mametz–Montauban inclines, which tapered from the Pozières–Longueval ridge. This was mostly because Below and Stein expected the main British attack further north, and the absence of major actions in this area since 1914 implied that the Allies attributed little importance to it. Probably all of these factors contributed to XIV Reserve Corps attaching less tactical and strategic importance to the Mametz–Montauban area than others further north, and as a result it was comparatively under-developed as a defensive stronghold.

By mid-May 1916, Stein's headquarters was circulating doctrine that expanded on Falkenhayn's original guidance.[50] Emphasis remained on using the front line to blunt an enemy attack. Stein's guidelines laid down the best defensive practices for infantry, artillery, machine-gunners, signallers, engineers and so forth. They also detailed the construction of trenches, strongpoints, dugouts and communication lines, the use of barbed wire and the conversion of villages into defensive obstacles, among myriad other subjects. This was a common-sense guide based on experience.[51] Soden, for instance, later noted that the Battle of Serre against the French in June 1915 had been 'extremely instructive preparation for the Battle of the Somme,'[52] and also that his defences reflected the lessons of fighting at Arras, Champagne and Verdun,[53] namely in their ability to withstand heavy artillery fire. Châles de Beaulieu — who had a talent for talking up his own game ahead of practising it — said the Arras battles of 1915 showed that well-constructed positions could, even if heavily shelled, 'be held against repeated assaults.'[54] Stein's directives became the benchmark for the construction of defensive positions throughout most of his corps, and broadly encapsulated practices already well established in many of his divisions.

The eight-day Battle of Serre against the French in June 1915 offered particularly valuable insights for Below, Stein, Soden, Borries and Hahn in preparing their defences. The 6–13 June attack by the French was presaged by a massive bombardment west of Serre, followed by infantry breaking into 52nd's and 26th's lines. Fighting devolved into costly thrust and counterthrust. It ended with XIV Reserve Corps retaining the high ground around Serre and on Redan Ridge, and the French clinging to lower ground to the west. From this battle, Below, Stein and several of their divisional commanders learned how to prepare their positions to withstand attack and bombardment, use defensive artillery, locate and apply reinforcements to battle, seal off enemy break-ins, and maintain lines of communication and command. Soden said these lessons were of the greatest value:[55] 'At the time nobody fully appreciated the devastating effect of concentrated artillery fire against the forward trenches.'[56] Below further noted the importance of spotting attacks early, and giving defenders enough warning to exit their dugouts and man the parapet quickly.[57] These lessons were emphasised in Stein's directive and formed the basis of Soden's, Borries', Hahn's and, later on, Süsskind-Schwendi's defensive schemes.

In his document, Stein said all trenches were to be suitable for firing from, and that the first defensive line must not yield in the event of an enemy attack. He insisted that the front-line position comprise three separate trenches, rather than two, and that each should have two rows of barbed wire in front as an impediment to enemy infantry. Each infantry company sector should have communication trenches linking these three first-position trenches, and each battalion sector should have separate communication trenches for troops coming into and leaving the line. The intermediate and second-line trench systems should consist of two trenches, each with two rows of wire and the same number of communication trenches as in the first line, while the third line should be dug to the depth of a spade head, and several strongpoints housing machine guns established. The 'thin' defensive lines of 1914 and early 1915 were soon replaced by increasingly deep, sophisticated networks of trenches, strongpoints, fortified villages and obstacles.

Carefully deployed machine guns were integral to XIV Reserve Corps' defences. By 30 June each of Stein's regiments had at least 12 guns operated by specialist companies, often supplemented by independent machine-gun units, captured weapons and at least 30 *Musketen* (light machine guns) per division. The 26th, for instance, had at least 90 heavy machine guns and 30 *Musketen* distributed throughout its sector.[58] These were to be employed at commanding points in the second and third trenches of the front-line system, and fired over the front-line trench into no-man's-land.[59] 'The possibility of delivering both frontal and flanking fire must not be forgotten,' wrote Stein of deploying water-cooled MG08 machine guns that fired 500–600 rounds a minute to an observable range of about 1900 yards.[60] 'The better the first trench is defended by flanking fire, especially that of machine guns, the more can the infantry garrison be reduced.'[61] Machine-gun posts were camouflaged and dummy positions created to conceal the exact location of weapons, which were to be kept in dugouts during bombardments and only deployed when an enemy attack began. 'It is taken for granted that the crews are trained in firing without the sledge [base for the gun], on a pedestal built up of sand bags.'[62] Stein wanted his positions protected by multiple killing zones, or areas of no-man's-land where multiple machine guns co-ordinated their fire to devastate any enemy infantry attack.

At La Boisselle, for instance, *Hauptmann* Otto Wagener, a specialist machine-gun officer in Reserve Infantry Regiment 110 (RIR110), set up the notorious killing zones of Mash and Sausage Valleys. Wagener, who in the 1930s became a confidant to Adolf Hitler, possessed a keen eye, understood how to adapt defences to the land, and searched out the best machine-gun sites for achieving interlocking and flanking fields of fire.[63] It was this architect of death's crossfire killing traps that caused thousands of British casualties in 8th and 34th Divisions in an unwavering fusillade of bullets on the first day of the Somme.

Stein set XIV Reserve Corps to implementing his defensive doctrine, the hefty workload falling squarely on the rank and file, as well as men such as Wagener. 'Men are not eager to take part in this kind of work; they must be kept to it with a firm hand,' wrote Stein.[64] 'This task becomes less difficult when the men have once realised from experience how important the work is to their own personal safety.' Stein insisted that no effort was to be spared in ensuring his corps could fend off a major attack and believed the results would be realised when the Allied offensive arrived.[65]

WORK BEGAN WITH revitalising the existing positions as winter faded into spring in 1916. Dugouts, headquarters and observation posts were mined into the ground and camouflaged, as were machine-gun posts. Trench walls were lined with chicken mesh, woven brushwood and planks of timber to reduce the likelihood of their collapsing under shellfire or rain. Duckboards were laid, more trenches were dug with steel loopholes for sentries built into their parapets. Barbed-wire entanglements were thickened, and further back more artillery gun pits were dug. Soden said there was a 'feverish development of the positions, including the Intermediate Position and the Second and Third Positions.'[66] The number of microphone-equipped 'Moritz' underground telephone interception stations was increased. 'Church bells, sirens and gongs were installed to warn of gas attacks.'[67] Large stores of ammunition, including hand grenades, were placed in shell-proof shelters, as far forward as the front line itself.[68] This labour-intensive, spring–summer programme consumed large volumes of materiel, time and labour.

Leutnant-der-Reserve Paul Heizmann, RIR109, recalled the toil at La Boiselle. He wrote of lugging timber, knife rests, trench mortars and ammunition, sandbags, coils of wire and pickets into the trenches:

> Over time, at the cost of strenuous labour, which robbed us of
> our nights, we produced a first-class trench system ... which
> in our sector, not including the long communication trench
> to Contalmaison, eventually reached twenty-seven kilometres
> [16.8 miles]. ... How we sweated, what labour it cost, to link up the
> saps in the left-hand sector! What care we took over dugouts for
> the regiment, battalion, kitchens, aid post and the mortar pits! We
> made every piece of ground into a fortress.[69]

Unteroffizier Otto Lais, a machine-gunner in Infantry Regiment 169, laboured through the spring of 1916 on the gentle slopes before Serre, which he later said became an 'ingeniously organised infantry fortress' that would be deadly to the attacker:[70]

> 'Curse and work' was our trench-motto in the positions in front
> of Bapaume in the Artois! This motto was a reference to the
> 'endless' digging, to the drawing of wire entanglements, and to the
> never-ending construction of dugouts. One swore, one grumbled,
> one groaned at the nightly hauling of the rolls of barbed wire,
> the barricades, the wooden frames and all the other 'treasured'
> things in the life of an infantryman. Particularly 'popular'
> was the enjoyment we infantrymen had hauling the hundred-
> weight mines [for mortars]. We have the feeling that nowhere
> on the whole Western Front is there as much graft, digging and
> tunnelling as here.[71]

Vizefeldwebel Albert Fickendey, Infantry Regiment 66 (IR66), described the months leading up to Stein's directive and immediately after as 'der Maulwurfskrieg,' or 'the mole's war.' He said spades and picks were used so frequently there was no time for the blades to rust. The men soon became accustomed to the graft: 'Some, who previously sat behind desks in educational institutions and had enlisted voluntarily now spat in their hands in despair. Where had their well-manicured hands of study gone? They had been replaced by hard, calloused German fists that were not afraid of work!'[72]

Materials used in the building of these trench systems were the domain of construction companies, which comprised up to several hundred infantrymen-cum-tradesmen. Their rate of work was phenomenal. RIR109's records for April 1915–January 1916 revealed that its construction company provided, among many other items: 2560 ladders for climbing out of trenches, 9819 beds for dugouts, 13,049 planks, 41,276 boards, 27,060 wooden posts, 212,965 sandbags, 25,175 pounds of nails, 38,010 duckboards, 13,394 barbed-wire balls and coils, 3309 rolls of barbed wire and 27,452 iron rods.[73] Additionally, the company supplied 30,000 workshop-made tallow candles to provide light inside dugouts that were constructed in April–August 1915.[74] Tons of ammunition were also hauled forward. These supplies were for just one of Stein's 20 infantry regiments and excluded the often competing demands of independent pioneer, engineer, artillery, machine-gun and trench mortar units. Construction companies put in incalculable hours to keep pace with requirements, and Stein drove them and his other soldiers hard to complete the work.

'The extent of the position was far beyond the level one normally expected from a division,' said Stein of the 26th's lines,[75] although he might as easily have been speaking of those belonging to 2nd Guards Reserve, 52nd Infantry or 28th Reserve Divisions. 'The general situation forced us to do so,' he said, referring to the expected offensive.

Stein held his subordinates responsible for transforming his corps' defences.[76] He repeatedly visited the front during 1915 and 1916 and noted various issues that needed attention. 'We were at first reduced to making up the number of machine-guns, and even batteries of artillery, from the reserves, from captured materiel, and by begging them from other depots.'[77] But Stein's eyes could not be everywhere and he was reliant on his divisional commanders. Borries, the 52nd's dynamic commander, padded daily through his trenches. *Unteroffizier* Lais wrote of Borries: 'Usually unaccompanied, wearing a shabby windcheater, he went along the trenches, climbed down into the dugouts, clambered over the spoil, squeezed at night through the lanes of barbed wire, was here, was there, was everywhere.'[78] Lais continued: 'The divisional commander [Borries] checks everything! In the opinion of us other ranks, His Excellency just has a "digging-mania."'[79] Soden, Süsskind-Schwendi and Hahn were also relentless critics of their men's work. Soden was another who risked death or injury by stalking through the trenches, redoubts and artillery lines, chatting with officers and startling private soldiers with unheralded arrivals. *Leutnant-der-Reserve* Eugen Rueff, RIR119, later recalled Soden's purpose:

> The cooperation between artillery and infantry was encouraged. Nearly every day he [Soden] was in the front line, monitoring the fortifications with his own eyes, not just on paper. No major enterprise [to improve the defences] was carried out without the divisional commander assessing the terrain and possible employment of artillery and infantry fire.[80]

By contrast, Châles de Beaulieu appears to have been hands-off at Montauban,[81] his headquarters acting more as a clearing house for Stein's orders rather than driving their implementation. Commanders who actively evaluated their defences and engaged with their men were more effective in ensuring the work met or even exceeded Stein's standards.

Not all of XIV Reserve Corps' defences were created equal. North of Hill 110 they were progressed by motivated commanders who appreciated the ground's tactical and strategic value. Those around Mametz and particularly Montauban, however, were not built with anywhere near the same level of determination or foresight. The root cause was hidden by a corps-wide reorganisation in May 1916, and also by numerous regiments being revolved through this part of the line. While Hill 110 had been converted into a stronghold,[82] this did not apply to the trenches running east through Carnoy Valley and past Montauban towards the Somme. None of the units in these trenches in 1915–16 appear to have attached much tactical value to them.[83] During the warmer months of 1915 they were developed for static trench warfare, rather than to the more rigorous standards required for withstanding a determined infantry–artillery attack, such as that experienced at Serre.[84] Work effectively ceased in the autumn and winter,[85] and from early spring 1916 these trenches were again maintained rather than materially improved according to Stein's guidance.[86] When RIR109 inherited these positions around Mametz just before 1 July it was too late for remedial work; the regiment was thereby condemned to military disaster and heavy casualties on the first day of the Somme.

Responsibility for these tactical-level failings belonged to the formation commanders involved. For those of the trenches in Carnoy Valley and in front of Mametz this was Châles de Beaulieu and not Hahn; the latter simply had the misfortune of taking over his predecessor's tardy work. For those before Montauban it was Châles de Beaulieu, again, and, before him, *General-der-Infanterie* Albert *Ritter* von Schoch, commander of 1st Bavarian Infantry Division, which was not part of Stein's corps. RIR109, a regiment noted for building excellent defensive positions,[87] received the Mametz trenches in mid-June 1916 from IR23, which was in Châles de Beaulieu's division, and found them unfit for purpose, with the second and third defensive lines not properly developed.[88] There were insufficient telephone lines, a shortage of forward ammunition and food depots, and inadequate barbed wire. The number of dugouts was insufficient and their shallowness meant they were unable to withstand concerted shellfire.[89] It was much the same story in the positions that Bavarian Reserve Infantry Regiment 6 took over from Infantry Regiment 62 (IR62) on the eve of battle.[90] IR62 had received them from Schoch. Moreover, because large sweeps of the ground between Mametz and Montauban were open to British observers, the weeks of maintenance work undertaken were frequently unpicked by shellfire.[91] One solution was to construct a robust line further back, perhaps on the southern crest of Caterpillar Valley, with ground-holding trenches before it, but such an idea was ahead of its time and precluded by the German army-wide focus on front-loaded defences. Châles de Beaulieu's and Schoch's failures to convert their positions into defensive fortresses had a lot to do with their shortcomings as commanders, frequent unit changes, failure to attach appropriate strategic and tactical value to the task at hand, and Below and Stein's belief that the Allied vanguard would attack further north.

STEIN AND BELOW allocated their limited number of artillery batteries according to the military value they attached to specific ground. In total,

XIV Reserve Corps had about 147 batteries totalling about 570 field and heavy guns.[92] The vast majority supported the trenches that would be attacked by Third and Fourth Armies. The number of batteries and guns allocated to each division varied. The 52nd had about 28 batteries (106 guns), and to the south, the 28th had about 33 (125–130 guns).[93] On either flank, 2nd Guards Reserve Division and the 12th had about 22 batteries (80 guns) and 25 batteries (95–100 guns) respectively.[94] The 26th had 39 batteries (154 guns), by far the most of any division; the fact that about a quarter (26.5%) of Stein's artillery was deployed in support of this division between Ovillers and just south of Serre underlined the fact that this was regarded as must-hold ground to XIV Reserve Corps and Second Army.

Less obvious problems included the quality of guns available. Bavarian Foot Artillery Regiment 10 reported a 'serious' lack of heavy artillery in the 28th's area, meaning the number of guns with the range to shoot at targets well behind enemy lines was limited, and that other heavy guns were lower-quality captured weapons.[95] Crewing bigger guns was a matter of pride among artillerymen. It was with this in mind that *Unteroffizier* Willi Traumüller, Foot Artillery Battery 550, excitedly wrote home 'Guess who is going to be working on a heavy gun!'[96] This lack of bigger-calibre weapons reported in the 28th's area was a story repeated across XIV Reserve Corps and Second Army.[97] Soden's barrel inventory was broadly representative. Of his division's 154 guns, only 96 (62.3%) were either modern 7.7-centimetre field guns or 10.5-centimetre light field howitzers.[98] Thirty-eight (24.7%) were older, obsolete or captured guns, among them Russian heavy field howitzers that were prone to breaking down after only a short period of firing. A further 20 (13%) older 9-centimetre German guns lacked recoil mechanisms, meaning they were prone to lurching out of position with each shot and needed to be constantly re-aimed. Stein's concentration of guns was barely sufficient for the defensive role he had allocated to them and even then, based on the 26th's figures,[99] more than a third were unreliable and unsuited to that work before a single shot was fired.

Stein nevertheless resolved to conserve and make the best possible use of his limited and ageing pool of artillery. He said there were to be at least twice as many battery positions as guns, and each position was to have at least two shell-proof observation posts and separate dugouts for the gun crew and ammunition.[100] Most of the artillery was deployed at least 2000 yards behind the front line,[101] and each battery was to be protected by belts of wire and equipped with stores of hand grenades and demolition charges in the event of an enemy break-in.[102] Liaison officers were attached to infantry headquarters. Buried telephone cables connected batteries with various headquarters and calls for artillery support on these had priority.[103] Infantry could also use flares to call down a barrage or vary its range. 'When an infantry attack is threatening, intense artillery fire will be directed on the enemy's trenches. ... When the assault is launched, barrage fire will be opened,' wrote Stein.[104] He insisted artillery officers use initiative and open fire when the intensity of British shellfire suggested an imminent attack:[105]

> The artillery, so far from waiting for light signals or telephone
> messages from the infantry (both means of communication
> may fail), should shell the enemy's trenches with an intensity
> increasing in proportion to the enemy's fire, in order to prevent
> his infantry from leaving its trenches. Immediately it becomes
> evident, from the enemy's artillery fire, at what point he intends
> to break through, the fire of every battery ... will be directed on to
> the portion of the enemy's front line trench which is opposite the
> sector threatened.[106]

Even humble infantrymen in the trenches saw few shades of grey when it came to the role of the batteries behind them. 'The artillery is decisive,' wrote *Unteroffizier* Wilhelm Munz, RIR119.[107] Stein's guns were purposely grouped and deployed to provide close defensive fire support for XIV Reserve Corps' front line, breaking enemy attacks as they formed or crossed no-man's-land, and isolating any break-ins from reinforcement.[108]

Gunners used teams of surveyors and observers in tethered balloons and aircraft to register the fall of their shot. This data was used to improve the accuracy of defensive barrages and counter-battery work, the latter a systematic targeting of British artillery guns. As Stein's guidelines put it, 'The enemy's artillery must be constantly weakened by shelling individual battery positions which are known for certain to be occupied.'[109] Survey sections plotted the location of British guns by watching for their muzzle flashes at night, while observers in the kite balloons worked day and night. Several months into the Somme offensive, *Leutnant-der-Reserve* Martin Hieber, Artillery Air Detachment 229, described the view over the River Somme marshes and hinterland at the southern end of what had been XIV Reserve Corps' sector:

> The almost flat landscape here on the Somme is exceptionally beautiful from above. The broad valley with its shimmering marshes; the villages with their lush meadows; the yellowish-gold of cornfields; the roads pencilling delicate lines through this mosaic; the intervening shadows of hills: all this constitutes such a wealth of colour and from that one can hardly take in all the details at once.[110]

Hieber, a 25-year-old law student from Stuttgart, would be killed in 1917.

Aeroplanes were essential to the artillery's role. Artillery Air Detachment 221 flew 75 sorties over the British positions opposite 26th and 28th Reserve Divisions in April–June 1916.[111] Thirty-nine were for gun registration and target-spotting, and 27 were for reconnaissance.[112] This information helped planners segment the British lines into detailed artillery target zones from mid-1915, with guns allocated to each.[113] This meant shellfire could be landed accurately day or night, with repeated testing and increased infantry–artillery co-operation improving response times.

There were problems, as *Leutnant-der-Reserve* Georg Büsing, Reserve Field Artillery Regiment 20 (RFAR20), later lamented: 'Firing activity ranged from worthwhile targets, to retaliatory fire on settlements and identified enemy batteries. Ranging-in exercises were conducted with the help of our flying detachment, however, good results were seldom achieved and exercises mostly had to be cancelled due to the low number of aircraft available and enemy superiority in the air.'[114] Yet there were also benefits, as *Leutnant-der-Reserve* Gerster explained:

The importance of infantry–artillery links was recognised ever more. As a result the communications system was subject to constant improvement. Rocket signals, semaphore flags and light signals by night, which were received by artillery observation points, served this purpose. … Over the months these measures led to perfect co-operation between the two arms of service, to trust of the artillery by the infantry, which was not shaken by the occasional unavoidable dropping short of shells. In this way the foundation for the effective countering of an enemy attack was laid.[115]

The result was a responsive artillery scheme that complemented the corps- and army-wide emphasis on stopping an enemy attack at or well before the front line.

Two artillerymen in 28th Reserve Division have left us descriptions of their work. *Feldwebel* Karl Eiser, Reserve Field Artillery Regiment 29, peered over the British lines through binoculars from Contalmaison church spire: 'We watched endless columns of lorries making the journey between Bray-sur-Somme and Albert every day. These convoys often consisted of 100 lorries. We frequently saw great artillery convoys, so long that it would take three hours for each to pass a given point.'[116] This intelligence was fed back to headquarters, and target locations issued to the batteries covering those areas. *Leutnant-der-Reserve* August Bielefeld, commanding a 15-centimetre howitzer battery in Reserve Foot Artillery Regiment 16 near Mametz Wood, was involved in this type of work:

We bombarded distant targets including the approach road Bray–Albert, rest camps at Albert and Bécourt, as well as the approach roads Albert–La Boisselle, Albert–Fricourt and several others. For each gun the objective was targeted and determined in order to be able to fire by map reference in case of a failure of the observation. The battery had good success, particularly on the approach road Bray–Albert and the rest camps which lay at the side of the roads.[117]

This integration of observation, communication and target zones was mostly replicated throughout Stein's divisions.

In practice, there was considerable variance in the quality of Stein's artillery positions. Those north of Fricourt, and particularly beyond the Albert–Bapaume road, were generally better made than those south, where less tactical importance was attributed to the ground and also due to Châles de Beaulieu's failings. Many of the 26th's gun pits and observation posts were made of concrete, supported by hefty beams and lined with stout timber, while deep dugouts were sunk to protect gun crews and ammunition.[118] Reserve Field Artillery Regiment 27 described its gun lines as prepared by 'all [the] experiences of trench warfare,' with the best observation points selected.[119] Improvements continued until 24 June, when the British bombardment began.[120] At Gommecourt some under-developed gun positions of 2nd Guards Reserve and 52nd Infantry Divisions provoked a 'dubious shaking of the heads,'[121] but were quickly upgraded. 'All lines and levels of effectiveness were improved,' wrote *Leutnant-der-Reserve* Büsing.[122] 'The fire distribution plans were kept up to date taking into consideration all reinforcements that arrived, protection was checked, permanent observation posts were established in the fighting trenches, and signalling was systematically organised for the event that the telephones failed.'[123] South of Fricourt, particularly behind Mametz, the 28th's recently acquired gun pits were essentially earthworks supported by timber beams, devoid of any structural strengthening.[124] Photographs reveal that many of the 28th's guns were protected by nothing more than a canopy of foliage resting on flimsy wooden frames. Moreover, the 28th's artillery telephone lines were often laid over-ground and exposed to shellfire, which meant they were more easily severed.[125] The story was no different in the 12th's gun lines behind Montauban.[126] This north–south dichotomy in the build quality of XIV Reserve Corps' gun positions went unchanged prior to 1 July.

Against this backcloth the number of German guns and their battery positions were eroded by increasing British shellfire from early March. A four-gun battery of RFAR20 at Gommecourt was spotted by the RFC soon after it began firing.[127] Its camouflaged positions were shelled, three of four guns destroyed and the gun pits wrecked. As Büsing explained, 'The destroyed guns were replaced straight away; the emplacements were rebuilt again in one night using beams prepared in the pioneer park.'[128] *Oberst* Mack, commanding BFAR19, complained bitterly about British aerial superiority, the RFC's quick location of battery positions, and the subsequent loss of guns and men in poorly prepared positions:[129] 'The human losses were bearable, but it was impossible to replace the loss of material.'[130] Near Fricourt, *Feldwebel* Eiser said British artillery claimed gunners and observers in almost every battery of his regiment.[131] Over at Serre, *Reservist* Christian Eberle, Infantry Regiment 180 (IR180), complained that a brick building long used for observation was 'now almost completely gone.'[132] Further south, the observation benefits of Hill 110 were marginalised by the 'furious shelling, and the continuous trenches and long stretches of the main front were levelled,' Eiser said.[133] Another soldier grumbled that the 'enemy artillery does not forget to send us greetings at night as well as by day. They seem to know our dug-outs better than we do ourselves.'[134] This intensifying artillery activity through the spring months of 1916 not only began eroding the German artillery but also further signposted an attack.

As the spring of 1916 progressed it became increasingly obvious to Stein that a British attack was imminent. 'The fire of their artillery was gradually being increased in strength,' he wrote in his, at times self-aggrandising, autobiography. 'We knew fairly accurately the strength of the force that was opposed to us, and we had to reckon with a four- or five-fold numerical superiority.'[135] Soden noted the increasing activity opposite his division and concluded that an attack on XIV Reserve Corps' positions was inevitable:[136]

> The enemy attack preparations were seen mainly from aerial photographs. Numerous new approach roads, railways, assembly trenches, barracks huts were built. Many trees were felled. In many places the frontline trench had been brought forward. Gaps in the enemy wire [for attacking infantry to pass through] were identified. Behind enemy lines considerable traffic was noticeable. Enemy's artillery activity was increasingly strong.[137]

FEW GERMAN SOLDIERS ever forgot being on the receiving end of shellfire. *Unteroffizier* Schmid, Bavarian Field Artillery Regiment 1, recalled the face-blanching fear experienced by just-arrived reinforcements during a period of hostile shellfire near Fricourt:

None believed that he would escape with his life. I tried to keep their courage up by telling jokes and stories, but I was not very successful. As a last resort I took out my faithful harmonica and began to blow a tune: 'Muss i' denn zum Städtele hinaus.' ['Must I Leave This Town'] Some of them started to take notice and began to whistle along with me for all they were worth. Finally everything calmed down.[138]

Leutnant-der-Reserve Ernst Hibschenberger, RIR110, wrote that 'enemy mortar bombs and field artillery shells gave off a stink like phosphorous [sic], which irritated the mucous membranes and produced nausea.'[139] On that occasion — a 10-hour period on 19 July 1915 — he reckoned about 26,000 artillery and trench-mortar shells fell on a 220-yard-long stretch of Hill 110, presaging a French attack that failed. 'The whole position was a mass of craters and the trenches were completely flattened.'[140] Elsewhere, *Leutnant-der-Reserve* Rudolf Greisinger, IR180, remembered his men sitting 'shaken and agitated in their dark dugouts, trembling and wondering if the next moment they would be buried alive by a collapse.'[141] *Reservist* Wirth, RIR119, said deep underground infantrymen listened to the thick wooden frames of their dugouts creaking and groaning as a flurry of shells blew above in January 1916. 'No one spoke a word, but we were all aware of what was going on. Once again the English had tried and failed to collapse our dugouts and render us unable to fight.'[142] *Fahrer* Otto Maute, IR180, said his baptism of fire was while transporting ammunition to Ovillers. 'For the first time I heard the whistle of the shells which hit nearby. ... Naturally it was impossible to quieten the horses.'[143]

Shell-proof dugouts were the solution to protecting soldiers. Stein insisted that the number of dugouts was to be increased 'until there are sufficient to accommodate the infantry garrison that the Division considers necessary for the repulse of a prepared attack.'[144] These engineered catacombs were to be at least seven yards underground and have two entrances so the garrison could quickly sortie from the dugouts in the event of an attack alarm.[145] While much of the work involved in mining deep dugouts was the domain of pioneer units, infantrymen were also conscripted as labourers. *Unteroffizier* Wilhelm Munz explained:

'Such a shelter is built in the following way. First of all come fairly stout planks for the shoring-up, above them are arranged tree trunks for the roof, then three to four yards of natural earth and finally an earth/straw mixture. The shelters are a maximum of one yard wide to reduce the danger from direct hits.'[146] By the start of 1916, Soden's 26th had about 1500 mined dugouts across its seven-mile-wide sector, with Hahn's 28th having a similar number.[147] In May 1916, for instance, the 26th's Thiepval sector had sufficient dugouts to house 3900 men of the four-battalion Reserve Infantry Regiment 99 (RIR99), including 140 excavated under the front line itself, while at Ovillers there was enough subterranean accommodation for 2500 men of the three-battalion RIR109 in the first position.[148] Fifty-second Infantry and 2nd Guards Reserve Divisions likely had equivalent dugout shelters. Only in 12th Infantry Division's sector were there markedly fewer, and the unknown number of dugouts there were of lesser quality and prone to flooding due to the high water table resulting from the proximity of the Somme.[149] XIV Reserve Corps' dugouts, as with the quality of their infantry and artillery positions, became fewer and of poorer build south of Fricourt.

Wilhelm Munz, who died on 1 July, described his mole-like existence in a letter to his girlfriend:

> Steep steps lead down from the trench into the dug-outs. Just
> like the steps in your home from the glass doors down to the
> cellar, only our steps are steeper and so low that one has to go
> bent double. My dug-out is about as big as your verandah and
> five metres [5.5 yards] down. In the centre, like in a small garden
> outhouse, is a table with wooden trestles. We have fixed pictures
> on the panelled walls. Down there we sit and read and write by the
> light of a candle hung above the table by a wire. It is a shame that
> you cannot pay us a flying visit to see inside for yourself.[150]

The chief danger for dugout dwellers was artillery shells that collapsed their shelters, particularly man-sized beasts that burrowed deep into the soft earth before detonating. Occupants were often killed outright, or crushed, or trapped underground and asphyxiated. *Oberstabsarzt* Niedenthal, RIR110's doctor, remembered an April 1915 blast that trapped 14 men underground. Attempts to dig them out failed. *Leutnant-der-Landwehr* Karl Weymann, a 39-year-old professor of medicine from Karlsruhe in RIR110, was found dead. 'In his eyes, with their blank stare, could be read all the terror of death from asphyxiation.'[151] When rescuers finally broke into the dugout chamber they found the rest dead, a dozen 'sitting in a line along the wall, as though they were asleep.'[152]

If the fighting above ground was mired in stalemate, the high-stakes subterranean battle burrowed on. All along the battle front specialist gangs of sappers and infantrymen-cum-labourers toiled in shafts often 55–75 yards deep to blow the enemy skywards, enhance XIV Reserve Corps' defensive scheme and construct listening posts to gather intelligence. This was the case at La Boisselle, Beaumont Hamel, Serre, Fricourt, Hill 110 and Mametz. Galleries numbered in the hundreds. It was unforgiving graft, carried out in often darkened corridors with spades, picks and bayonets used to quietly scrape sod out to be hauled away in sandbags. Toiling noisily with a spade or pick was to risk detection by British underground listening posts, as was speaking too loudly or clattering along a narrow corridor. Both sides used microphones to home in on the other's mining activity, and at times it was plainly audible to the ear.[153] As one anonymous Bavarian pioneer officer wrote in late-May 1916: 'The chambering of Gallery 33b [on Hill 110] is being further accelerated as the behaviour of the enemy [miners] leads one to believe that he intends blowing in our working. ... As a blow is to be expected at any moment, the work is extraordinarily dangerous and calls for great courage and extreme devotion to duty.'[154] *Leutnant-der-Reserve* Gerster later described the detonation of a German mine near Beaumont Hamel:

> The very earth quakes. The ground heaves up like a wave above
> the seat of the explosion and falls back once more. A light cloud
> of dust seems to be hovering over the site [of the mine blast].
> Suddenly blue flames rush skywards out of the crater, dancing and
> flickering on the ground and roaring upwards into the sky. This
> lasts for several seconds! Over there in the enemy trench, two long
> blue flames like snakes' tongues, lunge forwards seeking victims.
> No Man's Land is lit up by this ghostly light. Shots crash out. A
> machine gun starts to chatter. Can we hear shrieks?[155]

The result was great white-jawed craters studding the ground between opposing trench lines. The scars from some of those mine blasts are still hidden among the trees on Hill 110 above Fricourt and at La Boiselle's Glory Hole (Granathof).

OBSERVERS THROUGHOUT XIV Reserve Corps' lines noticed increasing activity behind the enemy trenches from as early as August 1915. Columns of artillery and infantry were seen thick along the fretwork of roads feeding the British positions. Everything pointed to a large-scale relief of the French soldiers that the Württembergers and Badeners had faced since late 1914. The first sign that the British now occupied the ground from Gommecourt south to almost the River Somme was artillery shell fuses made in England or America. To the experienced ear these fuses sparked shell bursts that sounded entirely different from their French equivalents. Rumours raced along the line, everyone speculating on who their new foes were. Reports filtered back that British infantry now held the trenches — their serge-coloured uniforms, pleated pockets, puttees and peaked forage caps giveaways to those who had seen them before. The ubiquitous rimmed steel helmet that marked Tommy from French soldiers, the latter more commonly known as *poilus*, had yet to be introduced. That, as Gerster wrote, meant hard proof was required to confirm the nationality of the enemy: 'The [26th] divisional order to bring in a prisoner dead or alive was hardly necessary. Even without it, our patrols were as hell bent as the devil after some poor soul, on running to earth the slightest shred of evidence.'[156] Soon a trickle of British prisoners and equipment captured by patrols or raiding parties confirmed the enemy's identity. The British army had arrived on the Somme.

Sentries peering through steel trench loopholes were on the lookout for any hint of British activity. 'In no circumstances may observation of the front suffer interruption. There will nevertheless be casualties among the sentries,' wrote Stein.[157] Just as importantly, the front-line garrison had to be ready to race up from its dugouts at the shout of a sentry to repulse an enemy attack.[158] That assumed the 'men reach the parapet in time.'[159] Thus, said Stein, infantry had to be alert and practised in responding to a sentry's alarm or listening for the instant the enemy's shellfire lifted further back, a tell-tale sign of an imminent attack. 'Above all, every group commander and every man must realise that the success or failure of an [enemy] assault depends on his timely appearance at the parapet.'[160] Support and reserve troops were to be applied to battle as required, whether in specialist bombing teams to eject a break-in or as infantry reinforcements.[161] Stein believed ground lost to or contested by the enemy was often easily recaptured or held if swift counterattacks were launched by infantry commanders on the spot.[162] Stein demanded his infantry be constantly alert and well drilled in responding to an enemy attack, and the onus of responsibility fell squarely on the sentries.

Unteroffizier Wilhelm Munz described sentry work in more detail:

> Between the two lines of trenches the British and Germans have
> huge wire obstructions. They are simple wire and iron frames
> strung with barbed wire. ... Now you can see why simply coming
> across to us is not so easy? For with every step the wire twangs,
> and the sentries who hear it shoot at once, while flares are fired
> which light the terrain bright as day.'[163]

There were also false alarms, wrote *Unteroffizier* Schultz, Reserve Infantry Regiment 40: 'A patrol of volunteers was sent forward in the direction of the sound and everyone waited, nerves strained, for its return. The "captured item" which they brought back was only an old umbrella, which ... had been blown into the obstacle by a gust of wind!'[164]

Front-line regiments also undertook the often-vicious business of patrolling no-man's-land and raiding enemy trenches. Their aims ranged from gathering intelligence and capturing, killing or wounding enemy soldiers, to destroying, damaging or seizing enemy equipment and securing mastery of no-man's-land by night. *Unteroffizier* Peter Collet, IR66, noted the surge in British activity near Serre in April 1916 and said 'it was quite natural that we wanted to know what was behind this.'[165] Stein had endorsed aggressive action in no-man's-land and issued a guide for raiding and patrolling in early 1916.[166] Successful raids were usually supported by artillery and trench-mortar barrages of up to 10,000 shells that pared the enemy's wire, isolated the portion of trench to be entered, covered the subsequent withdrawal, and suppressed hostile shellfire.[167] Dozens of such night-time endeavours took place throughout 1915 and the first half of 1916. Most involved fewer than five men, but others comprised several dozen and some up to 200.[168] Smaller operations were often ad hoc; bigger enterprises were planned and rehearsed behind the lines.[169] Soldiers were armed with daggers, grenades, sharpened entrenching tools, pistols and rifles, and blackened their faces with boot polish before striking out. *Vizefeldwebel* Hermann Klotz, IR180, was part of a patrol in no-man's-land at Ovillers when eight British soldiers stumbled out of the darkness:

> On the first shot the [British] officer fell into the arms of another
> fellow who was immediately hit through the heart with a second
> shot. The others bolted. Three more shots at a range of 30 feet and
> two more Englishmen were dead. Two of the dead Englishmen
> were dragged back into our trench.[170]

Close-quarter fighting in enemy trenches often harked back to medieval times. *Oberleutnant* H. Reymann, IR62, recalled that his short-handled entrenching tool with its razor-sharp blade performed 'wonderfully' as a trench-fighting weapon.[171] Soon every regiment had a cadre of patrol and raiding veterans whose risky business often won accolades in the form of promotion or Iron Cross medals.

Those who survived for any length of time knew how to steal across fire-swept ground, make use of every scrap of cover and avoid detection. It was dangerous work. Mistakes and indecision could lead to death or injury. In early June 1916, *Unteroffizier* Walter Bönsel, RIR119, was caught unawares soon after his raiding party dropped into the British front line:

> A shadowy [British] figure stormed forward. The man blinked
> at me in the pitch black of night, and suddenly two pistol shots
> flashed past my head, one grazing my cheek. I had the presence of
> mind to shine my flashlight in his face, but my pistol shots did not
> hurt him. He fled around a trench corner.[172]

Bönsel lived. Others did not. *Vizefeldwebel* Hermann Bocker, RIR119, was a pre-war singing teacher and opera singer, and master in the art of trench raiding and patrolling. The 39-year-old — whose life said much about man's capacity to harbour both the sublime and the brutal — was mortally wounded when his patrol was ambushed in April 1916. On another occasion, *Unteroffizier* Matthias Dirr, RIR119's teenage king of no-man's-land, said a moment's pause in diving to dirt in no-man's-land cost two men their lives. One of the men's 'brain, his sinews and fibres were hanging out of his head,' wrote the apprentice engineer, himself killed aged 18 in February 1916.[173] The femoral artery of the second was cut: 'Bright red blood shot out like a river, like a fountain.'[174] Dirr and his surviving men snaked belly-to-ground to safety. 'We used each tuft of grass, each thistle and each turnip stem as cover.'[175]

Leutnant-der-Reserve Roland Vulpius, RIR110, watched the luminous hands on his wristwatch hit 5.50 p.m. on a late-December night in 1915. 'Go!' A storm of artillery shells slammed onto the enemy trenches. Within seconds Vulpius's men were inside the hostile ditch. Hand grenades were tossed down inky dugout entrances. Thirteen prisoners were nabbed and a torch pointed into their faces. Vulpius called out in English, 'If anyone makes a wrong move he's a dead man!'[176] The captives were trotted back to German lines to be interrogated and then sent to prisoner-of-war camps.

Stein's ever-evolving patrolling and raiding guide produced results. In the period 1 January–23 June 1916, no fewer than 207 British soldiers were caught by patrols and raiding parties across the whole of XIV Reserve Corps' sector.[177] Seventy-six were captured in January–March, with a further 131 taken in the remainder of the period. That the number of prisoners taken increased alongside the likelihood of a British attack was unsurprising given the demand for up-to-date intelligence from Stein. Prisoners were questioned by regimental, divisional and corps intelligence officers, sometimes in the trenches but mostly at headquarters behind the lines. Stein wanted information that could pinpoint the date, place and time of the British attack, and any snippet that fleshed out the details of enemy infantry and artillery units opposite. 'Times were rough,' wrote *Unteroffizier* Paul Scheytt, a trainee teacher serving in RIR109. 'The revolver was the best interpreter.'[178] Numerous sources, including Below and Stein, revealed that prisoners either directly or indirectly suggested a late-June attack date. Prisoners also disclosed that multiple British battalions were arriving on the Somme front and promptly undergoing tactical training for an offensive.

This and other information was evaluated by Below's and Stein's intelligence staffs. Reports from patrols, raiding parties and observation and listening posts were supplemented by aerial photographs and transcripts of British conversations picked up by underground telephone intercept stations. Aerial photographs, for instance, revealed enemy approach routes to the front line, recently dug assembly trenches, just-laid light-gauge railway tracks, and new buildings and huts, among myriad other developments in hostile territory. As Soden put it:

> Sources of intelligence improved. These included radio intercept
> and listening in to telephone conversations by means of the
> installation of 'Moritz' and 'Arend' stations. All the time that the
> enemy was unaware of the potential of these stations, we were in
> a position to listen in to every enemy order and we got to know
> every company commander by name.[179]

Soon enough XIV Reserve Corps built up a detailed picture of the British units and their activities. Command structures, orders and instructions, military routine, officer names and inter-unit reliefs were all part of the intelligence jigsaw. But, even after months of surveillance, there were still gaps. By 23 June, Stein and Below still only had a general idea of when the British attack would be launched.

Grubby, sleep-deprived soldiers in the trenches joined the dots of their own accord. Near Thiepval in late-March 1916, *Leutnant-der-Reserve* Friedrich Kassel, RIR99, heard 'trains roll across the valley of the Ancre and speculated what they [the British] were transporting. Three months later we should get the answer to our queries.'[180] At Mametz, *Vizefeldwebel* Frisch, RIR109, said while soldiers were given no explanation of the expected offensive, everyone 'could draw the correct conclusions from his own observations. Everyone felt that decisive events were nearing.'[181]

THESE SAME SOLDIERS were exhausted by chronic night-time labouring, daily military bunkum and the rigours of living in a ditch. 'I remember my first day in the trenches,' wrote *Unteroffizier* Wilhelm Munz. 'I moved here and there very cautiously, avoiding every puddle and carefully removing immediately every tiny piece of mud from my uniform. Yet now when I see myself covered from head to toe with earth and filth I am content and happy, for it is better "camouflage" than our field-grey.'[182]

Infantrymen lived and slept in their numerous dugouts when off duty. Hot food was lugged forward in metal canisters by ration parties, but was often tepid by the time it arrived forward. *Fahrer* Maute said the fare was simply 'adequate,' suggesting much room for improvement.[183] Each soldier was issued a loaf of bread every two days; limited spices were available to add taste to thinly peeled potatoes and a daily meat ration of 288 grams.[184] *Grenadier* Emil Goebelbecker, RIR109, explained: 'We had one hot meal a day. It consisted of beans, peas, lentils and dehydrated vegetables. These were cooked with meat and tasted very good. We also had bread with jam and made coffee and tea in the trenches. We also had emergency rations — canned meat, bottled [mineral] water and first-aid supplies.'[185] Downtime was spent shucking lice from clothing seams, or cleaning weapons and equipment. *Vizefeldwebel* Karl Schuler, a 20-year-old in RIR110, wrote home that 'we have an awful lot of "pets" here. Those lousy lice are eating us up completely.'[186] Shaving and haircuts were group affairs, four or five men at a time with cutthroat razors and scissors. Entertainment was had from chatting with mates, card games, writing home, reading, and playing or listening to the music made with a meagre few instruments such as harmonicas, zithers and violins. Here and there makeshift altars were carved into dugouts and trench walls. Boredom was rife and many a grimy soldier became an inveterate smoker as a distraction from the mundane.

As *Leutnant-der-Reserve* Friedrich Conzelmann, RIR121, explained:

We old soldiers grumble about this and that. On one occasion it is about women, then our children, or possibly even about the money we should have. This is all ridiculously small in relation to what we have experienced and endured outdoors. Our homes [in Germany] seem like paradise. We often do not cope well with little things when we have overcome so much.[187]

As with British soldiers a few hundred yards away, nobody got used to the plump corpse rats lurking in and around the trenches and dugouts. *Leutnant-der-Reserve* Franz Demmel, Bavarian Infantry Leib Regiment, was revolted by the plague of pink-tailed rats. 'They came creeping up to sniff around for anything edible in our knapsacks, which we used as pillows. They were not shy about using our faces as a shortcut. They scrabbled their way up the sleeves of our jackets and began to nibble away wherever they liked. These bloody creatures could drive a man to despair.'[188] *Unteroffizier* Albrecht Munz, IR180, said the deep underground dugouts were a 'playground for rats' and that 'hatred for them rose to gigantic proportions.'[189] He decided to do something about the plague in his small corner of the front and suspended a loaf of bread from his dugout ceiling, just a couple of inches above a water-filled tin pot. Soon enough, 'I heard the squealing as the rat frantically tried to climb up the smooth metal [pot] walls. A sharp French bayonet brought his swimming lesson to an end. ... The night ended with another two of these rodents in the same water bath and now we had our 750 grams of bread for our own use.'[190]

The wettest months of the year turned the German soldiers' daily ordeal of toil, boredom and rats into one of degradation.[191] They referred to these months as a so-called 'mud offensive,' reflecting their ongoing stuggle against the elements. *Leutnant* Fiedel said the surfeit of rainwater resulted in numerous trenches becoming knee-deep sloughs.[192] Trench walls lined with wicker revetments held their form longer than those without, but inevitably slithered into the ditch.[193] Stein complained that this filthy weather quickly destroyed weeks of labouring work.[194] Soldiers stuck fast in the gloop — it 'clung to boots in great clumps that looked like an elephant's feet'[195] — had to be dug free. *Leutnant-der-Reserve* Vulpius remembered that the 'damp, west wind, which has been blowing gas back over us, obstinately refused to slacken.'[196] Life in the trenches was dismal, wrote *Oberleutnant* Reymann, adding 'many dugouts ran so full of water that they could no longer be used.'[197] Some trenches had crude sumps; in others water was splashed out with pails or squeaky hand pumps. Uniforms were sodden for weeks on end, and soldiers became ill.[198] In January 1916, RIR99 sent a total of 200 men to hospital suffering from influenza, colds, upset stomachs and leg cramps.[199] More were ill but stayed with their units.[200] It was some consolation that 'the Englishman is no better off. At various points in his position we could watch him bailing the water out.'[201] War-fighting and labouring ebbed in the October–March period, but snipers, shellfire and gas still claimed lives.

It was with this in mind that *Gefreiter* Otto Klinkerfüss, Field Machine-gun Platoon 55 in 28th Reserve Division, wrote to his sister-in-law in November 1915: 'I don't know whether the war will end soon. I would like to know as I've had enough. We all hope it will be next year, when the enemy has overplayed his game. Then they will stop.'[202] As it turned out, Klinkerfüss was quite wrong. Behind the lines, XIV Reserve Corps' infrastructure network was centred on the rural service centre of Bapaume and its satellite villages. By late 1915 there were corps and divisional slaughterhouses, bakeries, cookhouses and mineral-water bottling plants to meet the corps' daily demands. Produce and livestock were acquired locally, or freighted in from Germany. There were also corps and divisional workshops, ironmongers and repair depots, dumps for all manner of materiel and ammunition, parks for vehicles and wagons, and schools converted to hospitals.

For soldiers out of the line, Bapaume, along with other villages nearby, became a rest centre where they could refresh body and mind.[203] There were shops selling civilian goods, sparsely stocked military canteens, cinemas, estaminets, and bars with German-brewed beer. *Reservist* Wilhelm Keller, IR180, complained that one bar was 'fun, but a bit thin on the spirits so I went for drinks with another guy elsewhere.'[204] *Hauptmann* Johann Heyberger, IR180, recalled bawdy nights in an officers' bar at Courcelette, which 'thanks to the care of my paymaster … never lacked a good drop of beer.'[205] Meantime, funeral services were held in regimental and divisional cemeteries, and church services in local chapels and billets. Concerts were staged periodically, often by musicians from the ranks, and supplemented by travelling opera and theatre companies. By early 1916, XIV Reserve Corps was almost entirely self-sufficient.

Unteroffizier Eugen Kaisser, Württemberg Reserve Dragoon Regiment, spent nine days out of the line in Bapaume in late-May 1916:

> The whole regimental staff had been billeted quite nicely in a brewery building and farmyard. It's a little cramped, but that doesn't matter. Nearby there's a nice garden, which I use in my

free time, so I am there at the moment. I made a table and chair from some wood in a workshop and so now I am quite alone and undisturbed, which is a real treat.[206]

Time out of the line was also used to train battalions in the latest infantry tactics, particularly from January 1916 as the expected Allied offensive neared. Regiments were revolved out of the line for seven- or eight-day periods during spring for this purpose. *Reservist* Friedrich Bauer, IR180, described the training as a 'holiday' from the trenches, adding 'we have been busy practising all sorts of things.'[207] He and others repeated bayonet exercises, gas-mask drills, and practised responding to attack and gas alarms, throwing live hand grenades and deploying machine guns at speed. Heyberger recalled a grenade training accident: 'One [soldier] died immediately with ghastly injuries. Another man's hands were cut off at the wrist and he lost both eyes.'[208] Rehearsals in quickly exiting dugouts and manning trench parapets were run through time and again, usually under the eye and stopwatch of an unforgiving NCO or subaltern.[209] Dummy trench systems were used to practise counterattack drills, one platoon playing the part of defenders and another that of the enemy. These exercises were replicated at platoon, company and battalion levels to ensure co-ordination, and would be repeatedly seen in XIV Reserve Corps' defensive tactics on 1 July.

Soldiers sending postcards home to families, sweethearts and friends generally revealed little of life at the front, as the cards might be read by anyone. *Musketier* August Opielka, IR23, penned a few lines to his girlfriend from a trench near Mametz: 'I am well and with all my heart I wish you the same.'[210] But, in an unusually direct comment, Opielka also said he feared a disfiguring wound: 'One does not know what will happen from one day to the next. Hopefully I won't be wounded like one man I saw.'[211] Bauer also wrote home after returning from leave: 'It's a shame that the holiday came to an end so quickly.'[212] He was killed at Ovillers on 3 July 1916. *Unteroffizier* Gotthilf Harr, RIR119, was 'healthy and so far alright in the trenches.'[213] *Kanonier* Heinrich Hartung, RFAR20, was pleased to receive parcels with sweets and tobacco: 'They arrived just at the right time. We are now labouring hard at night in the gun trenches.'[214] *Ersatz-Reservist* August Stegmaier, IR180, who was killed at Thiepval on

28 September 1916, apologised to his girlfriend for forgetting to write: 'You will certainly be a bit miffed as I didn't send you any news, but I totally forgot.'[215] *Reservist* Keller, who was lightly wounded on 1 July 1916, said he sent postcards home mostly 'as a sign of life. I'm still healthy and merry, thank God.'[216] These and other men obviously self-censored their words; they were doing well and were healthy, wanted family news from home, and were grateful for parcels of food, tobacco and socks and underwear.

Nevertheless, comforts from home and occasional reminders of life back in Germany provided only brief respite from trench-life drudgery and homesickness. *Musketier* Gustav Öschle, IR180, unexpectedly bumped into an old acquaintance while trench-digging at Serre. 'You can imagine the joy that was, two old school friends meeting one another in a place like this.'[217] Nearer Mametz, Opielka eagerly awaited his girlfriend's letters, but in May 1916 revealed that troubling thoughts were playing on his mind: 'Please don't forget me in these horrid far away shores from yours.'[218]

COME 23 JUNE, Second Army and XIV Reserve Corps had run out of time to finish preparing their defences for the anticipated British attack. If Falkenhayn remained distracted by Verdun and Galicia, Below and Stein were entirely focused on the Somme. The latter two generals had correctly — albeit late in the piece — anticipated an Anglo-French offensive on either side of the Somme. North of the waterway, they attached considerable tactical value to the ground between Fricourt and Serre, more specifically that between Ovillers and Serre. They also held hypothetical concerns that a breakthrough would be driven vigorously towards Arras, potentially undermining the German army's tenure of the Somme. Below and Stein had spent about 18 months converting Second Army's positions into a defensive fortress of barbed wire, earthworks and fortified villages. These, along with the infantry and artillery present, had been seamlessly integrated into a defensive system designed to stop any enemy attack with a tremendous weight of co-ordinated artillery and machine-gun firepower. The weak area was further south at Mametz–Montauban, because it was seen as less tactically important and it had consequently gone under-developed. Below, Stein and their subordinates were as ready and prepared to meet the Anglo-French offensive as they could be, but — in contrast with Falkenhayn — retained concerns about the adequacy of resources at their disposal to do so.

A day before the British bombardment began Soden was again in the forward area at Thiepval, chatting with his officers and inspecting his defensive positions. It was 23 June, and Soden knew he and his men now had to steel themselves for battle. As he told one officer, 'Good luck.'[219]

CHAPTER 4

Ballad of the Blind Gunners

The British preparatory bombardment, 24–30 June 1916

'It was as if the devil incarnate wielded the baton with diabolical delight in this hellish concert.'[1]
— *Major* Max Klaus, Reserve Field Artillery Regiment 26

'BOOM! ABSOLUTE SILENCE for a minute. Boom! Followed quickly by a more distant report from a fellow-gun,' wrote Second-Lieutenant Edward Liveing, 1/12th Londons (Rangers).[2] The bombardment had begun; hundreds of artillery guns cracked forth from behind the British lines in a concerted roar, belching muzzle flashes and smoke as they lobbed life-stealing shells over no-man's-land. Pillars of flame, chalkstone, clay and smoke of all colours rose and fell along the German line. Barbed-wire entanglements jangled and snapped, and shattered wooden trench revetments were tossed about. German soldiers scurried into their yards-deep engineered dugouts to escape the metal storm. The ground heaved and quaked and minute waterfalls of chalkstone dust trickled between dugout joists. 'Our whole line,' wrote *Feldwebel* Karl Eiser, Reserve Field Artillery Regiment 29, a lookout in Contalmaison's church spire, 'was lit up as innumerable lightning flashes soared over, a hissing and howling, gasping, splintering and exploding — all this filled the air.'[3]

British gunners belted out one shell after another to an exacting timetable, day in, day out. Lieutenant Frank Lushington, Royal Garrison

Artillery (RGA), said the 'whole of life seemed to merge into one clanging, clashing, roar of sound. Covered with sweat and grime, the slaves of the gun toiled and laboured, ate, lay down and slept, and toiled and laboured again, to the roar and rush and scream of hundreds of hurrying shells. Their horizon was bounded by the vast and insatiable engine which they continuously fed. Their minds were numbed and deafened by the never-ending clamour of their gods.'[4]

The bombardment was supposed to have lasted five days, 24–28 June, these known to planners respectively as U, V, W, X and Y. The attack was to have gone in on Z day, 29 June. Rain and poor visibility saw the shellfire extended two days — officially Y1 and Y2, 29–30 June — with the attack deferred until 1 July. Weather conditions were far from perfect. Of the five-day period only one was fine; the rest — along with the two additional days — saw rain, mist and low cloud. Bad weather or not, the artillery's job was to smash German defensive obstacles and mechanisms, kill or otherwise subdue the enemy garrison, destroy or neutralise the hostile artillery, and break or harass German communication lines and logistics networks.

In practice, the first two days of the bombardment were for wire-cutting and registering the guns on selected targets to ensure accuracy of shot.[5] They were followed by three more, subsequently extended to five, for wire-cutting and the systematic destruction of defences such as trenches, fortified localities, strongpoints, observation posts and machine-gun emplacements, along with the targeting of billets, lines of communication and villages. The rump of the destructive fire was the responsibility of the heavy guns and howitzers, because of their greater range and larger shells.[6] However, the late arrival of many batteries meant that time was lost registering their fire for accuracy, and that most of their shellfire was weighted to the second half of the bombardment. Of the field guns, 18-pounders were to cut wire, and sweep trenches, villages, woods and hollows with their fire. The 4.5-inch howitzers were tasked with destroying trenches and assisting in the bombardment of villages and woods, and with completing the destruction of machine-gun emplacements. The British gunners, wrote *Leutnant-der-Reserve* Friedrich Kassel, Reserve Infantry Regiment 99 (RIR99), 'wanted to be sure of overkill. Nobody should be alive when their infantry left their trenches.'[7]

Haig had 1769 artillery guns and howitzers to support his two attacking armies. Fourth Army, responsible for the lion's share of the operation, had 1537 artillery pieces spread more or less evenly along a frontage of about 25,000 yards (14.2 miles). There was one field gun for every 21 yards, while the heavy barrels equated to about one to 57 yards.[8] The 232 guns spread across the 4000 yards of VII Corps' net battle front equated to about one field gun per 27 yards and one heavy for every 47 yards. Two-thirds (1158, or 65.5%) of the total gunstock was field artillery — 18-pounders and 4.5-inch howitzers — with the rest heavier guns and howitzers (511, or 28.9%) and French artillery pieces mostly for firing gas shells (100, or 5.6%).[9] Among the 511 barrels comprising the heavy ironmongery were 60-pounder guns (140, 27.4%), plus 4.7- (44, 8.6%), 6- (22, 4.3%), 9.2- (3) and 12-inch (1) guns.[10] Additionally there were 6- (132, 25.8%), 8- (64, 12.5%), 9.2- (84, 16.4%), 12- (13, 2.5%) and 15-inch (8, 1.6%) howitzers.[11] This concentration was impressive to those who had not seen the like before.[12]

Fourth Army allocated its artillery about 3 million shells for the bombardment and attack, most for 18-pounders (2.6 million shells) and 4.5-inch howitzers (260,000). About half, or 1.5 million, were loosed off on 24–30 June.[13] Average daily expenditure was 215,521, ranging from 138,118 on 24 June to 375,760 on 30 June.[14] General Sir Henry Rawlinson, commander of Fourth Army, said this worked out at roughly 150,000 shells each day, with a further 50,000 nightly.[15] His data showed that, between 24 June and 1 July, Fourth Army fired 1.64 million shells.[16] Of these, 1.29 million (78.8%) were fired by the army's field artillery and 348,603 (21.2%) by its heavy guns. He noted that ammunition accumulated for the five-day bombardment alone totalled 40,000 tons, and reckoned there 'should not be much left of his [the enemy's] defences at the end of it.'[17] The problem was the vast majority of Fourth Army's stockpiled ammunition was for field artillery not suited to laying destructive shellfire of the type needed to obliterate German-engineered dugouts, fortified villages and formidable redoubts.

Nevertheless, the concerted roar of these guns was deafening.[18] Lieutenant-Colonel Neil Fraser-Tytler, Royal Field Artillery (RFA), said his dugout was 'fairly rocking with the roar of the bombardment,' and when he was on the telephone 'I had to smother my head and phone under the bed-bag before I could hear a word.'[19] Orders had to be written, it being 'impossible to make anyone hear the spoken word.'[20] In the gun pits, artillerymen blocked their ears with cotton wool, paper plugs, or grimy palms; in the trenches, infantrymen gradually acclimatised to the din. Lieutenant Derick Capper, 8th Royal Sussex, found 'gunfire when not directed at one definitely stimulating and morale raising to the extent that one felt almost exhilarated by it.'[21] Lieutenant Lushington said the 'tumult of Hell' grew in force and volume until the 'whole world seemed to rock with sound.'[22] Infantrymen in the trenches and billets found no respite from the noise. 'Practically all the time, too, the air reverberates to the drum of our cannonade,' wrote Major James Jack, 2nd Scottish Rifles, complaining that 'we get scarcely any sleep.'[23] Private George Ashurst, 1st Lancashire Fusiliers, likened the sound to 'ghostlike express trains hurtling through the sky.'[24] Gunners and infantrymen alike struggled to communicate in the noise, the aural assault quite likely storing up hearing issues for later life.

By day many were fascinated by the sight of massive shells labouring up their parabolic arcs.[25] 'I would stand behind the guns and watch the shells in flight; sometimes I could see where they were bursting,' wrote Private Leonard Price, 8th Royal Sussex.[26] Fraser-Tytler observed one shell climbing at a 'very steep angle, and when about half-way on its downward path it gradually becomes invisible.'[27] Rumour had it, said Lieutenant Robin Rowell, 12th Squadron, Royal Flying Corps (RFC), that one pilot saw a 'shell come up, look at him, and turn at the top of its parabolic path to go down again and blow up the Hun. I have often wondered why the idle gunners chalk ugly faces on the noses of their shell. Now I know.'[28]

The sight of shellfire slamming into the German lines was equally captivating. Second-Lieutenant Liveing said the projectiles 'crashed into strong points and gun emplacements and hurled them skywards.'[29] Fraser-Tytler thought shell blasts a 'wonderful sight' with their 'smoke of every colour, black, white, grey, yellow and brown, rising often hundreds of feet in the air.'[30] Midway through the bombardment he said 'the Hun trenches have become merely one vast shell-ploughed field.'[31] Lushington likened the sprays of earth and smoke thrown up by big shells to waves crashing against boulders. 'The white chalk line of a piece of trench would appear through the billowing smoke, then a giant breaker would strike it, flinging up a cloud of black spray.'[32] Lieutenant-General Sir Thomas Morland, commander of X Corps, said 'we are pounding them properly.'[33] Lieutenant-General Sir Walter Congreve, VC, commander of XIII Corps, simply 'saw & heard a great many shells.'[34] Ashurst said the larger howitzer shells 'dug deep into his [the German] line before they exploded, shaking the very ground under our feet four or five hundred yards away, lifting tons of debris into the air and leaving a gaping hole in which a house could be placed.'[35] To most observers it looked as though the German positions were being transformed into a desolate moonscape of shell craters and debris.

By night the staccato symphony continued. Captain David Kelly, Leicestershire Regiment, watched the 'endless line of gun flashes and bursting shells.'[36] Ashurst saw the 'sky illuminated with hundreds of large and small flashes like lightning dancing on the distant ridges.'[37] Rifleman Aubrey Smith, 1/5th Londons (London Rifle Brigade), remembered that night firing at Gommecourt 'afforded such a marvellous display of flickerings and flashes in the heavens,' which he likened to a 'terrific thunder-storm.'[38] One evening, high above the German lines, Lieutenant Cecil Lewis, 3rd Squadron, RFC, peered back across no-man's-land: 'Below, the gloomy earth glittered under the continual scintillation of gunfire. Right round the salient down to the Somme, where the mists backed up the ghostly effect, was this sequined veil of greenish flashes, quivering. Thousands of guns were spitting high explosive, and the invisible projectiles were screaming past us on every side.'[39] Near Maricourt, Lieutenant Robert Kelly, RFA, said the muzzle flashes of French guns 'ran up and down the far slopes of the darkening valley, and the soft barks of their 75's mingled like the tappings on giant kettle-drums. ... We used to stand and watch the growing heaps of empty cartridge-cases dwarf the faint figures of the gunners until dusk veiled all things save the orange flashes of the guns.'[40] The sheer scale of the surreal light show was novel to many, and at least temporarily held their attention.

German positions were pounded, pummelled, pulverised. 'Artillery fire continues to a depth of ten kilometres [6.2 miles] behind the trenches; everything is blown to bits,' said one German soldier.[41] *Unteroffizier* Felix Kircher, Reserve Field Artillery Regiment 26 (RFAR26), assessed the trenches as 'drumfire flattened,'[42] as did an officer in Reserve Field

Artillery Regiment 20 (RFAR20) who wrote of an 'incalculable field of craters.'[43] *Kanonier* Hermann Heinrich, Field Artillery Regiment 21 (FAR21), thought the shellfire a 'travelling Hell, this whining, crashing and bursting of exploding shells.'[44] *Oberstleutnant* Alfred Vischer, commander of Infantry Regiment 180 (IR180), said he and his men saw 'smoke and masses of earth flying up like a shroud into the air above them and the incessant flashes of the shrapnel shells was like being in the mouth of Hell.'[45] *Leutnant-der-Reserve* Matthaus Gerster, Reserve Infantry Regiment 119 (RIR119), described the scene:

> All around there was howling, snarling and hissing. With a sharp ringing sound, the death-dealing shells burst, spewing their leaden fragments against our line. The [shrapnel] balls fell like hail on the roofs of the half-destroyed villages, whistled through the branches of the still-green trees and beat down hard on the parched ground, whipping up small clouds of smoke and dust from the earth.
> Large calibre shells droned through the air like giant bumblebees, crashing, smashing and boring down into the earth. Occasionally small calibre high explosive shells broke the pattern.[46]

Numerous villages, whether part of the forward defences or further back, were reduced to chaotic piles of wood and masonry. Some civilians were killed, the tearful living evacuated. *Feldwebel* Eiser said the resultant 'red cloud of disintegrating brickwork hindered visibility.'[47] *Fahrer* Otto Maute, IR180, saw Miraumont 'burning brightly.'[48] An ammunition train was blown up at Combles, while Ginchy, Guillemont, Longueval and a host of other villages were set ablaze and soon reduced to rubble.[49] Scarcely a wall stood in Beaumont Hamel,[50] Fricourt and surrounds were ploughed up,[51] Pozières was veiled in 'smoke and fumes.'[52] At Longueval, *Vizefeldwebel* Weickel, Reserve Infantry Regiment 109 (RIR109), described the shellfire as a 'most dreadful' overture:[53] 'One of the very first shells demonstrated their destructiveness, tearing down completely, as it did, the side wall of a tall house. Staircase, rooms, furniture, stoves; all were exposed to view. Two days later it was all one great heap of ruins.'[54] Once-orderly trenches became wastelands of loose earth, postcard villages collapsed into brickheaps and paddocks and roads were heavily dimpled. A pall of smoke and dust lingered over all. Gerster later wrote of the greyish veil:

> Was it chance or did the power of the endless shocks cause the dust in the air to coalesce? The clear sky soon clouded over and a light rain damped down the clouds of smoke from the exploding shells, thus making observation easier. At the same time the bombarded trenches, which were full of powdered, loose soil, were turned into muddy puddles, thus adding to the misery of the trench garrisons.[55]

Clouds of lethal chlorine gas were released from cylinders in the British lines from time to time, the idea being for the wind to carry its vapours across the long, rank, yellow grass of no-man's-land. These releases usually lasted an hour, but they were frequently stopped by erratic wind and technical problems.[56] Private William Senescall, 11th Suffolks, saw one gas cloud as it floated across no-man's-land. 'Low down on the ground you could see tree stumps, wire stakes etc sticking through it.'[57] Lieutenant-General Sir Aylmer Hunter-Weston, VIII Corps, described gas as 'nasty, tricky stuff' and hoped it would kill numerous Germans.[58] On 27 June, III Corps said 'gas from 1600 cylinders was liberated with smoke,'[59] while gas-mask-wearing enemy soldiers watched as the 'chlorine and phosgene plume clouds rolled in.'[60] German soldiers were generally well equipped with gas masks, meaning casualties were few,[61] and the gas clouds often dissipated before reaching the German gun lines.[62] A German officer at Fricourt said 'the pressure in the [British] gas cylinders is too low and the wind too weak for the men occupying the trenches to be much affected.'[63] Reserve Field Artillery Regiment 28 (RFAR28) said humidity and long grass worked as natural filters on the gas clouds.[64] Gas shells fired by the French 75-millimetre field guns produced negligible results.[65] A German Second Army report said because of 'technical mistakes, the enemy has so far achieved little through the use [of gas].'[66] Environmental and technical factors rendered Fourth Army's gas releases essentially useless.[67]

German soldiers sat out the gas clouds and shellfire tornado in their deep dugouts. *Leutnant-der-Reserve* Emil Geiger, Reserve Infantry

Regiment 121 (RIR121), described this period as 'terrible days of gruelling barrage.'[68] *Leutnant-der-Reserve* Rudolf Greisinger, IR180, remembered 'shaken and agitated men sitting in their dark shelters trembling and wondering if their [dugout] shelter will collapse.'[69] At Beaumont Hamel, *Leutnant* Stefan Westmann, RIR119, said the 'ground shook under the constant impact of light and heavy shells.'[70] *Feldwebel* Eiser felt the 'tremendous jolt and tremor of the "moling" shells with which they were showering the village. Heavy shells howled and wobbled high overhead.'[71] At Thiepval, *Gefreiter* Peter Kuster, RIR99, said heavy-calibre shells known as 'marmalade buckets' sounded 'like an InterCity train' and the earth trembled when they blew.[72] Kassel recalled a dud shell buckled his dugout's joists: 'My heart seemed to stop, now comes the end. ... But the catastrophe did not come.' *Grenadier* Walter Peeck, RIR119, agreed: 'Our dugouts were 8–10 metres [9–11 yards] deep and had been strengthened with heavy wooden beams and railroad ties. Lucky for us this provided quite adequate shelter.'[73] As *Leutnant-der-Reserve* Gerster explained: 'Half collapsed holes indicated where the dugouts which still remained were located. The staircases were buried beneath piles of earth, which had fallen down from above. As a result the troops had to scramble up a smooth steep slope, which offered almost no footholds, in order to climb up to daylight.'[74] Whatever the appearance of the German trenches between Montauban and Gommecourt, their garrisons, as we shall soon see, were mostly safely holed up yards below.

Some were not so lucky. Westmann repeatedly dug others 'out of masses of blackened earth and splintered wooden beams. Often we found bodies crushed to pulp, or bunks full of suffocated soldiers.'[75] He was writing of shallower dugouts, ones not designed to withstand direct hits.[76] Others told of how dreaded 38-centimetre shells slammed down, man-sized monsters that burrowed deep into the soft earth before detonating.[77] *Leutnant-der-Reserve* Wilhelm Geiger, Reserve Infantry Regiment 111 (RIR111), wrote of one such strike near Fricourt: 'All the lights went out. There were shouts in the dark and a choking cloud of explosive gases.'[78] Gerster was at Beaumont Hamel:

Their mighty explosions blew a crater three metres [3.3 yards] deep and 4–5 metres [4.4–5.5 yards] in diameter. Weaker dugouts were crushed by the force of these evil monsters. Soldiers sat in their dugouts and listened to the devilish whistling as these shells rushed down, all their senses alert and every nerve stretched to breaking point, and then the shell hit with a dull thud and exploded with a gruesome roar. ... Weak tallow candles and acetylene flames were extinguished by the blast. The walls rocked like a boat. Black and toxic smoke crept down the stairs. Soil and rock flew high in the air, and for a long time after the explosion the pelting down of stones and clods could be heard.[79]

Survivors were often left stunned, disoriented and shell-shocked.

Fourteenth Reserve Corps suffered an estimated 2500 casualties in the period 24–30 June,[80] and almost certainly no more than 3000. This from the corps' ration strength of about 95,000 men, which suggested a casualty rate of about 2.6–3.2%. This was a small loss given the thousands of British shells raining down. The oversized RIR99 at Thiepval was worst affected, with at least 472 men killed, wounded or missing. Infantry Regiment 62 (IR62) around Montauban suffered a total of 350 casualties, while Reserve Infantry Regiment 55 (RIR55) at Gommecourt booked losses totalling just 50. RIR121 at Redan Ridge and Heidenkopf, RIR119 around Beaumont Hamel and RIR111 around Fricourt lost 147, 103 and 87 officers and men respectively. Available data suggests the other infantry regiments comprising the corps suffered losses within this broad range, but precise figures for its numerous machine-gun, pioneering, artillery, transport and ancillary units are unavailable. Although XIV Reserve Corps had lost the equivalent of one infantry regiment, the overall low casualty rate proves that the vast majority of its men were safely housed in underground dugouts.

General-der-Infanterie Fritz von Below, commander of Second Army on the Somme, grew increasingly alarmed by the British preparations for what he expected to be an offensive of attrition. After five days' intensive shellfire he concluded that it would continue for some time:[81] 'Because of the procedure which he has adopted, the enemy is in a position to flatten our positions and smash our dugouts, through the application of days of fire with 280 and 300 millimetre guns. This means that our infantry is suffering heavy losses day after day, whilst the enemy is able to preserve his manpower.'[82] Below knew the shellfire would be followed by an infantry attack, and rightly determined that there was only so much shellfire his positions could withstand and so many casualties his units could suffer.

BRITISH SOLDIERS GENERALLY believed the bombardment effective. Private Alfred Askew, 7th Yorkshires, said he 'didn't think there would be any of them [German soldiers] left alive.'[83] Rifleman Frederick Conyers, 1st Rifle Brigade, was 'quite happily singing away, thinking, I did, that it would be a walkover.'[84] Private Howard Wide, 9th Devons, believed 'there would be little opposition to reaching our objective.'[85] Private Arthur Ward, 1/5th Lincolns, had 'visions of the enemy being devastated' and hoped this would 'achieve a miracle, perhaps collapse of the enemy.'[86] Lieutenant Philip Heath, 55th Trench Mortar Battery, said his men were 'so confident that many of them had taken to sitting on the parapet of their trenches to watch what was going on.'[87] Lieutenant Billy Goodwin, 8th York & Lancasters, was 'most excessively cheerful' and thought 'Mr Fritz won't know or dare to look for us until we're on top of him. Everybody is feeling gloriously confident.'[88] Rifleman Herbert Williams, London Rifle Brigade, said a 'break-through was confidently expected.'[89] Private Arthur England, 8th Norfolks, wrote: 'We were told that the Great Push would be a walkover, and we believed it, for surely no one could have survived such punishment.'[90] Captain John Collis-Browne, 2nd Lancashire Fusiliers, said, 'this must be the start of the end of the war!!!'[91] Most believed the infantry attack would be nothing less than an outstanding success, the epitaph to a bombardment whose scale and fury they had not seen before.[92]

A much smaller number of soldiers were sceptical. Second-Lieutenant Archibald Laporte, RFA, bade a fellow officer at La Boisselle good luck: 'You know as well as I do we shall never get across.'[93] Major Alfred Gibbs, RFA, later said Thiepval was 'inadequately bombarded by Heavy Artillery before the battle, and I expect most of those concerned thought the same. I remember having very grave misgivings as to the chances of our attack succeeding.'[94] Brigadier-General Henry Croft, 68th Brigade, said during training the 'usual joke went round that we were being "fed up for slaughter."'[95] Others were convinced that the relative quiescence of the German guns was by design rather than because they had been destroyed.[96] Lieutenant Aubrey Moore, 1/5th Leicesters, doubted the 'trenches would be full of dead Boche — a few, perhaps.'[97] Ashurst noted that 'Fritz kept strangely quiet. ... He knew that later on he would need every bit of ammunition and patiently reserved his fire.'[98] Lieutenant Jocelyn Buxton, 2nd Rifle Brigade, imagined that 'the German generals opposite are having to think furiously.'[99] Rifleman Henry Barber, London Rifle Brigade, held a similar view when he said the bombardment unsurprisingly led to the 'Germans scenting that something was brewing.'[100] Fraser-Tytler wondered if 'the Hun has any surprise devilry in store; he has been suspiciously quiet on the whole, but, of course, as the whole line is strafing he may think that it is only a bluff on this sector.'[101] Major Jack was cynical about optimistic senior staff officers.[102] He pondered, 'how much of this admirable spirit will survive the German fusillade?'[103] Lieutenant Capper thought the surge in artillery activity 'must have given the Germans warning of an impending attack.'[104] These soldiers all expected the attacking infantry to encounter at least some organised resistance after the impressive bombardment lifted.

Perhaps it was with a view to quieting any such murmurings, along with generally boosting morale, that numerous formation commanders assembled their men for a series of sabre-rattling talks. Most were convened in the days immediately before battle, and several on 30 June. In 50th Brigade, Brigadier-General William Glasgow told the Yorkshires to 'give them hell, no prisoners. ... Now is the time to get your own back.'[105] Hunter-Weston fronted various battalions of VIII Corps and told his men the attack would be a walkover. 'What a load of bullshit he talked,' said a less-than-convinced Private Donald Cameron, 12th York & Lancasters.[106] Such reactions, whatever their pithy appeal, were extreme even at the time. The widespread absence of such comments in literally hundreds of soldiers' memoirs and diaries from the day suggests this disgruntled soldier — and several others like him in VIII Corps — were responding more to 'Hunter Bunter' and his reputation as a bungler than to Haig and Rawlinson's battle plan. Even then, there were exceptions within VIII Corps. As Captain Collis-Browne wrote, Hunter-Weston's message was 'conveyed to my men, it gave us all good heart.'[107] Lieutenant Lewis was upbeat after Temporary Major-General Hugh Trenchard, head of the RFC, gave a pep talk to his squadron. 'We were all sure that victory was certain. That the [German] line would be broken, the cavalry put through, and the Allies sweep on to Berlin.'[108] Most servicemen remained reticent, however; they well knew death and injury were very real risks in battle, regardless of how impressive the shellfire appeared or what some jawboning officer had said beforehand.

Back in the danger zone, empathy for German soldiers varied. Lieutenant Goodwin, who would be shot dead on 1 July while snared in barbed wire near Ovillers, told a friend that 'I wouldn't be a Bosche just now for a good deal.'[109] Lieutenant Lushington doubted whether a 'human being could live under that terrible blasting and hammering!'[110] Rifleman Smith noted the comments of men in his platoon: '"Let 'em have it." ... "Give them a dose of their own medicine." ... "Keep it up, boys."'[111] And later, 'fellows were laughing for joy as they contemplated the shaking this bombardment was giving the Germans.'[112] Hunter-Weston, a 'rubicund little man,'[113] wrote that it was 'very satisfactory that we are now able to repay them in their own coin.'[114] Private England was one of several 'almost moved to be sorry for the Hun.'[115] Some regarded the bombardment as payback for hostile shellfire past, others contemplated the suffering foisted upon their enemies; all were pleased that they were not on the receiving end of the metal tornado themselves.

Across the other side of no-man's-land, Baden, Württemberg, Prussian and Bavarian dugout dwellers were short of food, water and sleep. Many lived on coffee, and the occasional tepid stew brought up by ration parties at night.[116] Not all of the ration parties made it through the shellfire, though.[117] Drinking water was scarce, let alone water for bathing or shaving in the hot, candle-lit chambers. *Gefreiter* Kuster said no provisions reached his parched platoon near Thiepval: 'We collected rain water from the trench and made coffee on the little spirit burner.'[118] Another complained that the 'English offensive has been known long enough to permit more arrangements being made to prevent this.'[119] Toilets were buckets, run upstairs and slopped out into a shell hole when full. Within days the dugouts were ripe with stale air, tobacco smoke and body odour. One soldier said his bunker was a 'beastly hole.'[120] *Oberleutnant-der-Reserve* Heinrich Vogler, IR180, said 'my men's mood was low, but they were in no way lacking in courage or determination.

Many were still writing letters to their loved ones at home.'[121] Privations compounded as the shellfire continued. 'We are getting no rest day or night,' said one soldier, 'sleep is quite a secondary thing, and as for food, that is the same.'[122] Wilhelm Geiger, RIR111, was ready to 'drop with tiredness and wanted to snatch some sleep.'[123] *Leutnant-der-Reserve* Gerster said the 'uninterrupted high state of readiness, which had to be maintained because of the entire situation ... hindered the troops from getting the sleep that they needed because of the nerve-shattering artillery fire.'[124] *Leutnant-der-Landwehr* Max Lazarus, RIR109, wrote: 'Every one of us in these five days has become years older. We hardly know ourselves.'[125]

Starvation, thirst, exhaustion and shellfire brought fatigue, which soon became chronic. Gerster described the mood in his dugout:

> Tired and indifferent to everything, the troops sat it out on wooden benches or lay on the hard metal beds, staring into the darkness when the tallow lights were extinguished by the overpressure of the explosions. Nobody had washed for days. Black stubble stood out on the pale haggard faces, whilst the eyes of some flashed strangely as though they had looked beyond the portals of the other side. Some trembled when the sound of death roared around the underground protected places. Whose heart was not in his mouth at times during this appalling storm of steel?[126]

This maddening existence was commonplace.

Soldiers' moods worsened as fatigue set in. *Feldwebel* Eiser pondered how many 'men would a battalion or infantry regiment still have who were fit to fight?'[127] One despairing soldier of RIR111 concluded, 'we cannot hold out much longer.'[128] *Leutnant-der-Reserve* August Bielefeld, Reserve Foot Artillery Regiment 16 (RFtAR16), said the 'continuous artillery bombardment got on our nerves,'[129] aggravated by dugout claustrophobia and a lack of contact with the outside world. *Leutnant* Westmann saw that men 'became hysterical and their comrades had to knock them out, so as to prevent them from running away and exposing themselves to the deadly shell splinters.'[130] *Unteroffizier* Friedrich Hinkel, RIR99, found the 'torture and the fatigue, not to mention the strain on the nerves, were indescribable!'[131] *Infanterist* Theodor Eversmann, RIR99, recorded his mood decline, from 'uncertainty is hard to bear' to a despairing 'How long will it go on?'[132] Finally, Eversmann, who was killed on 1 July, contemplated his own mortality:

> One's head is a madman's; the tongue sticks to the roof of the mouth. Five days and five nights, a long time, to us an eternity. Almost nothing to eat and nothing to drink. No sleep, always wakened again. All contact with the outer world cut off. No sign of life from home, nor can we send any news to our loved ones. What anxiety they must feel about us. How long is this going to last? Still there is no use thinking about it. If I may not see my loved ones again, I greet them with a last farewell.[133]

Heavily fatigued soldiers who were unable to cope with the stress succumbed to nervous exhaustion and, less frequently, breakdown.

Nobody doubted what the shellfire meant. *Fahrer* Maute thought 'the British are going to open an offensive and this seems to be starting.'[134] Others were more expansive. *Soldat* Wilhelm Lange, RIR99, knew the 'big attack that had been expected for a long time would now follow.'[135] *Generalleutnant* Franz *Freiherr* von Soden, whose 26th Reserve Division held almost half of the besieged ground, realised it heralded the 'beginning of the long-expected attack.'[136] Eversmann wondered when the attack would begin: 'tomorrow or the day after? Who knows?'[137] A soldier in RIR111 commented midway through the bombardment that although no British attack had yet materialised, 'we are prepared.'[138] An officer in RIR121 said it was 'a deliverance as you finally knew where you stood,' meaning he expected an imminent attack.[139] *Vizefeldwebel* Weickel felt there 'could no longer be any doubt. This was deadly serious. It was a matter of life and death and the enemy was going all out for destruction.'[140] German soldiers expected an attack, and soon, but the exact date and time remained unknown to them.

These soldiers remained generally willing to defend their positions. *Oberstleutnant* Vischer overstated the case when he claimed the mood in IR180 was 'excellent' and that his men 'look forward to the coming attack.'[141] *Leutnant-der-Reserve* Gerster was nearer the mark when he said many were 'seized by a deep bitterness at the inhuman machine of destruction which hammered endlessly. A searing rage against the enemy burned in their minds.'[142] *Leutnant-der-Reserve* Friedrich Stutz, RIR121, felt similarly: 'This thought completely dominated our mood. Everything else, danger to life, food shortages, hardships and suffering combined into anger towards the English.'[143] Hinkel shared these opinions:

> There was just one single heartfelt prayer on our lips: 'Oh God, free us from this ordeal; give us release through battle, grant us victory; Lord God! Just let them come!' and this determination increased with the fall of each shell. You made a good job of it, you British! Seven days and nights you rapped and hammered on our door! Now your reception was going to match your turbulent longing to enter![144]

Other veterans, however, were more measured. One simply said that when the bombardment ended 'we will have it out between us.'[145] *Leutnant-der-Reserve* Kassel later recalled that he and his dull, apathetic men were 'prepared to defend ourselves whatever the cost.'[146] A battery commander in RFAR20 said the British 'expected to reap the success of the fire that was designed to wear us down — and were [to be] badly disappointed.'[147] There were exceptions, of course: near Mametz some soldiers of RIR109 mulled the merits of surrendering over resistance and likely death.[148] German soldiers were, overall, well prepared to meet the British attack when it eventually came, and many were motivated by a desire to exact bloody payback for their ordeal by shellfire.

Back in the British lines, gunners were frustrated by equipment failures. Among the heavy batteries numerous guns broke down through overuse or shoddy manufacture. No fewer than 29 (7%) of Fourth Army's 427 heavy artillery pieces failed during the bombardment, usually due to damaged bores, wear and tear and a host of other reasons.[149] Failures among the 6-inch, 9.2-inch and 60-pounder guns were commonplace, as they were among the 4.7-, 6- and 15-inch howitzers.[150] Often these guns were out of action for at least one day, possibly more. Moreover, the 4.7-inch guns were obsolete, and many of the 6-inch howitzers were limited in range and lacked hydraulic recoil systems, meaning they had to be repeatedly re-aimed.[151] The 8-inch howitzers were bastardised coastal guns that also lacked hydraulic recoil systems. No wonder that Lieutenant Heath thought such weapons to be 'antediluvian monsters.'[152] Field artillery batteries also struggled with breakdowns. Buffer-spring trouble among 18-pounders was rife. No fewer than 64 (6%) of Fourth Army's 1010 field artillery barrels were sidelined for at least one day, if not more.[153] 'We had never expected to have to fire so many shells in such a short space of time and the guns had become overheated,' said Sergeant Robert Sutterby, RFA.[154] The number of guns out of action for at least one day was probably closer to 10%, if not more, which was a sizeable dilution of the firepower on which so much depended.

Weapons were repaired with whatever parts were to hand or could be scrounged. Eighteenth (Eastern) Division had exhausted its supplies of 18-pounder buffer springs by the end of June.[155] 'I had to improvise,' wrote Sutterby of salvaging parts from derelict weapons. 'With the aid of a few gunners some drag ropes and a few stumps of trees, I lashed the [derelict] gun to a tree stump and the men held on to the ropes. As I released the tension on the recuperator front nut, they let the gun piece move steadily until it had expended all its savage rebound.'[156] Twenty-four hours later Sutterby's 18-pounders were again contributing to the bombardment. 'The boys were surprised at seeing how it was done.'[157]

Many of the shells, fuses and cartridges were faulty, unreliable or unusable. Numerous reports referred to them as 'not so good,' 'unsatisfactory,' or simply 'bad.'[158] Problematic fuses were the most common cause of 'dud' shells, meaning those that failed to detonate.[159] Lieutenant-Colonel Arthur Jenour, RGA, complained that American-made ammunition 'was not very good, quite an appreciable proportion being duds.'[160] Fuses exposed to moisture often failed to detonate, or threw accuracy out by hundreds of yards.[161] Third Corps said 2000 rounds for its 6-inch howitzers lacked model-44 fuses or adaptors.[162] Thirteenth Corps' artillery was plagued by numerous bad-quality fuses, its 6-, 4.5- and 8-inch howitzers firing numerous duds.[163] Fuses for 8-inch howitzers so frequently failed that the battlefield was in places littered with unexploded munitions; attempts to fix the problem flopped when the fuses unscrewed themselves in flight.[164] Model-100 fuses for explosive shells were supposed to blow on impact and cut barbed wire, but the wet ground absorbed the shells and reduced blast effectiveness. Had the 'quality of the ammunition been good [which even then suggests plenty of room for improvement], the quantity might have sufficed,' wrote the British official historian.[165] The number of dud shells might have totalled as much as 10–20% — it is difficult to estimate precisely — meaning the bombardment's effectiveness was reduced by at least this much.

One German soldier used a sliver of chalk to scrawl 'I don't want war!' on the belly of a dud British 38-centimetre shell. Soon a smaller-calibre missile landed nearby and also failed to blow. Someone scribbled 'Neither do I!' on its side. 'This childish little joke,' wrote a German soldier, 'stood out against the seriousness, horror and death.'[166]

The preparatory bombardment provided a steep learning curve for many gunners. Captain Innes Ware, RGA, learned a 'certain amount about the intricacies of gunnery' on the Somme.[167] The different shell diameters, the multitude of fuses each with different purposes, and the variety of brass-cased cartridges to fire the projectiles made the job a complex one: 'These charges had varying degrees of velocity attached to them. They had something on our range tables and we had to make allowances for that. Really it was quite a complicated matter.'[168] Inevitably some gunners either did not fully understand the charts, or simply did not attach sufficient importance to them. Major Musard Nanson, RGA, said many artillery officers failed 'to make accurate use of the data then supplied in the range tables of their guns for the purpose of the correction of their shooting to allow for changes in the meteorological conditions since a registration of accurate shooting had been obtained.'[169] As another artillery officer later said, 'In truth the problem of semi-siege warfare and the large concentration of guns necessary for the work had never been studied by the General Staff in peace, nor by any of the leading gunners, or gunnery schools, [so] we had to learn our lesson in the pitiless school of war.'[170] Pitiless, indeed, and with so very much riding on the success of the bombardment and on the gunners providing it.

Problems with ground observation added to the difficulties in assessing the field artillery's wire-cutting. This was important work, noted Lieutenant Moore, who said the German wire — with a thick core and razor-sharp one-and-a-half-inch barbs — was a serious obstacle for infantry. It was mostly 'held up by wooden stakes, the depth or width of this carpet of wire was seldom less than 20 yards and about three feet high, and it was very dense. In many of the enemy's more important strategic positions a double row was put down.'[171] It was no surprise that the British parapet 'was lined like the dress circle at a theatre' with forward observation officers (FOO), said one, but the dense shellfire 'did not conduce to accurate observation.'[172] Third and XIII Corps discovered long grass made assessing damage to the enemy wire difficult.[173] Bad weather also affected ground observation.[174] Thirteenth Corps said on 26 June that observation was difficult 'owing to weather and smoke discharge,'[175] while XV Corps noted on 27 June that visibility was 'difficult owing to storms & bad light.'[176] On 28 June, X Corps said rain and bad light for most of the day 'made observation at times impossible,'[177] a problem also noted by VIII Corps.[178] In spite of these difficulties, FOO reports retained a positive bias. In the northern part of the battlefield, where the lie of the land afforded limited observation, III, VIII and X Corps often described their gunners' work as 'satisfactory' or 'good.'[179] In the southern area, where the British positions yielded better views, FOO reports were couched in strikingly similar language. Fifteenth Corps referred to the wire's being cut with 'fairly satisfactory results' and 'well and satisfactorily cut', while XIII Corps said its results were 'very' and 'quite' satisfactory.[180] At times other phrases such as 'progress made,'[181] 'very effective,'[182] 'everything going well,'[183] and 'successfully completed'[184] were used. The theme of these corps' reports suggested wire-cutting was — despite marked observational difficulties — going broadly to plan, but in truth they offered no meaningful assessment.

Infantry patrols probing the German lines under veil of darkness discovered all was not well, as records from about 50 patrols in the period 24–30 June reveal. These covered about 20% of the German front line facing Fourth Army.[185] At best these presented an ambiguous picture of the state of the enemy's front-line wire; at worst they suggested significant problems. Of the 50 patrols, 24 (48%) said the wire in their sectors was not cut, 20 (40%) reported it was cut, and six (12%) that it was only cut in some places.[186] This ratio did not appreciably improve as the bombardment progressed.[187] On a corps-by-corps basis, the wire facing XV and XIII Corps in the Fricourt–Mametz–Montauban area was cut considerably better than that elsewhere, presumably because of the better observation there. Further north, the reports lacked consistency and showed that III and X Corps' wire-cutting was almost evenly split between positive and negative results.[188] In VIII Corps' area, the wire was intact before 31st Division, reasonably well cut in front of 4th Division and varied from non-existent to strong before 29th Division.[189] Rawlinson said on 30 June that he was 'not quite satisfied that all the wire has been thoroughly cut,'[190] but General Sir Douglas Haig firmly believed the job had been done well.[191] Rawlinson and Haig were, however, concerned by VIII Corps' progress, largely because of disquieting patrol reports from that area, and Major-General Beauvoir de Lisle, commanding 29th Division, who was 'anxious about the success of the attack north of the Ancre.'[192] While patrol reports implied almost two-thirds of the wire-cutting had failed outright or in part, Haig — beguiled by generally optimistic corps' artillery summaries — believed otherwise.

To most corps-level observers the enemy front-line trench system seemed heavily battered. Tenth Corps said on 28 June that its heavy howitzers had been effective in destroying the opposing German defences,[193] and two days later that 'as far as results could be seen', concentrated shellfire had done satisfactory damage.[194] Thirteenth Corps was even more upbeat on 26 June, reporting the German front line was 'very badly damaged, also much of [the] second line.'[195] A day later it noted that 'Practically whole [German] front line done in except in a few places.'[196] Fifteenth Corps reported on 28 June that 'many strong points and MG Emplacements destroyed,'[197] and on the eve of battle that the 'whole of the hostile trench system appears to be very knocked about.'[198] Seventh Corps assessed the German trenches as 'very much knocked about,'[199] adding the bombardment had been 'very effective.'[200] Eighth Corps said the shelling of opposing German trenches was progressing satisfactorily by 27 June, and just 48 hours later that its 4.5-inch howitzers had 'done considerable damage to front and second line trenches. Judging by [aerial] photographs trenches have been badly battered.'[201] Third Corps said its two front-line divisions 'appeared satisfied with wire & bombardment,'[202] and on other occasions that there was 'noticeable' and 'considerable' damage done.[203] From the other side of no-man's-land, the smoke- and dust-shrouded jumble of debris that was the German line looked increasingly indefensible.

General Sir Douglas Haig, commander of the British army, was optimistic and bullish, and believed his Third and Fourth Armies would punch through the German lines on the first day of the Somme, bringing a return to mobile warfare. His attack was focused on the strongest portion of the German Second Army's positions and was significantly under-resourced. *(Te Papa)*

General-der-Infanterie Erich von Falkenhayn, the German Chief of General Staff, Supreme Army Command, was focused on operations at Verdun and Galicia, and believed his Second Army had the resources to ward off an Anglo-French offensive on the Somme. Falkenhayn under-estimated the French component, however, and was forced to rethink his Somme strategy going forward. *(Period postcard)*

Lieutenant-General Sir Henry Rawlinson, commanding Fourth Army, preferred a step-by-step approach to operations on the Somme and doubted a breakthrough would be achieved on the offensive's first day.
(Imperial War Museum [IWM])

General-der-Infanterie Fritz von Below, commanding the under-resourced German Second Army, expected a strong British offensive north of the Somme, but underestimated the strength of the French attack.
(Author's collection)

Lieutenant-General Sir Edmund Allenby, commanding Third Army, went along with plans for an operation at Gommecourt salient to divert German artillery and infantry reserves, despite his initial reservations. *(IWM)*

Generalleutnant Hermann von Stein, commanding the German XIV Reserve Corps, expected the Allied offensive, but the outcome of battle revealed his failure to create defences of uniform strength north of the River Somme.
(Period postcard)

Lieutenant-General Sir Thomas D'Oyly Snow did not understand the difference between diversions and feints, which explains why his VII Corps became a magnet for German machine-gun and artillery fire at Gommecourt. *(IWM)*

Generalleutnant Richard *Freiherr* von Süsskind-Schwendi was the aloof and ruthless commander of 2nd Guards Reserve Division at Gommecourt, where his men annihilated VII Corps.
(Author's collection)

Lieutenant-General Sir Aylmer Hunter-Weston condemned his VIII Corps to disaster around Serre and Beaumont Hamel after bungling his artillery plan and the timing of the Hawthorn Ridge mine blast prior to battle. *(IWM)*

Generalleutnant Karl von Borries oversaw his 52nd Infantry Division's construction of bespoke and robust defences between Gommecourt and Serre, which defeated VII and VIII Corps. *(Courtesy of Infantry Regiment 170)*

Lieutenant-General Sir Thomas Morland's X Corps mostly failed bloodily because of his linear thinking around Thiepval, while dithered command decisions on his part resulted in missed opportunities at Schwaben Redoubt. *(IWM)*

Generalleutnant Franz *Freiherr* von Soden drove his 26th Reserve Division hard to develop a lethal network of defensive killing zones between Serre and Ovillers, which mostly repulsed III, VIII and X Corps' attacks. *(Courtesy of 26th Reserve Division)*

Lieutenant-General Sir William Pulteney was guileless and ignorant of the strength of the German defences his III Corps faced at Ovillers and La Boisselle, which was why it failed so tragically in a maelstrom of machine-gun fire. *(IWM)*

Generalleutnant Ferdinand von Hahn, the head of 28th Reserve Division, successfully defended La Boisselle against III Corps, but lesser-quality positions at Fricourt and Mametz saw both lost to XV Corps by 2 July 1916. *(Courtesy of Reserve Infantry Regiment 221)*

Lieutenant-General Sir Walter Congreve, VC, was professionally minded and prepared, which was why his XIII Corps triumphed over German positions at Montauban. He focused on consolidating gains rather than exploiting them. *(IWM)*

Generalleutnant Martin Châles de Beaulieu's hands-off command of 12th Infantry Division between Montauban and the River Somme condemned his men to failure against the British XIII Corps and French XX Corps. *(Courtesy of Infantry Regiment 23)*

Lieutenant-General Sir Henry Horne had a ruthless, nimble mind and produced partial victory by his XV Corps at Fricourt and Mametz, but his opportunist streak caused unnecessary casualties when he attempted to force Fricourt's early capture. *(IWM)*

General Sir Hubert Gough was the bullish, attack-minded commander of Reserve Army, which was to come into play after German lines were breached. He was to be frustrated throughout the opening day of the Somme. *(Te Papa)*

Officers and men of 15th West Yorkshires take a break from practising trench digging in England. This battalion was destroyed by German machine-gun fire near Serre on 1 July 1916. *(Peter Smith Collection)*

Württemberg soldiers of all ages stop work for a cigarette and a crafty swig of wine in a trench near Beaucourt, in the River Ancre valley. *(Author's collection)*

Tin hats, puttees, gas masks and Lee Enfields — soldiers from a York and Lancasters' battalion scrubbed up well for a behind-the-lines studio photograph to be sent home to their families in England. *(Peter Smith Collection)*

'You will certainly be a bit miffed as I didn't send you any news, but I totally forgot,' wrote *Ersatz-Reservist* August Stegmaier, Infantry Regiment 180, from the trenches at Serre. Stegmaier, pictured at top left, was killed on 28 September 1916. *(Author's collection)*

Dig, dig, dig! Württemberg soldiers from Pioneer Battalion 13 take a breather from excavating what appears to be either a deep dugout to withstand British shellfire or a mine chamber under no-man's-land. *(Author's collection)*

Gas-mask-wearing British soldiers rehearse the job of clearing a mock German trench under the watchful eye of trainers in England. Fist-sized beanbags were used as substitutes for hand grenades during training. *(Peter Smith Collection)*

'I was terribly worried,' wrote Lieutenant-Colonel Robert Collins, 17th (Northern) Division headquarters, of the 10th West Yorkshires' role on the first day of the Somme. The battalion suffered galling casualties advancing from trenches like these near Fricourt. *(IWM)*

Several tumbled-down red-brick villages hemmed into the forward German defensive system remained formidable infantry obstacles. These fortified villages totalled nine across the entire battle front, all engineered to hold multiple shell-proofed machine-gun posts in their mazes of interconnected cellars and ruins. These posts were difficult to pinpoint before the bombardment, and near impossible when their camouflaged firing apertures looked pretty much like any other dark void in the piles of rubble. It did not matter much whether that was at Gommecourt, Serre, Beaumont Hamel, Ovillers, Mametz or Montauban, which were all a jot behind the front line, or at Thiepval, La Boisselle and Fricourt, which were part of it. Machine-gunners sat out the bombardment in their dugouts and more than likely were under orders to stay their fire to avoid detection. At La Boisselle, for example, all of its 35 cottages were wrecked save a few lonely walls and topsy-turvy roofs. As one historian has noted, 'To all appearances, therefore, La Boisselle was but a rubble heap, which afforded poor protection against an attacking force; actually it was a terribly strong position in which a small garrison of brave and determined men could offer a stout resistance for a considerable length of time, causing heavy casualties amongst assaulting troops.'[204] These razed villages received nothing like the dead weight of shell needed to neutralise their firepower, and each successive blast only made it more difficult to locate machine-gun posts hidden among their ruins.

German infantrymen who chanced death by shell blast for a look above ground found their earthworks devastated. All line regiments reported their trenches flattened, reduced to shallow scrapes or pitted wastelands of overlapping shell holes and quite unrecognisable, while barbed-wire entanglements were damaged.[205] *Leutnant-der-Reserve* Gerster outlined the scene in his typically vivid manner: 'Tangles of wire wrapped around steel supports still showed in some places. ... Where the front line trench once ran, shreds of corrugated iron, splinters of timber shuttering, empty food tins, smashed weapons and the kit and equipment of the dead and wounded lay everywhere.'[206]

RFC aerial photographs, however, showed that many heavily shell-pocked trench lines retained at least some of their pre-bombardment form, more so between Gommecourt and La Boisselle than between Fricourt and Montauban. Evidently some of these German regimental writers — several of whom published their books as propaganda during the First World War, others during the more nationalistic 1930s — over-wrote the hardships and difficulties to emphasise the victory of 1 July. Soden was closer to the mark when he said his 26th Reserve Division's positions initially withstood the shellfire well, but were soon severely damaged.[207] The inevitable conclusion among German officers and men was that their positions were increasingly ripe for attack,[208] but that did not mean they were indefensible.

The acid test was whether enough deep dugouts had been destroyed, killing or incapacitating their occupants. If sufficient German soldiers lived and won the race to their parapet, British infantry would be met with a storm of bullets in no-man's-land and their attack would almost certainly fail. Intelligence gathering fell to night-time patrols that stole into the hostile ditches, inspecting damage and nabbing prisoners. The large tracts of uncut or partially broken wire before VIII, X and III Corps — between Serre and Leipzig Redoubt — frequently blocked the raiders. In places they were driven off by rifle fire from an alert garrison, suggesting either that the dugouts were intact or that the shellfire had not hit the trenches sheltering enemy infantry.[209] Before XV and XIII Corps, the wire was better cut and patrols frequently breached the enemy parapet, finding several dugouts blown in.[210] Even in this area, on the eve of battle, several patrols were forced back by heavy German machine-gun and rifle fire, implying that here too enemy soldiers had been sheltering underground.[211] Twelve prisoner interrogations were published by Fourth Army in the period 25–30 June, nine from XV Corps' area and one each from III, X and XIII Corps' sectors.[212] These suggested some dugouts had been destroyed around Fricourt, Mametz and Montauban, but negligible intelligence for the ground between Leipzig Redoubt and Serre meant no such conclusions could be drawn for that part of the battlefield.[213]

German casualty figures provide a telling insight. That the preparatory bombardment caused 2500–3000 casualties, or 2.6–3.2% of XIV Reserve Corps' strength, meant the remaining 92,000–92,500 officers and men, or 96.8–97.4%, were alive and able to defend their positions. This survival rate very obviously reveals that the vast majority of German dugouts across XIV Reserve Corps' sector were intact at the end of the preparatory bombardment.

Senior British intelligence officers, who were unaware of this data at the time, ignored the abundance of available warning signs that the shellfire-torn German positions remained not only defensible, but also defended. 'From the examination of prisoners,' said Fourth Army Intelligence, 'it is apparent that our artillery fire has been most effective. Most of the dug-outs in the [enemy] front line have been blown in or blocked up. Even the deep dug-outs of a Battalion H.Q. were not proof against our big shells.'[214] This singular optimism was shared by Brigadier-General John Charteris, Haig's toadying chief of intelligence. 'So far as I can see, the Germans have no real idea of any attack in force being imminent,' he wrote on 28 June, entirely out of touch with reality. 'The chief danger I fear is that they should leave their front-line trenches practically empty and hold in strength their second and third lines. Evidence to-day tends to show that this has not been done as yet.'[215] Was Charteris implying he knew the enemy front line remained well defended with its infantry holed up in dugouts, or was he suggesting more worryingly that distant German trenches remained intact and defensible? Charteris was also well aware that the German artillery and infantry had not been silenced.[216] A day earlier he had assessed that there 'must be heavy [British] casualties,' referring more to the overall scale of Haig's attack than hinting at pending disaster, 'but everything looks well for success.'[217] With hindsight, Fourth Army Intelligence's and Charteris's conclusions can be seen as vacuous — but at the time they were the official line given to Haig and Rawlinson.

German accounts reveal that infantrymen all along the line were waiting for Haig's attack to begin, which did not bode well for its chances of success. Sentries sheltered in dugout entrances, popping out to nose around, or using a mirror to peer into no-man's-land.[218] It was harrowing work; death and injury were commonplace.[219] 'Many a time,' wrote *Feldwebel* Schumacher, RIR119, 'I came across a man on sentry, his rosary in his hand and his thoughts directed to the strict fulfilment of his duties.'[220] Near Ovillers on 25 June a sentry of IR180 alerted his company to an enemy patrol, which was shot into retreat.[221] Patrols near Beaumont Hamel and Thiepval on the nights of 26 and 29 June were also thwarted by vigilant lookouts; dugout dwellers raced up into fresh air and drove the raiders back.[222] South of Serre, RIR121 said repeated British patrols were fended off by alert soldiers who rushed from their dugouts at a moment's notice.[223] Referring to 26th Reserve Division's sector north of the Albert–Bapaume road, *Leutnant-der-Reserve* Gerster was correct when he said the battered 'German positions were ripe for attack, but not the crew!'[224] Further south, at Montauban, IR62 believed that 'although the position was battered, the garrison was still prepared to defend it.'[225] The message was clear: the broken forward German positions remained at least defensible, their garrisons largely intact and responsive to enemy activity.

The shellfire had little physical impact on the German chain of command, but severely disrupted its communication network. Fourteenth Reserve Corps commander *Generalleutnant* Hermann von Stein's headquarters at Bapaume was tested by long-range shellfire, but stayed put and in contact with its subordinate divisions via telephone. Two regimental headquarters were destroyed — those of RIR110 and RIR121, the latter's commanding officer killed — but brigade and divisional headquarters remained operational. Officer losses were few. RIR99 recorded 16 officer casualties during the bombardment, or about 3% of its total losses during that period.[226] More worrying were the frequently cut telephone links in the forward battle zone.[227] Front-line infantry companies and platoons were all too often isolated from their own battalion and regimental headquarters, and crucially their supporting artillery.[228] Runners took too long to convey messages, and emergency flares to call down defensive shellfire often went unseen in the shroud of smoke. Light-signalling equipment was equally ineffective, and risked revealing headquarters' locations.[229] This patchy communication in Stein's forward battle zone meant he was dependent on infantry units standing firm when the enemy attacked, relying on rehearsed defensive tactics and on his artillery chiming in independently with a defensive barrage.

MUCH DEPENDED ON how effective Haig's counter-battery fire was in pinpointing and destroying the guns and artillery positions of XIV Reserve Corps. Most commonly these German batteries were located in some valley, ruined building or shot-through wood, or otherwise simply dug into the ground and camouflaged. They were supposed to be spotted by eyes-peeled observers in aircraft or tethered kite balloons, the latter likened to 'great gorged leeches of the air,'[230] 'yellow dragons in the blue skies'[231] or 'pensive and somewhat inebriated tadpoles.'[232] The giveaways were muzzle flashes, piles of shell casings or the wicker baskets that held them, and poorly disguised earthworks. Sound-ranging was nascent, and in any case the ballad of shellfire rendered that technology more or less useless.[233] The idea of counter-battery fire was to destroy or neutralise a sufficient number of German artillery batteries to either prevent or reduce their ability to fire a defensive barrage that could break up Haig's infantry attack.

The problem was that Haig simply did not have big enough guns — 60-pounder guns and howitzers with bores of six inches or greater — for the job. There were only about 441 (24.9%) of these artillery pieces suitable for counter-battery fire across the attack fronts of Fourth and Third Armies.[234] Available data suggests these fired roughly 226,300 high-explosive shells on Fourth Army's front, or an estimated 15% of the 1.5 million released.[235] But shellfire from these big, vital weapons was neutered from the outset by being apportioned over seven days, spread across Fourth Army's 25,000-yard-wide (14.2-mile-wide) sector, diluted throughout XIV Reserve Corps' depth positions and split by a variety of destructive tasks beyond counter-battery. 'There were not sufficient guns on the [VIII] Corps front to attend to the hostile batteries,'[236] said Captain James McDiarmid, RGA, adding that the 'importance of efficient Counter Battery Work had not been fully realised.'[237] Emphasis on this type of fire varied between corps: XIII Corps gave it greater priority than XV Corps, the others falling somewhere in between. Even then, competing target priorities, wet weather, poor observation and limited ammunition supply meant the volume of this fire could vary from one day to the next, even within a single corps. Fortunately for Stein the planners at Fourth Army headquarters attached less priority to counter-battery work, which was already far too thinly spread, than to wire-cutting and trench destruction.[238]

On the face of it, Fourth Army's counter-battery gunners appeared to make progress. Corps artillery war diarists recorded alleged success in their counter-battery work almost daily, but the data and the way in which it was compiled varied considerably.[239] By 30 June it was clear from German shellfire that the counter-battery work had not gone to plan.

Fourth Army's five corps variously assessed hostile fire that day as 'heavy,' 'active,' 'moderate,' 'considerable' and 'fairly active.'[240] Two days earlier Rawlinson noted the destruction of German guns was not going well.[241] It was this that Major William Dobbie, VIII Corps headquarters, referred to when he later said the 'reports received at first were very rosy and it was not for some time that we realised that something was amiss.'[242]

RFC reports confirmed Rawlinson's counter-battery worries. Of the 571 active battery positions and gun emplacements the RFC claimed to have spotted in the period 24–30 June, just 59 (10.3%) were alleged to have been hit by shells.[243] Part of the difficulty lay in the artillery's accuracy. Captain Ware said of every 800 shells his gun fired only a 'very small number' landed on target, and the number of misses 'must have been very large really.'[244] The rest of the problem lay in faulty munitions and unreliable measuring of the counter-battery gunners' effectiveness. During the bombardment the RFC logged at least 1120 hours of flying time in the battle zone by a total of 468 pilots, many flying multiple sorties.[245] Unfortunately these sorties were often ineffectual: the foul weather undermined RFC–artillery co-operation,[246] severely crimping aerial observation and frequently forcing counter-battery gunners — already encumbered with poor-quality weapons and shells — to fire blind. As the RFC's official historian wrote years after the war:

> Every hour of bad weather that kept aeroplanes away from the front brought respite to some German battery, and the full effect of the lost hours must be borne by the infantry when they advanced to the assault. No one realised this better than the airmen. Pilots flew in and under the low clouds and took advantage of every bright interval to continue their work of helping the artillery to destroy the enemy guns, but the grey days took their toll of flying time, and the effect on the day of attack, although it cannot be estimated, was none the less important.[247]

Even when the weather allowed, aerial observation did not always function smoothly, at least according to the artillery. RFC observers were often unable to distinguish the shellfire they were directing from that of other guns.[248] Artillerymen on the ground were flooded with too many and often vague target locations from their eyes in the sky,[249] and at other times were either unable to locate aeroplanes for the work or were plagued by patchy ground-to-air communication.[250] Inexperienced and inefficient observers were also a problem.[251] Most of these issues would have been resolvable with time, but immediately prior to 1 July there was no slack and they became just further drains on the quality of British counter-battery fire.

German soldiers were ignorant of the RFC's difficulties but understood the dangers of aviators' prying eyes.[252] *Major* Max Klaus, RFAR26, described the British airmen as vultures,[253] while *Leutnant-der-Reserve* Ernst Moos, Reserve Field Artillery Regiment 27 (RFAR27), thought them a plague.[254] 'These British arimen,' wrote one German historian of the Somme, 'observed for their batteries, dropped bombs on troop quarters, harassed artillery batteries and columns of infantry with machine-gun fire, and photographed the German defences down to the smallest detail.'[255] *Leutnant-der-Reserve* Gerster was one of many who lamented the loss of air superiority,[256] and when several German tethered balloons were shot down on 25 June he said the situation worsened.[257] As the German historian of the Somme noted: 'The aerial reconnaissance of the XIV Reserve Corps was hereafter almost paralysed. ... The enemy completely dominated the air.'[258] Klaus said that without observation balloons the German gunners were figuratively blindfolded and the 'air was almost purely English.'[259] The only option to conserve lives and guns, said Gerster, was to avoid detection: 'Soon no infantryman dared to be outside his dugout when an aircraft was circling overhead. With brown, clay and earth-stained tarpaulins they tried to camouflage the dark holes that marked the entrances to dugouts from the keen eyes of observers.'[260] Sometimes these efforts were successful;[261] other times not.[262] Many German soldiers were angry at their own lack of aerial support ahead of the looming battle.

With this in mind, Stein ordered restraint among his artillery batteries to preserve their ability to provide essential close defensive support for his infantry. The order probably went out in May or June; the exact date is unknown. Stein realised he needed functional guns to destroy or neutralise enemy infantrymen as they attempted to cross no-man's-land when their preparatory bombardment and supporting barrage lifted. As *Leutnant-der-Reserve* Georg Büsing, with RFAR20 at Gommecourt, explained: 'The artillery commander issued orders to maintain a certain level of restraint, as the British seemed, in the first stage of their preparatory fire, to be trying to tempt us to fire in defence so that they could identify our positions, to induce us to expend a lot of ammunition, to find our batteries by aerial observation.'[263] Artillery-officer Moos agreed, as did Gerster, who noted the order was enforced across 26th Reserve Division's sector.[264] In practice, however, the order was not followed to the letter across XIV Reserve Corps. In general terms it was implemented between Gommecourt and Ovillers, to a lesser extent around La Boisselle and Fricourt, and virtually not at all between Mametz and Montauban, the latter two areas also having the poorest quality gun positions to begin with. Unsurprisingly, those divisions exercising caution in retaliatory artillery fire suffered fewer barrel losses than others.

Fourteenth Reserve Corps' gun losses during the bombardment are known to some extent. The corps, as noted earlier, had roughly 570 field and heavy guns spread across 147 batteries.[265] One of the worst-hit divisions was the 28th in the southern part of the battlefield. Its supporting artillery was reduced by about 10 (30.3%) batteries to just 23 during the 24–30 June bombardment, but among those guns left were many 'useless' weapons, implying the rate of attrition might have been considerably higher, perhaps even 40–50%.[266] Moreover, these weapons were 'unable to provide sufficient support,' either being substandard or temporarily broken.[267] Twelfth Infantry Division's guns behind Montauban and Curlu — about 25 batteries totalling 95–100 barrels — suffered much the same fate, if not worse.[268] Between Gommecourt and Serre, 2nd Guards Reserve Division and 52nd Infantry Divisions are thought to have lost few of their combined 50 batteries, totalling 186 guns. Twenty-sixth Reserve Division, which had a nominal 39 batteries totalling 154 guns spread between Serre and Ovillers, possibly lost about 20–30% of its guns, although one artillery group lost half of its 28 barrels.[269] In practical terms, XIV Reserve Corps had an estimated 450 nominally active guns at dawn on 1 July, but in actuality that number could have varied between 400 and 500, and those batteries deployed behind Fricourt, Mametz and Montauban had suffered much greater losses than those between Ovillers and Gommecourt.

Below, commander of Second Army, was troubled by his gun losses; his reaction had a lot do with the central role they played in his defensive scheme. 'The enormous enemy superiority in heavy and long-range batteries, which the Army has so far been unable to counter, is proving very painful. Our artillery would have been adequate to respond to an assault launched after a one-day heavy bombardment of our trenches.'[270] Without doubt Below considered his artillery losses heavy, and was concerned — perhaps unduly, with the benefit of hindsight — about whether or not they would be able to lay down a thick curtain of defensive shellfire when the expected British attack came.

HAIG ACKNOWLEDGED none of the problems with the bombardment and instead focused on the positive. He said his men were in splendid spirits and several had told him they had never before been so well instructed and briefed on an upcoming operation.[271] 'The wire has never been so well cut, nor the artillery preparation so thorough.'[272] In the two days before battle Haig spoke to his corps commanders — Lieutenant-Generals Henry Horne, William Pulteney, Thomas D'Oyly Snow, Morland and Congreve — who were apparently all brimming with confidence.[273] Of those responsible for the northern part of the battlefield, where question marks surrounding the artillery's effectiveness were greatest, Morland was 'quietly confident of success' and Pulteney was 'quite satisfied with the artillery bombardment and wire cutting.'[274] Hunter-Weston — who expected success, but added that this was 'in the hands of God'[275] — was, in Haig's words, 'quite satisfied and confident.'[276] Pulteney later said he believed the German trenches 'obliterated.'[277] Snow thought all the German soldiers 'will have been killed by our artillery barrage.'[278] Further south, where the shellfire was more effective, Horne was 'very pleased with the situation' and 'in high hopes.'[279] Congreve and 'all about him expressed themselves full of confidence.'[280] Everyone was telling Haig what he wanted to hear: everything was going very well, actually, and a positive outcome was to be expected.

Haig was not entirely without reservations. He apparently sent Charteris to Hunter-Weston's headquarters not long before battle with authority to cancel VIII Corps' attack. 'It had little chance of complete success and there was a certainty of many casualties. But even partial success might mean much to other parts of the line,' wrote Charteris.[281] He decided to let VIII Corps proceed, and his rationale — cruel as it seems with knowledge of subsequent events — provided the ever-profligate Hunter-Weston with a bespoke excuse. Charteris's claim must be treated with caution. Eighth Corps' job had always been to provide flank support for Fourth Army and, while Haig might have considered limiting part of its operation, cancellation of its role so close to battle, as Charteris suggests, seems highly improbable.

Haig and Rawlinson were nevertheless cautiously confident on the eve of battle. 'I feel that everything possible for us to do to achieve success has been done,' wrote Haig on 30 June. 'Whether or not we are successful lies in the Power above. But I do feel that in my plans I have been helped by a Power that is not my own. So I am easy in my mind and ready to do my best whatever happens tomorrow.'[282] By 'success,' Haig was referring to a breakthrough battle and deployment of Reserve Army. He continued: 'With God's help, I feel hopeful for tomorrow.'[283] Rawlinson, too, was generally pleased with Fourth Army's preparations, but his operational hopes were considerably more measured than Haig's. On the eve of battle he confided in his private diary:

> What the actual results will be no one can say, but I feel pretty confident of success myself though only after heavy fighting. That the Bosche will break, and that a debacle will supervene, I do not believe; but should this be the case I am quite ready to take full advantage of it. The weather has greatly improved and all looks hopeful but the issues are in the hands of the Bon Dieu God.[284]

Haig and Rawlinson were rightly anxious going into their first major battle as C-in-C and army commander respectively, but it was altogether more troubling that their operational expectations were still very much polarised after seven days' shellfire and just hours before the infantry went in.

FAR BEYOND POZIÈRES Ridge senior German commanders were also assessing the state of their defensive positions. *General-der-Infanterie* Erich von Falkenhayn, Chief of General Staff, Supreme Army

Command, was still chiefly focused on the offensives in Verdun and Galicia. He acknowledged Second Army's positions astride the Somme had been flayed, but attached less strategic value to these and thus remained sparing with reinforcements of men, guns and aeroplanes.[285] By contrast, an increasingly worried Below had predicted a major combined Anglo-French attack either side of the river, and was troubled that the bombardment resembled the 'tactics of wearing down and attrition.'[286] The 'enormous enemy superiority in heavy and long-range batteries, which the Army has so far been unable to counter, is proving very painful,' he said, noting the loss of men and materiel, and damage to his defensive positions.[287] Six months later he would appraise the shellfire, referring to 28th Reserve Division at Fricourt–Mametz, 12th Infantry Division at Montauban and XVII Army Corps further south.[288] With hindsight, and in reference to these areas, he would write of insufficient artillery, the loss of air superiority, a failure to properly distribute infantry in depth, inadequately constructed defence-in-depth positions, and the general damage caused by days of shellfire.[289] His concerns about the artillery and aeroplane shortages predated the bombardment by weeks, but on the other points his position in late-June 1916 was less clear. At the time Below well knew his army was reliant on stretched resources in defending the Somme battlefield, but there is nothing to suggest he realised how vulnerable XIV Reserve Corps' left flank was to a concerted Anglo-French attack.

Stein and the other tactical-level commanders were far from bullish in their outlooks. Stein was silent on the period 24–30 June in his faux-breezy memoir,[290] but probably shared Below's worries. His post-war writings suggest he was concerned by the damage to his defences and British aerial supremacy, but was confident that his men would hold their positions.[291] At Gommecourt, *Generalleutnants* Richard *Freiherr* von Süsskind-Schwendi and Karl von Borries, commanders respectively of 2nd Guards Reserve and 52nd Infantry Divisions, were prepared for a defensive battle and realised the looming attack on the salient would be an attempted British diversion from operations further south. An out-of-time *Generalleutnant* Ferdinand von Hahn was rightly bothered by the quality and depth of his 28th Reserve Division's just-inherited defences, more so around Fricourt–Mametz than at La Boisselle, and was almost certainly troubled by his severe gun losses in the former. *Generalleutnant* Martin Châles de Beaulieu, 12th Infantry Division, was so worried about the state of his front-line infantry at Montauban that he foolishly revolved in last-minute replacements, but appears to have been less concerned by gun losses and his pulverised trenches. Soden was by far the most confident of the divisional commanders: he simply expected his 26th would hold its ground between Serre and Ovillers by repulsing any attack.[292] He wrote in a divisional order of the day dated 26 June:

> The effort and work in the course of the last two years that were
> made in the extension of our positions, may already have to endure
> a powerful test in the next few days. Now it requires everyone
> to be firm, to courageously persist, to do your duty, to shun no
> sacrifice and no exertion, so that the enemy is refused victory. And
> everyone must be conscious that it is necessary that we hold the
> bloody embattled ground and that no Englishman or Frenchman
> who penetrates into our lines might remain unpunished. I know
> that I am united in these convictions with the entire division and I
> look forward to the coming events with full confidence.[293]

Stein must have known his generals' views, but he never commented on them, or on his failure to construct corps-wide defences of uniform depth and strength. Instead, after the war, he reverted to stating the obvious: 'After extensive preparations the enemy believed he had made the [German] positions defenceless and could step forward over them unhindered.'[294]

COLUMNS OF equipment-laden British soldiers trudged along traffic-clogged roads late on 30 June and into the early hours of 1 July before filing through the crowded trench maze towards their jumping-off lines. 'All the valleys were filled with troops moving softly up to the assembly trenches, their winding ranks looking like grey-green snakes at a distance,' wrote Lieutenant Kelly.[295] Many had penned a few words in case they died on 1 July, perhaps a last note to somebody back home or a will bequeathing their few worldly possessions. 'I am writing a letter home, Sir, it will be my last,' a grim-faced Ulsterman told Lieutenant-Colonel Frank Crozier,

9th Royal Irish Rifles, the night before battle.[296] Equipment had been checked and rechecked. Water bottles were full, bayonets sharpened, rifles cleaned and oiled, ammunition pouches rammed and haversacks bulging with rations. Some strapped an entrenching tool across their chest as a crude form of body armour; others struggled under the added dead weight of trench mortars, machine guns, stretchers, wooden ladders for scaling parapets and 101 other apparently essential items. Each man knew exactly the part he had to play; jittery platoon commanders briefed their men once more. But, now, just hours from battle, there was no sign of any overt optimism.

'No one got, or tried to get much sleep, but there was no sign of nervousness or apprehension; we just talked … through the night,' wrote Lieutenant Heath, the trench mortar officer.[297] Another officer said he 'sat in a shelter with some of my men and tried to keep up their spirits by playing my tin whistle to them. But it was a long night.'[298] Second-Lieutenant Liveing, the 1/12th Londons (Rangers) officer, pondered whether the next day he would be lying out 'stiff and cold in that land beyond the trees.'[299] Second-Lieutenant Laporte, the artillery subaltern, was in the trenches opposite La Boisselle. As night faded into the dawn of 1 July he watched a string of Northumberland Fusiliers squeeze past knots of soldiers in a narrow communication trench behind Tara and Usna hills:

> In single file they went steadily by, silently save for the sound of
> equipment knocking against the trench and of their feet on the
> soft earth, burdened with rifles, belts of ammunition, bombs,
> picks, shovels, iron rations, water-bottles, haversacks, gas-bags
> and tin helmets. … At intervals there were halts as they were held
> up ahead. Hardly a word was spoken. Some by slight nervous
> movements showed signs of strain, but most were steady-eyed
> enough. Then they were gone.[300]

CHAPTER 5

Hunter Bunter's Folly

VIII Corps' pre-ordained failure at Serre and Beaumont Hamel

'You see for young lads like me, those that were left, it was like a bad dream. We couldn't take in what was happening around us. The shock of it hit us later.'[1]
— Private Noel Peters, 16th Middlesex

HAWTHORN MINE BLEW like a giant earthen carbuncle, heaving great slabs of clay and chalkstone skyward, along with one-score German soldiers. Debris flopped to the ground within about 20 seconds, leaving clouds of fine grey dust and smoke billowing over Hawthorn Ridge. All that remained of the redoubt that once stood there was a crater that measured 130 feet wide and 58 feet deep, including an 18-foot-high lip of chalkstone spoil that tapered off into the surrounding land. 'The field was white, as if it had snowed,' wrote *Leutnant-der-Reserve* Matthaus Gerster, of Reserve Infantry Regiment 119 (RIR119), adding the gigantic divot 'gaped like an open wound in the side of the hill.'[2] The blast of 40,600 pounds of ammonal collapsed nearby German dugouts, crushing occupants and entombing others. Some clawed their way out; others suffocated. Above ground several German soldiers were stunned by a cocktail of concussion and fear. The eruption, wrote Gerster, heralded the start of the anticipated British attack.

Lieutenant Geoffrey Malins, a British army cinematographer and shameless self-promoter, immortalised the moment with a hand-cranked movie camera. Moments before 7.20 a.m., he worried about how much film he had left. Then the ground convulsed. 'It rocked and swayed. I gripped hold of my tripod to steady myself. Then, for all the world like a gigantic sponge, the earth rose in the air to the height of hundreds of feet. Higher and higher it rose, and with a horrible, grinding roar the earth fell back upon itself.'[3] British soldiers nearby watched in awe. Many felt the shock waves ripple through their trenches.[4] Several German soldiers felt the judder in their dugouts more than a mile away and wondered if it was an earthquake.[5] Some in the Newfoundland Regiment mistakenly thought the village of Beaumont Hamel had been razed.[6]

Stand at the edge of the Hawthorn Ridge crater today and you can see for miles around. Its tactical value back in 1916 is obvious. German machine-gunners here could sweep no-man's-land and the British assembly trenches from the Beaumont Hamel–Auchonvillers road valley around to the northern edge of today's Newfoundland Memorial Park.

This danger was recognised by Lieutenant-General Sir Aylmer Hunter-Weston and his VIII Corps headquarters. Their concerns were centred on whether German infantry would occupy the crater first, something they had form in. But, in effect, the timing of the Hawthorn Ridge Redoubt blast at 7.20 a.m. served as a giant clapperboard that signalled the pending attack 10 minutes before it began. 'Hunter Bunter's folly'[7] — as the blast timing became known — would have devastating consequences for VIII Corps' infantry, which explained why pretty much everyone involved in the decision-making later scrambled for cover.

Fifty-two-year-old Hunter-Weston had served on the Indian North-West Frontier and in Egypt and South Africa before the First World War. He fought in France in 1914, and then at Gallipoli in 1915. He liked horses and hunting, wore a bushy moustache and occasionally used a walking stick. He liked posing for formal photographs, but often made candid snaps look awkward. He saw himself as a 'plain, blunt soldier,'[8] and never shied from imparting pearls of wisdom to subordinates: 'I was given the power to strike the right note & to enthouse [sic] the men.'[9] Some thought Hunter-Weston intelligent and rich in human sympathy.[10] More said he was over-optimistic, often patronising or brutal in tone, unable to delegate

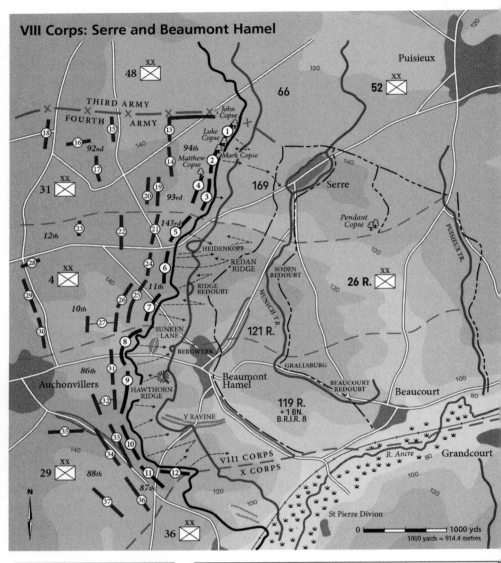

VIII Corps: Serre and Beaumont Hamel

48 XX

Puisieux

52 XX

John Copse

66

THIRD ARMY

FOURTH ARMY

18

15

16

92nd

17

Luke Copse

94th

Matthew Copse

13

14

1

2

Mark Copse

140

169

Serre

140

31 XX

93rd

19

20

21

143rd

4

3

5

Pendant Copse

12th

23

22

24

6

HEIDENKOPF

REDAN RIDGE

SODEN REDOUBT

120

26 R. XX

PUISIEUX TR.

4 XX

11th

RIDGE REDOUBT

MUNICH TR.

120

10th

26

25

7

SUNKEN LANE

8

BERGWERK

121 R.

GRALLSBURG

28

140

27

29

30

86th

31

9

HAWTHORN RIDGE

Beaumont Hamel

BEAUCOURT REDOUBT

Beaucourt

100

80

Auchonvillers

32

Y RAVINE

119 R.
+ 1 BN.
B.R.I.R. 8

35

33

10

34

VIII CORPS

X CORPS

R. Ancre

80

Grandcourt

29 XX

88th

11

12

87th

36

100

100

120

N

37

36

St Pierre Divion

0   1000 yds
1000 yards = 914.4 metres

36 XX

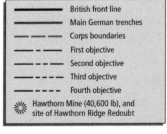

British front line			
Main German trenches			
Corps boundaries			
First objective			
Second objective			
Third objective			
Fourth objective			
Hawthorn Mine (40,600 lb), and site of Hawthorn Ridge Redoubt			

1	12 Y. & L.	11	1 K.O.S.B.	21	6 R. WAR.	31	16 MIDDX.
2	11 E. LANCS.	12	1 R. INNIS. FUS.	22	1 KING'S OWN	32	1 R. DUB. FUS.
3	15 W. YORKS.	13	14 Y. & L.	23	2 ESSEX	33	1 BORD. R.
4	16 W. YORKS.	14	13 Y. & L.	24	1 SOM. L.I.	34	1 NFLD.
5	8 R. WAR.	15	12 E. YORKS.	25	1 HANTS.	35	4 WORC.
6	1 RIF. BDE.	16	10 E. YORKS.	26	2 SEA. H.	36	1 ESSEX
7	1 E. LANCS.	17	11 E. YORKS.	27	2 R. DUB. FUS.	37	2 HANTS.
8	1 L. FUS.	18	13 E. YORKS.	28	2 DUKE'S		
9	2 R. FUS.	19	18 W. YORKS.	29	1 R. IR. FUS.		
10	2 S.W.B.	20	18 D.L.I.	30	1 R. WAR.		

and — the most extreme view — a charlatan.[11] His penchant for inspecting latrines was no more coincidental than the 'magnificent, gleaming' boots and buttons at his headquarters.[12] The moniker 'Hunter Bunter' had much to do with his pushy, self-important character. Hunter-Weston's personality was authoritarian; he was obsessed with order, control and hygiene.[13]

Hunter-Weston carried a well-earned reputation for bloody daylight attacks that lacked imagination and artillery support. That dated back to Gallipoli, when the Scot was said to have been willing to 'contend in open debate that, provided the objective was gained, casualties were of no importance.'[14] This 'logician of war' saw few shades of grey when it came to justifying casualties in successful attacks, but, as we shall see, saw many more when it came to accounting for industrial-scale military failure and its cost.

Eighth Corps opposed a trinity of formidable German defensive networks crisscrossing the high ground north of the River Ancre. From above, the German front line looked a bit like an oversized 'L'. The down-stroke of the L blocked the uphill approaches to Serre village at its top end, and thereafter meandered southwards across a series of low-lying ridges and road valleys before arriving at Beaumont Hamel, which sat in the angle formed by the horizontal bar, then headed east to the river valley fens. No-man's-land was 200–600 yards across, the distance generally narrower north of Beaumont Hamel than south. As we shall see, each of the attacking divisions — north to south, 31st, 4th and 29th — used a variety of tactics to help them cross the open ground between the opposing lines. Forty-eighth (South Midland) Division, less two battalions attached to the 4th, was in corps reserve.

The strength of the German defences lay in their co-ordinated redoubts and fortified villages. In the front-line system, Hawthorn Ridge Redoubt (Weissdornfeste), Ridge Redoubt and the Bergwerk covered the northern approaches to Beaumont Hamel, while Y-Ravine (Leiling Schlucht) blocked access from the south. Heidenkopf — known to the British as the Quadrilateral, and more an elbow of trenches that jutted out into no-man's-land as a defensive feature than a redoubt — was nestled in a natural amphitheatre just south of Serre. Further back 1000–2000 yards, the intermediate position, known to the British as Munich Trench, was on higher ground again. It included Soden (Feste Soden), Grallsburg and

Beaucourt (Feste-Alt-Württemberg) Redoubts, along with the fortified villages of Serre and Beaucourt. Back another 1000–2000 yards, but mostly the latter, was the second position, or Puisieux Trench, which included more redoubts and Grandcourt village on the southern bank of the Ancre. These layered defences were designed to stop any enemy attacks with a significant volume of co-ordinated machine-gun and rifle fire.

Most of this land was held by 26th Reserve Division. Its Württemberg-recruited RIR119 and Reserve Infantry Regiment 121 (RIR121) occupied the trenches from the Ancre to just south of Serre. Thereafter, the trenches belonged to soldiers of 52nd Infantry Division, with the Baden-drawn Infantry Regiment 169 (IR169) defending Serre. These three German infantry regiments, all in XIV Reserve Corps, totalled about 9000 men. These faced an estimated 25,000 infantry, pioneer and engineer officers and men of Hunter-Weston's corps who actually participated in the attack, from the total 96,794 soldiers of all ranks and units in VIII Corps.[15]

As mentioned earlier, German commanders regarded the subtle west-facing salient between Hamel, Beaumont Hamel and Serre as must-hold ground.[16] Defences here were based on two spurs that curved behind and overlooked the front-line positions as they faded into the northern banks of the River Ancre. Fourteenth Reserve Corps and Second Army treated the Serre–Grandcourt (Serre Heights) and Redan Ridge–Beaucourt Spurs as essential because of the southeasterly views they afforded over Thiepval Plateau and Pozières,[17] and also east over a string of villages towards Bapaume. Loss of this ground would render Beaumont Hamel, Beaucourt, Grandcourt, Miraumont and Thiepval untenable.[18] Moreover, the 26th's artillery lines just north of the Ancre would be lost, denuding Thiepval and Pozières of northern flank support. If this happened, the 26th's positions around Pozières, Ovillers and La Boisselle would subsequently be jeopardised and potentially rolled up by the British.[19] None of this had escaped the 26th's commander, *Generalleutnant* Franz *Freiherr* von Soden, or his superiors at XIV Reserve Corps and Second Army, who knew the loss of the elevations behind Beaumont Hamel and Serre, and in particular Serre Heights, had significant tactical ramifications for the tenability of his divisional sector and thus spared no effort in making it impregnable.[20]

Hunter-Weston planned to break this German fortress with a frontal infantry assault supported by artillery. His three divisions would attack to a depth of 3000–3500 yards and link up side by side on Serre–Grandcourt Spur, its final objective, by midday. In so doing it would provide flank support for Fourth Army's main thrust towards Pozières. This spur also had a wider value in that it provided a foundation from which the under-construction German third defensive line and a handful of villages could later be assaulted.[21] The initial stages of Hunter-Weston's advance were the toughest to complete as these involved a mostly uphill operation against the multiple fortified villages and redoubts. Furthest north, 31st Division would capture Serre before moving onto the high ground beyond, while immediately south 4th Division would attack astride Redan Ridge and seize Ridge Redoubt, Heidenkopf and Soden Redoubt before coming up alongside the 31st. Twenty-ninth Division was to take Bergwerk, Beaumont Hamel, Y-Ravine, Grallsburg, Beaucourt Redoubt and Beaucourt village before arriving at the southern end of the spur. Attainment of these ambitious objectives was reliant on VIII Corps' artillery nullifying resistance during both the seven-day bombardment and the battle-day barrage.[22]

Eighth Corps' gunners had three tasks. They had to kill or neutralise Württemberg and Baden infantry, destroy defensive obstacles and mechanisms such as barbed wire and machine-gun posts, and also suppress hostile artillery grouped further back. Prior to Zero hour, this was the purpose of the prolonged bombardment, and during the attack it was the job of the supporting barrage. In the period 24–30 June, VIII Corps' artillery fired almost 363,000 heavy and field artillery shells at the German positions.[23] On 1 July they would fire about 61,500 shells.[24] Impressive as these figures appear, they do not take into account the number of duds, the dilution of shellfire over a wide area, the weighting to shrapnel over explosive shells, or the difficulties in locating and then destroying distant targets given the technology of 1916. There were other problems, too. In Hunter-Weston's battle sector, Fourth Army had allocated the equivalent of about one field gun to every 20 yards of attack frontage, and about one heavy barrel for every 44 yards.[25] This concentration was, even a year later, considered ridiculously low.[26] At the time Hunter-Weston waxed lyrical about the cut wire, which in many places remained intact, and German trenches that were 'blown to pieces.'[27] He reckoned his corps had only to 'walk into Serre.'[28] As events would show, Hunter-Weston's optimism was entirely misplaced because VIII Corps' artillery had failed in all three of its essential tasks.

Brigadier-General John Charteris, General Sir Douglas Haig's chief of intelligence, visited Hunter-Weston late on 28 June. As mentioned previously, he had Haig's authority to stop VIII Corps' attack if he thought it wise.[29] He found Hunter-Weston and his divisional chiefs convinced they would achieve a great success and approved the attack. 'The Corps Commander said he felt "like Napoleon before the battle of Austerlitz!"'[30] It was a careless line that revealed much about Hunter-Weston's delusions.

There were more troubling problems in that VIII Corps' artillery programme for 1 July was unfit for purpose. The plan was for Hunter-Weston's infantry to be presaged by a timetabled barrage. It was to start on the German front line and step back at six set intervals until the final objective was taken. But Hunter-Weston fiddled with the timetable to accommodate the mine-blast timing: infantry could not seize the crater if heavy artillery was shelling the area.[31] Astoundingly, he ordered his corps' heavy artillery to lift its shellfire off the entire German front line opposite his corps at 7.20 a.m. to targets further back, rather than just that opposite 29th Division.[32] Field artillery would step its 'thin' fire further back at 7.30 a.m., but in the 29th's sector it would be halved from 7.27 a.m.[33] Gunnery officers tweaked their fire plans, but infantry planners were oblivious.[34] It was a classic case of left hand not knowing what the right was doing. The result would be thousands of British infantrymen stranded in no-man's-land for up to 10 minutes before their attack began and exposed to the enemy's defensive artillery and machine-gun fire. As far as blunders went, this one was pretty big and, as we shall see, guaranteed disaster for Hunter-Weston's infantry.

Eighth Corps had at first wanted the mine blown at 6 p.m. on 30 June,[35] and then changed the timing to 3.30 a.m. on 1 July, so that the crater could be seized before the main attack.[36] General Headquarters (GHQ) wanted it shifted to 7.30 a.m.[37] Hunter-Weston said the blast was advanced to 7.20 a.m. at the request of 29th Division to avoid having infantrymen hit by falling debris as they crossed no-man's-land.[38] The 29th's commander, Major-General Beauvoir de Lisle, denied this.[39] He blamed the mining officers. The mining officers blamed VIII Corps and one another. So it continued. Most pointed an accusatory finger at Hunter-Weston. It turned out nobody in VIII Corps had wanted the 7.20 a.m. time slot, but somehow that was what they got.[40] It is damning to find Hunter-Weston begrudgingly admitting responsibility later.[41]

Hunter-Weston's mine-timing decision was apparently queried several times by concerned senior artillery officers.[42] But the general was 'not to be moved from his scheme,' wrote Major John Gibbon, Royal Artillery.[43] 'We knew [the attack] was foredoomed to failure.'[44]

'EVERYONE KNEW ... IT was important not to miss the moment that the [British shell] fire moved back [to more distant targets] and the infantry assault began,' wrote *Leutnant-der-Reserve* Gerster, RIR119.[45] That signalled the start of the so-called race for the parapet. The winner was whoever reached the German front line first; the greater the margin the better. As it turned out, both the shelling debacle and the mine explosion gave German defenders an unrecoverable head start as Hunter-Weston's infantry were deploying hundreds of yards away in no-man's-land. At the same time, as a German officer just south of Serre recalled, the British barrage 'lifted onto our rear positions and we felt the earth shake violently — this was caused by a mine going off near Beaumont. In no time flat the slope opposite resembled an ant heap.'[46] German infantrymen raced up from dugouts and into the shellfire-torn trenches, propping rifles and machine guns on broken parapets and shell-crater rims; they were ready and waiting, 5–10 minutes before the British attack even began.[47] Hunter-Weston's meddling had lost his infantry the parapet foot race by quite some distance.

One British soldier chanced a peek towards the enemy parapet as the barrage lifted. 'Out on the top [of the trench] came scrambling a German machine-gun team. They fixed their gun in front of their parapet and opened out a slow and deadly fire on our front.'[48] At that moment many soldiers realised they were doomed. Heavy casualties were inevitable. Here and there some machine guns were chattering away before the bombardment even lifted.

Disaster, if not massacre, followed. Within moments a lopsided battle was raging.[49] German machine-gunners fired staccato bursts. Riflemen drew careful bead. Shellfire tore down whole groups of British soldiers.[50] 'Despite the protection of the wooden rifle stock [around the gun barrel], the skin on their left hands burned,'[51] said Gerster, who fought on Hawthorn Ridge. There were 'shouted commands, cries for help, messages, death screams, shouts of joy, wheezing, whining, pleading, gun shots, machine gun fire crackling, and shell explosions.'[52] He continued: 'Everywhere the [British] skirmishing line crumples. Khaki-brown spots cover the broken earth. Arms are thrown in the air, indicating death. We can see people rushing back wounded, or sheltering in shell craters. The severely wounded are rolling on the ground.'[53] VIII Corps' attack was irretrievably faltering before it had even really begun.

Red flares rising skyward from the German front line and urgent calls from artillery observers quickly brought down a hurricane of shrapnel and explosive shellfire. In some places it began around 7.20 a.m. In others, such as in 31st Division's area, it started at about 7 a.m.[54] Bigger German guns systematically pummelled the British trenches. Lighter-calibre weapons threw down a curtain of shellfire on no-man's-land to impede successive waves of attacking infantry. Nominally about 61 guns, or 40% of 26th Reserve Division's 154 artillery pieces, were deployed between the River Ancre and Heidenkopf.[55] These were complemented by an estimated 35 guns of 52nd Infantry Division behind and to the north of Serre.[56] While many guns had been damaged or destroyed by the British bombardment, plenty had survived, were stocked with ammunition and now began shooting at pre-allocated target zones.[57] 'On the morning of 1 July virtually all batteries [surviving the bombardment] are fully ready to fire,' said *Major* Max Klaus, Reserve Field Artillery Regiment 26 (RFAR26).[58] This was the benefit of XIV Reserve Corps having insisted that its gunners preserve firepower through fire discipline.

'This barrage which fell at Zero was one of the most consistently severe I have seen,' said Brigadier-General Hubert Rees, commanding 94th Brigade, of the scene in no-man's-land and within the British lines.[59] 'It gave me the impression of a thick belt of poplar trees from the cones of the explosions. As soon as I saw it I ordered every man within reach to halt and lie down but only managed to stop about 2 companies because all troops had to move at once in order to capture their objectives on time. It was impossible for any but a few men to get through it.'

The botched mine blast and initial barrage lift comprised the first element of a three-act tragedy. The second act, which had yet to begin, was all about 4th, 29th and 31st Divisions' generally disastrous attacks in the two-and-a-half hours to about 10 a.m. The third was played out on Hawthorn Ridge and at Heidenkopf, where destined-to-fail British incursions took on the qualities of epics that belied their actual importance. In truth, few soldiers would have recognised these distinctions; for them it was mostly a day-long horror story bare of any redeeming qualities.

THE SECOND ACT began with 29th Division's attacks across a 200–600 yards-wide no-man's-land around Beaumont Hamel failing by about 8 a.m. Here — in keeping with the popular imagery of soldiers advancing in unwavering lines — all of the 29th's attacking battalions were ordered to press forward in columns of sections, although some minor tactical variations were used in places.[60] Overall, however, the tactics used by the 29th to get its infantry across no-man's-land and into RIR119's trenches did precisely nothing to lessen the slaughter that was about to follow.

Each of the 29th's three brigades had a section from either 1/1st West Riding, 1/3rd Kent or 1/2nd Field Companies, Royal Engineers (RE) attached for consolidating gains.[61] Two companies of 1/2nd Monmouths* were split up across the 29th's leading attack battalions for carrying and consolidation work. Two Russian Saps in the 29th's area — First Avenue and Mary, both well out into no-man's-land — were used as Stokes-mortar emplacements. These tunnels were quickly clogged with wounded and battle stragglers, and repeated efforts to link and extend them to the German line by the remaining half of 1/2nd Monmouths failed under a torrent of bullets.[62]

Twenty-ninth Division's 86th and 87th Brigades, respectively commanded by Brigadier-Generals Weir Williams and Cuthbert Lucas, attacked side by side. The 86th was astride the shallow Beaumont Hamel–Auchonvillers road valley. To the north, 1st Lancashire Fusiliers† — two of its companies racing forward in extended order at 7.30 a.m. from a sunken lane in no-man's-land and the rest overland in columns of sections from

---

*   1/2nd Battalion Monmouthshire Regiment (Territorial Force). Battalion war diary states 106 casualties — 11 k (killed), 85 w (wounded) and 10 m (missing) — 1–3 July. SDGW notes 28 deaths.

†   1st Battalion Lancashire Fusiliers. *Official History* states 483 casualties (164 k, 308 w and 11 m). SDGW notes 148 deaths.

the British front line behind them — was dropped by machine-gun and rifle fire.[63] Sap 7, an unopened Russian Sap linking the sunken lane and the British front line, was soon filled with wounded trying to get back. It was a similar story for the rump of 2nd Royal Fusiliers* immediately south, with less than 120 from one of its companies having raced forward minutes before Zero to find German infantry already at the smouldering Hawthorn Ridge crater.[64] Support battalions 16th Middlesex† and 1st Royal Dublin Fusiliers‡ were similarly swept down as they crossed the front line just before 8 a.m. and attempted to pass through their own wire and move forward.[65] Further south, again, the 87th's 2nd South Wales Borderers§ began deploying at 7.20 a.m. in the area now known as Newfoundland Memorial Park and was taking casualties around its own front line and as men bunched to pass through gaps in their own wire.[66] None made it across the bullet-swept no-man's-land and into the German trenches.[67] The same fate befell 1st Borders¶ as it followed immediately behind.[68] Opposite Mary Redan salient, closer to the River Ancre, the decimation of 1st Royal Inniskilling Fusiliers** began as it left the British front line at 7.30 a.m. under heavy machine-gun fire.[69] A few apparently won their way into the hostile trench, but these were driven out, captured or killed.[70] First King's Own Scottish Borderers (KOSB)†† followed and made no headway.[71] Virtually none of 29th's initial attack battalions reached the German lines; their dead, dying and wounded lay thick around the British trenches and in no-man's-land.[72]

---

*   2nd Battalion Royal Fusiliers (City of London Regiment). *Official History* states 561 casualties (164 k, 349 w and 48 m). SDGW notes 167 deaths.

†   16th (Service) Battalion (Public Schools) Duke of Cambridge's Own (Middlesex Regiment). Also known as Public Schools Battalion. Official History states 539 casualties (187 k, 309 w, 14 m and 29 p). SDGW notes 163 deaths.

‡   1st Battalion Royal Dublin Fusiliers. *Official History* states 305 casualties (76 k and 229 w). SDGW notes 56 deaths.

§   2nd Battalion South Wales Borderers. *Official History* states 372 casualties (150 k, 218 w and 4 m). SDGW notes 127 deaths.

¶   1st Battalion Border Regiment. *Official History* states 575 casualties (183 k, 368 w, 22 m and 2 p). SDGW notes 201 deaths.

**   1st Battalion Royal Inniskilling Fusiliers. *Official History* states 568 casualties (245 k, 319 w, 3 m and 1 p). SDGW notes 229 deaths.

††   1st Battalion King's Own Scottish Borderers. *Official History* states 552 casualties (156 k and 396 w). SDGW notes 129 deaths.

One officer of 1st KOSB complained bitterly about the lack of secrecy in preparing his battalion's attack. This applied equally across the combined fronts of 86th and 87th Brigades. 'The advertisement of the attack on our front was absurd. Paths were cut and marked through our wire days before. Bridges over our trenches for the 2nd and 3rd waves to cross by were put up days in advance. Small wonder the M.G. [machine-gun] fire was directed with such fatal precision.'[73] The result, as 1st Borders' war diarist noted, was that multiple battalions advanced at a slow walk 'until only little groups of half a dozen men were left here and there, and these ... took cover in shell holes or where ever they could. The advance was brought entirely to a standstill.'[74] These grim themes were repeated in the battle reports of multiple battalions,[75] and it was evident, too, in the diaries and memoirs of those lucky enough to survive the machine-gun maelstrom.

Sergeant George Osborn, 2nd South Wales Borderers, expected to die:[76] 'My word, we found ourselves in a hot shop.'[77] He ducked into a shell hole and knew it was 'certain death to move.'[78] A bullet carried away Private Derek McCullock's right eye, and soon afterwards shrapnel caught the 16th Middlesex soldier in the torso and legs. 'My collar bone, shoulder blade and two ribs were broken and I had a bullet in my left lung. I managed to crawl back to our lines.'[79] Private Peter Smith, 1st Borders, miraculously reached the intact German wire where he, too, ducked into a shell crater. 'The Jerries started throwing bombs, we had to retire.'[80] He and four others later scampered back over a field of corpses: 'It was pure bloody murder.'[81] Sergeant Alexander Fraser, 1st Borders, said seven men of his 34-strong platoon were wounded as they clambered out of a support trench well behind the British front line: 'All I could do was lay these [seven] chaps on the fire step [of the trench]. We weren't allowed to do anything for them and make sure the next chaps went up. Seven hit out of one Platoon going out and I still had to go up [the trench ladder].'[82]

It was a story repeated all around the 29th's lines and is reflected in the division's casualty roll for 1 July. The 29th booked about 5240 casualties, among them 1628 dead, 3107 wounded, 220 missing, 32 prisoners and 253 unspecified. Across no-man's-land, RIR119 suffered 292 casualties on 1 July, these comprising 101 dead and 191 wounded.[83] In brief, for every one German casualty opposite the 29th, there were 17.9 British: a ratio that includes a premium for Hunter Bunter's meddling.

Shortly after 7.30 a.m., Major Edward Packe, 15th Squadron, Royal Flying Corps, was 2000 feet above the Beaumont Hamel battlefield in an open-cockpit BE2c. The sight of numerous dead in no-man's-land horrified him: 'Only in two places did I see any of our troops reach the German trenches, and only a handful at each.'[84] Soon enough, Packe himself copped a bullet in the buttocks from ground fire and returned to base.

Somewhere out among the dead was 24-year-old Private John McDonnell, 1st Royal Inniskilling Fusiliers. The married man and father from County Tyrone is today buried at Ancre British Cemetery. His wife, Mary, later chose the epitaph upon his headstone:

At our fireside,
Sad and lonely,
The children I do tell,
How their noble father fell.

FOURTH DIVISION'S INITIAL attack was eastbound on a 1500-yard front between Redan Ridge and Heidenkopf. Here, immediately north of 29th Division, there was plenty of failure, but also some initial gains. 'We sprang like cats on the [trench parapet] top, and then we had to walk,' said Private Thomas Kirby, 1st East Lancashires.[85] The assault was led by three battalions — south to north, 1st East Lancashires, 1st Rifle Brigade (both of 11th Brigade) and the 1/8th Royal Warwicks, this last attached from 48th (South Midland) Division's 143rd Brigade — going over abreast and moving forward in linear successive waves.[86] Three more — 1st Hampshires, 1st Somerset Light Infantry and 1/6th Royal Warwicks, also of the 143rd — followed in section columns to mitigate the effect of an expected defensive barrage.[87]

Sections from 7th, 1/1st Durham and 1/1st Renfrew Field Companies, RE, were to help with consolidation.[88] Four Russian Saps in 4th Division's patch had Lewis-gun teams at their respective heads in no-man's-land. The men at the heads of these saps — north to south, Delaunay and Bess Street in 1/8th Royal Warwicks' sector, and Cat Street and Beet Street in 1st Rifle Brigade's zone — quickly fell prey to so-called 'friendly' shellfire or enemy infantry.

German machine guns in the front and support trenches spat lead directly at the attackers. 'When the Germans saw us coming they did not half open out with [artillery] heavies and machine guns,' said Kirby.[89] Machine guns to the north around the ruins of Serre, where 31st Division's attack was a failure in progress, and south at Ridge Redoubt, caught 4th Division in brutal enfilade.[90]

As it turned out, 4th Division's two northern-most lead battalions made limited gains around Heidenkopf, whereas the third met with outright failure on the camber of the east–west running Redan Ridge. Eleventh Brigade's 1st East Lancashires* moved into no-man's-land on the ridge shortly before Zero and met with heavy machine-gun fire.[91] About 40 men fought their way into the hostile line and were killed or captured.[92] Following behind, 1st Hampshires† was confronted by a storm of metal and said it was 'impossible even to reach the German front line.'[93] The division's two other lead battalions did better. Adjoining companies of 1st Rifle Brigade‡ and 1/8th Royal Warwicks,§ of 11th and 143rd Brigades respectively, found the enemy wire cut and separately fought their way into the enemy front line and the scarcely defended Heidenkopf. This group of trenches was a jot north of today's Serre Road Cemetery No. 2 and projecting from the main German line. These battalions' outer-most companies — 1st Rifle Brigade's right company on the ridge and the 1/8th's left company nearer to Serre — were mostly stopped either by frontal and enfilade machine-gun fire, or both.[94] Survivors from the following 1st Somerset Light Infantry¶ and 1/6th Royal Warwicks,** of 11th and 143rd Brigades respectively, pressed forward. They suffered from machine guns around Serre and in Ridge Redoubt, the 1/6th losing 80 men

---

* 1st Battalion East Lancashire Regiment. 4th Division states 502 casualties (68 k, 257 w and 177 m). SDGW notes 171 deaths.

† 1st Battalion Hampshire Regiment. 4th Division states 585 casualties (123 k, 265 w and 197 m). SDGW notes 218 fatalities.

‡ 1st Battalion Rifle Brigade (The Prince Consort's Own). 4th Division states 474 casualties (59 k, 246 w and 169 m). SDGW notes 158 deaths.

§ 1/8th Battalion (Territorial Force) Royal Warwickshire Regiment. 4th Division states 588 casualties (58 k, 254 w and 276 m). SDGW notes 228 deaths.

¶ 1st Battalion Prince Albert's (Somerset Light Infantry). 4th Division states 476 casualties (51 k, 180 w and 245 m). SDGW notes 156 fatalities.

** 1/6th Battalion (Territorial Force) Royal Warwickshire Regiment. 4th Division states 472 casualties (48 k, 184 w and 240 m). SDGW notes 157 deaths.

before reaching its own parapet.[95] Some reached the German lines, but in insufficient numbers to do anything other than help consolidation.[96] By 9 a.m., 11th Brigade had penetrated the German front line behind Heidenkopf on a frontage of about 600 yards and to a depth of 250–500 yards, but their early gains were already taking on the characteristics of a siege rather than an advance.[97]

Captain Douglas Adams, 1/8th Royal Warwicks, said the enemy enfilade was initially too high as his battalion crossed over. The triggermen soon shortened their range.[98] 'Casualties became so heavy that by the time that isolated parties had reached the German support trench (about 200 yards behind the front line) further advance was impossible.'[99] It was a question of numbers. Even if 11th Brigade had forced a limited entry into the German line it was still a long way short of Hunter-Weston's objectives and never of sufficient scale or momentum to be expanded upon.

Leutnant-der-Reserve Friedrich Stutz, RIR121, was in the Redan Ridge front line as the 1st Rifle Brigade attempted to advance:

'The English had pushed underground tunnels [Russian Saps] forward, close to our front line. They broke the surface just before the attack and positioned Lewis guns at these. The name of the tunnel in front of us was "The Cat." They tried to force us to keep our heads down [while the infantry crossed no-man's-land]. A hand grenade salvo silenced the Lewis gun and we rushed forward. *Reservist* Fischer did great work with the bayonet. The Lewis gun is ours. Now our machine guns prove devastating to the enemy's [infantry] columns and an artillery battery behind sends shells into them.'[100]

Private Ralph Miller, 1/8th Royal Warwicks, remembered 'hundreds of fellows, shouting and swearing, going over with fixed bayonets.'[101] Second-Lieutenant George Glover, 1st Rifle Brigade, said his battalion's first wave bunched at the German wire and a 'most fearsome hail of rifle and machine gun fire with continuous shelling opened on us. Most of us seemed to be knocked out.'[102] Private Fred Lewis, 1/8th Royal Warwicks, prayed 'to Almighty God that if I got wounded that it would be light.'[103] He got his wish: a bullet pierced his left foot. His battalion commander was nearby: 'We'd only gone over the top a few yards and he [the commander] was killed instantly — right at my side — a bullet through his head. Colonel [Edgar] Innes his name was.' Others, wrote Lewis, were less fortunate and died slowly and in pain. 'You'd look at them lying there all gashed, legs off, arms off, and stomach all ripped open. You'd think "Poor bugger!" and that was it. It was a matter of being used to it.'[104] Second-Lieutenant William Page, 1st East Lancashires, saw some German soldiers atop their parapet waving their caps. 'Come on English,' they taunted, before being killed by a shell burst.[105] Private John Kerr, 1st Somerset Light Infantry, reached the German trenches. A bullet grazed his head and he was taken prisoner. Among all of the carnage and death it bothered him more that his captors 'stole our money and valuables.'[106]

Fourth Division, including the two Royal Warwicks battalions attached, would run up a total of 5752 casualties for 1 July, among them 1883 dead, 3563 wounded, 218 missing and 88 prisoners. Meanwhile, RIR121 recorded 179 dead, 291 wounded and 70 missing for the period 1–10 July, although mostly on the first day of that period.[107] In short, for every one German casualty opposite the 4th, there were 10.7 British.

Nobody knows exactly what happened to Private Harry Woodward, 1/6th Royal Warwicks, except that he was probably killed by machine-gun fire. The Birmingham teenager, whose 15th birthday was just a few weeks before he hopped the sandbags and went forward into battle, is named on the Thiepval Memorial. At the time of his death Woodward had been in France for more than a year, which meant he had been in the trenches since the age of 13. Another among 1/6th Royal Warwicks' dead was 21-year-old Private Fred Andrews. He penned a letter to his mother in late June: 'Do not worry I hope the war will soon be over now. Things are looking up here.'[108] A few weeks later his mother wrote back: 'Oh son I do hope you are all right. I have not had a line for nearly three weeks. ... My own dear boy I am quite sure it is not your fault I do not know what is preventing you from writing if I could only get a line in your hand writing I should feel better.'[109] Andrews is buried at Serre Road Cemetery No. 2.

Such was the noise and confusion of battle that nobody really noticed four underground German mines detonating at the head of Heidenkopf. The idea was to blow up British infantry as they entered the trenches. The mines were fired at about 7.45 a.m., some probably later in the morning.

British and German sources are equally vague. One detonated as 1/8th Royal Warwicks entered the German line, two smaller mines were apparently fired as 1st King's Own* crossed at about 9.30 a.m., while around the same time 2nd Lancashire Fusiliers had a couple of mines blown 'under our first wave.'[110] Four craters were seen after battle, but German observers shied from saying they had seen the blasts.[111] Apparently the British attack 'suddenly faltered' near the mines, and many corpses were later found nearby.[112] Quite how quadruple explosions — each with a charge of 1250–1600 kilograms (2750–3500 pounds), according to German records, and leaving a crater about 10 metres (11 yards) deep and roughly 25 metres (27 yards) across — could go unmentioned in the memoirs of so many men in the area remains unknown. The only certainty is that these four mine blasts were nowhere near as effective as had been expected.[113]

AT THE EXTREME north of VIII Corps, 31st Division's attack eastwards up the exposed grassy incline leading towards Serre village and positions held by IR169 was a disaster from the outset. Thirty-first Division's leading waves moved through their wire and into no-man's-land at about 7.20 a.m. and lay down waiting for Zero.[114] The first two waves were to advance in extended order, with subsequent ones in columns of sections.[115] German shells were already bursting, soon joined by grazing machine-gun fire.[116] A company of the 12th King's Own Yorkshire Light Infantry (KOYLI)† was attached to each of the 31st's 93rd and 94th Brigades. Three sections of 210th Field Company, RE, were attached to 94th Brigade, which hoped to consolidate its gains by day, while the 93rd planned to deploy sections from 211th and 223rd Field Companies later that night.[117] Five Russian Saps on the 31st's front — north to south, John, Mark, Excema, Gray and Bleneau, the latter containing a Stokes mortar that quickly spent its ammunition when it began firing at 7.28 a.m. — were opened at 6.30 a.m. Once the attack began, the remaining two companies of 12th KOYLI were to dig these saps across to the German lines. All of the opened Russian Saps in the 31st's sector would to some extent become havens for wounded men throughout the day.

---

*   1st Battalion King's Own (Royal Lancaster Regiment). 4th Division states 445 casualties (43 k, 222 w and 180 m). SDGW notes 115 deaths.
†   12th (Service) Battalion (Miners) (Pioneers) King's Own (Yorkshire Light Infantry). Battalion war diary states 189 casualties of all ranks. SDGW notes 38 deaths.

By day's end, the 31st had accrued about 3600 casualties, including 1349 dead, 2169 wounded, 74 missing and 8 prisoners. Opposite, IR169 sustained 141 dead, 219 wounded and 2 missing.[118] That worked out at a rate of one German casualty for every 9.9 British.

In 93rd Brigade's patch, just north of 4th Division, 15th West Yorkshires* was almost annihilated by 'severe' frontal and flanking machine-gun and rifle fire.[119] Following, 16th West Yorkshires,† along with one company of 18th Durham Light Infantry,‡ suffered appalling casualties even before reaching their own front line. Numerous men were killed and wounded as they clambered from their assembly trenches, and still more fell as they pressed towards the British wire to begin their attack. Against the odds a small number, incredibly, made it across no-man's-land and into enemy lines, fewer still to Munich Trench immediately south of Serre and some of these, allegedly, to Pendant Copse, about a mile behind the German front line.[120] Eighteenth West Yorkshires,§ coming on behind, made no headway, and incurred most of its casualties before even reaching its own wire.[121] The remaining three companies of 18th Durham Light Infantry were held in reserve.

Ninety-fourth Brigade, to the north, advanced on a two-battalion frontage from trenches lacing Mark, Luke and John Copses just west of Serre. The attack of 11th East Lancashires¶ and 12th York & Lancasters** also faltered in withering machine-gun crossfire,[122] as well as a heavy

---

* 15th (Service) Battalion (1st Leeds) Prince of Wales's Own (West Yorkshire Regiment). Also known as 1st Leeds Pals. 93rd Brigade recorded 528 casualties (67 k, 279 w and 182 m). SDGW notes 222 deaths.

† 16th (Service) Battalion (1st Bradford) Prince of Wales's Own (West Yorkshire Regiment). Also known as 1st Bradford Pals. 93rd Brigade noted 527 casualties (67 k, 311 w and 149 m). SDGW notes 149 deaths.

‡ 18th (Service) Battalion (1st County) Durham Light Infantry. 93rd Brigade states 252 casualties (29 k, 189 w and 34 m). SDGW notes 67 deaths.

§ 18th (Service) Battalion (2nd Bradford) Prince of Wales's Own (West Yorkshire Regiment). Also known as 2nd Bradford Pals. 93rd Brigade tallied 441 casualties (53 k, 288 w and 100 m). SDGW notes 100 deaths.

¶ 11th (Service) Battalion (Accrington) East Lancashire Regiment. Also known as Accrington Pals. 94th Brigade noted 621 casualties (77 k, 463 w and 81 m). SDGW notes 118 deaths.

** 12th (Service) Battalion (Sheffield) York & Lancaster Regiment. Also known as Sheffield Pals or Sheffield City Battalion. 94th Brigade recorded 511 casualties (48 k, 147 w and 316 m). SDGW notes 248 deaths.

curtain of shellfire. That shellfire, the blasts of which Brigadier-General Rees earlier likened to poplar trees, began on the brigade's rear-most assembly trenches and worked its way forward to the British front line.[123] Twelfth York & Lancasters later reported: 'As soon as our [preparatory] barrage lifted from their front line, the Germans, who had been sheltering in Dug-outs immediately came out and opened rapid fire with their machine guns.'[124] Most of these two battalions were stopped in no-man's-land. However, up to 100 men of 11th East Lancashires surprisingly reached the ruins of Serre, only to be killed or captured there, with very few of the 12th York & Lancasters making it that far, too.[125] In the wake of these battalions, the leading companies of 13th* and 14th York & Lancasters† were also fired on before reaching no-man's-land, and were then mauled by a 'perfect tornado' of shell- and machine-gun fire when attempting the cross.[126] Again, a very small number of men of the 14th reached the enemy line.[127] It was with bloody and good reason that the 94th's attacks were immediately suspended.[128] On 94th Brigade's extreme northern flank, the Russian Sap known as John jutted into no-man's-land to provide northern flank protection. It was soon clogged with bloody, broken men and others sheltering from German defensive fire.

If a few isolated parties of the 31st had breached the German trenches, the overall theme was of multiple battalions effectively destroyed as effective fighting units around and behind their own front line, or as they attempted to cross the barren no-man's-land. Supporting battalions of the 93rd and 94th all 'suffered heavily from the German artillery barrage, which was at once put down when they made any movement and was obviously directed by observation.'[129] Those small groups of survivors who miraculously made it further were all too often confronted by intact coils of German wire, sections of patchy entanglements that were essentially impassable, and gaps defended by German infantry. As 12th York & Lancasters' war diarist bleakly noted:

---

* 13th (Service) Battalion (1st Barnsley) York & Lancaster Regiment. Also known as 1st Barnsley Pals. 94th Brigade totted up 275 casualties (46 k, 169 w and 60 m). SDGW notes 81 deaths.

† 14th (Service) Battalion (2nd Barnsley) York & Lancaster Regiment. Also known as 2nd Barnsley Pals. 94th Brigade noted 270 casualties (27 k, 141 w and 102 m). SDGW notes 92 deaths.

In view of the fact that the enemy artillery became active as soon as it was daylight, it would appear likely that the enemy was warned of the attack by observing gaps cut in our own wire [for infantry to pass through] and tapes laid out in No Man's Land [to aid deployment], thus obtaining at least three and a half hours warning of the attack. … Our intention to attack must have been quite obvious.[130]

He might have been writing for the whole of 31st Division, with 29th Division further south having failed for strikingly similar reasons.

Survivors of the 31st's leading waves told of an operation that was shot into submission from the outset.[131] Lance-Corporal James Glenn, 12th York & Lancasters, remembered the attackers 'hadn't gone but a few steps when they went down again.'[132] He said the 'funny thing about being in a barrage was being frightened and trying not to show it to your mates.'[133] Corporal Douglas Cattell, 12th York & Lancasters, said he 'never saw a German and I never fired at one. Yet all this firing was coming at us.'[134] Private Alfred Howard, 15th West Yorkshires, had brazened his way to the intact German wire when a bullet smashed his rifle and he went to ground. 'Away on the left a party of Germans climbed out of the trench, they kicked one or two bodies, any showing signs of life were shot or bayonetted.'[135] After a few hours under the blazing sun surrounded by corpses, Howard bolted back whence he came. A bullet clipped his leg and he collapsed into a shell hole. 'I got out of the hole and crawled to our line, all was quiet, except for the groans of dead and dying. You could not tell what had been trenches from shell holes, but all were full, bodies one on top of the other.'[136] Most did not get close enough to the hostile parapet even to see a German soldier, let alone squeeze off a pot shot.

Those in follow-up battalions saw the grisly fate of those before them. It was with good reason that Private Tommy Oughton, 13th York & Lancasters, said he felt 'very mixed as we waited to go over.'[137] Then his battalion moved towards the British front line. 'You could see bodies dropping here, there and wondering, is it you next?' Nearby, Lance-Corporal Charles Moss, 18th Durham Light Infantry, saw a soldier resting a piece of raw meat on his left forearm: 'It was the remains of his right forearm.'[138] Private Frank Raine, 18th Durham Light Infantry, reached a 'stage where you get beyond being frightened, but I felt guilty at dropping into a shell hole.'[139] Lieutenant Robert Heptonstall, 13th York & Lancasters, made good distance before being wounded and going to ground. He saw a 'dead man propped up against the German wire in a sitting position. He was sniped at during the day until his head was completely shot away.'[140] Corporal Arthur Durrant, 18th Durham Light Infantry, was wounded a few paces into no-man's-land. 'I started dragging myself along again over bodies. Dead bodies and bits of bodies and I came to a shallow trench and I was on my back and I thought well if this is the end it is the end and that is that and I lay there looking at the sky.'[141]

ALL ALONG VIII Corps' line German machine-gunners were deciding the outcome of the battle. Few British soldiers saw the muzzle flashes of those machine guns firing from the intermediate position, about 1500 yards away. But they could definitely see and hear the damage they were doing, and take an educated guess at where the welter of bullets was coming from. One soldier, at least a mile behind the front line, described the sound as a 'tearing rattle' within the battle symphony.[142] Raine was in no-man's-land: 'Oh my God, the ground in front of me was just like heavy rain, that was the machine-gun bullets.'[143] Private Wilfred Crook, 1st Somerset Light Infantry, was met with a 'murderous burst' just south of Heidenkopf: 'I knew we were doomed. Bullets flew everywhere and dust spurted near our feet and all around as they hit the ground. Near misses in passing whispered of death, while others plucked at our sleeves or hissed and spat viciously to ricochet. The noise was deafening.'[144] Private Bert Ellis, in the yet-to-attack Newfoundland Regiment, later described the fusillade tearing across the open sweeps of what is now Newfoundland Memorial Park:

> No doubt you know what a noise the 'air hammer' makes at the
> dock when they are working; well, that's something like a machine
> gun sounds when in action. They played havoc with our men and
> to make matters worse they had, practically on both sides, what is
> called enfilading fire, which is the worst kind of fire to be under.
> You could almost see the bullets coming, they came so thick and
> fast.[145]

All of these machine guns between Serre and the River Ancre had pre-registered and interlocking arcs of fire that covered no-man's-land, as well as the British front line and the latticework of ditches behind.

'We just had to load and reload. They went down in their hundreds,' wrote *Musketier* Karl Blenk, IR169, who was among those pelting 31st Division's infantry with bullets before Serre.[146] 'We just fired into them.' He later surveyed the carnage: 'There was a wailing and lamentation in No Man's Land and much shouting for stretcher-bearers. ... When the English tried again, they weren't walking this time, they were running as fast as they could but when they reached the piles of bodies they got no farther.'[147] Blenk was describing the killing zone, the area of no-man's-land in which the cones of fire from multiple machine guns overlapped and created a concentration of bullets essentially impassable for infantry, no matter what small-unit tactics they were using.

Wounded staggering back along the roads behind the battlefield told artillerymen of the horror. Lieutenant Frank Lushington, Royal Garrison Artillery, said he heard of 'whole companies mown down as they stood, of dead men hung up on the uncut German wire like washing, of the wounded and dying lying out in No Man's Land in heaps.'[148]

Early battle reports reaching Hunter-Weston's headquarters at Marieux, 10 miles west of Serre, gave a false picture of events. He described these reports as 'very rosy, to the effect that all the German front line had been taken.'[149] In fact, not one report received by VIII Corps before 8.40 a.m. even suggested anything had gone wrong. But neither scandal nor cover-up was afoot. The problem lay with a confluence of factors: heavy casualties among regimental officers who normally sent the reports; delayed and intermittent communication between headquarters; and over-optimistic observers whose visibility was obscured by the smoke of battle. Hunter-Weston believed the 31st had obtained a footing in Serre, the 4th had nabbed two lines of German trenches, the 29th was through Beaumont Hamel, and X Corps to the south had snatched a vital German stronghold known as Schwaben Redoubt, near Thiepval.[150] The only interpretation an optimistic Hunter-Weston could have formed on the basis of this information was that VIII Corps was progressing not quite to plan and very slowly, which was actually very different from the the disaster unfolding.

Back on the battlefield, the mechanical nature of the attack guaranteed the killing would continue. It was a point Captain Stair Gillon, 1st KOSB, later seized upon: 'If the G.O.C. [General Officer Commanding, Major-General de Lisle of the 29th] could have flown or rather hovered over the scene for ten seconds the attack would have been countermanded. ... But the terrible thing about war is that an attack once launched can rarely be broken off. Those in control don't and can't know what is going on in front.'[151] So it was that several follow-up battalions in 4th, 29th and 31st Divisions were destined to repeat the tragedies of the leading battalions, despite desperate attempts to stop them.

Fourth Division headquarters told 10th and 12th Brigades to stop their infantry from crossing into no-man's-land until a clearer picture of events was established.[152] These brigades were timed to cross into no-man's-land at about 9.30 a.m.; the message from divisional headquarters — sent in view of the manifestly heavy losses — went out at 8.35 a.m. Already there was some confusion at brigade headquarters over the flares seen rising skyward — one white flare meant the attack had been stopped, and three signalled objectives reached — and thus over how 11th and 143rd Brigades had actually performed. It was against this backcloth and with gradual realisation of the 11th's heavy early losses that 4th Division headquarters issued its order, which began slowly filtering down the chain of command. Captain William Carden Roe, adjutant, 1st Royal Irish Fusiliers, received an urgent telephone call from Brigadier-General Charles Wilding's 10th Brigade headquarters to stop his reserve battalion's attack:

'But,' I stammered, 'what about the white lights?'
    'Those ruddy white lights mean "Held up by machine gun fire," and the damned things are going up everywhere.'
    The whole rotten truth suddenly dawned on me.[153]

Unfortunately, technology, the confusion of the day and some broken telephone links meant circulation of the divisional order did not get through in time, or at all, to the next lot of battalions pressing forward.

This tranche of 4th Division pushed forward on a combined frontage of about 1500 yards under heavy artillery and machine-gun fire from about 9.30 a.m. These battalions included 2nd Royal Dublin Fusiliers and 2nd

Seaforth Highlanders, both of 10th Brigade, and used a blend of section columns and artillery formation.[154] Also going forward were 1st King's Own, 2nd Essex, 2nd Lancashire Fusiliers and 2nd Duke of Wellington's, which were all in Brigadier-General James Crosbie's 12th Brigade and all moving forward in artillery formation.[155] Attempts to stop the attack of 2nd Royal Dublin Fusiliers* were partially successful, but some platoons went forward.[156] Without exception, these became casualties.[157] The kilted 2nd Seaforth Highlanders† received no word to stop its advance.[158] Some of its much-depleted ranks crossed over and joined in the Heidenkopf fighting.[159] Elements of the casualty-thinned 2nd Essex‡ and 1st King's Own also defied the odds and made it into the German lines.[160] Behind them, word to halt the advance reached 2nd Lancashire Fusiliers§ and 2nd Duke of Wellington's⁵ a fraction too late to stop two companies of the former and three of the latter from entering the no-man's-land welter.[161] Those who survived the passage and reached Heidenkopf participated in the fighting there.[162] The remaining companies of these battalions went over shortly before 11 a.m.[163] The besieged wedge around Heidenkopf now comprised the thinned-out ranks of all of 4th Division's brigades, but there would be no more reinforcements of men and munitions for hours.

'Our machineguns did excellent work,' wrote *Leutnant-der-Reserve* Riegel, Machine-gun Sharp-shooter Troop 198.[164] He was on Redan Ridge shooting head-on at 2nd Royal Dublin Fusiliers. 'The entire line of skirmishers falls before us. Some try to come forward alone, but our infantry are on the parapet and mop up the individuals who come too close.'[165] Lieutenant William Colyer, 2nd Royal Dublin Fusiliers, later grieved for friends killed: 'I can scarcely grasp the fact that I shall never see some of them again. It is such a short while ago that I left them in

---

*   2nd Battalion Royal Dublin Fusiliers. 4th Division states 328 casualties (54 k, 234 w and 40 m). SDGW notes 61 deaths.
†   2nd Battalion Seaforth Highlanders (Ross-Shire Buffs, The Duke of Albany's). 4th Division states 398 casualties (68 k, 228 w and 102 m). SDGW notes 119 deaths.
‡   2nd Battalion Essex Regiment. 4th Division states 437 casualties (48 k, 180 w and 209 m). SDGW notes 139 deaths.
§   2nd Battalion Lancashire Fusiliers. 4th Division states 382 casualties (26 k, 253 w and 103 m). SDGW notes 67 deaths.
⁵   2nd Battalion Duke of Wellington's (West Riding Regiment). 4th Division states 394 casualties (24 k, 309 w and 61 m). SDGW notes 52 deaths.

the height of good spirits, and now in the freshness of youth they have suddenly gone off to another world.'[166]

Around this time Brigadier-General Charles Prowse, commanding 11th Brigade, stepped into no-man's-land. He was on his way forward to get a handle on events at Heidenkopf, and probably also to arrange an attack to silence the Ridge Redoubt machine-gunners. He did not get far. A bullet slammed into his stomach. He died a few hours later in a medical station and is today buried at Louvencourt Military Cemetery. Across VIII Corps' battle front, nine battalion commanders were killed or died of wounds, and nine more were wounded.[167] Casualties among junior officers and NCOs were alarmingly heavy, which meant organised command and control within the British lines quickly began to fragment, and even more so in the Heidenkopf toehold.

On the south side of Beaumont Hamel, Major-General de Lisle now committed Newfoundland Regiment* and 1st Essex,† both in Brigadier-General Douglas Cayley's 88th Brigade. It was 8.37 a.m., and de Lisle wrongly believed the advance by its infantry was only temporarily held up and that parties of its infantry were fighting in the German trenches.[168] Major Richard Spencer-Smith, second in command of reserve battalion 2nd Hampshires, considered the attack a 'grave error of judgement, being preordained to failure and having no chance of success.'[169] German machine-gunners were in no way subdued.

First Essex was initially delayed; communication trenches were clogged with casualties. The Newfoundlanders advanced overland in columns of sections at 9.15 a.m. As Private Walter Day, Newfoundland Regiment, later said, 'We knew we were in for it. Everybody knew we were in for it.'[170] Within 30 minutes, the battalion lost 233 men dead, 386 wounded and 91 missing.[171] Attacking from trenches well behind the front line, mostly north of today's memorial park, many Newfoundlanders were felled long before entering its present-day grounds. Others made it into no-man's-land and proceeded down the long incline towards Y Ravine. One said the 'air seemed full of hissing pieces of lead all bent on the same grim

---

* 1st Battalion Newfoundland Regiment. *Official History* states 710 casualties (233 k, 386 w and 91 m). SDGW notes 272 deaths.

† 1st Battalion Essex Regiment. *Official History* states 229 casualties (60 k, 167 w and 2 m). SDGW notes 33 deaths.

errand. Our comrades began to fall all round us, and now a man stood alone where before a section had stood.'[172] First Essex came up 40 minutes later, deployed in columns of sections and attacked.[173] It, too, failed in a storm of artillery and machine-gun fire. 'The fire was hellish and many men were not able to get back from No Man's Land until twenty-four hours after the attack died down,' wrote Captain George Paxton, 1st Essex.[174]

Divisional headquarters learned of these disasters at about 10 a.m., and five minutes later de Lisle, who now had a better handle on the fate of his division, wisely decided no more of the 29th should be sent forward.[175] It was too late; most of the killing had already been done.

Hunter-Weston's rose-tinted knowledge of events abated alongside worsening situation reports, but his outlook remained upbeat. At about 10.25 a.m, he ordered the 29th's 4th Worcesters* and 2nd Hampshires,[†] along with the rest of the 4th's 10th Brigade — 1st Royal Warwicks and 1st Royal Irish Fusiliers — to renew the attack at 12.30 p.m. and take Beaumont Hamel and the German intermediate line, or Munich Trench, behind it. This was far too optimistic, but revealed Hunter-Weston knew his corps had no hope of reaching its final objective, Serre–Grandcourt Spur.[176] He contemplated using 48th (South Midland) Division, and brought it up to Mailly Maillet. A 12.30 p.m. rush forward by 1st Lancashire Fusiliers was gunned down. The 88th's part in the planned operation was delayed, postponed and finally cancelled at 1.45 p.m. In the 10th's sector, between about 1 p.m. and 2 p.m., attempts by a strong patrol from 1st Royal Warwicks[‡] and then a company of 1st Royal Irish Fusiliers[§] to cross the British front-line trenches into no-man's-land faltered under intense machine-gun fire.[177] At about 2.55 p.m., Major-General Sir William Lambton, 4th Division's commander, told VIII Corps his division had suffered too many casualties to attack again.[178] Casualties, confusion and communication and organisational difficulties

---

*   4th Battalion Worcester Regiment. 29th Division states 53 casualties. SDGW notes 6 deaths.

†   2nd Battalion Hampshire Regiment. 29th Division notes 25 casualties. SDGW notes 3 deaths.

‡   1st Battalion Royal Warwickshire Regiment. 4th Division states 77 casualties (15 k, 59 w and 3 m). SDGW notes 12 deaths.

§   1st Battalion Princess Victoria's (Royal Irish Fusiliers). 4th Division states 141 casualties (14 k, 116 w and 11 m). SDGW notes 10 deaths.

saw the 10th's part in the planned attack postponed and then abandoned mid-afternoon.[179] Hunter-Weston now reflected on events: 'The result of the day's fighting up to the present 3pm has been disappointing. We have gained very little ground & our hold on what we have got is precarious. It is very probable that the result of the VIIIth Corps attack will be that we shall find ourselves back on our original line.'[180] Regardless of this mid-afternoon epiphany, Hunter Bunter was not quite done yet. His profligate thoughts returned to Serre and 31st Division.

Just after midday, Brigadier-General Rees' 94th Brigade was ordered by Major-General Robert Wanless-O'Gowan, commanding the 31st, to attack and confirm the British footing at Serre, which was behind enemy lines.[181] Rees suggested postponing until more detailed information on the situation could be gathered, implying he had nil appetite for any operation of the type suggested.[182] Wanless-O'Gowan was back in touch at about 5.20 p.m. asking Rees and Brigadier-General John Ingles, of the 93rd, if they were arranging an operation to establish communications with 'our troops in Serre.'[183] Wanless-O'Gowan — almost certainly at Hunter-Weston's behest — offered up some fresh troops. Rees and Ingles rightly opposed any such endeavour, as their brigades were not 'in a fit state,' which was a polite way of saying they had been shot to pieces.[184] Rees doubted whether any British troops were in Serre, barring the dead and prisoners. This seemed to be supported by the latest Royal Flying Corps observation report.[185] Wanless-O'Gowan listened to his men on the spot. He told Hunter-Weston their concerns and proposed using his 92nd Brigade to hold the front line in case of a German counterattack, and suggested a prepared operation on 2 July with fresh troops might be a better course of action.

Hunter-Weston seized upon Wanless-O'Gowan's suggestions even though he knew all was not going remotely well. At 6 p.m. he ordered the 92nd forward for a two-battalion attack at 2 a.m. on 2 July to clear up 'the situation' in Serre.[186] Almost four hours later, Hunter-Weston realised the folly of this operation — one wonders exactly how much politely worded lobbying from his subordinates was required — and cancelled it.[187] Hunter-Weston had finally conceded defeat, seven hours after stating that it was the most likely outcome of the battle for VIII Corps.

From Soden's mid-morning perspective the fighting between Serre and Beaumont Hamel had gone mostly to plan. Reports arriving at his

Biefvillers headquarters led him to identify 36th (Ulster) Division's unexpected and troubling break-in around Schwaben Redoubt (fully discussed in Chapter 6, which deals with X Corps' operations) as a priority. Soden realised that the loss of this ground posed a significant threat to the tenability of his divisional sector if left unchecked. Comparatively speaking, the tactical situations around Ovillers, further south and also in his divisional sector, and in the Beaumont Hamel–Serre area, to the north, were under control. Other reports would have told him that RIR119's and RIR121's co-ordinated defences were broadly functional and had mostly blunted the enemy's attacks within one-and-a-half hours.[188] The Hawthorn Ridge break-in was obviously minor and already fading. The wedge of land yielded around Heidenkopf had been contained and was being gradually squeezed out by organised counterattacks that began late morning. By about 9 a.m., Soden knew his on-the-spot commanders were controlling the battle between the River Ancre and Serre, and that he could focus his attention on remedying the tenuous and troubling situation at Schwaben Redoubt.[189]

'EVERY BATTLE HAS shown that trenches which are either lost or in dispute may be comparatively easily cleared or recaptured, when this is undertaken immediately,' said *Generalleutnant* Hermann von Stein, XIV Reserve Corps' commander.[190] 'I expect leaders to show the greatest determination and initiative in such cases.' So it was that the third and final act of the day, the German reclamation of ground lost to Hunter–Weston's Corps, was set in train.

It began at about 10. a.m. on Hawthorn Ridge, where a small group of 2nd Royal Fusiliers, joined by some men of 16th Middlesex, had held the crater rim nearest the British lines for almost three hours, while German infantry occupied the other side. British and German machine-gunners and riflemen traded shots from opposite sides. A few of the up to 120 men of the 2nd Royal Fusiliers who made it there had even entered the trenches of RIR119, engaging the enemy with bayonet, grenade, rifle and pistol. It was always a one-outcome battle. For those fusiliers who chanced a look back at their own lines, the sight was of 86th Brigade's main attack being clinically gunned down, which meant they would be neither reinforced nor supplied with ammunition.[191] Moreover, they were outnumbered and casualties were increasing. As small, well-armed RIR119 counterattack groups worked in from each flank, this casualty-depleted, beleaguered group of British soldiers was gradually pushed back; they retreated to the crater before survivors ran a gauntlet of machine-gun fire as they dashed away overland. Few made it back. By 10.30 a.m., the crater on Hawthorn Ridge was lost for good, meaning 29th Division had failed to make a single lasting gain.

Private Noel Peters, 16th Middlesex, watched a blood-covered soldier of 29th Division race back towards safety amid the no-man's-land fusillade. Occasionally he stumbled, fell, picked himself up and continued on. 'And then he took a run and a dive and landed on the parapet. We grabbed his arms and hauled him over. ... He kept patting his legs to see where he was hit. "I don't know, I think they got my legs." But do you know what? He didn't have a scratch on him.'[192]

One-and-a-quarter miles away at Heidenkopf, 4th Division's break-in quickly took on the characteristics of a smaller-scale trench raid. During the day soldiers from some nine battalions found their way to the German trenches here and beyond, but probably no more than about 1000. Effectively, the break-in had taken three successive trenches of the enemy front-line system on a 600-yard frontage. Men from different units were mixed up, officer and NCO casualties were heavy, and nobody really knew the layout of the heavily shellfire-damaged German trenches. In places consolidation had got underway quickly, in others not. One critic later said those in Heidenkopf had not grasped the 'difference between a battle and a raid.'[193] He meant that order had not been imposed upon chaos and that the captured trenches were never really made fit for defence against the organised counterattacks that were certain to follow.

The initial German fightback was implemented by on-the-spot NCOs and subalterns of RIR121. Patrols probed for weak spots in the British perimeter, and bombing parties began concentric counterattacks, both along trenches and overland.[194] Soon the regiment's commander, *Oberstleutnant* Adolf Josenhans, ordered more counterattacks without delay.[195] His junior commanders led small, well-armed groups of infantry — usually 10–20 men, sometimes more — who worked from one corpse-littered trench bay or shell hole to the next. Supplies of grenades and bullets were brought up behind them. Where required, company- and battalion-sized units were applied to the job. The Rifle Brigade's historian said an 'attempt was made to hold out in the German second line [of the front line system]; but the German supply of bombs was apparently inexhaustible, and after fifteen minutes, this was found to be impossible.'[196] Josenhans committed his regiment's 3rd Battalion piecemeal: 'Step-by-step the tenacious enemy was pushed back. Again and again they barricaded themselves with sandbags with a machine gun or mortar, so it was hard to get at them with grenades.'[197] By 11 a.m. the most advanced 4th Division parties had been driven from Munich Trench, and by 5 p.m. 'all that could be retained was the trench [150–200 yards in length] across the base of the Quadrilateral [Heidenkopf]. Blocks were made.'[198] By dusk, several hours later, the British had been forced back into the Heidenkopf trenches.[199] The struggle continued into the night and, barring one company of 1st Royal Irish Fusiliers that went over that night and held out until about noon on 2 July, the bridgehead was eventually yielded around midnight as the last defenders stole away.

Sergeant Arthur Cook, 1st Somerset Light Infantry, recalled the chaos as officers and NCOs tried to organise the Heidenkopf defences.[200] 'Jerry was popping up all over the place, behind and on our flanks and throwing grenades at us from all angles.' Somebody panicked and 400–500 men bolted, at first in dribs and drabs. Drummer Walter Ritchie, 2nd Seaforth Highlanders, stood in plain view atop the parapet and repeatedly bugled 'Charge', which stemmed the flood. Ritchie, a professional soldier, won the Victoria Cross for this, and for carrying messages over fire-swept ground. He lived. The situation remained touch and go. Cook's group collected grenades from the dead but soon these were spent. 'The Germans then gradually drove us back inch by inch, through their superior supply of bombs.' The uninjured trampled over the dead and wounded. Bombs were scarce, as was water. 'Jerry took advantage of the maze of communication trenches to follow up every yard we gave.' Soon all that remained in Cook's immediate area was a stretch of the old German front line, held by about 50 parched soldiers. 'Shells were now falling thick and fast, the enemy had apparently retired and asked for artillery support to try to dislodge us.' It worked. Shortly before midnight, Cook's party withdrew, stumbling over corpses and into shell holes. 'How I escaped I do not know.'

Leutnant-der-Reserve Emil Geiger, RIR121, was thinking much the same as he led a counterattack group into Heidenkopf that afternoon. 'I seemed to be invincible on this day.'[201] All around him men were killed — an NCO shot in the heart, two just-arrived reinforcements shot through the head, along with plenty of others killed or wounded in the fighting. 'We ran into English machine-gun fire at a distance of a few metres. Two of my men were almost torn to pieces. I was, strange as it may sound, unscathed.' Geiger continued: 'We attacked the enemy concentrically using our grenades and they had to withdraw from traverse to traverse. We had very heavy losses.'[202] Here and there the resistance firmed, and Geiger's group had to consolidate their gains. 'We were forced to put a barricade between us and the enemy, sandbags on top of our dead friends and enemies.' That night the trenches were back in German hands. Geiger was 'quite exhausted by the excitement of the day, apathetic and [cradling a] half dislocated arm through the many throwings of hand grenades.' Earlier that afternoon, a parched *Leutnant-der-Reserve* Friedrich Conzelmann, RIR121, guzzled greedily at his water bottle: 'The sun shone so beautifully over the slaughter of 1 July. The heat beating down on us was such that we nearly died of thirst.'[203]

German soldiers returning to Heidenkopf described it as a charnel-house. One said British and German dead lay heaped up in piles of five or six, all horribly mutilated by hand-grenade blasts.[204] Another said about 150 German soldiers lay dead in the trenches — witnesses said their bodies ranged from severely mangled to badly charred — and at least three times as many British.[205] The scene of carnage around RIR121's positions spilled into no-man's-land where about 1800 British soldiers lay.[206] 'The lines of English dead,' wrote one German eyewitness, 'are like tide-marks, like flotsam washed up on the sand.'[207]

Eighth Corps' bloody destruction north of the River Ancre was guaranteed before a single man stepped into no-man's-land. The seven-day bombardment's failure was compounded by the botched timings of the Hawthorn Mine blast and initial barrage lift. German defenders had up to 10 minutes' warning to meet an attack from their battered but defensible network of trenches, redoubts and fortified villages, with help from multiple operational artillery batteries. Unsurprisingly, numerous British battalions were destroyed behind and around their own front line, as well as in no-man's-land. This was exactly as Soden had planned. The mechanical nature of the attack — despite efforts to stop it in places — only added to the slaughter. Fourth Division's Heidenkopf epic was destined to fail, as was the 29th Division's toehold at the Hawthorn Ridge crater. The few men of 31st Division who made it to Serre proved to be red herrings who enticed profligate Hunter-Weston towards ill-considered salvage operations even after he had admitted any hope of success was lost. By contrast, in a division-wide context, Soden's regiments, defensive line and counterattack scheme north of the Ancre had performed as he expected. From an early hour, as we shall see in the next chapter, he was able to rely on his men on the spot to organise the defence and counterattacks, and focus his attentions, reserves and artillery on erasing X Corps' very troubling break-in at Schwaben Redoubt, near Thiepval. In short, Hunter-Weston's pre-battle blunders had handed Soden the tactical advantage and victory over VIII Corps. The tactical ramifications of this quickly extended south of the meandering waterway and affected the outcome of the neighbouring X Corps' operation.

A SWATHE OF lumpy ground and a ditch half filled with rotting leaves in what is today known as Sheffield Memorial Park, near Serre, are all that remain of the front-line trench from which 94th Brigade set out. Few got far beyond this defile, which edges a stand of trees that in 1916 was known severally as Mark, Luke and John Copses. Nowadays the park holds a handful of stone memorials and ageing plaques. In December 2014 it is muddy and cold, and several of the memorials are draped with British north-country football tat and made-in-China wreathes with fading poppies. It was somewhere near here that war poet Sergeant John 'Will' Streets, 12th York & Lancasters, was wounded then killed while trying to rescue a wounded soldier. Some of his verses were probably roughed out in these trenches, as he explained: 'They were inspired while I was in the trenches, where I have been so busy that I have had little time to polish them. I have tried to picture some thoughts that pass through a man's brain when he dies. I may not see the end of the poems, but hope to live to do so.'[208] The 31-year-old is thought to be buried in Euston Road Military Cemetery, which back in the day probably was not all that different from another soldiers' plot that Streets saw not long before his death:

When war shall cease this lonely, unknown spot,
Of many a pilgrimage will be the end,
And flowers will bloom in this now barren plot,
And fame upon it through the years descend,
But many a heart upon each simple cross,
Will hang the grief, the memory of its loss.

FROM HIS POSITION on the outskirts of Serre, *Unteroffizier* Otto Lais, IR169, saw successive lines of 31st Division's infantry advancing into a swarm of bullets from multiple chattering machine guns. Belt after belt of gleaming Spandau ammunition clattered through Lais's weapon; its water coolant boiled and piping-hot barrels were repeatedly changed. The gun's steam overflow pipe broke loose: 'With a great hiss, a jet of steam goes up, providing a superb target for the enemy. It is the greatest good fortune that they have the sun in their eyes. ... We fire on endlessly.'[209] Soon the water ran out. Lais's mates urinated in the coolant container as an alternative. Ammunition stoppages were cleared. He saw British soldiers go to ground, hiding behind the dead and wounded. 'Many hang, mortally wounded, whimpering in the remains of the barbed wire.'[210] All told, his gun loosed off about 18,000 rounds, and another nearby about 20,000: 'That is the hard, unrelenting tempo of the morning of 1st July 1916.'[211] Lais continued: 'Skin hangs in ribbons from the fingers of the burnt hands of the gunners and gun commanders! Constant pressure by their left thumbs on the triggers has turned them into swollen, shapeless lumps of flesh. Their hands rest, as though cramped, on the vibrating weapons.'[212] Using those same hands, Lais, the killer, later became an artist known for his brush and charcoal celebrations of women and sexuality.

'Impressions came back later, in flashes, very clear, like photos,' said Private Alfred Damon, 16th Middlesex. 'But then? No, nothing.'[213] He remembered that soldiers of 29th Division advanced with tin triangles fixed to their haversacks, which meant British observers could see them more clearly from a distance. Now he could see those 'tin triangles glittering in the sun' on the backs of the numerous dead.[214] Soon enough, Damon's platoon hopped the bags, and after about 100 yards a bullet thudded into his shoulder.[215] The former public schoolboy did not like swearing, said he had had a pious upbringing.[216] With bullets and shrapnel flying those values did not seem to matter so much. 'I let go with a stream of filthy language; words that would have made a Cockney Eastender blush. I suppose I must have heard all those words and retained them in my subconscious mind.'[217] He crawled back to the British trenches and then to a dressing station where he met a blood-covered friend whose scalp had been creased by a bullet: 'The only thing he told me about it was that the impact was so great that he thought he was dead. I remember being surprised that a person's thoughts can travel at such speed between the impact of the bullet and unconsciousness.'[218]

Damon was quite likely one of the soldiers in Lieutenant Malins' film of the attack across the Beaumont Hamel–Auchonvillers road. At the time a somewhat detached Malins was watching shells burst, listening to the swelling machine-gun fire and worrying whether his camera's lens was clean:[219] 'I looked upon all that followed from the purely pictorial point of view, and even felt annoyed if a shell burst outside the range of my camera. Why couldn't Bosche put the shell a little nearer? It would make a better picture. And so my thoughts ran on.'[220] This was Malins at his most high-handed. Soon enough a chunk of German shrapnel cleaved his tripod leg, which Malins fixed. A few hundred yards away through the viewfinder he saw shellfire doing the same thing to men, except that they were not quite so easily repaired and returned to action.

'This certainly provided me with what would be called a traumatic experience,' wrote Private William Slater, 18th West Yorkshires, of advancing from a trench 500 yards behind the British front line opposite Serre.[221] He saw men hit by machine-gun bullets fall in a 'curious manner,' and sheltered in a shell crater with others, most likely still behind British lines. As explosive shells blew and shrapnel whirred, he pondered his own mortality:

> What would it be like to be obliterated like an insect under
> someone's foot? Would there be a sudden blackness like the
> switching off of a light, and if so would it continue forever, and in
> that case how should I know that I was dead? Although I was not
> unduly afraid of being killed outright, I certainly shrank from the
> possibility of being grievously wounded and left there to die in
> agony.[222]

Leutnant-der-Reserve Adolf Beck's memories were mostly of soldiers dying horrible deaths. The RIR121 officer saw British soldiers cut down by machine guns 'as if by mowing machines,' and by the explosion of 'diabolical' shells that penetrated the soft ground before detonating.[223] One explosion sent bodies flying in all directions. One of the victims, a tall Scot, came down on an iron stake and 'was spitted straight under his lower jaw. Thereafter I was faced with the gruesome sight of a death's head staring at me.'[224] Beck soon found that his observation post, near Heidenkopf, was behind enemy lines. A British soldier called out 'Germans?' into the darkness of its entrance — as if he was ever going to get an answer — and tossed two hand grenades down the stair well. 'They exploded wrecking the timber and doing my hearing no good.'[225] At dusk, Beck slipped past some British outposts until he linked up with other soldiers of RIR121. Soon enough Heidenkopf was retaken and Beck found himself among an exhausted group of German soldiers: 'Sitting amongst comrades from the other companies, tired out and emotionally drained, were the remnants of my 3rd Company — thirty men and five *Unteroffiziers*. They slumped there, dog tired and spent. It had all been too much!'[226]

Private Francis 'Mayo' Lind of Little Bay, Newfoundland, was not so lucky. The nickname 'Mayo' came after he complained about a shortage of tobacco of that brand at the front,[227] in one letter among a bunch of his published in a Newfoundland newspaper. The community rallied; the boys at the front were inundated with tobacco.[228] In 1916 it was a patriotic act — not so now — and made Lind something of a Newfoundland celebrity. On 29 June he promised to send 'a very interesting letter' soon.[229] But, just before 9 a.m. on 1 July, Lind's promise was about all used up. He was killed in what is now Newfoundland Memorial Park, probably by machine-gun fire. Someone saw him 'doubled up as though he had been hit in the stomach.'[230] The affable 37-year-old with pale blue eyes and a boyish turn of phrase was gone. Newfoundland had lost its most famous war scribe. Years later, Lind's body and that of another Newfoundlander were found and buried together at Y Ravine Cemetery in the memorial park. Lind's cryptic epitaph on the shared headstone: 'How closely bravery and modesty are entwined.'

THREE DAYS AFTER the battle, Hunter-Weston penned a farrago of fiction and fact for his soldiers.[231] It was rich with the adjectives of heroism and the word 'failure' was conspicuous for its absence; it was not something he would publicly admit to. Instead he wrote of the 'splendid courage, determination and discipline' of his divisions and of the glorious dead who had 'preceded us across the Great Divide.' The next part of his message was mostly a lie: 'By your splendid attack you held these enemy forces here in the North and so enabled our friends in the South, both British and French, to achieve the brilliant success they have.' The British and French had certainly made gains well south of the Albert–Bapaume road, but Hunter-Weston was very obviously seeking to divert attention away from the tragedy that had befallen his corps. He knew full well that VIII Corps' job was never to provide any kind of diversionary attack for the areas where gains had been made, but rather to provide flank support for Fourth Army's main thrust around the Albert–Bapaume road.[232] In brief, his message was a paean to the virtues of duty and gallantry, and was designed to dress his failure as something it never was, a success.

Hunter-Weston's semi-literate letters to his wife reveal much of the man behind the façade. 'Our attack, though carried out with wonderful gallantry, discipline & determination failed to get home, & though we inflicted heavy losses on the enemy, our losses also were severe, & we are still in our old positions.'[233] Privately, he could admit his corps' failure, but he was incapable of accepting responsibility for having set the tactical parameters of battle in favour of the enemy. He was disappointed that his corps' 'splendid preparations, excellent discipline & magnificent courage in attack, have not had the result we all hoped for.'[234] In Hunter-Weston's mind it was better to veil the big picture of catastrophe with the adjective-rich language of heroism, propped up with the crackpot eugenics of his message to the troops: 'It was a magnificent display of disciplined courage worthy of the best traditions of the British race.'[235] If casualties held no importance to Hunter-Weston in victory, he attached some higher moral value to them in defeat; in this logician's mind, anything could figure as anything else.

Eighth Corps' casualties ran to at least 14,592: by far the most of any army corps on 1 July. This included 4860 dead, 8839 wounded, 512 missing, 128 prisoners of war and 253 unspecified.[236] Losses among the opposing German regiments totalled about 1194, including 421 dead, 701 wounded and at least 70 missing. For every German casualty opposite

VIII Corps, there were about 12.2 British, this skewed ratio revealing the true extent of Hunter-Weston's defeat.

BRIGADIER-GENERAL WALTER Ludlow hiked over Heidenkopf in March 1918 looking for his son's corpse. Captain Stratford Ludlow, 1/8th Royal Warwicks, was last seen deep in the German lines, shouting encouragement to his men and puffing on a cigarette. The 22-year-old Solihull officer's body was finally found in the 1930s and buried at Serre Road Cemetery No. 2. In 1918, his father found the slopes there covered with thick, brown grass and the occasional head of wild broccoli. Old trenches were collapsing, and scattered about were corroding bombs, bayonets, helmets and rifles. He saw not a living soul, but spied plenty of bones and nameless graves marked by crude wooden crosses already falling into disrepair:

> I sat on the edge of a shell hole opposite to the German position in No Man's Land, and wondered how it was possible that any troops in the world could attack such a position in broad daylight on a lovely July morning. There was not sufficient cover for a mouse except that which was afforded by shell holes in moving forward to the attack.[237]

Stand at the foot of Serre Road Cemetery No. 2 when a bitterly cold December gale belts across the amphitheatre and it is easy to see what he meant. There is nowhere to hide.

CHAPTER 6

Loitering without Intent

X Corps, squandered opportunities and failure
at Thiepval

'Every now and then another straggler came in and we got
talking about those who had been hit. Many of us broke
down and started howling.'[1]
— Lance-Corporal James Henderson, 14th Royal Irish Rifles

LIEUTENANT-GENERAL SIR Thomas Morland was a man of paradoxical empathies and simple views. As the rag-tag remnants of an infantry battalion attached to his X Corps withdrew from the Somme in July 1916, one soldier spied him on horseback: 'I had a lump in my throat as I saw him there with tears in his eyes.'[2] And, yet, seven days after his corps was martyred on the dog-legged battlefield around Thiepval, with more than 3000 of its dead rotting in the summer sun, Morland was having his likeness immortalised: 'I have now got the plaister [sic] cast of my head and the bronze me is in the process of construction.'[3] Clearly, in commissioning such a work, Morland had expected a different outcome to the 1 July battle for his corps. Perhaps that was because he saw few shades of grey when it came to the art of attack. 'The Bosches have had a good hammering and we shall go on punching them, I hope for a long time yet,' he wrote the following week.[4] Here was Morland in a nutshell: by turns intimate and callous, and quite guileless when it came to managing a battle.

Morland wore a monocle and smoked fat cigars. He liked horse-riding and polo and fox hunting. 'To the end of his days he was a true type of the old Army,' stated his 1925 obituary.[5] He was well liked by his staff, old-fashioned in his opinions and methods, and 'hardly left much impress on the men whom he commanded.'[6] His career had been built on obscure West African spats, but by 1916 his health and mental vigour had declined. As his obituary said, 'the virile personality of the tropical campaigns was becoming hard to recognize under the almost nonchalant habits of mind, which Morland [had] assumed when the Great War came to a close.'[7] What *were* these nonchalant habits of mind? General Sir Douglas Haig wrote in May 1917 that he thought the 50-year-old descendant of William the Conqueror lacked knowledge and confidence in the summer of 1916;[8] he might as well have said that Morland was not up to the job.

Tenth Corps faced fortress-like German defences that followed the rolling downs around the ruins of Thiepval. From the air, the German front line in X Corps' sector formed a giant numeral '7'. The cross bar of the 7 began just north of the River Ancre and ran southeast over the camber of sharply rising ground that held Thiepval Plateau and Schwaben Redoubt (Feste Schwaben), and thence down to Thiepval. The down stroke of the 7 ran along Thiepval Spur before ending at Leipzig Redoubt (Granatloch), a leafy former quarry now home to a silage barn facing Authuille Wood. As elsewhere, this defensive network comprised three successive arteries — the interconnected front, intermediate and second trench lines, each separated by about 1000 yards, but more to the south and east of Thiepval — that were sited to command the slopes as they tapered down towards the British lines. The British assembly trenches for the attack — wrote Major Austin Girdwood, a staff officer at 32nd Division headquarters — were 'dug a few days before the attack and being in chalk only advertised the fact that the attack was imminent. They should have been dug at a much earlier stage and properly camouflaged.'[9]

Once again the backbone of the German defences lay in their string of mutually supporting redoubts, strongpoints and fortified villages. In the front-line system, the houses and cellars of St Pierre Divion and Thiepval were turned into mini-fortresses with numerous machine guns, while Leipzig Redoubt salient became a latticework of trenches and machine-gun posts. Further back, Wonderwork (Wundtwerk) strongpoint covered

X Corps: Schwaben Redoubt and Thiepval

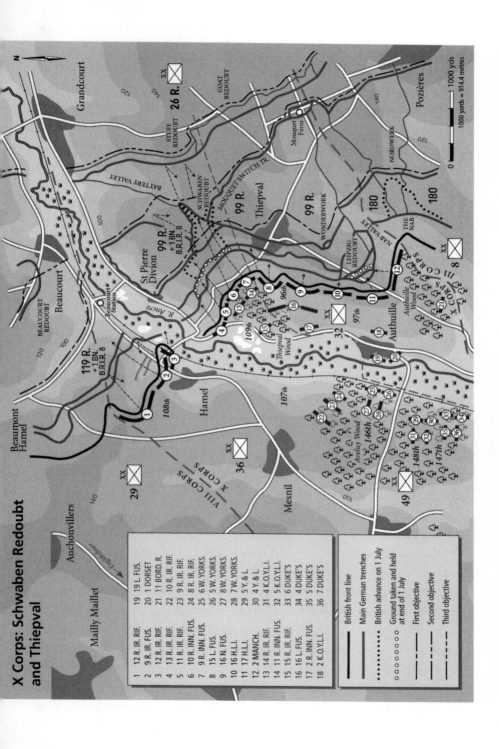

1	12 R. IR. RIF.	19	L. FUS.
2	9 R. IR. FUS.	20	1 DORSET
3	12 R. IR. RIF.	21	11 BORD. R.
4	13 R. IR. RIF.	22	10 R. IR. RIF.
5	11 R. IR. RIF.	23	9 R. IR. RIF.
6	10 R. INN. FUS.	24	8 R. IR. RIF.
7	9 R. INN. FUS.	25	6 W. YORKS.
8	15 L. FUS.	26	5 W. YORKS.
9	16 N. FUS.	27	8 W. YORKS.
10	16 H.L.I.	28	7 W. YORKS.
11	17 H.L.I.	29	5 Y. & L.
12	2 MANCH.	30	4 Y. & L.
13	14 R. IR. RIF.	31	4 K.O.Y.L.I.
14	11 R. INN. FUS.	32	5 K.O.Y.L.I.
15	15 R. IR. RIF.	33	6 DUKE'S
16	16 L. FUS.	34	4 DUKE'S
17	2 R. INN. FUS.	35	5 DUKE'S
18	2 K.O.Y.L.I.	36	7 DUKE'S

——	British front line
——	Main German trenches
oooooo	British advance on 1 July
ooooooo	Ground taken and held at end of 1 July
——	First objective
——	Second objective
– – –	Third objective

0   1000 yards = 914.4 metres   1000 yds

Thiepval and the redoubt. It was also sited to defend the roughly 2250 yards of ground between the German front line at the tip of the redoubt and the intermediate trench system due east of Thiepval. The intermediate trench ran southeast from near Beaucourt, in the River Ancre valley, via Schwaben Redoubt and Mouquet Switch Trench to Mouquet Farm, near Pozières. It held regularly spaced machine-gun posts and was crowned by Thiepval Plateau and Schwaben Redoubt, about 500 feet above sea level. Machine-gunners at Beaucourt could enfilade the plateau from the north, while the Nordwerk strongpoint to the south, outside X Corps' sector, could cover both Leipzig Redoubt and Wonderwork. The second position ran southeast from Grandcourt in the river valley towards Pozières and included Stuff (Feste Staufen) and Goat Redoubts (Feste Zollern), which offered further fire support to Schwaben Redoubt and Thiepval respectively. These co-ordinated defences were designed to block enemy attacks in no-man's-land with a significant volume of firepower, as well as to stop any penetration beyond the German front line.

Trudge over the wind-swept Thiepval Plateau today and its military value in 1916 is obvious. From a German viewpoint, Stuff and Schwaben Redoubts afforded sweeping panoramas over the patchwork of farmland from Beaumont Hamel to the northwest, around to Leipzig Redoubt in the south. If the British held this ground, they could observe large portions of the German defensive network as it zigzagged over the undulating land from Beaumont Hamel, via Beaucourt and Grandcourt, to Thiepval. German artillery positions north and south of the Ancre would become immediately untenable.[10] Whoever held the heights had the power of observation over, and well beyond, the other's front line, and with it the ability to accurately direct artillery fire. This was vital ground to Second Army commander *General-der-Infanterie* Fritz von Below and *Generalleutnant* Hermann von Stein, commanding XIV Reserve Corps, because they realised its loss would see their defences astride the Ancre and then, by extension, those north of the River Somme quickly unravelled.[11]

Morland's plan to crack this stronghold with a frontal infantry attack supported by artillery lacked imagination. He ordered an advance to a depth of 3000–3500 yards, with three objectives achieved by mid-morning, taking X Corps onto Thiepval Plateau.[12] On 27 June, he said the barrage on the German lines was 'pounding them properly,'[13] implying he expected any resistance to be crushed. Tenth Corps had a total ration roll of 93,796 soldiers of all ranks and branches of service, but the estimated number of infantry officers and men directly involved in the attack, along with those from various pioneer and engineer units, was about 21,000.[14] On the corps' left, 36th (Ulster) Division would attack astride the slow-moving waters of the Ancre, capturing Schwaben Redoubt and the plateau, both north of Thiepval. On the right, 32nd Division would assault the western face of Thiepval Spur, capturing the village and Leipzig Redoubt, before moving on to the plateau to the northeast of the village. The 32nd's infantry was supplemented by a total of three sections attached from 206th, 218th and 219th Field Companies, Royal Engineers (RE), while the 36th had a total of five sections furnished by 121st, 122nd and 150th Field Companies.[15] Forty-ninth (West Riding) Division was in corps reserve at Aveluy Wood and about a mile behind the lines. Morland's objectives were ambitious, and even he believed them a 'very hard task.'[16] But none of his paperwork suggests he appreciated the wider tactical importance of the plateau, or how it might be used to outflank and capture Thiepval village and spur. Morland's objectives simply required a succession of irrepressible steps through to completion and relied on his artillery to smash a path for his infantry.

Morland's field and heavy gunners had three essential jobs. These were to neutralise the German infantry in its trenches and dugouts, nullify German artillery, and sweep away defensive obstacles such as barbed wire and machine-gun posts. Excluding the Ancre swamps, which for obvious reasons were not being attacked, there was one heavy gun in X Corps' sector to every 57 yards of attack frontage, and one field gun to every 28 yards.[17] These had fired an estimated 330,400 shells at the German positions in the period 24–30 June.[18] On 1 July, the corps would fire an estimated 56,000 shells,[19] with the barrage lifting from the German front line at Zero hour and stepping deeper into the German positions, six strides for the heavy guns and 10 for the field guns.[20] In practice there were insufficient guns, their fire was diluted across too wide an area and there were plenty of dud shells. It was easier to observe the fall of shellfire in some places than in others, which meant that gauging the guns' overall effectiveness was difficult. As events would show, X Corps' counter-battery, destructive and neutralising shellfire was, both prior to and on battle day, largely ineffectual.

Major Alfred Gibbs, whose Royal Field Artillery battery supported 96th Brigade's attack on Thiepval, later said he thought the village was inadequately bombarded by heavy guns and confessed to 'very grave misgivings as to the chances of our attack succeeding.'[21] He reckoned the speed at which Morland's barrage stepped back from the German front line was too quick. 'It should have combed the ground by moving back 50 yards at a time,' he said,[22] referring to the denser shellfire of creeping barrages that characterised later attacks on the Somme.

It was sadly ironic that many British soldiers were impressed by the final hour of Morland's preparatory bombardment. 'As the shells passed over our heads the air hummed like a swarm of a hundred million hornets,' said Second-Lieutenant John Stewart-Moore, 107th Trench Mortar Battery.[23] Then, at 7.30 a.m., there was an audible pause as sweating artillerymen lifted their fire onto more distant targets.[24]

THIRTY-SECOND Division's attack along an 1800-yard length of Thiepval Spur was mostly a failure. Thick pickets of German barbed wire had survived the barrage; only at Leipzig Redoubt was it sufficiently cut. Here, the 17th Highland Light Infantry* stole into no-man's-land minutes before Zero to get closer to the enemy parapet, and when the barrage lifted at 7.30 a.m., its successive lines won into the German trenches before the garrison emerged from its dugouts.[25] 'The leading lines pressed on, while moppers-up proceeded to clear the dugouts.'[26] Brigadier-General James Jardine, commanding 97th Brigade, said the 17th benefitted from 'some rising ground on their left in no man's land that interfered with any enfilade there was [from Thiepval].'[27] Although the 17th's limited gains were later reinforced by elements from other battalions — including men of 16th Highland Light Infantry, the right platoons of the following 2nd King's Own Yorkshire Light Infantry (KOYLI), 2nd Manchesters† and that night a section of 219th Field Company, RE[28] — its progress was limited by stout resistance and machine-gun fire from Wonderwork.

---

* 17th (Service) Battalion (3rd Glasgow) Highland Light Infantry. Also known as Glasgow Commercials or Glasgow Chamber of Commerce Battalion. 97th Brigade states 469 casualties (87 k, 254 w and 128 m). SDGW notes 182 deaths.

† 2nd Battalion Manchester Regiment. 14th Brigade states 464 casualties for July (29 k, 411 w and 24 m). SDGW notes 11 deaths.

The theme for the remainder of the 32nd's 14th, 96th and 97th Brigades was one of carnage. Their men were shot down 'as soon as', 'immediately,' and 'the moment' they left their trenches.[29] One battalion commander blamed this on the 'complete failure' of Morland's artillery, noting he had 'distinctly' heard German machine guns firing before the 7.30 a.m. start time.[30] On the left, closest to Thiepval, about 100 of the 15th Lancashire Fusiliers* surprisingly entered the hostile front line before defenders manned the parapet, and pushed north of the village. The rump of that battalion, 16th Northumberland Fusiliers[†] and 16th Highland Light Infantry[‡] — the latter with the left platoons of 2nd KOYLI[§] behind — made little if any impression with their linear waves, all suffering heavily.[31] The Northumberlands went forward behind a football drop-kicked into no-man's-land. As 2nd KOYLI's war diarist noted the 'hostile machine gun and shell fire was so intense that all efforts to cross the fire swept zone between the opposing [trench] lines failed.'[32] It was essentially the same story for the other two battalions.[33] Private Stanley Henderson, 16th Northumberland Fusiliers, recalled that his battalion commander, Lieutenant-Colonel William Ritson, repeatedly wailed '"My men, my men, what can I do?"'[34]

A trinity of uphill advances from Authuille Wood towards their own front line and then the southern face of Leipzig Redoubt by 11th Borders,[⁋] 1st Dorsets** and 19th Lancashire Fusiliers[††] either side of 9 a.m. were pelted by the Nordwerk machine-gunners. As the war diarist of 17th Highland

---

* 15th (Service) Battalion (1st Salford) Lancashire Fusiliers. Also known as 1st Salford Pals. Battalion war diary states 470 casualties (19 k, 148 w and 303 m). SDGW notes 268 deaths.

† 16th (Service) Battalion (Newcastle) Northumberland Fusiliers. Also known as Newcastle Commercials. SDGW notes 124 deaths.

‡ 16th (Service) Battalion (2nd Glasgow) Highland Light Infantry. Also known as Glasgow Boys' Brigade. 97th Brigade states 537 casualties (90 k, 276 w and 171 m). SDGW notes 252 deaths.

§ 2nd Battalion King's Own (Yorkshire Light Infantry). 97th Brigade states 322 casualties (46 k, 216 w and 60 m). SDGW notes 74 deaths.

⁋ 11th (Service) Battalion (Lonsdale) Border Regiment. Also known as Lonsdale Pals or Lonsdales. 97th Brigade states 544 casualties (93 k, 341 w and 110 m). SDGW notes 181 deaths.

** 1st Battalion Dorsetshire Regiment. 14th Brigade states 523 casualties for July, most on 1 July (22 k, 404 w and 97 m). SDGW notes 68 deaths.

†† 19th (Service) Battalion (3rd Salford) Lancashire Fusiliers. Also known as 3rd Salford Pals. Battalion war diary notes 268 casualties on 1 July. SDGW notes 40 deaths.

Light Infantry remarked, 11th Borders, 97th Brigade, was 'absolutely wiped out by Enemy Machine Gun fire,' and 1st Dorsets, 14th Brigade, was 'unable to make any progress.'[35] The Dorsets' ordeal, as told by the battalion's war diarist, was representative:

> It was during the dash across country from Authuille Wood to our own front line trench about 100 yds ahead that at least half our total casualties were sustained. By the time half the Battalion had left the wood, the end of Dumbarton Track and the ground up to our front line trench was covered with our killed and wounded; yet the men continued to jump up and advance over their fallen comrades as the word to go was given.[36]

Lance-Corporal William Bush, 1st Dorsets, said one bullet grazed his waist: 'I lay flat on the ground with my head to the Huns, as the steel helmet was a good protector for me.'[37] A second bullet clipped his hand, followed by a 'corker through the left elbow.'[38] Only about 66 of the 400-odd 1st Dorsets reached the redoubt.[39] Private George Ingham, 19th Lancashire Fusiliers, was probably among the 42 of his battalion in 14th Brigade who made it over: 'The German bayonets are awful things — one edge is like a razor and the other like a double saw. The sight of them makes you ratty!'[40] Ingham, 19, was killed two weeks later and is today buried at Warloy-Baillon Communal Cemetery Extension. Private John Farrer, 11th Borders, was among the dead outside Authuille Wood. The Carlisle coalminer enlisted in 1915 when his wife, Mary, was pregnant with their fourth child. He has no known grave and is today named on the Thiepval Memorial. A year later Mary penned a poem to her late husband that included the line: 'We think we see his smiling face as he bade his last good-bye.'[41]

Lieutenant-Colonel James Graham, 19th Lancashire Fusiliers, said even a smoke screen failed to lessen the effectiveness of the German machine-gun fire, which remained 'so annihilating' on the ground outside Authuille Wood.[42] Fifteenth Highland Light Infantry* was supporting 14th Brigade, commanded by Brigadier-General Charles Compton, but

---

*   15th (Service) Battalion (1st Glasgow) Highland Light Infantry. Also known as Glasgow Tramways Battalion. Battalion war diary states about 40 casualties. SDGW notes 8 deaths.

at about 9 a.m. was 'checked' in Authuille Wood, where it spent the rest of the day.[43] At 10.30 a.m. the 14th's advance was wisely stopped, but the damage had already been done.[44]

Wounded and living alike on the bullet-swept land between Authuille Wood and Leipzig Redoubt sheltered in shell holes or in Sanda, an opened Russian Sap. By about 4.30 p.m., Sanda had been dug through to the redoubt.[45] 'A good deal of the traffic which had originally to go over the top [to Leipzig Redoubt] was diverted down this passage. This was fortunate, as the overland track had by now been marked down by Machine Guns and snipers, and we were incurring considerable losses.'[46] Apparently a second Russian Sap in the area, this one named Inverary, was also opened and used as a means of communication.[47]

Elsewhere, at about 9.15 a.m., two companies of the 96th's 16th Lancashire Fusiliers,* attacking the trenches outside the northwest corner of Thiepval, met a similarly bloody fate as they attempted to reach the 100-odd 15th Lancashire Fusiliers believed to be in or near the village:[48] 'All were mowed down; a few men crawling met the same fate.'[49] Remnants of the two companies were forced back into their own line.[50]

Thiepval Spur's no-man's-land was a graveyard in progress: 'Occasionally I can see the hands thrown up and then a body flops to the ground,' wrote one eyewitness.[51] Worse yet, the killing zone of machine guns and artillery covering no-man's-land extended hundreds of yards behind the British front line. Many of the 32nd's follow-up battalions took heavy casualties as they moved forward from their own support and reserve trenches, or while waiting to advance.[52] Private Henderson, 16th Northumberland Fusiliers, described the scene in and just behind the British lines as that of a massacre: 'The cries from the wounded and dying were horrible to remember!'[53] By 9.30 a.m., the 32nd's initial attack was almost entirely cowed — stopped dead in no-man's-land and within its own lines — and its toehold in Leipzig Redoubt sealed off.

Five months later, as autumn rain lashed the ground, Lieutenant-Colonel Charles Abercrombie returned to the 96th's battlefield. 'The dead [of the 15th Lancashire Fusiliers] were still lying in the long grass, thickly scattered all the way from our front line right up to the enemy's wire. We

---

* 16th (Service) Battalion (2nd Salford) Lancashire Fusiliers. Also known as 2nd Salford Pals. SDGW notes 16 deaths.

could trace also the hopeless effort that my men [of the 16th Lancashire Fusiliers] made.'[54] One of the dead there was Private Harold Stephenson, 15th Lancashire Fusiliers, who today rests at Connaught Cemetery. His two brothers were also killed on 1 July. Private Edward Stephenson, a father of six in 1st Lancashire Fusiliers, killed near Beaumont Hamel, and Rifleman Ernest Stephenson, 2nd Rifle Brigade, killed near Ovillers, are named on the Thiepval Memorial. No wonder Brigadier-General Clement Yatman, commanding 96th Brigade, said 'only bullet proof soldiers' could have taken Thiepval.[55] He was correct: the 32nd's 1200-plus dead were proof enough.

Gefreiter Peter Kuster, Reserve Infantry Regiment 99 (RIR99), said the shell-pocked German front line near Thiepval 'came alive' with defenders when the attack began. 'My company was about 120 men before the attack, when we were relieved only 35 men were left.'[56] *Soldat* Wilhelm Lange, RIR99, a 28-year-old farmer's son from Magdeburg, stood atop a trench parapet, firing indiscriminately at British infantry in no-man's-land. 'You fool, can't you hear the bullets whistling?' shouted his officer.[57] *Leutnant-der-Reserve* Friedrich Kassel, RIR99, was in the line just north of Leipzig Redoubt, his trench and dugout steps quickly bloody with the gore of dead men.[58] Over the parapet, 20 yards away, Kassel saw the leading waves of 16th Highland Light Infantry heaving into sight: 'No boys, we are still alive, the moles come out of their holes. Machine-gun fire tears holes in their rows. They discover our presence [and] throw themselves on the ground, now a mass of craters, welcomed by hand-grenades and gun fire.'[59] Later, Kassel led a patrol into Leipzig Redoubt, working gingerly from one breastwork to the next, winkling Scotsmen out with grenades and bayonets. Lange, meantime, was caught in a brutal bomb duel with some of the Highlanders.[60] 'We threw grenades for all we were worth. I've no idea how many.'[61] The savagery was veiled in smoke and dust, and rent with shots, shouts and grenade blasts. Kassel again takes up the story:

I felt my right hand hit by a heavy stroke, a bullet from a distance of 20 metres [22 yards]. The gun fell out of my hand, blood is running. I can still see how a [British] rifleman tries to throw himself out of reach of a hand grenade thrown by Kühnel. In vain. It explodes and will probably have finished him.[62]

Killing took place around trench corners, over blockades and in shell craters. 'Badly wounded "Tommies" fall into our hands and their rations provide something to satisfy our hunger and thirst.'[63] Kassel's patrol, and others like it, soon ran into stout resistance and consolidated its limited gains. While part of Leipzig Redoubt had been lost, the fortress of Thiepval and Nordwerk, Wonderwork and Goat Redoubts remained defiant.

THIRTY-SIXTH (ULSTER) Division's six leading attack battalions produced vastly different outcomes from one another in their initial charge. On the Ancre's northern bank, half of 108th Brigade failed. Leading elements of 12th Royal Irish Rifles,* on the left, and 9th Royal Irish Fusiliers† clambered from their trenches two minutes before Zero in an attempt to get some distance across the unusually wide no-man's-land. Their linear waves[64] were immediately under fire. Their supporting barrage was too thin and German machine-gunners fired on 'our people going through our own wire.'[65] Few made it across the up to 600-yard-wide no-man's-land, which included a ravine on the 9th's front. Sergeant Sam McKeever, 12th Royal Irish Rifles, was there:

> Our ranks were getting very thin, but we had to go on. ... We had about 300 yards to cross before we reached the German trenches, which gave the Germans a temporary advantage. We were now running forward in order to get the job done. ... There were two brothers Smith. I remember seeing these two brothers in contact with the Germans. They were using their bayonets.[66]

In places, German riflemen laden with ammunition and festooned with stick grenades clambered atop their parapets to get a better shot. 'They were all full of anger,' wrote *Reservist* Gottlob Mauss, Reserve

---

* 12th (Service) Battalion (Central Antrim) Royal Irish Rifles. Also known as Central Antrim Volunteers. 108th Brigade states 403 casualties (62 k, 246 w and 95 m). SDGW notes 139 deaths.
† 9th (Service) Battalion (Armagh, Monaghan and Cavan) Royal Irish Fusiliers. Also known as Armagh, Monaghan and Cavan Volunteers. 108th Brigade states 535 casualties (58 k, 312 w and 165 m). SDGW notes 222 deaths.

Infantry Regiment 119 (RIR119), referring to the commonplace desire among German infantrymen for payback after living through the prolonged British bombardment.[67]

Against the odds, remnants of both the 9th and the 12th breached the German lines here and there along a stretch of about 1000 yards. The enemy wire was little impaired, but better cut before the 9th than the 12th.[68] German shrapnel fire was now bursting over no-man's-land. Some of the 9th made it a few hundred yards beyond the parapet of RIR119, and were allegedly 'last seen advancing upon Beaucourt Station.'[69] All were killed, captured or squeezed out by counterattacks. By 8 a.m. the 36th's attack north of the Ancre was over.[70] Two minor attacks — one late morning, another at 12.30 p.m. — to support operations by the 29th Division failed in tempests of bullets. Lieutenant-Colonel Stewart Blacker, 9th Royal Irish Fusiliers, was unsurprised. He had told Major-General Sir Oliver Nugent, commanding the 36th, of his worries about poor artillery preparation on the morning before battle: 'I remarked to him "Morituri te Salutant" realising full well the hopelessness of the task allotted to the two battalions.'[71] 'We who are about to die salute you,' indeed.

On the sharply rising ground south of the Ancre that today holds the Ulster Tower memorial it was an altogether different story. Here, the remainder of 108th and 109th Brigades comprised the first assault wave heading for Thiepval Plateau, with 107th Brigade to subsequently leap-frog the latter for more distant objectives. The 108th's and 109th's leading elements left their trenches at 7.15 a.m. and crept to within 100 yards of the German line before buglers sounded the advance at Zero.[72] In this area better observation meant that X Corps' artillery had, helped by French 75-millimetre field guns, cut the enemy wire along about 1000 yards. Mortars firing from at least six of 10 saps pushed out into no-man's-land prior to 1 July opened fire on the German line at 7.25 a.m.

On the left, the 108th's 13th Royal Irish Rifles,* followed by the 107th's 15th Royal Irish Rifles,† adopted a blend of extended lines followed

---

*   13th (Service) Battalion (1st Co. Down) Royal Irish Rifles. Also known as 1st County Down Volunteers. 108th Brigade states 530 casualties (53 k, 226 w and 251 m). SDGW notes 226 deaths.

†   15th (Service) Battalion (North Belfast) Royal Irish Rifles. Also known as North Belfast Volunteers. 36th Division states 275 casualties. SDGW notes 78 deaths.

by columns of platoons to move forward, but heavy machine-gun fire from St Pierre Divion caused 'terrible' casualties and limited gains.[73] The 108th's 11th Royal Irish Rifles* — using a similar mix of extended lines and columns of platoons — and the 109th's 9th[†] and 10th Royal Inniskilling Fusiliers[‡] — obscured by a smoke screen as they moved forward in columns of platoons with elements following in artillery formation — dashed into the German front trench system when the barrage lifted and overwhelmed the garrison.[74] Within minutes of 7.30 a.m., the door to Schwaben Redoubt and Thiepval Plateau was ever so slightly ajar.

German infantrymen were quickly overrun by the 36th. The front-line system was held by a company of Bavarian Reserve Infantry Regiment 8 (BRIR8) and three companies of RIR99, with Schwaben Redoubt garrisoned by another company from each of those regiments. The company of BRIR8 holding the redoubt was effectively destroyed as a fighting force by the Ulstermen. From a nominal strength of about 200 it recorded 187 casualties: 57 killed, four dying later of wounds, 113 prisoners and 13 wounded.[75] This company's fate — the large number of prisoners a reflection of how quickly the 36th was into the German trenches — was more than likely shared by those companies of RIR99 similarly swamped in and before Schwaben Redoubt.

The Ulstermen's promising start continued as they pushed further northeast, beyond the area broadly marked today by Ulster Tower and Mill Road Cemetery. Support battalions 11th Royal Inniskilling Fusiliers[§] and 14th Royal Irish Rifles[¶] followed on in columns of platoons, with some elements in artillery formation,[76] at 7.30 a.m. 'No sooner were they clear

---

*   11th (Service) Battalion (South Antrim) Royal Irish Rifles. Also known as South Antrim Volunteers. 108th Brigade states 387 casualties (59 k, 222 w and 106 m). SDGW notes 134 deaths.

†   9th (Service) Battalion (Co. Tyrone) Royal Inniskilling Fusiliers. Also known as County Tyrone Volunteers. Battalion war diary states 477 casualties (59 k, 260 w and 158 m). SDGW notes 218 deaths.

‡   10th (Service) Battalion (Derry) Royal Inniskilling Fusiliers. Also known as Derry Volunteers. 36th Division states 431 casualties. SDGW notes 128 deaths.

§   11th (Service) Battalion (Donegal and Fermanagh) Royal Inniskilling Fusiliers. Also known as Donegal & Fermanagh Volunteers. 36th Division states 594 casualties. SDGW notes 229 deaths.

¶   14th (Service) Battalion (Young Citizens) Royal Irish Rifles. Also known as Belfast Young Citizens. 36th Division states 316 casualties. SDGW notes 90 deaths.

of our own wire,' noted 14th Royal Irish Rifles, 'when the slow tat tat of the Hun machine guns from Thiepval village and [also from the general direction of] Beaumont-Hamel caught the advance under a deadly cross fire, but nothing could stop this advance and so on they went.'[77]

These machine-gunners continued to enfilade the 109th's exposed right as it pressed into the high ground towards Schwaben Redoubt. Casualties in the right-most battalion, the 9th, were heavy, but 'the advance was not checked and by 8 a.m. the [German] reserve trench, including the front face of Schwaben Redoubt, had been entered.'[78] A sizeable portion of 36th (Ulster) Division's first objective had fallen. More than 400 prisoners were sent scampering across the old no-man's-land. Hereafter, concentric and increasingly heavy long-range machine-gun and rifle fire — from Thiepval to the south, and St Pierre Divion, Grandcourt and Beaucourt in the River Ancre valley to the north — played over the 109th's advance, which continued until all of the redoubt was taken by about 8.50 a.m.[79] The 36th's forward-most elements had advanced about a mile and were now consolidating a bullet-swept finger of land deep in German territory.

Private Lindsay Hall, 10th Royal Inniskilling Fusiliers, was quickly into the German trenches: 'All that could be seen was a few twisted iron spikes and splinters of wire lying in the bottom of shell holes.'[80] He jumped into the cratered trench and 'done for' some German soldiers exiting their dugouts.[81] His platoon moved forward overland. 'The wounded were crying in agony, and a few chaps lying dead with head or legs blown off. Oh it was terrible.'[82] The advance was exhausting. 'I was terrible thirsty. I never knew how dry I could be. Some chaps took the water bottles off the dead men.'[83] Hall was later hit by shrapnel above the knee, but made it back to the British lines. Private Edward Brownlee, a machine-gunner in 108th Brigade, had reached the German wire, 'when I got hit in the jaw, breaking it at the joint [with the bullet] passing through my tongue and coming out at the left of my Adam's Apple. I also had one through my left arm above the elbow. I lay from 7.30 [a.m.] to 12 noon with terrible loss of blood and bothered with flies and mosquitoes.'[84]

Following behind, 107th Brigade had moved up through Thiepval Wood, suffering numerous casualties from shellfire along the way. It began crossing no-man's-land around 8 a.m. Ninth[*] and 10th Royal Irish Rifles[†] advanced abreast, with their lead companies in extended order and those behind in columns of platoons, followed by 8th Royal Irish Rifles[‡] in the same formation, into the tempest of shrapnel and bullets.[85] Major George Gaffiken, a 30-year-old teetotaller in the 9th, waved an orange handkerchief and shouted to his men: 'Come on, boys. This is the 1st of July. Let the enemy have it.'[86] One sergeant wore an Orangeman's sash.[87] Lieutenant-Colonel Frank Crozier, commanding the 9th, rushed his men forward one company at a time during a lull in the shellfire. Machine-gunners in Thiepval had the range and bowled many of the 107th: 'The majority lie out all day, sun-baked, parched, uncared for, often delirious and at any rate in great pain.'[88] One of Crozier's soldiers was later reported dead. 'Men in battle see fairies — and devils,' Crozier said. The soldier was, in fact, a prisoner, and his family was annoyed that he had wrongly been reported killed. Crozier wrote to them: 'Why not count your blessings?'[89] By about 10 a.m., the rump of the 107th had pushed through Schwaben Redoubt and suffered heavy casualties from the British barrage still falling on the German second defensive position.[90] It went to ground in knee-length rank grass about 100 yards shy of this trench, the 36th's final objective, until the shellfire lifted at 10.10 a.m.[91]

This delay gave a recruit battalion of Infantry Regiment 180 (IR180) rushing up from Grandcourt just enough time to man the line, and a machine-gun company in that village time to get the Ulstermen's range.[92] Machine-gunners about 2000 yards northwest in Beaucourt Redoubt (Feste-Alt-Württemberg) also opened up. So far, 8th, 9th and 10th Royal Irish Rifles had advanced more than 1000 yards beyond the old German front line. North of Schwaben Redoubt they were approaching Battery Valley, which held some abandoned artillery gun pits, and eased down towards Grandcourt. Northeast, they were approaching Stuff Redoubt on the edge of Thiepval Plateau. Here, *Unteroffizier* Felix Kircher, Reserve

---

[*] 9th (Service) Battalion (West Belfast) Royal Irish Rifles. Also known as West Belfast Volunteers. 36th Division states 319 casualties. SDGW notes 95 deaths.

[†] 10th (Service) Battalion (South Belfast) Royal Irish Rifles. Also known as South Belfast Volunteers. 36th Division states 417 casualties. SDGW notes 104 deaths.

[‡] 8th (Service) Battalion (East Belfast) Royal Irish Rifles. 36th Division states 367 casualties. Also known as East Belfast Volunteers. SDGW notes 5 deaths.

Field Artillery Regiment 26 (RFAR26), saw 'khaki-clothed men with flat steel helmets run up and down our barbed wire.'[93] German observers further back spotted the danger and soon their shells joined the British ones screaming down onto the 107th's leading elements.[94] *Major* Max Klaus, RFAR26, said the gunners' intervention averted a 'serious danger.'[95] Kircher said it was a decisive moment, but overstated the case when he said the path to Grandcourt, about a mile away, lay open.[96]

A small number of men from the 107th entered the German second-line trenches after the brigade started forward again, at about 10.10 a.m.[97] At least two platoons went forward towards Stuff Redoubt, maybe more, and some of these men got into the enemy trenches in at least two places.[98] One group of 50 dropped into an empty trench, near the redoubt. Of the others: 'About 35 [of 9th Royal Irish Rifles] men got into "D" line [immediately before Stuff Redoubt] … they found "D" line strongly held and a great number of them became casualties through hand grenades.'[99] Most of the survivors fell back, but a small group under Corporal Robert Short, 9th Royal Irish Rifles, held out until he was killed in 'desperate hand-to-hand fighting.'[100] Short is named on the Thiepval Memorial. About 500 yards east, some 200 more of the 107th and other units reached the head of Battery Valley.[101] The 107th had done well to get even this far, particularly around Stuff Redoubt, but it was over-extended, had suffered heavily, was encountering stiffening resistance and remained exposed to shrapnel and machine-gun fire. Remnants of the 107th had no choice but to retire onto Schwaben Redoubt before noon.

Fighting in Schwaben Redoubt and on Thiepval Plateau was savage. It took place in narrow, tumbled-down trench bays, around corners and in unlit, foul-smelling dugouts. One man likened it to a 'Belfast riot on the top of Mount Vesuvius.'[102] Soldiers were speckled in chalk dust and blood, and were sticky with sweat. 'The blood had got about the tongue of our boots and our socks were soaked with it.'[103] To strike out alone or chance a glance over the parapet was to court death. 'I peeped over to have a look and found myself looking down the barrel of a German rifle, only twenty yards away. I got the hell out of it as fast as I could,' said Private Robert Irwin, 9th Royal Inniskilling Fusiliers.[104] Killing and maiming were done with grenades, bayonets, rifle butts, pistols and clubs. As Private Hugh Stewart, a machine-gunner-cum-infantryman in 109th Brigade, explained:

I had a bayonet in one hand and a revolver in the other. You see
I used to shoe horses before I joined up and had powerful strong
wrists and it was not a great hardship for me to fire one of them big
heavy revolvers. They had a kick like a horse but if you hit a man
with a bullet from one of them he gave no more trouble.[105]

Life and death could be measured in seconds. One Bavarian soldier
aimed his rifle at a nearby Ulsterman, but 'that man was a second quicker
than he.'[106] The Bavarian died. Few would forget their ordeal: as Stewart
recalled, 'I had never killed a man with a bayonet before and it sent cold
shivers up and down my spine many's a night afterwards just thinking
about it.'[107]

Living were felled by shrapnel balls and bullets and jagged splinters
of red-hot metal. Others were eviscerated, blown apart or vaporised by
shell bursts. 'There was a loud explosion near me and part of the torso of a
man, clothed in a khaki jacket, landed just in front of my Lewis gun,' said
Irwin.[108] Lance-Corporal James Henderson, 14th Royal Irish Rifles, found
a man with his leg nearly blown off: 'He begged me to kill him but I couldn't
do it.'[109] Private James Devennie, 10th Royal Inniskilling Fusiliers, saw a
shell hit a man 'in the throat and his head disappeared.'[110] Private Jim
Donaghy, same battalion, found a man whose arm had been flayed open
from shoulder to wrist, and applied a puttee-cum-tourniquet.[111] Soon
Donaghy himself was hit in the thigh and throat, and within seconds 'lost
so much blood that I looked like a red-tunicked soldier.'[112] Rifleman John
Hope, 14th Royal Irish Rifles, found a man shot in the head: 'His brain is
oozing out of the side of his head and he is calling for his pal. … In a short
time all is quiet, he is dead.'[113] Rifleman Davie Starrett, 9th Royal Irish
Rifles, took an altogether more brutal opinion of the wounded and dead:
'On days like that there's no sympathy in your heart. Over them you go.'[114]

Many had never seen enemy soldiers up close before. Reactions
were situational. In 14th Royal Irish Rifles, Rifleman John Grange saw
a wounded German sniper clubbed with his own rifle,[115] while Rifleman
James Megaw, same battalion, promised to shoot another soldier who
had threatened to kill an unarmed prisoner.[116] Captives who resisted
were often killed:[117] 'Something happened which caused [Sergeant
James] Porter's men to open fire killing some [surrendering Germans]

and wounding others.'[118] Corporal George Lloyd, 9th Royal Irish Rifles, was captured and covered in blood after bandaging a wounded officer: 'One of the Germans thought it was German blood and came at me with his bayonet. He would have let me have it if one of their N.C.O.s hadn't stopped him.'[119] Others responded differently: 'As soon as they [Bavarian soldiers] saw I was badly wounded they passed on, some of them stooping down to shake my hand,' said Lieutenant James Shannon, 10th Royal Inniskilling Fusiliers.[120] And then there was pity for enemy soldiers badly wounded and beyond medical help. Starrett later remembered a dying Bavarian: 'Half of his face was blown away.'[121] Donaghy saw another young German clasping a gaping stomach together with his hands: 'He was dying and as he looked up at us he kept repeating, ... "No bon, ... No bon." It really upset us.'[122]

SEVEN MILES AWAY, *Generalleutnant* Franz *Freiherr* von Soden knew quick thinking and decisive action were everything at critical moments such as this. News of the attacks all along his divisional sector quickly reached the headquarters of his 26th Reserve Division at Biefvillers.[123] At first, the balding 60-year-old's picture of events at Thiepval was obscure, hindered by intermittent, delayed and often confusing battle reports. In the hour to around 8.30 a.m., more accurate messages arrived and these confirmed that alarming events were unfolding around Schwaben Redoubt. Soden now knew the redoubt had fallen and that elements of 36th (Ulster) Division threatened to advance further, testing his second defensive line and most advanced artillery positions. 'The enemy had recognised the great value of the heights,' wrote one German historian[124] — mistakenly, as it turned out. Soden himself said retaking the redoubt was 'of particular importance for the course of the battle.'[125] If the Ulstermen retained even a corner of the high ground above Thiepval, the 26th's entire position was at risk.[126] At 8.55 a.m., Soden ordered a counterattack and began committing his reserves.

Soden's artillery now became a decisive factor in the battle. Tenth Corps' pre-battle counter-battery work had simply not destroyed enough of the German guns sited to provide close defensive fire. Soden had long insisted that his divisional gunners conceal their positions, conserve ammunition and retain their pre-allocated defensive capabilities.[127] Sufficient German guns had survived the British preparatory bombardment and battle-day barrage. From shortly after 7 a.m. some were dropping six shells a minute on the British trenches in Thiepval Wood.[128] 'Plomp, plomp — it is "good-bye," I think,' wrote Lieutenant-Colonel Crozier.[129] At 7.10 a.m., 20 minutes before Zero, 10th Royal Irish Rifles' commanding officer, Lieutenant-Colonel Herbert Bernard, was killed when his battalion came under simultaneous machine-gun fire from the front, right and rear before even reaching its own front line.[130] The 50-year-old is buried at Martinsart British Cemetery. The battalion war diarist set the scene: 'The Battalion continued to advance [through the wood towards the British front line] suffering heavily from shell and machine-gun fire, the ground being much cut up and difficult to cross.'[131] From about 7.30 a.m. the German gunners intensified their fire on two key areas. The first was the ribbon of ground between the old German front line and Thiepval Wood, where a curtain of shellfire cut off the Ulstermen in Schwaben Redoubt and slowed reinforcements pushing forward. By around 9 a.m. the former no-man's-land was impassable to all but the luckiest of souls. In the second area, German observers had spied the dangerous break-in on Thiepval Plateau and directed gunners to pour shells onto this ground to limit the enemy's gains there. Within one-and-a-half hours of the start of the Ulstermen's attack, Soden's gunners had isolated the breach.

The shellfire on Thiepval Wood stripped trees bare. Boughs were broken, stumps overturned. Splinters of bark, wood chaff and leaves flew. Lachrymatory gas shells added to the smoke-laden horror. Telephone lines run forward from the wood were frequently cut. Attempts by elements of pioneer battalion 16th Royal Irish Rifles* to dig a communication trench across no-man's-land were shot into submission.[132] This shellfire, in concert with the machine guns in Thiepval, turned the northern fringes of the wood and the former no-man's-land into a metal barrier.[133] One machine gun at Thiepval fired something like 18,000 rounds at this small area. By day's end, the sunken Thiepval–Hamel road, passing between the present-day Mill Road and Connaught Cemeteries, was a 'mass of dead heaped up.'[134]

---

* 16th (Service) Battalion (2nd County Down) (Pioneers) Royal Irish Rifles. Also known as 2nd County Down Volunteers. Battalion war diary states at least 32 casualties. SDGW notes 2 deaths.

French road workers found the remains of Sergeant David Blakey, 11th Royal Inniskilling Fusiliers, beside this road in November 2013. The 26-year-old coalminer turned rugby league player's bones lay beneath six inches of dirt. A metal identity disc gave up the Gateshead-born man's name. The married father of two joined the 36th because his wife was from Londonderry. In December 1916 he was posthumously awarded the Military Medal for bravery in the field. 'None of us can believe it,' said one relative of the 2013 find.[135] Other families were not so lucky: walk through Connaught Cemetery and you will find one headstone marking the single grave of 15 unidentified British soldiers, and another for 12. The single-line epitaph on both of these two headstones: 'Known unto God.'

Stuttgart-born Soden's chief frustration throughout the morning was the time it took to organise his counterattack. 'An over-hasty insufficiently prepared countermove could easily fail,' a German historian later wrote.[136] 'The attack had to take place as quickly, but as comprehensively as possible, so as not to allow the enemy time either to settle in or orientate himself, nor to give him the advantage of defending against a purely frontal attack.'[137] The attack would comprise about 2500 men organised into three groups, recapturing the lost ground with co-ordinated and strong counterattacks closing in from multiple directions. Eight infantry companies of BRIR8 formed its backbone, supported by two recruit companies of IR180, two machine-gun companies, and another of engineers. The problem was that numerous telephone lines were cut, and Soden's orders had to be run out to these scattered units, which then had to be marched forward and familiarised with the ground and their objectives. All of this was to be achieved under heavy British shellfire, on broken ground and in the midst of battle; lengthy delays were inevitable. Even a direct order from corps commander Stein that Schwaben Redoubt be 'recaptured at all costs' could not alter the reality of the situation.[138] It would be mid-afternoon before any kind of semi-organised counterattack was launched. For the meantime, Soden would be left to stalk impatiently around his operations room, poring over situation reports and awaiting confirmation that the counterattack had gone in.

Back in the British lines, Major-General Sir Edward Perceval, commanding 49th (West Riding) Division, had quickly realised the potential for developing the 36th's break-in. He was with Nugent, the

36th's commander, when reports of its initial success and the 32nd's initial failure arrived soon after 8 a.m.[139] Perceval believed the 49th should be used immediately to support and exploit the 36th's gains.[140] Nugent was concerned about over-extending the salient northwards, flanking divisions having made no supporting gains, and feared such a scenario would see his men go to 'their own destruction.'[141] Nugent favoured consolidation and to this end, at about 8.30 a.m., told X Corps headquarters he was interested in deploying the 107th, but queried whether it might be 'stopped from advancing upon the last [German] line.'[142] Nugent and Perceval understood the value of the high ground and that victory, or at least retention of the heights, rested in bold action. But, neither Perceval, Nugent nor X Corps headquarters staff had the authority to commit the 49th without Morland's blessing. 'Feeling that there was not a moment to be lost, he [Perceval] himself went to Englebelmer, two miles away, to urge this course on General Morland.'[143] Regrettably, he failed to convince Morland, who was already at the start of a day-long fixation on Thiepval and resuming the 32nd's moribund attack.[144]

Much has been made of Morland's piecemeal use of the 49th. At 8.35 a.m., contrary to Perceval's request, he decided only its 146th Brigade would go to Thiepval Wood to support either the 36th or the left of the 32nd.[145] The leading elements of the 146th would not arrive until about 11.35 a.m., two-and-a-half hours too late to have a hope of reaching Schwaben Redoubt through the German shellfire. Later, 147th Brigade was sent to the Authuille–Aveluy area, while much of the 148th remained in Aveluy Wood. Major Frank Watson, 146th Brigade headquarters, said the 49th was 'frittered away in a series of minor operations, based on either misinformation or misjudgement on the part of the higher staff responsible for that part of the battle.'[146] Lieutenant-Colonel Abercrombie, commanding 16th Lancashire Fusiliers, was haunted by the failure to develop the 36th's initial success, but said once the attack lost momentum 'it seems to have been impossible to repair it.'[147] Brigadier-General Archibald Cameron, X Corps' chief of staff, later attempted to shift the blame for this away from Morland, alleging that the 49th seemed 'terribly slow. It was most difficult at Corps HQ to find out where they had got to and what they were doing.'[148]

If only Morland had used the 49th to develop, or at the very least consolidate, the 36th's gains. If only Morland had not deployed the 49th piecemeal; if only he had set that division in train earlier. If only, indeed. These propositions all assumed that the 49th was close enough to the battlefield to be deployed effectively in any scenario, which it was not.

Morland had deployed the 49th in Aveluy Wood, about a mile behind the front line, with a view to it following up a corps-wide break-in. That had not happened. If 146th Brigade was to have had any influence on the battle for the heights, it would have had to have been much closer to Thiepval Wood, or heading there well before 6.30 a.m. At that time it was still in Aveluy Wood. The 146th's warning message to move forward arrived from Morland at 8.35 a.m., and it was in train by 8.55 a.m. There was no hope that the 146th would get forward before the former no-man's-land became impassable. In this light, Perceval's dash to Englebelmer was a pointless exercise: he could not turn the clock back. Events had unfolded contrary to Morland's expectation of a uniform, wide-scale advance, and this effectively confined the 49th, by dint of its location, to the sidelines of battle. Morland now had to adapt to events in and around Schwaben Redoubt and a half-failed corps attack, but his focus was elsewhere.

This point was not lost on critics. Major Watson and Brigadier-General Michael Goring-Jones, commander of the 146th, thought the 49th was 'too far back at Zero hour, and that it was moved up too late' to be of any use.[149] 'A vigorous use of the Corps Reserve in support of the 36th Division would have changed the whole aspect of July 1st 1916, and resulted in a very great success at a point of vital importance.'[150] Soldiers of the 49th also thought their division was left to loiter without intent. Corporal Herbert Allen, 1/8th West Yorkshires,* passed time playing cards in Aveluy Wood until his battalion moved off: 'To us it seemed a proper mix up. No one seemed to know what was happening.'[151] Perceval and Nugent would have agreed. The British official historian added that the 'delay in taking advantage of the favourable situation created by the success of one portion of the assault was, as on so many other occasions, utilized by the enemy.'[152] Morland should have considered long before

---

* 1/8th Battalion (Leeds Rifles) (Territorial Force) Prince of Wales's Own (West Yorkshire Regiment). SDGW states 5 deaths.

1 July how the 49th might be applied to battle without delay in any given scenario, and specifically in the case of partial success on his corps' battle front. That Morland did not revealed his inability to think laterally, which, given the events that had unfolded, handed the initiative to Soden and ultimately consigned the 36th to failure. Haig was correct; Morland was not up to the job.

Morland, who was up his observation tree near Englebelmer, had a fair enough picture of events by 9 a.m. He knew that the 36th was in and round Schwaben Redoubt in some strength, but north of the Ancre it had failed. He also knew that the 32nd had nabbed a corner of Leipzig Redoubt, but that 14th, 96th and 97th Brigades' morning had mostly been one of failure. Other reports indicated elements of 15th Lancashire Fusiliers were fighting around Thiepval; in reality these few men were already dead or had miraculously linked up with the 36th. Morland also knew the neighbouring III and VIII Corps had not made any progress on his flanks. For these reasons, at 9.10 a.m., almost 40 minutes after Nugent's request to consolidate the 36th's gains, he attempted to delay the 107th's tilt at its final objective, but it had already advanced beyond recall.[153] In contrast to Nugent and Perceval, Major-General Sir William Rycroft, commander of the 32nd, now proposed a convoluted uphill operation by his division that involved a change in direction of attack to force the spur between Thiepval and Leipzig Redoubt and bring the division up alongside the 36th. It would begin with precisely the same style of frontal assault that had already failed. Morland's endorsement of this latter course was predictable, unimaginative and in keeping with his bent for a neat advance across his corps' frontage.

'The plan of attack was doomed to failure from the start,' wrote Major Girdwood at 32nd Division headquarters. He told Rycroft the proposed change in direction mid-attack was a mistake as 'men will always turn in the direction from which the hostile fire is coming. At that point I was told to mind my own business.'[154]

In reality, Morland had only one viable option to capitalise on the 36th's gains with the purpose of restarting the 32nd's advance and achieving a uniform advance across his corps' sector. That was to push the 107th forward and then east behind Thiepval,[155] rather than further northeast towards Battery Valley and Stuff Redoubt as planned. *Leutnant-*

der-Reserve Matthaus Gerster, RIR119, later said that such a move might have 'rolled up' the companies of RIR99 immediately north and east of Thiepval that had so far fended off the frontal attacks in their sectors.[156] It also promised to render Thiepval village and spur untenable for German defenders,[157] only then potentially allowing the 32nd to renew its attack. As Gerster explained, nothing less than the 'fate of the day' hung on what happened next at Schwaben Redoubt.[158]

Against this backcloth, one 36th patrol found Mouquet Switch Trench, leading behind Thiepval, vacant. But there was nobody on the spot to sanction such a shift of direction. Brigade commanders had been told to remain within British lines: neither Brigadier-Generals William Withycombe, Charles Griffith nor Reginald Shuter went forward after their commands, respectively 107th, 108th and 109th Brigades. 'No provision had been made for such a movement in the rehearsals, no reserves were sent up to carry it out,' wrote the British official historian.[159] In truth, Morland never considered this option, and Nugent allegedly did not raise the idea. Brigadier-General Cameron, Morland's selectively minded chief of staff, who was later knighted and promoted to general, said this: 'If 36th Division had been of [the] opinion that a move down the Mouquet Switch [behind Thiepval] would have been of assistance to it, the corps [headquarters] would have been quite ready to provide the troops.'[160] Cameron was lying. He well knew that Morland had dithered over the 107th's application for about 40 minutes, had never grasped the potential of the situation before him, and was already bent on more frontal attacks at Thiepval. In the event, the 107th's advance on the German second line, heavy casualties and subsequent fragmentation rendered any hopes for a lateral expansion redundant. Gerster's subsequent criticism that British senior commanders had badly misjudged the potential of their gains around Schwaben Redoubt was correct,[161] and for this Morland was to blame.

Morland's Thiepval myopia now produced a predictably bloody string of attacks throughout the afternoon. Each was preceded by an ineffectual barrage that did nothing to lessen German machine-gun fire. 'It was impossible to show a head above the parapet without drawing a storm of M.G. fire,' said Lieutenant-Colonel Abercrombie.[162] At about 1.50 p.m., the remaining two companies of 16th Lancashire Fusiliers and two more from 2nd Royal Inniskilling Fusiliers* were shot to a standstill while attacking towards the northwest corner of Thiepval.[163] Another attack by 146th's 1/6th West Yorkshires[†] at 4 p.m. met a similar fate. As one officer eyewitness wrote: 'It is impossible to describe the angry despair which filled every man at this unspeakable moment.'[164] Only with difficulty was 1/5th West Yorkshires'[‡] part in this operation called off. At 5.10 p.m., Morland — still believing that some 15th Lancashire Fusiliers were in Thiepval and that a few 2nd Royal Inniskilling Fusiliers were in a position to assault the village from the north — ordered more attacks.[165] It was time for a reality check. Rycroft, who now realised the futility of his earlier plan, and that no British troops were in or near Thiepval, phoned Morland and told him so. Morland then placed the remainder of the 49th's 146th and 148th Brigades at the disposal of the 36th but, unbelievably, also planned a midnight tilt at Thiepval, which was later cancelled. As dusk crept over the battlefield, Morland finally began to see the potential of the 36th's break-in, but he was altogether out of time.

FROM ABOUT MIDDAY the 36th was consolidating a wedge driven deep behind the German front line. This wedge was about 1000 yards wide at the old German parapet and tapered to a point about 1200 yards into enemy territory before ending at the northeast corner of Schwaben Redoubt. The first 500–600 yards of the wedge included the old German front-line trench system and a portion of the intermediate position, with the remainder taking in the whole of the isosceles-shaped redoubt. Plotted on a map, the 36th's stronghold even looked a bit like a wonky triangle, the right axis tracing some of the carriageway between Grandcourt and the Thiepval crossroads. The perimeter line was lumpy rather than smooth due to zigzagging German trenches and Ulster outposts sited to make best defensive use of the undulating ground and potential German counterattack approach routes. As the 36th later reported, 'Between

---

*   2nd Royal Inniskilling Fusiliers. Regimental history states 162 casualties (10 k, 135 w and 17 m). SDGW notes 16 deaths.

†   1/6th Battalion (Territorial Force) Prince of Wales's Own (West Yorkshire Regiment). SDGW states 35 deaths.

‡   1/5th Battalion (Territorial Force) Prince of Wales's Own (West Yorkshire Regiment). Battalion war diary notes 61 casualties (5 k and 56 w). SDGW states 12 deaths.

11.30 a.m. and 2.00 p.m. there was a comparatively quiet time whilst consolidation was going on. Ammunition, bombs and water were short, and the men were gradually getting exhausted.'[166]

Soden's first semi-organised counterthrusts went in shortly after 2 p.m. and continued through the afternoon against both flanks of the 36th's wedge. They worked their way in via trenches, across dead ground, up the sharp inclines from the River Ancre valley and overland. Lewis gunners in 8th Royal Irish Rifles and field artillery destroyed two companies of enemy infantry advancing up the slope from Beaucourt.[167] It was a success that ran against the grain. First the 36th's outposts fell, then vulnerable sections of trench and next pressure was put on the main defensive perimeter. The barrage of shell- and machine-gun fire outside Thiepval Wood meant supplies of ammunition, hand grenades and water coming forward were negligible. Communications with the British front line were fragmentary, and reliant on runners who were all too frequently killed or wounded as they ducked and dived their way across the battlefield. Throughout the bridgehead it was a case of resisting until forced to withdraw. Casualties among officers and NCOs added to the confusion. 'After their fine start in the morning they were thoroughly disheartened at receiving no support, and very unsteady.'[168] A composite company of 1/5th York & Lancasters,* of 148th Brigade, made it over to the Ulstermen at about 4.30 p.m. and participated in the fighting.[169] Of 150th Field Company, RE, which went forward with 11th Royal Inniskilling Fusiliers to help with consolidation, none of the sappers returned.[170] By 5 p.m. the 36th had lost Schwaben Redoubt, barring its southwest face, and held no more than a 500-yard-deep rectangle of the German front-line system and intermediate trench on a frontage of 1000 yards.[171] The situation was desperate and the fighting extraordinarily bloody.[172] As one eyewitness told it, 'In one part of the B line [intermediate trench] near the [Ancre] river there was a carpet of dead and dying Ulstermen and Germans. Blood lay like a layer of mud.'[173]

Only now were elements of 146th Brigade arriving forward and only thanks to some slack in the German shellfire. Their orders: make

---

*   1/5th Battalion York & Lancaster Regiment. 148th Brigade records 99 casualties (12 k, 67 w and 20 m). SDGW notes 14 deaths.

good and consolidate.[174] First across were three companies of 1/7th West Yorkshires,* at about 7.30 p.m.[175] These were later joined by a small party of 1/5th West Yorkshires, the remainder of that battalion not going forward, while at about 8.30 p.m. a company from each of 1/7th and 1/8th West Yorkshires were 'sent over to the German line to form a defensive flank facing north to cover the operation at Fort Schwaben & to reinforce the 107th Brigade.'[176] Lance-Corporal Henderson, 14th Royal Irish Rifles, was struggling back when he ran into some of the West Yorkshire soldiers: 'I have never seen such a look of terror on the faces of human beings.'[177] The war diaries of 1/5th, 1/7th and 1/8th West Yorkshires are scant,[178] while 146th Brigade's states that subsequent events in Schwaben Redoubt were shrouded in the 'general confusion and darkness [and] it is not possible to draw conclusions.'[179] Some conclusions, however, *can* be drawn, and these are that the West Yorkshires — exhausted by their day-long traipse from Aveluy Wood, changing orders and the effects of the heavy shellfire on Thiepval Wood — were caught up in the scrap alongside the 36th and suffered a 'good many casualties.'[180]

A few hours earlier Soden had finally lost patience and roughed his subordinates into action. Eight hours had lapsed since he had first ordered a counterattack, and still the enemy retained a footing in Schwaben Redoubt and the old German front line. Shortly after 5 p.m., Soden, confident that the rest of his divisional sector between Serre and Ovillers was intact, excluding a handful of isolated incursions, told BRIR8 to storm the redoubt. There were no shades of grey in his words: 'This is a direct order.'[181] Available artillery would provide fire support.[182] Once again the concentric counterattacks began, starting at about 8.30 p.m., some at 6.30 p.m. 'An enemy counter [attack] developed from Grandcourt direction in lines in extended order. Machine guns and artillery made them disappear in the dead ground [of Battery Valley].'[183] Two battle groups — now totalling no more than 1000 men, probably far fewer — closed in from the north and northeast, along with a smaller force from the east. 'From this time onwards,' recorded the 36th in an after-battle report, 'the enemy never relaxed his pressure.'[184]

---

*   1/7th Battalion (Leeds Rifles) (Territorial Force) Prince of Wales's Own (West Yorkshire Regiment). SDGW states 11 deaths.

German gains were made one trench bay at a time with grenade and bayonet. Reinforcements from Infantry Regiment 185 (IR185) were fed into battle. The 36th's collapse was relatively swift, even though elements of the 146th and fewer of the 148th had arrived forward with limited supplies of ammunition and grenades. Soon after 8.30 p.m., the wedge won by the Ulstermen had contracted to a 1000-yard-long length of the old German front line and the support trench immediately behind it.[185] It was probably defended by no more than about 500 men, likely far fewer. The only men now remaining between these trenches and the redoubt were dead and wounded; isolated pockets were surrounded then killed off or captured, or forced to retire.[186] Fifty-year-old *Oberstleutnant* Alfons *Ritter* von Bram, commanding BRIR8, was Soden's man on the spot organising the counterattacks. He now planned a final push; it would start at 10 p.m., with the infantry assault preceded by a 60-minute barrage.

Hauptmann Herbert *Ritter* von Wurmb led one of the battle groups. Of the roughly 800 men in Wurmb's band, about 200, or one in four, was killed or wounded on 1 July. That figure is misleading. It does not consider the fragmented nature of his force, which had, by dint of the fighting, been broken into smaller groups. Progress was slow and bloody, and co-ordination with the other assault groups problematic in the darkness and confusion of battle. Wurmb's men shouted 'Hurra!' a lot and fired their weapons freely, pretending to be a much larger force. Such was their confidence that they located other German units by shouting and singing '*Die Wacht am Rhein*' ('The Watch on the Rhine'). Finally, at about 10.30 p.m., under the flickering light of flares, Wurmb — who later wrote a book and completed doctorates in medicine and dentistry — saw dense lines of Ulster and Leeds soldiers withdrawing from the redoubt under a hail of machine-gun and small-arms fire. The battle was won: 'The enemy had been thrown back. Schwaben Redoubt was ours! A tiny band had succeeded in throwing out a much stronger force. It demonstrated that old truth in the *Art of War*: "Only the will to win gains victory."'[187] One wonders what Morland would have made of such thinking.

All that now remained were a few isolated pockets of British and Ulster soldiers. Most would fall back overnight on 1 July; one small band of Leeds soldiers resisted for longer. Private Stewart of the 109th was there, somewhere, helping collect ammunition from the dead and resting while sentries kept watch: 'It was hard for we kept seeing the bits and pieces of the dead bodies and the terrible bleeding of the wounded, and the smell of sweat and hunger kept us from sleeping.'[188] Another was Corporal George Sanders, whose band of about 30 men of 1/7th West Yorkshires held out in a separate corner of the enemy front line till 3 July without food or water after the first night. Sanders organised and led the rag-tag, fatigued defence, fighting off several German attacks. Sanders — who won the VC for courage, determination and leadership — and his men were eventually pulled back to British lines. By that time they numbered just 19.

The butcher's bill for X Corps was horrendous. The corps sustained 9643 casualties for the day, including 3270 dead, 5733 wounded, 326 missing, 172 prisoners and 142 unspecified other casualties.[189] The 36th suffered 5104 casualties, among them 1856 dead, 2728 wounded, 213 missing, 165 prisoners and 142 unspecified others. Thirty-second Division's 3949 casualties comprised 1283 dead, 2552 wounded, 108 missing and 6 prisoners, while the 49th accrued 590 casualties, with 131 of these dead, 453 wounded, 5 missing and 1 prisoner. These figures included five battalion commanders, two of them killed and three wounded.[190] On average, then, X Corps suffered more than nine casualties a minute between 7.30 a.m. and midnight on 1 July, and all Morland really had to show for this bloodletting was an isolated toehold at Leipzig Redoubt.

The network of medical stations, trenches, woods and roads behind the British front line was clogged with wounded, dying and exhausted soldiers. One witness to the horror later reported:

As one approached Paisley Dump [at the southeast edge of Thiepval Wood] one became aware of noise — a noise inhuman. A wail as of enormous wet fingers on an enormous glass; a wail that rose and fell, interminable, unbearable. Then suddenly one became aware whence that wail came. All along the muddy roadway they lay — the wounded; hundreds of them; brown blanket shapes; some shouting, some moaning, some singing in delirium, some quite still.[191]

Casualties in the German units involved in the fighting numbered roughly 2400. BRIR8 recorded 835 casualties for the period 1–3 July.[192] Of these, 533 were incurred on 1 July, including 178 dead, 217 wounded and 138 prisoners of war.[193] RIR99's casualties for the period 23 June–31 July totalled 2541.[194] Those for 1 July, albeit based on fragmentary data, were an estimated 1800–2000.[195] This range sits well with an estimate by a German veteran who said RIR99 suffered about 50% casualties on 1 July.[196] Thus, for every German casualty opposite X Corps, there were about four British, a ratio that reflects the tough fighting at both Schwaben Redoubt and Leipzig Redoubt.

Tenth Corps' failure was the result of Morland's bungled corps command. This included his artillery's failure to neutralise German defensive obstacles and mechanisms, his deployment of the 49th too far back, and his myopic planning. All of these factors were decided before a single X Corps soldier even stepped into no-man's-land on 1 July; Morland had handed the pre-battle tactical advantage to Soden. His subsequent and bloody Thiepval fixation and a missed opportunity to potentially flank that village with 107th Brigade were avoidable. Intelligent use of the 107th would have required quick, lateral thinking on Morland's part, but he did not appreciate the high ground's tactical value. This led to the 36th's pointless sacrifice. It was obvious to German commanders, wrote *Major* Klaus, that their X Corps counterparts 'did not recognise or understand how to use their great success.'[197] On the other side of the hill, Soden simply relied on his largely intact defensive network and decentralised command, both of which functioned more or less as planned. Nevertheless, his delayed counterattack was also the result of having reserves too far back, as well as severed telephone lines, but these factors were more than offset by Morland's bungling. Morland had missed an opportunity to take advantage of the 36th's success and with it a chance to force Soden and Stein into rethinking the tenability of their defences between Thiepval and Beaumont Hamel, potentially altering the short-term course of the Somme offensive.

Unsurprisingly, Morland distanced himself from the fiasco within days:

I am sorry to say my Corps has made little progress & has lost very heavily. The Ulster Division did magnificently to start with but got driven back later. ... Swift advances cannot be expected in this sort of warfare & I expect we shall go on for a long time like the Germans at Verdun, perhaps not as long as that.[198]

In his mind the Somme offensive was always one of attrition.

IN THE CROWDED assembly trenches Sergeant Jim Maultsaid's thoughts were alive with memories of his home and family. Others looked at photographs of their mothers, wives and children. A few sobbed quietly. Those singing hymns or praying were drowned out by the shellfire. Here and there minor scuffles broke out as tensions rose. Maultsaid worried about losing a limb, but the prospect of other injuries horrified him more. 'God save me from the loss of my sight. How I dreaded blindness — anything but that.'[199] Soon, Maultsaid, 14th Royal Irish Rifles, was scrambling up a rough trench ladder and into no-man's-land, which was seething with advancing Ulstermen and exploding shells: 'A wall of flame meets us. We stagger and gasp from shock. My very hair seems to scorch under the impact. The air is full of hissing, burning metal and the ground rocks beneath our feet as we tear our way through our own wire defences.'[200]

Maultsaid saw men fall, writhing in loud agony: 'May I never hear such cries again!'[201] He pressed on into Schwaben Redoubt, and with a small group set to digging in. 'Shells screeched overhead, shrapnel burst above us. Big black "coalboxes" came over with the noise like an express train.'[202] Soon a bullet ripped a chunk of flesh and bone from Maultsaid's right shoulder. Eventually he made it back to the British lines. Fifty years later he pondered the memory of his friends killed that day: a generation that by then existed only in his mind. It was an existential conundrum, 'For, had I not seen them fall?'[203]

Unteroffizier Friedrich Hinkel, RIR99, had a grandstand-like view of no-man's-land from his trench, just north of Thiepval and on the southern fringes of Schwaben Redoubt. To his left, he saw British infantry attacking Thiepval Spur caught in a 'finely meshed net' of crossfire:[204] 'The range is great, set sights at 600 metres [656 yards]! And now the enemy leaped and turned somersaults over there. ... Soon, without their leader [i.e. officer] to rely upon they became a mass.'[205] To the right, the situation in Schwaben

Redoubt was critical; Thiepval was at risk of being flanked and captured. Forceful, on-the-spot leadership was needed. A thin, ad-hoc defensive line was thrown up just north of Thiepval to try to stop 36th (Ulster) Division pushing eastwards and forcing the village's capture from behind. Hinkel was there, 'thirsty, hungry, listless and played out.'[206] Artillery fire from a cacophony of guns firing on the lost trenches was 'hellish.'[207] But the Westphalian and his gang in a blockaded trench bay resolved to fight on: 'Wherever a [British] steel helmet showed itself, it was dealt with, just as in a hare shoot. These lads did not seem to know where they were in our trenches and so we allowed some groups to approach us calmly before despatching them with hand grenades.'[208] Under the flickering light of shell bursts and flares, the fighting reignited on Thiepval Plateau. Hinkel could see the enemy's hazy forms, and opened fire on the fleeting targets in the half light. 'Once more our machine guns clattered away and our rifles glowed red hot. Many an Irish mother's son lay down to the eternal sleep from which there is no awakening.'[209] He rued a shortage of hand grenades, which meant the British could not be fully evicted that night. 'The dawn of a new day revealed to us, in the form of great piles of dead and wounded, some of the success of the violent work we had achieved in conjunction with our machine guns.'[210]

The dead of BRIR8 also lay thick around the blood-spattered trenches of Schwaben Redoubt. They had been recruited from the Pirmasens area of Rhineland-Palatinate and had worked as farmers, clerks, labourers, miners and students, and in 101 other jobs. Roll books reveal much about these men. Many were in their 20s, single and still finding their way in life. Others were in their 30s, married men and fathers. Among them, brothers, co-workers and classmates who enlisted together. Had they met under different circumstances, these Rhine River valley soldiers would have had a lot in common with the Ulstermen. But such ideas were phantasms that would never be: in the maze atop the heights they were trying their very best to kill one another.

Occasionally the plough still brings the Somme dead to the surface, but mostly not. *Vizefeldwebel* Karl Losch, RIR119, rests somewhere in these fields. The former Stuttgart businessman was in the trenches just north of the River Ancre, opposite elements of 36th (Ulster) Division's 108th Brigade. At about 8 a.m. he stood atop the parapet to get a better shot at the Ulstermen. A bullet caught the unmarried Losch. The 20-year-old fell, staggered to his feet and was shot twice more, once in the head. He lost consciousness, died 10 minutes later and was buried in a now-lost mass grave. Several months later, Losch's parents learned he was dead via letters from his acquaintances still at the front. *Leutnant-der-Reserve* Richard Seeger, a friend serving in the neighbouring Reserve Infantry Regiment 121 who was killed at war's end, wrote that he was grief-stricken: 'Such a loyal friend I have lost with his death, I will probably not find anyone like him.'[211]

Seasoned walkers over the former battlefields occasionally find dentures that once belonged to soldiers in the plough lines. The spot where they are found can be where a soldier died, but that is not always the case. Late on 1 July, Private Henderson, 16th Northumberland Fusiliers, and chum Freddie were blown sprawling into the mud of a front-line trench by a shell blast. Freddie lay face down, motionless and apparently dead. After a while, though, he stirred and stood up with a muddy face and broad frown: 'Oh Man, I couldn't find my false teeth.'[212]

SIX OF THE nine Victoria Crosses awarded for 1 July were for actions around Thiepval. Four of the six were posthumous. Only one of the four has a known grave. What does it take to win the Victoria Cross? Who qualifies for immortality? On 1 July 1916 the six were aged 20–32. Four were rankers and working-class: two in the linen trade, one a farm labourer and the fourth a fitter. The others were middle-class and officers, one a student and the other a tea merchant. They liked rugby, rowing and music, and went to church. But for their brave deeds they might have been anybody.

Glasgow-born Sergeant James Turnbull, 17th Highland Light Infantry, won his bronze cross for a hand-grenade epic that spluttered on and off in Leipzig Redoubt. Almost single-handedly he kept German infantry at bay from an isolated post, thanks to a powerful throwing arm that allowed him to outrange enemy bombers. Eventually a sniper got Turnbull, shot him dead, but only as he defiantly hurled still more bombs. The powerfully built 32-year-old who worked in the Scottish rag trade before the war was later buried at Lonsdale Cemetery, Authuille, where about one in three of the 726 identified burials are for 1 July.

The other Victoria Crosses in X Corps' sector were for gallantry around Schwaben Redoubt, or north of the Ancre. Early on 1 July,

Rifleman Billy McFadzean, 14th Royal Irish Rifles, was blown to pieces when, in a crowded trench in Thiepval Wood, he threw himself onto an upset box of grenades that blew up, the safety pins in two having dislodged as they fell. McFadzean's selfless act saved the lives of several soldiers nearby. His mates wept when his gore was carried away. Captain Eric Bell, 9th Royal Inniskilling Fusiliers, earned his posthumous award south of the Ancre for rallying knots of leaderless infantrymen. He had earlier gone forward alone, tossing mortar bombs into the German front line. His supply spent, Bell stood on the parapet under fire and coolly shot enemy soldiers until himself killed. Foundry worker Corporal Sanders, 1/7th West Yorkshires, won his VC at Schwaben Redoubt for acts of gallantry mentioned earlier. He died aged 56 in 1950. Lieutenant Geoffrey Cather, 9th Royal Irish Fusiliers, won his for lugging four wounded soldiers in from the north-bank no-man's-land overnight on 1 July, and tending to others. He was shot dead on another such errand on 2 July.

Rifleman Robert Quigg won his Victoria Cross for hauling seven wounded soldiers in from no-man's-land north of the Ancre. The 31-year-old farm labourer from County Antrim was looking for Second-Lieutenant Sir Edward Macnaghten, 6th Baronet Macnaghten, who owned the estate on which he worked. Time and again Quigg, 12th Royal Irish Rifles, struck out to find the 20-year-old, Eton-educated baronet, each time hauling in another wounded man in his stead. Quigg, who died aged 70 in 1955, eventually bowed to exhaustion. Macnaghten was presumed dead on 1 July and his name appears on the Thiepval Memorial. As a soldier Quigg was reckless, wanted to kill Germans, and had been told by Lady Macnaghten not to return home without her beloved son. As an old man he wore black trousers, braces and a collarless shirt, and rarely ventured beyond his garden.[213] Such is the nature of yarns built up around war heroes. The story has it that King George V asked if Quigg was married when he presented the VC at York Cottage, Sandringham. The gruff rejoinder: 'No Sir, but after what has happened to me I suppose I soon will be.'[214] As it happens, he died a bachelor, as had so many of his friends on the altar of Thiepval and surrounds nearly 40 years earlier.

CHAPTER 7

Ovillers, La Boisselle or Bust

III Corps' charge into the valleys of death

*'They flung everything at us but half-croons. ... I saw one
lad putting his hands in front of his face as if to shield
himself from the hail.'*[1]
— Private Jimmy McEvoy, 16th Royal Scots

'NO INDICATION THAT Ovillers, Contalmaison or La Boisselle had
been captured,' wrote Major Lanoe Hawker, VC, of the Royal Flying
Corps (RFC), after a midday sortie over the battlefield. In the cloudless
sky above the shell-pocked Albert–Bapaume road Hawker spied twin
mine craters, one on either side of the carriageway, near the ruins of La
Boisselle. The Y-Sap crater to the north was clear of British infantry, but,
from his lattice-tailed DH2, Hawker observed minor gains around the
chalkstone jaws of the massive Lochnagar cavity. 'Many dead lying on the
Eastern slopes [of Sausage Valley] outside this crater,'[2] wrote the pilot who
was commander of 24th Squadron.

Five hours earlier, Lieutenant Cecil Lewis, 3rd Squadron, RFC, had
been 8000 feet above the old Roman road that runs between Albert and
Bapaume. At 7.28 a.m. Y-Sap mine blew with a heave and flash, vaulting
an earthen pillar some 4000 feet into the air. 'A moment later came the
second [Lochnagar] mine. Again the roar, the upflung machine, the
strange gaunt silhouette invading the sky.'[3] Through the mist and smoke

Lewis watched the British barrage lift off the German trenches and lines of khaki-clad infantrymen of III Corps move forward. It had begun.

A pilot flying overhead might have likened this part of the battlefield to the splayed fingers of his left hand, the digits being spurs and the gaps between valleys. Today, looking towards Albert from outside Ovillers Military Cemetery, you are standing just below the crest of Ovillers Spur, the middle finger. Off to the immediate left — beyond the scoop of Mash Valley and the die-straight highway — is La Boisselle Spur, the ring finger. Beyond that swell are Sausage Valley and then Fricourt Spur, the little finger. Over to the right, hidden by the summit of Ovillers Spur, are Nab Valley and then Thiepval Spur, which is the index finger, with Leipzig Redoubt at its tip. Thiepval sits in the crook between that finger and your thumb.

Twenty-sixth Reserve and 28th Reserve Divisions' trenches, redoubts and strongpoints crisscrossed the spurs overlooking III Corps' approach routes from the lower ground towards Albert, and blocked off the grassy valleys in between. The 26th's Infantry Regiment 180 (IR180) held the trenches from Ovillers north to Leipzig Redoubt, while the 28th's Reserve Infantry Regiment 110 (RIR110) defended the ground between La Boisselle and Fricourt Spur. Machine-gunners in Ovillers and La Boisselle covered Mash Valley with formidable defensive firepower. South of La Boisselle, a swell of ground known as Schwabenhöhe dominated the approaches to that village and, along with Sausage Redoubt, those to Sausage Valley. A series of trenches 1000–1500 yards beyond were designed to scotch any break-ins, as was the intermediate line proper, about the same distance back again and running from Mouquet Farm to Pozières and thence to Contalmaison. In between, Nordwerk and Mouquet Farm Redoubts covered the area north of Ovillers, while Scots Redoubt supported Sausage Redoubt and La Boisselle. A second position, 1500–2000 yards further back again, prevented access to Pozières Plateau on the main ridge. These defences conformed to the ground and were formidable; forcing them would require careful application of thought, artillery and infantry.

The task fell to Lieutenant-General Sir William Pulteney, whose corps command owed more to seniority than either professional or intellectual ability.[4] He had served in Egypt and Northern Ireland before the war,

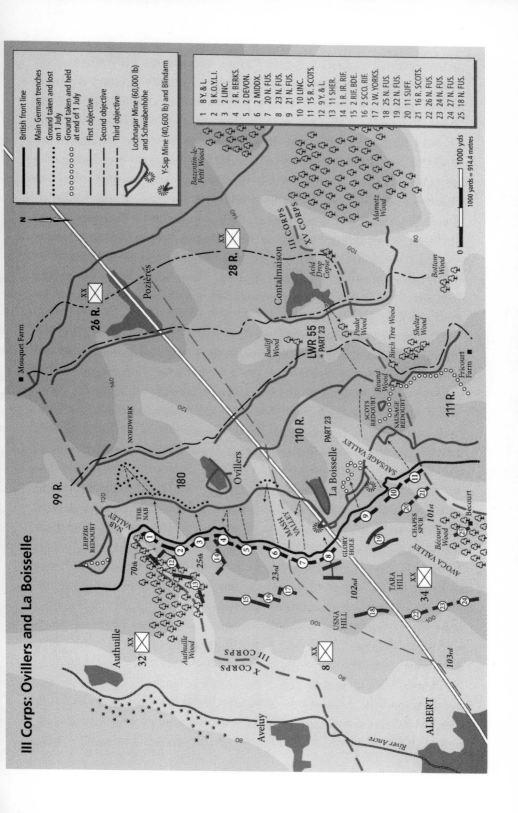

III Corps: Ovillers and La Boisselle

Legend:

- British front line
- Main German trenches
- Ground taken and lost on 1 July
- Ground taken and held at end of 1 July
- First objective
- Second objective
- Third objective
- Lochnagar Mine (60,000 lb) and Schwabenhöhe
- Y-Sap Mine (40,600 lb) and Blindarm

1 8 Y. & L.
2 8 K.O.Y.L.I.
3 2 LINC.
4 2 R. BERKS.
5 2 DEVON.
6 2 MIDDX.
7 20 N. FUS.
8 23 N. FUS.
9 21 N. FUS.
10 10 LINC.
11 15 R. SCOTS.
12 9 Y. & L.
13 11 SHER.
14 1 R. IR. RIF.
15 2 RIF. BDE.
16 2 SCO. RIF.
17 2 W. YORKS.
18 25 N. FUS.
19 22 N. FUS.
20 11 SUFF.
21 16 R. SCOTS.
22 26 N. FUS.
23 24 N. FUS.
24 27 N. FUS.
25 18 N. FUS.

0   1000 yards = 914.4 metres   1000 yds

Bazentin-le-Petit Wood

Mametz Wood

Mouquet Farm

Pozières

26 R.

XX

28 R.

XX

Contalmaison

III CORPS
XV CORPS

Acid Drop Copse

Bottom Wood

Batiff Wood

LWR 55 + PART 23

Peake Wood

Birch Tree Wood

Shelter Wood

Fricourt Farm

NORDWERK

110 R.

Round Wood

SCOTS REDOUBT

SAUSAGE VALLEY

SAUSAGE REDOUBT

111 R.

Ovillers

180

La Boisselle

PART 23

Becourt

LEIPZIG REDOUBT

NAB VALLEY

THE NAB

99 R.

MASH VALLEY

GLORY HOLE

CHAPES SPUR

Becourt Wood

AVOCA VALLEY

101st

32

XX

Authuille

Authuille Wood

X CORPS
III CORPS

8

XX

USNA HILL

TARA HILL

34

XX

102nd

103rd

Aveluy

River Ancre

ALBERT

with stints in Uganda, Congo and South Africa suiting this marksman's taste for big-game hunting. By 1916 'Putty,' a peaceful country squire in appearance,[5] had advanced well beyond his limited abilities thanks to the wartime demand for experienced senior officers. The 55-year-old Eton alumnus had attended neither Royal Military Academy at Sandhurst, nor Staff College, which explained why he lacked the professional skillset of his peers and was probably the basis for his reputation as a bungler. One officer thought him the 'most completely ignorant general I served during the war.'[6] General Sir Douglas Haig had this to say about Pulteney in May 1916: 'He seemed very fit and cheery. But after listening to his views on the proposed operations of his Corps, I felt he had quite reached the limits of his capacity as a commander. A plucky leader of a Brigade or even a Division, he has not however, studied his profession sufficiently to be really a good corps commander.'[7]

The story goes that talented staff officers were appointed to III Corps to offset Pulteney's muddling, which was all about ill-thought-out operations and buck-passing when they turned sour.[8] Eventually it would get him sacked, but not until 1918. Later he served as Gentleman Usher of the Black Rod, and his 1941 obituary said he had never been 'known to make a mistake in the ritual and ceremonies of Parliament.'[9] Pulteney's bent for 'ritual and ceremonies' was all about hiding behind a mask of competence.

Pulteney planned to break the Ovillers and La Boisselle stronghold with a frontal and uphill assault towards Pozières Ridge. Success here was central to Haig's strategy, and would open the way to Bapaume then Arras for the cavalry, and then the infantry of General Sir Hubert Gough's Reserve Army. Failure would bust Haig's Somme plans. Pulteney committed two whole divisions to the attack: the 8th and the 34th, with 19th (Western) Division in corps reserve. Third Corps had a total nominal strength of 94,460, but the estimated number of infantrymen actually involved in the battle, along with elements of various other units, was about 16,700.[10]

Mash Valley, which holds the Albert–Bapaume road, was the demarcation line between the two attacking divisions, the 8th's area being to the north and the 34th's to the south. They were to advance to a total depth of 2500–3700 yards behind the German front line. The 34th, its infantrymen wearing yellow-coloured triangles on their backs so they could be seen by observers, would attack in four distinct columns. Its 101st and 102nd (Tyneside Scottish) Brigades formed the vanguard, followed by 103rd (Tyneside Irish) Brigade.[11] To his credit, Putty opted to try to pinch off the salient at the head of La Boisselle Spur, with the two columns of the 102nd taking it and the village that sat atop it from either side. There were two big mines in the 34th's sector to help its infantry: Y-Sap and Lochnagar mines respectively totalled 40,600 and 60,000 pounds.[12] Y-Sap mine was to erase the Blindarm, a small grouping of German trenches overlooking Mash Valley, and Lochnagar was to obliterate the strongpoint Schwabenhöhe overlooking Sausage Valley and no-man's-land. By contrast, the 8th was spread out over a much wider frontage, with its three brigades — north to south, the 70th, 25th and 23rd — attacking abreast. While some of the 8th's and 34th's lead battalions would attack directly up Ovillers and Fricourt Spurs, most were condemned to advance along the death traps of Mash, Sausage and Nab Valleys.

Everything hinged on the ability of III Corps' artillery to shell the German positions and resistance into submission. Pulteney had a comparatively rich concentration of artillery that included 98 heavy guns and howitzers, or about one to every 40 yards of attack frontage, and about 175 field guns, or roughly one to every 23 yards.[13] A dozen attached French guns would fire gas shells. But there were significant problems with the artillery's pre-battle work: too many dud shells, a lack of ammunition and shellfire diluted over a wide area undermined its efforts to break down German defences and resistance, both in the front line and further back.[14] Moreover, Pulteney did not have anything like the number of guns required to produce a German collapse and open the way for Gough's army. His own gunners warned that their attempts to cut the enemy's more distant wire defences would likely be unsuccessful.[15] Even so, Ovillers and La Boisselle were razed, trenches collapsed and wire was mostly pared away. As one German soldier said, 'Whoever went above [ground] as a sentry could barely still recognise the position. Instead of well-developed trenches he saw one crater alongside another; the last wall remnants of La Boisselle became crushed into powder in these days of innumerable shells.'[16] Yet, even as a pulverised warren, the Ovillers and La Boisselle moonscape was defensible by German soldiers who were holed up in dugouts and listening to muffled explosions 30–40 feet above. They just had to race up from their bunkers, take positions in the shellfire-torn wasteland and open fire.

None of this squared with Pulteney's belief that the ruined villages and Schwabenhöhe would be untenable and the enemy wiped out.[17] Not everyone agreed. Lieutenant-Colonel John Shakespear, 18th Northumberland Fusiliers,* was well aware that La Boiselle's garrison was 'very much on the alert.'[18] Lieutenant-Colonel Godfrey Steward, 27th Northumberland Fusiliers, was astounded by the optimism at Pulteney's headquarters: 'Their Intelligence must have been atrocious.'[19] Captain Reginald Leetham, 2nd Rifle Brigade,† said the bombardment of Ovillers was impressive, but pondered whether it was 'doing us much good' given that most German soldiers were safe underground.[20] Major James Jack, 2nd Scottish Rifles, also doubted whether German infantry in Ovillers had been cowed.[21] While Pulteney optimistically believed the bombardment was fit for purpose, several battalion and company commanders whose men would be involved in the attack held significant doubts.

As it turned out, German morale withstood the bombardment, which caused few casualties. The 2570-strong RIR110 had anticipated the attack after 'long days and nights of unbearable tension.'[22] One soldier claimed he felt 'extreme joy that the deep dugouts constructed by us with hard work also protected us against the heavy calibre shells.'[23] Another said British hopes that life in the German trenches would be extinguished were 'very false.'[24] One officer in the roughly 2800-strong IR180 alleged that the mood in its dugouts was 'exceedingly' encouraging:[25] 'The bombardment can't last for too long; we expect the attack from one day to another.' Another officer, *Oberleutnant-der-Reserve* Heinrich Vogler, IR180, recalled nearly 55 years later that while his 'men's mood was low,' they were not lacking in 'courage or determination.'[26] So it was that the soldiers of IR180 and RIR110 waited deep underground, with rifles to hand and the flickering light of candles playing across their stubbly faces as they waited to exact bloody payback.

---

* 18th (Service) Battalion (1st Tyneside Pioneers) Northumberland Fusiliers. SDGW notes 13 deaths.
† 2nd Battalion Rifle Brigade (The Prince Consort's Own). Battalion war diary states 133 casualties. SDGW notes 26 deaths.

These soldiers knew full well that the British attack would begin early on 1 July. Late on 30 June, an underground Moritz listening device in the La Boisselle salient had intercepted a British message suggesting the attack was due the next day.[27] This news was forwarded to Second Army and thereafter circulated among front-line regiments, which notified their companies two to three hours before Zero.[28] As *Schütze* Christian Fischer, a machine-gunner in IR180 opposite the increasingly splintered ruins of Authuille Wood, remembered:

> Early in the morning of 1 July word filtered through to us that the
> enemy would attack that morning. ... Some of us said the English
> would attack at 7.30 a.m. At 5.30 a.m. the *Vizefeldwebel* stood at
> the dugout entrance and waited for the enemy's attack, while we
> stood ready with our guns in the dugout. We all looked at the
> clock and waited anxiously for the enemy attack. We wanted to get
> back at the Englishmen.[29]

Those brave lookouts who ventured up into the trenches found them destroyed, wrote another soldier, but across no-man's-land 'everything was full of life and the British trenches were a mass of steel helmets.'[30] Most everyone had an ear cocked for the audible moment when the British shellfire moved further back, confirming the infantry attack was beginning.[31]

From 6.25 a.m., III Corps' artillery and mortars spiked to a crescendo, raining shells onto the German front line. The barrage should have been maintained consistently until Zero or, as Brigadier-General John Pollard, 25th Brigade, preferred, co-ordinated with the attacking infantry.[32] That would at least have forced enemy soldiers to remain underground while Pulteney's crossed no-man's-land. It did not happen. After just 35 minutes the heavy guns stepped their fire back, leaving only the field artillery's lighter shells to play over the German front trench until 7.30 a.m.[33] This dilution of shellfire gave Württemberg and Baden soldiers further notice, and ample time to rush some men into ground-holding positions. Several German machine guns began firing at 7 a.m.[34] Twenty-eight minutes later the mine blasts sent shock waves pulsing through the subterranean German city, and two minutes later the field guns lifted their fire further back.[35] This confluence of factors pinpointed the attack almost to the minute. At 7.30 a.m., 'The Swabians poured forth out of every mined dugout. The trench was barely still able to be recognised, but each man, each group, each platoon knows their place and their defensive field. Nestled behind the destroyed breastworks and in shell craters, they awaited the superior strength of the approaching enemy.'[36]

Worse still, 26th Reserve and 28th Reserve Divisions' artillery in this area was far from destroyed. In nominal terms the 26th had at least 29 guns directly supporting the Ovillers sector and providing close defensive fire for IR180, plus a further 28 nearby that could shoot into this area if needed. Divisional commander *Generalleutnant* Franz *Freiherr* von Soden had insisted on preserving his limited artillery resources through fire restraint, which meant many of his batteries went undetected by RFC and artillery spotters, and survived counter-battery shoots. A large portion remained intact, concealed and good to open defensive fire when the British attack began. *Generalleutnant* Ferdinand von Hahn's gunners in the 28th had not shown the same restraint. Many of its estimated 60 barrels behind La Boisselle and the summit of Fricourt Spur had been knocked out, leaving an estimated 42, of which many were apparently useless.[37] But Hahn's guns in this part of the line remained capable of supporting the front-line infantry, according to British battle accounts,[38] although never to the same extent as Soden's.[39] While large portions of IR180's and RIR110's positions were flattened, the garrisons were intact and their supporting artillery was ready to lay down close defensive fire, stopping enemy infantry from crossing no-man's-land and also sealing off any breaches of the German lines.

In the event that any enemy infantry did break into the German positions, someone had circulated a pamphlet through the dugouts and gun pits of RIR110 outlining several phonetic translations of useful English-language phrases. The obviously English-speaking writer had a sense of humour:

> *Hands up you fool! (Honds opp ju fuhl!)...*
> *Hands up, come on Tommy! (Honds opp, kom on Tomy!)*[40]

'JUST BEFORE ZERO hour, I was sat on a fire step, three of us pressed close together,' recalled Lance-Corporal Archibald Turner, 10th Lincolns, of a conversation about the shellfire in 34th Division's sector.[41] 'Chap on one side said: "If there's a bugger for you, you'll get it." Just then a shrapnel shell burst just above us and he got a shrapnel ball through his helmet and was killed outright.' The third man's leg hung by a sinew. 'He asked me to cut it off but I only had a knife and I didn't want to give him gangrene and, anyway, it was time to go over.' Private William Senescall, 11th Suffolks, recalled German shellfire — 'Wouf, Wouf, all around' — and the throaty crackle of machine guns. 'I now for some reason began to feel panicky. I just felt like bolting or something.'[42] Private Michael Manley, 26th Northumberland Fusiliers, wanted the ordeal over. 'You know it's going to be rough. I was scared when the shells came over it didn't half put the wind up you.'[43] Private William Corbett, 15th Royal Scots, recalled 'the expression of expectancy on the faces of these men standing side by side with thoughts of home and their loved ones whom most of them would never see again.'[44]

Walk around the duckboard track circling Lochnagar crater today and the military value of the German redoubt that once stood here is plain to see. From this place — Schwabenhöhe — you have a more than 180-degree panorama over 34th Division's assembly trenches from Sausage Valley around to Avoca Valley, which runs between the Albert–Bapaume road and Bécourt Wood. Lieutenant-Colonel Charles Somerset, 11th Suffolks, said that, unless destroyed or suppressed, this redoubt would inflict heavy casualties as infantry crossed the grassland expanses of no-man's-land.[45] That was why III Corps opted to blow it sky high — the trenches, machine-gun posts and dugouts occupied by a company of RIR110 vaporised in one fell swoop — and send the infantry in once the debris had settled. Nobody knows how many the blast killed, but the number was not great, probably a couple of dozen.[46] 'When the English infantry began their mass attack with the huge explosion at the 5th Company [sector] ... we immediately made ourselves ready to be deployed,' said *Vizefeldwebel* Theodor Laasch, RIR110,[47] whose platoon was in reserve dugouts just behind La Boisselle and would participate in the fighting against both 8th and 34th Divisions.

Thirty-fourth Division's lead battalions were mostly swept down by machine-gun fire. They each moved forward on a frontage of 250–400 yards. To the north, the 102nd attacked either side of La Boisselle Spur, some battalions up Mash Valley and others between the village and Lochnagar crater. Further to the south, 101st Brigade attacked along Sausage Valley and along the northern slopes of Fricourt Spur. Each of these brigades had two battalions of the 103rd attached. Within 10 minutes 80% of the men in the leading battalions — from left to right, 20th,[*] 23rd[†] and 21st Northumberland Fusiliers,[‡] 10th Lincolns[§] and 15th Royal Scots,[¶] all of which advanced in linear waves[48] — were casualties. This was the result of ready-and-waiting German machine-gunners and riflemen generally winning the race for their parapets and spraying no-man's-land with tens of thousands of bullets.[49] There were no fewer than 30 machine guns with interlocking fields of fire spread across RIR110's sector.[50] Follow-up battalions moved forward — 22nd Northumberland Fusiliers,[**] 11th Suffolks[††] and 16th Royal Scots[‡‡] in the

---

[*] 20th (Service) Battalion (1st Tyneside Scottish) Northumberland Fusiliers. Also known as 1st Tyneside Scottish. Battalion war diary states 661 casualties (72 k, 315 w and 274 m). SDGW notes 317 deaths.

[†] 23rd (Service) Battalion (4th Tyneside Scottish) Northumberland Fusiliers. Also known as 4th Tyneside Scottish. Divisional history states 640 casualties 1–3 July (187 k, 451 w and 2 m). SDGW notes 239 deaths.

[‡] 21st (Service) Battalion (2nd Tyneside Scottish) Northumberland Fusiliers. Also known as 2nd Tyneside Scottish. Divisional history states 478 casualties 1–3 July (172 k and 306 w). SDGW notes 131 deaths.

[§] 10th (Service) Battalion (Grimsby) Lincolnshire Regiment. Also known as Grimsby Chums. Battalion war diary states 502 casualties (70 k, 269 w and 163 m). SDGW notes 162 deaths.

[¶] 15th (Service) Battalion (1st Edinburgh) Royal Scots (Lothian Regiment). Also known as 1st Edinburgh City Battalion. *Official History* states 513 casualties (241 k, 269 w and 3 m). SDGW notes 226 deaths.

[**] 22nd (Service) Battalion (3rd Tyneside Scottish) Northumberland Fusiliers. Also known as 3rd Tyneside Scottish. Divisional history states 539 casualties 1–3 July (205 k, 333 w and 1 m). SDGW notes 160 deaths.

[††] 11th (Service) Battalion (Cambridgeshire) Suffolk Regiment. Also known as the Cambridge Battalion. Divisional History states 691 casualties 1–3 July (6 k, 402 w and 283 m). SDGW notes 196 deaths.

[‡‡] 16th (Service) Battalion (2nd Edinburgh) Royal Scots (Lothian Regiment). Also known as 2nd Edinburgh City Battalion. Divisional history states 472 casualties 1–3 July (31 k, 79 w and 362 m). SDGW notes 221 deaths.

second wave in extended order,[51] with the 103rd's 25th,* 26th,† 24th‡ and 27th Northumberland Fusiliers§ in the third and deployed in waves of columns of platoons.[52] The result was multiple battalions concertinaed in no-man's-land, confusion, failing command structures and appalling casualties.

In the 101st's right column, 15th Royal Scots moved within 200 yards of the German line before the barrage lifted and, with a skirling of bagpipes, was over and beyond the flattened enemy parapet on the southern slopes of Sausage Valley, and soon atop Fricourt Spur. It was followed forward by 16th Royal Scots. Private Frank Scott, 16th Royal Scots, found the German trenches to be 'absolutely battered to bits, practically just chalk heaps and hardly anybody in it. Those left were so demoralised that they hadn't a fight left in them but surrendered right away.'[53] A Royal Scots officer watched the attackers from the assembly trenches: 'They move about deliberately, taking steady aim at the foe crowning the slope [of Fricourt Spur], and pushing upward slowly but surely. ... The little clusters of men gradually fall into the [trench] line towards the top of the slope.'[54] Both battalions suffered under machine-gun fire in Sausage Redoubt and La Boisselle, briefly veered into the neighbouring XV Corps' sector and were pushed from their most advanced gains, which were around Birch Tree Wood and a trench running northeast towards Peake Wood.[55] Scots Redoubt was taken. Sausage Redoubt remained defiant; flame throwers incinerated a small party trying to storm its defences. A few groups of the following battalion, 27th Northumberland Fusiliers, made it across no-man's-land behind the Royal Scots. The 101st's right column had done well to force an entry to the German line, but come noon its most

---

* 25th (Service) Battalion (2nd Tyneside Irish) Northumberland Fusiliers. Also known as 2nd Tyneside Irish. Divisional history states 491 casualties 1–3 July (9 k, 13 w and 469 m). SDGW notes 139 deaths.

† 26th (Service) Battalion (3rd Tyneside Irish) Northumberland Fusiliers. Also known as 3rd Tyneside Irish. Divisional history states 247 casualties 1–3 July (59 k, 23 w and 165 m). SDGW notes 168 deaths.

‡ 24th (Service) Battalion (1st Tyneside Irish) Northumberland Fusiliers. Also known as 1st Tyneside Irish. Divisional history states 620 casualties 1–3 July (17 k, 319 w and 284 m). SDGW notes 157 deaths.

§ 27th (Service) Battalion (4th Tyneside Irish) Northumberland Fusiliers. Also known as 4th Tyneside Irish. Battalion war diary states 550 casualties (104 k, 388 w and 58 m). SDGW notes 143 deaths.

advanced line was a 250-yard-long stretch of Wood Alley trench between Scots Redoubt and Round Wood atop Fricourt Spur.

Incredibly, some small groups of soldiers progressed much further, towards Contalmaison, roughly 2000 yards behind the German front line. A mixed bag of 15th and 16th Royal Scots and 27th Northumberland Fusiliers, along with some 10th Lincolns and 11th Suffolks, whose ordeal will soon be discussed, had fought determinedly to hold the trench between Birch Tree Wood and Peake Wood, which was on the approach to Contalmaison. They were forced to retire after desperate close-quarter fighting.[56] Corporal George Lowery, 27th Northumberland Fusiliers, came face to face with a German officer in the enemy trenches: 'He fired at me with his revolver and missed me. Just as he was going to fire a second time I threw the bomb, which blew his head off.'[57] Private Tom Hunter, 16th Royal Scots, saw a friend killed as he peeped round a trench corner. 'I threw my bomb round the corner and the lads followed up with the bayonet. It [the ensuing fight] did not last long.'[58]

One small band of 16th Royal Scots actually entered Contalmaison,[59] the furthest advance achieved on 1 July. A few of the 27th Northumberland Fusiliers also reached the shellfire-damaged village, while several of the 24th Northumberland Fusiliers almost made it that far, too.[60] Roughly 14 wounded soldiers from several of these units were captured and held in Contalmaison until they and the village were liberated several days later.[61] One of these soldiers later described his experience:

> There were eight or nine other Englishmen, all wounded, lying there; and I was in front, right in the mouth of the [German] dug-out, where I could see the trench, where a lot o' Boches was sitting, smoking cigarettes, an' talking in their own lingo. By an' by a German officer comes along. I knew he was coming by the way these chaps jumped an' dropped their smokin' and talkin'. They came to attention pretty smart; I'll say that for 'em.[62]

The 101st's left column, meantime, suffered heavily as it advanced along Sausage Valley. Tenth Lincolns and the following 11th Suffolks were swept down by machine-gunners in Sausage Redoubt and around La Boisselle; they were destroyed as effective units within 30 minutes.[63]

'In spite of the fact that wave after wave were mown down by machine-gun fire, all pushed on,' wrote 11th Suffolks' war diarist.[64] 'We often saw entire platoons bunch together so long until one after the other was shot down,' wrote one German observer.[65] Precious few from the left-flank platoons made it to the Lochnagar crater and adjacent ground.[66] Some 24th Northumberland Fusiliers, coming forward behind the 11th Suffolks, now went forward under 'intense machine gun fire' and, while a number did get across no-man's-land, the battalion's attack was otherwise halted.[67] A few hundred soldiers from all three battalions had snatched a limited footing in and around the crater, but further up Sausage Valley the formidable Sausage Redoubt, which had wreaked so much havoc, remained resistant and deadly.

Oberleutant-der-Reserve Kienitz, a machine-gun officer in RIR110 near Sausage Redoubt described the attack:

> The serried ranks of the enemy were only a few metres away from the trenches when they were sprayed with a hurricane of defensive fire. Some individuals stood exposed on the parapet and hurled hand grenades at the enemy who had taken cover to the front. Then, initially in small groups, but later in huge masses, the enemy began to pull back towards Bécourt [opposite the entrance to Sausage Valley] until finally it seemed as though every man in the entire field was attempting to flee back to his jumping off point. The fire of our infantrymen and machine guns pursued them, hitting them hard. … Our weapons fired away ceaselessly for two hours, then the battle died away.[68]

Lieutenant-Colonel Somerset's grim forecast had proved correct. 'The bombardment had by no means extinguished the German machine guns which increased their fire as the waves advanced, and our Artillery barrage moved off the front line of the German system,' he wrote.[69] 'They were almost wiped out & very few reached the German front line.' An artillery smoke screen on La Boisselle was largely unsuccessful, due to the direction and weakness of the wind, and failed to obscure German machine-gunners' views.[70] 'The Germans put down a terrific barrage on our front line directly the assault commenced & opposite La Boisselle it was doubled. Chapes Spur & the forward slopes of Tara & Usna [Hills] were swept by machine gun fire,'[71] Somerset said. 'The 11th Suffolks in the support line had further to go & walked straight into the German barrage.'[72] This was the ghastly experience of all of the 34th's follow-up battalions, not just 11th Suffolks.

Attempts to cross no-man's-land by the three sections of 207th Field Company, Royal Engineers (RE), at about 10 a.m. faltered in the face of 'impossible' machine-gun fire.[73] At 1 p.m., a single company of 18th Northumberland Fusiliers (with about 30 bombers from 10th Lincolns) attempting to reinforce the Royal Scots also failed to get across.

Survivors recalled chattering machine guns and likened the patter of bullets to heavy rain or hail. They told of friends falling face down, one after another, and wondered when they themselves would be hit. 'It shook my faith in every certainty. Your officers, your pals, maybe even men you didn't care for much, all falling in front of you,' wrote Lance-Sergeant Jerry Mowatt, 16th Royal Scots.[74] Private Lew Shaugnessy, 27th Northumberland Fusiliers, was at first curious when he saw scores of soldiers falling around him: 'I wanted to find out what they were looking for, it didn't occur to me that they were men in their death agonies kicking and screaming.'[75] Others spoke of near misses, shot-through tunics and equipment, fractured bones, arterial spurts, gunshot wounds to limb or torso and of bullets slamming into corpses. Some veterans even remembered the smell of battle: Private Corbett, 15th Royal Scots, said the stench of cordite 'resulted in an atmosphere that was choking to the throat.'[76] Those who advanced furthest often felt isolated and put their progress down to luck. The wounded spoke of terrible injuries and prolonged, parched agony.

Machine-gun fire almost tore Captain Peter Ross, 16th Royal Scots, in two at the waist. The mathematics teacher was in unimaginable pain and begged somebody to end his misery. It came down to an order; two of his men reluctantly obliged.[77]

No-man's-land was covered with hundreds of soldiers, the living motionless and pressed hard to the ground to avoid snipers' bullets. Private Senescall saw a man shot in the head. 'I distinctly heard, in spite of the other noises, him give a loud groan.'[78] He saw 'Gerry hats moving about' in trenches further up Sausage Valley. A shell landed nearby:

With all the bits and pieces flying up was a body. The legs had been blown off right up to his crutch. I have never seen a body lifted so high. It sailed up and towards me. I can still see the deadpan look on his face under the tin hat, which was still on, held by the chin strap. He still kept coming and landed with a bonk a few yards to my left. Lucky me that he missed me.[79]

More shells burst near Senescall, followed by a spatter of bullets. A delirious soldier sobbed for his mother: 'He sounded like one of the fifteen or sixteen year olds of which there was a sprinkling in the battalions.'[80] Dusk fell, and, after a testing 13 hours in no-man's-land, Senescall bolted roughshod over bodies until he made it back to the British lines. Private Edward Dyke, 26th Northumberland Fusiliers, chanced his arm, too: 'The return to safety was as bad as the charge. We came down a slope, which we had now to ascend. Machine guns were rattling, and German snipers from the opposite hill were picking off the wounded.'[81]

The mixed bag of 10th Lincolns, 11th Suffolks and 24th Northumberland Fusiliers who had reached the crater held its still-warm rim closest to the German trenches. Soon enough, machine-gun fire played along the chalkstone lip; the wounded and dead rolled down into its still-steaming core. 'It was as hot as an oven after just being blown up,' said Lieutenant Ambrose Dickinson, 10th Lincolns.[82] Nearby, Lieutenant John Turnbull, same battalion, was wounded in the spine as he crawled for the crater: 'There were 50–100 unwounded men. We consolidated around the lip of the crater; our parapet was of uncertain thickness and very crumbly. There was a certain amount of cover for all but very shallow,' he later wrote.[83] Turnbull continued: 'I found my flow of language very useful several times; especially when the fit men wanted to bolt for it and leave a good hundred wounded who couldn't walk. I asked them what the — — they thought they were doing and they all meekly went back, much to my surprise.'[84] Private Frank Stubley, 10th Lincolns, made it beyond the crater but said machine-gun fire 'cut us a bit thick just as we got over his second line. That is where he stopped most of us. He gave me one through my nose and out by the cheek.'[85] These soldiers would hold the ground around and just beyond the crater rim for the rest of the day, incurring a constant trickle of casualties in the process.

A Russian Sap known as Kerriemuir Street extended almost up to the German front line near Lochnagar crater and was used as a forward supply route for bombs, ammunition and water.[86] Two other Russian Saps on III Corps' front were Waltney in 2nd Lincolns' sector and Rivington in 2nd Royal Berkshires' area; the former was opened on 1 July but apparently went unused, while the latter remained unopened. Meantime, Kerriemuir Street was 12–14 feet below ground, its 410-foot-long corridor being almost 9 feet high and roughly 3 feet wide.[87] It finished about 180 feet short of the German line, a jot northwest of the crater, and had its head opened late on 30 June.[88] From about 10 a.m., it was clogged with wounded men heading back and supply parties moving forward. By about 7 p.m. it had been extended to the old German front line.[89] It was via this route that 18th Northumberland Fusiliers and 209th Field Company, RE, lugged forward bombs, ammunition, water and so forth. 'It was due to their exertions that the men in the front line were able to hold on,' wrote 34th Division's war diarist.[90] As one soldier who plied this course later wrote: 'A small [Russian] Sap head had been blown [open] not many yards from the German front line and through this came supplies and we also got a telephone cable from it and we signals [sic] fixed up a telephone to Advanced Brigade H.Q. & this was fixed up at the bottom of some stairs of a German front line dugout.'[91]

Through the afternoon German officers and NCOs set to reorganising RIR110's garrison, particularly in the areas where 101st Brigade had broken into its lines. That meant organising counterattack groups, establishing which ground was still German-held and, most importantly, working out exactly where the enemy was. *Unteroffizier* Gustav Brachat, RIR110, tried to make contact with parties of German soldiers near Scots Redoubt. 'I suddenly heard "Halt". I stood in front of a barricade and firmly determined through listening and observing that it was occupied by Englishmen. I went back to relate the news to my platoon.'[92]

CLOSER TO THE Albert–Bapaume road the 102nd made limited, bloody headway. In the right column, 21st Northumberland Fusiliers began crossing the 200-yards-wide no-man's-land about two minutes before Zero and quickly overran the pulverised trenches between La Boisselle and the Lochnagar crater. It linked up with the 101st to its right at Schwabenhöhe.

The 21st was followed by 22nd and then 26th Northumberland Fusiliers, which both suffered severely on the exposed eastern slopes of Tara Hill at the hands of the La Boisselle machine-gunners and the German defensive barrage.[93] The fusiliers' few survivors made it some 500 yards beyond the German front line, running into increasingly stiff resistance from support companies of RIR110 and Infantry Regiment 23 (IR23). *Leutnant* Paul Fiedel, IR23, likened the experience for his men to rifle-range shooting: 'They grinned at their *Leutnants* with pipes in their mouths and were happy. This was an opportunity to do something other than the endless entrenching. A machine-gun crew of the 2nd Company, RIR110, smoked at their guns.'[94]

Whistles blew and Private Thomas Easton's platoon of 21st Northumberland Fusiliers began moving towards the Lochnagar crater area. He was in one of the battalion's later waves and noticed German machine-gun fire passing overhead: 'This was so until we passed our own front line and started to cross no-man's-land, then trench machine guns began the slaughter. Men fell on every side, screaming with the severity of there [sic] wounds, those who were unwounded dare not attend to them.'[95] Dead lay on the enemy's wire, and 'their bodies formed a bridge for others to pass over and into the German front line.' Small groups of bombers worked their way up communication trenches between La Boisselle and the crater. Grenades were tossed into dugouts and nests of resistance were bombed into submission:

> There was [sic] fewer still of us but we consolidated the lines we
> had taken by preparing firing positions on the rear of the trenches
> gained, and fighting went ok all morning and gradually died
> down, as men & munitions on both sides became exhausted. Some
> of our Battalion troop got consolidated on the edge of the Great
> Crater on our right, but little further progress was made.[96]

The severely wounded lay in a 30-foot-deep dugout in the old German front line, but 'many of them just died, for nothing much could be done until darkness set in.' Easton recalled sitting briefly with an older soldier named Jack in the captured trench. Jack was delirious; he reckoned he could hear a band playing. 'This man finally flopped forward and he had no back. He had been hit by an explosive bullet which blew out the whole of his back between the shoulders and he was dead.' Easton continued, 'the day wore on, no rest, no let up, wounded men pleaded for water to make up the blood they had lost, but water was at a premium for the day had been hot.' Company Quartermaster Sergeant Gawen Wild, 26th Northumberland Fusiliers, was wounded and hauled into a shell hole by a friend who was killed in the act. 'You can imagine my feelings, lying there with one of my best chums who'd given his life to save mine,' he wrote.[97]

Surprisingly, a few fusiliers made it to Bailiff Wood, near Contalmaison, about 2000 yards behind the German front line. As *Leutnant-der-Landwehr* Alfred Frick, Reserve Field Artillery Regiment 28 (RFAR28), told it: 'Runners, telephonists and men from the Construction Company were formed into a defence platoon and set off under the command of *Leutnant* Strüvy [of Reserve Field Artillery Regiment 29 (RFAR29)]. This little united force succeeded in ejecting the bold intruders.'[98] These endeavours towards Contalmaison, along with those mentioned earlier, were exceptions to the rule. The overall pattern was scores of Northumberland Fusiliers being shot down as they closed on the trenches held by IR23 a couple of hundred yards beyond the crater. Local counterattacks and limited bomb supplies saw the 102nd's early gains halved within hours, and of the roughly 2100 officers and men of the 21st, 22nd and 26th Northumberland Fusiliers who set out, only several hundred remained in the German lines.

'In the event of my death I leave all of my property and effects to My Wife Mrs Norah Nugent,'[99] wrote Private George Nugent, 22nd Northumberland Fusiliers, before battle. He was killed within an ace of Lochnagar crater, likely by a bullet or shrapnel. The 28-year-old labourer's bones were found there in 1998 and identified by an engraved cutthroat razor. A weathered oak cross with metal plaque now stands near the spot. Nugent — then a married father of a one-year-old girl — is now buried at Ovillers Military Cemetery. His epitaph's opening line: 'Lost. Found.'[100] Captain William Herries, same battalion, made it further than Nugent but found his progress blocked by the support companies of IR23 and RIR110:

Most of the men were killed, and the only thing to do was to get a machine gun up, which we were fortunate enough to do. Then we gave them it hot. Further along [Captain John] Forster, [Lieutenant William] McIntosh and [Lieutenant Walter] Lamb got over with a party of men, but the whole lot were mown down with a machine gun. In the meantime our bombers were at work and reached their [German] third line, which they held for a short time, but out of which we were bombed step by step — all our bombs having been used. I won't tell you of any of the scenes in the trenches, but I had to pull myself together with a mouthful of brandy once or twice. We were now busy digging the Bosches out of their dugouts. They all threw up their hands and yelled, 'Mercy Kamerade!' and seemed very surprised that they were not killed off.[101]

Forster and Lamb have no known grave and are today named on the Thiepval Memorial. McIntosh died of wounds on 6 July 1916 and is buried at St Sever Cemetery, Rouen.

Back in the British lines, battery commander Captain Ivan Pery-Knox-Gore, 152nd Brigade, Royal Field Artillery (RFA), saw a machine gun firing from La Boisselle's southern outskirts, and resolved to break orders. 'Took the law into my own hands, stopped firing per [barrage] time table and turned our gun onto the M.G. [machine gun]'[102] His gun silenced that machine gun and several others nearby, and blew a sniper 'to bits.'[103] Pery-Knox-Gore then directed his guns to support the infantry's limited gains just south of La Boisselle. 'Turned our guns onto the points where M.G. & rifle fire were coming from & eventually silenced all & our men were left in peace & started consolidating. It was nervous work strafing the [German] bombers as at times they were only about 50 yards from ours.'[104] Nervous work, too, for the infantry, as Lieutenant Turnbull recalled: 'For some unknown reason, our artillery started shelling us with whizz-bangs.'[105] He lit a red flare, signalling to an artillery-spotting aircraft, which flew off and alerted the batteries. The barrage was stopped. 'Of course,' wrote Turnbull, 'the Boche redoubled his efforts, though we escaped without further casualties.' Generally, though, the RFC's contact patrols were a complete failure in III Corps' sector, wrote Lewis of 3rd Squadron: 'No flares or any ground signals seen. Nothing whatever to report to corps.'[106]

In Mash Valley the 102nd's leading 20th and 23rd Northumberland Fusiliers were almost annihilated by machine-gun crossfire from Ovillers and La Boisselle.[107] Here the width of no-man's-land varied greatly, at the extremes 100–800 yards wide but mostly 500–750 yards. Fantastic as the Y-Sap mine blast appeared, it — along with two smaller ones at the Glory Hole — utterly failed to shatter resistance close to La Boisselle, or even provide piles of spoil high enough to reduce observation and enfilade from its ruins. Barely any of the 23rd reached the crater after starting off at 7.35 a.m. to avoid falling debris from the explosion. But some, along with disorganised groups of the neighbouring 20th, which began at 7.30 a.m. and had the widest stretch of open ground to cross, breached the German trenches north of La Boisselle. Fewer made it a hundred or so yards behind its piles: 'It was seen later from the position of the dead that some [of the 20th and 23rd] had crossed the [German] front trench and moved on to the second before they were shot down, and that flanking parties had tried in vain to force an entrance to La Boisselle.'[108]

One officer amazingly walked unseen up the Albert–Bapaume road, into La Boisselle, collected some souvenirs from a German dugout and returned them to the headquarters of 102nd Brigade, which was commanded by Brigadier-General Trevor Ternan.[109] Further back, Lieutenant James Hately recalled how the 25th Northumberland Fusiliers, coming on behind the 23rd, formed up in the western lee of Usna Hill, swapping 'cheer'o's and 'good luck's before moving up the slope:[110] 'I could see the men stumble and fall headlong or see others go up in the air, but still the remainder went steadily forward, till I lost them when they crested the hill.'[111] Once over the crest, the exposed 25th, like the 103rd's three other battalions, was briskly destroyed by the overworked Ovillers and La Boisselle machine-gunners: 'Heavy fire from machine guns and rifles was opened on [the] battalion from the moment the assembly trenches were left also a considerable artillery barrage. ... The forward movement was maintained until only a few scattered soldiers were left standing,' wrote 25th Northumberland Fusiliers' war diarist in his matter-of-fact after-battle report.[112]

A horrified *Vizefeldwebel* Laasch saw clusters of British soldiers behind his trench at the northeast end of La Boisselle, most likely some of the very few 20th or 23rd Northumberland Fusiliers who made it that far:

We fired, partly standing upright, into the Englishmen at close
range. Did the excitement race through my veins or was our

success still not damning enough for me? I staggered around between the groups and shouted: 'Blast it, fire at them, fire at them!' until an annoyed *Landwehrmann* yelled at me while loading: 'By thunder Herr *Feldwebel*, I am firing!' I fired there with him and it grew quieter. How we knocked them over like hares![113]

Laasch ventured gingerly down a communication trench towards the front line. Suddenly he was confronted by three British soldiers: 'I threw my hand grenade in front of their feet and jumped back as fast as lightning.' Later he found the grenade had killed a British officer with red hair and freckles.

Thirty-fourth Division's attack was effectively over by 10 a.m., although localised fighting would continue for the rest of the day. The division's only meaningful gains were atop Fricourt Spur, around Scots Redoubt and Round Wood, where it was in contact with XV Corps, and a besieged footing around and slightly beyond Lochnagar crater. None of the 34th's battalions came close to achieving even their first objectives, even though a few isolated groups advanced good distances beyond the German front line. 'It was no fault of theirs that they did not reach their allotted objective,' said Brigadier-General Robert Gore, commander of the 101st.[114] The advances directly along Mash and Sausage Valleys were predictable failures. The wounded and unscathed alike sheltered in no-man's-land among the dead, under the blazing sun. Their chance to slip back unseen to the British front line — itself jammed with bloodied, broken men — would only come in the half light of dusk or under the cover of night. Until then they risked adding to what was an already swollen casualty roll: 'Exposure of the head meant certain death. None of our men were visible but in all directions came pitiful groans and cries of pain,' said one officer stranded in the Mash Valley no-man's-land.[115]

Major-General Edward Ingouville-Williams, commander of the 34th, had gone forward to watch the attack begin. Most likely he saw the 103rd deploy and move over the Tara–Usna ridge where it was 'met by machine gun and rifle fire.'[116] 'Inky Bill,' as Ingouville-Williams was known, returned to his headquarters at 8.30 a.m. Thereafter the 34th's battle log is studded with increasingly disturbing reports of heavy losses and an impassable no-man's-land: carrying parties could not lug supplies forward to the most advanced infantry.[117] 'I reported, very bluntly I'm afraid, to General [Ingouville-]Williams that no objectives had been gained and the left wing (102nd Brigade) had suffered heavily,' said Captain David James, 34th Trench Mortar Battery.[118] Ingouville-Williams had no reserves, and telegraphed Pulteney late in the morning asking for 19th (Western) Division to help clear the area south of La Boisselle and allow the attack to proceed.[119] Ninth Welsh was placed at his disposal, but it was insufficient for the job and not employed.[120]

The 34th's bill: 6380 casualties, including 2480 dead, 3587 wounded and 313 prisoners or missing. Of the attacking battalions of 101st and 102nd Brigades, not one suffered fewer than 472 casualties. The undeniable conclusion is that the 34th had practically ceased to exist as an effective fighting formation by 8.30 a.m., probably much earlier. The Tyneside-recruited 102nd and 103rd were hit particularly hard. Their 20th, 23rd and 24th Northumberland Fusiliers losing 661, 640 and 630 officers and men respectively. Losses in the 103rd were particularly disturbing as its four battalions were shredded by bullet and shell on the exposed slopes of Tara and Usna Hills, well behind the British front-line trenches from which the attack began. Seven battalion commanders were casualties, five of them dead and two wounded.[121] Brigadier-General Neville Cameron, commander of 103rd Brigade, was shot in the stomach at about 7.50 a.m. and hauled back to safety. 'He smiled in that nice way of his, told me to carry on, he'd be alright,' said Captain James. Cameron lived.

Casualty figures for the German units directly opposite the 34th cannot yet be determined with precision. For the period 23 June–3 July, RIR110 recorded 1089 casualties, including 193 dead, 397 wounded and 499 missing.[122] Among these were a total of 195 fatalities for the periods 23–30 June and 2–3 July.[123] The regiment's casualty list for 1 July must therefore be no more than 894, and is almost certainly lower if non-fatal casualties on those other days are considered.[124] This figure includes 235 soldiers who are confirmed 1 July deaths, the 659 others who were wounded, declared missing or taken prisoner.[125] IR23 recorded just nine fatalities among its two companies attached to RIR110.[126] Casualties in Landwehr Brigade Replacement Battalion 55, which was grouped around Contalmaison, were few, but precise figures are unavailable. Altogether the 28th suffered about 903 casualties against 34th Division's 6380, this conservative ratio equating to at least one German casualty for every 7.1 British and emphasising the lopsided nature of the battle.

As far as 28th Reserve Division commander Hahn was concerned, the initial fighting around Mash and Sausage Valleys and La Boisselle went rather more than less to plan. First news of the British attack had reached his headquarters at about 8 a.m.[127] Hahn's artillery in this part of the battlefield had survived the bombardment in sufficient numbers to lay down defensive fire in support of the infantry positions to block enemy reinforcements coming forward.[128] Overall, north of Fricourt Spur, the enemy had essentially been brought to a standstill from the outset, with heavy casualties inflicted. Any incursions were limited — such as astride the Lochnagar mine crater, or beyond Scots Redoubt and briefly towards Contalmaison. Company and battalion commanders were already organising the fightback with long-standing and well-rehearsed counterattack tactics. Wagon-loads of ammunition were already being brought forward to resupply the infantry.[129] Available evidence suggests Hahn left his subordinate commanders to get on with the job, and that was because his focus and worries were already much further south, between Fricourt Spur and Mametz where the British XV and XIII Corps had made significant and critical inroads against his divisional sector.[130]

'I COULD SEE nothing of what was going on in front. ... Time and again we were covered with soil and debris thrown up by the [German] shells,' wrote Major Jack, 2nd Scottish Rifles, of the assembly trenches before Ovillers where 8th Division was about to begin its attack:[131]

> The strain on the waiting men was very great, so I took to joking about the dirt scattered over my well-cut uniform, while dusting it off with a handkerchief. We knew at 7.30 that the assault had started through hearing the murderous rattle of German machine guns, served without a break, notwithstanding our intense bombardment which had been expected to silence them.

Lieutenant Alfred Bundy, 2nd Middlesex, said the moments before Zero were an 'interminable period of terrible apprehension.'[132] Captain Alan Hanbury-Sparrow, 2nd Royal Berkshires, remembered the smoke of shellfire and that a 'reddish dust was over everything. There was a mist, too, and hardly anything was visible.'[133]

North of the Albert–Bapaume road, 8th Division committed all three of its brigades to the attack across the camber of Ovillers Spur, with its left and right flanks dipping into Nab and Mash Valleys respectively. It would come up against machine-gun fire from Leipzig, Nordwerk and Mouquet Farm Redoubts to the north, Ovillers centrally and La Boisselle to the south. Leipzig Redoubt and La Boisselle were outside the 8th's sector. For these reasons it seemed to the divisional commander, Major-General Havelock Hudson — who was 'quick enough to see what was going to go wrong' but lacked the personality to challenge his superiors[134] — that the 8th had little chance of success unless neighbouring divisions advanced a little ahead of his own.[135] Hudson's request to postpone the 8th's Zero hour was rejected by Fourth Army,[136] which meant his division was condemned to Pulteney's generally guileless attack scheme.

All three of the 8th's brigades would cross a steadily rising no-man's-land that was 200–800 yards wide, but mostly 200–400 yards. In theory their objectives, including Ovillers, ran 2500–3500 yards behind the German line before finishing around Pozières on the main ridgeline. In reality, the survivors of the 8th's heavily casualty-depleted battalions who made it across no-man's-land were ejected within hours. Some lingered until mid-afternoon. By day's end all that remained of the 8th's limited gains were numerous bloody khaki bundles scattered between the scarlet poppies and grass of no-man's-land, and in and around the German trenches.

Eighth Division's leading battalions crept closer to the German trenches a few minutes before Zero, while the last of the intensive shellfire rained down. Their attack was to start at 7.30 a.m., each battalion on a frontage of 250–400 yards. Machine-gun fire from Ovillers, the German first and second trenches, and in enfilade from La Boisselle tore into the infantry on the bare no-man's-land. Survivors pressed forward. Within 80 yards of the German parapet the machine-gun and rifle fire rose to a crescendo, while 26th Reserve Division's intact field guns threw down a curtain of shellfire on no-man's-land and also on the British front and support lines. Casualties were predictably heavy. Survivors charged forward and soon the 'excellent' waves were gone, jumbled together in chaos: 'Companies became mixed together, making a mass of men, among which the German fire played havoc.'[137] Only isolated parties reached the German lines, and never in sufficient strength to alter the one-way course of battle.

'The attack on our part of the line was immediately recognised by the lifting back of the enemy's artillery fire,' said *Oberstleutnant* Alfred Vischer, commander of IR180.[138] 'Everyone rushed out of their deep dugouts and occupied the crater ground and trenches, if they were still recognisable and usable. Machine guns were in position and red flares demanded our artillery barrage. A raging infantry, machine gun and artillery fire brought the attack to a halt.' IR180 had about 24 machine guns across its sector sited to co-operate with one another and provide direct fire and enfilade in support of the front-line infantry.[139] Captain Hanbury-Sparrow watched the leading companies of 2nd Royal Berkshires fade into the mist, and 'as they did so, so did the first shots ring out from the other side.'[140] Later, as the mist cleared, he saw 'heaps of dead, with Germans almost standing up in their trenches, well over the top — firing and sniping at those who had taken refuge in shell holes.'

The attacks of 23rd and 25th Brigades produced depressingly similar outcomes. On the Mash Valley slopes of Ovillers Spur, few of the 23rd's 2nd Middlesex* and 2nd Devons,† which both advanced in linear-wave formations and began deploying at 7.23 a.m.,[141] beat the crossfire odds after clearing the parapet and creeping through lanes cut in the wire: 'The enemy opened with a terrific machine gun fire from the front and both flanks which mowed down our troops,' wrote 2nd Devons' war diarist in an entry that applied equally to 2nd Middlesex.[142] Some miraculously made it to the German line just south of Ovillers, fewer of them a couple of hundred yards beyond, before being pushed back, killed or captured.[143] A bit to the north, as Ovillers Spur fades into Nab Valley, the 25th's 2nd Royal Berkshires,‡ advancing in a mix of linear waves and columns of

---

* 2nd Battalion Duke of Cambridge's Own (Middlesex Regiment). *Official History* states 623 casualties. SDGW notes 265 deaths.

† 2nd Battalion Devonshire Regiment. Battalion war diary states 431 casualties (50 k, 200 w and 181 m). SDGW notes 172 deaths.

‡ 2nd Battalion Princess Charlotte of Wales's (Royal Berkshire Regiment). *Official History* states 374 casualties. SDGW notes 158 deaths.

sections from 7.30 a.m., and 2nd Lincolns,* which began deploying at 7.25 a.m. and likely used a similar attack structure,[144] met a storm of machine-gun fire from the front and in enfilade.[145] 'The machine guns were in good condition and did deadly trade,' wrote *Oberleutnant-der-Reserve* Vogler in a succinct after-battle summary.[146]

Directly in front of Ovillers, 2nd Devons' left companies and those on 2nd Royal Berkshires' right were gunned down. Stand on the old German front line here, atop the spur behind Ovillers Military Cemetery, and you can still find scores of 1916 Spandau bullet casings oxidised to green. 'The enemy had exceptionally high losses,' said *Oberstleutnant* Vischer.[147]

A jot further north some 2nd Lincolns worked their way into the wrecked German trenches at about 7.50 a.m. by short rushes from one shell crater to the next.[148] In places they progressed a little further, but these men were soon forced back. Follow-up battalions — the 23rd's 2nd West Yorkshires,[†] likely in linear waves, and the 25th's 1st Royal Irish Rifles[‡] in columns of platoons[149] — suffered in the German defensive shellfire, and then in the machine-gun fire sweeping no-man's-land. Just 10 men of 1st Royal Irish Rifles managed to cross.[150] The 2nd West Yorkshires later estimated it suffered 250 casualties behind the British front line: just shy of half its casualties for the day.[151] One of that battalion's companies lost 146 of the 169 men who went into action behind 2nd Middlesex.[152] Shortly after 9 a.m. both brigades' toeholds in the German lines collapsed under concentric bomb and bayonet counterattacks. With heavy casualties, limited ammunition and essentially no prospects of being reinforced, it was only a matter of time before those few men in the German trenches were forced back into no-man's-land to skulk in crowded shell holes.

'I struggled on and seemed to be quite alone, when I was bowled over and smothered by debris from the mine,' remembered Private Frank Lobel, 2nd Middlesex,[153] more likely referring to a large shell burst as he was too far away to be hit by mine debris. 'I tried to find some comrades,

---

* 2nd Battalion Lincolnshire Regiment. Battalion war diary notes 463 casualties (32 k, 311 w and 120 m). SDGW notes 125 deaths.

† 2nd Battalion Prince of Wales's Own (West Yorkshire Regiment). *Official History* states 429 casualties. SDGW notes 102 deaths.

‡ 1st Battalion Royal Irish Rifles. *Official History* states 446 casualties. SDGW notes 58 deaths.

but could not do so. ... To this day I can only think of it [1 July] in sorrow.' Lieutenant Bundy wrote of the din, acrid fumes and smoke and dust that limited visibility: 'Suddenly an appalling rifle and machine-gun fire opened against us and my men commenced to fall. I shouted "Down!" but most of those who were still not hit had already taken what cover they could.'[154] After a series of dashes, Bundy was back within an ace of the British parapet. He watched helplessly as 'sparks flew from the wire continuously as it was struck by bullets.'[155] Eventually the fusillade abated and he scrambled into the trench. Major Henry Savile, 2nd Middlesex, said mutually supporting enfilade from Ovillers and La Boisselle caused most of the Mash Valley casualties: 'Any sign of movement in No Man's Land was immediately met with a burst of fire.'[156] Those who made it across were reorganised in some 300 yards of the German front line, and this was 'held for two hours until their numbers very greatly reduced they were driven out by German counter attacks from both flanks.'[157] Meantime, Major Jack readied his company of 2nd Scottish Rifles* to reinforce Savile's men in the German line: 'I stepped back several paces to take a running jump on the parapet, sound my hunting horn and wave my waiting men on.' Just then a message cancelling the attack arrived: 'What a relief to be rid of such a grim responsibility.'[158]

Vizefeldwebel Laasch, who was commissioned after the Somme, was one of the La Boisselle machine-gunners firing at the 2nd Devons and 2nd Middlesex in Mash Valley, among them Lobel, Bundy and Savile: 'Tightly packed lines poured out of the English trenches, strode across the wide foreground [of Mash Valley] and ended up in the heavy defensive fire of Regiment 180. I also fired one belt after another into the flank of the ever-advancing English battalions with our machine gun. Never in the war have I experienced a more devastating effect of our fire: the fallen were tightly packed in the entire hollow up to Ovillers!'[159]

Twenty-fifth Brigade's break-in just north of Ovillers lasted only a couple of hours. Private Fred Perry, 2nd Lincolns, said 'few of us got to the German front line and all our team got wounded. We made our way back as well as we could, when we arrived in our trenches we had to walk over dead soldiers.'[160] About 70 of Perry's battalion made it to the German

---

* 2nd Battalion Cameronians (Scottish Rifles). SDGW notes five deaths.

trenches, where *Reservist* Gottlob Trost, IR180, saw a friend locked in a vicious punch-up with a soldier of 2nd Lincolns: 'The 180th man finally incapacitated his opponent with a stiletto knife he carried with him in the shaft of his boot. The fight was over. The Englishman was seriously wounded.'[161] Trost does not state whether the wounded soldier died or was taken into captivity. Among the other 2nd Lincolns in the German line was Lieutenant-Colonel Reginald Bastard: 'We drove off a counter attack from the German 2nd line Trench, but were bombed out when we had exhausted our own bombs and all the German ones we could find, we only retired to the shell holes in no man's land.'[162] Further attempts would have been a 'useless sacrifice of life,' and in any case brigade headquarters had already ruled against it. Bastard later made it back to the British lines and reorganised the 100-man garrison for defence: 'Captain [Robert] Leslie and myself were the only two not hit of the officers, I had 3 bullet holes through my clothes and Leslie 2.'[163]

In Nab Valley, 70th Brigade's attack in successive linear waves was a bloody disaster that included yet another short-lived breach of the German line.[164] Thirty-second Division's quick gains at Leipzig Redoubt, about 1000 yards northwest, briefly occupied the attention of machine-gunners in Nordwerk Redoubt. It was all that remnants of 8th King's Own Yorkshire Light Infantry's (KOYLI)* and 8th York & Lancasters'† leading waves needed to cross the levelled German front line, having deployed at 7.27 a.m. and started their attack at 7.30 a.m.[165] Some elements of these battalions reached the German front-line system's second trench and beyond. *Schütze* Fischer had hauled his machine gun up to the parapet to meet 8th KOYLI's attack head-on: 'At a distance of only 40–50 metres [44–55 yards] I could see figures in English uniforms with sparkling bayonets.'[166] His weapon dealt 'death and destruction' to the incoming waves of men, but small parties broke in to the left and right of his position and closed in with rifle fire and grenades: 'After a short bayonet fight we retreated back into our dugout. ... The English fired a few shots into the dugout but didn't have the guts to come down. They

---

*   8th (Service) Battalion King's Own (Yorkshire Light Infantry). *Official History* states 539 casualties. SDGW notes 276 deaths.

†   8th (Service) Battalion York & Lancaster Regiment. *Official History* states 597 casualties. SDGW notes 289 deaths.

called then something like "Gom on," which probably meant "Come up!" We did not react to it.'[167]

It was somewhere near here that *Gefreiter* Karl Walz, IR180, was killed. The 25-year-old Swiss, who had volunteered to fight in the German army, wrote home not long before the battle that he had tired of trench life, but had some good news: 'We have been fitted out with new uniforms, which was really necessary. Now we look very smart again.'[168] He has no known grave.

Seventieth Brigade's always limited progress into the German lines petered out due to heavy casualties and loss of momentum in the face of increasing resistance. Support battalions were mauled by the German shellfire and machine guns, few getting across no-man's-land and through the partially cut wire. Eighth KOYLI estimated 60% of the men in its two follow-up waves became casualties before reaching the German wire.[169] Much the same bloody fate was meted out to 9th York & Lancasters* and 11th Sherwood Foresters,† which followed at 8.40 a.m. and about 8.56 a.m respectively.[170] Ninth York & Lancasters lost more than half its strength either in its assembly trenches or between there and the British front line. The battalion suffered further casualties when it actually began its attack. The killing-zone ordeal of 11th Sherwood Foresters was noted by brigade headquarters: 'It was impossible to stand at all in No Man's Land and the Battalion crawled forward on hands and knees to the help of the Battalions in front.'[171] Few got there.

Corporal Don Murray, 8th KOYLI, recalled his passage across no-man's-land: 'It seemed to me, eventually, I was the only man left. I couldn't see anybody at all. All I could see were men lying dead, men screaming, men on the barbed wire with their bowels hanging down, shrieking, and I thought, "What can I do?" I was alone in a hell of fire and smoke and stink.'[172] Sergeant William Cole, 11th Sherwood Foresters, made it about 50 yards into no-man's-land: 'I had a shock like a thousand volts of electricity going through my shoulder and out at the top of my right arm, and I knew I was finished for a bit, but not done.'[173]

---

* 9th (Service) Battalion York & Lancaster Regiment. *Official History* states 423 casualties. SDGW notes 163 deaths.

† 11th (Service) Battalion Sherwood Foresters (Nottinghamshire and Derbyshire Regiment). *Official History* states 437 casualties. SDGW notes 119 deaths.

By now the Nordwerk machine-gunners had returned their focus to Nab Valley. Their fire sweeping over the northern slope of Ovillers Spur and the valley bottom was so intense that all communication between the British assembly trenches and 70th Brigade's soldiers in the German lines was lost. *Oberstleutnant* Vischer saw 150–200 British soldiers 'mowed down' on the Nab Valley–Thiepval road. In no time the 70th's footing was besieged by machine-gun and rifle fire, while hastily organised German bombing parties forced its men back with co-ordinated counterattacks closing from multiple directions. It was here, in Nab Valley, that *Vizefeldwebel* Albert Hauff, IR180, led one such group of bombers forward, as one of his men later recalled:

> Now it was time to drive the enemy out. We went in over piles of corpses and used hand grenades to clean up the position. Those Englishmen who weren't dead or wounded crept back into the shell holes [of no-man's-land]. Any sign of resistance from them was showered with grenades. ... Immediately we began to dig out collapsed shelters and make the trench defensible again. Some reinforcements came forward.[174]

Hauff was decorated for his bravery, but was killed in September 1916. Meanwhile, by 3 p.m. the 70th's survivors had pulled back into the Nab Valley no-man's-land. 'I brought my machine gun back into position and shot at the fleeing English,' wrote *Schütze* Fischer.[175]

'Well, Martin, we will have lunch in the German trenches,' said Lieutenant Billy Goodwin, 8th York & Lancasters.[176] The 23-year-old, Tralee-born Corpus Christi College graduate was liked by subordinates because he 'always looked after them before he looked after himself,' said Private Patrick Martin, same battalion. Before the war Goodwin had enjoyed golf, tennis, rugby and racing around leafy country lanes on his motorcycle. But in Nab Valley on the warm morning of 1 July those days came to an abrupt end, as Corporal George Booth, 8th York & Lancasters, explained: 'He advanced towards the German lines — was shot and fell on the barbed wire (German). ... He seemed quite fearless in the attack. I went over the top at the same time, was slightly wounded and lay in the open for about 12 hours. Lt. Goodwin was still on the wire when I got away.'[177] Goodwin's body was found and he is today buried at Blighty Valley Cemetery, Authuille Wood, where 227 of the 491 identified burials are for 1 July. *Schütze* Fischer remembered another horribly wounded British soldier snared in the entanglement: 'He shot at me a few times but the bullets just missed my head.'[178] Fischer does not state this soldier's fate, but he was likely shot.

Attempts to renew 8th Division's attack amounted to nothing. Shortly after 9 a.m., Brigadier-Generals Harry Tuson of the 23rd and John Pollard of the 25th asked divisional headquarters to bring the barrage back to the German reserve trench line and Ovillers as a defensive measure:[179] 'It could not well be turned on to the front system, which the Germans had manned again at most places, as our men were lying close up to it, even where they were not thought to be in it.'[180] Divisional commander Hudson sanctioned a half-hour shoot, and told Tuson and Pollard to organise a fresh attack. They and the 70th's Brigadier-General Herbert Gordon said they had too few men — his portion of the British front line was held by fewer than 100 men as well as the 15th Field Company, RE — given that the German trenches were now fully manned, also noting a fresh bombardment would likely hit British infantry sheltering nearby in no-man's-land.[181] This was relayed to III Corps' Montigny headquarters at 12.15 p.m.[182] Pulteney, aware the 23rd and 25th were 'hung up', but believing more favourably that the 70th was 'holding' the German front line,[183] decided to rejuvenate the attack north of Ovillers at 5 p.m., prefaced with 30 minutes' shellfire. The 70th would continue its advance in conjunction with 19th (Western) Division's 56th Brigade closer to Ovillers.[184] The decisive factor in Pulteney's thinking was the 70th's presence in the German lines that afternoon, which led him to believe that regrouping and applying fresh troops would produce results.

It is not clear whether Hudson challenged Pulteney's decision on the basis of his brigadiers' refusal, but it seems improbable. Hudson lacked the 'personality to be insubordinate & refuse' pressure from higher office.[185] Events rendered the matter moot: the 70th's eviction forced Pulteney to cancel the planned attack. The field companies of 1st and 2nd Home Counties (Territorial Force), RE, were sent up to help hold the British front line, and were later put to work bringing in wounded. 'Wiser counsels,' wrote the official historian somewhat cryptically of Pulteney's fruitless attempts to renew the attack, had 'prevailed.'[186]

Eighth Division ran up 5121 casualties, including 1927 dead, 3095 wounded, 86 missing and 13 prisoners.[187] 'The experience of this day had been bitter, and its losses terrible,' wrote the division's historians.[188] Ten of its 12 infantry battalions lost more than 374 men each, with the six that led the attack off suffering an average of 505 men killed, wounded and missing.[189] *Schütze* Fischer, the machine-gunner, later said British dead lay thick in no-man's-land outside Authuille Wood: 'Not only were they laying [sic] side by side but also one on top of the other.'[190] Several battalions lost all their officers, while seven battalion commanders became casualties — two of them killed, two died of wounds and three more wounded.[191] Second Middlesex was worst hit, with 623 (92.6%) of the 673 officers and men who went into battle becoming casualties. Only 50 turned up at roll call the next day. Its commander, Lieutenant-Colonel Edwin Sandys, was wounded and evacuated to England. Two months later the 40-year-old shot himself dead: 'I have come to London today to take my life. I have never had a moment's peace since July 1.'[192]

IR180's casualties totalled 280, or about 10% of its nominal strength, including 83 dead, 184 wounded and 13 missing.[193] For every one German casualty there were about 18 British, this ratio reflecting IR180's total dominance across its battle sector: 'The losses of the enemy were atrociously heavy. Fifteen hundred to 2000 corpses were mown down in entire rows lying there in the evening in front of the sector of the Württemberg regiment. On the other hand, the losses of the regiment were fortunately small,' wrote one German historian.[194]

'I drove like the wind,' wrote *Fahrer* Otto Maute, IR180, of his evening journey towards the front line with an ammunition-laden wagon and under shellfire.[195] He was on the Albert–Bapaume road and showered by shrapnel fragments the 'size of your fist.' Maute pondered the consequences of being wounded: 'What would it be like to receive a direct hit from a ship's thirty-centimetre gun?' He dumped the ammunition in a forward collection zone and raced back to Warlencourt, where the walking wounded were already filtering back with predictably alarmist stories: 'Our regiment had heavy losses in the attack, but [on Thiepval Spur, the neighbouring] Regt. 99 [RIR99] came off worse, they say fifty per cent.' He wrote to his family of the devastation: burning and smashed villages, and aircraft shot out of the sky. 'At home you simply have no idea of what war is like.'

From Soden's viewpoint, the fighting between Leipzig Redoubt and Ovillers paled in comparison with the danger caused by 36th (Ulster) Division's break-in above Thiepval. His attention rightly lay on that latter part of the battlefield, which was the most tactically important feature within the 26th's entire defensive scheme. Soden's thinking was based on battle reports that showed IR180 had quickly gained control of its sector, with any break-ins either already ejected or in the process of being evicted. The few short-lived enemy incursions into IR180's territory were never going to unravel Soden's southern-most regimental position, let alone test Pozières Ridge further back. Soden knew his Nab Valley–Ovillers defence-in-depth scheme had been battered by shellfire, but crucially that mutually supporting redoubts, strongpoints and trench systems remained functional and defensible. Most of IR180's infantry and machine-gunners had survived the bombardment and responded quickly to the lifting of the British barrage. Moreover, 26th's artillery provided effective defensive fire as required. 'The enemy's plan of attack was thwarted,' wrote Soden in a crisp summary of the fighting around Ovillers, also noting the artillery's 'outstanding achievements' in helping secure the victory.[196]

SUCH INSIGHTS WERE lost on Pulteney who, in the 1930s, coughed up a facile explanation. 'The main thing overlooked was the fact of the trenches being obliterated giving no cover for the attackers when reached, no one realised the depth of the German "Dug Outs", our own Dug outs were miserable attempts, the ground was absolutely strewn with our own 8-inch dud shells.'[197] Fair enough, there were too many dud shells. But it was risible to state that 'the main thing' behind III Corps' failure was obliterated German trenches, as well as the unrealised depth of the German dugouts. Pulteney's corps had known of the deep dugouts since early June. And what had he expected from the seven-day bombardment — scores of dead German soldiers and pristine trenches awaiting new tenants? He was also well aware of the functional German defence-in-depth scheme, the failure of his counter-battery fire, faulty intelligence and the numerous unsuppressed machine guns. These factors were all addressed in the British *Official History*, which does not directly apportion blame. 'I heartily congratulate you on the work, I can find nothing to criticise,' a grateful Pulteney enthused to the official historian after critiquing a draft copy.[198] It was not much of an admission, but it was the closest Pulteney came to conceding that he had turned up for battle unprepared and been wholly outclassed by Soden and Hahn before Ovillers and La Boisselle.

Proof lay in the butcher's bill. Pulteney's III Corps racked up 11,501 casualties.[199] This included 4407 killed, 6682 wounded, 380 missing and 32 prisoners. By contrast, Soden's and Hahn's regiments opposing 8th and 34th Divisions suffered at least a combined 1183 casualties, including 327 dead and 856 others wounded and missing.[200] That equated to about one German casualty for every 9.7 British, a grim ratio by anyone's maths.

Pulteney tried to gloss over the tragedy at the time by feting the 34th's survivors with tributes.[201] As Lieutenant-Colonel Somerset bitterly told it, four days after battle Pulteney 'inspected the remnant of the 101st Brigade & complimented them on their bravery & tenacity.'[202] Lieutenant-Colonel Shakespear continued:

> He [Pulteney] specially referred to valuable service that they had performed in guarding the left flank of the 21st Division, which, had our small isolated detachments not held firmly on to the positions they had seized, might have been seriously endangered, and in fact the whole attack would have been in jeopardy, and all our line down to the French might have been rolled up.[203]

Pulteney was dealing exaggeration and lies. The 21st's flank was not exposed to anything like the kind of danger Pulteney suggested, and XV and XIII Corps' gains were never going to be rolled by a German counterattack from III Corps' sector. Hahn and Soden did not have the resources for such a stroke, and never considered it.[204] But in Pulteney's mind pretty much anything could be dressed as its own opposite; his after-battle pep talk was all about hawking black as its own inverse and the outright defeat his corps had just suffered as nothing less than an aspect of victory.

Survivors knew the truth. In 8th KOYLI, for instance, just 25 of its 685 officers and men who went into battle turned up at the quartermaster's depot afterwards. As Corporal Murray recalled, 'The quartermaster was an acting captain, and he said "Is the battalion on the march back?" A lance corporal was in charge, and he said, "They're here."'[205] The rest were dead, wounded, missing or stragglers yet to turn up. Walk over the fields and among the headstones at Commonwealth War Graves Commission cemeteries around Ovillers and La Boisselle and the dead are still there, still mute witnesses to Pulteney's incompetence.

CHAPTER 8

Fluttering for Fricourt

XV Corps, the Fricourt–Mametz salient and a complex attack

'The enemy's superiority was great, but the English
wasted an enormous amount of large and small-
calibre ammunition, and one must wonder why greater
devastation wasn't caused by such superior firepower.'[1]
— *Feldwebel* Robert Hauschild, Reserve Infantry Regiment 111

JOURNALIST PHILIP GIBBS' typewriter rattled steadily towards the midnight hour as he belted out one paragraph after another, in utter exhaustion of body and brain.[2] At dawn that morning, 1 July, the scribe and other pressmen were motored to an observation post on a hillock near Albert that afforded sweeping views of the Thiepval–Morval ridge, which was where the first day of the Somme would be fought out. At first mist and smoke shrouded the ground, and Gibbs said he 'stood like a blind man, only listening.'[3] The veil broke; the gilded statue of the Virgin Mary and infant Jesus atop Albert's basilica leaned at a near-horizontal angle and sparkled in the sun. It had hung that way since being hit by a shell in January 1915. British soldiers believed that when the statue fell the war would end. It eventually toppled in April 1918, with the Armistice following after much more fighting in November 1918. All that, though, was in the future; for the moment Gibbs watched as aeroplanes darted across the azure sky, artillery shells slamming into the German lines.[4] Nobody spoke much. Gibbs confessed to feeling an 'unreal sense of safety.'[5] The seasoned hack planned to get an overview of the battle from afar and then move forward to gather colour from the soldiers of XV Corps. By day's end he knew Mametz and Montauban were captured, and Fricourt threatened.[6] He also knew his coverage was partial at best; battlefield visibility had been limited and reports from the front were incomplete.[7] His jaunty copy conveyed events seen from a distance and alleged British-soldier interviews:

'They went across toppingly,' said a wounded boy of the West Yorkshires, who was in the first attack on Fricourt. 'The fellows were glorious,' said another young officer who could hardly speak for the pain in his left shoulder, where a piece of shell struck him down in Mametz Wood. 'Wonderful chaps!' said a lieutenant of the Manchesters. 'They went cheering through machine-gun fire as though it were just the splashing of rain.'[8]

'Toppingly,' 'glorious,' 'wonderful' and 'cheering'. Rot. Who spoke like that? Gibbs' colour looked false because it probably was; the propagandist had finally vanquished the pressman. As Gibbs later confessed, he and other uniformed wordsmiths were not only 'subject to the general rules of censorship' at the time, but shockingly 'were in agreement' with them.[9]

Fifteenth Corps faced a German-held salient that skirted the fortified villages of Fricourt and Mametz. It was split by the southwest-running Willow Stream. Both villages were nestled among the tangle of spurs either side of the stream valley in the sleepy southern foothills of the Thiepval–Morval ridge. Fricourt, to the north, was within a few hundred yards of the German front line, with Fricourt Wood immediately behind. To the south, about 1000 yards further up the valley, Mametz lay exposed on the western tip of the Mametz–Montauban ridge and just behind the German front line in the Mametz–Carnoy valley. The curve of the salient meant approach routes to Mametz and Fricourt were an awkward mix of up-hill-and-down-dale, studded with a handful of increasingly shot-through copses. The battle for this bulge and the villages it contained would be fought out on the main ridge's gentle southern fells rather than its highest ground.

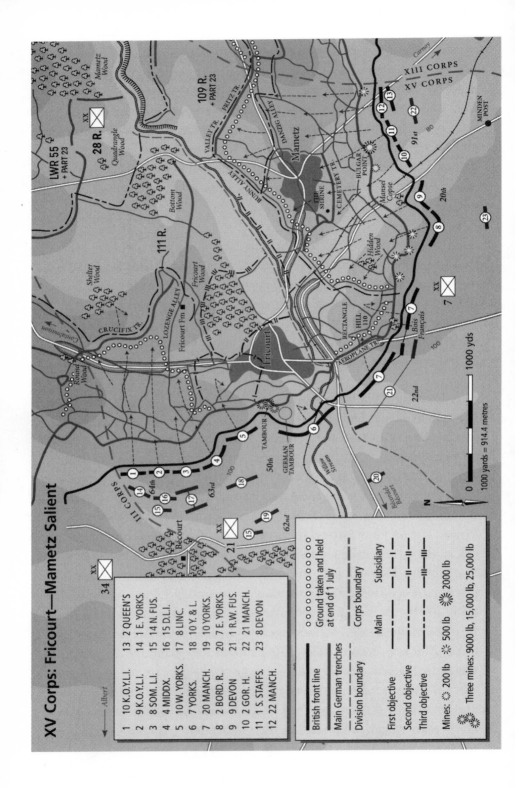

XV Corps: Fricourt—Mametz Salient

← Albert

1	10 K.O.Y.L.I.	13 2 QUEEN'S
2	9 K.O.Y.L.I.	14 1 E. YORKS.
3	8 SOM. L.I.	15 14 N. FUS.
4	4 MIDDX.	16 15 D.L.I.
5	10 W. YORKS.	17 8 LINC.
6	7 YORKS.	18 10 Y. & L.
7	20 MANCH.	19 10 YORKS.
8	2 BORD. R.	20 7 E. YORKS.
9	9 DEVON	21 1 R.W. FUS.
10	2 GOR. H.	22 21 MANCH.
11	1 S. STAFFS.	23 8 DEVON
12	22 MANCH.	

British front line

Main German trenches

Division boundary

○○○○○○○○○ Ground taken and held at end of 1 July

‒ ‒ ‒ Corps boundary

	Main	Subsidiary
First objective	—·—	— I —
Second objective	—··—	— II —
Third objective	—···—	— III —

Mines: ☀ 200 lb ☀ 500 lb ☀ 2000 lb

☀ Three mines: 9000 lb, 15,000 lb, 25,000 lb

0   1000 yards = 914.4 metres

1000 yds

N

XIII CORPS
XV CORPS

MINDEN POST

Drive northeast along the road from Bécordel-Bécourt towards Fricourt and soon enough the latter's rooftops and church spire appear over the lush paddocks. The village sits in the cleft formed by two low-lying rises. Off to the front left are the gentle inclines of Fricourt Spur, with the Albert–Bapaume road some distance beyond and out of sight. To the front right is the high ground of Hill 110, topped with a shock of trees that is Bois Français and looks like an ill-fitted toupee, with Mametz hidden beyond. Fricourt stands mute guard at the mouth of Willow Stream valley, which provides access to a string of other villages and woods that ultimately lead to High Wood and Longueval more than three miles away on the main ridge. Whichever side held the high ground around Fricourt overlooked and controlled the village; for the British, this would potentially open the way to subsequent German defences, and then, with time, planning and sufficient infantry and artillery resources, the way to Bapaume and Arras beyond.

The German 28th Reserve Division's defences here differed from those of 26th Reserve Division further north. *Generalleutnant* Ferdinand von Hahn's 28th enjoyed none of the mutually supporting spurs that characterised the 26th's positions and were ideally suited to a co-ordinated defence-in-depth scheme.[10] More worryingly, the re-engineering of defences in this area had not been driven forward with anywhere near the same urgency as the 26th's.[11] Hahn's men were less than pleased at having only just inherited these under-developed positions from *Generalleutnant* Martin Châles de Beaulieu's 12th Infantry Division, and had no time for meaningful improvements before Fourth Army's seven-day bombardment began. The 28th's positions, particularly the deep dugouts to protect soldiers from shellfire, were insufficient, largely confined to the front-line system and crammed with soldiers.[12]

The ruins of Fricourt and Mametz were nevertheless converted into machine-gun fortresses to bolster the front-line system. Between 1000 and 2000 yards back, the first intermediate line supported the forward battle zone, and blocked advances up the Willow Stream and the Mametz–Carnoy valley. This line took in a handful of woods and Fricourt Farm, all of which held or could hold machine-gun strongpoints. Roughly 1000 yards further on, the fragmented second intermediate position was sited to seal off any breach of the first two. The striking omission in the 28th's defences was a network of carefully sited redoubts and strongpoints with anything like the firepower that would wreak so much carnage further north between La Boisselle and Gommecourt.

The job of busting this defensive network fell to 55-year-old details man Lieutenant-General Sir Henry Horne.[13] Before the war Horne had served in India and South Africa, where he burned Afrikaaner farms in a failed attempt to quell resistance.[14] His previously non-descript career bloomed in 1914–16. Being a Haig protégé helped, as did the fact that both men were devoutly religious. Horne sometimes went to church twice on a Sunday. But his rise to corps command in 1916 had more to do with Haig's and Fourth Army commander General Sir Henry Rawlinson's appreciation of his scientific, open-minded approach to warfare and a 'meticulous and indefatigable personal attention to details of organisation and execution.'[15] Colleagues thought Horne courteous, charming, modest, honest and unpretentious,[16] but Afrikaaner families probably still saw him as a war criminal. While artilleryman Horne was said to be sociable and even humorous among friends, outsiders thought him sparing with words.[17] He possessed a 'wise, kindly look, with a suspicion of a smile coming through his seriousness.'[18] He liked horse-riding, hunting and fishing, found coarse language distasteful and later hypocritically raged against German scorched-earth tactics.[19] Horne had a 'spare, almost gaunt, figure, his sharp quasi-aquiline features were the very personification of dynamic energy.'[20] There were many shades of grey to Horne's nimble, ruthless mind.

Horne was quick to spy opportunity, open to taking calculated risks and prone to impatience. This last characteristic can be seen in Horne's sacking of Major-Generals Thomas Pilcher, 17th (Northern) Division, and Ivor Philipps, 38th (Welsh) Division, in early July 1916 after they failed to produce results to his satisfaction.[21] He said Pilcher could not get the 17th to 'advance quickly,'[22] while he thought politically appointed Philipps ignorant and incompetent.[23] Horne's eye for opportunity and measured risk-taking was all about securing operational success based on an objective assessment of facts, which was helped by his temperament being 'always under complete control.'[24] This would be seen in his plans to tackle the Fricourt–Mametz salient, and was present still in September 1918 when he approved Lieutenant-General Sir Arthur Currie's daring and ultimately successful scheme to break through Canal du Nord.[25] 'I don't believe I ought to let them do it,' he said of the Canadian Corps,[26] but agreed after balancing potential risks against rewards.[27] Within Horne's results-driven character there lurked a calculating, dispassionate opportunist with an eye to securing battlefield victory.

Horne's battle plans wisely treated Fricourt village and wood as significant obstacles to a frontal attack. His final orders proposed a three-phase flanking manoeuvre to envelop them and render them untenable by seizing the high ground on either side.[28] From a total corps of 76,671 officers and men, an estimated 18,000 infantry, along with assorted engineers and pioneers, would be directly involved in the attack.[29] The first phase of Horne's plan would see 21st Division take Fricourt Spur, while 7th Division would seize Hill 110 and Mametz. They would then each form defensive flanks facing Willow Stream valley. In the second phase, the divisions would push on to more distant objectives, further isolating Fricourt village and wood. These would be captured in a third phase carried out by 50th Brigade of 17th (Northern) Division, which was otherwise in corps reserve. On paper, Horne's plan appeared intelligent, conformed to the difficult ground, bypassed the strongest German defences and gave his infantry a fighting chance at producing results.

Even so, valid concerns lingered around the effect that unsilenced German machine-gunners in Fricourt would have on the attack by 21st Division northwest and north of its ruins. Concerns centred on whether 10th West Yorkshires*, of 50th Brigade, would be caught in machine-gun enfilade, wrote Temporary Lieutenant-Colonel Robert Collins, 17th (Northern) Division headquarters.[30] Collins and the 50th's commander, Brigadier-General William Glasgow, held significant reservations along these lines, as did Major-General Sir David 'Soarer' Campbell, the 21st's commander from May 1916.[31] As Collins explained, 'It was obvious that machine guns sheltering behind the crater area [known as The Tambour] just west of Fricourt had a glacis slope to shoot up north-west.'[32] If not destroyed these weapons could enfilade Glasgow's 10th West Yorkshires and, further north, 63rd and 64th Brigades as they crossed the exposed no-man's-land on Fricourt Spur. Collins set out his concerns further: 'Attack on the machine guns behind the craters was terribly difficult owing to the broken state of the ground. ... I was terribly worried about

---

*   10th (Service) Battalion Prince of Wales's Own (West Yorkshire Regiment). Battalion war diary states 710 casualties. SDGW notes 306 deaths.

the role allotted the 10th West Yorks; the whole of this portion of the attack [by 50th Brigade] did not sound right.'[33]

Against this backcloth, XV Corps' artillery had the threefold job of neutralising and destroying enemy infantry, artillery and defensive obstacles. It had gathered about one heavy barrel for every 58 yards of attack frontage, and one field or howitzer barrel for every 25 yards.[34] Across the corps' 5000-yard frontage there were an estimated 200 field guns and howitzers[35] and 78 British heavy guns,[36] plus an assortment of French field artillery. Because the corps had devoted fewer heavy guns to counter-battery work than others, a greater proportion of its shellfire had been used to break down German defences and resistance.[37] Several other factors meant Horne's gunners were more effective than those further to the north. First, higher ground behind the British lines afforded better observation over the German lines and allowed shellfire to be directed and assessed more accurately. Second, French and XIII Corps' gunners further south fired into the salient as a safeguard for their own operations, effectively improving Horne's artillery concentration, bolstering his counter-battery fire and destroying more enemy guns.[38] Third, in this part of the battlefield 28th Reserve Division's gunners had not shown sufficient fire restraint, meaning their batteries behind the salient had been more easily located and destroyed prior to 1 July, undermining their ability to provide defensive shellfire for front-line infantry. On the eve of battle the 28th probably had fewer than 30 guns actually firing in direct support of the Fricourt–Mametz salient,[39] and many of these were 'useless' weapons.[40]

All of this meant the 28th's artillery was unable to effectively seal off no-man's-land and stop attacking British infantry and reinforcements from moving forward, or limit any break-ins. By dawn on 1 July, XV Corps' gunners had effectively robbed the 28th of its artillery support in the salient and placed the defensive workload squarely on German infantry.

The point was not lost on Lieutenant-Colonel Henry Bicknell, 4th Middlesex: 'Another remarkable point, due either to the efficiency of our counter battery work or to the demoralization of the enemy, was the absence of a [defensive] German artillery barrage.'[41]

Fricourt–Mametz salient was primarily held by Reserve Infantry Regiments 111 (RIR111) and 109 (RIR109). RIR111 was ensconced around

Fricourt, while a large portion of RIR109 was around Mametz. Their positions were also sprinkled with soldiers from Infantry Regiment 23 (IR23), several Bavarian pioneer companies and at least three machine-gun sharp-shooter detachments. RIR111 had no fewer than 24 machine guns spread throughout its sector, but mostly in the forward and intermediate trench systems. Around Mametz there were fewer, probably about 16. All told there were about 7000 infantrymen defending the salient.[42] RIR109 and RIR111 hailed from the towns, cities and farmlands that now line Baden-Württemberg's borders with France and Switzerland. RIR109 was drawn from around the industrial cities of Freiburg and Karlsruhe, while RIR111 was recruited from the rural service centres on the northern shores of Lake Konstanz's satin waters. IR23's soldiers were from Silesia, now southern Poland, and at times must have struggled to understand the more numerous Badeners and their unfamiliar Swabian dialect.

IN THE 65 minutes before Zero, the ferocity of XV Corps' barrage escalated sharply. The intensive pummelling of the German front-line system began at 6.25 a.m., with a hurricane bombardment from Stokes mortars starting about an hour later. Gas was released at Fricourt at 7.15 a.m. for 10 minutes, and at 7.26 a.m. smoke discharges took place around the village to screen the Willow Stream–facing flanks of 21st and 7th Divisions from the prying eyes of machine-gunners in Fricourt village and wood. As one German historian, a veteran of RIR111, later wrote: 'As it began to get light everything was shrouded in mist, which grew thicker and thicker as [British] gas and smoke were released in several places. … Behind this wall [of smoke] the Englishmen prepared to attack.'[43] Two minutes before Zero several mines were blown at points along the German line. Two of the largest mines[44] — a third in the series failed to blow — were detonated just west of Fricourt to distract the enemy's attention there and form piles of debris that shielded the 21st's right flank from machine-gunners in and around the village and a cratered area of no-man's-land known as the German Tambour (Kniewerk). Private Cyril Stubbs, 10th West Yorkshires, saw the columns of earth rise skyward: 'The German trenches for a length of 300 yards were sent aloft, and the smoke and chalk dust hung around for several minutes after, for all the world like a thick, fat cloud.'[45] German accounts are dismissive of the mines' effectiveness, however, simply stating that they did not significantly damage their positions.[46]

In their deep dugouts German soldiers listened for the seven-day barrage to lift, a clear signal that the attack was starting. Some companies were forewarned thanks to a listening device at La Boisselle that intercepted British communications.[47] That information was circulated: 'We got our machine-gun ready on the top step of the dug-out and we put all our equipment on; then we waited,' said *Grenadier* Emil Kury, RIR109.[48] Morale between dugouts varied. Some soldiers expected to die and prayed;[49] others waited patiently to exact revenge for having endured so much shellfire.[50] Morale was said to be splendid among soldiers in dugouts further back.[51] One Baden soldier noted that there were many infantrymen aged more than 40 in his regiment who were more inclined to surrender and return to their families than risk death.[52] Whatever the mood, the audible lifting of the barrage at 7.30 a.m. and the muffled explosions of multiple underground mines across the salient signalled the attack.[53]

Kury, who was in the trenches at Mametz, recalled the flurry of activity at 7.30 a.m.: 'Someone shouted, "They're coming! They're coming!" We rushed up and got our machine-gun in position. We could see the English soldiers pouring out at us, thousands and thousands of them.'[54] So it began.

British infantry had to cross a no-man's-land 100–400 yards wide, but mostly about 200 yards. Nine of the 10 battalions comprising XV Corps' vanguard advanced in successive linear waves.[55] Two battalions — 9th* and 10th King's Own Yorkshire Light Infantry (KOYLI)† — adopted a column formation of successive two-platoon waves because of their narrower attack frontages, while another, 8th Somerset Light Infantry,‡ used a modified linear formation with some elements in artillery formation. Six of the 10 battalions began three to five minutes before Zero, with the remainder stepping forward at 7.30 a.m. The 7th's five leading battalions progressed either 'steadily' or at a 'walk.' The 21st's five lead battalions moved in

---

*   9th (Service) Battalion King's Own (Yorkshire Light Infantry). Battalion war diary states 497 casualties (158 k and 339 w). SDGW notes 174 deaths.

†   10th (Service) Battalion King's Own (Yorkshire Light Infantry). Battalion war diary states 502 casualties (59 k, 308 w and 135 m). SDGW notes 162 deaths.

‡   8th (Service) Battalion Prince Albert's (Somerset Light Infantry). 63rd Brigade states 443 casualties for 1–6 July (73 k, 289 w and 81 m). SDGW notes 115 deaths on 1 July.

either 'quick succession,' 'quick time' or a 'rush.' All followed a 50-yards-a-minute creeping barrage that stepped deeper into enemy territory.[56] The 21st's orders said 'success of the operation will largely depend on troops following up the barrages as closely as possible,' something not emphasised in the 7th. As it turned out, the creeping barrage provided some cover during the no-man's-land crossover but it was too thin to suppress all resistance and thereafter moved too quickly for the attacking infantry to keep up.[57] Bicknell later assessed the creeping barrage: 'Owing to severe fighting in and around the German front and support trenches and the heavy losses there the infantry never got near enough to it [the barrage] again for it to be the slightest use. We saw it getting further and further away whilst the intervening ground was full of Germans who were as safe from it as we were.'[58]

British soldiers generally expected an easy crossover after their artillery had destroyed or suppressed German resistance.[59] A 50th Brigade machine-gunner said it 'seemed impossible for anything to survive in Jerry's lines.'[60] Lieutenant Wilfred Sansom, 174th Tunnelling Company, was in a Russian Sap dubbed L25 beneath no-man's-land when the 65-minute intensive bombardment began: 'It was awful, just one terrible roar and the sap wobbled as though drunk.'[61] Private George Wilkinson, 10th Yorkshires, thought the 'whole world seemed to be on fire.'[62] Corporal Victor King, 1st Royal Welsh Fusiliers, said the bombardment was 'like hell let loose.'[63] Amid the din one Devonshire soldier distinctly heard 'larks singing in heaven above, and it lifted my spirits.'[64] Stubbs wondered 'how I would feel when I went over — not frightened, mind you, but puzzled. Well, when I got on to the top it was just like field day.'[65]

Fifteenth Corps' operations around the Fricourt–Mametz salient played out as two interrelated acts, each with multiple scenes. The first involved the opening attacks of 7th and 21st Divisions to about 2 p.m. The second was about those divisions' renewal of operations from 2.30 p.m., with the capture of Fricourt the central focus. As it happened, XV Corps turned in a relatively successful performance when compared with III, X, VIII and VII Corps, but the thread was that battalions attacking furthest from Fricourt advanced deeper into enemy lines than those nearest to the village's red-brick ruins and fortified cellars, which held German infantrymen and numerous machine guns.

THE CURTAIN LIFTED on the first act with 50th Brigade suffering galling casualties on the western fringes of Fricourt. Tenth West Yorkshires, ordered to wear 'gas helmets rolled upon the head,' attacked just northwest of the village, a tickle beyond the two just-blown craters of The Tambour, whose piles of chalkstone spoil were not high enough to screen their advance as intended.[66] While two companies crossed the German front line before the defenders could man the parapet, the pair following was annihilated by machine guns in Fricourt and in enfilade from the south and, further away, the southeast.[67] The dead lay in rows. A few of the living that reached the German trenches held out until nightfall. Others were isolated and killed near the northwest outskirts of Fricourt. Some hid in a cellar and lived.[68] With 710 casualties by day's end, the battalion practically ceased to exist.[69] Nearby, at 7.45 a.m., one company of 7th Yorkshires* was destroyed within moments when its commander, Major Ralph Kent, directed it — for reasons still unknown — to advance directly at Fricourt. It was an error; the company was not supposed to have attacked at this time at all. 'This seemed so incredible that I could hardly believe it was true,' said Lieutenant-Colonel Ronald Fife, commanding 7th Yorkshires, of his subordinate's blunder.[70] Of the 140 officers and men of A Company who went forward, 108 were dead or wounded at the hands of at least one German machine-gun team, probably more.[71] This company, noted RIR111, evidently did not anticipate resistance and suffered 'huge losses' as it attempted to leave its own trenches in wave formation.[72]

The dead of 7th Yorkshires and 10th West Yorkshires lay in heaps; the wounded and unscathed hid in shell holes or tried to crawl back. Among the ripening corpses was Bradford-born Private Sam Tomlinson, 10th West Yorkshires. The 19-year-old's body was later interred at Dantzig Alley British Cemetery with an epitaph chosen by his parents: 'Too far away thy grave to see, but not too far to think of thee.'

One German machine-gun team on Hill 110 had a clear view over the ribbon of ground that was the scene of the 50th's tragedy. From more than 1000 yards away, the gun, said one of its five-man team, 'put down a hail of fire on the attacking enemy. Two companies of British [probably

---

*   7th (Service) Battalion Alexandra, Princess of Wales's Own (Yorkshire Regiment). Battalion war diary states 351 casualties. SDGW notes 104 deaths. Casualty figures are for whole battalion.

7th Yorkshires] who attempted to assault from the area of Fricourt Station were quickly caught by our machine gun and suffered dreadful casualties.'[73] The gun rattled through some 22,000 rounds during the day. Three of its crew became casualties:[74] a small loss in relation to the casualties they had inflicted.

Twenty-first Division's break-in came high on Fricourt Spur, on the demarcation line between two German regiments. Here, the defences were pulverised, the wire cut, and several machine guns put out of action during the barrage.[75] A roughly 170-yard gap had opened between RIR111 and Reserve Infantry Regiment 110.[76] Even so, 64th Brigade's 9th and 10th KOYLI came under machine-gun fire from the front, Fricourt to the southeast and high ground nearer La Boisselle as it crossed no-man's-land from 7.25 a.m. One MG08 machine gun began firing even before the British bombardment ceased. The two battalions' initial waves advanced from a secret Russian Sap known as Dinnet Street, just outside the British wire and about 180 yards from the German line.[77] This sap ran parallel to the German parapet and was opened overnight on 30 June. Two other Russian Saps northwest of Fricourt — Balmoral Street and Purfleet, originally intended to be used as flame-thrower emplacements to hose the German front line with liquid fire — appear to have gone unused.[78] Crucially, Horne's effective pre-battle counter-battery fire meant German gunners were only able to lay down the weakest of defensive barrages on no-man's-land, and were insufficient to stop the British infantry.[79]

Ninth and 10th KOYLI were met with a flurry of stick grenades on reaching the hostile parapet but nonetheless broke into the trench 'with little delay,' and quickly pushed the German defenders back.[80] Sir Basil Liddle Hart, then a captain in 9th KOYLI and later a military historian and theorist, was there, face to face with the enemy:

> They were mostly six footers and they hauled their remaining
> machine-guns out of the dug-outs and lying in shell-holes fired
> point blank at us, despite our terrible barrage of shell-fire. Their fire
> was so deadly that our men were forced to crawl, and this slowed
> down our advance so that the barrage lifted off the German trenches
> before we had nearly reached their front line. Our battalion lost
> about 500 men crossing the 180 yards of No Man's Land, of whom

the majority were only slightly wounded, but unhappily we had 14 officers killed before we reached the German trenches.[81]

Support battalions 15th Durham Light Infantry* and 1st East Yorkshires† followed behind the two KOYLI battalions. They, too, suffered in the German defensive machine-gun and rifle fire, but with 'magnificent dash' made the crossing and were soon at close quarters with the enemy.[82]

Feldwebel Karl Eiser, Reserve Field Artillery Regiment 29 (RFAR29), was near what would become the high-tide mark of 64th Brigade's advance on Fricourt Spur, where two machine guns hammered a 'long drawn-out' fire.[83] He saw an officer whose 'reckless spirit and black humour was well known to everybody,' but who soon looked 'pale and bleary-eyed.'[84] Two field guns were lost before being retaken and then inflicting an 'appalling harvest' among the enemy.[85] 'At least our division [on Fricourt Spur] had warded off the breakthrough for today.'[86]

Closer to Fricourt, the lead battalions of Brigadier-General Edward Hill's 63rd Brigade, 4th Middlesex‡ and 8th Somerset Light Infantry, were also punished by machine-gun fire when they began at 7.25 a.m. The 8th's lead platoons suffered about 50% casualties and the 4th's leading wave stalled in the fusillade before restarting four or five minutes later.[87] The 4th's ordeal might also be linked to Bavarian pioneers apparently detonating a mined dugout in the area moments after the Tambour blasts, allegedly burying 80 British soldiers and forcing the rest back into their own trench under heavy fire.[88] Elements of both 8th Somerset and 4th Middlesex, the latter now moving forward again, breached the German front line. 'Survivors pushed on in small groups beyond the [German] support line,' recorded 4th Middlesex's war diarist.[89] Eighth Lincolns§ and 10th York & Lancasters¶ followed from about 8.40 a.m. and also suffered in the crossover.[90]

---

* 15th (Service) Battalion Durham Light Infantry. Battalion war diary states 459 casualties (63 k, 323 w and 73 m). SDGW notes 137 deaths.
† 1st Battalion East Yorkshire Regiment. SDGW notes 119 deaths.
‡ 4th Battalion Duke of Cambridge's Own (Middlesex Regiment). 63rd Brigade states 546 casualties for 1–6 July (117 k, 283 w and 146 m). SDGW notes 63 deaths on 1 July.
§ 8th (Service) Battalion Lincolnshire Regiment. 63rd Brigade states 248 casualties for 1–6 July (34 k, 180 w and 34 m). SDGW notes 8 deaths on 1 July.
¶ 10th (Service) Battalion York & Lancaster Regiment. 63rd Brigade states 293 casualties for 1–6 July (30 k, 192 w and 71 m). SDGW notes 13 deaths on 1 July.

'I'm for it this time,' shouted one soon-to-die 10th York & Lancasters company commander to Constantinople-born Major Arthur Willis, of the same battalion, who turned left and then right to wave his men forward. Within moments a German sniper shot Willis through the chest: 'I was knocked over and lay for some time before a stretcher-bearer came. ... On the way a H.E. [high explosive] shell dropped near us and covered me with earth etc. However I was able to get my hands to uncover my face and the bearers did the rest.'[91] Lieutenant-Colonel Robert Johnston, 8th Lincolns, was one of those caught up in fighting through the fretwork of trenches west of the sunken Fricourt–Contalmaison road. He and his men repeatedly engaged small German counterattack parties with bombs and rifle grenades. 'If these bombing attacks had been successful, and the Germans had got a foothold in Lozenge Alley [running between the German front line and Fricourt Farm] at this point ... they would have taken our troops in Sunken Road to the north of Lozenge Alley in flank as well as in rear, and turned them out.'[92]

German efforts to eject the break-in with immediate local counterattacks failed. Too many of the 21st were in their trenches. Resistance slowly fragmented and casualties mounted. The 21st's gains were made one trench bay at a time with grenade, bayonet and rifle. Both brigades reached the sunken lane north of Fricourt by about 8 a.m., with the 64th moving a couple of hundred yards on and taking some of Crucifix Trench. Sixty-second Brigade's four battalions — 12th* and 13th Northumberland Fusiliers,† 1st Lincolns‡ and 10th Yorkshires§ — were committed throughout the day, sometimes piecemeal, first as ammunition carriers and then as reinforcements for the 64th. Several companies of 14th Northumberland Fusiliers¶ went forward to help with consolidation.[93] By 9 a.m., the 21st held a tactically important mini-salient high on Fricourt Spur; this was in keeping with Horne's plan to outflank and capture the village below.

---

* 12th (Service) Battalion Northumberland Fusiliers. SDGW notes 13 deaths.

† 13th (Service) Battalion Northumberland Fusiliers. SDGW notes 7 deaths.

‡ 1st Battalion Lincolnshire Regiment. Battalion war diary states 119 casualties (3 k, 114 w and 2 m). SDGW notes 11 deaths.

§ 10th (Service) Battalion Alexandra, Princess of Wales's Own (Yorkshire Regiment). SDGW notes 41 deaths.

¶ 14th (Service) Battalion (Pioneers) Northumberland Fusiliers. SDGW notes 4 deaths.

From his observation post on a knoll of high ground near Bécourt, Major Musard Nanson, Royal Garrison Artillery (RGA), watched the progress of 64th Brigade through a telescope:

> I saw the occupation of the Sunken Road [running north across Fricourt Spur] by our infantry; I saw reinforcements enter the sunken road until it was packed close with men. Later I saw a fairly dense line advance from the Sunken Road to Crucifix Trench, from my telescope point of view apparently without resistance or casualty. As soon as Crucifix Trench was occupied a large mass of Germans in long overcoats rose out of a trench higher-up, Shelter Trench, and descended towards Crucifix Trench. As it was too far away for me to see that they were surrendering I concluded that they were and withheld the order to fire on them.[94]

Approaching midday, the 21st's mini-salient was far from secure. This worried Brigadier-General Hugh Headlam, commanding 64th Brigade, who had followed his men forward. At about 11 a.m. he told divisional headquarters that there were 'none of our troops west of [the] sunken road within supporting distance. ... Both of his [64th Brigade's] flanks were in the air, except for such local protection as he himself had arranged.'[95] Fifteen minutes later Major-General Campbell committed two battalions. First Lincolns went up to the old German front line in the 64th's sector, while 10th Yorkshires were placed under Headlam's command and dispatched in the wake of 8th Somerset Light Infantry and 8th Lincolns to join the Fricourt Spur fighting. The arrival of 10th Yorkshires was 'considerably delayed by congestion in the communication trenches. Two Coys [companies] were sent to Crucifix Trench with orders to work along this trench towards Fricourt Farm.'[96] Such were the understated words of Campbell's report on this Victoria Cross action, revisited below. For the minute, Private Matthew Watkin, 10th Yorkshires, struggled through the clogged-with-wounded British trenches. He thought it ironic: 'people at home will be going to the beaches, unaware of the carnage.'[97]

Well-to-do Temporary-Major Stewart Loudoun-Shand enjoyed adventure and travel and believed in serving his country. The former banker and merchant had worked between London, Ceylon and South Africa.

His battalion, 10th Yorkshires, was stopped by a tornado of bullets as its soldiers scrambled into the open.[98] The 36-year-old officer and veteran of the South African War did what few others would: he stood on the parapet, helped his men up and rallied them forward. Soon he was shot. Propped up against a trench wall, he died offering up still more encouragement to his men. He won a posthumous Victoria Cross and is buried in Norfolk Cemetery, near Bécordel-Bécourt. As eyewitness Corporal Harry Fellows, 12th Northumberland Fusiliers, said of Loudoun-Shand's bravery, 'Since that day he has remained my hero of the Great War.'[99]

The fortunes of war ... Sergeant Alex Fisher, 10th KOYLI, steeled himself for battle by entering 'some sort of mental coma that enabled me to carry on and think clearly.'[100] He darted from one shell crater to the next, betting a second shell would not land there:[101] 'I quickly formed the opinion that by observing these particular hazards I could overcome my terror and anticipate what the next thing would be in the way of shellfire or even rifle fire.'[102] Private Maurice Symes, 8th Somerset Light Infantry, was wounded early in the attack. He did not make it across no-man's-land, did not see a single enemy soldier, and did not see the machine guns firing at him: 'You could see people going down all the way around, you know, getting shot.'[103] Private John Mortimer, 10th York & Lancasters, was sickened by the sight of mutilated soldiers. 'The fact that it could happen to me I did not realise straight away, but when I did I trembled with fear. I forced myself to keep up with the others and as I became a fatalist in my mind, the trembling ceased to a degree.'[104] Captain Robin Money, 15th Durham Light Infantry, saw 'all these poor fellows lying there in rows' as he stalked across no-man's-land. A splinter of shrapnel broke his wrist and left him unable to cock his revolver: 'So, one wonders what to do.'[105]

ON THE OTHER side of the salient, German positions facing 7th Division ran down from Hill 110 into the Mametz–Carnoy valley before ascending the western shoulder of the Mametz–Montauban ridge. Brigadier-General Cyril Deverell — then commanding 20th Brigade, later at the helm of 3rd Division and after the war Field Marshal and Chief of Imperial General Staff (1936–37) — identified enemy positions on the eastern inclines of Hill 110 as key ground; these had to be captured, stopping RIR109's machine-gunners and riflemen there from enfilading and potentially breaking the neighbouring 91st Brigade's drive towards Mametz along the scoop of the valley. 'Unless the German position opposite Mansel Copse was engaged, the success of the whole of the 7th Division to the right [of its 20th Brigade] was jeopardised.'[106] Other German machine-gunners in and around Mametz, such as at The Shrine strongpoint in the cemetery just southwest of the village, and in Fricourt Wood further away, had fields of fire either along or across the Mametz–Carnoy valley, or both. It was essential for British gunners providing the artillery to support, destroy or suppress the streams of fire from these points to facilitate the infantry's advance and minimise its casualties.

The 7th was spread across a roughly 3000-yard, three-brigade front around Mametz. Seven mines were blown here, three around the front-line trenches held by elements of RIR109 just south of Hidden Wood and not under direct attack. On the right, 91st Brigade's 22nd Manchesters* shouldered the spur east of Mametz after a 700-yard uphill advance against a company of IR23 that had suffered 'exceedingly large' losses thanks to the British barrage[107] and a 500-pound mine blast.[108] The neighbouring 1st South Staffords,† its passage facilitated by the 2000-pound Bulgar Point mine under a German front-line strongpoint, also attacked uphill and entered the village's southeast outskirts, before being forced back to Cemetery Trench on its south side.[109] Both had begun at 7.30 a.m., and suffered heavily crossing no-man's-land and pushing beyond the German front line. Reinforcements from 2nd Queen's‡ and 21st Manchesters§ initially failed to alter the impasse.[110] This impasse was, explained Major Frank More-Molyneux, 2nd Queen's, 'owing to the bombardment having had very little effect' on Dantzig Alley (North) and machine guns there 'causing severe casualties to the leading battalions.'[111] In the centre, spread out across the Mametz–Carnoy valley, 20th Brigade's 2nd Gordon

---

*   22nd (Service) Battalion (7th City) Manchester Regiment. Also known as 7th Manchester Pals. Battalion war diary states 490 casualties (130 k, 249 w and 111 m). SDGW notes 200 deaths.

†   1st Battalion South Staffordshire Regiment. Battalion war diary estimates 310 casualties. SDGW notes 86 deaths.

‡   2nd Battalion Queen's (Royal West Surrey Regiment). 7th Division history estimates 300 casualties. SDGW notes 54 deaths.

§   21st (Service) Battalion (6th City) Manchester Regiment. Also known as 6th Manchester Pals. 7th Division history estimates 250 casualties. SDGW notes 63 deaths.

Highlanders[*] and 9th Devons,[†] the former helped by a 200-pound mine blast under German lines, suffered heavy losses as they set off at 7.30 a.m. and 7.27 a.m respectively.[112] Both penetrated a few hundred yards beyond the German line to the south and southwest of the village. Eighth Devons[‡] was punished as three of its companies went forward separately — to support either the 9th Devons or Gordons, or both — at about 10.30 a.m.[113] Deverell, who saw tactical value in securing the German positions beyond Mansel Copse, concluded that the Devons had done the job at great cost from machine guns in The Shrine and thus 'permitted the troops on their flanks to get on.'[114] On the left, atop Hill 110, 2nd Borders[§] began at 7.27 a.m. and, helped by yet another 500-pound mine, quickly entered the line held by RIR109, swung northwest towards Bois Français and was caught up in close-quarter fighting.[115] 'From here we advanced in short rushes, all companies and lines by this time mixed up,' wrote Lieutenant George Prynne, 2nd Borders.[116] While 7th Division was short of its initial objective and casualties were heavy, it had made solid inroads into the high ground east of Mametz and on Hill 110, and needed to develop these footings if that village then Fricourt were to fall later as planned.

Private James McCauley, 2nd Borders, watched horrified in a captured German dugout as a British infantryman swung a slime-covered sandbag onto a Baden soldier's hideous, gaping stomach wound and then stomped it in: 'Years after the war, I still sit by my fireside and see in the flickering flames that poor German boy with his hands outstretched in tearful appeal.'[117] Private Charles Wicks, 2nd Queen's, had spent the night of 30 June sitting on a trench fire-step wondering what fortunes the following day would bring. Years later he remembered a spick-and-span second-lieutenant with gleaming boots and Sam Browne belt. 'I can always see him going over the top when we did get out [of the assembly trench] and just in front of me, he caught it, he hadn't gone two steps before he was killed.'[118]

---

[*] 2nd Battalion Gordon Highlanders. 20th Brigade states 457 casualties (125 k, 293 w and 39 m). SDGW notes 122 deaths.

[†] 9th (Service) Battalion Devonshire Regiment. 20th Brigade states 480 casualties (149 k, 276 w and 55 m). SDGW notes 158 deaths.

[‡] 8th (Service) Battalion Devonshire Regiment. 20th Brigade states 207 casualties (40 k, 160 w and 7 m). SDGW notes 40 deaths.

[§] 2nd Battalion Border Regiment. 20th Brigade states 327 casualties (81 k, 180 w and 66 m). SDGW notes 88 deaths.

Private Howard Wide, 9th Devons, saw numerous men hit by the stream of lead coming from The Shrine. It intrigued him that some wounded read their Bibles, 'as if they knew they faced a lingering death, and desired some comfort of hope.'[119]

Sergeant Richard Tawney, 22nd Manchesters, saw some German infantrymen kneeling atop their parapet to get a better shot. One was even standing. He was just 100 yards away: 'It was insane. It seemed one couldn't miss them. Every man I fired at dropped, except one. Him, the boldest of the lot, I missed more than once. I was puzzled and angry. Three hundred years ago I should have tried a silver bullet. Not that I wanted to hurt him or anyone else. It was missing I hated.'[120] The Calcutta-born soldier, later a seminal lecturer in economics, saw his platoon commander lying prone, with his breathing laboured and face blanched: 'His soul was gone. He was really dead already; in a minute or two he was what the doctors called "dead".' Then a bullet slammed into Tawney's chest:

> What I felt was that I had been hit by a tremendous iron hammer,
> swung by a giant of inconceivable strength, and then twisted with
> a sickening sort of wrench so that my head and back banged on
> the ground, and my feet struggled as though they didn't belong to
> me. For a second or two my breath wouldn't come. I thought — if
> that's the right word — 'This is death', and hoped it wouldn't take
> long. By-and-by, as nothing happened, it seemed I couldn't be
> dying.[121]

Tawney lay for 30 hours in no-man's-land before being rescued.

Grenadier Emil Goebelbecker, RIR109, was on sentry duty just east of Mametz when the attack began. He recalled that his regiment's forward-most companies were in the dugouts of the front-line system's second and third trenches, not the first: 'The British troops left their trenches and attacked *en masse*. Our front lines gave in immediately. There were very few defenders left and with no NCOs or commissioned officers to take command, everyone dropped back on their own.'[122] Just south of the village, *Grenadier* Kury, RIR109, was shot in the chest and felt blood flow from the exit wound in his back.[123] He recalled 'lying semi-conscious and seeing British soldiers jumping over our trench.'[124] Somewhere near Bois

Français, *Leutnant-der-Reserve* Georg Bauer's men of Bavarian Pioneer Regiment clashed with the 2nd Borders in a brutal fight with bomb and bayonet.[125] Bauer snatched a glance down the hill towards Mametz and saw the Devons and Gordon Highlanders advancing: 'Wave upon wave of Englishmen penetrated forward through the Carnoy Valley on the left of us, so that the danger of being surrounded became ever greater.'[126] This was the benefit of Deverell's plan to engage and then take the German defences on the eastern slopes of Hill 110, helping the neighbouring 91st Brigade's advance. As Bauer put it, the 'difficulties of my own defence grew from minute to minute' and his outnumbered men slowly yielded ground.[127]

'The Devonshires held this trench; The Devonshires hold it still.' So reads the dedication stone at Devonshire Cemetery, Mansel Copse. Among the dead here are 30-year-old Captain Duncan Martin and 23-year-old Lieutenant William Noel Hodgson, respectively artist and poet, killed by machine-gun fire from The Shrine. Martin had made a plasticine model of the land and correctly predicted that 9th Devons would be raked by a fusillade of bullets from the strongpoint. A fellow officer later wrote that 'Iscariot [Martin] was shot through the heart below Mansel Copse and all his staff killed round him; Smiler [Hodgson] killed about the same place, getting his bombs up. He was smiling in death when they found him.'[128] Two days before battle, Hodgson — a Cambridge University contemporary of dead war poet Rupert Brooke, minus the naivety — had expected death: 'Must say good-bye to all of this; By all delights that I shall miss.'[129] Weeks earlier Private Albert Conn, a former dockworker in the same battalion, saw a corporal shoot a warbling lark out of a tree: 'A couple of the lads told him to fuck off out of it.'[130] Not everyone possessed the silky talents of Martin and Hodgson; think of those other men, too, when you walk among the headstones in this cemetery and others on the Somme.

Aerial patrols by the Royal Flying Corps (RFC) further unpicked the 28th's defences. Several machine-gun positions were spotted by observers of 3rd and 9th Squadrons, RFC, and destroyed by targeted shellfire.[131] 'This was all the more serious because the shellfire-damaged positions of RIR109 required artillery protection,' wrote one German historian.[132] Further back, the artillery lost more guns as the RFC accurately directed counter-battery fire.[133] These gun losses, which were in addition to those suffered during the pre-battle bombardment and artillery barrage supporting the attack, further undermined the 28th's already negligible artillery capabilities. One German historian said the 28th's 'few guns still firing could not prevent enemy reinforcements moving up.'[134] *Leutnant-der-Reserve* August Bielefeld, Reserve Foot Artillery Regiment 16 (RFtAR16), remembered that an RFC spotter plane located his 15-centimetre heavy gun hidden in the southern fringes of Mametz Wood: 'We were subjected to aimed fire. After every shot we fled into the adjacent dugout [and then from the British guns] we received a heavy shell, which pushed in the entrance and trapped the whole gun crew in the dugout.'[135] Six hours later, Bielefeld's men had managed to dig their way free, only to find their gun's barrel and aiming mechanism wrecked by shrapnel.

Twenty-eighth Reserve Division's front-line positions on the high ground either side of Fricourt had been quickly overrun, and casualties were heavy. RIR111 was still fighting on Fricourt Spur and Hill 110, while RIR109 was fully engaged around Mametz. In all three locations crude defensive lines were thrown up. Local reserves were applied to battle piecemeal, and counterattack groups were quickly depleted in number.[136] Telephone links between headquarters were cut.[137] Multiple runners became casualties and battle haze made semaphore unreliable.[138] Organised resistance and the work of ejecting British infantry fell to junior commanders with whatever men they could organise on the spot,[139] but these officers and NCOs were being spent at an alarming rate. Numerous small-scale counterattacks failed through lack of manpower and organisation. There was insufficient artillery left either to cast down a defensive barrage on no-man's-land, or to limit the enemy's advance.[140] Surviving machine-gunners had to fulfil both roles.[141] Supplies of ammunition and hand grenades were limited and dwindling quickly.[142] One Badener said it 'was heart-breaking to have no guns or reinforcements worth mentioning.'[143] Retention of the 28th's positions now depended on how Hahn deployed his negligible reserves to battle.

Darmstadt-born Hahn had already established a bleak picture of events across the 28th's positions south of Fricourt Spur. Telephone lines between front-line battalions and the 58-year-old's headquarters were severed.[144] By about 8 a.m., reports from observers well behind the front line left Hahn in no doubt as to the developing danger.[145] He set to strengthening his second intermediate position, up to 3000 yards behind the front line, with elements of IR23, ancillary divisional troops and machine-gun teams. Around this time RIR109 and RIR111 requested urgent reinforcements via signal lamp.[146] Hahn's rejoinder: 'Persevere, reinforcements are approaching.'[147] Another influx of reports before 9.30 a.m. told Hahn that Fricourt Spur was all but lost, that Mametz was under concerted attack and that further east Montauban had probably already fallen.[148] Hahn was by now well aware that the Fricourt–Mametz salient was under threat on both flanks, and that the British were making steady gains.[149] It was a crucial moment. Hahn now decided against attempting to retake the lost ground:[150] he was more concerned by significant British gains closer to Montauban. It was a concession that ran against orders and reduced RIR109 and RIR111 to ground-holding formations, but it did buy time to bolster the 28th's line further back.

The significance of Hahn's decision should not be overlooked. It meant he had conceded not only that Fricourt and Mametz would be lost, but also that he no longer had the resources on hand to defend them properly, or reclaim them after they inevitably fell. It was a judgement call that flew in the face of a dictate from *General-der-Infanterie* Erich von Falkenhayn, Chief of General Staff, Supreme Army Command, that not an inch of territory should be ceded, even if doing so would result in better-placed defensive positions.[151] Although Hahn would escape without penalty, he was almost certainly rebuked, as Second Army's chief of staff, *Generalmajor* Paul Grünert, was sacked for sanctioning such tactical moves elsewhere.[152] Hahn's decision likely reflected his annoyance with the salient's poor-quality defensive positions and his division's increasingly tenuous footing there. It also amounted to a tacit criticism of the army-wide emphasis on front-loaded defensive schemes, and further suggested that he already believed the British offensive would become one of attrition.

Soldiers on the battlefield saw no such shades of grey, as an embittered *Feldwebel* Eiser, the NCO in RFAR29, later revealed: 'We were deeply disappointed: why had we been abandoned with no reinforcements or relief? Was that our reward for what we had given up and sacrificed?'[153]

HORNE HAD AN optimistic summary of events by 11 a.m.,[154] and no idea of Hahn's tactical thinking. He knew 7th and 21st Divisions were approaching their first objectives, but had no knowledge of 50th Brigade's failure.[155] The first two elements of Horne's plan were incomplete: it was too early to assault Fricourt head-on. Fifteen minutes later, believing III and XIII Corps' infantry were progressing on his flanks, Horne decided to renew his attack by ordering 91st Brigade's first objective, Dantzig Alley (North) on the spur east of and overlooking Mametz, and the unimaginatively named Fritz Trench just beyond, to be captured. An earlier attempt by 91st Brigade to seize these objectives at 10.30 a.m., after 30 minutes' shellfire, had failed to produce results.[156] At 11.15 a.m., Horne, aware XIII Corps had now taken the nearby Pommiers Redoubt and Beetle Alley to the east, ordered a fresh attempt to force Dantzig Alley (North) and Fritz Trench. An hour later, the 7th's commander, Major-General Herbert Watts, said somewhat bullishly that he wanted to 'push straight through' to his objectives.[157] A further 30 minutes' bombardment was ordered at 12.25 p.m., on the same objectives as previously and at the request of Brigadier-General John Minshull-Ford, the 91st's commander, to break up a German counterattack that was forming. The infantry would follow the bombardment, which was to lift at about 12.55 p.m. Earlier, at 11.45 a.m., Horne told 21st Division to advance its left flank on Fricourt Spur and keep in touch with III Corps.[158] At midday, Horne's focus was very much on developing the 7th's and 21st's gains, retaining contact with neighbouring corps and continuing to build a platform from which Fricourt could be enveloped and then taken.

The 91st's attack east of Mametz went in as planned. The bombardment broke down some, but by no means all, resistance. One advanced section of German field guns fired over open sights until their crews were killed.[159] The remaining companies of 2nd Queen's took Dantzig Alley (North) soon after 1 p.m., thereafter bombing their way westward down its traverses and reaching the outskirts of Mametz.[160] About 45 minutes later they linked up with 1st South Staffords and the remaining three companies of 21st Manchesters, which had worked their way into the ruined village's southeast corner around the same time.[161] The 91st had finally captured a sizeable chunk of its first objective, but its second, a few hundred yards beyond, remained outstanding and its left flank was vulnerable to local counterattack as the 20th Brigade had yet to come up alongside. Seventh Division was still a long way from forming a defensive flank facing Willow Stream valley.

At least 25 minutes before the 91st's attack began, an impatient Horne was already betting on a positive outcome. By 12.30 p.m. he was even more convinced that III and XIII Corps were advancing on his flanks, with their reports suggesting German resistance was collapsing.[162] Apparently German artillery was 'running away' in III Corps' sector, while the enemy was in 'full retreat' in XIII Corps area.[163] In III Corps' case this information would turn out to be almost entirely incorrect; not so for XIII Corps.[164] At the time, both pieces of news were what an optimistic Horne wanted to hear. He resolved to force an outcome to the battle by launching more of 50th Brigade directly at Fricourt, hoping to capitalise on what he believed was widespread crumbling resistance. Orders went out at 12.50 p.m. The attack would begin at 2.30 p.m. It would be preceded by a half-hour artillery bombardment that jerked back 500 yards at Zero, and 15 minutes later a further 250 yards, at which point it would remain for one-and-a-half hours. Horne was enacting the final phase of his attack scheme, the capture of Fricourt, despite the fact that neither of its two preconditions had been met. In his mind, this was a measured risk founded on positive battlefield reports;[165] in reality it was a flutter based on incorrect or overly optimistic information.

Mid-afternoon, Horne, now aware of the 91st's gains, revealed he expected the 50th's attack on Fricourt to produce results:

Up to now, 2.30 p.m., the attack generally has been very successful.
I am a bit backward still as the two villages in front of me have
proved very difficult. Villages are always a difficult problem as the
houses and cellars give cover for machine guns &c. I hope however
that before long now we shall be able to get on better & make a
good job of it.[166]

The problem was that nothing had changed at Fricourt. German machine-gunners were still there, still dug in amid the ruins with ample stores of ammunition to hand and very much motivated to continue the fight.

Horne's flutter around the mouth of Willow Stream valley produced a predictable sacrifice on the altar of Fricourt. Attempts to have the attack called off by the 50th's commander, Glasgow, fell on deaf ears at divisional and corps headquarters.[167] So it was that the remaining three 7th Yorkshires companies were destroyed by 'murderous' machine-gun and rifle fire.[168] In three minutes and 50 yards these companies ran up 176 casualties, or about one a second.[169] At 2.33 p.m., two companies of 7th East Yorkshires,* attacking on the same stretch of ground as 10th West Yorkshires that morning, were shot down within yards of their own parapet, losing 155 men. Further operations by the 50th were stopped.[170] German accounts acknowledge that Horne was attempting to force what he perceived as a favourable position, and recorded bluntly that these British afternoon attacks were simply 'smashed with heavy losses.'[171] As the swathe of still-warm Yorkshire corpses proved, machine-gunners still lurking in Fricourt's ruins and possibly opening in long-range enfilade from the western slopes of Hill 110 to the southeast made the village impervious to direct assault at this time.

'Three hundred yards away I saw the enemy's trenches bristling with bayonets and lined with steel helmets,' said Lieutenant-Colonel Ronald Fife, 7th Yorkshires, of the German trenches in front of Fricourt:[172] 'The deafening cracking of the enemy's machine guns and rifles, which began the moment that the first wave of men crossed the parapet, showed clearly what was happening. ... It was evident that the assault was under enfilade from both flanks and that it would be a miracle if it succeeded against such a storm of bullets.'[173] Nobody made it as far as the barbed wire outside the British front line, said Private Alfred Askew, 7th Yorkshires: 'We were mown down like ninepins.' Two bullets caught his left arm and his nickel razor case stopped a third: 'What a nice souvenir.'[174] Later that night, Brigadier-General Robert Fell, commanding 51st Brigade, went to Meaulte, where he found Glasgow 'quite broken down by his losses — Pilcher [the 17th (Northern) Division's commander] and I talked with him till after midnight.'[175]

IT IS THE height of summer. The track down to Fricourt New Military Cemetery is lined with six-foot-tall corn, which rustles in a gentle, balmy breeze. It feels like you are walking along an open-topped corridor, which opens out onto a small cemetery clearing, also surrounded by

---

* 7th (Service) Battalion East Yorkshire Regiment. 50th Brigade states 437 casualties 1–11 July (69 k, 311 w and 57 m). SDGW notes 40 deaths.

cornstalks and close to the still-visible mine craters of the Tambour area west of Fricourt. Here rest 210 soldiers, most of them in mass graves, which is why so many headstones carry multiple names from the 7th East Yorkshires and 10th West Yorkshires. Among their epitaphs: 23-year-old Lieutenant William Keighley, 'Love, laughter, life'; 29-year-old Lieutenant Alfred Ratcliffe, 'A very dearly loved son and brother'; and 16-year-old Private Albert Barker, 'Beyond Recall. ... So dear'. Before the war, Keighley, 10th West Yorkshires, was a teacher. Barker, 7th East Yorkshires, was a schoolboy. Ratcliffe, also 10th West Yorkshires, was a barrister, and yet another would-be poet and Cambridge University chum of Brooke. Then, there is another headstone that forces you to stop and think:

Six Privates of the Great War
West Yorkshire Regiment

In death, six men bereft of names — stripped of the one constant in their young lives: identity itself.

WHILE THE 2.30 P.M. direct attacks on Fricourt were a disaster, a more successful sequel by 7th Division was afoot on Hill 110 and at Mametz, foreshadowed by a 30-minute bombardment. The Russian Sap on Hill 110's west-facing camber just south of Fricourt — known as L25, with twin Vickers-gun emplacements at its head, near the German-held Aeroplane Trench — was opened along its length at 2.30 p.m. The machine-gun officer failed to turn up and his sergeant had no orders; the Vickers emplacements at the saphead, which had been opened at 7.30 a.m., went unused. Lieutenant Sansom, the tunnelling officer, was there: 'We waited anxiously until 2.30 p.m. expecting to go and we opened up the sap. Enemy had MG [machine gun] on it at once and half men getting out were dropped.'[176]

On 7th Division's left flank, just south of Willow Stream, Brigadier-General Julian Steele's 22nd Brigade went in. Twentieth Manchesters,*

---

* 20th (Service) Battalion (5th City) Manchester Regiment. Also known as 5th Manchester Pals. Battalion war diary states 325 casualties 1–5 July, most on 1 July (120 k, 176 w and 29 m). SDGW notes 124 deaths.

followed by half of 1st Royal Welsh Fusiliers,* crossed over on an extended three-company front. Private Pat Burke, 20th Manchesters, watched his battalion commander Lieutenant-Colonel Harold Lewis, who was later killed, wave his men forward with the words 'Isn't it wonderful.'[177] The battalion's two left companies in the vicinity of the L25, the Russian Sap, were raked by Fricourt's machine-gunners as they reached the sunken road leading from the ruined village up to Hill 110.[178] They were soon caught in a bitter bomb fight for the group of trenches known as the Rectangle, just behind the German front line.[179] Support waves lost heavily.

War poet Siegfried Sassoon, 1st Royal Welsh Fusiliers, watched the 'sun flashes on bayonets, and the tiny figures advance steadily and disappear behind the mounds of trench debris.'[180] At about 9.30 a.m., he nipped off for a shave and returned: 'Fricourt was half-hidden by clouds of drifting smoke — brown, blue, pinkish, and grey; shrapnel bursting in small blue white puffs, with tiny flashes.'[181] Larks appeared bewildered, flitting along with querulous cries and weak on the wing, reluctant to rise into the iron sky. Around midday Second-Lieutenant Sassoon ate his last orange in contemplation: 'I am looking at a sunlit picture of Hell. And still the breeze shakes the yellow charlock, and the poppies glow below Crawley ridge.'[182] It was 2.30 p.m. and the 20th Manchesters were advancing: 'Many walked across with sloped arms. About twenty-five casualties on the left (from a machine-gun in Fricourt). I could see one man moving his left arm up and down as he lay on his side: his head was a crimson patch. The others lay still. Then the swarm of ants disappeared over the hill.'[183] Private Stephen Smith, 20th Manchesters, was one of Sassoon's 'ants.' The 39-year-old Mancunian cloth beetler was killed. He left behind a wife, Sarah, and two children aged seven and five. He has no known grave and is today named on the Thiepval Memorial.

The German collapse at Mametz now came on swiftly as 7th Division renewed its attack mid-afternoon. Ninety-first Brigade's 2nd Queen's and elements of 21st Manchesters had, between 3 p.m. and 6.30 p.m., moved beyond Dantzig Alley (North) and cleared their Fritz Trench objective after a hard fight under 'covering fire from Lewis guns and rifles.'[184] They

---

*   1st Battalion Royal Welsh Fusiliers. SDGW notes 4 deaths.

linked up with XIII Corps to the east. To the west, they remained in contact with 1st South Staffords and more elements of 21st Manchesters, which had expanded their footing in the village's southeastern ruins by this time, and now forged ahead to reach their Bunny Alley objective about 7.40 p.m. Captured machine guns 'were turned on the then retreating enemy.'[185] In 20th Brigade's patch, at 3.30 p.m. after 30-minutes' shellfire, two companies from reserve battalion 2nd Royal Warwicks,* tracing the Gordons' path that morning, and several companies of 8th Devons, following 9th Devons' footsteps, were sent forward to break the impasse southwest of Mametz. Before they reached their start line several hundred German soldiers in and around Mametz and The Shrine surrendered, more fleeing towards Fricourt Wood. Eighth Devons, 2nd Gordons and 2nd Royal Warwicks now pushed beyond Hidden Wood, Dantzig Alley (South) and Mametz to reach their Bunny Alley and Orchard Trench objectives soon after 4 p.m. Bombing parties worked through Mametz to 'tackle each house in turn, and very soon they were clear of all but dead Germans.'[186] Around Hidden Wood, 2nd Borders advanced and made contact with 22nd Brigade just west of Bois Français about 5 p.m. By dusk the 7th had taken most of its first two objectives and held a 2000-yard defensive flank facing Willow Stream, isolating Fricourt and its wood from the south.

It was during this fighting that The Shrine fell to a cobbled-together group of Devonshire bombers who worked around its flanks via shell holes and half-collapsed trenches before silencing its machine guns: 'A vast pile of empty cartridges around them told their tale hardly less plainly than the lines of dead and wounded lying out in No Man's Land near Mansel Copse.'[187]

At least three 7th Division officers believed failing German resistance around Mametz should be exploited. At about 6 p.m., Lieutenant-Colonel William Norman, 21st Manchesters, began preparing Mametz to withstand counterattack, later walking out to Bunny Alley, which overlooked Willow Stream valley: 'I was at once strongly convinced that the enemy had abandoned the neighbourhood.'[188] Norman asked brigade headquarters for reinforcements to exploit the gains. He received

---

* 2nd Battalion Royal Warwickshire Regiment. SDGW notes 3 deaths.

a company of 2nd Royal Irish Regiment,* which he thought insufficient for the job.[189] Major Guy Drake-Brockman, a staff officer, remembered a 'feeling at H.Q. 7 Div. that a great opportunity was being let slip' that evening:[190] 'Certain localities outside the final objective could have been captured with very small loss, which subsequently were very costly to take.'[191] Whatever the case, there was no further attempt to take Fricourt that evening and XV Corps' focus shifted to consolidating its gains.

Private Frank Cloudsdale, 21st Manchesters, found the German trenches full of dead and wounded. 'The Battalion was now split up and the position became confused. ... As the day wore on we began to dig in and tried to form a line in order to get cover. When darkness came we were still bogged down.'[192] Fifty-fourth and 95th Field Companies, Royal Engineers (RE), went forward overland at about 4.30 p.m., followed later by 1/3rd Durham Field Company and pioneer battalion 24th Manchesters, and wired the whole new front line, built four strongpoints, duckboarded tracks and repaired roads.[193] Private Wicks' group of 2nd Queen's was led by a sergeant, all the officers being dead or wounded: 'It was rather confused because so many regiments had been cut up and battalions decimated and they were wandering about spare. ... So we had to dig in there in front of Mametz and wait for reinforcements.'[194] Second-Lieutenant Arthur Walsh, 24th Manchesters,† and his pioneers spent the night filling shell holes, dragging coils of barbed wire and 'very cautiously' clearing unexploded shells:[195] 'Stretcher bearers moved the corpses and tended any wounded still alive but not [yet] brought in. I was as usual apprehensive, but it was a quiet night on this patch, as though tired out by the preceding inferno.'[196]

Hours earlier, the first batches of stumbling, dishevelled German prisoners had begun filing through Minden Post, roughly 1000 yards behind the old British front line and near Carnoy. Cinematographer John McDowell, attached to 7th Division, filmed their bewildered march into captivity. The route was thronged with curious British soldiers; some played to the camera, others were less inclined. The seriously

---

* 2nd Battalion Royal Irish Regiment. Battalion war diary states 50 casualties. SDGW notes 4 deaths.
† 24th (Service) Battalion (Oldham) (Pioneers) Manchester Regiment. Also known as Oldham Pals. Battalion war diary states 8 casualties. SDGW notes 1 death.

injured were carried supine on stretchers with a prisoner at each corner. Walking wounded hobbled back, their fatigued, pain-creased faces often nonplussed by the cameraman's presence. The next day McDowell went forward to film the captured ground, which was a corpse-littered wilderness of gravel and shell holes. He rolled off some footage of British and German dead. A Manchester soldier and dog, the battalion's mascot, lay side by side and made for an interesting shot. McDowell must have filmed late in the afternoon, as his reel shows many of the fly-blown dead already stiff with rigor mortis as burial parties set to work.

Back over on Fricourt Spur, a small afternoon attack towards Shelter Wood by elements of the 21st's 10th KOYLI and 15th Durham Light Infantry was a predicable failure. Orders arrived late. It began 10 minutes after British shellfire lifted off the wood at 1.30 p.m. Captain Liddle Hart, 9th KOYLI, explained why the attack was swiftly broken up:

> The Germans swept the open [ground] between Crucifix Trench [just west of Shelter Wood] and Shelter Wood with a fire that it was impossible to live in, and a captain of the [15th] Durhams [Captain Denis Ely] who called on a few men to follow him in an attempt to reach the wood was shot down before he had gone many yards.[197]

The sniper who got Ely did not have long to live: 'One of our [15th Durham Light Infantry] men, Private J[ohn] Jolley, saw him. They saw each other and fired. The German's bullet grazed Jolley's nose. Jolley's bullet struck fair and square in the head.' Ely is named on the Thiepval Memorial.

Consolidation of the 21st's gains was quickly underway. Such limited German shellfire as there was continued to kill, maim and bury soldiers in Crucifix Trench and other forward positions, but the Sunken Road received rather more machine-gun fire in enfilade from both north and south along its length. 'The majority of the survivors of the [64th] Brigade were digging themselves into shallow holes on the [road] bank nearest the Germans,' wrote Liddle Hart.[198] As the war diarist of 15th Durham Light Infantry noted, the Sunken Road soon formed a 'line of resistance should the parties who had advanced in Shelter Wood have to withdraw.'[199] Although 21st Division was still well short of its final objectives, its infantry had gone quite some way towards fulfilling Horne's plan by isolating Fricourt and Fricourt Wood from the north.

That night Lieutenant Lancelot Spicer, 9th KOYLI, later a Liberal politician, dodged shellfire and snipers' bullets on his way up Fricourt Spur: 'Sure enough I heard the "ping" of a bullet behind me.'[200] At about 9 p.m. he found the sunken Fricourt–Contalmaison road 'simply full of men,' which was 'distinctly comforting.'[201] Knots of soldiers sheltered in the lee of the road's banks, which were 12–15 feet high. Here and there consolidation was underway. Captured dugouts became headquarters and dressing stations: 'It was very difficult to get in without treading on the wounded.'[202] He learned that two battalions of 62nd Brigade — 12th and 13th Northumberland Fusiliers — were on their way, but Spicer and the rest of the 64th had to remain until the fresh battalions had taken over. German shellfire was light. 'At 3 a.m. we got all the men on to work at a systematic consolidation, and also served them out with bread and seltzer water.'[203] Nearby, Major Nanson, RGA, had reached Lozenge Alley, which he found 'so packed with our troops that you had to climb over men in places to get along it.'[204] Ninety-seventh, 98th and 126th Field Companies, RE, had little work to do that night, Fricourt not having fallen, although sections of the 98th were involved in fighting throughout the day and were used to bolster 63rd Brigade's right flank closest to the village.[205]

Feldwebel Robert Hauschild, RIR111, led a small group of men towards the front line through Mametz Wood and shellfire that screamed 'like a herd of demons.' He arrived at a trench just north of Fricourt, and there met some men from his home city of Pforzheim: 'For a few moments one forgot all danger.' The trench was shallow, almost devoid of shelter from shrapnel and bullet. Casualties quickly totted up. 'Finally, as shadows lengthened it became darker, the shellfire lessened.' An officer turned up and said the trench had to be held. 'Oh, fine!' Hauschild doubted the odds of success, but his men began digging in with bayonets regardless: 'Not too far away we could hear the English likewise entrenching.'[206]

THE GERMAN DECISION to abandon Fricourt came with the realisation that RIR111 and RIR109 simply could not hold their forward battle zones any longer. There was no artillery support to speak of, and there were no reinforcements coming forward to either defend the ground still held or retake that lost. To stay would invite still more casualties in what was very obviously a one-outcome battle.[207] RIR111 would withdraw to the first intermediate position, which was between 1000 and 2000 yards behind the old German front line, at about 11 p.m. and effectively surrender Fricourt, while RIR109 had abandoned Mametz in the early evening for positions further back. Runners darted from one shell hole to the next alerting the infantry, which filtered back silently in small groups, in some cases having to fight through British outposts. Walking wounded struggled along. The more seriously injured were lugged in tarpaulins, or abandoned.[208] Hours before dawn on 2 July, the remnants of RIR111 held a crude defensive line that curved between Round Wood on Fricourt Spur, and Bottom Wood just north of Mametz, with a support line about 1000 yards further back held by elements of IR23, Landwehr Brigade Replacement Battalion 55 and more remnants of RIR111.[209]

In some parts of the battle zone German defenders continued to hold out. This was the case on Hill 110, where resistance continued until early on 2 July. It was a choice of risking death or injury while attempting to slip back, or surrendering. *Oberstleutnant* L. Knies, Pioneer Battalion 13, said his 2nd Reserve Company on Hill 110 was gradually fragmented, surrounded and then 'overtaken by fate after a hard, fair fight.'[210] *Unteroffizier* Rudolf Stadelbacher and *Unteroffizier* Otto Schüsle, both RIR111 and based on Hill 110, said the British were 'so close that we could hear them talking.'[211] *Leutnant-der-Reserve* Bauer, the Munich pioneer officer also fighting on Hill 110, was collared at about 9 p.m.: 'The superior strength of the enemy had been so overwhelming that there was no longer a need for a formal surrender, but we were simply assembled in the middle under masses of Englishmen who then took us away.'[212]

Wilhelm Seebacher's day was one of brushes with captivity and death. The *Musketier* in RIR111 raced up from his dugout near Bois Français on Hill 110 as the British barrage lifted, but ducked into another when he saw enemy soldiers approaching. Two British sentries were soon patrolling the trench, pacing a two-minute beat past his nook: 'Fortunately it had not occurred at all to both Tommies to look in my dugout.'[213] After watching and timing the sentries for more than an hour he chanced a late-afternoon dash for freedom:[214] 'Quickly I took to both of my legs and vanished in the opposite direction.'[215] Seebacher soon linked up with a Bavarian soldier and returned to attack the British sentries: 'They were probably not particularly pleasantly surprised when our first hand-grenades came flittering past.'[216] More German soldiers arrived: 'The fighting surged back and forth, but we maintained the position.'[217] Overall, however, Hill 110 had become untenable, and shortly before midnight Seebacher's rag-tag band decided all was lost and struck out for the new German line.[218]

Most of those German soldiers who made it back were pleased to be out of the inferno and sipping mineral water. Others were bitter at having yielded ground they believed would have been defensible with proper artillery and infantry support.[219] *Unteroffizier* Friedrich Thomas, RIR109, said that Mametz and its surrounds were no longer tenable by mid-evening: 'Exceedingly heavy losses forced a withdrawal via the road to Bazentin-le-Petit. A last attempt to face the enemy was made at 11 p.m., but it was in vain.'[220] At an after-battle roll call the Karlsruhe law clerk counted just six survivors from a company of about 250 men. Similarly, the normally 2800-strong RIR111 comprised just 1000 men by 4 July,[221] most of its losses having been incurred on 1 July. *Feldwebel* Eiser watched a haggard, stubble-faced string of parched soldiers straggle into Contalmaison: 'They recounted the most appalling crimes committed by the British against their prisoners. We had to listen to the most terrible stories although we had no head for it.'[222]

Back in the British lines, Captain Brian Reeves, 1st Royal Welsh Fusiliers, believed Fricourt could have been taken that night, after the German withdrawal, rather than on 2 July as was already being planned. Bombing parties creeping along the sunken road from Hill 110 down into Fricourt found the carriageway littered with 20th Manchesters' dead. They arrived in the village's ruins about midnight. They found 'little resistance, and were able to pass through the village from end to end, reporting the capture of Fricourt in the early hours of the morning 2nd July. It was some hours after this that patrols from the 17th [Northern] Division also penetrated the village.'[223]

Eight miles further back at Heilly, Horne appraised his corps' performance in a letter laden with subtext and understatement. He made no direct comment on his abortive mid-afternoon Fricourt gamble, but did offer up some kind of oblique explanation: 'The [III] Corps to the north of us have not got on too well. Not as well as I first heard. We have done pretty well — very hard fighting. The [XIII] Corps to the south [sic, should be east] of us has done very well. We shall have to stick on hard tonight and tomorrow against counterattacks, I expect.'[224] Horne was obviously frustrated that III Corps had materially overstated its performance earlier in the day, this information having tempted him into a casualty-heavy and failed attempt to take Fricourt much earlier than planned. Horne's statement that his corps had done 'pretty well' went to his moderate satisfaction with the results achieved, but also suggested he saw much room for improvement, although he never did expand fully on either that viewpoint or his decision to implement the attack on Fricourt ahead of schedule.

Horne's XV Corps had done well overall, but had only partially achieved its objectives. Twenty-first Division had advanced about 1000 yards beyond the German front line on the upper slopes of Fricourt Spur, while the 7th had progressed 1000–1500 yards and taken Mametz. Together they had effectively outflanked Fricourt, which would effectively fall the next day. Some 1625 prisoners had been taken. The seven-day bombardment had mostly destroyed or neutralised Hahn's supporting artillery, robbing the 28th of defensive shellfire. In places north of Fricourt and around Mametz the British artillery had wreaked enough destruction to facilitate localised break-ins, which were subsequently exploited. The creeping barrage had helped initial waves cross over — more so the 21st's quick-time vanguard than the 7th, advancing at walking pace — but had thereafter outpaced the infantry. Sufficient enemy machine guns had survived the shellfire to either slow or, in the case of 50th Brigade before Fricourt, absolutely stop progress. Horne's artillery had done well, but it had needed more guns, more shells and more-focused fire for the infantry to achieve an emphatic outcome. All of this said, Hahn's command on 1 July amounted to a successful but costly salvage operation in positions that had been frequently poorly developed to begin with and then wrecked by shellfire.[225] His tactical decision-making in a fluid situation — using RIR109 and RIR111 as ground-holding units while reinforcing intermediate positions further back — was timely and forward-looking, even if it ran counter to prevailing German defensive doctrine. Horne's corps had managed a convincing break-in at Fricourt–Mametz, but Hahn was correct when he said that the British 'attempt to break through failed due to the tenacious bravery of our troops.'[226]

Partial victory came at a bloody price. Early on 2 July, Sapper Francis Palmer-Cook, RE, saw a padre plucking identity discs from the dead of the previous day: 'His arm was full of them, from his wrist right up past his elbow.'[227] Seven battalion commanders were casualties — three killed, two dead from wounds and two wounded.[228] The 7th recorded 3380 casualties, of whom 1032 were killed, 2321 were wounded and 27 were missing. The 21st suffered 4256 casualties, among them 1182 dead, 2962 wounded and 112 missing. Fiftieth Brigade's two attacking battalions amassed 557 dead including one battalion commander,[229] 565 wounded and 33 missing, all for no gains of military value. Altogether, XV Corps ran up 8791 casualties, and of these 2771 were dead, 5848 were wounded and 172 were missing.

Horne later summed up his corps' losses as 'not very great, I am thankful to say.'[230] It was a conclusion that — in light of the negligible gains and galling British losses elsewhere this same day — does not seem entirely unfounded. But this ignores the 50th's sacrifice and the corps' avoidable losses, particularly in 20th Brigade, by known German strongpoints that should have been destroyed or suppressed before battle. Horne's assessment of the casualties was slippery, and his use of the phrase 'not very great' suggests they were much higher than he was comfortable with and certainly neither light nor moderate.

Losses among the German units facing XV Corps are more challenging to pin down. This has a lot to do with the difficulties in piecing together what happened to the shattered regiments involved, and the way in which German casualty statistics were compiled. RIR109 suffered up to 2089 casualties on 1 July, this number including about 556 dead and a further 943 prisoners.[231] The other 590 soldiers were temporarily missing, wounded or both, mostly on 1 July. Broadly speaking, about 1044 of RIR109's casualties were opposite XV Corps, of which about a quarter were dead.[232] RIR111's losses totalled 1826 for the period 24 June–4 July, among them 252 dead, 453 wounded and 1121 missing. Post-war tallies revealed that up to 1703 of the casualties occurred on 1 July,[233] including 265 dead and the remaining 1438 either wounded, missing-to-return or prisoners.[234] Pioneer Battalion 13's 2nd Reserve Company lost 111 men,[235] and the IR23 company near

Mametz recorded 168 missing, including 43 dead.[236] Bavarian Pioneer Regiment suffered at least 182 casualties, with 17 dead, 150 prisoners and 15 wounded.[237] German casualties for the defence of Fricourt–Mametz salient therefore totalled up to 3208, or one for every 2.7 British.

Such bald statistics were of little interest to Baden, Bavarian and Prussian veterans who years later remembered close friends killed in battle:

A bullet came a-flying;
For me, or was it you?
It tore him clean away,
And at my feet he lay,
So part of me fell too.[238]

THE BONES OF 17,027 German soldiers are buried at the Soldatenfriedhof (Soldiers' Cemetery) just north of Fricourt. Some 5057 are buried in graves marked by a simple metal cross, each with multiple names or the words '*Ein Unbekannter Deutscher Soldat*' ('An Unknown German Soldier'). Another 11,970 men are in four mass graves at the back of the cemetery, each plot fronted with zinc panels naming those buried or thought buried within. No fewer than 6477 are unidentified. It takes about three minutes to meander the length of the mass graves without reading the names. Year-round this is a sombre, dark place that sits in semiotic contrast with the triumphalism of the Thiepval Memorial and the white Portland stone of Commonwealth War Graves Commission headstones.

Pad up and down the moss-infested grass rides and you will find several 1 July casualties interred from various parts of the battlefield. Back in 1916 their corpses were dumped in shell holes and trenches, or lost in the bowels of deep underground dugouts. Some were later disinterred and reburied at Fricourt or one of the other German war cemeteries in the general area. Most of the pre–1 July burials at German cemeteries behind the lines have long since vanished. Several of these graves appear to have been cleared, but more were simply forgotten or ploughed into the ground as French landowners reclaimed their properties after the war.

The thought rankled with grief-stricken Mannheim veteran Waldemar Stöckle in 1926, when he returned to RIR111's regimental cemetery at

Le Sars, on the Albert–Bapaume road. There, with dusk upon him, the former *Unteroffizier* found the regiment's war memorial broken and overgrown with nettles and shrubs as finches twittered hidden in the trees:

> I searched around trying to discover if at least one of the gravestones, which had been carved so carefully by their comrades, was still there. But not one single little cross could be found. If only the sole surviving stone could have spoken and told me what had happened in the meantime and where our fallen now lay; but it remained dumb.[239]

The crumbling German memorial is still there, still forgotten and still circled by nettles as finches chirrup the evening in.

CHAPTER 9

The Straw Man of Montauban

XIII Corps' two-speed operation around Montauban

'Every man had had his job explained to him, and each battalion had its objective, and so everything was prepared for a real advance.'[1]
— Corporal Norman Menzies, 2nd Royal Scots Fusiliers

'THE GUNS WERE blazing away; great black mushrooms were shooting up out of the surface of the white sea [of mist] in front as the big shells burst in the German trenches,' wrote Lieutenant-Colonel Harold Bidder, 21st Machine-Gun Company.[2] It was about 5 a.m. as he watched the first sunrays spill over the crater land before Montauban, catching dewdrops on the knee-length grass and throwing down long shadows from rusting barbed-wire pickets. 'It was a strange scene & we stood about on the grass round our position, apparently alone in the world on this brilliant morning, only disturbed by the crashing of the guns behind & weird upheavals in the mist surface.'[3] By 7 a.m. the silver-grey swirl was dissipating and the British trenches were alive with soldiers of 18th (Eastern) and 30th Divisions steeling themselves for battle, which was now just 30 minutes away.

Thirteenth Corps' success around Montauban now depended on the preparations made by its commander, a 53-year-old asthmatic and

Victoria Cross winner. Details-conscious Lieutenant-General Sir Walter Congreve, VC, had served in India and South Africa, winning the famed bronze cross for valour in the latter. He liked to go forward, see the lie of the land, speak with his men and assess the flow of battle.[4] A shell blast in 1917 would snatch Congreve's left hand away, the stump later crowned by a prosthetic hook, which made his hobby of solo yacht sailing much more challenging. Congreve's obituary described him as a 'perfect gentleman,' but somewhat paradoxically added that he spoke in the 'plainest language.'[5] His lack of interest in courting popularity[6] posed difficulties and produced several clashes with Fourth Army commander General Sir Henry Rawlinson, who always did prefer toadying subordinates. General Hubert Gough, Reserve Army commander, held a different view of Congreve: 'Very spare and lightly built, a frame giving evidence of the fragility of his constitution, a firm and very English countenance, with an indomitable and courageous will, a character which could remain outwardly unmoved at times of great personal sorrow or of immense responsibility and danger, an energy which made him active of body in spite of ill-health.'[7] But bullish Gough, with a polarising personality and no stranger to controversy, was biased. He inclined towards bold, decisive men like Congreve. His father, uncle and brother had all won the VC too.

Congreve's job was to storm German defences on the Mametz–Montauban ridge, providing flank support for Fourth Army's main thrust around Ovillers and La Boisselle and keeping contact with the French XX Corps immediately to the east. To the north, the ridge faded into the generous scoop of Caterpillar Valley, with a string of woods, villages and undulations thereafter leading to the Thiepval–Morval ridge. The Mametz–Montauban ridge's southern incline tapered towards the British front line, which was 400–700 yards in front of the villages of Carnoy and Maricourt. British observers could plainly see the chalkstone zigzags of the east–west-running German front line and, 700–1000 yards behind, its support network. Further back, the intermediate trench line of Montauban Alley ran roughly parallel to the Mametz–Montauban road and was tucked out of sight in Caterpillar Valley. Neither this trench, nor the unfinished second position, about 3000 yards behind the German front line on the valley's far lip, held any defensive fortifications of note. Further forward, Pommiers, Glatz and Dublin Redoubts — along with

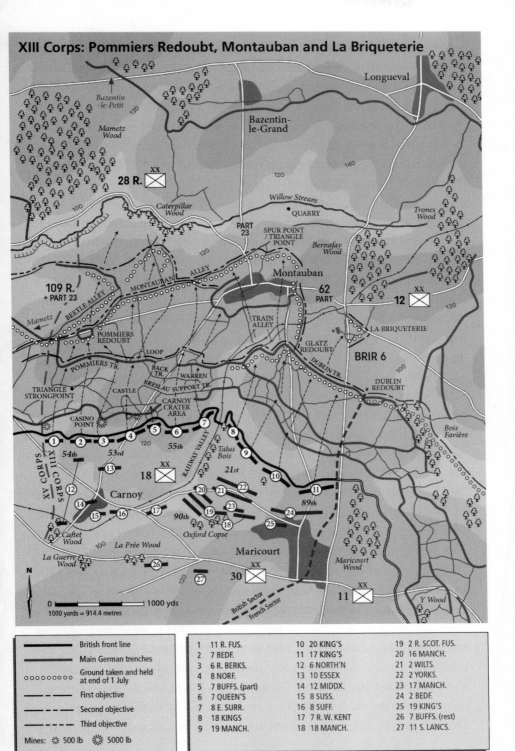

XIII Corps: Pommiers Redoubt, Montauban and La Briqueterie

Longueval

Bazentin-le-Petit

Mametz Wood

Bazentin-le-Grand

28 R. ⊠

Caterpillar Wood

Willow Stream

QUARRY

Trones Wood

PART 23

SPUR POINT / TRIANGLE POINT

Bernafay Wood

12 ⊠

109 R. + PART 23

MONTAUBAN ALLEY

BEETLE ALLEY

Mametz

Montauban

62 PART

TRAIN ALLEY

LA BRIQUETERIE

POMMIERS REDOUBT

LOOP

GLATZ REDOUBT

DUBLIN TR.

BRIR 6

POMMIERS TR.

BACK TR.

WARREN

DUBLIN REDOUBT

BRESLAU SUPPORT TR.

TRIANGLE STRONGPOINT

CASTLE

CARNOY CRATER AREA

CASINO POINT

Bois Favière

① ② ③ ④ ⑤ ⑥ ⑦ ⑧

XIII CORPS

54th

53rd

120

55th

RAILWAY VALLEY

Talus Bois

⑨

21st

⑩

XV CORPS

⑬

18 ⊠

Carnoy

⑫

⑭

⑮ ⑯

⑰

90th

⑳ ㉑ ㉒

㉓

⑲

⑱

Oxford Copse

㉔ ㉕

89th

⑪

Caftet Wood

La Prée Wood

Maricourt

Maricourt Wood

La Guerre Wood

㉖

N

㉗

30 ⊠

11 ⊠

Y Wood

0   1000 yds
1000 yards = 914.4 metres

British Sector
French Sector

British front line		
Main German trenches		
Ground taken and held at end of 1 July		
First objective		
Second objective		
Third objective		
Mines: ❋ 500 lb ❊ 5000 lb		

1	11 R. FUS.	10	20 KING'S	19	2 R. SCOT. FUS.
2	7 BEDF.	11	17 KING'S	20	16 MANCH.
3	6 R. BERKS.	12	6 NORTH'N	21	2 WILTS.
4	8 NORF.	13	10 ESSEX	22	2 YORKS.
5	7 BUFFS. (part)	14	12 MIDDX.	23	17 MANCH.
6	7 QUEEN'S	15	8 SUSS.	24	2 BEDF.
7	8 E. SURR.	16	8 SUFF.	25	19 KING'S
8	18 KINGS	17	7 R. W. KENT	26	7 BUFFS. (rest)
9	19 MANCH.	18	18 MANCH.	27	11 S. LANCS.

strongpoints The Loop, The Castle and The Warren — all overlooked large sweeps of no-man's-land, and were in turn watched over by British observers from high ground near Maricourt. Encouragingly, most of this German defensive network was in plain view, and each successive line was weaker than the one preceding it. This point was not lost on Congreve, who — albeit writing late on 1 July — noted that Fourth Army's attacks between La Boisselle and Serre 'did not get on so well but they had a much harder job.'[8] It was a fair assessment.

A further complicating factor was the German order of battle opposing XIII Corps. Here, running obliquely west of Montauban, was the demarcation line between 28th Reserve and 12th Infantry Divisions. The 28th's sector was roughly west of the Carnoy–Montauban road and held by a battalion of Reserve Infantry Regiment 109 (RIR109) and elements of Infantry Regiment 23 (IR23). East of the carriageway, before and around Montauban, the 12th's patch was held by five companies of Bavarian Reserve Infantry Regiment 6 (BRIR6), in the front line, and elements of Infantry Regiment 62 (IR62) in support.[9] These units, along with others sprinkled throughout, numbered about 3000 men, among them Bavarians, Badeners, Württembergers and Prussians. The Bavarians, exhausted from labouring, had been revolved into the front line barely 24 hours before the attack to relieve fatigued, food-deprived Prussians suffering from poor morale. *Generalleutnant* Martin Châles de Beaulieu, commanding the 12th, and his boss, *Generalleutnant* Hermann von Stein, commanding XIV Reserve Corps, were responsible for this. Châles de Beaulieu had insisted the 62nd be replaced, even though he knew full well that a British attack was imminent.[10] Stein's error was in allowing this needless reshuffle — the Prussians' lot was not much different from that of any other front-line unit during 24–30 June — which robbed 12th and 28th divisions of essential local reserves. It was a prospect that did not sit well with *Hauptmann-der-Reserve* Ernst Klug, BRIR6: 'As hard as it sounds, we should not have replaced them. Our unweakened division [sic] could have then led a counter-attack with full strength following the attack on 1 July.'[11] Klug was more likely referring to his regiment rather than 10th Bavarian Infantry Division, which had already been split up due to a corps-wide shortage of manpower. The point, however, was that Châles de Beaulieu and Stein's eleventh-hour meddling with the composition of the front-line garrison would become a decisive factor in the looming battle.

Exposed German defences bore the brunt of British shellfire. Congreve said the 15–20-yards-wide German wire entanglements were 'splendidly cut everywhere' by the 60,000 tons of shells dropped on them.[12] As *Oberleutnant* H. Reymann, IR62, recalled: 'All three of the front line trenches were levelled and the whole area formed a large crater-field. Where our once broad wire obstacles stood you could only see shattered piles and fragments lying around.'[13] *Offizierstellvertreter* Joseph Busl, BRIR6, added that the just-inherited positions were hardly fit for purpose. His platoon had only three or four dugouts.[14] One of these collapsed with the loss of eight men.[15] There were also fewer deep dugouts than elsewhere in XIV Reserve Corps' battle front, and these were mostly under the front-line system, overcrowded, exposed to shellfire and in generally poor condition.[16] In places the German front-line system had been so comprehensively destroyed that it was difficult to tell whether it even had dugouts.[17] Telephone links between regimental headquarters, battalion sectors and the artillery were virtually non-existent, meaning communication was reliant on runners.[18] Moreover, several Bavarian companies were under the tactical command of unfamiliar Prussian officers,[19] and, because of the reshuffle, unit boundary lines were confused. *Oberst* Jakob Leibrock, commanding BRIR6, was concerned that Châles de Beaulieu and Stein had disregarded Supreme Army Command's prevailing defensive doctrine of the day: 'The independent and automatic cooperation of all departments, on which rightly so much emphasis and value had been placed during training and in the past year of war, and which had to be considered a main factor of our combat capability, was altogether absent.'[20] Another factor was the lack of import that Châles de Beaulieu's headquarters attached to the warning signals flowing in from subordinates on the ground about the disrepair of the divisional sector.[21] There can be no doubt that German defences between Montauban and Mametz were vulnerable to a rehearsed infantry attack that was well supported by artillery.

Congreve's gunners had pummelled the 12th's and 28th's artillery into submission, with assistance from some French heavy batteries. Thirteenth Corps had accumulated about 76 heavy guns, or about one for every 47 yards of front, and about 205 field guns, or one to every 17 yards.[22] Multiple trench mortars would join the last few minutes of the bombardment from Russian Saps opened in no-man's-land overnight on 30 June. This firepower — combined with effective location of enemy batteries by Royal Flying Corps (RFC) observers — resulted in numerous German guns being destroyed during 24–30 June and then on 1 July. Due to the lack of tactical and strategic value attached to this ground by successive German commanders, it held a comparatively poor concentration of artillery, perhaps about 50 field and heavy guns.[23] Twenty-eighth Reserve Division was supposed to have 25 guns supporting its positions east of Mametz, while the 12th probably had a similar number behind Montauban.[24] But, lack of fire restraint, poor camouflage and low-quality battery positions meant that this already-sparse barrel stock was quickly eroded by counter-battery fire. German accounts state that artillery in the Mametz–Montauban area suffered 'considerable losses' and that its 'fighting power fell off more and more'[25] as 1 July approached: 'Numerous guns were lost, especially among the stationary batteries in Caterpillar Valley Wood and at Bazentin-le-Grand. ... This was all the more serious because [of] the shellfire-torn positions.'[26] This applied equally to RIR109 and BRIR6. Come dawn on 1 July, neither the 12th nor the 28th had sufficient surviving guns to provide close defensive shellfire for the front-line system that would destroy, impede or isolate any British attack, let alone one that broke into their positions.

Congreve's plan to tackle these shellfire-shattered German defences with 18th (Eastern) and 30th Divisions was bold and relatively straightforward. Thirteenth Corps had a total ration strength of 74,615 all ranks, but of these an estimated 15,220 infantry officers and men, including elements from various divisional units, were directly involved in the attack.[27] Congreve's plan comprised three phases, each a progression of the one preceding it. The first phase took in the capture of the German front and reserve lines, the Mametz–Montauban ridge, Montauban village and Montauban Alley. The 18th and 30th would then establish a long flank and link up with the infantry of the French XX Corps at Dublin Redoubt, which was just east of the Maricourt–Longueval road and about halfway between Bernafay and Maricourt Woods. The second and third phases, conditional on Fourth Army's gains north of Fricourt, would see XIII Corps' advance swinging firmly northeast to take Bernafay and Trônes Woods, Falfemont Farm and Guillemont in combination with the neighbouring French XX Corps' seizure of Hardecourt and Maurepas. Thirteenth Corps was to provide flank support to Rawlinson's main thrust around Ovillers and La Boisselle, but the proposed latter phases were never a carte-blanche licence for exploitation.

The 18th and 30th would attack uphill from the low ground in front of Carnoy and Maricourt. Their respective attack frontages were about 2000 yards and 1500 yards. No fewer than six Russian Saps had been carved out beneath no-man's-land; these were to provide covered passage for infantry once their heads were blown open shortly after Zero hour. The 18th, commanded by Major-General Sir Ivor Maxse, would advance 1500–2000 yards to capture the Mametz–Montauban ridge and then Montauban Alley. The 30th, commanded by Major-General Sir John Shea, would, on its left, advance 2000–2500 yards, take Montauban and come up alongside the 18th, while its right would press forward 1000–1500 yards to take Dublin Trench and maintain contact with the French. Both divisions would use all three of their infantry brigades. They would follow a timetabled artillery barrage — the heavy guns lifting their shellfire from one trench line to the next, while the field guns stepped their fire back in short lifts from one German trench to the next.[28] This was not a pure creeping barrage, as the timed curtain of shellfire would not creep over the German positions at consistent intervals of time and distance. Ninth (Scottish) Division was about two miles away, in corps reserve, and tucked behind Maricourt Ridge.

At dawn on 1 July, all of the pieces were in place, but Congreve was a tad unsettled: 'Daylight hours before [Zero] very anxious as I had the Infantry of 2 Divisions packed into Carnoy Valley where every shell must have told on it but the Bosch did nothing.'[29]

'IT IS A strange feeling you get just in the couple of minutes before going over, but once over, everything is alright,' wrote Private James Smith, 17th King's, of the moments before 30th Division's attack began.[30] Corporal Joseph Quinn, 20th King's, downed a tot of rum in the 30th's assembly trenches: 'I can assure you, you don't get enough to make you feel like telling anyone the history of your past life, let alone getting to the stage of being drunk.'[31] One soldier recalled that 'Five minutes to go' was whispered along crowded assembly trenches.[32] 'There was much handshaking and wishing one another good luck. I think we all made silent prayer.'[33] Then it was 'Get ready,' and the whistle blew. The same soldier, whose name is unknown, continued:

> I had just got one foot against the side of the trench and my hand
> on my rifle to climb over, when two shells burst immediately above
> me, covering me with dust. I was dazed for a few seconds. One
> shell had carried the [trench] bridge away above me; the other
> shattered my rifle and blew the bayonet to pieces. I picked up a
> wounded man's rifle and went over.[34]

The 30th's leading four battalions, two each from 21st and 89th Brigades, were swiftly across the up-to-500-yards-wide no-man's-land, moving quick time through the mist, rifles at the slope. Nineteenth Manchesters* and 17th[†] and 20th King's[‡] advanced on frontages of roughly 375 yards each, while 18th King's[§] was spread across 250 yards, its left pressed up hard against Railway Valley, which along with Talus Bois was roughly the boundary between XIII Corps' two attacking divisions. Eighty-ninth Brigade's 17th and 20th King's used four-wave formations, each comprising four platoons abreast,[35] with 2nd Bedfords in support and committed piecemeal to the battle, and some of its number attached to the lead battalions as mopping-up parties.[36] The leading waves of 21st Brigade's 18th King's and 19th Manchesters moved forward in extended order.[37] The 18th's fourth line was in columns of sections, while the 19th, which expected a tough fight to capture the fortified and well-defended Glatz Redoubt, sent its final waves forward in lines of half platoons.[38]

---

*   19th (Service) Battalion (4th City) Manchester Regiment. Also known as 4th Manchester Pals. 21st Brigade states 210 casualties 1–4 July (37 k, 126 w and 47 m). SDGW notes 61 deaths.

†   17th (Service) Battalion (1st City) King's (Liverpool Regiment). Also known as 1st Liverpool Pals. *Official History* records 103 casualties for 1 July. SDGW notes 2 deaths.

‡   20th (Service) Battalion (4th City) King's (Liverpool Regiment). Also known as 4th Liverpool Pals. Battalion war diary states 80 casualties. SDGW notes 23 deaths.

§   18th (Service) Battalion (2nd City) King's (Liverpool Regiment). Also known as 2nd Liverpool Pals. Battalion war diary estimates casualties at 500. SDGW notes 170 deaths.

Two platoons of 2nd Yorkshires* accompanied 18th King's and 19th Manchesters as mopping-up teams,[39] with the remainder advancing in columns of sections to occupy and consolidate the German front line, while much of 2nd Wiltshires† was used as carrying parties.[40]

The crossover was, said Private Thomas Pringle, 18th King's, 'no rush forward with wild Indian-like whoops' and nothing 'less than the execution of a set military movement.'[41] Seventeenth King's encountered only slight infantry resistance due to XIII Corps' artillery work 'having been very effective on the German trenches.'[42] Nineteenth Manchesters noted that the 'only checks to our advance were our own artillery barrages and these pauses were utilized for reorganisation of the lines.'[43] So effective had the bombardment been that the 30th's four-battalion vanguard was into the battered German trenches before the garrison could react. Stubbly-faced Bavarian soldiers were trapped in their dugouts with the 'spirit knocked out of them,'[44] said Lieutenant Edgar Willmer, 17th King's. The artillery had 'done their work well.'[45] One Liverpool officer stood between two German dugout exits and turned alternately left and right, shooting the occupants as they raced out 'just as if he were in a shooting saloon.'[46]

Advancing abreast, 89th Brigade's 20th and 17th King's and 21st Brigade's 18th King's and 19th Manchesters pressed on, pausing about 200 yards behind the German front line for their barrage to step back, some men sparking up cigarettes as they waited.[47] The experience by 17th King's of 'some shelling,' 'very slight infantry resistance' and 'little machine-gun fire' was broadly shared by 20th King's and 19th Manchesters.[48] By contrast, 18th King's met with 'heavy shelling and machine-gun fire enfilade.'[49] The few knots of resistance encountered by Brigadier-General the Honourable Ferdinand Stanley's 89th were overwhelmed and by 8.30 a.m. the 89th had advanced about 750 yards behind the German front line and was digging in at Dublin Trench, its final objective. The brigade's casualties were relatively light. Not so for Brigadier-General the Honourable Charles Sackville-West's 21st. The

---

*   2nd Battalion Alexandra, Princess of Wales's Own (Yorkshire Regiment). 21st Brigade states 260 casualties 1–4 July (56 k, 185 w and 19 m). SDGW notes 66 deaths.

†   2nd Battalion Duke of Edinburgh's (Wiltshire Regiment). 21st Brigade states 52 casualties 1–4 July (8 k, 43 w and 1 m). SDGW notes 3 deaths.

crammed-together 18th King's was briefly slowed by local resistance and suffered most of its 500 casualties from a machine gun away to its left in 18th (Eastern) Division's sector. Bombers broke the impasse, and by 8.35 a.m. the 21st had taken Train Alley and then Glatz Redoubt, which, said Private William Gregory, 18th King's, had been hurriedly evacuated:

> When we got to the Glatz Redoubt it was in a right mess. There were bodies everywhere, in all kinds of attitudes, some on fire and burning from the British bombardment. Debris and deserted equipment littered the area, and papers were fluttering round in the breeze. There were only two of us at the start, and then we met with others coming in.[50]

It had taken the 30th about an hour to secure its first objective; the attack was so far going rather more than less to plan thanks to the effectiveness of the pre-battle bombardment and the barrage supporting the infantry's advance across no-man's-land and then into the German positions.

Poor visibility, broken communications and the effective British shellfire consigned German infantry facing the 30th to failure. 'The attack,' wrote *Oberleutnant* Reymann, IR62, 'was probably recognised too late by the companies of BRIR6 due to the dense fog, and the first trench was in the enemy's hands right at the beginning of the attack.'[51] Two Bavarian companies holding this part of the line ran up 286 casualties, including 151 prisoners, of whom many were wounded. The other 135 were killed or wounded.[52] Clouds of mist, smoke and dust limited visibility to a matter of yards. Few apparently heard the bombardment step back, and broken telephone lines meant surviving artillery batteries could not be contacted. Red flares calling for support went unseen, and in any case there were too few guns to provide any meaningful defensive fire. The two German regiments defending Montauban were rapidly overrun and their soldiers promptly killed or taken prisoner.

'I was very badly wounded during a struggle with hand grenades at the beginning of the attack when British troops advanced into our trenches,' wrote *Reservist* Michael Theurlein, BRIR6.[53] 'My right leg was smashed and my arms and head were bleeding from many wounds.'[54] A few hundred yards behind the Bavarians, a 'weak' company of IR62 was wiped out.[55] The headquarters staff of Second Battalion, IR62 was killed or captured, while that of BRIR6 near Bernafay Wood was isolated by broken communications and had no idea of the unfolding rout.[56]

Offizierstellvertreter Busl, the officer deputy, claimed that the 'joy of battle shone out of everyone's eyes.'[57] He meant his men were wide-eyed with adrenaline and fear. 'Where the bombardment had torn large gaps [in the wire], the enemy was successful in penetrating. However our men soon fell on these Englishmen with hand-grenades and annihilated them after some time. Nevertheless the platoon was at the end of its power to resist because of the Englishmen's superior strength.'[58] Twice-wounded Busl surrendered. Others extricated themselves, making for Bernafay and Trônes Woods. *Kanonier* Hermann Heinrich, Field Artillery Regiment 21 (FAR21), was in Bernafay Wood: 'Due to the constant barrage our guns were unusable. … Retreating infantry told us that the English were on their heels.'[59] The remnants of Heinrich's battery later pulled back to Guillemont and he found himself in an ad-hoc command post. 'I heard nothing other than the crash of exploding shells, I was repeatedly covered with dirt from shell blasts,' he wrote.[60]

'I felt as if an elephant had kicked me,' said Private Charles Healey, 19th Manchesters, of the advance by 21st Brigade.[61] He was shot in the chest, right thumb, left thigh and genitals. 'As the sun was sinking I thought it was near the end.'[62] Stretcher bearers later picked him up. Back in the assembly trenches, machine-gun officer Lieutenant-Colonel Bidder watched the wounded raising their tin hats on entrenching-tool handles, 'giving the effect of a field of gigantic mushrooms.'[63] Private Thomas Frank, in follow-up battalion 2nd Yorkshires, said his company was mostly 'shot down before we got over. We only had to put our heads over the top and we got it.'[64] Although the German wire was well cut, 'you had to watch yourself from not getting tripped up.'[65] Private Pringle recalled 'rivalry, you know, between the different companies, and it proves a fine incentive in an attack.'[66] He said 18th King's encountered 'no opposition at the first trench. Our artillery had peppered it far too well, and we saw German bodies lying all along.'[67] Further on, German machine-gunners sprayed the left flank of the 18th King's with a stream of bullets. 'You could see the flash as it passed,' said Private Gregory, his friends felled all around him.[68] Most of the battalion's casualties lay beyond the German support line, said Private Sydney Steele, also 18th King's, who saw 'fellows just lying there, higgledy-piggledy all over the place, some two, three and four high — one mass of dead men as far as you could see.'[69]

Over in 89th Brigade's sector, adjacent to the French, Lieutenant Willmer noted 'some mist about but the sun broke through and glinted on the men's bayonets' as they began moving forward. 'There was no hurry and so far as our battalion was concerned, very little resistance.'[70] Private Francis Woods, 17th King's, said he 'bombed and searched dugouts, cleared trenches of prisoners and dead, and held on.'[71] Some German soldiers were pleased to be captives: 'They were in a fearfully unkempt condition, with days of growth on their faces, and some of them looked to be quite fifty-nine years of age.'[72] One diminutive Liverpudlian held 16 Germans prisoner at the point of a bayonet and unloaded rifle; another thought the scene 'too funny for words, and I'd have given anything to have had a camera.'[73] Private Robert Fleetwood, 20th King's, was hooked in some barbed wire and dropped his rifle to free himself. 'When I turned around to pick up my rifle, I got a shock. A German had it, and he was pointing it right at me. I thought my last day had come.'[74] The German did not shoot; he bolted. 'I took a rifle from a dead German but found I didn't know how to use it!'[75] Corporal Quinn, not far away, was bemused by the language of soldiers snared in wire: 'It was such glowing hot language that the wire should have melted away.'[76] He soon reached Dublin Trench. 'It all seemed too easy, much easier than when we had practised it behind the lines. Of course shells were dropping all about us, but we took them philosophically.'[77]

Ninetieth Brigade moved forward at about 8.30 a.m. with orders to leapfrog 21st Brigade and take Montauban. It took the 90th about an hour to get to the Train Alley area, its three attack battalions also suffering heavy casualties from machine guns in 18th (Eastern) Division's sector and occasional shrapnel bursts overhead.[78] Sixteenth* and 17th Manchesters† advanced in linear waves.[79] They were followed by the

---

* 16th (Service) Battalion (1st City) Manchester Regiment. Also known as 1st Manchester Pals. 90th Brigade states 351 casualties 1–3 July (40 k, 281 w and 30 m). SDGW notes 81 deaths.

† 17th (Service) Battalion (2nd City) Manchester Regiment. Also known as 2nd Manchester Pals. 90th Brigade states 342 casualties 1–3 July (67 k, 225 w and 50 m). SDGW notes 116 deaths.

rump of 2nd Royal Scots Fusiliers,[*] which had some platoons attached to the 16th and 17th for mopping-up.[80] Eighteenth Manchesters[†] provided carrying parties.[81] German shellfire did 'little damage owing to the formation adopted and to the soft nature of the ground.'[82] Captain Ernest Sotham, 16th Manchesters, wrote: 'The advance took place in quick time with rifles slung & the Trench bridges were carried & each man carried in addition to his extra S.A.A. [small-arms ammunition], several bombs, sandbags, full marching order with the next day's ration.'[83]

Ninetieth Brigade's attacking battalions arrived at their battlefield jumping-off line about 15 minutes early, before the barrage 'plastering' Montauban had lifted.[84] Leading waves sheltered in the trench; the rest waited bellies to ground a little behind. The German machine gun in 18th (Eastern) Division's sector was finally silenced. Officer casualties in the Manchester battalions meant the 90th's advance was delayed. It finally began at about 10 a.m. when the shellfire lifted off brickheap-like Montauban and a fusillade from a solitary machine gun broke the inertia. Orderly attack structure was lost; men from 16th and 17th Manchesters, along with 2nd Royal Scots Fusiliers, bunched into two dense lines about 400 yards apart and continued ahead quick time, although some walked.[85] A smoke screen on the open ground before Montauban hid their vulnerability. The trench around the village's southern outskirts was undefended and overrun, with the Manchesters and Royal Scots Fusiliers entering the tumbled-down village and ratting its ruins for enemy soldiers from about 10.05 a.m. Second-Lieutenant Alfred Fraser-Harris, an observation officer for Brigadier-General the Honourable Charles Steavenson's 90th Brigade headquarters, looked on: 'I plodded on keeping my eyes on Montauban which seemed hundreds of miles away. Eventually I got near enough to see the first line of troops entering the village. And they had not had much trouble. Then I ran back as fast as I could and reported to the Brigadier.'[86] Within the hour the Manchesters had moved through the village, and at about 10.30 a.m. seized their portion of

---

[*]   2nd Battalion Royal Scots Fusiliers. Battalion war diary states 178 casualties (20 k, 100 w and 58 m). SDGW notes 46 deaths.

[†]   18th (Service) Battalion (3rd City) Manchester Regiment. Also known as 3rd Manchester Pals. Battalion war diary states killed, wounded and missing totalled 176 on 1 July. SDGW notes 38 deaths.

Montauban Alley, a few hundred yards beyond its northern houses, and with it the 30th's final objective.

'Shells were exploding all round us & there was a steady drone of small arms fire,' said Private Squire Brookes, 16th Manchesters, of the advance to Montauban.[87] 'Men went down with increasing frequency.'[88] Lance-Corporal Frank Gudgeon, 16th Manchesters, thought someone had kicked him in the right calf muscle. It was a bullet. Another cut through the instep of his boot, a third lodged itself in his field dressing and two more passed between his tunic and pack. Gudgeon sheltered in Montauban Alley and chatted to a silent German soldier sitting on the fire-step nearby: 'I touched him and he fell off the fire step. I then saw his shirt front was open and [he had] a bullet wound near the heart. He had some photos in his hand, evidently of his wife and family.'[89] Private Allan Bell, 17th Manchesters, thought the attack so well planned that the 'actual thing was like another rehearsal.'[90] He saw an officer shot in the head who 'must have died that instant.' He also saw a 'Jock' of the 2nd Royal Scots Fusiliers shot through the jaw and in lingering pain. 'When I got to the far end of Montauban I at once lay down and fired at a retreating German gun team who were dragging a field gun by a rope. I well remember adjusting my aim for the weight of the bayonet, as taught.'[91] A bullet punched through Bell's helmet and creased his scalp. 'Yer wanna be more careful,' he was told a few days later when issued a replacement helmet, as if he needed the advice.

'I didn't get far,' recalled Corporal Norman Menzies, 2nd Royal Scots Fusiliers, who was shot in the left thigh near the old German front line.[92] 'I lay on "Fritz's old firing step" waiting on the stretcher-bearers to come for me, the sun burning tremendously and the "whiz-bangs" coming over every three minutes.' At about 3 p.m. Menzies struck out for safety. 'I managed to roll off the firing step into the bottom of the trench, and with the aid of a rifle used as a crutch hobbled painfully towards the dressing station.' It took him five hours to get there.

Montauban was a ruin of skeletal buildings and piles of bricks, with all kinds of debris and corpses strewn about. Captain Hubert Worthington, 16th Manchesters, thought it a 'scene of complete devastation so that even the alignment of the streets could scarcely be traced.'[93] Enemy soldiers who resisted were 'driven into cellars and dug outs & bombed.' Hundreds of enemy soldiers surrendered to the leading wave as it passed through the ruined village. Another Mancunian said that 'most of the houses had been knocked head-over-heels. The only ones I saw standing were a couple of cafes.'[94] He added that while plenty of German soldiers had fled, others were 'monkeying about the ruins.'[95] Small groups of Manchesters worked from one collapsed building to the next, bombing nests of resistance into silence. The same soldier contined: 'We saw some Huns in a ground-floor room, so we dropped a Mills bomb through the window, and didn't wait for an answer.'[96] A Sergeant Watkins, Manchester Regiment, was in one of the Montauban mopping-up parties:

The Germans put up a better fight here than they had done in the first three lines of trenches. They had constructed a veritable rabbit warren of communication trenches until they formed a regular ring around the village. Each house was connected with the other, so that the British had a terror of a time in rounding them up. No sooner did we enter into one cellar than they ran into the next and sniped at us all the time. But our men were not to be beaten like that. They became like bloomin' ferrets and drove them out. Fritz doesn't like cold steel.[97]

Although the attack's vanguard had moved on through Montauban to secure the final objective, it was several hours before all resistance in the village was cowed and its ruins cleared of enemy soldiers.

The view from Montauban Alley was over the deep east–west-running scoop of Caterpillar Valley. On the far side, the British soldiers could see the infamous horseshoe of woods — Caterpillar, Mametz, Bazentin, High, Delville, Trônes and Bernafay Woods — that would later become notorious death traps, as well as, and all a mile or more away, Longueval to the northeast, the two Bazentin villages to the north and Contalmaison to the west.[98] A stream of German infantry was retreating down the Montauban–Bazentin-le-Grand road and artillery observers who reached the forward area quickly enough lost no time in directing shellfire onto them. A trinity of advanced German field guns in Caterpillar Valley was rushed and captured at about 11 a.m., the first of the Somme offensive. For any weary, sweaty foot sloggers taking all of this in from the outskirts of Montauban, it looked as if much more could be achieved, but — as we shall soon see — it was never going to be quite that simple.

Oberst Leibrock, commanding BRIR6, was surprised when a lone British soldier demanded the surrender of his regimental headquarters staff at La Briqueterie, near Bernafay Wood.[99] The stray soldier was himself taken prisoner by Leibrock's men at about 10 a.m. He told his captors that Montauban was under attack and that the situation for the Germans at Mametz further west was grim.[100] It was the first indication that Leibrock had of 'something bad' being afoot.[101] Two-and-a-half hours later, La Briqueterie was under attack by a company of 20th King's. It went forward at 12.30 p.m., after a 30-minute bombardment, to clear the brickwork's ruins, which were strewn with dead, and whose chimney had previously been used as an observation tower. Attempts by Leibrock and his staff to bring a machine gun into action failed; they were cornered in their dugout. Grenades were tossed down the stairs, casualties increased.[102] As Leibrock told it:

> An English breakthrough, such as the one described by the captive Englishman, appeared to me ever more likely. Under these circumstances I considered further sacrifice to be pointless and I also could not expect a counter attack in view of the total silence of the German artillery, therefore I decided after still further discussion with remarks to the officers to surrender.[103]

The company of 20th King's held the pulverised ground of La Briqueterie throughout the afternoon under shellfire, its casualties steadily mounting. Patrols went forward to probe the southern outskirts of Bernafay Wood, about 250 yards away, there finding 'many German corpses and bringing back a good many prisoners.'[104] *Kanonier* Heinrich, the gunner in FAR21, said when these patrols reached the wood they 'appeared to have a leisurely walk around' before withdrawing.[105] Bernafay Wood remained in German hands.

British infantry quickly began consolidation ahead of an anticipated German counterattack. Montauban Alley was converted into a crude front-line trench with a fire-step facing Caterpillar Valley, while defensive strongpoints were pushed forward at pre-allocated points.[106] 'The digging of trenches was very difficult owing to the fact that the village was a mass of shell holes & loose crumbling earth. The total inadequacy of trenches in such soil was abundantly proved in the next 48 hours,' wrote the battalion war diarist for 17th Manchesters.[107] Sniper, machine-gun and sporadic shellfire caused a constant trickle of casualties, which increased from early afternoon as retreating German gunners regrouped and began shelling the eastern half of the village and surrounds with shrapnel and high-explosive projectiles.[108] The 201st Field Company, Royal Engineers (RE), suffered heavy casualties while working in Montauban's ruins throughout the afternoon.[109] Captain Worthington, wounded that afternoon, described the tactical situation:

> The field of fire from Montauban Alley was limited as the ground
> in front fell away rapidly into Caterpillar Wood Valley. Spur
> Point [better known as Triangle Point], an important position in
> advance of Montauban Alley which commanded the valley, could
> not be occupied, as our guns were shelling the spot. ... Unlike
> the 16th, the 17th Manchesters on the right had an excellent field
> of fire with clear vision down and up to Longueval and across
> to Bernafay Wood. It had been expected that the counter attack
> would come from Bernafay Wood but this did not happen [at this
> time].[110]

Sixteenth and 17th Manchesters held an exposed salient. To the left, 18th (Eastern) Division had yet to come up alongside them, while to the right approaches from Bernafay Wood a few hundred yards away were also open. It would be another five to six hours before the 30th's left flank was shored up, and even then sporadic hostile shellfire continued.[111]

Shea, the 'smart fellow' with 'plenty of brains and energy' at the helm of 30th Division,[112] found little cause for complaint with his division's performance. The divisional war diary is studded with entries outlining its quick gains. Reports confirmed that the French were also progressing well to the east, but that Maxse's 18th (Eastern) Division was lagging behind in the two-and-a-half hours to 11.45 a.m.[113] 'Once the [enfilade] fire from the left was neglected [sic] and the advance pushed on, the village of Montauban fell an easy victim,' Shea wrote in an after-battle report.[114] The 30th had performed so well and — barring the casualties and temporary hold-ups here and there — so closely to plan that Shea was largely surplus to requirements: there simply was no reason for him to intervene in the flow of a battle that his men had prepared for, rehearsed and executed so thoroughly and effectively.

The 30th racked up 3011 casualties. These comprised 828 fatalities (including one battalion commander),[115] 2118 wounded, 53 missing and 12 prisoners.[116] BRIR6 incurred 1809 casualties between arriving on the Somme and withdrawing overnight on 1 July.[117] Of these, 806 were in its five front-line companies facing XIII Corps on battle day, and included 308 dead, 418 prisoners, 77 wounded and 3 missing.[118] IR62 recorded 737 casualties for 1 July, with an estimated 250 fighting against the 30th.[119] The rest of IR62's and BRIR6's casualties were suffered against the French further south. Thirtieth Division's victory cost 2.9 casualties for every one German, although the German figure included a significant number of prisoners.

Lugging tools and coils of gleaming barbed wire forward to consolidate the captured ground was no easy task. Corporal Quinn, 20th King's, watched supply columns labour forward: 'Suddenly a "Jack Johnson" would scream over our heads and appear to burst within twenty yards of the carrier. At any rate, the smoke from it would clear away and you would again see him like the man "off to Philadelphia," striding forward.'[120] Private Ernest Grindley, 19th Manchesters, had a kerosene tin of water in one hand, a bag of corned beef in the other, semaphore flags tucked into his backpack, and a rifle slung over his shoulder: 'How we managed to get the food to them in the face of all the gun fire without becoming victims was just a case of "You were lucky, mate."'[121] Private Harold Dunn, 19th King's,* found the haul up to Dublin Trench heavy work. 'The heat of the sun was intense, and we were like grease spots.'[122] Dunn and his group were soon digging a strongpoint, their tunics and webbing off while they swung pick and spade. Then some shrapnel shells burst overhead and a few high-explosive projectiles landed nearby:[123] 'It was just about then that I received my first wound. It [was] a piece of

---

* 19th (Service) Battalion (3rd City) King's (Liverpool Regiment). Also known as 3rd Liverpool Pals. 89th Brigade states 70 casualties 1–4 July (12 k, 55 w and 3 m). SDGW notes 13 deaths.

shrapnel entering my right leg above the knee. At the same time three of my pals were killed (blown to atoms) and two more wounded.'[124]

'I CAN'T TELL you the feeling I had. It was a mixture of all kinds of madness,' recalled Private Clifford Barden, 7th Royal West Kents, of the minutes before 18th (Eastern) Division began its attack.[125] Second-Lieutenant William Tullock, 53rd Machine-Gun Company, remembered a 'great deal of jesting' about the likely mortality rate:[126] 'Clearly there was a tension which none could wholly conceal.'[127] Tullock, killed on 20 July and buried at Péronne Road Cemetery near Maricourt, said the intense shellfire provided a 'memory never to be erased from the mind.'[128] Private Norman Norton, 8th Norfolks, had a 'nasty feeling in the stomach.'[129] Lieutenant Philip Heath, 55th Trench Mortar Battery, wondered 'how much more of it I could stand without bursting my eardrums or going crazy.'[130] Private Clarrie Jarman, 7th Queen's, said with the 'blast of whistles and after wishing our chums the best of luck, over the top we went expecting, as we had been told, just a walkover.'[131] Lance-Corporal John Cousins, 7th Bedfords, was impatient: 'For God's sake let us get going, it's a relief to hear the whistle signal. We start to scramble out of our trenches through the gaps previously cut in the barbed wire and start to trot forward.'[132]

No-man's-land was 100–400 yards wide, but mostly about 250 yards, and the 18th deployed about six battalions abreast across its divisional sector, on varying frontages of 200–400 yards. All would push forward in a slight northeasterly direction. Those with less distance to travel to the German line — 11th Royal Fusiliers and two platoons of 7th Buffs — began at 7.30 a.m, the rest two to three minutes before Zero, when their leading companies moved into no-man's-land to form up before formally starting.[133] All used variations of the standard four-wave formation. The leading waves of 11th Royal Fusiliers, 7th Bedfords, 6th Royal Berkshires, 7th Queen's and 8th East Surreys went forward in extended lines, with at least some of those following deployed in artillery formation to mitigate the damage caused by anticipated German defensive shellfire.[134] Only 8th Norfolks advanced in four linear waves, and it is probable that the half company of 7th Buffs at the Carnoy craters used a similar formation.[135] The Carnoy craters was an area of no-man's-land east of the Carnoy–Montauban road that was heavily dimpled with cavities from the blasts of multiple mines in the 18 months to 1 July. Meantime, support battalions — 10th Essex, 6th Northamptons and the remainder of 7th Buffs — provided one or two platoons to work as mopping-up teams for the battalions leading the attack, the remainder being used to hold the old front line, provide carrying parties or act as reinforcements.[136]

Fifty-third and 54th Brigades reached their initial objectives in just 30 minutes, following a barrage of artillery and machine-gun fire. Two mine blasts preceded Zero by about three minutes. On the left, 54th's 11th Royal Fusiliers* and 7th Bedfords† advanced broadly between the two craters. Both were smartly across the German front and support lines with, respectively, 'few' and 'extremely small' losses.[137] Lance-Corporal Cousins found the advance hard work: 'I am carrying a Lewis gun and a pannier of 2 drums of ammunition. I find it impossible to keep up with the fast-moving men with rifles only.'[138] Further on, the Bedfords suffered heavily from a machine gun at The Triangle strongpoint, which was overpowered with rifle and grenade. Eleventh Royal Fusiliers made good time, bombers overcoming pockets of resistance. So rapid was the advance that the 11th had to pause just prior to Pommiers Trench, its first objective, and wait for the barrage to step back further.[139] After it lifted, 11th Royal Fusiliers and 7th Bedfords seized their objective, which was 750–1000 yards from their jumping-off lines, at about 8 a.m.[140]

One of the dead was Lance-Corporal Richard Goebel, a 40-year-old in 7th Bedfords. The electric gas-stoking machine driver from Fulham, London, had served in the Royal Marines before the war. He is buried at Dantzig Alley British Cemetery near Mametz. Several years later his family — wife Edith, 42, and school-age daughters Edith and Alfreda — penned a simple epitaph for his headstone: 'In loving memory of our dad.' But, Goebel was just one among many casualties. Lance-Corporal Cousins, also 7th Bedfords, confessed to a 'callous indifference to what happened to other people as long as it doesn't touch you so why worry.'[141]

Unteroffizier Friedrich Thomas, a pre-war paralegal from Karlsruhe in RIR109, watched 54th Brigade storm forward in 'great masses' towards

---

* 11th (Service) Battalion Royal Fusiliers (City of London Regiment). Battalion war diary states 222 casualties (53 k, 152 w and 17 m). SDGW notes 59 deaths.

† 7th (Service) Battalion Bedfordshire Regiment. Battalion war diary states 321 casualties (90 k, 225 w and 6 m). SDGW notes 87 deaths.

Pommiers Redoubt, which he knew as Jaminwerk: 'Our defence position was not as good as at La Boisselle and Ovillers, we had no protection against the enemy's fire and had to move towards the village [of] Mametz, leaving wounded and dead behind.'[142]

The advance on Pommiers Redoubt, the second objective and about 250 yards further on, began at about 8.30 a.m. Eleventh Royal Fusiliers, 7th Bedfords and a company of 10th Essex, from the neighbouring 54th Brigade, moved forward.[143] They faltered under frontal rifle and machine-gun fire while crossing the flat of the Mametz–Montauban ridge, with many soldiers shot down in the redoubt's partially cut wire. Cousins thought the fusillade murderous: 'Men were falling right & left of me screaming above the noise of shellfire and machine guns.'[144] Captain Wilfred Bull, 7th Bedfords, reckoned the 30 minutes outside the redoubt 'will be a nightmare for years to come.'[145] The redoubt was soon outflanked and rushed. Its defenders were killed or taken prisoner by 9.30 a.m. after a bruising, hour-long hand-to-hand scrap through trench bays and in dugouts.[146] Seventh Bedfords' war diarist later wrote of the heavy losses: 'Many of the dead lay round the front and flanks of the redoubt. It is unquestionable that the Germans who remained in the redoubt were either ordered or fully prepared to defend this last vital point in their line of defence to the last.'[147] Not all of the defenders there were prepared to fight to the end, as *Unteroffizier* Gustav Luttgers, RIR109, explained:[148]

> We realised it was the English who were behind us, so we jumped back into our trench. ... We tied a handkerchief to a rifle and waved it and the English came and rounded us up. We were very depressed but we knew that once we had surrendered the English wouldn't shoot us. We could see from their faces that they were as pleased as we were that it was all over, but they took all our watches from us.[149]

With Pommiers Redoubt captured, the now-mingled 11th Royal Fusiliers and 7th Bedfords, reinforced by 6th Northamptons,* pressed on to Beetle Alley, 100 yards on. They seized that trench at about 10.15 a.m.

---

* 6th (Service) Battalion Northamptonshire Regiment. Battalion war diary states 160 casualties (29 k, 127 w and 4 m). SDGW notes 32 deaths.

Attempts to bomb east along Montauban Alley towards the village 1000 yards away were thwarted by trench blocks of wire and wood, and devolved into fitful bomb-throwing contests that failed to produce results. This advanced line would be the high-tide mark of the 54th's advance for some hours, the exhausted and thirsty soldiers preparing their new positions for defence. Cousins recalled the 'frantic efforts to get organised, to find friends, the cessation of gun fire, an uncanny silence. Neither side knew where each other were [sic] for sure so artillery was out.'[150] Lieutenant Derick Capper, 8th Royal Sussex,* led his platoon of pioneers forward in artillery formation behind 11th Royal Fusiliers and up to the new front line:

> We were eventually able to get to work on making 'strong points' and I spent the rest of the day moving between them to supervise the work and see the sections had all the necessary equipment etc. By evening the fighting had died down and the Germans had been driven back across Caterpillar Valley well behind their original trench system. It was a fine night. ... I was pretty soon moving around after dark. Corpses were lying around and could not easily be seen so one was constantly treading on them — a very unpleasant sensation.[151]

The 54th had advanced 1000–1500 yards and secured its portion of the Mametz–Montauban ridge, but the 18th's other brigades were lagging.

Fifty-third Brigade attacked uphill, at first partially astride the Carnoy–Montauban road, to the right of the 54th. Initial progress on its right flank, where 8th Norfolks was attacking, was helped by bursts of liquid fire from two Livens Large Gallery Flame Projectors. These oil-fuelled metal dragons, 56 feet long and weighing 2.5 tons, lay hidden in more Russian Saps, just west of the road and the Carnoy craters.[152] They were about 60 yards from the German front line, but had a range of about 110 yards. Their nozzles had been pushed up overnight on 30 June. 'With a roar,' wrote Colonel Charles Foulkes, Special Brigade, RE, 'the streams of oil became ignited [at 7.30 a.m.] and shot forward towards the enemy,

---

* 8th (Service) Battalion (Pioneers) Royal Sussex Regiment. Battalion war diary states 95 casualties (11 k, 82 w and 2 m). SDGW notes 12 deaths.

being traversed slowly from side to side, while dense clouds of black smoke, flecked with flame, rose a hundred feet into the air.'[153] Second-Lieutenant Tullock, who was just behind the British front line, watched the khaki-clad figures of 8th Norfolks move forward:

> Spouts of liquid fire, accompanied by vast volumes of black
> smoke, shrouded the German trenches in a mantle of death.
> At the appointed hour crowds of small figures leaped into the
> battlefield. My heart stood still to see them. They seemed to move
> about in a confused manner — now appearing, now disappearing.
> How feeble and tiny they looked in that ghastly reek?! 'None
> will survive,' I said to myself. But the event gave me the lie, for
> gradually they passed and entered into the shell clouds, and as
> they passed others came. The smoke swallowed up the heroes in its
> folds.[154]

On the left, 6th Royal Berkshires* suffered some casualties from the 5000-pound Casino Point mine blast. As Captain Richard Rochfort of that battalion explained, 'There was a blinding flash, the whole of the earth seemed to shake and the mine went up. The earth was filled with huge lumps of earth. ... One man was killed by a sphere of earth five feet in diameter which fell on him.'[155] Lance-Corporal Edward Fisher, 10th Essex,† reckoned the mine sent up a fountain of earth as tall as Nelson's Column in Trafalgar Square, London: 'I saw huge slabs of earth and chalk thudding down, some with flames attached, onto the troops as they advanced.'[156] The blast obliterated a German machine-gun strongpoint, destroyed three dugouts and four sniper posts and resulted in shell-shocked enemy soldiers surrendering.[157] It also left a crater 97 feet wide and 30 feet deep, surrounded by a doily of brilliant-white chalkstone spoil.[158]

With the wire cut the Berkshires and 8th Norfolks‡ were promptly into the German front line and beyond.[159] Eighth Norfolks' right was

---

*   6th (Service) Battalion Princess Charlotte of Wales's (Royal Berkshire Regiment). Battalion war diary states 350 casualties. SDGW notes 91 deaths.

†   10th (Service) Battalion Essex Regiment. SDGW notes 29 deaths.

‡   8th (Service) Battalion Norfolk Regiment. Battalion war diary states 345 casualties (105 k, 227 w and 13 m). SDGW notes 108 deaths.

subsequently slowed by nests of resistance and enfilade from further east, but the advance of its left companies and 6th Royal Berkshires was unaffected, and it pressed on towards their first objective, Pommiers Trench.[160] Three machine guns slowed the advance; one crew was surprised by a small bombing party and charged, and the other crews retreated. Pommiers Trench was taken at about 7.50 a.m., but machine-gun strongpoint The Loop held out at its eastern end and caused many casualties. A company of 10th Essex was sent up as reinforcements. Bombing squads and Lewis guns sent to silence the strongpoint were held up by blocked trenches and failed. The rump of the 53rd was at its first objective on time, but casualties were heavy and on the right it was still held up by pockets of determined resistance.

'One fellow quite near me carrying a bag of bombs was hit & his bombs exploded giving him a terrible wound,' said Private Norton, a Lewis gunner.[161] 'We occupied Jerry's front line. One dug out enemy still firing up the shaft. One or two "mills" hand grenades after warning thrown down the shaft. No result. Then an officer of trench mortars threw down a football [of] 56lbs of high explosives, which blew in the entrance.'[162] Norton and a friend hauled a British officer whose knees had been smashed by bullets to safety. 'Heard later that he lived although crippled.'[163] Thirty-six-year-old *Landsturmann* August Kind, RIR109, was killed somewhere around the Casino Point crater, just a few weeks after writing a last postcard home to his sister. 'I'm still well, hope you are too. Hope to see you soon.'[164] Kind has no known grave.

Progress was slower again for 55th Brigade, which attacked up the incline east of the Carnoy–Montauban road behind a barrage of artillery and machine-gun fire. More than two battalions — from left to right, two platoons of 7th Buffs[*] and the 7th Queen's[†] and 8th East Surreys[‡] battalions — began to cross the up-to-250-yards-wide no-man's-land. Private Jarman later recalled: 'We had been drilled to go over in Star

---

[*]   7th (Service) Battalion Buffs (East Kent Regiment). 55th Brigade war diary states 205 casualties 1–2 July (52 k, 146 w and 7 m). SDGW notes 49 deaths.

[†]   7th (Service) Battalion Queen's (Royal West Surrey Regiment). Battalion war diary states 532 casualties (181 k, 293 w and 58 m). SDGW notes 159 deaths.

[‡]   8th (Service) Battalion East Surrey Regiment. Battalion war diary states 538 casualties (133 k and 405 w). SDGW notes 138 deaths.

Formation, the four sections of each platoon forming a star and then on approaching the German line to spread out in extended order.'[165] One of the Livens projectors apparently suppressed the garrison at the western end of the 150-yard-long Carnoy craters,[166] but not at its eastern extremity where the two 7th Buffs platoons made little impression. A machine-gun here tore into 7th Queen's and 8th East Surreys in enfilade. Casualties were heavy, 7th Queen's suffering 'very severely' in the welter of bullets.[167] The ensuing confusion and delay gave German defenders time to man their support line, held as the front line, and other positions further back. When the British barrage lifted, 7th Queen's was checked by small-arms fire and 'all advantage was lost.'[168] Eighth East Surreys had better luck and crossed the enemy front-line system, but was held up at a tangle of trenches known as The Warren until the neighbouring 30th Division's progress forced German infantry to retire. By 10 a.m., 8th East Surreys, helped by elements of two 7th Buffs companies, had bombed their way forward to just shy of Train Alley, their first objective. Fifty-fifth Brigade's progress, though, was alarmingly slow.

A bullet tore a chunk of Private Jarman's right calf muscle away early in the 7th Queen's attack: 'In the few minutes in which I remained conscious I had a look round and the ground was just covered with lads in khaki, dead, wounded and dying. The ground was being spattered with shrapnel, high explosives and bullets — it was almost impossible not to get hit and the noise of it was deafening. It was like being in a daze — the last thing I remember is seeing a Woking lad, [Lance-Corporal] Tommy Lomax, blown to nothing.'[169] Lomax is named on the Thiepval Memorial. Meantime, Lieutenant Heath watched 8th East Surreys go forward: 'Here, a single soldier would fall; there, a whole group would be mowed down by a machine gun, or disintegrate when a shell burst among them: but the lines still moved steadily forward. To me it seemed that these brave men were marching straight to victory, and I was tremendously elated.'[170] An hour later he was in the old German front line, whose 'sole inhabitants at this point were three dead, extremely dead, Germans with two or three other corpses round the traverse on each side.'[171] Perhaps these bodies were evidence of the vicious work done by Captain Claude Janion, 8th East Surreys. Janion reached the German front line and, as Heath recalled, had 'gone completely berserk; armed with a rifle and bayonet he was seen to kill ten Germans, most of them with the latter weapon.'[172] After the war, Janion, whose bravery on this day won him a Distinguished Service Order, became a school teacher in Johannesburg who taught his pupils of Camelot, the Knights of the Round Table and, somewhat ironically given his actions on 1 July, chivalry.

Captain Wilfred 'Billie' Nevill, 8th East Surreys, won fame of a different stripe. The 21-year-old Cambridge University student — keen on rugby, cricket, hockey and running — had bought a pair of footballs when on leave in London. The idea was to provide at least some mental distraction for men faced with hopping the parapet sandbags and moving forward to cross a bullet-swept no-man's-land. One of the footballs he bought was inscribed:

> The Great European Cup-Tie Final,
> East Surreys v Bavarians,
> Kick Off at Zero.

'I saw an officer climb into No Man's Land, a football under his left arm. He was beckoning the others to follow, as they came out he kicked off the football,' wrote Private Leonard Price, 8th Royal Sussex, whose platoon was nearby.[173] Nevill, who had heard the opening whistle, was not alive to see the contest end: he was shot dead within 20 yards of the British line. He is buried at Carnoy Military Cemetery.

By mid-morning, the 18th's attack was far from uniform across its roughly 2000-yard-wide frontage. Only the 54th had attained its second objective of the Mametz–Montauban ridge. The adjoining flanks of the neighbouring 53rd and 55th, broadly centred on the Carnoy–Montauban road, had stalled near the German front line. The result was a large south-pointing wedge of still-German-held trenches and strongpoints that jutted defiantly into the 18th's path of advance, its apex at the Carnoy craters. Shortly after 8 a.m., Brigadier-General Thomas Jackson's 55th Brigade headquarters knew all was not going to plan.[174] As the 7th Royal West Kents' war diarist explained, 'The [55th] Brigade informed us by telephone that all appeared to be going well, but that the leading Battalions had met with more opposition than was anticipated, and had suffered considerable casualties.'[175] It was about 9.30 a.m. before the craters fell to Captain

Arthur Kenchington's B Company, 7th Buffs, and about 200 Bavarians were taken prisoner, several of them badly scorched by the Livens flame projectors.[176] Kenchington wrote: 'In the end, a gallant dash by a Subaltern and a Sergeant into a wire-filled sap and thence round the flank of the [crater] M.G's [machine guns] succeeded and allowed the survivors to clear the area. The crew of the M.G. were clubbed. Heaps of used [bullet] cases testified to the stout way they had served their gun.'[177] Even so, the wedge of German resistance opposite the 53rd and 55th held out. Maxse's attack had stalled, which meant the neighbouring 90th Brigade, of 30th Division, would advance on Montauban with its left flank open to enfilade and potentially a locally organised counterattack.

Resistance slowly unravelled as the German defenders realised they were outflanked. With Pommiers Redoubt lost to the west and Montauban having fallen to the east, German infantry was in danger of being cut off if the Mametz–Montauban road was rolled up behind them from east and west. One by one and then in knots they retreated overland and along communication trenches from Breslau Support Trench, which was impeding 7th Queen's, and The Loop, which was holding up 6th Royal Berkshires. British patrols and bombing parties followed, kept contact and occupied the evacuated ground. German rear-guard positions were bombed and rushed, grenades were tossed down dugout steps and large groups of surrendering Badeners, Prussians and Bavarians were rounded up, disarmed and sent trotting into captivity. Seventh Queen's nabbed 90 enemy soldiers, while 60 more surrendered to 6th Royal Berkshires.[178] 'They would not face the bayonet and took to their heels. But few escaped,' said Sergeant William Lambourne, 6th Royal Berkshires.[179] Resistance at Back Trench, opposite 8th Norfolks and elements of 7th Queen's, lasted until 1 p.m., when about 160 Bavarians clambered atop their parapet with their hands held high.[180] On the extreme right of Maxse's sector, the leading elements of 8th East Surreys, 7th Royal West Kents and some 7th Buffs had reached Montauban Alley shortly after noon, German resistance before them fragmenting comparatively quickly. But it was 2 p.m. before 7th Queen's, reinforced by more 7th Buffs, arrived at the Mametz–Montauban road and 5.15 p.m. when they took their portion of Montauban Alley. Sixth Royal Berkshires and 8th Norfolks arrived alongside 25 minutes later, after a gruelling fight north from The Loop. By

6 p.m., and after a hard-fought contest, the 18th (Eastern) Division finally held Montauban Alley in its entirety and had achieved almost all of its battle objectives.

Fifty-third and 54th Brigades now sent a few hundred men forward a further 400 yards to their third and final objective in the western depths of Caterpillar Valley. These soldiers — a total of three casualty-thinned platoons from 7th Bedfords and 11th Royal Fusiliers, along with a company of 8th Norfolks — held their advanced line until relieved on 2 July. Before then, as dusk began settling in on 1 July, they sent patrols out to probe for enemy positions. One small band of 8th Norfolks actually reached the fringes of Caterpillar Valley Wood, meaning they had covered an impressive 2300 yards since setting out at 7.30 a.m. that morning.

'I came across [Private] Roger Waghorn [of 7th Royal West Kents] ... and he remarked that we should never forget the 1st of July, 1916, when we met in the enemy's trenches and had a smoke,' said Lance-Corporal Clarence Burnett, whose platoon of 7th Royal West Kents had gone forward as reinforcements late that morning.[181] Meanwhile, 12th Middlesex[*] advanced in artillery formation at about midday to occupy and consolidate the old German front overrun by the 54th. The war diarist of the 12th explained: 'The German trenches were very much damaged and in places obliterated. There were many German dead ... and prisoners taken appeared very dazed and shaken, testifying to the intensity of our Bombardment.'[182]

Earlier that morning, from his position on the Mametz–Montauban road, *Unteroffizier* Paul Scheytt, RIR109, had watched the British advance.[183] At midday, word was passed along the German ranks that Montauban had fallen. By early evening casualty numbers were rising and ammunition dwindling. Resistance was fragmenting in the face of advancing British infantry, which outnumbered the defenders:

> Although we took all the ammunition from wounded & dead
> we realised that if the British had made a fresh attack we could
> not hold our position. The day closed with another heavy

---

*   12th (Service) Battalion Duke of Cambridge's Own (Middlesex Regiment). Battalion war diary states 38 casualties (4 k, 30 w and 4 m). SDGW notes 6 deaths.

attack by the British, partly standing up in an open field we fought the attack. When our last cartridge had been fired we retreated through Artillerieschlucht [Caterpillar Valley Wood] to Bazentin-le-Petit.[184]

Once there, Scheytt and other parched survivors guzzled mineral water and nodded off as battle fatigue overtook them. On the other side of Caterpillar Valley the men of the 18th were similarly downing bottles of liberated soda water, puffing on captured cigars, ratting dugouts for souvenirs and shaking hands with one another, after what most saw as a fine day's work.[185]

'Our boys were amongst the first to meet and get to our objective,' wrote Private Barden, 7th Royal West Kents,* of the advance to Montauban Alley.[186] 'God only knows how any of us got there, but we did, and held it, too. It was a terrible night of suspense, and we waited for the demoralised Fritz to get together again and come at us in a counter-attack.'[187] A few hundred yards away, Private Norton's platoon of 8th Norfolks was digging a strongpoint overlooking Caterpillar Valley and out towards Longueval.[188] In the early evening, Norton saw the enemy 'dragging out his guns & transport as if moving back, it was then very quiet with only an occasional long range shell from Jerry coming over.'[189] Sections of the 79th, 80th and 92nd Field Companies, RE, were also helping dig strongpoints and wire defences around Montauban Alley.[190] All along the new line exhausted soldiers toiled to make their positions defensible: 'If a man ceased digging for a moment he dropped off to sleep where he stood or fell.'[191] Major Lanoe Hawker, VC, 24th Squadron, RFC, was overhead at about 8 p.m. and said the attack had gone well: 'Very heavy shelling along ravine from Caterpillar [Valley] Wood to North of Bois de Bernafay [Bernafay Wood] followed by white and red [flare] lights along the same ravine.'[192] Lieutenant Heath, who was now at Montauban Alley, spied a German field-gun emplacement about 300 yards away in Caterpillar Valley. He fired a single trench mortar round to encourage any crew nearby to surrender:

---

* 7th (Service) Battalion Queen's Own (Royal West Kent Regiment). 55th Brigade states 179 casualties 1–2 July (36 k, 142 w and 1 m). SDGW notes 29 deaths.

In a few seconds, a white handkerchief was hoisted, tied to the end of a rifle. I ceased fire. A Pickelhaube (German spiked helmet), then made its appearance, but, to our astonishment, its wearer who climbed out of the trench was seen to be wearing khaki [i.e. a British uniform]. He then cheered at the top of his voice, and after executing an extempore war dance, ran briskly over to us amid roars of laughter from the men.[193]

From Maxse's viewpoint the debut attack of his 18th (Eastern) Division had been one of frustratingly slow progress capped off with eventual success. At first all appeared to go rather well.[194] But by 11 a.m. if not earlier, Maxse was well aware that his infantry were not consolidating Montauban Alley at the scheduled time of 10 a.m. Progress reports revealed that the centre and right of the 18th's sector were held up; there can have been no doubt in Maxse's mind that his attack was stalling. He was well aware that his brigadier-generals — Harold Higginson of the 53rd, Thomas Shoubridge of the 54th and Jackson of the 55th — were committing their attack and support battalions to break the impasse. He also knew the 18th's objectives needed to be achieved alongside those of 30th Division. Maxse had spent ample time training his men to overcome unplanned tactical setbacks and unexpectedly strong resistance. More reinforcements were sent in, but come 1.30 p.m. the central portion of the 18th's sector still held out, even if the German grip was weakening. At 3.15 p.m. Maxse intervened, ordering the re-bombardment of a 300-yard stretch of Montauban Alley. At 4.30 p.m. another bombardment was ordered for 30 minutes from 5.15 p.m., but this was postponed to 6.15 p.m. and then cancelled at 5.50 p.m., as progress was finally being made against now-collapsing German resistance. Maxse said in-touch-with-events Higginson did 'not now consider it [the bombardment] necessary.'[195] Finally, at 7.40 p.m., a relieved Maxse got word that all of Montauban Alley had been taken and that consolidation was afoot; his well-trained men on the battlefield and brigade staffs had proved themselves equal to the job set them. 'Well done. It's what I expected,' wrote Maxse in a message to his men that night. 'Now hold on to what you have gained so splendidly.'[196]

Captain Maurice Grove-White, an RE staff officer with XIII Corps, described the 18th's achievement as 'no mean feat in any battle, and certainly an extraordinary performance in their first battle.'[197] He explained that Maxse's mopping-up parties had been a key element of the victory, as had the pre-battle training in open-warfare methods, with infantry 'working forward by fire and manoeuvre without artillery support.'[198] It was a point echoed repeatedly in the post-war divisional history, which attributed rather less import to the flank gains of 55th Brigade and 30th Division in eventually forcing a German collapse within the wedge.[199]

Casualties in the 18th totalled 3115, among them 912 dead, 2157 wounded and 46 missing.[200] German units opposite suffered about 1060 casualties. Among these were about 1044 casualties in RIR109, with a little less than a third of these dead.[201] The company of IR23 involved lost 16 killed and missing and an unknown number of wounded.[202] That is, for every one German casualty there were 2.9 British.

Back in the British assembly trenches, soldiers of reserve battalions spent the day amid a grisly scene. Here, sporadic German shellfire collapsed trench walls, wounded soldiers struggling in from no-man's-land and eviscerated others. Private Sydney Fuller, 8th Suffolks,* was in the ditches vacated by 55th Brigade. It was about 11 a.m. 'I stepped on something, and looking down I saw a piece of a man's backbone, and pieces of flesh strewn about the trench. Hanging down from the parapet, in the corner of the traverse, was a mass of entrails, already swarming with flies.'[203]

NEWS OF THE attack reached the headquarters of *Generalleutnant* Ferdinand von Hahn, commander of 28th Reserve Division, and 12th Infantry Division's Châles de Beaulieu at about 8 a.m. Confusion in the battle zone and broken telephone links meant it was another two-and-a-half hours before they had a clearer picture of events.[204] The two officers, in telephone contact with one another, were aware of British gains around Montauban and had received vague reports that the village was lost.[205] They still did not know that their units to the south and west of Montauban were disintegrating under XIII Corps' attack.[206] Both realised the 'uncertain situation around Montauban meant that the second position north of the village [between Bazentin-le-Petit and

---

* 8th (Service) Battalion Suffolk Regiment. Battalion war diary states 21 casualties (7 k and 14 w). SDGW notes 10 deaths.

Longueval] needed to be strengthened,' with more troops held ready to garrison Mametz Wood.[207] By noon Châles de Beaulieu and Hahn were certain Montauban was lost and knew British infantry was overlooking Caterpillar Valley and not far from the German second defensive position on its opposite side. Châles de Beaulieu must have now realised his error in moving the Bavarians into the line just before battle. With no local reserves to speak of, and confronted by British gains around Fricourt and Mametz and French progress closer to the River Somme, he and Hahn were forced to abandon any idea of an immediate counterattack to reclaim lost ground and set to shoring up what little their men still retained.[208]

Hahn and Châles de Beaulieu's tactical defeat between Mametz and Montauban resulted from a lack of defensive artillery firepower. They each had fewer guns than 26th Reserve Division to begin with, and many of those they had were destroyed during 24–30 June. Come 1 July, artillery–infantry communication links had failed, numerous observation officers had beome casualties, and the fluid battle meant surviving artillerymen either lacked reliable target co-ordinates or were firing blind in the mist and smoke of battle.[209] By mid-afternoon on 1 July, even more guns had been destroyed, neutralised or were out of ammunition.[210] Dust- and smoke-shrouded gun pits were peppered with shrapnel and explosives.[211] Casualties were heavy.[212] RFC observers raked German batteries with machine-gun fire and pinpointed them for British counter-battery gunners.[213] As one German historian wrote, 'An English flyer circling low over the [Bernafay] wood quickly discovered the batteries and soon 28-cm shells began landing.'[214] As XIII Corps sent patrols forward from Montauban Alley during the afternoon and evening, several more guns were lost — either abandoned or disabled.[215] In this part of the battlefield Hahn and Châles de Beaulieu had lost the artillery duel both prior to and on battle day, and with it the ability to lay down any kind of meaningful defensive shellfire that might have slowed or broken Congreve's attack.

At midday, the German second position between Bazentin-le-Grand and Longueval was held by a battalion of IR23 and a hotchpotch of non-combatant troops totalling about 1000 men, plus a handful of machine guns.[216] IR23's most advanced position was a quarry in Caterpillar Valley, about 800 yards due north of Montauban, garrisoned by a jumble of its soldiers, some from IR62 and some Bavarian battle stragglers. In total they numbered about 150, of whom many were wounded. In theory this position would block any British advance down into the valley, and the approaches from Caterpillar Valley Wood to the west; in reality the quarry's few defenders did not have the means to resist a concerted attack. Between the quarry and Bernafay Wood was a single platoon of IR23. From mid- to late-afternoon, four companies of IR62, a company of pioneers and four infantry companies from the divisional training depot — all together probably numbering fewer than 2000 — arrived forward at Bernafay and Trônes Woods, and Bois Favière.[217] The western and southern fringes of Bernafay Wood were held by about half these men. There were, in brief, insufficient troops to launch a counterattack, and in any case battle reports were sketchy on where exactly the forward-most British infantry was. As one German historian wrote: 'A daylight attack on Montauban from the north [Bazentin-le-Grand–Longueval area] was hopeless. The village could only be attacked with any chance of success from the east. But the enemy had probably also reached Bernafay and Trônes Woods. That was not the case, as it was later revealed. ... Nightfall had to be awaited.'[218] *Oberleutnant* Reymann later put an overtly positive slant on events, alleging that the 'front was held and a big breakthrough prevented.'[219] Others such as *Grenadier* Goebelbecker, who was closer to Mametz, were surprised: 'What puzzled me most all day was the lack of further forward movement by the British troops after the initial attack. The whole German line had collapsed & it would have been a simple matter for them to make a much larger advance than they did.'[220]

Seven miles away at Bapaume, an increasingly alarmed Stein realised the danger on his corps' left flank. An Anglo-French breakthrough between Montauban and the River Somme had the potential for catastrophe if extended northwest towards Thiepval and 36th (Ulster) Division's break-in, roughly north in the direction of Bapaume, or northeast in conjunction with the French break-in immediately to the east. He had already sent a regiment to close down the Thiepval incursion, and at 1.30 p.m. committed Bavarian Infantry Regiment 16 (BIR16), the last of his on-the-spot reserves, to Hahn as a precautionary measure to bolster the Bazentin-le-Grand–Longueval line.[221] Stein also expected Bernafay and Trônes Woods to have fallen, which was incorrect, and he began moving 12th Reserve Division forward from Rancourt to slot into the line between Longueval and Hardecourt in Châles de Beaulieu's divisional area, the latter village being among the objectives of the French XX Corps.[222] It would be hours before these units arrived forward and — despite best attempts and numerous orders — early on 2 July before any meaningful and then unsuccessful counterattack began.[223] Stein realised the implications of Congreve's break-in, especially in combination with events elsewhere, and moved to comply with Supreme Army Command orders that no ground be yielded. But, as we shall see, Stein, whose second defensive line was threadbare but still intact, need not have worried about the British and French attempting a Montauban–Hardecourt breakthrough at all.

One story has it that Congreve went up to the Mametz–Montauban ridge early in the evening and saw an opportunity to extend his corps' advance.[224] He allegedly dashed back to his headquarters some miles away, telephoned Rawlinson and sought consent.[225] While Congreve did go forward the next day, his diary makes no reference to his leaving his headquarters at any time before 10 p.m on 1 July.[226] Corps and divisional war diaries and reports make no mention of Congreve's alleged going forward on 1 July.[227] The official history is no different, and no known officers on the battlefield witnessed Congreve anywhere near Montauban that day.[228] None of these sources logged Congreve's alleged telephone call, and neither did Haig's, Rawlinson's nor Gough's accounts.[229] There is nothing in the Fourth Army headquarters telephone log remotely akin to a request from either Congreve or his headquarters to exploit its gains.[230] In fact, Fourth Army had 'nil' telephone contact with XIII Corps between 4 and 8 p.m.[231] It is incredibly difficult to believe that Congreve either went forward or put in his urgent call seeking to extend XIII Corps' attack after the fall of Montauban.

If Congreve ever flirted with ideas of additional operations around Montauban, he definitely quit them quickly. Shea was ordered to delay the conditional phases of the 30th's operation due to failures elsewhere along the British battle line, and instead help the lagging 18th.[232] Congreve was also well aware that the neighbouring XV Corps was still fighting hard around Hill 110, Fricourt and Mametz, while to his right the French 39th Division had some interest around midday in pressing its gains towards Hardecourt. These operations were apparently abandoned by the 39th's commander, General Antoine Nourrisson, on the grounds that Hardecourt was not guaranteed to be empty of enemy infantry, and also because Congreve's corps was not proceeding to its second-phase operations.[233] It was a combination of all these factors, along with fears of a German counterattack, that prompted Captain Ernest Sotham, 16th Manchesters, to note that the defence of Montauban was the 'main & only thought' that afternoon.[234] This was emphasised to subalterns on the battlefield.[235] However, at least one officer noted that the 9th (Scottish) Division was in corps reserve, and pondered 'could not they have used them?'[236] Congreve did have the 9th to deploy, but his afternoon focus was on completing all of his corps' primary objectives and consolidating them rather than launching an ad-hoc exploitative operation.

Even if Rawlinson and Congreve had opted to take extra ground at Montauban, potentially in combination with Nourrisson's division at Hardecourt, it would have been considerably more difficult than is often stated. Stein's defences between Bazentin-le-Grand, Longueval and Bernafay Wood were definitely thin but they were certainly not toothless. As we have seen, there were about 1000 men, plus a handful of machine guns, holding the under-developed Bazentin-le-Grand–Longueval line from midday.[237] Within 12 hours it would be heavily reinforced by BIR16. From mid- to late-afternoon, Bernafay Wood was held by another 1000 men with an unknown number of machine guns. After dusk, the troops in this wood would be supported by Reserve Infantry Regiment 51 (RIR51).[238] There were also several German artillery guns firing on Montauban during the afternoon that could be re-aimed to help break up any renewed British attack. The obvious point is that any exploitation of gains by XIII Corps during the afternoon would have had to have been co-ordinated and organised, comprise fresh troops of the still-hours-away 9th and be properly supported by artillery. It was never just a matter of Congreve sending a few battalions sauntering across Caterpillar Valley towards Bazentin-le-Grand and Longueval, or east in the direction of Bernafay Wood, to take up occupancy.

Taking all of this into account, the sentiments of some British soldiers in response to the lack of further forward movement can be seen as those of men flushed with the thrill of victory. Private Norton said a cavalry force could have 'inflicted enormous damage to the Germans' lines of communications.'[239] Lieutenant Heath recalled that the decision for consolidation over exploitation was met with 'unutterable disappointment' and anger.[240] A somewhat optimistic Heath continued, outlining his plan for a push beyond Caterpillar Valley: 'Even a comparatively small, determined, fast moving force pushed through the fifteen-kilometre-wide [9.3-mile-wide] gap and advancing north east towards the Ancre, while the Germans were off their balance, could capture their artillery in the Ancre Valley and attacking from their rear, might well surround them and destroy them.'[241] Captain Edward Spears, a liaison officer attached to the French Sixth Army, was 'almost biting my nails down to the palms with frustration.'[242] Sergeant Thomas Bennett, 2nd Bedfords,* commented that 'if only we had attacked at dawn instead of 7.30 a.m. we could have done much better.'[243] If only, indeed. Tempting as many of these propositions may be to believe, they remain straw-man arguments founded on XIII Corps' gains rather than an appreciation of Fourth Army's overall attack framework and performance, its decision-making to that time and a marked under-estimation of the German forces still holding XIV Reserve Corps' line in the Bazentin-le-Grand–Longueval–Bernafay Wood area.

None of this was lost on Captain Hugh Cornes, Royal Field Artillery, who years later noted a perennial problem associated with grassroots battlefield tacticians' casting judgement on what might have been: 'My outlook at the time was frightfully local.'[244]

IT IS SUMMER and fields either side of the road from Montauban down into Caterpillar Valley are alive with wheat swishing in the breeze. In the heart of the valley, adjacent to an abrupt cutting, is Quarry Cemetery. It was here that the 150-strong band of Prussian and Bavarian battle stragglers was holed up throughout the afternoon of 1 July in what was then no-man's-land. The cemetery holds 583 graves, five dating from the Somme's first day. It is one of the lesser-visited cemeteries in the area, perhaps because it is hidden by the fold of the ground and all but invisible from the outskirts of Montauban. Twenty-three-year-old former shop assistant Lance-Corporal Horace Brown, 16th Manchesters, who died on 1 July, rests here. His epitaph: 'Far Away Yet Ever Near.'

---

*   2nd Battalion Bedford Regiment. 89th Brigade states 66 casualties 1–4 July (7 k, 53 w and 6 m). SDGW notes 6 deaths.

'The air reverberates to the drum of our cannonade,' wrote Major James Jack, 2nd Scottish Rifles, of British shellfire on enemy positions. Pictured is a 9.2-inch gun immediately after belting out its high-explosive payload sometime on 1 July 1916. *(IWM)*

'What would it be like to receive a direct hit from a ship's 30-centimetre gun?' pondered *Fahrer* Otto Maute, Infantry Regiment 180. The road shown here being struck by a high-explosive shell, near Miraumont in June 1916, was on Maute's wagon route. *(Author's collection)*

'Down there we sit and read and write by the light of a candle,' said *Unteroffizier* Wilhelm Munz, Reserve Infantry Regiment 119. These Württemberg artillerymen are holed up in a shell-proof dugout, and using a salvaged house door as a table. *(Author's collection)*

This well-camouflaged Bavarian field gun at Montauban may have gone unseen by the probing eyes of Royal Flying Corps observers, but its flimsy shelter did nothing to protect it from searching British counter-battery fire. *(Author's collection)*

'The earth rose in the air to the height of hundreds of feet,' wrote Lieutenant Geoffrey Malins, who filmed the massive Hawthorn Ridge mine blast. Its detonation at 7.20 a.m., 10 minutes before VIII Corps' advance was due to begin, alerted German soldiers that they were about to be attacked. *(IWM)*

'The field was white, as if it had snowed,' wrote *Leutnant-der-Reserve* Matthaus Gerster, Reserve Infantry Regiment 119, of the Hawthorn Ridge mine explosion. It was no different at La Boisselle, as evidenced by the chalkstone jaws and spoil of the huge Y-Sap crater. *(IWM)*

'How feeble and tiny they looked in that ghastly reek,' thought Second-Lieutenant William Tullock, 53rd Machine-Gun Company, of British infantry advancing on the German front line near Montauban behind great spurts of liquid fire from Livens flame projectors. *(IWM)*

'My heart seemed to stop; now comes the end,' wrote *Leutnant-der-Reserve* Friedrich Kassel, Reserve Infantry Regiment 99, of a British shell that landed above his dugout. Pictured are Bavarian gunners in their dugout at Montauban early in the British preparatory bombardment. *(Author's collection)*

'Anyway, it was time to go over,' wrote Lance-Corporal Archibald Turner, 10th Lincolns. Equipment-laden infantrymen of 34th Division trudge slowly towards the tornado of German machine-gun and artillery fire near La Boisselle. (*IWM*)

'I wanted to find out what they were looking for,' noted a perplexed Private Lew Shaugnessy, 27th Northumberland Fusiliers, of soldiers he saw going to ground on the La Boisselle no-man's-land. Many of them were dead or wounded, or seeking respite from the German fusillade. (*IWM*)

'Never in the war have I experienced a more devastating effect of our fire,' stated *Vizefeldwebel* Theodor Laasch, Reserve Infantry Regiment 110 (RIR110). He was writing about Mash Valley, where British dead lay thickly (above). Mash Valley's killing zone was designed by *Hauptmann* Otto Wagener, RIR110 (above right). (*IWM; courtesy of Reserve Infantry Regiment 110*)

A Bavarian machine-gun team set up for business on a shellfire-hammered trench parapet, having raced up from their dugout beneath. Even heavily damaged positions were defensible, as this photo taken later in the summer of 1916 illustrates. *(Author's collection)*

Barbed-wire pickets and fields of fire — a German view of no-man's-land through a metal observer's shield, said to have been taken near La Boisselle. British infantry relied on their artillery sweeping away the wire and at least suppressing enemy resistance. *(Author's collection)*

'By thunder *Herr Feldwebel*, I am firing!' yelled a Baden soldier to *Vizefeldwebel* Theodor Laasch, Reserve Infantry Regiment 110. Here soldiers of Laasch's regiment draw bead on British infantry stranded in no-man's-land near La Boisselle on 1 July 1916. *(Courtesy of Reserve Infantry Regiment 110)*

'If the British had made a fresh attack we could not have held our position,' wrote *Unteroffizier* Paul Scheytt, Reserve Infantry Regiment 109. Soldiers of 7th Queen's and 7th Buffs pause on the Mametz–Montauban road on 1 July 1916, before their final attack on Montauban Alley. *(IWM)*

'God only knows how any of us got there, but we did,' recalled Private Clifford Barden, 7th Royal West Kents, of reaching his battalion's objective, Montauban Alley. Soldiers of 55th Brigade (above) began consolidating that trench for defence soon after its capture. *(IWM)*

'I considered further sacrifice to be pointless,' said *Oberst* Jakob Leibrock, commander of Bavarian Reserve Infantry Regiment 16, whose headquarters' dugout was hidden among the ruins of La Briqueterie (above), a brickworks east of Montauban. He and his staff soon surrendered. *(IWM)*

'It was pure bloody murder,' remembered Private Peter Smith, 1st Borders. This unidentified British soldier, found dead in the trenches near Montauban, is slumped on his rifle and wearing a haversack of hand grenades. *(IWM)*

'Hands up, you fool!' A dishevelled and wounded British prisoner, said to have been nabbed during the brutal close-quarter Heidenkopf fighting, manages a weary smile as his triumphant captor from Württemberg looks on. *(Author's collection)*

'I cannot now see the features in a person's face,' wrote Private Sidney Smith, 1/5th Sherwood Foresters, of being wounded on 1 July 1916. Here, a badly injured British soldier, with his eyes crudely bandaged, lies in the German trenches at Gommecourt. *(Author's collection)*

'We will have lunch in the German trenches,' said Lieutenant Billy Goodwin, 8th York and Lancasters, to one of his soldiers just before battle. The Corpus Christi College graduate was highly regarded by his platoon. He died snared in German wire in Nab Valley on 1 July 1916. The 23-year-old, who liked golf, tennis and motorcycles, is buried at Blighty Valley Cemetery. *(Liddle Collection, University of Leeds)*

'It's a shame the holiday came to an end so quickly,' wrote *Reservist* Friedrich Bauer, Infantry Regiment 180, after returning to the Somme trenches from leave. The 25-year-old, from Rudersberg in Württemberg, had been an orchard worker and liked to sing on his way to and from work. He was killed on 3 July 1916 at Ovillers and has no known grave. *(Author's collection)*

Thirteenth Corps ran up 6126 casualties on 1 July. This included 1740 dead, 4275 wounded, 99 missing and 12 prisoners.[245] Opposing units of 12th Infantry and 28th Reserve Divisions suffered exceptional losses of about 2116 officers and men. In other words, XIII Corps suffered about 2.9 casualties for every one German, a ratio that reveals just how casualty-heavy the fighting was for Congreve's men in achieving their objectives.

Congreve's XIII Corps had turned in a stunning success. Prior to battle his gunners had swept away most of the German wire, levelled many trenches and strongpoints, broken communication links and almost entirely neutralised the hostile artillery. All of these factors helped the 18th's and 30th's well-rehearsed soldiers. The morning mist, along with smoke discharges, obscured advancing infantry, but their supporting artillery barrage was too quick. The 18th's slower advance was due to the artillery's failure to suppress resistance at the Carnoy craters, allowing German defenders there and further back time to organise and to hold out. Pockets of resistance were eventually outmanoeuvred and bombed into submission, mopping-up teams following behind. Meantime, too many German soldiers of the 12th Infantry and 28th Reserve Divisions were jammed into the forward area and the garrison had been foolishly reorganised at the last minute. In truth, the Mametz–Montauban defences, unlike those in XIV Reserve Corps' other divisional sectors, became weaker with each successive line. Châles de Beaulieu was primarily responsible: he was short on foresight and did not drive defensive development with the same verve as other divisional commanders in XIV Reserve Corps. Stein should have picked up on this, but did not. For this and allowing BRIR6 to be revolved into the line at the last minute he, too, must bear responsibility. Thus, Congreve's success owed much to his artillery's effectiveness, the lie of the ground, implementation of an intelligent attack scheme by infantrymen who knew their jobs, and tactical blunders by German commanders in organising Montauban's defence.

It was these factors that Captain Grove-White referred to when he attributed Congreve's victory to thorough preparations prior to battle:[246] 'The success of the XIII Corps in contrast to the failure of other Corps was in my opinion ... due to the extreme care that was taken to foresee and provide for every possible eventuality and not to rely solely on a set piece attack worked out according to programme.'[247] It was a fair assessment.

Congreve penned an open message to his men late on 1 July. Unlike his other corps commanders further north, he did not have to lie or window-dress defeat as some kind of moral victory. He somewhat unusually just had to write the truth, and even then he was sparing with words: 'Please convey to all ranks my intense appreciation of their splendid fighting which has attained all asked of them.'[248] Nothing else needed to be said. Congreve was to the point and sincere, and his men loved him for it.

CHAPTER 10

'This Tragic Adventure'

VII Corps' clinical destruction at Gommecourt

'I just hate to think of it all, and am afraid, if I think more,
that I should have a nervous breakdown. Sorry, I can write
no more of it.'[1]

— Rifleman Noel Lockhart, 1/5th Londons (London Rifle Brigade)

'IT IS DOUBTFUL if any point in the line in France was stronger than this point of Gommecourt,' wrote poet laureate John Masefield after walking there in 1917, as wildflowers took root and slivers of metal crunched underfoot. It was an overstatement, of course, as German positions all the way south to La Boisselle had been just as formidable and deadly to the attacker, in some places more so. But Masefield's silky mind and untrained eyes were on a flight of poetic licence. 'There is nothing now to show that this quiet landscape was one of the tragical places of this war.'[2] Not quite then, not quite now, as it happens.

Walk along the old battle line outside Gommecourt salient today and the metal of war is still there: slivers of rusted iron that flake away in your palm, and the brass of bullet casings and shrapnel both oxidised to green. Look closely enough just after a rainstorm, with a bit of wind and luck and just the right light, and it can appear as if someone has cast a few handfuls of emeralds into the plough lines.

Back in the summer of 1916 this elbow of land nine miles north of Albert belonged to the ruthlessly minded *Generalleutnant* Richard *Freiherr* von Süsskind-Schwendi, commander of 2nd Guards Reserve Division. Sixty-one-year-old, Württemberg-born Süsskind-Schwendi was a Prussian Staff College graduate, and one-time personal adjutant to Prince Alexander of Prussia. Every inch the polished guardsman, he exercised daily to keep fit.[3] He was a practical man and appreciated bespoke defensive schemes that made the best use of ground, machine guns and artillery.[4] His top-flight division had inherited the Gommecourt fortress in late-May 1916.[5] Until then, 61-year-old *Generalleutnant* Karl von Borries had been estate manager, and his 52nd Infantry Division still held the salient's southern flank.[6] Borries was another Prussian Staff College alumnus, and everything about the Gommecourt earthworks reflected his dynamic character and ever-critical eye. Süsskind-Schwendi liked Borries' work because it conformed with his own grim mission statement: 'It is not a question of merely repelling the enemy's attack; the object should be to annihilate him.'[7]

This position's strength lay in the mutually supporting defences of the salient's head and shoulders, which were held by at least 12,000 men. The snout, where the northwest- (Gommecourt North) and southwest-facing (Gommecourt South) front lines met, was bounded by the roads from Gommceoucrt to Foncquevillers and Hébuterne. Just behind was Gommecourt Park, a large stand of trees laced with strongpoints and trenches, then Kernwerk, a redoubt of earthworks, fortified buildings and dugouts enveloping the core of the village. A head-on tilt here was guaranteed to be a bloody slog over bough and brick. The adjacent stretches of no-man's-land — respectively north and south of the two roads — had been converted into machine-gun and artillery shooting galleries laced with thick pickets of barbed wire. Behind were the serried trenches of the front-line system, all with excellent fields of fire.[8] The trenches further back were sited to blunt break-ins from either side.[9] Multiple machine guns were housed in trenches, redoubts, strongpoints and fortified woods, among them Schwalbenneste (The Z and Little Z Redoubts), Gommecourt and Pigeon Woods, Nameless Farm and also The Maze and Quadrilateral groupings of trenches. If the strength of the salient's apex was daunting enough to provoke flanking attacks, its shoulders were equally tailored to repulse them.

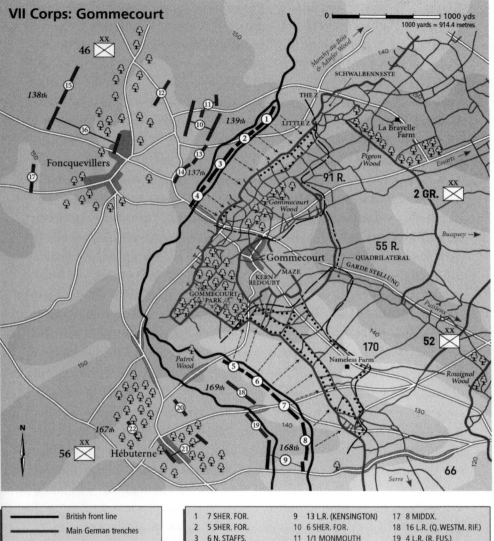

VII Corps: Gommecourt

0 [scale bar] 1000 yds
1000 yards = 914.4 metres

46 XX

138th

15

12

139th

11

10

16

Foncquevillers

14 137th

13

1

2

3

4

LITTLE Z

THE Z

Gommecourt
Wood

Gommecourt

MAZE

KERN
REDOUBT

GOMMECOURT
PARK

Patrol
Wood

5

6

18

169th

20

167th

22

56 XX

Hébuterne

21

19

168th

9

8

7

Nameless Farm

170

QUADRILATERAL

GARDE STELLUNG

55 R.

91 R.

SCHWALBENNESTE

Monchy-au-Bois
& Adinfer Wood

La Brayelle
Farm

Pigeon
Wood

Essarts

2 GR. XX

Bucquoy →

Puisieux

52 XX

Rossignol
Wood

66

Serre ↓

150

140

130

120

140

N

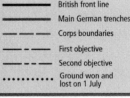

	British front line
	Main German trenches
	Corps boundaries
	First objective
	Second objective
	Ground won and lost on 1 July

1	7 SHER. FOR.	9	13 L.R. (KENSINGTON)	17 8 MIDDX.
2	5 SHER. FOR.	10	6 SHER. FOR.	18 16 L.R. (Q. WESTM. RIF.)
3	6 N. STAFFS.	11	1/1 MONMOUTH	19 4 L.R. (R. FUS.)
4	6 S. STAFFS.	12	8 SHER. FOR.	20 2 L.R. (R. FUS.)
5	5 L.R. (LOND. RIF. BDE.)	13	5 N. STAFFS.	21 1 L.R. (R. FUS.)
6	9 L.R. (Q. VICT. RIF.)	14	5 S. STAFFS.	22 7 MIDDX.
7	12 L.R. (RANGERS)	15	5 LINC.	
8	14 L.R. (LOND. SCOTS.)	16	5 LEIC.	NB: L.R. = LONDON REGT.

Artillery positions were further back, secreted away in valleys and folds in the ground, and among pockets of foliage. Second Guards Reserve Division was supported by about 80 field, heavy and captured guns.[10] Half (Gruppe Süd) were deployed behind Gommecourt North and the salient head, with the remainder (Gruppe Nord) around Essarts, closer to Monchy-au-Bois. Gruppe Nord's guns could enfilade no-man's-land opposite Foncquevillers, along with those batteries of 111th Infantry Division around Adinfer Wood, also near Monchy-au-Bois. Gommecourt South was backed by up to a third of 52nd Infantry Division's estimated 100 artillery barrels.[11] Further south, around Puisieux, artillery supporting Infantry Regiment 66 (IR66), another third of the 52nd's complement, could enfilade no-man's-land facing Hébuterne if called upon, as well as that before Serre.[12] Most of these guns survived the seven-day British bombardment and their crews waited patiently to loose off a tornado of defensive shellfire and destroy the expected British attack.[13]

The job of cracking the Gommecourt fortress belonged to Lieutenant-General Sir Thomas D'Oyly Snow, the portly 58-year-old at the helm of Third Army's VII Corps. To some, the square-jawed, white-haired general was 'Snowball.' Others gave him the suggestive moniker 'Slush.' He had scraped out his career as an infantry subaltern on the African continent, first in South Africa against the Zulus, then in Sudan and Egypt. Promotion and Staff College, Camberley, were tailed by more time in Egypt, Sudan and then India. By the outbreak of the First World War, the perennially upbeat Snow — whose stock phrase was 'all goes well' — was back in England commanding 4th Division, which he took to France in August 1914 before taking the helm of 27th Division. Snow fought the retreat of 1914 at Le Cateau and Marne, and also commanded his division in 1915 at the Second Battle of Ypres. Several times he was nearly killed or injured by German fire.[14] Early in the war he was seriously injured when a horse rolled on him, which was why he returned to Britain frequently for treatment. He was promoted to corps command in July 1915.

Snow professed awareness of the challenges posed by fighting on the Western Front, namely adapting to a war of materiel, static positions, the growing importance of artillery and tactical cohesion between artillery, infantry and engineers. Nevertheless, Snow also confessed that he and other senior British officers suffered from 'a total lack of imagination' when it came to actually breaking the tactical impasse.[15] Come 1916, Snow was a long-serving campaigner whose moments of acute professional introspection promised much when it came to his ability to adapt to the nature of fighting stalemate warfare on the Western Front.

The problem was that Snow habitually talked a better game than he delivered. Field-Marshal Viscount Bernard Montgomery, who was Brigade Major of 104th Brigade in 1916, later said Snow did not really have a grasp on what was afoot at the front.[16] That might have had something to do with his occasionally contemptuous opinion of the average fighting man: 'Unless driven to it by his officers, wrote Snow, the British soldier would sooner die than dig, but whether the reason for this was stupidity, lack of imagination or laziness I don't know, but probably it was a little of all three.'[17] As a corps commander the work he put into planning and preparing operations was said to be 'quite useless.'[18] At Arras in 1917, he 'merely told his Divisions to get on with it' and provided no corps-tailored, co-ordinated artillery plan.[19] Snow's speciality was frontal assaults with little effort made to reduce casualties.[20] Others criticised the profligate general as being more frightened of GHQ than the enemy.[21] His diary reveals a man unduly concerned about his seniors' perception of him, and whether or not he would be fired as a result:[22] 'One was never sure whether for some particular action one would be promoted or stellanbosched [i.e. sacked].'[23] At best there were significant questions surrounding Snow's abilities as a corps commander; he undoubtedly lacked empathy, confessed to a lack of imagination and was more concerned about appeasing General Sir Douglas Haig than husbanding his men's lives in battle.

This explains why Snow did not stand behind his valid concerns about Gommecourt's being a poor location for a diversionary operation on 1 July. He and Third Army commander Lieutenant-General Sir Edmund Allenby warned Haig about the salient's formidable defences and artillery.[24] They proposed attacking further north at Arras, where German positions were weaker, the terrain more favourable and enemy infantry and artillery reserves more likely to be drawn in.[25] Their words fell on deaf ears. Haig briefly flirted with Monchy-au-Bois as a location but soon settled on Gommecourt. He told the duo to help Fourth Army by 'diverting against itself the fire of the artillery and infantry which might otherwise be directed against the [neighbouring] left flank of the main attack near Serre.'[26] Haig was being literal and eager-to-please Snow acquiesced; any hope of implementing a feint on 1 July, rather than a diversion, was lost.

By early June Snow had unsurprisingly swapped his initial concerns for optimism. Gommecourt was now a 'favourable' spot for a pincer operation to snip off the salient because the geography and opposing trench lines were ideal for artillery preparation. Snow now watered down his and Allenby's earlier reservations to a set of lesser disadvantages, which suggested they would be easily overcome. Gains made by his corps would not be exploited. In effect Snow had agreed that VII Corps would take a hit for 'Team Haig', and hopefully facilitate the progress of the neighbouring VIII Corps by soaking up any slack in the German shellfire and drawing in any enemy infantry reserves that might otherwise be deployed closer to Serre.

Critics were everywhere. Brigadier-General Sir Archibald Home, a senior staff officer in 46th (North Midland) Division, confided in his diary at the time that a diversionary operation at Arras would 'probably have been the best.'[27] He believed the Gommecourt plan too ambitious, and thought Snow a 'fusser' whose pre-battle conferences were 'futile.'[28] He added that VII Corps' headquarters 'wants ginger [livening up] badly' and 'it ought to take the thing in hand and issue quite definite orders as to what it wants. They will not take responsibility.'[29] Snow's reputation at Third Army headquarters was worse. Brigadier-General Spencer Hollond, an officer on Allenby's staff, said that Snow's 'arrangements for this attack were monstrously bad.'[30] Hollond's character assassination continued:

He never co-ordinated the plan of his divisions, neither did he supervise their individual arrangements. He went on [health] leave to England for ten days during the preparation and arrived back only a few days before the attack. I thought his supervisions so bad that I tried to get Allenby to degommer [i.e. sack] him, but Allenby wasn't sure of getting G.H.Q. support.[31]

It boded ill for VII Corps' operation that two senior staff officers directly involved in the planning believed Snow unfit for command, and that he and his headquarters were not up to the job.

Snow proposed a three-phase operation to pinch off the salient and straighten the line. There would be no direct attack on the salient head, with the ground opposite it separating 46th (North Midland) and 56th (1st London) Divisions and held by 1/4th Lincolns* and half 1/3rd Londons.† The first phase would see 46th and 56th converge after breaching the salient's flanking defences with unimaginative head-on attacks that conformed with Haig's orders for the diversion. The second would see them link behind Gommecourt village, isolating it, Kernwerk and Gommecourt Park. The infantry had just 30 minutes from 7.30 a.m. to achieve these objectives. Shellfire would cut the German wire for the infantry, which would be covered by a smoke discharge from just before Zero. There would be no underground mine blasts to obliterate key German strongpoints and redoubts; time was too short to tunnel across. Capture of the salient's core would start at 10.30 a.m. after VII Corps' biggest howitzers had pulverised it for three hours. Snow anticipated quick completion of the flanking phases, followed by a breather then a mop-up of the shattered salient head; everything hinged on the British artillery getting infantry into the German lines and allowing it to consolidate gains.

'This looked such an easy, simple operation, especially on the map in an HQ some 20 miles behind the line,' said Lieutenant Aubrey Moore, 1/5th Leicesters.[32] 'Whether it would lead to success or failure, it had been a colossal feat of organisation.' Lieutenant-Colonel Lionel Southam, Royal Field Artillery (RFA), thought Snow's orders were 'inspired with unusual optimism and did not provide for any hitch. I have some recollection of the ease with which it was anticipated the clearing of the particularly formidable [Gommecourt] park would be affected [sic].'[33]

The first difficulty was getting infantry across the wide no-man's-lands. In late May, the 56th's most advanced trenches were pushed forward until 250–400 yards from the German front line, from 600–800 yards previously. Even then, the 56th's commander, Major-General Sir Charles Hull, thought the distance should have been cut to 150–250 yards, but time was too short.[34] Subsequent weeks saw a latticework of

---

*   1/4th Battalion (Territorial Force) Lincolnshire Regiment. SDGW notes 6 deaths.
†   1/3rd Battalion (Royal Fusiliers) London Regiment (Territorial Force). 56th Division states 152 casualties (20 k, 127 w and 5 m). SDGW notes 26 deaths.

trenches link these advanced ditches back to the old front line. On the 46th's front, no-man's-land was 400–500 yards wide, but soft ground, wet weather and hostile shellfire meant attempts to tunnel out and dig an advanced assembly trench beyond a bramble of old French wire produced mediocre results. At best it was just three to four feet deep. Rain in the week before 1 July turned these and other defiles into barely negotiable mires, but they would nonetheless be used as jumping-off lines for most of the 46th's leading attack battalions. On the first day of battle, 1/1st Monmouths* were to improve and dig communication trenches. For the meantime, the deadly ground between the opposing front lines had been narrowed, but Snow's infantry still had to travel at least two-and-a-half end-on-end football fields before even reaching the German parapet.

Seventh Corps' artillery was supposed to have cut the wire, run up enemy casualties, silenced hostile artillery and blasted a path for the infantry. For this it had 84 heavy guns, or one for every 47 yards of its 4000 yards sector, which included the not-to-be-attacked salient head.[35] Its 148 field guns and howitzers equated to one every 27 yards.[36] These ratios were consistent with Fourth Army's. But more than a third of the heavy guns did not have the range to hit German batteries opposite,[37] and certainly not those in adjacent sectors.[38] Those enemy batteries within range had suffered few gun losses prior to 1 July. Worse yet, the corps-controlled artillery produced varied results with its shooting, which had a lot to do with the shellfire's composition. The 56th's gunners, for instance, had allocated nearly three times more 18-pounder shells for wire-cutting than the 46th.[39] Many of these and numerous trench-mortar shells failed to detonate. In places across the corps front the wire was cleared — more so in the 56th's sector than the 46th's — but in some others it was intact, or had merely been cleaved into tangles that remained obstacles.[40] Moreover, the 46th's commander, Major-General Edward Montagu-Stuart-Wortley, had alarmingly decided not to shell the German front line opposite as he wanted it taken intact. German accounts reveal that numerous trenches were damaged by the shellfire but not rendered indefensible, and that, as elsewhere, deep dugouts mostly protected their occupants.[41] German casualties totalled about 200 for the whole salient

---

*   1/1st Battalion (North Midland) Monmouthshire Regiment (Territorial Force). SDGW notes 22 deaths.

during the bombardment.[42] Snow's gunners could hardly have done any worse: German artillery remained active, wire-cutting was inconsistent and enemy infantry was safe underground waiting for the attack to begin.

German soldiers well knew that British preparations opposite the salient meant an attack was being prepared for. *Leutnant-der-Reserve* Adolf Kümmel, Reserve Infantry Regiment 91 (RIR91), explained why: 'The new British assault trenches, the pushing forward of saps, the frequent bombardment of important points, the appearance of heavy trench-mortars, and the increasing artillery fire, which from time to time rose to "drum-fire," left no doubt as to the intention of the enemy.'[43] The precise location of the attack could not have been flagged more clearly. That neither neighbouring division — 37th and 48th (South Midlands) Divisions, respectively north and south — undertook any meaningful activity to suggest they would be participating only served to concentrate German attention on the salient. These points were not lost on Süsskind-Schwendi, noted *Oberleutnant* Alfred Wohlenberg, Reserve Infantry Regiment 77 (RIR77): 'When on 29 June a deserter confirmed the major attack we suspected the enemy would make, the division issued orders for an increased state of alarm.'[44] Rifleman Aubrey Smith, 1/5th Londons (London Rifle Brigade), recalled that German prisoners said the attack was expected.[45] One afternoon a placard was hoisted above the German parapet with the scrawled challenge 'Come On.'[46]

'They know we are coming all right,' said a chipper Snow before battle.[47] It was a pithy one-liner to please Haig, who had agreed that no attempt should be made to hide VII Corps' preparations for its diversionary attack.[48] The British official historian wrote that the outcome of this decision was 'immediate and satisfactory,' citing the arrival of 2nd Guards Reserve Division at Gommecourt as proof that VII Corps' diversion was succeeding in drawing in German reserves.[49] As it happened, that division had arrived at the salient on 23 May, several days before the 56th began digging its assembly trenches, and almost two weeks before Snow even submitted his final attack plans to Haig for approval.[50] The official historian's language was curious: 'satisfactory' implied plenty of room for improvement. A more obvious conclusion was that 2nd Guards Reserve's arrival intentionally strengthened XIV Reserve Corps' order of battle by reducing the sector sizes of each of its four other front-line divisions. Front-line battalions all along the corps' front were more concentrated rather than over-extended and the cast of supporting artillery south to Montauban increased as a ratio of guns per yard of front line defended. If anything, 2nd Guards Reserve's arrival effectively served to bolster XIV Reserve Corps' entire battle front, which was actually quite unsatisfactory.

All of this, along with the preparatory bombardment's failure, meant that Snow's infantry was entirely reliant on whatever artillery support it had on battle day. Soldiers had no idea that the last moments of the final intense bombardment, which began at 6.25 a.m., were flawed. Half of the heavy guns were to lift their fire off the German front-line system onto second-phase objectives at 7.28 a.m., with the remainder following at 7.30 a.m., before both shifted their metal curtain further on.[51] Field artillery either side of the salient would step its fire back at 7.30 a.m. to either the German support or reserve trench, and then at intervals beginning at three to four minutes jump increasingly further back. This meant the German front-line trench would be free of suppressive shellfire from 7.30 a.m., just as the 46th's and 56th's leading waves began to cross over no-man's-land, and within 10–20 minutes the entire front-line system would be clear. At this point all Snow's infantry had for cover in the open expanse of no-man's-land was smoke, which was no kind of barrier to either bullets or shrapnel.

'It was hard at first to recognise individual [British] figures in the dense smoke clouds,' said *Leutnant-der-Reserve* Kümmel of the moments immediately after 7.30 a.m.[52] Ten minutes earlier, German front-line infantrymen had been roused by shock waves rippling through their dugouts from the massive Hawthorn Ridge mine blast three miles away. In the trenches, when the British attack began, shellfire-dodging sentries frantically belted alarm gongs and roared 'They're coming!' into shadowy dugout entrances. It was now a tickle after 7.30 a.m. and several minutes had passed since the first throaty bursts of range-finding German machine-gun fire had raced towards the British lines, while shrapnel shells coughed overhead and dispatched their cargo of marble-sized lead balls. Within moments the cacophony travelled to the ears of *Hauptmann* Kurt *Freiherr* von Forstner, Reserve Infantry Regiment 15 (RIR15), at Bucquoy:[53] 'There was the clatter and thump of rifles, the "Tack-Tack" of machine guns and the crash of hand grenades, intermingled with the howling, roaring, barking and bursting of red-hot iron shells.'[54]

'WHAT WAS THE difference between twenty minutes and twenty years? Really and truly what was the difference?' pondered Second-Lieutenant Edward Liveing, 1/12th Londons (Rangers) as he and other infantrymen counted down the last few minutes before the attack began in 56th (1st London) Division's sector.[55] 'I was living at present, and that was enough.'[56] Rifleman Reg Mason, also Rangers, said those around him in the assembly trenches were 'trembling with a mixture of fear, noise and the long sitting in a cramped position.'[57] Mason said that at this time his 'mental concentration was impaired, and the automatic soldier moved forward.'[58]

Two brigades of the 56th were to attack on a frontage of about 1250 yards with a total of about 5820 men.[59] All of its lead battalions and those following in support were ordered to advance in successive linear waves.[60] The 169th, on the left adjacent to the salient's head and with two battalions advancing abreast, had the toughest job. The brigade's London Rifle Brigade,[*] at left, and 1/9th Londons (Queen Victoria's Rifles)[†] would lead off, followed immediately by 1/16th Londons (Queen's Westminster Rifles)[‡] and then 1/2nd Londons (Royal Fusiliers).[§] The 169th — with a company of 1/5th Cheshires[¶] and 2/2nd London Field Company, Royal Engineers (RE), attached — was to finish up to 800 yards behind the German front line, isolating the salient head from the south. On the division's right, the 168th would provide flank support by storming the German front-line system to a depth of 300–500 yards. This brigade, also

---

[*]   1/5th London Battalion (London Rifle Brigade) London Regiment (Territorial Force). 56th Division states 584 casualties (63 k, 220 w and 301 m). SDGW notes 276 deaths.

[†]   1/9th Battalion (Queen Victoria's Rifles) London Regiment (Territorial Force). 56th Division states 526 casualties (45 k, 266 w and 215 m). SDGW notes 221 deaths.

[‡]   1/16th Battalion (Queen's Westminster Rifles) London Regiment (Territorial Force). 56th Division states 520 casualties (14 k, 249 w and 257 m). SDGW notes 172 deaths.

[§]   1/2nd Battalion (Royal Fusiliers) London Regiment (Territorial Force). 56th Division states 256 casualties (44 k, 211 w and 1 m). SDGW notes 178 deaths.

[¶]   1/5th (Earl of Chester's) Battalion (Territorial Force) Cheshire Regiment. Pioneer battalion. 56th Division states 178 casualties (14 k, 115 w and 49 m). SDGW notes 48 deaths.

with two battalions advancing side by side, was led by 1/12th Londons (Rangers),* on the left, and 1/14th Londons (London Scottish),† with 1/4th Londons (Royal Fusiliers)‡ and 1/13th Londons (Kensington)§ in support. The 168th also had 2/1st London Field Company and a company of 1/5th Cheshires attached. Meanwhile, 167th Brigade's 1/1st Londons¶ and 1/7th Middlesex** remained in reserve all day, while the remaining half of 1/3rd Londons and 1/8th Middlesex†† were to hold the assembly trenches and supply working and carrying parties. Smoke was discharged from the British lines at 7.25 a.m. Its light-grey-to-white tints billowed along no-man's-land, sparking immediate German shellfire there and on the assembly trenches. Then the attack began.

'Everything stood still for a second, as a panorama painted with three colours — the white of the smoke, the red of the shrapnel and blood, the green of the grass,' wrote Second-Lieutenant Lieving.[61] 'I felt as if I was in a dream, but I had all my wits about me.'[62] Corporal Arthur Schuman, London Rifle Brigade, heard the stutter of machine guns: 'I kept my head down as low as possible, helmet tilted to protect my eyes, but I could still see men dropping all around me.'[63] Rifleman Henry Russell, same battalion, sheltered in a scoop of dead ground: 'I believed that I would be dead within seconds and would be rotting on the ground, food for the rats next day. I am now convinced that when it comes to the last crunch nobody has any fear at all.'[64] Away to the right, onlooker Major Charles Carrington, of 1/5th Royal Warwicks, 48th (South Midland) Division, which was holding the trenches south of VII Corps, glimpsed a few

---

*   1/12th Battalion (The Rangers) London Regiment (Territorial Force). 56th Division states 515 casualties (28 k, 258 w and 229 m). SDGW notes 151 deaths.
†   1/14th Battalion (London Scottish) London Regiment (Territorial Force). 56th Division states 558 casualties (50 k, 242 w and 266 m). SDGW notes 220 deaths.
‡   1/4th Battalion (Royal Fusiliers) London Regiment (Territorial Force). 56th Division states 275 casualties (30 k, 186 w and 59 m). SDGW notes 53 deaths.
§   1/13th Battalion (Kensington) London Regiment. 56th Division states 317 casualties (37 k, 195 w and 85 m). SDGW notes 55 deaths.
¶   1/1st London Battalion (Royal Fusiliers) London Regiment (Territorial Force). 56th Division states 80 casualties (3 k, 69 w and 8 m). SDGW notes 18 deaths.
** 1/7th Battalion (Territorial Force) The Duke of Cambridge's Own (Middlesex Regiment). 56th Division states 41 casualties (2 k and 39 w). SDGW notes 0 deaths.
†† 1/8th Middlesex (Territorial Force) The Duke of Cambridge's Own (Middlesex Regiment). 56th Division states 30 casualties (30 w). SDGW notes 10 deaths.

London Scottish 'in their hodden-grey kilts' dashing into the smoke: 'That was all. That and a growing hullabaloo of noise.'[65] Rifleman Noel Lockhart, London Rifle Brigade, felt there was 'not enough air to breathe, so many shells were bursting. Small bodies of men simply disappeared when a shell burst near them.'[66]

Beneath the silver smoke swirls, bullet and shrapnel ripped, eviscerated, pierced, severed and shattered. Men fell. Some lay still. Others, wracked with pain, stumbled through the knee-length grass looking for shelter, or lay writhing.[67] A young Londoner staggered back, cut about the face, bleeding, his limp arm broken in several places. 'Is there a dressing station down there, mate?' he asked Signaller William Smith, RE, who offered to collar a stretcher bearer. 'Oh,' said the private, 'I don't want him for me. I want someone to come back with me to get my mate. He's hurt!'[68]

The Londoners' steady walk accelerated as German artillery and machine-gun fire roared. Depleted leading waves increasingly lost formation in the smoke and confusion. Small groups blundered forward. On the left, 169th's London Rifle Brigade benefitted from mostly cut wire at the southern corner of Gommecourt Park and several collapsed German dugouts. Two companies ventured into the jagged wood towards Kernwerk and Gommecourt village, but were blunted by a scratch force of 2nd Guards Reserve Division's pioneers and engineers. Some British troops are alleged to have made it to the Quadrilateral grouping of trenches, which was 800 yards behind the German front line and east of Gommecourt. At the southern end of the battle front, the 168th's London Scottish won into the German line, although its right was heavily enfiladed. Mostly intact wire slowed the Queen Victoria's Rifles and Rangers, the two central battalions of the attack, and soldiers of Infantry Regiment 170 (IR170) were soon at their parapet, firing. Eyewitnesses told of 'mangled barbed-wire with parts of human beings hanging on them.'[69]

London Rifle Brigade groups that had made it into the German front line now struck southeast along the trench and rolled up its defenders holding the Queen Victoria's Rifles and Queen's Westminster Rifles at bay.[70] The impasse broken, these men — like those of the London Scottish, who lacerated 'shins, legs & things' on loose wire[71] — pushed into the third trench of the German front-line system, several small parties advancing even further on. Some Rangers, reinforced by two companies of 1/4th Londons, now managed to get through the wire, and a few filtered through to the German second trench, but the rest of that battalion's attack failed. Smoke, speed of advance, patchy wire and some collapsed German dugouts had allowed the depleted 56th limited initial gains, albeit far short of its final objectives. Its infantrymen found the German trenches a shambles of piled-up chalkstone, splintered planks, frayed wicker revetments and bloodied corpses.

Smoke and dust clouds shrouding no-man's-land obscured the attacking infantry.[72] A *Leutnant* Koch, of Machine-gun Sharp-shooter Troop 73, told of a 'first rush' of London Rifle Brigade, which 'suddenly' materialised from the smoke.[73] He said five of a seven-man machine-gun team at the southern corner of Gommecourt Park were killed or wounded within minutes by shadowy forms amid the pall. Its two unscathed survivors were surrounded; *Unteroffizier* Gustav Schultheiss and *Gefreiter* August Berkefeld resisted until killed by a storm of hand grenades.[74] Nearby, in another gun team, cut-off-but-calm machine-gunner *Gefreiter* August Niemeyer held out until shot in the face.[75] The trio are buried at the Neuville-St Vaast Kriegsgräberstatte (German War Cemetery), Berkefeld and Niemeyer side by side and Schultheiss nearby.[76] Further back, German artillery observers reported that the Londoners had 'over-run' Gommecourt South's forward trenches, which were held by IR170 and Reserve Infantry Regiment 55 (RIR55).[77]

Rifleman Frank Hawkings, Queen Victoria's Rifles, lay wounded in no-man's-land and saw a 'medley of Huns and QVRs [Queen Victoria's Rifles] at close quarters with bomb and bayonet. The tide of battle rolled on as our fellows forced their way to the Hun trench.'[78] Second-Lieutenant Liveing later remembered a hare, eyes bulbous with fear, bounding towards him. Men dropped all around; others kneeled to draw bead on German infantry at their parapet. Liveing moved towards a defile in the wire: 'There was a pile of our wounded here on the German parapet.'[79] Corporal Schuman thought the journey endless, but eventually fell into the German trench: 'I sat on the firing platform to regain my breath. I felt something very soft. Looking under a groundsheet I saw the body of a German officer.'[80] Private Arthur Hubbard, London Scottish, emptied his rifle 'on three Germans that came out of their dug outs bleeding badly and put them out of their misery. They cried for mercy, but I had my orders.'[81] Sergeant Henry Smith, same battalion, killed 'my first German — shot him clean through the forehead and sent his helmet spinning in the air.'[82] Others took prisoners who were sent jogging back towards the British lines; several were killed or wounded by their own defensive shellfire.[83]

This metal curtain on no-man's-land grew in ferocity, and by 8 a.m. was essentially impassable. Machine-gunners belted out two-second taps of bullets from Garde Stellung, 750–1000 yards behind their old front line, Nameless Farm further forward, the Quadrilateral closer to Gommecourt and also the Kernwerk. IR66 further south and elements of RIR55 in the unassailed salient head enfiladed no-man's-land lengthwise from north and south. Shellfire further thwarted subsequent waves of the 56th's leading battalions, and those following, while they were either forming up or attempting to cross.[84] *Hauptmann* Ulrich Lademann, IR66, said that 'only isolated parts of the attack waves arrived at the [wire] obstacles.'[85] *Leutnant-der-Reserve* Georg Büsing, Reserve Field Artillery Regiment 20 (RFAR20), said that 2nd Guards Reserve Division's guns in Gruppe Süd alternated between 'blocking fire' and a 'rolling barrage,' stopping successive masses of enemy infantry all day: 'Troops gathering for fresh attacks, particularly at Patrol Wood [in 169th Brigade's sector] … were identified and engaged with complete success.'[86] Major John Bowles, Royal Garrison Artillery, at VII Corps headquarters, agreed that when these guns joined the defensive fire, 'hopes of success were finished.'[87] German bombardiers and machine-gunners alike fired to pre-ranged target zones, meaning they did not even need to see their targets to be sure of hitting them. Second Guards Reserve's 80 artillery guns fired 22,603 shells on 1 July, most on no-man's-land and the British assembly trenches.[88] This no-man's-land maelstrom effectively isolated men of the 56th that had made it into the German lines and guaranteed it would only be a matter of time before their limited, unsupported gains were lost.[89]

German junior commanders of RIR55 and IR170 on the spot knew their work. They immediately organised their men and resistance, and reinforced key points, such as Kernwerk, with support companies. London Rifle Brigade later reported that shortly after 8 a.m. the 'first serious opposition was encountered in the shape of strong enemy bombing parties, whose advance was covered by snipers, some of whom were even up trees.'[90] Rifleman Percy Harris, Queen Victoria's Rifles, explained how this played out: 'I did not feel a bit frightened as the Germans gave very little resistance, and seemed to be retiring, and they were until we took their first two trenches, and then they started to throw over hand grenades.'[91] Progress slowed. It was the beginning of the end. By about 8.30 a.m. the 56th had been blocked along a 1500-yard front of Gommecourt South by three battalions of RIR55, IR170 and assorted engineer and pioneer units. Ground between Garde Stellung and the front-line system's third trench was the flotsam mark, with to-and-fro bomb battles sputtering in the handful of communication trenches between. For the rest of the day Garde Stellung became a defensive perimeter for RIR55 and IR170, and also a staging line for units coming forward and launching counterattacks.[92]

Probably no more than 500–700 men of the 56th had made it into the German lines. The exact number will never be known. Small groups led by NCOs and subalterns pressed deeper into the foreign trenches and linked up with others. Lewis guns were sited, ammunition totted up, sandbags filled, new firing steps cut, and coils of wire, wood and whatever could be scrounged from dugouts and trenches used to block ditches running back to the still-German-held ground. Rifleman Frank Jacobs, London Rifle Brigade, was near Kernwerk and said consolidating the 'smashed' ground was an 'awful job.'[93] Lance-Corporal John Foaden, same battalion, saw snipers kill three of his 10 men in two minutes. He thereafter filled sandbags 'whilst lying down, until there was sufficient cover to work our Lewis gun.'[94] Corporal Roland Ebbetts' posse of London Rifle Brigade men was in 'isolated groups in [shell] holes with heaps of earth between them. These heaps were very large, but communication was maintained between them by men crawling over the top.'[95] Their priority was to form a defensive line that would not be easily penetrated by German soldiers.

Chaos reigned in the British trenches from which the attack had begun as explosive shells pitched to earth and heaved soil, debris and men skyward. Shrapnel shells burst overhead, issuing their lethal cargo. It continued all day. '1.10 p.m.: Shelling fearful. [Second-Lieutenant Noel] Mackenzie killed. Trench practically untenable, full of dead and wounded. Very few men indeed left,' wrote Major Cedric Dickens, Kensingtons, in a staccato message. Nineteen-year-old Mackenzie, of Dickens' battalion, is named on the Thiepval Memorial. Dickens continued, this time at 2.40 p.m.: 'Trenches unrecognisable. Quite impossible to hold. Bombardment fearful for two hours. I am the only officer left.' If his words oozed urgency and the terror of those in the British trenches, they were also a stark contrast to the easy turn of his grandfather, novelist Charles Dickens. Soldiers all along the 56th's front line experienced similar ordeals to Dickens'. Orderly Sergeant Harry Coates, London Scottish, described his section of the British assembly trenches as 'all knocked in and chaps buried underneath. We were treading over dead bodies and all sorts of things going along.'[96]

Attempts to run bombs, ammunition, extra machine guns and reinforcements across no-man's-land were cut down amid the 'merry hell' of defensive fire.[97] Throughout the late morning and afternoon such sorties by the remnants and support elements of London Rifle Brigade, 1/4th Londons, Queen's Westminster Rifles, Kensingtons, Queen Victoria's Rifles and 1/2nd Londons, among others, were shot into submission. A few made it over, but never in high enough numbers or with sufficient munitions to help the bridgehead's defence.

'The only thing to do was to crawl back,' wrote Lance-Corporal Sidney Appleyard, Queen Victoria's Rifles, of being wounded in no-man's-land.[98] Lieutenant-Colonel Vernon Dickins, same battalion, said his reserve company made a trinity of attempts to get across the fire-swept ground, but 'all who started became casualties.'[99] Rifleman Henry Barber, London Rifle Brigade, prayed 'we would not have to go over in the face of that murderous fire,' and was saved by a shrapnel ball that puckered several inches of flesh along his spine.[100] Not far away, a grievously wounded Captain Arthur Moore, 1/4th Londons, wept in the lee of the Hébuterne–Bucquoy road when he overheard someone carelessly say he was going to die.[101] The 32-year-old has no known grave and is named on the Thiepval Memorial. Numerous efforts to dig communication trenches across no-man's-land failed for precisely the same reason: 'After three splendid efforts in the face of the overwhelming gun-fire we had to desist,' wrote Private Sydney Newman, 1/3rd Londons (Royal Fusiliers), of attempting to dig one such trench.[102] 'This murderous fire continued.'[103]

Ten miles away at his Henu headquarters, the 56th's commander, Major-General Hull, knew from about 8.15 a.m. that his leading battalions had got into the German trenches but that all was not going smoothly.[104] By 9.30 a.m., he reported the German defensive fire as severe and noted that heavy fighting continued in the just-captured enemy trenches. His division's exact footprint remained unclear, however, with fragments of frequently out-of-date information coming in from a variety of sources.[105] By midday he had ordered up a fresh bombardment on the Quadrilateral group of trenches east of Gommecourt to help the 169th 'push on' and link up with the 46th (North Midland) Division on the other side of the salient. He knew the 46th had experienced difficulties early on, but that it had men inside the German lines and planned to renew its attack.[106] Still the German shellfire rained onto no-man's-land.

Süsskind-Schwendi and Borries were by this time well aware from battle reports arriving at their headquarters that VII Corps was attempting a pincer movement. They also knew Major-General Hull's 56th had snatched a footing in the German front-line system of Gommecourt South.[107] On the other hand, the 56th's attack was already being disrupted by defensive shell- and machine-gun fire. All that remained was for the British gains to be squeezed out by concerted counterattacks. Süsskind-Schwendi and Borries probably did what most generals in such situations do: they told their subordinates to get on with the job and report back when done.[108]

As German front-line infantry absorbed the attack, their officers were independently marshalling reserves forward.[109] Fifty-one-year-old *Major* Otto von Ihlenfeld, commanding IR170, organised his regiment's counterattacks, joined by 45-year-old *Major* Paul Tauscher's battalion of RIR55. Their respective headquarters were in contact via one of the few remaining telephone wires.[110] Tauscher was ordered to 'drive out the enemy.'[111] Ihlenfeld's orders were probably no different. Tauscher had arrived forward east of Gommecourt at about 10 a.m. — his battalion marched through a seemingly endless warren of communication trenches running forward from Bucquoy — and learned the enemy was still ensconced in Gommecourt South.[112] He and Ihlenfeld ordered up multi-pronged counterattacks, with no fewer than 11 companies of RIR55, IR170 and reserve regiment RIR15 converging on the 56th's bridgehead from the east, north and west, joined by elements of mortar, pioneer and machine-gun units. They totalled about 2000 men,[113] who were well armed, festooned with 'potato masher' grenades and extensively trained in counterattack tactics. The first organised groups tasked with retaking the lost ground set off at around 11.30 a.m., with more following over subsequent hours.[114]

Rifleman Basil Houle, a teenage sniper in London Rifle Brigade, was there. In 1910 this chorister at St George's Chapel, Windsor, sang at the funeral of Edward VII, and then the Coronation of George V and Queen Mary. 'We could see the Germans moving up the trenches towards us. I shot one and he went down shouting. Another one looked round and I got him in the back. I got so mad and excited. ... But they came back and absolutely showered us with bombs so we all scrambled back towards our own lines.'[115]

By mid-afternoon the 56th's vanguard had been driven back to the old German front line and split in two. The collapse had been swift. The third German trench was yielded from about 1 p.m., with the London line tightening further still as more counterattack groups closed, probing for weak points and exploiting gaps. Soldiers of IR170 held captive in dugouts were freed and recycled into the battle. The Londoners repeatedly used lamps to flash the signal 'SOS BOMBS — SOS BOMBS' towards their old front line.[116] These were seen by observers. 'But,' wrote Rifleman Herbert Williams, London Rifle Brigade, it was 'still quite impossible for anyone to get across [no-man's-land], though several tried more than once.'[117]

Back in the bridgehead, rifle ammunition was low, grenade supplies exhausted and casualties were still mounting. The Rangers' thinly held niche was lost by 3.10 p.m., survivors fleeing into the metal storm of no-man's-land.[118] What remained was a rag-tag 200 of the 169th wedged into about 400 yards of the trench adjacent to Gommecourt Park and, further south, probably no more than 50 of the 168th's London Scottish in a besieged pocket with open flanks. Captain Hubert Sparks, London Scottish, walked overland, rallying his men in an act of signal bravery that 'beggars the power of eulogy.'[119] Come 4 p.m., the defiant Sparks' choices were to stay and be killed, surrender or bolt: 'Either of these first two alternatives is distasteful to me. I propose to adopt the latter.'[120] Small groups of kilt-wearing men peeling away were pelted with bullets, the wounded and the so-far unscathed scrambling for the haven of shell holes or chancing a foot race against lead across no-man's-land.

Leutnant Wilhelm Kaiser's counterattack group of RIR15 tackled the pocket of London Scottish behind a five-minute ad-hoc barrage:[121] 'We made no progress at all when we attempted to use the rolling up procedure [working from one trench bay to the next]. Instead we went up over the parapet and parados and attacked across country with hand grenades. At that the enemy pulled back rapidly and some Tommies surrendered.' Within 30 minutes — with lots of shouts of 'Hurra!' — the trench was clear of London Scottish and back in German hands.[122]

A thousand yards further north, Corporal Schuman and his small band of Londoners continued to fight on:

> Germans were in the same trench slinging over stick-bombs
> from both flanks. I must have been really mad, for in the heat of
> the moment, I quickly picked up a stick-bomb, certain that I had
> sufficient time to throw it back. But the trench being so high, it hit
> the top and fell back. With two or three others who were near me,
> we had to nip into the next bay very smartly.[123]

After 10 hours of sweat-soaked killing all that remained by 5.30 p.m. was a 100-yard-long wedge of trench held by about 70 grubby-faced officers and men.[124] One-and-a-half hours later their footprint was smaller still, thanks to trench-mortar fire, machine guns in enfilade and showers of stick grenades. Come 8.20 p.m. just 30 men were capable of defending what was now probably only 50 yards of the old German front line. Their choices: death, surrender or flight. The decision was made. Survivors dropped excess equipment, shook hands with the wounded they had to leave behind, bade good luck to their pals and drew breath for their dash back into no-man's-land. The wedge was about to blow. Schuman was still there:

> I was just petrified. I knew that if I stayed in the trench I would
> have most certainly been killed. I hardly waited for the order,
> but it came — 'Every man for himself.' I did not wait to argue —
> over the top I went like greased-lightning — surviving a hail of
> bullets. I immediately fell flat. Then trying to imagine I was part
> of the earth, I wriggled along on my belly. Dead, dying, wounded,

feigning death, who knows? The ground was covered with them. I sped from shell-hole to shell-hole. Never had I run faster.[125]

As RIR55's war diarist somewhat blandly told it, there was violent close-quarter fighting that saw the enemy take to his heels pursued by rifle, machine-gun and artillery fire.[126]

Teddy Bovill made it back, slithering, crawling and running across the 300-yard-wide graveyard that was no-man's-land. Bullets buzzed about. Anxious soldiers watched. Some shouted the Queen's Westminster Rifles' subaltern on. Thirty minutes it took the bloody-faced central London corn merchant to reach the parapet. Then, bang! Sniper! Bovill fell fatally wounded into the trench. He died within minutes. His body was lost and he is today named on the Thiepval Memorial.

Throughout the afternoon Major-General Hull was a bystander to the tragedy due to communication delays, difficulties with observation and the curtain of German shellfire. His battle log is laden with frustration at the steadily worsening situation in the German lines, his men's successive withdrawals until jammed into a small section of enemy trench, multiple failed attempts to get munitions and reinforcements over, and the 46th's repeatedly delayed and then stopped second attack.[127] Hull could do nothing to alter the outcome, even with the late reallocation of artillery to provide defensive fire for the bridgehead and limited counter-battery work.[128] By mid-afternoon he was thinking about protecting his own front line in case of a German counterattack, and this took precedence as evening faded in. Come 7.15 p.m., Hull had written off the 56th's gains. He ordered the barely 100 men still in the German lines to be withdrawn after dark — they withdrew before receiving any such instruction — and the consolidation of his own shellfire-battered front line.[129]

The 56th's failure was essentially the story of Snow's gunners having failed to suppress or destroy German artillery during the seven-day bombardment, and on battle day, when it put just three of 80 enemy guns out of action. If smoke cover, advanced assembly trenches, partially cut wire and speed of attack allowed the 56th's leading battalions into the enemy lines, the quick defensive rejoinder from German gunners entirely isolated them from reinforcements and supplies of ammunition. It also annihilated subsequent waves of attacking infantry. This was exactly as Süsskind-Schwendi and Borries had intended, and their infantry fightback was organised by on-the-spot platoon, company and battalion commanders operating to a long-standing counterattack template. Hull later claimed that the 56th had reached the majority of its objectives. This was a moot point: Snow, Allenby and Haig had seen the division's specific role — along with that of the 46th — as diverting German shellfire and infantry reserves away from VIII Corps' advance at Serre rather than achieving any nominal gain in ground. That Hunter-Weston's corps had failed almost immediately meant the 56th no longer had any tactical objectives of import to achieve and that its thousands of casualties were essentially for nothing.

'This tragic adventure,' was how Lieutenant-Colonel Southam, RFA, summed up the 56th's ordeal.[130] The division ran up 4314 casualties. Among them were 1353 killed, 2355 wounded, 373 missing and 233 prisoners. Its lasting gains were nil. Casualties in the three German regiments directly involved in Gommecourt South's defence ran to at least 1072. This included about 282 casualties in RIR55, namely 92 dead, 154 wounded and 36 missing.[131] IR170 lost 242 dead, 272 wounded and 136 missing, giving it a total 1 July casualty roll of 650.[132] IR66 recorded 36 dead and 92 wounded,[133] while RIR15 accrued at least 12 losses.[134] Thus, for every German casualty opposite the 56th there were about four British. One officer, a *Leutnant* Petersen of RIR15, observed after battle that British dead in the sweep of land between the opposing lines lay 'stretched out in rows.'[135] Even he realised they had been 'sacrificed for absolutely nothing.'[136] Decades later, *Gefreiter* Hugo van Egeren, RIR55, reflected on it all: 'We were hardened, experienced soldiers. It wasn't fair to send these young soldiers against us. Some of them were only students and we felt very sorry for them.'[137]

'FIX BAYONETS' WAS the cry all along 46th (North Midland) Division's assembly trenches just minutes before its attack began, remembered Private Thomas Higgins, 1/5th North Staffords.[138] Bullets grazed the parapet, and in no-man's-land scores of shrapnel and explosive shells erupted. 'The Officer yelled at the top of his voice: "One. Two. Three." Over we went.'[139] Lieutenant Moore, 1/5th Leicesters, recalled that while few 'expected to see the next day dawn,'[140] one nervous wag hoped there 'was a pub in Gommecourt and that it would be open!'[141] What followed was an ordeal not really that much different from the 56th's bloodletting. The 46th was to advance on a two-brigade frontage. Right to left, 137th and 139th Brigades would attack southeast towards the German front line in Gommecourt North, the former brigade's right flank resting on the Foncquevillers–Gommecourt road.

The leading waves of 137th Brigade advanced into the pall of dust and smoke blanketing no-man's-land with some German artillery and machine guns already firing. On the left, 1/6th North Staffords[*] led off from the advanced assembly ditch, to which it had moved at about 7.27 a.m. To the right, 1/6th South Staffords[†] advanced from their original front line, as the forward jumping-off trench was too shallow and a mud slough. These two battalions were followed respectively by 1/5th North Staffords[‡] and 1/5th South Staffords,[§] and then, behind these, 1/5th Lincolns.[¶] Together, they comprised nine waves across a frontage of about 650 yards. Their roughly 2500 soldiers were supposed to advance up to 700 yards behind the German front line before reaching their final objective. Each man was weighed down with no less than 66 pounds of kit and equipment. Those in support waves stumbled forward with all manner of hefty materiel for consolidating the captured ground. The 137th's first wave moved forward at varying times at or just after 7.30 a.m. to the shrill of pea whistles, shouts and the wave of officers' arms.

Within moments the khaki of their uniforms had melted into the light-grey smoke swirl. Platoons and companies were soon jumbled. Equipment-laden soldiers squelching over the greasy pasture of no-man's-land were caught midway as soldiers of RIR91 and elements of RIR55 scurried from dugouts when the British shellfire stepped back.[142] Within eight minutes the entire German front-line system was free of harassing

---

[*]   1/6th Battalion (Territorial Force) The Prince of Wales's (North Staffordshire Regiment). 137th Brigade states 373 casualties (42 k, 161 w and 170 m). SDGW notes 170 deaths.

[†]   1/6th Battalion (Territorial Force) South Staffordshire Regiment. 137th Brigade states 252 casualties (20 k, 138 w and 94 m). SDGW notes 88 deaths.

[‡]   1/5th Battalion (Territorial Force) The Prince of Wales's (North Staffordshire Regiment). 137th Brigade states 219 casualties (24 k, 124 w and 71 m). SDGW notes 28 deaths.

[§]   1/5th Battalion (Territorial Force) South Staffordshire Regiment. 137th Brigade states 186 casualties (17 k, 112 w and 57 m). SDGW notes 49 deaths.

[¶]   1/5th Battalion (Territorial Force) Lincolnshire Regiment. SDGW notes 1 death.

shellfire, and, within 15 minutes, so was Gommecourt Wood. Riflemen and machine-gunners here and in the front line immediately south of the Foncquevillers road had free rein and shot the Staffords into the grassy mire as the southwest breeze swiftly dissipated the smoke. Machine guns in Schwalbenneste, which was about 1200 yards northeast of that road and could enfilade the entire length of Gommecourt North's no-man's-land, probably inflicted casualties, too. Red flares fired skywards from the German trenches immediately invigorated the defensive barrage, which had begun a few minutes before 7.30 a.m. with the smoke release.[143] *Leutnant-der-Reserve* Kümmel was there: 'The dense veil of smoke gradually lifted, and the view became better, whereby the appearance of new English Storm troops was recognised and could be taken under well-aimed fire. Thereby through the well-placed barrage fire from our artillery any further attack was made impossible.'[144]

British assembly and communication trenches were already jammed with wounded, dead and battle stragglers. Among them were men of subsequent waves trying to push along crowded communication trenches to their jumping-off lines, after their orders to deploy overland were changed as soon as the German shellfire thickened.[145] This alteration to the plan derailed the forward flow of men in the rear waves and ultimately stalled the whole attack, but it did save lives.

In no-man's-land the living went to ground as bullets and shrapnel whirred overhead. Others continued amid the welter until cut down; the very few who made it beyond the mostly intact German wire and into the trench beyond were evicted, taken prisoner or killed. Still others sheltered in a 50-square-yard rectangle of shallow, collapsing trenches overgrown with nettles that had once marked the foundation of a sugar factory. All that was left of that factory were a few bullet-riddled old boilers and scraps of metal and wood. The 137th's attack was over by 8 a.m. thanks to Süsskind-Schwendi's crossfire death trap of artillery and machine guns.

Survival was all about luck. 'After having proceeded no more than 20 paces the whole line fell as one man, leaving me running,' said Lance-Corporal Reg Tivey, 1/5th North Staffords.[146] 'I did not know what had happened really, and surmised the line had been wiped out, since deliberate rifle fire and Maxim [machine-gun] fire was concentrated on us.'[147] In the assembly trenches, Lieutenant-Colonel Robert Raymer,

1/5th South Staffords, said it was soon obvious the 'attack had come to a standstill.'[148] He told the 137th's headquarters at 9.01 a.m.[149] Private Harry Loake, 1/5th South Staffords, had made it halfway across: 'A shell burst overhead, and, [shrapnel] striking my trenching tool, knocked me sick for a minute or two. If it had not been for that tool I should have been killed. Although slightly wounded, I got up again and made for the German trenches.'[150] An ammunition pouch just above his heart also stopped a bullet. Then a shell splinter bruised his arm. He dived belly-to-earth near some other soldiers: 'A shell burst over us, killing some of them and breaking my rifle, so I thought it was time to get somewhere a bit safe.' Another bullet ripped Loake's haversack as he rolled into a shell crater. Five near misses in 30 minutes: 'I don't think there is a luckier chap.'

Others fared much worse. Private Thomas Tunnicliffe, 1/6th North Staffords, watched horrified as a German stick grenade blew near a Lewis gunner burdened with an ammunition haversack: 'It set the pack on fire, exploded and the ammunition killed the man.'[151] A wounded Lieutenant George Adams, 1/6th South Staffords, saw bullets pare off part of Lieutenant Samuel Evans' nose, then his ear, while a third slammed into his left shoulder.[152] Lieutenant Douglas Robinson was blown spread-eagled into the air and left deaf and mute.[153] 'Oh, I don't know who else,' wrote an overwrought Adams.[154] Lieutenant Gavin Knowles, 1/5th South Staffords, was shot in the head within the German lines, collapsing into a soldier's arms. Another, Private Alfred Hosell, same battalion, shook and shouted at Knowles' corpse, hoping in vain that the usually cheerful officer might be revived.[155] Knowles is named on the Thiepval Memorial. In the British lines the shellfire was equally indiscriminate. Next day, Lieutenant Moore saw the gore cleared: 'A staggering number of bodies were unearthed.'[156]

German accounts outlined the fate of the few Staffords who made it into their trenches in chillingly brief detail. Small counterattack groups of RIR91 squeezed the North Staffords out with repeated concentric skirmishes and then chased them 'over the first line with hand grenades and infantry fire, so that only a few Englishmen escaped.'[157] Adjacent to the Foncquevillers–Gommecourt road it was the same. Two companies of RIR55 killed, captured or ejected any South Staffords with the same tactics. By 8 a.m. the only Staffords still in the German front line opposite the 137th were corpses or prisoners. They were supposed to be at their final objective.

For most, the 137th's high-tide mark began about halfway across no-man's-land and petered out at the frequently intact thicket of German wire. Private John Atkins, 1/6th North Staffords, recalled that 'most of us got shot down there [at the wire].'[158] One officer remembered the battalion's first two waves were heavily depleted before even reaching the wire, noting that few of the third wave got that far.[159] Shell-hole dwellers and those in the open clawed at the earth with hands, bayonets and entrenching tools to improve their cover. Private Higgins, 1/5th North Staffords, lay winded by shrapnel under the broiling sun: 'I was parched with thirst, my water bottle had been knocked off somehow coming over. The smell of blood and dead bodies was sickening. I mentally said goodbye to those I loved, as I did not seem to have the ghost of a chance of living through that day.'[160] Once at the wire, said Lance-Corporal Jack Maycock, 1/6th North Staffords, the 'Germans threw bombs at us and opened rapid rifle fire from their front trench, which was strongly manned. They had grey uniforms and little round grey caps.'[161] Some stood atop their parapet to get a better shot.[162] It continued into the evening. Any sign of life or resistance was quietened with bomb and bullet. Lieutenant John Stansby, 1/6th North Staffords, lay thrice wounded: 'When darkness fell the Germans threw volleys of hand grenades into the wire, and then came out to pick up the pieces.'[163] He was taken prisoner.[164]

A jot further north, 139th Brigade made better initial progress. Its leading battalions snatched a toehold in the enemy line, also under cover of smoke. The attack was led by 1/5th* and 1/7th Sherwood Foresters† abreast, the latter on the left. Behind were 1/6th‡ and 1/8th Sherwood Foresters,§ respectively support and reserve battalion. Altogether these battalions

---

* 1/5th Battalion (Territorial Force) Sherwood Foresters (Notts & Derby Regiment). 139th Brigade states 432 casualties (33 k, 153 w and 246 m). SDGW notes 195 deaths.

† 1/7th (Robin Hood) Battalion (Territorial Force) Sherwood Foresters (Notts & Derby Regiment). 139th Brigade states 463 casualties (35 k, 237 w and 191 m). SDGW notes 199 deaths.

‡ 1/6th Battalion (Territorial Force) Sherwood Foresters (Notts & Derby Regiment). 139th Brigade states 154 casualties (17 k, 133 w and 4 m). SDGW notes 30 deaths.

§ 1/8th Battalion (Territorial Force) Sherwood Foresters (Notts & Derby Regiment). 139th Brigade states 46 casualties (1 k and 45 w). SDGW notes 7 deaths.

were to comprise nine waves, all of their soldiers burdened with much the same equipment as the 137th and the rear-most lines again lugging heavier supplies. The attacking battalions totalled about 1700 men, excluding the 1/8th, which did not actually attack, and were to advance up to 300 yards behind the German parapet on a 550-yard frontage, protecting the 137th's left flank in the process. Minutes before Zero, German artillerymen and machine-gunners — once again forewarned by the smoke and audible dilution of the shellfire as the British barrage stepped off their front line to targets further back — began sweeping the path of advance.

Casualty-depleted leading waves made it to the German wire, fewer still filtering through occasional gaps towards the enemy parapet. Some of RIR91's front-line infantry had yet to sortie from its dugouts: perhaps the entrances were blocked or the soldiers had not heard the spoiler of lifting shellfire. Small groups of Sherwood Foresters dropped into the hostile ditch unopposed, fewer still ventured further on. On the far left a few of the 1/7th veered into Schwalbenneste, where they were spied by RFC observers. Shellfire to suppress the redoubt's multiple machine guns was stopped, which proved disastrous for subsequent waves of the 139th and the 137th, these respectively having 2/1st North Midland and 1/2nd North Midland Field Companies, RE, attached. Soon numerous soldiers of RIR91 were at their parapet,[165] many tossing stick grenades at Sherwood Foresters still scrambling to get through stretches of intact wire. *Leutnant-der-Reserve* Kümmel said machine guns were brought into position and 'directed a murderous fire on the English.'[166] This and defensive shellfire 'crushed' the attack.[167] Only elements of the 139th's fourth, fifth and sixth waves stepped beyond their jumping-off line.[168] Battlefield communications failed. No-man's-land was alive with metal. Forward movement faltered; the 250-odd Sherwood Foresters in German lines were cut off.

'It was like driving sheep to the slaughter,' said Private Joseph Singleton, 1/7th Sherwood Foresters, who was shot in the calf while in the German trenches.[169] Singleton, together with 17-year-old Private Donald McAllister, of the same battalion, hobbled back to no-man's-land. Just as he dived into a crater he saw German soldiers in the trench he had just left. 'Fuck 'em!' said McAllister as a bullet smacked fatally into his head.[170] Singleton crawled to safety that night. McAllister was later buried at Hannescamps New Military Cemetery. Eighteen-year-old

Private Auberon Tomlinson, 1/7th Sherwood Foresters, saw someone fall wounded and shrieking into the barbed-wire web, and his commanding officer, Lieutenant-Colonel Lawrence Hind, shot through the head. 'He was beyond help,' said Tomlinson, who lay among corpses, 'pretending to be dead all day.'[171] Second-Lieutenant Sydney Banwell, also 1/7th Sherwood Foresters, was shot and fell, and over the next four days was wounded six more times before managing to crawl back. He had survived on water and food scavenged from the dead. Private Herbert Ulyatt, same battalion, saw a wounded officer grasp at his chest and fall to his knees, as if praying amid the fusillade. He saw a bullet thud into another officer, who 'turned a somersault and lay still.'[172] Nearby, a shrapnel splinter ruptured Private Sidney Smith's left eye and scored his right. The 1/5th Sherwood Foresters soldier was taken prisoner just outside the German lines: 'I cannot now see the features in a person's face.'[173]

Captain John Green, Royal Army Medical Corps, attached to 1/5th Sherwood Foresters, won a posthumous Victoria Cross for half dragging, half carrying a wounded officer back from the German wire against orders. Twice the keen rower and all-round sportsman stopped to bind Captain Frank Robinson's wounds; the second time he was killed by a bullet to the brain. Green, a 27-year-old surgeon, lies at Foncquevillers Military Cemetery under the shadow of a catalpa tree. Twenty-three-year-old 'Bubbles' Robinson, the 139th's machine-gun officer, died and was buried at Warlincourt Halte British Cemetery.

Sherwood Foresters who had made it into the German line pressed deeper into the labyrinth of trenches, some of which were 8–12 feet deep, while others were little more than mounds of loose chalkstone. Soon they ran into RIR91's support companies. Behind them the just-bypassed front-line garrison exited its dugouts and fired into their backs. The 35 men of 1/7th Sherwood Foresters who made it into Schwalbenneste were forced back into the wire and killed. A break-in just south of the redoubt by a further 25 was 'destroyed through bitter close combat' in a matter of minutes.[174] Between this point and the northern corner of Gommecourt Wood small groups of the 1/5th and 1/7th, likely totalling no more than 200, had made it to the German second trench and attempted to bring a machine gun into action. Fighting spluttered back and forth for three or four hours. The Sherwood Foresters were always going to lose: they were fewer in number, and short of bullets and bombs. German shellfire meant that neither reinforcements nor ammunition could be run over. RIR91's counterattack companies rushed the machine gun, thereafter snatching successive trench bays until any still-living Sherwood Foresters had fled.[175] By 11 a.m. the 139th's gains had been lost.[176]

The German trenches were rent by gunshots and grenade blasts and hobnailed boots clattering along duckboards. 'I threw three bombs. I did not wait to see the result,' said Private Frank Bates, 1/5th Sherwood Foresters, of encountering a German soldier.[177] Corporal Peter Murphy's band of 1/5th Sherwood Foresters rumbled a group of nine enemy soldiers. One was shot. The rest bolted. 'I bayoneted the last two while the remainder of the enemy was shot down by our party.'[178] They then ran into a strong counterattack group:

A German ran up along the parados from the left. Captain [Arthur] Naylor [of 1/5th Sherwood Foresters] shouted 'That man — shoot him,' but we were too late for as we raised our rifles the German dropped his bomb and jumped into [the] far end of [the] next [trench] bay. We were now subjected to bombing from both flanks, and having exhausted our own bombs we replied with the German 'potato-mashers' [grenades]. We held the bay while the store of bombs lasted.[179]

Not far away, half a dozen bullets thudded into a trench wall near Lieutenant Theodore Downman, 1/5th Sherwood Foresters. He moved on, made it to the second German trench and linked up with a dozen others. Bombs were spent fighting off German soldiers who snatched pot shots around trench corners before darting away. Downman saw Second-Lieutenant John McInnes, 1/5th Sherwood Foresters, stagger dazed when a bullet glanced off his helmet: 'He was hit again, this time right through the helmet and into the brain. He died immediately.'[180] McInnes is named on the Thiepval Memorial. At about 8 a.m. Downman's left arm and hip were pierced by grenade splinters:

The men scattered immediately and Bosch opened with rifles from the direction in which we had been going. I was hit by a bullet in the left arm, through the bicep, the bullet then struck a steel shaving mirror which I carried in my left breast pocket, and so being turned made a shallow groove across my solar plexus and landed in a box of safety matches in my right breast pocket, igniting them. ... Almost immediately after the bombs the trench filled with Germans from both sides, and before I could offer any resistance I was pounced on.[181]

Downman, who died aged 88 in 1970 at Penzance, was collared. Six weeks later his family received word he was a prisoner of war.

Mid-morning, Brigadier-Generals Hugh Williams of the 137th and Charles Shipley of the 139th were mulling over their next moves. Both knew their gore-spattered trenches were clogged with battle stragglers, knots of men whose units had yet to attack, and discarded equipment. Hostile shellfire was still falling and machine-gun bullets kicked up parapet dust or whistled overhead by the thousands. By 9.01 a.m., Williams had been told the 137th's attack had failed, but he wanted to stop any freed-up German infantry and artillery from being deployed against the 139th's and 56th (1st London) Division's gains. He sanctioned an attack comprising any available men of 1/5th South Staffords and 1/5th North Staffords, followed by elements of 1/5th Leicesters.[*] Lieutenant-Colonel Raymer, 1/5th South Staffords, was wounded while organising the operation and the job then fell to Lieutenant-Colonel Charles Jones, 1/5th Leicesters. Jones later commented on the proposed operation: 'A second attack by the same troops is always very difficult to organise, and in this case the difficulties were many.'[182] By contrast, Shipley, aware that the 139th's role was to provide flank support for the 137th, wanted to run ammunition across to any Sherwood Foresters still in the German lines. He saw anything else as futile.[183] Dwindling supplies of trench-mortar smoke bombs needed to be restocked if the infantry's move across no-man's-land was to be masked with smoke. Based on these reasons, and common sense, both brigadiers realised further operations were not immediately possible.

A 'worn-out' and 'incapable of inspiring any enthusiasm'[184] Montagu-Stuart-Wortley, the 46th's commander, was not dissuaded. He

---

[*] 1/5th Battalion (Territorial Force) Leicestershire Regiment. SDGW notes 13 deaths.

ordered an attack involving his two brigades to be carried out as soon as possible.[185] The 137th would attack afresh and the 139th would send over one company to support its men still thought to be in the German lines. It was about 9.30 a.m., and Snow, who was at the 46th's headquarters, had already confirmed the 56th's break-in. It was probably on the strength of Snow's words that Montagu-Stuart-Wortley now told Williams the 'success of the whole [VII Corps] operation depends on your pushing on as soon as possible.'[186] It suggested Snow saw any hold-up of the 46th as transient. At about 10 a.m., Montagu-Stuart-Wortley insisted Williams' brigade take 'Gommecourt Wood at all costs.'[187] This was an interim objective, and clarified that he and Snow were thinking in terms of a salvage operation that just might have a spill-over benefit for the 56th. Even then, the pair was plainly out of touch with events and interpreting the clutch of increasingly grim battle reports in their possession far too charitably. They did not appreciate the 46th's operation was already in its final stages. Snow sanctioned the attack.[188]

A truculent Shipley wanted none of it, as Lieutenant Claude Good, 1/7th Sherwood Foresters attached to 46th's headquarters, recalled of a telephone call he overheard:[189]

The GOC [General Officer Commanding, Montagu-Stuart-Wortley] said, 'The 5th Battalion must go over and regain contact.' The Brigadier [Shipley] said it was impossible. The gunfire & machinegun fire was so intense nothing could get across, also, the enemy wire was not cut, [and] no-man's-land was three hundred yards across. The GOC said: 'They must go over under a smoke screen.' General Shipley replied that it would blow back over our own lines. I cannot remember the details of the row which followed. I recall that Shipley said 'I stand by my decision and am willing to face the consequences.'[190]

At 11.20 a.m. Montagu-Stuart-Wortley — impatient, growing in resolve and unaware the last Sherwood Foresters had finally been evicted from the German line — stipulated a 12.15 p.m. start.[191] Remnants of the 137th — two waves of 1/5th North and South Staffords followed by two of 1/5th Leicesters — would attack under smoke, as would one company and ammunition-carrying parties of the 139th's 1/6th Sherwood Foresters. The Staffords men had to be side-stepped left through congested trenches to attack opposite the northern end of Gommecourt Wood, roughly where the 1/6th North Staffords had gone over that morning. Delays, disorganisation, confusion and lack of smoke bombs saw the attack delayed a trinity of times to 3.30 p.m. British artillery shelled the German lines in the 30 minutes before Zero. The thin veil of smoke provided by the trench mortars from 3.20 p.m. provoked an instant reflux of German shell- and machine-gun fire. Shipley cancelled the 139th's operation,[192] Williams following suit with the 137th as officer casualties and confusion within the attacking battalions caused more delays.[193] Snow, now knowing the 56th's gains were being fast eroded on the south side of the salient, finally called off the attack.

'I was, and am, quite satisfied that there was no possible chance of reaching the objective and no result could have been achieved,' wrote Lieutenant-Colonel Godfrey Goodman, 1/6th Sherwood Foresters, of the attempts to restart the attack.[194] Twenty of his men did not get word that it had been cancelled. Eighteen were felled by shrapnel and bullet within 20–30 yards of their own parapet. One made it back. Others, too, had seen the writing on the wall. Lieutenant Moore, 1/5th Leicesters, thought orders for the afternoon flutter would produce 'sheer murder' and had contemplated refusing the order.[195] 'I gave myself a metaphorical kick up the bottom and pulled myself together,' he said.[196] It was fortunate for him that the attack was cancelled.

Not so lucky were the 1/5th Lincolns, 138th Brigade. Snow and Allenby, the commander of Third Army, wanted to provide a 2.30 a.m. diversion on 2 July to support a renewed attack by Hunter-Weston's derelict VIII Corps at the same time. Hunter-Weston hoped to reach and evacuate any of his men then mistakenly still believed to be at Serre, but VIII Corps cancelled this operation shortly before 10 p.m. Meantime, Allenby's supporting plan was essentially a watered-down version of VII Corps' already failed operation that would see one brigade of the 46th and two battalions of the 56th link up behind Gommecourt. On receiving word that VIII Corps was not going ahead, Allenby dropped these plans: 'The general situation does not appear to me to demand the sacrifice.'[197] But he, Snow and Montagu-Stuart-Wortley were still keen to reach and extract Sherwood Foresters still believed to be in the German lines around and just south of Schwalbenneste. Plans for this 11 p.m. operation had bubbled along throughout the evening, and were eventually signed off by Snow's headquarters. Hull of the 56th wanted no part in either this or the now-cancelled plan for early on 2 July; Montagu-Stuart-Wortley was as game as ever. So it was that, at about midnight, a much-delayed company of 1/5th Lincolns ventured towards the German line just north of Gommecourt Wood, which had been attacked by 1/5 Sherwood Foresters that morning. They lost direction and were rumbled outside the enemy wire. German infantry once again blazed away with machine guns and rifles, and called down defensive shellfire in the flickering light of flares. Forty-eight Lincolns were casualties. Survivors went to ground and were eventually ordered to retire.

The commander of 1/5th Lincolns, Lieutenant-Colonel Thomas Sandall, later described the night-time operation as a 'forlorn hope,' citing lack of organisation and time, and assembly trenches clogged with wounded, dead and battle stragglers. 'It is obvious that failure was inevitable.'[198] Neither was the futility of the operation lost on Private Arthur Ward, 1/5th Lincolns, whose platoon was one of several that did not go forward. Ward's sergeant thought the orders vague and demanded definite instructions. He wanted to know whether his men were to gain and defend a foothold in German lines or bring prisoners back. Neither Sandall, who obviously harboured reservations of his own, nor his adjutant could provide answers to the platoon commander's question. 'They informed the sergeant that his action might be looked on as mutiny,' wrote Ward. 'Still he remained firm stating that the men would follow willingly, but they must have a fair chance. We were recalled and that was the end of that incident.'[199]

It was a pathetic epitaph to a day-long tragedy. The 46th's failure was the result of mostly intact German wire, numerous defenders who sat out the preparatory bombardment in shell-proof dugouts, and large numbers of operational enemy artillery batteries that intervened when the attack began and ultimately decided the outcome of the battle. Cosmetic damage to the German positions had scarcely interfered with 2nd Guards Reserve Division's pre-planned defensive scheme and any British incursions were efficiently eliminated by long-standing counterattack tactics. Smoke cover offered no protection to Montagu-Stuart-Wortley's infantry, and its pre-Zero release only flagged the pending attack to already-alert German observers. It was then quickly dissipated in this part of the battlefield by wind. The barrage supporting the 46th was fundamentally flawed, in that it lifted off the German front line too quickly and for the most part allowed defenders to man their parapets and begin shooting into no-man's-land. The message was clear: the 46th had been categorically defeated by poor planning in the face of an intelligent and flexible German defensive scheme that was almost entirely intact on battle day.

The bloody price of failure: the 46th racked up 2455 casualties, for no lasting gains. Included were 853 killed, 1411 wounded, 186 missing and five prisoners. Among the division's casualties were five battalion commanders, three of them killed, one dead from wounds and another wounded.[200] Most of the killing was over by 8.30 a.m. German casualties totalled 265.[201] RIR91's dead, wounded and missing ran to about 150, while those of the battalion of RIR55 deployed in the northern half of the salient totalled about 115, including 18 killed, 95 wounded and two others missing.[202] For every German casualty north of the Foncquevillers–Gommecourt road there were 9.2 British, a ratio that emphasises the impact of the in-form German artillery and machine-gunners and resultant one-sided nature of the fighting.

Montagu-Stuart-Wortley was sacked a few days later. In Snow's words to Haig, the 46th had shown a 'lack of offensive spirit.'[203] The implication was that VII Corps' attack might have achieved more but for the 46th. This was a serious allegation and revealed that Snow had no concept of the 1 July battlefield, or of how the 46th's ordeal had been framed by his and corps headquarters' failings. He said Montagu-Stuart-Wortley was too old and lacked the constitution required for command, and that a younger man would be preferable. On every count Snow was lobbing stones from a glass house. He probably wanted to appease Haig, who was already fuming over the mistaken belief that few of the neighbouring VIII Corps' men had left their trenches on 1 July. Montagu-Stuart-Wortley was the obvious fall guy for the 46th's failure. Allenby agreed. Haig already disliked Montagu-Stuart-Wortley and blamed him for the Hohenzollern Redoubt debacle on 13–19 October 1915, an action that had resulted in the useless slaughter of British infantry for no lasting military gains. That

Montagu-Stuart-Wortley had previously corresponded with King George V, at the latter's request, only fuelled Haig's distrust. As Home, a senior staff officer at 46th headquarters, said, 'they meant getting rid of him and I suppose this was the opportunity.'[204] Montagu-Stuart-Wortley's career was over. He died an embittered old man in 1934.

Walk among the headstones at Foncquevillers Military Cemetery and you will find some of the 46th's dead. There are 600 named headstones; 115 of the 124 soldiers killed on 1 July and buried here rest in a mass grave beneath 59 headstones. They were shoemakers, errand boys, colliery labourers and rag-trade workers. Nine were husbands, the rest probably single. Private George Palmer, 1/4th Leicesters,* was also buried at this cemetery. The 21-year-old bookbinder, who stood just five feet and two-and-a-half inches, was treated for debility and concussion before the Somme. He survived the carnage of 1 July, but his luck expired at the end of a shell burst on 28 February 1917. His effects — some letters and photos, a Bible, a few coins and a badge — were sent to his mother, Harriett. She chose her son's epitaph knowing she would likely never visit France: 'Will some kind hand in a foreign land place a flower on my son's grave.'

'JULY 1ST TERMINATED in a complete victory,' crowed Süsskind-Schwendi in his after-battle report.[205] He had good reason to gloat. Gommecourt salient remained entirely in German hands after VII Corps' incursions were destroyed according to established artillery and infantry defensive doctrine. The tremendous firepower deployed by 2nd Guards Reserve and 52nd Infantry Divisions' largely intact artillery was the decisive factor. These gunners first disrupted VII Corps' advance by cutting off infantry that made it into the German lines, and then destroyed the attack by stopping supporting waves from crossing over. As the morning progressed and VIII Corps' attack at Serre failed, more of the 52nd's batteries opened up in enfilade, along with those of 111th Infantry Division further north. On-the-spot officers and their men erased the isolated London and North Midland pockets of resistance with template concentric counterattacks. The situation was always under control; there was simply never any need for either Süsskind-Schwendi

---

* 1/4th Battalion (Territorial Force) Leicestershire Regiment. SDGW notes 1 death.

or Borries to request reinforcements from XIV Reserve Corps. 'Every man in the Division is proud of this result and of the success won,' wrote Süsskind-Schwendi.[206]

Thousands of crumpled khaki bundles in plain view to all outside Gommecourt were evidence of the killing. Seventh Corps recorded 6769 casualties, including 2206 dead, 3766 wounded, 559 missing and 238 prisoners. The regiments of Süsskind-Schwendi's 2nd Guards Reserve and Borries' 52nd used to some extent or another in the fighting around Gommecourt lost a combined total of about 1391 men,[207] among them at least 463 dead, 746 wounded and 160 missing from RIR55, RIR91, IR170 and IR66.[208] Additionally, RIR15 and RIR77, the latter in the line further north and not under direct attack, suffered a combined 22 losses.[209] Those figures equated to one German casualty for every 4.9 British: a ratio that confirmed Süsskind-Schwendi had well and truly achieved his mission statement of annihilation, although not without cost.

Snow somewhat surprisingly also claimed the operation as a success. He alleged his corps had drawn in enemy troops to 'oppose it, which might otherwise have been used against Fourth Army.'[210] He was referring to the arrival of Süsskind-Schwendi's division back in May, of which he amazingly only learned some time on 30 June. This division was slotted into XIV Reserve Corps' order of battle to strengthen the entire line north of the Somme, not, as Snow suggested, in response to the visible battle preparations by VII Corps. He never knew this, but in any case his self-professed success in this sense related only to one element of VII Corps' objectives. Snow had been wholly committed to the other, which was to literally draw German artillery and infantry fire away from Serre and onto his own battalions in the hope that it might benefit VIII Corps' attack. While VII Corps certainly acted as a magnet for German fire, it produced no tactical benefit whatsoever for VIII Corps. When the assault on Gommecourt failed, Snow blamed the large number of active German guns, the breadth of no-man's-land and the 46th's delayed rear waves.[211] He said VII Corps' counter-battery work had been 'inadequate,'[212] which was a serious understatement. Most of these failings were, in fact, directly attributable to his corps-controlled artillery. Snow was touting his faulty understanding of 2nd Guards Reserve's arrival as proof of success, but avoiding directly incriminating his headquarters for the bungled artillery and other preparations that led directly to his infantry's failure.

In the days afterwards Snow and Haig went on a morale-boosting exercise. Snow — who on battle day thought all was 'going alright'[213] — stuck to his story. 'Although Gommecourt has not fallen into our hands,' he said in an open message to the men of his corps, 'the purpose of the attack, which was mainly to kill and contain Germans, was accomplished.'[214] Haig chimed in with a declaration that he deplored the casualties, but that VII Corps' operation had 'proved of material assistance to the success of the general plan of operations.'[215] Allenby no doubt thought much the same. There was no substance to any of it. VII Corps had neither contained Süsskind-Schwendi's or Borries' divisions, nor drawn in any of XIV Reserve Corps' reserves from Bapaume or elsewhere. Snow's corps had not even provided any kind of useful diversion for VIII Corps, or killed many Germans at all, whether in military or comparative terms. Moreover, the theme of Fourth Army's operations on 1 July was mostly one of unmitigated failure, which was really quite difficult to confuse with success. Snow, Allenby and Haig were on a spin exercise to buff tactical defeat into the intangible strategic victory it never was with bunkum and falsehoods.

Careless-with-words Snow did not have the skillset to sell lies. 'When I heard that you had been driven back,' he later told the remnants of the 56th, 'I did not care a damn. It did not matter whether you took your objective or not. Our attack was only a feint to keep the German Guards Divisions [sic] occupied whilst the main attack was being made down south.'[216] There it was. Callous 'Slush' still did not understand the difference between a feint and a diversion, falsely implied VII Corps' objectives had had some kind of direct link to the gains made at Fricourt, Mametz and Montauban, and revealed he knew absolutely nothing about working a crowd of grieving soldiers. An embittered Captain Ferdinand Wallis, London Rifle Brigade, thought Snow tactless given the 56th's survivors had 'been through Hell' and, insightfully, that their friends had been 'deliberately sacrificed.'[217] Plenty of others felt that way, too. Sergeant Isaac Read, 7th Leicesters, 37th Division, was behind the battlefield as a scarecrow column of South Staffords trudged by late on 1 July:[218] '"How d'you go on mates?" No one took the slightest notice, save a corporal carrying three rifles, who was bringing up the rear of the party. He half-turned, and, indicating the weary straggling figures before him, shrugged expressively. "General f... up in command again!" and he went on. Then he turned again. "Back where they f... well started!"[219]

By no means all of them, though.

CHAPTER 11

The Earth Abideth

A British defeat and coalition positive

'I have been waiting for years to put on record items of horror, ineptitude of commanders, callous indifference to the suffering of the infantryman.'[1]
— Rifleman Henry Barber, 1/5th Londons (London Rifle Brigade)

ALMOST TWENTY THOUSAND British and Newfoundland soldiers lay dead or dying around the Somme battlefield at midnight on 1 July. Observers that day and thereafter, until the bloodied khaki bundles disintegrated into the earth or were buried, looked upon the grisly evidence of an almost complete German victory over General Sir Douglas Haig's British army. It was certainly far more that than a singularly British tactical defeat, which deftly airbrushes out the work of skilled German commanders, infantrymen and gunners who inflicted the bloodletting. Lieutenant-General Sir Henry Rawlinson, the prone-to-highs-and-lows commander of Fourth Army, well knew it, too. Come 2 July he was beginning to realise the scale of the tragedy between Montauban and Gommecourt. According to one historian: 'Frequently, he [Rawlinson] walked about the garden of his headquarters [at Querrieu], slashing at nothing with his stick, the round dome of his bald head bent forward.'[2] Rawlinson was a troubled man, mired in one of his funks as the enormity of British losses for negligible gains slowly dawned on him.

Officially, Third and Fourth Armies suffered a combined 57,470 casualties on the first day of the Somme.[3] This included 19,240 dead, along with 35,493 wounded, 2152 missing and 585 taken prisoner.[*] Blood from the dead alone would fill about two-and-a-half Olympic-sized swimming pools. By anyone's maths these numbers jar the mind — more so if one realises that most of these deaths took place in the one or two hours from about 7.30 a.m., as was the case.

This grim statistical palette was not available to Haig, Rawlinson or Lieutenant-General Sir Edmund Allenby, commander of Third Army, on battle day. Provisional casualty numbers reached their headquarters several days later, and certainly not before 3 July. One must not be too hard on them about this: these were days before calculators and databases, where ledgers, typewriters and manual arithmetic were everything. Battlefield confusion, delays in reporting casualties and technology limitations simply did not allow for instant data compilation at General Headquarters (GHQ). Late on 1 July, Rawlinson estimated casualties in Fourth Army at 16,000–20,000.[4] On 2 July, Haig, who was a man more interested in evaluating the tactical situation and planning his next moves than totting up casualties, said: 'Total casualties are estimated at over 40,000 to date. This cannot be considered severe in view of the numbers engaged, and the length of front attacked.'[5] He was out by a whopping 17,470, or about 30% of the eventual total.[6] Nowadays the Commander-in-Chief's (C-in-C) unempathetic diary comment is a magnet for epithets; not so then, when it went unread by others. Without doubt Haig's primary military concern on the night of 1 July and morning of 2 July was to clarify the ground his two armies actually held and then develop the Anglo-French offensive accordingly;[7] the optimist was still very much looking towards what could yet be.

---

*   The figure of 19,240 dead on 1 July is higher than in CWGC (18,480 for France, refined for UK and Canadian forces, and adjusted for army, airforce and aliases) and SDGW (17,125 for France and Flanders) databases. Deductions for non-Somme fatalities and additions for soldiers who died in a period including 1 July only lower these numbers. Work on the official figures ended after six months for 'reasons of economy,' not because they were complete. It should not be presumed that the *Official History*'s 2152 missing soldiers were dead, or that the figures stated would have remained materially unchanged if work on them had continued to completion.

By midnight on 1 July, roughly two-thirds of the British army's attack on the Somme had ended in disaster. The diversionary operation by VII Corps at Gommecourt and the assaults by III, VIII and X Corps broadly between Serre and La Boisselle had failed. Notable footings at Gommecourt, Heidenkopf near Serre, Hawthorn Ridge at Beaumont Hamel and Schwaben Redoubt above Thiepval were either lost, or about to be lost. An unsure footing remained at Schwabenhöhe, just south of La Boisselle, while the tip of Leipzig Redoubt near Thiepval was still in British hands. Fricourt had been outflanked by XV Corps' gains on Fricourt Spur, Hill 110 and around the captured village of Mametz. Brickheap-like Montauban and the ridge between that village and Mametz had fallen to XIII Corps. But, Haig and Rawlinson's infantry had scarcely broken into the German positions around Ovillers and La Boisselle, the focal point of the British army's operation, the infantry and cavalry of Reserve Army had not been pushed through, the high ground of Pozières Ridge was no closer than it had been that morning and there was no hint of mobile warfare out towards Bapaume and beyond. Haig's first day of the Somme was, on sum of parts, an abysmal tactical failure accompanied by industrial-scale casualties.

Even given the hefty casualty rate and negligible gains in ground, there was no possibility that Haig would close the Somme operations down. As General Sir William Robertson, Chief of Imperial General Staff, explained in August 1916, the coalition of Allies was 'under a mutual obligation to go on' and 'we could not tell Paris that we had had enough and meant to stop.'[8] The same was true on 1–2 July, and — even if Haig had grasped the extent of the tragedy more quickly — there were still the matters of the late-1915 Chantilly agreement, and the broader coalition aim of evicting the German army from France and Belgium, along with supporting the French army at Verdun and the Russian army's Brusilov Offensive in western Ukraine to consider. In short, the Somme's continuation after 1 July — it coughed and spluttered on until mid-November and produced more than a million casualties — was all about the necessity of coalition politics, plans and strategy. Quite apart from that, it really was not that easy for Haig to turn a big battle off just as one might flip a light switch at night before heading off to bed.[9]

Haig began 1 July at his advanced headquarters at Chateau Valvion, near Beauquesne, admiring the sunny morning, gentle breeze and mist that shrouded his assembled infantry. At 8 a.m., half an hour after the battle began, he assessed incoming reports as 'most satisfactory' and noted his infantry had 'everywhere crossed the Enemy's front trenches.'[10] By 9 a.m., his troops were 'in many places' advancing to timetable.[11] Evidence exists that Haig at this time hoped to achieve big gains in the northern part of the battlefield, specifically at 9.10 a.m. This can be seen in the war diary of II Corps, which was in Haig's GHQ reserve and grouped around Villers-Bocage, about 14 miles west of Albert as the crow flies. It directed the 23rd and 38th (Welsh) Divisions to 'reconnoitre roads to NE [broadly towards Serre, Beaumont Hamel and Thiepval] in case a move in that direction has to be carried out.'[12] More specific information arrived at Haig's headquarters. Twenty-ninth Division was held up south of Hawthorn Ridge, 31st Division was moving into Serre, VII Corps' attack at Gommecourt was progressing well even if part of 46th (North Midland) Division had not pressed on, and while some of X Corps was held up north of Authuille Wood other elements were apparently entering Thiepval.[13] Haig later said the reports of infantry in Serre and Thiepval were wrong, but on this point he was rather sanguine:[14] 'On a sixteen-mile front of attack varying fortune must be expected! It is difficult to summarise all that was reported.'[15] Haig's understanding of events was improving as the minutes ticked steadily by, and his hopes were increasingly focused on the central and southern parts of the battlefield. This can be seen, again, in II Corps' war diary. At 11.55 a.m., 23rd and 38th Divisions were directed to 'consider [the] possibility of a move to areas to [the] east at present occupied by 12th [(Eastern)] and 25th Divisions [both in Fourth Army reserve].'[16] Such a move to the ground immediately east of Albert would imply those latter two divisions had already moved further forward, something they were only to do if the cavalry had advanced before them.[17] As the morning progressed Haig formed an overall positive if marginally worsening impression of events and was still anticipating the cavalry might be deployed to battle.

At midday, four-and-a-half hours after the killing began, Haig wrote an upbeat letter to a politician in London. 'The wire has been more thoroughly cut than ever before, and also the Artillery bombardment has been methodical and continuous,' he wrote.[18] One must not be too harsh on Haig for the tone of this letter; he was very obviously writing in a general sense about battle preparations. We know now that Haig realised his infantry was making better progress in the southern part of Fourth Army's sector. Overall he remained positive. GHQ's reserve divisions were, as we have seen, still mulling moves closer to Albert that first required Reserve Army's cavalry to be deployed. Haig also likely knew General Marie-Emile Fayolle's French Sixth Army was making excellent gains astride the Somme, between Hardecourt and Estrées, the latter about 5.5 miles southwest of Péronne. But he was unaware of the extent to which his artillery had failed to perform, the negligible benefits produced by the massive mines and that most of his infantry had been caught in the open by an alert and unsurprised enemy. Come noon, Haig very much retained 'great hopes of getting some measure of success,'[19] and he still had no idea that his opening masterstroke on the Somme was already moribund.

That the Fourth Army attack was effectively over by this time had a lot to do with senior German commanders expecting the Allied offensive to fall between Gommecourt and Estrées. *General-der-Infanterie* Fritz von Below, commanding Second Army, and *Generalleutnant* Hermann von Stein, commanding XIV Reserve Corps, had forecast that the focal point of the coalition offensive would be on the British front rather than the French, and more specifically directed at the high ground either side of the River Ancre valley, broadly between Serre and Ovillers. This was their vital ground; a British success here was seen as likely undermining XIV Reserve Corps' tenure on the Somme, with necessary implications for all of Second Army.

Stein, Below and *Generalleutnant* Franz *Freiherr* von Soden, 26th Reserve Division's dynamic commander, had started converting this terrain into a virtually impregnable stronghold of tiered machine guns, artillery, earthworks, barbed wire and fortified villages from at least early 1915. The neighbouring 2nd Guards Reserve, 52nd Infantry and 28th Reserve Divisions had similarly developed their flanking positions between Gommecourt and Serre, and also from Ovillers to Fricourt. But Below and Stein always attached less value to 12th Infantry Division's patch between Mametz and Curlu; it was too far forward of the main ridge, which made it difficult for an attacker to assemble resources, and thus the area went under-developed. If Below and Stein drove the creation of a formidable defensive network north of Fricourt, they were equally responsible for its weakness further south.

German statistics reveal much about the effectiveness of the British preparatory bombardment. Stein's corps suffered 2500–3000 casualties during the seven days of shellfire, or 2.6–3.2% of its total 95,000 men. That meant 96.8–97.4% of its infantry, machine-gunners and artillerymen were alive in their deep dugouts and ready to deploy when battle began. Even though numerous telephone lines had been severed, the infantry and artillery were trained to operate independently and in isolation of one another. An estimated 120 (21.1%) of the roughly 570 artillery barrels supporting Stein's line had been destroyed, which meant about 450 (78.9%) of XIV Reserve Corps' guns remained nominally active, but among these were many 'useless' weapons that were 'unable to provide sufficient support.'[20] Most of Stein's gun losses occurred between Mametz and Curlu, where the local divisional artillery had shown insufficient fire restraint, was consistently located and, also because of its under-developed positions, frequently destroyed. Artillery batteries north from Fricourt to Gommecourt, where greater fire discipline was practised, went comparatively undetected and survived in their better-constructed pits. Wire-cutting followed a similar pattern: about two-thirds of entanglements were reported either intact or partially intact between Serre and La Boisselle, and either absent or patchy in other places. Come 1 July the key elements of XIV Reserve Corps' defensive scheme north of Fricourt were almost wholly intact, but further south they were damaged and vulnerable to attack.

There were many reasons why the 24–30 June bombardment was mostly ineffective. Haig had 1769 artillery guns and howitzers to shatter the German defences and support his infantry. These were spread roughly evenly across battle fronts of his six attacking corps at a ratio of one field barrel for every 21 yards and one heavy barrel for every 57 yards. This gunstock was skewed to lighter-calibre field artillery, as was its supply of ammunition. Guns frequently failed due to overuse and poor manufacture, while many shell fuses were of dodgy quality. All of this was exacerbated by often inexperienced gunners who laboured against poor weather and visibility with nascent counter-battery techniques, inconsistent use of range charts and often questionable ground–air co-operation. Ground and air observers were impressed by the sights and sounds of the shellfire, and their reports were biased towards measuring cosmetic damage over assessing the effective breakdown of the German positions. Infantry patrol reports suggesting all was not well were marginalised, as was other naysayer commentary. Haig was seduced by upbeat observer reports summarising surface damage and did not realise his artillery lacked the firepower in terms of concentration, ammunition type and calibre to destroy or subdue the German defensive scheme.

It is painfully obvious with hindsight that Haig directed the main part of his assault at the strongest sections of Second Army's positions, which had emerged from the bombardment battered but very much functional. So it was, barring a few against-the-grain infantry epics, that VII, VIII, X and III Corps failed to make any lasting material gains between Gommecourt and La Boisselle. Thereafter, applying the same retrospective knowledge, it is scarcely surprising to find XV and XIII Corps, which also benefitted from a French artillery contribution, making successively better progress as the strength and defensive capabilities of German positions tapered off in their areas. The British corps-level outcomes of battle were defined not just by the ineffectiveness of Haig's bombardment, but very much also by the level of military value that German commanders attached to the ground, and its resultant development throughout 1915 and early 1916.

British corps commanders turned in polarised performances. Seventh Corps' Lieutenant-General Sir Thomas D'Oyly Snow at Gommecourt did not understand the difference between a diversion and a feint, sought to draw enemy shell- and machine-gun fire onto his men and was still unable to snatch German gunners' attention away from Serre. Lieutenant-General Sir Aylmer Hunter-Weston gave prior notice that VIII Corps was attacking between Serre and Beaumont Hamel thanks to the bungled timing of the Hawthorn Ridge mine explosion and supporting barrage. Lieutenant-General Sir Thomas Morland thought in straight lines at Thiepval, repeatedly trying to restart X Corps' dead attacks while ignoring promising gains at Schwaben Redoubt. Lieutenant-General Sir William Pulteney's III Corps paid severely before Ovillers and La Boisselle for his mask of competence and lack of imagination. Lieutenant-General Sir Henry Horne was typically opportunistic when he bloodily failed to force the early capture of Fricourt after XV Corps' initial gains on the back of a generally effective bombardment. Lieutenant-General Sir Walter Congreve, VC, was methodical and cautious as XIII Corps produced impressive gains against under-developed and shellfire-neutralised German positions around Montauban. These commanders' after-battle pep talks reflected this: Snow, Hunter-Weston, Morland and Pulteney spoke bunkum and lies to dress up military failure as something else, Horne was slippery in explaining partial success and Congreve was sincere after his victory.

A total of 175 battalions from Third and Fourth Armies, totalling about 133,175 officers and men, were involved in the 1 July fighting, whether they went over the top, remained in the British trenches or played a supporting role. A sample of 29 battalions whose bayonet strength on 1 July is accurately known reveals an average into-battle total of 761 officers and men for each, the range being 567–928.[21] (Bayonet strength is the number of officers and men who actually went into battle and is lower than nominal strength, which includes a portion of men left out of battle and other soldiers detailed to the transport work, cooking duties and other ancillary tasks.) The initial attack wave at 7.30 a.m. comprised 59 whole bayonet-strength battalions and totalled roughly 44,899 soldiers of all ranks who went over the top.[22] Of the remaining 116 battalions, about 75, comprising 57,075 soldiers, either followed immediately behind the first wave in direct support, or were involved in subsequent attacks throughout the course of the day. The remaining 31,201 men, across 41 battalions, were interleaved into the main attack waves, went forward piecemeal as carrying and consolidation parties or reinforcements, or remained in British lines, all too frequently under heavy German artillery and machine-gun fire.

Tactical formations used by attacking battalions varied. Of the 134 battalions that formally attacked, 108 (80.6%) did so using close-order tactics. Of these, 68 (50.7%) advanced in linear waves; 18 (13.4%) in linear waves followed by columns of platoons, sections or half platoons; 18 (13.4%) in columns of platoons or sections; and 4 (3%) in section columns. A further 9 (6.7%) adopted open-order artillery formation, with 14 (10.5%) a blend of linear wave, columns of platoon and sections, followed by some elements in artillery formation. The formation of advance used by 3 (2.3%) battalions is unknown. These figures do not include battalions committed piecemeal, whether providing reinforcements, or acting as carrying, consolidation or mopping-up parties. Nevertheless, the conventional imagery of unwavering lines of British infantry advancing into a tornado of German artillery, machine-gun and rifle fire[23] is more than 80% correct.

Of the 59 battalion units leading the attack, excluding minor elements of 7th Buffs, 51 (86.4%) did so in close-order formation. Of these, 38 (64.4%) advanced in linear-wave formations, with 9 (15.3%) progressing in linear waves followed by columns of platoons, sections or half platoons. Four (6.7%) moved forward in columns of sections. Eight (13.6%) of the 59 battalions led with linear-wave, or columns of platoons, or sections formations, followed by elements in artillery formation. Of the 59, 36 (61.8%) are known to have deployed in no-man's-land before 7.30 a.m. — 26 of them between 7.23 a.m. and 7.29 a.m., but on 10 occasions between 7.10 and 7.20 a.m. — with a view to getting closer to the German front line before the barrage lifted. Another 75 battalions went forward to the attack immediately behind the leading wave, or some hours later. Of these, 57 (76%) did so in close order, whether in linear waves, columns of platoons and sections or section columns. Nine (12%) advanced in artillery formation, while six (8%) used some form of close-order structure followed by at least some elements in artillery formation. A further 43 battalions were either partially interleaved into those attacking, worked on communication trenches, carried ammunition and supplies, consolidated captured ground, deployed piecemeal as reinforcements, or remained in British lines.

Where the preparatory shellfire had cut the German wire and substantially suppressed artillery–infantry resistance, these tactics produced results. This was the case for 7th, 21st, 18th (Eastern) and particularly 30th Divisions between Fricourt, Mametz and Montauban. Where German defensive obstacles remained there was no hope — as 29th and 31st Divisions' respective debacles at today's Newfoundland Memorial Park, near Beaumont Hamel, and Sheffield Memorial Park, near Serre, so painfully testified, along with the majority of 8th and 34th Divisions before Ovillers and La Boisselle, and most of 32nd Division at Thiepval. However, if the wire was either cut or patchy and the German infantry garrison and gunners further back were only briefly suppressed or slow in reacting, local break-ins were possible, at least until an organised enemy infantry–artillery fightback began. This was the lot of 46th (North Midland) and 56th Divisions at Gommecourt, 4th Division at Heidenkopf, 29th Division at Hawthorn Ridge, 36th (Ulster) Division at Schwaben Redoubt, and a portion of 8th Division at Nab Valley. The success or failure of British infantry tactics was not so much linked to the formation of advance alone, but rather to the level of the preparatory bombardment's effectiveness.

Barrages used to cover the infantry's passage across no-man's-land varied in effectiveness. Where the seven-day bombardment had left the wire cut or patchy, the infantry was often able to cross over and break into the German line, but only if the supporting barrage suppressed remaining enemy infantry, machine-gunners and artillerymen (including those further back and in neighbouring sectors) for long enough. This facilitated a handful of generally short-lived incursions by the northern III, VII, VIII and X Corps, and also the more substantial break-ins further south by XV and XIII Corps. Fifteenth Corps' infantry benefitted from a creeping barrage that rolled forward in consistent intervals of time and distance. XIII Corps' infantry was supported by a fire plan that involved a timed curtain of shellfire that stepped forward over the German positions, rather than creeping. In the case of XV and XIII Corps, the barrage mostly covered infantry until it reached the German parapet, but not always, as 7th, 18th (Eastern) and 21st Divisions discovered in places. In most cases the supporting barrage either lifted off the German front line too quickly, outpaced the infantry, or both.

Thereafter the men's fortunes were linked to how effective the pre-battle bombardment had been in suppressing or destroying enemy resistance and sweeping away defensive obstacles. This explains the German infantry's eradication of most of the initial gains by the four northern corps, and varying difficulties experienced by 7th, 18th and 21st Divisions, and to a much lesser extent 30th Division, in obtaining their objectives between Fricourt and Montauban. Providing artillery support for infantry as it moved forward was essential, but 1 July revealed that the success of that shellfire in breaking down obstacles and suppressing resistance was linked both to its own density and pace, and also very much to the preparatory bombardment's performance beforehand.

Nineteen mines of varying sizes were blown along Fourth Army's front, and these produced generally disappointing results. Of the massive mines, Hawthorn Ridge (40,600 pounds) facilitated a minor gain by 29th Division near Beaumont Hamel. However, its 7.20 a.m. detonation gave defenders in that area and much further afield a 10-minute warning of Third and Fourth Armies' attack. At La Boisselle, Y-Sap (40,600 pounds) had no discernible benefit for 34th Division, while the double-core Lochnagar blast (60,000 pounds) allowed a permanent footing against the overall grain of battle for that division just south of La Boisselle. Two 8000-pound mines designed to wreck German tunnels at the Glory Hole, just outside La Boisselle and not under direct attack, were of no benefit to the 34th. Several mines at The Tambour, east of Fricourt, probably helped 10th West Yorkshires' initial waves, but only two of three (9000 pounds, 15,000 pounds and 25,000 pounds) blew — the largest of the three failed to detonate because its chamber had flooded prior to battle. In each of these cases German casualties were considerably fewer than expected, and the defenders quickly recovered. Around Mametz, the Bulgar Point mine (2000 pounds) before 7th Division and Casino Point mine (5000 pounds) in front of 18th (Eastern) Division also helped the infantry forward, but better preparatory and supporting artillery work in this area was also a material factor. This was also the case for seven 200–500-pound mines blown around Mametz for the 7th, three of which were on ground not under direct attack, plus two more 500-pound mines north of Carnoy in the 18th's area. 'Though many mines were fired,' opined the official historian, 'they were too much scattered up and down the front to produce a noticeable effect on the enemy.'[24]

All of these factors, as well as a lack of surprise across the fronts of Third and Fourth Armies, profoundly affected the tactical outcome of the battle. German soldiers had observed the steady accumulation of men and materiel, which led to their commanders divining as early as February 1916 that a heavy British attack was being prepared. The beginning of the five- and then seven-day bombardment only flagged the attack's imminent arrival. The cutting of gaps in the British wire for infantry to pass through, the laying of rickety wooden bridges for infantry to cross their own trenches and the obvious digging of jumping-off ditches in some areas of no-man's-land further confirmed this. British soldiers taken captive in trench raids provided more details to their captors, and further information was intercepted by subterranean listening devices that tuned in to insecure and uncoded telephone communications. All of this meant German commanders very much expected Haig's attack, while the blowing of the Hawthorn Ridge mine alerted German defenders between Gommecourt and at least Ovillers and La Boisselle that the moment had arrived. The vast majority of German infantrymen and machine-gunners had survived the preparatory bombardment and were for the most part ready and waiting to meet the British attack up to 10 minutes before it began.

RAWLINSON AND HIS retinue began the day in an 'observation fort' known as the Grandstand on a hillock near Albert.[25] From here he had a sweeping view over the hazy battlefield. Rawlinson had returned to his Querrieu headquarters by 9.20 a.m.[26] Initial battle reports were already being telephoned in. From these calls a skeleton outline of progress was assembled.[27] 'The battle has begun well,' Rawlinson noted.[28] 'Bombardment was good and stokes [sic] mortars seem to have been a success. The villages of Serre, B. Hammel [sic] and Thiepvaal [sic] seem to be sticking us up but south the III, XV and XIII Corps seem to be getting on well. The French on our right are also going strong and have taken the Bois Favier [sic].'[29] In sum, Rawlinson was well aware by 9.20 a.m., almost two hours after Zero, that all was not going quite to plan: attempts to form a defensive left flank on Serre Heights were proving troublesome and positive progress already seemed to be skewed to the southern half of the battlefield, which was correct around Fricourt, Mametz and Montauban for XV and XIII Corps but not so for III Corps on the killing grounds before La Boisselle and Ovillers.

Shortly after noon Rawlinson had markedly tempered his initial assessment. He knew Montauban had fallen to XIII Corps, mistakenly believed Serre had been taken by VIII Corps and had been informed that Beaumont Hamel, Thiepval, Ovillers, Fricourt and Mametz were proving stubborn.[30] Further bombardments were needed.[31] 'The 18, 30, 31 and 36 Divisions seem to have done the best so far.'[32] These assessments are broadly confirmed by Fourth Army's summary of operations.[33] More specifically, 36th (Ulster) Division's stellar break-in at Schwaben Redoubt was known of, while it was believed 31st Division had men digging in around Serre. Fourth Division was in Heidenkopf, and 32nd Division was thought to have elements in Thiepval and definitely held Leipzig Redoubt. Third Corps apparently had men 'well over' the German second line, some bound for Contalmaison, Peake and Bailiff Woods or 'close in front of Pozières.'[34] La Boisselle was free of enemy, but the situation in Ovillers was unclear. Further south, XV Corps had effectively flanked Fricourt and was in the process of taking Mametz. Thirteenth Corps' 30th Division had seized Montauban. The neighbouring 18th (Eastern) Division was still some time away from pulling up alongside the 30th. From these reports Rawlinson noted at 12.15 p.m. that 'progress in the centre [of Fourth Army's battle front] is therefore slow whilst the flanks are secured.'[35]

It is probable that Rawlinson's actual understanding of progress was much bleaker than his personal diary suggests. In addition to normal army–corps communications, he was in private telephone contact with his subordinate corps commanders. What they told him of progress between Serre and La Boisselle, 'unofficially, as one comrade to another, seems to have been more disturbing than their official reports.'[36] The post-war memoir of *Sous-officier* Paul Maze tends to support this. The French liaison officer, attached to the staff of General Sir Hubert Gough, commander of Reserve Army, was in Rawlinson's operations room at Querrieu that day: 'Great tension was reigning in the office. I didn't envy the Generals their responsibilities as they pored over maps and messages, and faced at every moment the taking of grave decisions.'[37] And the key element of Maze's observations: 'At noon we knew that in front of Thiepval and Beaumont Hamel we had been severely checked. Of that, there was no more doubt — the attacks on the whole of the left front [being VIII and X Corps, and possibly including III Corps too] had failed. The casualties were very serious. The Reserve Army stood awaiting further developments.'[38] Gough was at Querrieu too: 'We could get as clear a grasp of the situation as was possible.'[39] It must be noted that Maze had the benefit of writing 15 years after the fact. However, at the time, Rawlinson wanted to believe 31st Division had made progress around Serre and that XV and XIII Corps had advanced around Fricourt–Montauban, but the lack of progress around Ovillers and La Boisselle led him to doubt whether Reserve Army would be deployed.

Proof of this can be seen in Reserve Army's orders to 3rd Cavalry Division either side of midday. At this time Reserve Army was taking orders from Rawlinson even though it was under Gough's command.[40] At 11.30 a.m., 3rd Cavalry Division was told that there was 'no chance' of it being 'required to move till 2 p.m. at earliest.'[41] This was followed by another order at 1.20 p.m. that said 3rd Cavalry should 'not make preparations to move till a warning message reaches them.'[42] These orders revealed that in the early afternoon Rawlinson doubted the cavalry would be sent into battle, suggested a decision on their deployment would be made mid-afternoon, but pulled up well short of actually standing these units down.

There were, broadly speaking, four ways in which battlefield gains could have been exploited. The first was for Rawlinson to decide whether or not to push Gough's Reserve Army — comprising 19th (Western) and 49th (West Riding) Divisions, plus three cavalry divisions — through a break in the German front-line system created by III and X Corps and thence on towards Bapaume, their flanks supported by VIII Corps and XV Corps' reserve 17th (Northern) Division. The second and third were for either Rawlinson or his corps commanders to use divisions in corps reserve locally, namely, north to south, 48th (South Midland), 49th (West Riding), 19th (Western), 17th (Northern) and 9th (Scottish) Divisions. Fourth, Haig had the authority to enact all the previous three options, envisaged them occurring and had previously told Rawlinson he anticipated a rapid-advance attack.[43] He expected subordinates to capitalise on emerging battlefield opportunities rather than let them slip.[44] By contrast, Rawlinson, whatever lip service he gave Haig prior to 1 July, always doubted a breakthrough and in particular lacked confidence in Congreve's 30th Division. He had already decided that use of Reserve Army's cavalry depended on the German front-line system falling before noon on 1 July, and saw little likelihood of corps reserves being deployed at all.[45] As it turned out, neither Rawlinson, nor his corps commanders, nor Haig would deploy any reserves to exploit any of the several opportunities that opened up.

By 3.15 p.m., Rawlinson had unsurprisingly decided Reserve Army's cavalry was highly unlikely to be deployed at all. 'On the South things are satisfactory on the North less so and there is of course no hope of getting Cavry [sic] through today,' he noted at this specific time.[46] The time stamp on this diary entry is critical to unravelling British command decisions on 1 July, as we shall soon see. At this time, Rawlinson was well aware that German infantry still held the vast majority of its trenches opposite VIII Corps, and that X Corps was still fighting in Schwaben Redoubt, was planning more attacks towards Thiepval and had a limited footing at Leipzig Redoubt.[47] He also believed III Corps had reached the outskirts of Contalmaison, but importantly had not taken Ovillers and had 'suffered heavily' in front of La Boisselle.[48] XV Corps was close to surrounding Fricourt, while XIII Corps had apparently reached all of its objectives.[49] In short, Fourth Army's proposed drive up Pozières Ridge was not progressing at all to plan, which meant Rawlinson was correct in recognising there was 'no hope' of getting the cavalry through, but, by 3.15 p.m., he still had not ordered these units to stand down.

Even against a backcloth of widespread disaster there were two places where Fourth Army had opportunities to develop break-ins. The first was at Schwaben Redoubt above Thiepval, where 36th (Ulster) Division had driven a deep wedge into the German line as part of the operation by Morland's X Corps. The second was around Fricourt–Mametz–Montauban, where XV and XIII Corps were making good, but in places slow, progress. Fourth Division's incursion at Heidenkopf, near Serre, was an epic in its own right, but never had potential for development. In the event, the break-ins at Schwaben Redoubt, Fricourt, Mametz and Montauban slipped by, regardless of Haig's guidance that his subordinates actively seek to capitalise on such opportunities as and when they arose.

Thirty-six (Ulster) Division's break-in came shortly after 7.30 a.m., when it captured a slice of land around Schwaben Redoubt and briefly reached 26th Reserve Division's second defensive line. This was *the* vital ground for Stein and Soden, an acknowledged lynchpin of their defences and thus potentially for Second Army, too. It was no surprise that Soden's artillery and machine guns quickly made no-man's-land impassable with a tempest of defensive fire, while counterattack battalions began retaking the lost ground. By about 10.30 p.m. the Ulstermen had been essentially evicted. Morland's focus for most of the day was elsewhere. He wanted to restart 32nd Division's mostly failed attacks around Thiepval, discarding any notion of consolidation, let alone exploitation, at Schwaben Redoubt.

He still blindly hoped for a nice, neat linear advance across his corps' frontage, did not cotton on to the value of the 36th's gains and wasted time. Rawlinson apparently had no quibble with Morland's Thiepval myopia.[50] In any case, 49th (West Riding) Division, in corps reserve, was too far back to be deployed at anything like the speed required, and was subsequently frittered away piecemeal. Additionally, Morland's artillery scheme lacked the flexibility for a redeployment to even partially subdue the German defensive fire. The only hope was if the unsupported 36th could hold on to its gains or push east behind Thiepval, but Stein and Soden had different ideas. Only in the early evening did Morland realise the break-in's potential, but by then it was too late and the 36th was already being pushed steadily back. Without doubt the 36th's gains severely tested Stein and Soden, and probably Below too, but Morland let them off the hook. If Morland had been minded to win a lasting footprint around Schwaben Redoubt, it might just have provoked a series of German command decisions that produced an alternative short-term Somme narrative.

Further south, the potential of XV and XIII Corps' gains around Fricourt–Mametz–Montauban have been overcooked by historians. That Horne's corps was heavily engaged at Fricourt–Mametz into the night, along with his failed afternoon flutter to force the capture of Fricourt, ruled out any corps-level exploitation in that area. Around Montauban, Congreve's 30th Division captured its objectives by 10.30 a.m., but closer to Mametz his 18th (Eastern) Division lagged and only pulled up alongside the 30th on the Mametz–Montauban ridge early evening. Congreve, aware of Fourth Army's failure further north, was not nearly as interested in an exploitative operation as has often been suggested, and there is no immediately available evidence to suggest he either went forward on 1 July or subsequently lobbied Rawlinson for consent.[51] These factors ruled out a combined secondary operation by the casualty-thinned 18th and 30th, while 9th (Scottish) Division was still hours away in corps reserve. None of these divisions were warned on battle day that they might have to participate in such an operation because Congreve was focused on achieving his primary objectives and then consolidating them to defend against an expected German counterattack.

It is now the vogue to argue that the Bazentin-le-Grand–Longueval–Bernafay Woods line was open for the taking, potentially providing a base for future operations and saving lives later lost in taking it. But this is a straw-man argument based purely on XIII Corps' gains, specifically the 30th's, which hints at opportunity lost and paints Haig as a victim of his subordinates' decisions. Neither was the case, as we shall soon see. An additional operation in the Montauban area would never have been a simple matter: there were at least 2000 German soldiers from cobbled-together infantry, machine-gun and ancillary units holding the Bazentin-le-Grand–Longueval–Bernafay Woods line, plus two reinforcement regiments on their way forward. Any infantry exploitation by XIII Corps needed to be carefully planned, co-ordinated and supported by artillery, all of which took considerable time, and even then its outcome had rather a lot to do with some German chaps across the way.

German divisional commanders mostly developed their positions to a defensive doctrine that emphasised front-line retention with essential fire support from artillery and machine guns further back. The idea was to stop the enemy in a no-man's-land killing zone of direct and enfilade fire. Where there were break-ins, artillerymen and machine-gunners could block no-man's-land with a tornado of shrapnel and high-explosve shells, as well as bullets, and isolate the incursion. At the same time, concentric infantry counterattacks would seek to retake the lost ground. Soden and *Generalleutnants* Ferdinand von Hahn and Karl von Borries relentlessly drove their men in 26th Reserve, 28th Reserve and 52nd Infantry Divisions, respectively, during 1915–16 to convert their positions into fortresses. *Generalleutnant* Richard *Freiherr* von Süsskind-Schwendi took a similar approach when his 2nd Guards Reserve Division arrived at Gommecourt in May 1916. These generals were experts in defensive tactics, understood the ground and how to best use it, drew on the lessons from fighting in 1915, and demanded performance. Soden was well known for his frequent inspections of defensive positions, as were Borries and Süsskind-Schwendi. The exception was *Generalleutnant* Martin Châles de Beaulieu, commanding 12th Infantry Division in the Montauban–Curlu area. Hahn had the misfortune of inheriting Châles de Beaulieu's below-par work around Mametz just before battle. Below and Stein must be held to book for the consequences of overseeing development of a corps-wide defensive scheme that turned out not to be of uniform depth and strength.

The German artillery order of battle reflected the value Below and Stein apportioned to the ground held by each division. Twenty-sixth Reserve, 28th Reserve and 52nd Infantry Divisions possessed about 390 (68.4%) of the corps' roughly 570 guns north of the River Somme. This was because Below and Stein correctly expected the focal point of the British attack to broadly fall between Serre and Ovillers. Here, for example, the guns of 26th Reserve Artillery Brigade were divided into three large groups, with fire control centralised, ammunition stockpiled and detailed target zones worked out to the yard. The flanking 2nd Guards Reserve and 12th Infantry Divisions had a combined 180 (31.6%) guns, but crucially Borries and then Süsskind-Schwendi had spared no defensive effort at Gommecourt, whereas Châles de Beaulieu had been considerably more *laissez faire* between Mametz and the river. With the exception of Mametz–Montauban, Haig's plan directed his infantry into bespoke killing zones of bullet, shrapnel and explosive to attack an engineered defensive scheme backed by most of XIV Reserve Corps' artillery. It was thus no surprise, wrote one German historian, that 'despite localised successes, the enemy's intention of breaking through on a wide front had failed.'[52]

HAIG KNEW NONE of this when his dust-speckled motorcade pulled into Querrieu after lunch on 1 July. The drive from Chateau Valvion to Querrieu would have taken roughly 30 minutes in ideal conditions, but it probably took Haig longer given the traffic-clogged roads of 1 July. We do not know exactly when he arrived at the pulsing heart of command for the British army's first day of the Somme, but according to Rawlinson's time-stamped diary it was certainly after 3.15 p.m.[53] The precise amount of time Haig spent at Fourth Army headquarters is also unknown, but it cannot have been much more than an hour, as he subsequently drove about 30 minutes to be at Villers-Bocage by 5 p.m., meaning he must have left by about 4.30 p.m.[54] Haig's diary simply states that he 'saw' Rawlinson, the latter briefly noting the C-in-C's presence after 3.15 p.m.[55] When Haig arrived at Querrieu, Rawlinson well knew that battlefield events were not going remotely to plan between Serre and La Boisselle, and while he had already decided there was no hope of deploying cavalry that afternoon he still had not issued any orders to that effect.[56]

No notes of the discussion between Haig and Rawlinson in the hour to about 4.30 p.m. are known to exist. But subsequent events make it apparent that Rawlinson briefed Haig both on the battlefield situation, and on his non-deployment of Reserve Army's infantry and cavalry. The British official historian later explained their discussion:

> Without giving a definite order, he [Haig] expressed [to
> Rawlinson] the wish that the attack of the Fourth Army should
> be continued on the 2nd [of July]: the situation was as yet too
> obscure for any radical change of plan: the best that could be
> done for the moment was to keep up the pressure on the enemy,
> wear out his defence, and with a view to an attack on his 2nd
> Position, gain possession of all those parts of his front position
> and of the intermediate lines still in his hands. In particular, the
> Commander-in-Chief desired that Fricourt, already enveloped on
> both flanks, should be captured.[57]

What followed was a series of orders that both put the objectives decided at this meeting into effect, and sanctioned a series of formation and unit moves. Haig then drove to Villers-Bocage and gave II Corps the orders pertaining to his GHQ reserve divisions at 5 p.m., while Fourth and Reserve Armies circulated theirs at the same time. These orders guaranteed there would be no Fourth or Reserve Army development of gains between Fricourt and Montauban on 1 July, or anywhere along the line, and revealed that at this time Haig and Rawlinson were very much collaborating when it came to deciding on their next Somme step.

In practice, this all meant that GHQ and Fourth Army conceded that the rest of 1 July would be spent consolidating such gains as there were, and deploying reserves ahead of operations restarting on 2 July. From about 4 p.m., 12th (Eastern) Division was placed at the disposal of III Corps to relieve the casualty-depleted 8th Division, and 25th Division was moved nearer to X Corps.[58] At 5 p.m., and not a minute earlier, 1st Cavalry and 2nd Indian Cavalry Divisions were ordered by Reserve Army, still under Rawlinson, to return to their concentration area near Querrieu, and about three hours later these, along with 3rd Cavalry Division, were told they were highly unlikely to be used on 2 July.[59] Haig's visit to II Corps headquarters at Villers-Bocage saw 23rd and 38th (Welsh) Divisions ordered to move closer to the front at 7 p.m.[60] The 23rd moved up behind XV and III Corps to the area vacated by the 12th, while the 38th replaced the 25th behind X and VIII Corps.[61] The 23rd and 38th were now at Rawlinson's disposal, and Haig gave his Fourth Army commander a 'hint not to use them up too soon.'[62] In Haig's and Rawlinson's minds, all the pieces were in place to resume the offensive on 2 July, just as they had agreed that afternoon, but tellingly neither saw any immediate role for the cavalry. It was in the light of this that Congreve decided on consolidation. Rawlinson, far from wrecking Haig's plans on 1 July,[63] did not stand the cavalry down too early, and in actual fact collaborated closely with the C-in-C on this matter and in deciding how they might together develop the offensive going forward.

'I see now that General Haig realised the situation,' wrote Lieutenant-Colonel William Norman, 21st Manchesters, in 1930 with the benefit of 14 years' hindsight. This was in stark contrast to his battle-day thinking. On 1 July, Norman was at Mametz, and like many others, at the time and on the spot, had been initially unable to 'understand why advantage was not taken of what was obviously a far-flung success [in and around that part of the battlefield].'[64]

That night, at about 10 p.m., Rawlinson issued orders for operations on 2 July.[65] He believed, almost certainly paraphrasing Haig, that a 'large part of the German Reserves have now been drawn in and it is essential to keep up the pressure and wear out the defence.'[66] Important tactical points in the German front- and intermediate-line defences needed to be secured with a 'view to an ultimate attack on the German second line.'[67] Congreve's XIII Corps was told to continue consolidating its gains and prepare for an operation in conjunction with Horne's XV Corps against Mametz Wood. Fifteenth Corps was also to take Fricourt and the wood behind it, and push up Willow Stream valley to Bottom Wood. It was to make contact with III Corps, which was falsely still believed to be in Contalmaison. Pulteney's III Corps was to renew its attempt to take La Boisselle and Ovillers and secure Contalmaison. Hunter-Weston's VIII Corps and Morland's X Corps, both now allocated to Gough's Reserve Army, were to capture the whole German front-line position and advance to the intermediate line beyond. Haig's grand plans for the offensive were now devolving into something much less than he had hoped for, but they were still in keeping with the more conservative aspects and stated objectives in his pre-battle operational orders.

Haig wanted to keep the pressure on the enemy and still saw opportunities ahead. It was this that his chief of intelligence referred to when he wrote late on 1 July that the 'present situation offers great possibilities, if we can grasp them.'[68] He continued: 'On the whole, our interpretation of the information received has been fairly good.'[69] Gough disagreed. Late that night he found his new command, VIII and X Corps, in such a poor state that he cancelled Rawlinson's orders for them.[70] It was this, plus a growing awareness of the north–south battlefield divide, that led Haig, on 2 July, to focus his attentions on developing gains south of the Albert–Bapaume road, while limiting those to the north of Leipzig Redoubt. Haig thus told Rawlinson that day to take Fricourt and neighbouring villages so as to 'reduce the number of our flanks, and then advance on [the] Enemy's second line [in that area].'[71] Rawlinson reverted to 'bite-and-hold' type and placed undue emphasis on the former two elements. He told Haig he was not in favour of pressing on in the Montauban area.[72] The result was two frustrating weeks of small-scale, bloody operations to straighten Fourth Army's lines, which cost no fewer than 25,000 casualties, before the German second position was successfully attacked on 14 July. Come lunchtime on 2 July, though, Gough was reorganising the two shattered corps of his Reserve Army, Rawlinson was bent on imposing step-by-step linear order to his front, and the first kernels of frustration were seeded in Haig's mind as any hope of maintaining operational momentum in the southern part of his battlefield began to fade.

That night Haig sent a telegram to Rawlinson, Gough and Allenby:

The enemy has lost heavily and is severely shaken. We have not yet completely broken down his resistance on the front attacked, and there is still hard fighting to be done, but we have gone a long way towards beating him, and a considerable success is within our reach. He has few reserves available while we have many, and his power to resist successfully a continued and determined prosecution of our attack is limited.[73]

In brief, Haig had revisited his four-stage operational thinking, and, at this time, saw the Somme as very much a wearing-out battle, one of attrition. Gone for the moment were his hopes of a decisive blow that would ultimately lead to victory, but they would resurface again later in 1916.

For Gough this marked a disappointing shift in thinking: 'In one day my thoughts and ideas had to move from consideration of a victorious pursuit to those of rehabilitation of the shattered wing of an army.'[74] Keep in mind these words were penned by Gough, a man described by Haig's chief of staff, Lieutenant-General Sir Launcelot Kiggell, as a 'thruster' and widely regarded as one of the most bullish, attack-minded generals on the Western Front.[75]

By contrast, there was optimism aplenty among the top brass of the French Sixth Army. Contrary to the overall British experience, the French had made excellent gains astride the Somme. Fayolle's army had benefitted from a prolonged preparatory barrage that destroyed many German defensive works and artillery batteries and had inflicted heavy casualties. North of the waterway, the French XX Corps had advanced immediately south of Congreve's men. Suffering about 1398 casualties,[76] it had claimed a roughly 1500-yard-deep slice of land between Hardecourt and Curlu, capturing the latter village from Châles de Beaulieu's 12th Infantry Division. To the south, 1st Colonial and XXXV Corps had begun two hours later. Thanks to overwhelming artillery supremacy they had pushed 1800–2650 yards east against 121st Infantry Division and elements of 11th Infantry Division, capturing the villages of Bequincourt, Dompierre and Fay, but pulling up short of Frise, Herbécourt, Assevillers and Estrées. They suffered no fewer than 4337 casualties, probably around 4500.[77] The timing and strength of this attack surprised German defenders. Neither General-der-Infanterie Erich von Falkenhayn, Chief of General Staff, Supreme Army Command, nor Below believed the Verdun-weakened French had either the manpower or resources to launch a meaningful attack on the Somme. They were proved very wrong.[78] By 9.45 p.m. Fayolle's army had seized its objectives and was within reach of the German second defensive line. The contrast with Haig's performance in the northern half of the coalition battlefield was striking.

Grand-bellied General Joseph Joffre, France's C-in-C, turned up at Fayolle's headquarters that afternoon to get the news first-hand. Fayolle said 'Papa' Joffre was soon beaming,[79] but his elation was tempered by reports that the main British attack had faltered. It was this that prompted Joffre to tellingly assess that the 'British do not yet have the skill.' He continued:

> The Germans did not believe that the French, just emerging from the Verdun battle, would be capable of starting an offensive on the Somme. ... They had therefore taken more precautions along the line facing the British, and this accounts for the more violent reactions which took place on their part of the line. The British also suffered from the fact that their artillerymen were less skilful than ours and their infantry less experienced.[80]

As far as simple military explanations went, and despite an obvious reluctance to give any credit to the German defenders, Joffre was pretty much bang on the money.

GERMAN COMMANDERS WERE severely rattled by events on 1 July, particularly the stronger-than-expected blow from Fayolle's army and more generally the ground lost between Mametz and Estrées. Below was at his St Quentin headquarters all day. He had predicted the location of the Anglo-French attack. Early reports from his subordinates — Stein north of the River Somme, and to the south *General-der-Infanterie* Günther von Pannewitz of XVII Army Corps — confirmed his forecast as correct.[81] Below quickly told Falkenhayn the Anglo-French offensive was afoot. Early on, it appeared the most threatened parts of the line were Schwaben Redoubt, potentially Fricourt, also Mametz and thereafter the defences running from Montauban, across the Somme and down to the Amiens–St Quentin road.

Even before midday Below began committing his reserves to meet the threat. North of the Somme, 12th Reserve Division was dispatched forward to the Ginchy–Combles area, where 12th Infantry Division was in the process of being mauled. The 185th Infantry Division was committed from around Bapaume towards 26th Reserve Division's sector, where the Schwaben Redoubt scrap was in full flight, and 11th Reserve Division began moving in behind XIV Reserve Corps' battle front from

Marcoing. South of the river, 22nd Reserve Division and the composite Division Frentz were moved into the line. Fifth Infantry Division was entrained from St Quentin, but was held up for 18 hours after several of its train carriages were destroyed in a bombing raid. If Below was uncertain about the fine detail of the fighting to midday, the headlines from Stein and particularly Pannewitz told him that from at least Mametz south his Second Army's front-line system had been overrun in places, particularly south of the Somme, and that locally organised fightbacks were afoot.[82] Everything about Below's actions late in the morning revealed an anxious but quick-thinking general focused on propping up the tottering portions of his line to avoid the Anglo-French attempt at a breakthrough he had long feared.

Below established a more reliable narrative of events throughout the afternoon. Between Gommecourt and La Boisselle, Stein's corps had blocked the British attack, barring the troubling Schwaben Redoubt incursion and several smaller break-ins here and there. South of there — and then more south of Mametz than Fricourt — he viewed the situation as considerably more serious.[83] Here the forward-most divisions — the 12th under Châles de Beaulieu, and the 121st — had yielded their entire front-line positions to the Anglo-French offensive on a front of about 12.4 miles, to a depth of about 1.6 miles. They had suffered numerous casualties and lost most of their artillery. Stein's corps recorded 109 (19.1%) of its roughly 450 remaining field and heavy guns were 'lost' on 1 July,[84] in addition to the 120 destroyed during the preparatory bombardment, and then mostly between Mametz and Curlu. South of Péronne, almost all of 121st Infantry Division's remaining guns, from an estimated 130, were 'put out of action' on 1 July.[85] 'The situation west of Péronne [between Mametz and Estrées] was very uncertain,' wrote the German official historian.[86] Throughout the afternoon Below was anxiously clock-watching as his reserves slowly worked their way forward. What Below did not know, and could not know, was that he had plenty of time to shore up his buckled defensive line thanks to Haig and Rawlinson's late-afternoon decision against any British attempt at exploiting their few limited gains that day.

Below's first reserve divisions arrived forward around Montauban before dusk. During the afternoon, 12th Reserve Division advanced up to Châles de Beaulieu's rag-tag new front line southeast of Ginchy and Combles. The division's three regiments would launch a bloody, mostly failed counterattack to reclaim the lost ground on 2 July. As part of this operation, Reserve Infantry Regiment 51, from Second Army reserve, and Bavarian Infantry Regiment 16, the last of Stein's corps reserves, arrived forward at the Bazentin-le-Grand–Longueval–Bernafay Wood line between about 9 p.m. and midnight.[87] Further north, Reserve Infantry Regiment 121 finally erased 4th Division's bridgehead at Heidenkopf. Thirty-six (Ulster) Division's gains at Schwaben Redoubt were lost to counterattacks by Bavarian Reserve Infantry Regiment 8 with assistance from other regiments. All that remained of the British initial gains on 1 July were death-sated bridgeheads at Leipzig Redoubt, Schwabenhöhe near La Boisselle, Fricourt Spur and Hill 110, plus the land between Mametz and Montauban, including the red-brick ruins of both villages. It would be three testing days before Below properly stiffened his second position with more men and artillery guns; until then he was reliant on an improvised, casualty-depleted but increasingly organised defensive line.

German losses for 1 July are difficult to pin down precisely. Partly this is because of the way in which unit casualty statistics were compiled, and also because surviving records are fragmentary and in some cases no longer exist.[88] Nevertheless, available data reveals XIV Reserve Corps reported no fewer than 15,000 (15.8%) of its nominal 95,000 men as killed, wounded or missing in the period from 23 June to at least 3 July, with up to about 12,000 (12.6%) on 1 July and roughly 3000 (3.2%) of these killed. Unsurprisingly, XIV Reserve Corps' casualties were skewed to the southern Fricourt–Curlu area, where Anglo-French gains were greatest and numerous soldiers in 28th Reserve and 12th Infantry Divisions were captured.

FALKENHAYN'S MEMOIRS SUGGEST a commander of calmness and objectivity, which was quite different from the puce-faced general who went looking for a scalp late on 1 July. On the chopping block was Below's chief of staff, *Generalmajor* Paul Grünert, who had approved chronically ill Pannewitz's request that day to shorten his defensive line south of the Somme.[89] This contravened Falkenhayn's doctrine of stubbornly clinging to ground. Pannewitz kept his job, but probably received a ticking off. Stein might have been rebuked, too, by Falkenhayn or Below, for approving the withdrawal of one regiment from besieged Fricourt, although there is no evidence of this. Grünert's replacement was *Oberst* Fritz von Lossberg, a Hesse-born, no-nonsense defensive expert who quickly set to work appraising Second Army's resources and positions. It is revealing that he first assessed the area attacked by Fayolle's army, rather than Rawlinson's, before divining the overall position of Second Army as 'extremely serious.'[90] One divisional commander at Péronne summed up the situation succinctly: 'Well, dear Lossberg, we constantly find ourselves in places where the shit is flowing in streams.'[91] Over time, Lossberg drove the implementation of a more elastic style of defence-in-depth on the Somme and across the Western Front, providing Allied commanders with more tactical questions to answer in 1917–18.

For the moment Verdun-obsessed Falkenhayn, who in the preceding months had ignored Second Army's pleas that more resources of men and guns and aircraft be diverted to the Somme front, was taking stock of the battle. As he saw it, the Anglo-French offensive had arrived with unanticipated ferocity; he had seemingly forgotten Below's numerous warnings. Falkenhayn appraised 1 July in goading language:

> With this superiority [in guns and men] it was inevitable that the enemy, when, on 1st of July, the storm at last broke, should score the initial successes. The gains of the English were even less than usual. North of the Bapaume–Albert road they did not advance a yard, south of the road not appreciably beyond the first German line. The French gains were greater: the whole of the German first line from Fay south of Hardecourt, north of the Somme, was lost. In several places the attack penetrated the second line. Even in this sector there was no question of the intended breakthrough having succeeded.[92]

Falkenhayn rightly concluded that overall, the Anglo-French attempt to produce a breakthrough had miscarried. But this was a complex man, talented at presenting himself and his decision-making favourably while marginalising enemy achievements. On the other hand, his actions revealed a general deeply troubled by the initial Anglo-French progress.

No fewer than 15 German infantry divisions were routed towards the Somme front within 10 days of 1 July. This was tacit admission that Falkenhayn believed the Haig–Joffre offensive retained breakthrough potential in its earliest days. In short, Falkenhayn recognised the looming danger, that his Somme defences were almost threadbare thanks to Verdun, and actively intervened.

Falkenhayn probably decided to reinforce the Somme some time late on 1 July, maybe even earlier that day, when he was in contact with Below. The necessity for this was emphasised by 48-year-old Lossberg the next day. At midnight on 2 July, stern-faced Lossberg turned up at Supreme Army Command's Mézières headquarters, and there spoke to a sleepy Falkenhayn, who had been woken for his star man's arrival:

> I told General von Falkenhayn that the 2nd Army was much in
> need of reinforcement divisions, artillery, aeroplanes and other
> ordnance for carrying out the enormous and heavy defensive
> struggle that lay ahead. Sufficient reinforcements for 2nd
> Army, however, were only available if the attack at Verdun was
> discontinued immediately. ... Only in this way would the supply
> of sufficient reinforcements to the Somme be possible, where the
> very broad and deeply indented French–English attack [between
> Fricourt and Estrées] was expected to continue with the objective
> of securing a breakthrough.[93]

It was on the strength of this assessment by Lossberg that Falkenhayn initially began dispatching limited numbers of artillery and infantry from Verdun.[94] Soon after, around 11 July, Falkenhayn introduced a 'strict defensive' policy on the Meuse, as opposed to ending the offensive there altogether, which allowed more resources to be committed to the Somme with a view to curbing the enemy's breakthrough hopes.

In this light, Below, who was distracted by stomach cramps and thrombosis during 1–3 July, was said to have viewed the situation 'very seriously indeed, but also confidently.'[95] Context is king. Everything about Below's rapid deployment of his Second Army reserves and quick communication with Supreme Army Command, given the scale of the Anglo-French offensive, revealed another German general deeply troubled by what course events might yet take, and how he might achieve a favourable outcome. His concerns centred on the Anglo-French gains between Fricourt and the Somme being steadily extended and gradually rendering Second Army's line between La Boisselle and Serre untenable. An enemy breakthrough in this general area purposefully driven towards Arras would have 'far-reaching consequences' for Second Army's tenure on the Somme,[96] and necessarily also for *Kronprinz* Rupprecht of Bavaria's Sixth Army, which would be caught on its exposed southern flank. Below's uptick in confidence only followed Falkenhayn's limited allocation of reinforcements, Lossberg's appointment and the arrival of reserves.

It was these factors that prompted Below to state on 3 July that the outcome of the war, no less, depended on Second Army's holding firm, irrespective of the enemy's superiority in numbers and materiel. Lost ground would be retaken by reinforcements: 'For the time being, we must hold our current positions without fail and improve on them by means of minor counterattacks. I forbid the voluntary relinquishment of positions. Every commander is responsible for making each man in the Army aware about this determination to fight it out. The enemy must be made to pick his way forward over corpses.'[97] Here, Below was parroting Falkenhayn's hard-line defensive doctrine. More than that, though, he was signalling that for Supreme Army Command and Second Army the Somme was no longer just a defensive battle, it was officially and swiftly moving towards an offensive of attrition and all of its implied horror.[98]

On the British side, Haig's grand plans for a breakthrough towards Arras were always too ambitious, as were the objectives set down in orders to facilitate this. Third and Fourth Armies simply did not have the resources to achieve their stated objectives. Meanwhile, German commanders predicted the British attack between Serre and Fricourt, but misread the strength of the French component. The lesser value they attached to the ground between Fricourt and the River Somme merely reflected this evaluation, as did the strength of their defences. It was this that led to the north–south dichotomy in the British artillery–infantry performance between 24 June and 1 July, and meant Haig threw the majority of his force at the most robust part of the German line. Break-ins that mattered at Schwaben Redoubt and, to a lesser extent, Montauban went unappreciated, and any potential they might have had was soon lost. Rawlinson, who harboured justifiable reservations throughout the planning process, made sensible command decisions on 1 July, particularly in collaborating with Haig that afternoon on the non-deployment of Reserve Army's cavalry and infantry. Haig's failure to achieve anything near his stated and hoped-for outcomes was due to a dislocation in his mind between his bullish strategic expectations and an under-appreciation of the tactical-level commitment needed to achieve them. Haig set the tactical parameters of battle between Gommecourt and La Boisselle in favour of Below and Stein, but they and Châles de Beaulieu reciprocated between Fricourt and Montauban, and the bitter-sweet tactical outcome to Britain's first day of the Somme merely reflected this failure in command on both sides of the hill.

The first day of the Somme should nonetheless be seen as a strategic positive for the Allied coalition, although definitely not a victory. German efforts at Verdun were crimped: some pressure was taken off French forces there and essential German resources were diverted northwest to the Somme. But Falkenhayn's response to ward off an Anglo-French breakthrough was always more of a knee-jerk reaction to the unexpectedly strong and successful French element than to the British performance. Falkenhayn was more troubled by Haig's accumulation of men and materiel as part of a larger coalition enterprise than his achievements in isolation, and the danger this posed in the future. If the British army had attacked alone its results would have been unlikely to have jolted Falkenhayn into diverting resources from the Meuse; he believed Below had men and materiel to shut down the Fricourt–Mametz–Montauban incursions. He would probably have been proved correct had there been no French operation. But there was; 1 July was always a coalition affair and its results must be measured in that broader context. Haig and Joffre had together achieved some of their intended strategic objectives, but the French army had very obviously outpaced the British army in terms of hoped-for tactical outcomes. If this pyrrhic sum-of-Somme-parts outcome mildly favoured the Anglo-French offensive going forward, it also, by dint of coalition necessity and direct German rejoinder, spawned one of the most notorious offensives of attrition the world has ever seen.

By the time that offensive ended in mid-November 1916 it had comprised no fewer than three distinct phases that took the British and

The Somme: Ground Gained, 1 July–19 November 1916

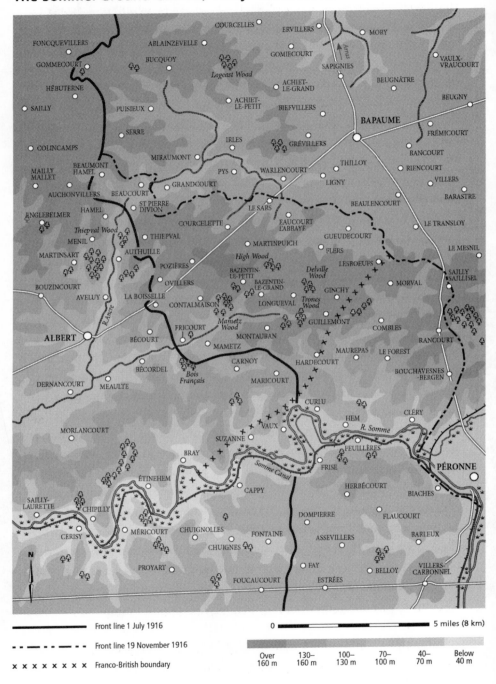

Front line 1 July 1916					
Front line 19 November 1916					
x x x x x x x x Franco-British boundary					

0 — 5 miles (8 km)

Over 160 m	130–160 m	100–130 m	70–100 m	40–70 m	Below 40 m

French armies over the Thiepval–Morval ridge. The breakthrough battle that Haig so hoped to produce had devolved into a slog forward, foot by bloody foot, studded with roughly a dozen component battles of varying magnitude, against a determined and well-armed enemy that clung stubbornly to its defensive positions. Bapaume, that lofty aim for the cavalry on 1 July, remained firmly in German hands. After four-and-a-half months, Haig's best gains were about seven miles from the jumping-off lines of 1 July — these skewed south of the Albert–Bapaume road — but were mostly more limited than this. The French army had continued to press forward, too, astride the Somme, managing a total advance of up to six miles. With the exceptions of Gommecourt and Serre, all of the villages built into the German front-line defences and earmarked for capture by Fourth and Third Armies on the opening day of the offensive had fallen, along with a string of others that broadly marked the high-tide line for Haig's offensive: Beaumont Hamel, Beaucourt, Courcelette, Le Sars, Pozières, Gueudecourt, Lesboeufs and Morval. There were plenty of other brickheap villages in between, too. Casualties (killed, wounded, missing and prisoners) totalled about 1.28 million officers and men of all armies involved in the fighting, this number including 419,654 British, 204,253 French and an estimated 660,000 German.[99]

The German army withdrew from the Somme to a new defensive line in late-February 1917, this amounting to a tacit admission of defeat.[100] Its then commander, *Generalfeldmarschall* Paul von Hindenburg, who took up the job after Falkenhayn's removal in August 1916, sanctioned the 'forced' withdrawal eastwards to the formidable position known as the Hindenburg Line (Siegfriedstellung), which ran between Arras, St Quentin and Soissons.[101] This move, which was conducted behind a brutal scorched-earth policy, clearly flagged that neither Hindenburg nor his deputy, *General-der-Infanterie* Erich von Ludendorff, wanted to undergo another attritional struggle on the Somme.[102] It further revealed that these generals realised the German army had suffered severely in quantitative and qualitative terms in 1916, on both the Western and Eastern Fronts. Hindenburg explained his outlook for 1917:

We had not the slightest doubt about what out enemies would do in the coming year. We had to anticipate a general hostile offensive, as soon as their preparations and the weather permitted it. It was to be assumed that, warned by the experiences of the past year, our enemies would endeavour to co-ordinate their attacks on all fronts, if we left them time and opportunity to do so. ... There was no doubt that, at the end of 1916, the position as regards relative numbers between us and our enemies had developed even more to our disadvantage than had been the case at the beginning of the year.[103]

It was obvious to Hindenburg and Ludendorff that their talent-thinned army would again be on the defensive in 1917 and that Germany would definitely not win the war on the Western Front that year.[104]

Haig firmly believed he had achieved a victory on the Somme. At year's end, in a dispatch summarising the fighting, he described the offensive as the opening of a wearing-out battle, which revealed at that time he saw plenty more campaigning before the British army and its Allies could deliver a decisive blow on the Western Front and so end the war. To this end, British command emerged from the Somme more skilled and experienced when it came to conducting operational-level set-piece engagements, and officers and soldiers on the ground were considerably more tactically adept. There was a closer alignment between and greater sophistication in the application of infantry, artillery, engineering and the air force. There were also technological advances, such as the introduction of tanks to the order of battle, and better-quality and more numerous munitions for the artillery, plus an overhaul of the governing infantry doctrine. These were the hard-won lessons of the Somme, but the grim process of converting Haig's untrained collection of divisions, as he assessed them in March 1916, into a war-winning legion of experienced and skilled battle technicians against a world-class opponent was by no means finished.[105] As Haig put it on the cusp of 1917:

The enemy's power has not yet been broken, nor is it yet possible to form an estimate of the time the war may last before the objects for which the Allies are fighting have been attained. But the Somme battle has placed beyond doubt the ability of the Allies to gain those objects. ... Our new Armies entered the battle with the determination to win and with confidence in their power to do so. They have proved to themselves, to the enemy, and to the world that this confidence was justified, and in the fierce struggle they have been through they have learned many valuable lessons which will help them in the future.[106]

WITH ITS BROAD sweeps of shingle and grass, the Thiepval Memorial to the missing looms over the former battlefields. There are few places on the Somme from which this stone giant cannot be seen, its adjacent car park being one. In the fields you can still find lumps of red brick from houses long gone. After the plough, spent bullets and rusted steel fragments occasionally stud the furrow lines. Neatly chiselled into the memorial's stone panels are the names of 72,255 British and South African soldiers who have no known graves.[107] The dog-eared memorial registers begin with 23-year-old James Aaron of Hull, killed on 1 July 1916. Tens of thousands of names later they end with 20-year-old Charles Zwisele of Clapton, London, who fell in August the same year. Between them is a legion of men who served in the British and South African forces who hailed from a multitude of places between Stornoway, Scotland, and Dunedin, New Zealand. Before the war they were labourers and linesmen and lawyers, married or single men. They were and are, in every sense of the phrase, a lost generation.

It is winter 2015, and a group of UK teenagers have been bussed to the memorial for a school trip. They are wearing ski gloves, which makes it difficult for them to snap photos with their mobile phones. Most give up. It is bitterly cold; everyone wants to get back into the warm bus. There will only be one group photo. 'What happened here, sir?' asks one of the teenagers. 'Well ...' begins the teacher, and his answer is swept away in an icy blast of Somme wind.

One generation passeth away, and another generation cometh: but that rich Somme earth abideth forever.

Endnotes

Abbreviations
BL British Library
NAUK UK National Archives
ULLC University of Leeds, Liddle Collection

Chapter 1: A Mother Named 'Attrition'
1. Rawlinson, Henry, diary, 21 June 1916, Rawlinson Papers, Churchill Archive.
2. Charteris, Brigadier-General John, *At G.H.Q.* (London: Cassell, 1931), p. 142.
3. Harris, J.P., *Douglas Haig and the First World War* (Cambridge: Cambridge University Press, 2008), p. 19.
4. Gibbs, Philip, *Now it Can be Told*, (London: Harper & Brothers, 1920), pp. 42–3.
5. *ibid.*
6. Dixon, Norman, *On the Psychology of Military Incompetence* (London: Pimlico, 1994), p. 380.
7. *ibid.*
8. *ibid.*, p. 375.
9. *ibid.*
10. *ibid.*, p. 254.
11. Sheffield, Gary, *The Chief: Douglas Haig and the British Army* (London: Aurum Press, 2011), p. 13.
12. Dunlop, John, *The Development of the British Army 1899–1914* (London: Methuen, 1938), p. 226.
13. Farrar-Hockley, A.H., *The Somme* (London: Pan Books, 1983), p. 32.
14. Sheffield, Gary, *The Somme* (London: Cassell, 2003), p. 1.
15. *ibid.*
16. Wilmott, H.P., *The First World War* (London: Dorling Kindersley, 2003), p. 11.
17. Balfour, Michael, *The Kaiser and his Times* (Boston: Houghton Mifflin, 1964), p. 355.
18. *ibid.*, pp. 350–1.
19. Sheffield, *The Somme*, p. 4.
20. Terraine, John, *Douglas Haig: The Educated Soldier* (London: Hutchinson, 1963), p. 149.
21. Haig, Douglas, diary, 14 December 1915, NAUK, WO/256/6.
22. Edmonds, Brigadier General Sir James E., *Military Operations, France and Belgium 1916: Sir Douglas Haig's Command to the 1st July: Battle of the Somme* (London: Macmillan, 1932), p. 7.
23. *ibid.*, pp. 7–8.
24. *ibid.*, p. 8.
25. War Committee, minutes, 28 December 1915, NAUK, CAB/42/6/14.
26. 'An Examination by the General Staff into the Factors Affecting the Choice of a Plan,' 16 December 1916, War Committee, appendices, 28 December 1915, *op. cit.*
27. Kitchener, Horatio, to Haig, Douglas, 28 December 1915, Appendix 5, *Military Operations France & Belgium 1916: Vol. 1, Appendices*, pp. 40–1.
28. Terraine, p. 182.
29. War Committee, subjects of discussion and conclusions, 13 January–8 March 1916, NAUK, CAB/42/7/6.
30. War Committee, minutes, 13 January 1916, NAUK, CAB/42/7/5.
31. Note by Secretary of State for War, NAUK, CAB/42/7/5.
32. War Committee, minutes, 7 April 1916, NAUK, CAB/42/12/15.

33. War Committee, extract from proceedings, 7 April 1916, *op. cit.*
34. Edmonds, p. 26.
35. *ibid.*, pp. 26–7.
36. *Douglas Haig: War Diaries and Letters 1914–1918*, ed. Gary Sheffield and John Bourne (London: Weidenfeld & Nicolson, 2005), p. 180.
37. Philpott, William, *Bloody Victory: The sacrifice on the Somme* (London: Abacus, 2011), p. 130.
38. Sheffield, *The Somme*, p. 14.
39. Passingham, Ian, *All the Kaiser's Men: The Life and Death of the German Soldier on the Western Front* (Stroud: The History Press, 2011), p. 93.
40. Edmonds, p. 31.
41. *ibid.*
42. *ibid.*, p. 32.
43. *ibid.*, p. 33.
44. Prior, Robin, and Wilson, Trevor, *Command on the Western Front: The Military Career of Sir Henry Rawlinson 1914–1918* (Barnsley: Pen & Sword, 2004), p. 7; Godley, Alexander, *Life of an Irish Soldier* (New York: EP Dutton, 1939), p. 33; de Lisle, Beauvoir, *Reminiscences of Sport & War* (London: Eyre & Spottiswoode, 1939), p. 131.
45. Malins, Geoffrey, *How I Filmed the War* (London: Imperial War Museum, 1993), p. 208.
46. Godley, p. 33.
47. Gibbs, *Now it Can be Told*, pp. 50–1.
48. *ibid.*, p. 51.
49. Charteris, *G.H.Q.*, p. 125.
50. Haig, diary, 12 December 1915, NAUK, *op. cit.*
51. Haig, diary, 18 April 1915, NAUK, WO/256/4.
52. Sheffield, *The Chief*, p. 168; Sheffield referred only to Rawlinson being ruthless and devious, the other assertions belonging to the author of this book.
53. *ibid.*
54. Prior and Wilson, *Command*, p. 25.
55. *ibid.*, pp. 72–9.
56. *ibid.*, pp. 72–9.
57. *ibid.*, p. 72.
58. Philpott, p. 130.
59. Prior and Wilson, *Command*, p. 31.
60. Griffith, Paddy, *Battle Tactics of the Western Front: The British Army's Art of Attack 1916–18* (New Haven: Yale University Press, 1994), p. 31.
61. *Haig: War Diaries and Letters*, ed. Sheffield and Bourne, p. 160.
62. Philpott, p. 107.
63. Haig, diary, 18 January 1916, NAUK, WO/256/7.
64. Maurice, Major-General Sir Frederick, *The Life of General Lord Rawlinson of Trent* (London: Cassell, 1928), p. 152.
65. Prior, Robin, and Wilson, Trevor, *The Somme* (Sydney: University of New South Wales Press, 2005), p. 39.
66. Rawlinson, diary, 2 March 1916, Rawlinson Papers, Churchill Archive.
67. *ibid.*
68. GHQ, 'The Opening of the Wearing-out Battle', 23 December 1916, in *Sir Douglas Haig's Despatches*, ed. Lt.-Col John H. Boraston (London: JM Dent & Sons, 1919), pp. 22–3.
69. *ibid.*
70. Rawlinson, Henry, diary, 30 March 1916, Rawlinson Papers, Churchill Archive.
71. *ibid.*
72. *ibid.*, 31 March 1916.
73. *Plan for Offensive by the Fourth Army, G.X.3/1*, 3 April 1916, Fourth Army Operations Papers, NAUK, WO/158/233.
74. *ibid.*
75. *ibid.*
76. *ibid.*
77. *ibid.*
78. *ibid.*
79. *ibid.*
80. *ibid.*
81. *ibid.*
82. *ibid.*
83. *ibid.*
84. Philpott, p. 98.
85. MacDonald, Alan, *Z Day: VIII Corps at Beaumont Hamel and Serre* (London: Iona Books, 2014), pp. 2–3.
86. *ibid.*
87. *ibid.*, p. 4.
88. Philpott, p. 99.
89. Haig, diary, 5 April 1916, NAUK, WO/256/9; Plan for Offensive by Fourth Army, 3 April 1916, Fourth Army Operations Papers, NAUK, WO/158/233; *OAD 710, op. cit.*; *OAD 710/1, op. cit.*
90. Plan for Offensive by Fourth Army, 3 April 1916, Fourth Army Operations Papers, NAUK, WO/158/233; Haig, diary 5 and 8 April 1916, *op. cit.*
91. Edmonds, p. 254.
92. *ibid.*, p. 255.
93. Philpott, p. 111.
94. *ibid.*, p. 110.
95. *ibid.*, pp. 110–11.
96. *OAD 710 Plans & Preparations for an Offensive*, 12 April 1916, Fourth Army Operations Papers, NAUK, WO/158/233.
97. *ibid.*
98. *OAD 710/1 Plan for Offensive Operations*, 13 April 1916, Fourth Army Operations Papers, *op. cit.*

99. *ibid.*
100. *Amended Plan Submitted by the Fourth Army to GHQ*, 19 April 1916, Fourth Army Operations Papers, *op. cit.*
101. Rawlinson, diary, 19 April 1916, *op. cit.*
102. *Amended Plan*, 19 April 1916, *op. cit.*
103. *ibid.*
104. *ibid.*
105. *ibid.*
106. *ibid.*
107. *OAD 876 to Sir H. Rawlinson*, 16 May 1916, Fourth Army Operations Papers, NAUK, WO 158/233.
108. *ibid.*
109. Kiggell, Launcelot, to Edmonds, James, letter, 2 December 1937, NAUK, CAB/45/135.
110. Edmonds, p. 46.
111. *ibid.*
112. Philpott, p. 104.
113. Edmonds, p. 47.
114. *OAD 12 to General Sir H. Rawlinson*, 16 June 1916, Fourth Army Operations Papers, *op. cit.*
115. Fourth Army Operation Order No. 2, 14 June 1916, Fourth Army Operations Papers, NAUK, WO/158/234.
116. *ibid.*
117. *ibid.*
118. *ibid.*
119. Rawlinson, diary, 18 June 1916, *op. cit.*
120. *ibid.*, 19 June 1916.
121. Philpott, pp. 116–17.
122. *ibid.*, p. 117.
123. *OAD 17 Commander-in-Chief's Instructions in Amplification of OAD 12*, 16 June 1916, Fourth Army Operations Papers, NAUK, WO/95/158/234.
124. *ibid.*
125. Prior and Wilson, *Somme*, p. 51.
126. *ibid.*
127. Philpott, p. 127.
128. *OAD 12, op. cit.*
129. *ibid.*
130. *OAD 17, op. cit.*
131. Philpott, p. 122.
132. *ibid.*, p. 123.
133. *ibid.*
134. Kiggell to Edmonds, 25 January 1938, NAUK, CAB/45/135.
135. *ibid.*
136. Charteris, *GHQ*, p. 137.
137. *ibid.*
138. Army Commander's Conference Remarks, 22 June 1916, Fourth Army Operations Papers, NAUK, WO/158/234.
139. *ibid.*
140. *ibid.*
141. Haig, diary, 27 June 1916, *op. cit.*
142. *ibid.*
143. *ibid.*
144. Haig, diary, 27 June 1916, NAUK, WO/256/10.
145. *Fourth Army Memorandum*, 28 June 1916, NAUK, WO/95/158/234.
146. *ibid.*
147. *ibid.*
148. Haig, diary, 27 June 1916, *op. cit.*
149. *Fourth Army Memorandum*, 28 June 1916, *op. cit.*
150. Rawlinson, diary, 28 June 1916, *op. cit.*
151. *ibid.*, 30 June 1916.
152. Edmonds, p. 44.
153. *ibid.*
154. *ibid.*, p. 45.
155. War Committee, minutes, 17 May 1916, NAUK, CAB/42/14/1.
156. Prior and Wilson, *Somme*, p. 30.
157. War Committee, minutes, 7 June 1916, NAUK, CAB/42/15/6.
158. War Committee, minutes, 30 June 1916, NAUK, CAB/42/15/15.
159. Prior and Wilson, *Somme*, p. 34.
160. War Committee, minutes, 21 June 1916, NAUK, CAB/42/15/10.

Chapter 2: 'I Learned to Hate the Place'
1. *To Fight Alongside Friends: The First World War Diaries of Charlie May* (London: William Collins, 2014), ed. Gerry Harrison, p. 126.
2. Capper, Derick, ULLC/WW1/GS/0267.
3. Pollard, George, ULLC/WW1/WF01/P/9.
4. Polack, Ernest, letter, 30 June 1916, ULLC/WW1/GS/1283.
5. Upcott, John, diary, 1 May 1916, ULLC/WW1/GS/1644.
6. Moakler, Frank, ULLC/WW1/WF01/M/21.
7. Fisher, Alex, ULLC/WW1/TR/02.
8. *ibid.*
9. Grindley, Ernest, ULLC/WW1/WF01/G/14.
10. *ibid.*
11. Capper, *op. cit.*
12. Pollard, *op. cit.*
13. Haig, Douglas, diary, 29 March 1916, NAUK, WO/256/9.
14. XIII c.3500 yards; XV c.4500; III c.3500; X c.5000; VIII c.4500; and VII c.4000. Tenth Corps' longer linear frontage included the River Ancre.
15. Bennett, Thomas, ULLC/WW1/MID01.
16. Osborn, George, diary, 6 April 1916, South Wales Borderers' (SWB) Museum.
17. Cousins, John, ULLC/WW1/MID01.
18. *ibid.*
19. Pollard, *op. cit.*

20. Brookes, Squire, ULLC/WW1/SEV01.
21. Falls, Cyril, *The History of the 36th (Ulster) Division* (London: M'Caw, Stevenson & Orr, 1922), p. 30.
22. Moore, Aubrey, ULLC/WW1/WF01/M/24.
23. Falls, *op. cit.*
24. Jarman, Clarrie, ULLC/WW1/WF01/J/5.
25. Cousins, *op. cit.*
26. Upcott, 3 May 1916.
27. Goodwin, William, diary, 19 March 1916, ULLC/WW1/GS/0644.
28. Allen, Henry, ULLC/WW1/MID01 & WF01/A/6.
29. Kirkland-Laman, Eric, diary, 3 May 1916, SWB Museum.
30. Jarman, *op. cit.*
31. Tennant, Cecil, ULLC/WW1/MID01.
32. Jarman, *op. cit.*
33. *ibid.*
34. Macdonald, Andrew, *On My Way to the Somme: New Zealanders and the Bloody Offensive of 1916* (Auckland: HarperCollins, 2005), p. 174.
35. Barber, Henry, ULLC/WW1/MID01.
36. Parker, Victor, interview with author, Christchurch, New Zealand, May 1991.
37. Lockhart, Noel, ULLC/WW1/MID01.
38. Aust, Walter, ULLC/WW1/MID01 & WF01/A/15.
39. England, Arthur, ULLC/WW1/WF01/E/7.
40. Pollard, *op. cit.*
41. *ibid.*
42. *ibid.*
43. Brew, James, ULLC/WW1/MID01.
44. Lockhart, *op. cit.*
45. Goodwin, 3 May 1916, *op. cit.*
46. Jarman, *op. cit.*
47. Archer-Houblon, Richard, ULLC/WW1/GS/0040.
48. Coom, Colin, ULLC/WW1/WF01/C/12.
49. Kirkland-Laman, 6 April 1916, *op. cit.*
50. Richardson, Roland, ULLC/WW1/WF02/R/8.
51. Moakler, *op. cit.*
52. Aust, *op. cit.*
53. Lockhart, *op. cit.*
54. Fourth Army Summary of Operations, March–June 1916, NAUK, WO/158/244; stated casualties totalled 9893, but no figures are given for the first week of March or the week ended 2 June.
55. 'Casualties – April,' Rawlinson Papers 1/6, Churchill Archive.
56. Bloye, Ben, ULLC/WW1/WF01/B/22.
57. Graü, Leo, postcard, 19 March 1916.
58. Edmonds, Sir James, *Military Operations France and Belgium, 1916, Vol. 1* (London: Imperial War Museum, 1992), pp. 268–9.
59. Hart, Peter, *Somme Success: the Royal Flying Corps and the Battle of the Somme, 1916* (London: Leo Cooper: 2001), p. 38.
60. Unknown correspondent, formerly of London Rifle Brigade, letter, 9 September 1929, NAUK, CAB/45/132.
61. Brownlow, Cecil, letter, 30 April 1930, NAUK, CAB/45/132.
62. Ounsworth, Leonard, ULLC/WW1/TR/05.
63. Laporte, Archibald, ULLC/WW1/GS/0920.
64. Beaumont, HW, ULLC/WW1/MID01.
65. The daily ration in early 1916 comprised: meat fresh/frozen (1 lb) or preserved (¾ lb); bread (1¼ lb) or biscuit or flour (¾ lb); bacon (4 oz); cheese (3 oz); vegetables fresh (8 oz) or dried (2 oz); tea (⅝ oz); jam (3 oz); sugar (3 oz); salt (½ oz); mustard (¹⁄₅₀ oz); pepper (¹⁄₃₆ oz); condensed milk (¹⁄₁₂ tin); pickles (weekly, 1 oz); oatmeal thrice weekly as an extra; and butter as an extra.
66. Jarman, *op. cit.*
67. Coom, *op. cit.*
68. *ibid.*
69. Lockhart, *op. cit.*
70. Senescall, William, ULLC/WW1/WF02/S/7.
71. Barber, *op. cit.*
72. Mawbey, Cyril, ULLC/WW1/MID01.
73. Grindley, *op. cit.*
74. Willmer, Edgar, ULLC/WW1/GS/1753.
75. Brookes, *op. cit.*
76. Tennant, *op. cit.*
77. England, *op. cit.*
78. Coom, *op. cit.*
79. Upcott, 11 April 1916, *op. cit.*
80. Barber, *op. cit.*
81. Brookes, *op. cit.*
82. Aust, *op. cit.*; Tennant, *op. cit.*
83. Richardson, *op. cit.*
84. *SS394: Notes on German Army Corps, XIV. Reserve Corps and 52nd Division* (March 1916); *Summary of Operations, Fourth Army,* periodic reports, April–June 1916, NAUK, WO/158/244.
85. England, *op. cit.*
86. *ibid.*
87. Garrand, Charles, ULLC/WW1/MID01.
88. Brookes, *op. cit.*
89. Kirkland-Laman, diary, 6 April 1916, SWB Museum.
90. Cousins, *op. cit.*
91. Reymann, H., *Das 3. Oberschlesische Infanterie-Regiment Nr. 62 im Kriege*

1914–1918 (Zeulenroda: Sporn, 1930), p. 84.

92. Corbett, William, ULLC/WW1/MID01.
93. Brookes, *op. cit.*
94. Aust, *op. cit.*
95. *Statistics of the Military Effort of the British Empire during the Great War 1914–1920* (London: The War Office, 1922), p. 666.
96. Pugsley, Christopher, *On the Fringe of Hell: New Zealanders and Military Discipline in the First World War* (Auckland: Hodder & Stoughton, 1991), p. 352.
97. *ibid.,* p. 354.
98. Allsop, John, ULLC/WW1/MID01.
99. Osborn, George, diary, 2 April 1916, *op. cit.*
100. Brookes, *op. cit.*
101. Archer-Houblon, *op. cit.*
102. Slater, William, ULLC/WW1/ MID01.
103. Good, Claude, ULLC/WW1/WF01.
104. Good, *op. cit.*; England, *op. cit.*
105. Coppard, George, *With a Machine Gun to Cambrai: The Tale of a Young Tommy in Kitchener's Army 1914–1918* (London: HMSO, 1969), p. 77.
106. Haig, Douglas, diary, 30 June 1916, NAUK, WO/256/10.
107. Rawlinson, diary, 30 June 1916, *op. cit.*; 'Total infantry in 4 Army on 26 June 1916,' Rawlinson Papers 1/6, Churchill Archive; 'Fourth Army Feeding Strength on 1st July 1916,' Rawlinson Papers 1/6, Churchill Archive; in addition there were 4459 French and 3189 Indian soldiers on the feeding list, plus 148,237 animals.
108. Charteris, Brigadier-General John, *At G.H.Q.* (London: Cassell, 1931), p. 147.
109. Capper, *op. cit.*
110. *ibid.*
111. Frank, Thomas, ULLC/WW1/ WF01/F/12.
112. Malins, Geoffrey, *How I Filmed the War* (London: Imperial War Museum, 1993), pp. 121–2.
113. 'Total infantry in 4 Army on 26 June 1916,' *op. cit.*; 'Total infantry in 4 Army on 10 June 1916,' Rawlinson Papers 1/6, Churchill Archive.
114. Barber, *op. cit.*
115. Capper, *op. cit.*
116. Easton, Thomas, ULLC/WW1/GS/0490.
117. Moore, *op. cit.*
118. Kelly, David, *39 Months: With the 'Tigers' 1915–1918* (London: Ernest Benn Ltd, 1930), p. 22.
119. Malins, *op. cit.*, p. 121.
120. Capper, *op. cit.*

121. Kirkland-Laman, 17 March 1916, *op. cit.*
122. Edmonds, p. 278.
123. Mawbey, *op. cit.*
124. Banks, T.M., and Chell, R.A., *With the 10th Essex in France* (London: Gay & Hancock, 1924), p. 103.
125. Croft, Henry, *Twenty-Two Months Under Fire* (London: John Murray, 1917), p. 199.
126. Coom, *op. cit.*
127. Archer-Houblon, *op. cit.*
128. Crozier, Frank, *Brass Hat in No Man's Land* (London: Jonathan Cape, 1930), pp. 57–8.
129. Stapleton-Smith, Private Cedric, interview with author, Christchurch, New Zealand, March 1992. He claimed he first heard such terms used by British soldiers in early 1916 at Armentieres.
130. Lockhart, *op. cit.*
131. *Report on Operations 21st June to 4th July, and from 8th to 15th July*, 32nd Division, war diary, July 1916, NAUK, WO/95/2368/1/2.
132. Beaumont, *op. cit.*
133. England, *op. cit.*
134. Durrant, Arthur, ULLC/WW1/ WF01/D/19.
135. Brookes, *op. cit.*
136. Capper, *op. cit.*
137. *The Great War Diaries of Brigadier Alexander Johnston 1914–1917*, ed. Edwin Astill (Barnsley: Pen & Sword, 2007), p. 137; Girdwood, Austin, letter, 30 June 1930, NAUK, CAB/45/134.
138. Edmonds, p. 286.
139. Grieve, Grant, and Newman, Bernard, *Tunnellers: The Story of the Tunnelling Companies, Royal Engineers, during the World War* (London: Herbert Jenkins, 1936), p. 116; the initial Somme establishment totalled seven companies, but the 184th and 185th were withdrawn in February 1916 and sent further north.
140. *ibid.,* p. 77; there were two establishments of tunnelling companies. One nominally comprised 569 officers and men, the other 344.
141. *ibid.,* p. 116; the example given is for 252nd Tunnelling Company, which was assisted by 1900 infantrymen in addition to its usual nominal strength in digging Hawthorne Mine and nearby galleries.
142. England, *op. cit.*
143. Williams, Frederick, ULLC/WW1/ WF02/W/19.
144. Levine, Joshua, *Forgotten Voices of the Somme* (London: Ebury Publishing, 2009), p. 87.
145. Edmonds, p. 272.
146. Rawlinson, diary, 7 April 1916, *op. cit.*

147. Edmonds, pp. 272–3.
148. *ibid.*, p. 273.
149. *ibid.*
150. *ibid.*
151. Edmonds, p. 274; Fourth Army's railheads were as follows — supplies: Méricourt, Heilly, Frechencourt, Edge Hill, Belle-Église and Acheux; ammunition: Puchevillers, Corbie, Authuille and Contay; engineer stores: Méricourt and Acheux; ambulance trains: Vecquemont.
152. *ibid.*; the assumption at the time was that motor transport columns could operate to a distance of 25 miles from railheads, and horse-drawn transports 32 miles.
153. Brown, Ian Malcolm, *British Logistics on the Western Front 1914–1919* (Westport: Praeger, 1998), p. 133.
154. Schreiber, Acton, 6 April 1930, NAUK, CAB/45/137.
155. Edmonds, p. 277.
156. Schreiber, *op. cit.*
157. Rawlinson, diary, 30 June 1916, *op. cit.*
158. Chateau Gate Traffic Report, Rawlinson Papers 1/6, Churchill Archive.
159. Edmonds, p. 283.
160. *ibid.*
161. *ibid.*
162. Codrington, Geoffrey, letter, 10 February 1930, NAUK, CAB/45/132.
163. Codrington, *op. cit.*; this was a common theme in all major offensives, and particularly when the weather closed in, such as at Third Ypres.
164. Fenton, George, letter, 23 August 1930, NAUK, CAB/45/133.
165. Binstead, Charles, ULLC/WW1/ WF01/B/18.
166. Cartwright, George, letter, 14 November 1929, NAUK, CAB/45/132.
167. Crozier, p. 96.
168. Prior, Robin, and Wilson, Trevor, *The Somme* (Sydney: University of New South Wales Press, 2005), p. 58.
169. *SS109: Training of Divisions for Offensive Action* (8 May 1916).
170. *ibid.*, p. 2.
171. *ibid.*, p. 1.
172. *ibid.*
173. *ibid.*, p. 2.
174. *ibid.*
175. *ibid.*, p. 1.
176. Banks and Chell, p. 105.
177. Burrows, John, *The Essex Regiment: 2nd Battalion (56th) (Pompadours)* (John H. Burrows & Sons, 1927), p. 140.
178. Barber, *op. cit.*; Brookes, *op. cit.*; Rowley, ECW, letter, 22 March 1930, NAUK,

CAB/45/137; Williams, F.J., *op. cit.*; Whitham, H., ULLC/WW1/TR/08; Burrowes, A.R., *The 1st Battalion, The Faugh-A-Ballaghs in the Great War* (London: Gale & Polden, 1925), p. 64.
179. Bax, Cyril, *The Eighth Division in War, 1914–1918* (London: The Medici Society, 1926), pp. 63–4.
180. Nichols, G.H.F., *The 18th Division in the Great War* (London: William Blackwood & Sons, 1922), p. 36; see also Falls, *op. cit.*, p. 41.
181. Moore, *op. cit.*
182. *Dundee Courier*, 11 July 1916.
183. Mitchell, Gardiner, *Three Cheers for the Derrys! A History of the 10th Royal Inniskilling Fusiliers in the 1914–18 War* (Derry: Yes! Publications, 1991), p. 74.
184. Tennant, *op. cit.*
185. Harris, Ruth, *Billie: the Neville Letters, 1914–1916* (London: Julia MacRae Books, 1991), p. 187.
186. Wyrall, Everard, *The History of the 19th Division 1914–1918* (London: Edward Arnold, 1932), p. 30.
187. Bell, Allan, ULLC/WW1/MID01; Williams, Herbert, ULLC/WW1/ GS/1745.
188. Wyrall, *19th Division*, p. 31.
189. Hart, Peter, *The Somme* (London: Weidenfeld & Nicholson, 2005), p. 55.
190. Senescall, *op. cit.*
191. Henderson, Stanley, ULLC/WW1/ WF01/H19 & MID01.
192. Pollard, *op. cit.*; see also Greenwell, Graham, *An Infant in Arms: War Letters of a Company Officer, 1914–1918* (London: The Penguin Press, 1972), p. 106.
193. Upcott, 1 June 1916, *op. cit.*
194. Jardine, James, letter, 13 June 1930, NAUK, CAB/45/135.
195. *The Great War Diaries*, p. 137.
196. Pollard, *op. cit.*
197. Burrows, John, *The Essex Regiment, 1st Battalion (44th)* (John H. Burrows & Sons, 1927), p. 205.
198. Branson, Douglas, ULLC/WW1/ GS/0187.
199. Burrows, *op. cit.*, p. 64; see also Hart, *Somme*, p. 55.
200. Coppard, p. 75.
201. Banks and Chell, p. 104.
202. Hart, *The Somme*, p. 55.
203. Middlebrook, Martin, *The First Day on the Somme* (London: Penguin Books, 1984), p. 86.
204. Crook, Wilfred, ULLC/WW1/ WF01/C/21 & MID01.
205. *Liverpool Daily Post*, 18 July 1916

206. Haig, diary, 30 June 1916, *op. cit.*
207. Crozier, p. 96.
208. Rawlinson, diary, 30 June 1916, *op. cit.*
209. *ibid.*
210. *The First World War Letters of General Lord Horne*, ed. Simon Robbins (Stroud: The Army Records Society, 2009), p. 168.
211. Congreve, Walter, diary, 1 May–23 June 1916, Congreve Papers, Hampshire Records Office.
212. Morland, Thomas, letter, 4 June 1916, Morland Papers, Imperial War Museum.
213. Hunter-Weston, Aylmer, letters, 21–30 June 1916, Hunter-Weston Papers, BL.
214. *ibid.*, 25 June 1916.
215. *Report on Operations on Fourth Army Front for Period Ending 6 p.m. Friday, 16th June, 1916*, Fourth Army, Summary of Operation, NAUK, WO/155/244.
216. Haig, diary, 30 June 1916, *op. cit.*

Chapter 3: 'Artillery is Decisive'
1. Collet, Peter, ULLC/WW1/GE/29.
2. A coalscuttle helmet was captured by III Corps in April 1916 at Ovillers and La Boiselle. It was the subject of a special report (NAUK/WO/157/171). At least one German regiment confirmed the very limited presence of these steel helmets prior to 1 July. Frisch, George, *Das Reserve-Infanterie-Regiment Nr. 109 im Weltkrieg 1914 bis 1918* (Karlsruhe: F. Thiergarten, 1931), p. 109.
3. Frisch, p. 123.
4. Dellmensingen, Konrad von, and Feeser, Friedrichfranz, *Das Bayernbuch vom Weltkriege 1914–1918* (Stuttgart: Belser, 1930), p. 300.
5. Reichsarchiv, *Der Weltkrieg 1914 bis 1918: Die Operationen des Jahres 1916* (Berlin: Mittler & Sohn, 1936), p. 343.
6. Fiedel, Paul, *Geschichte des Infanterie-Regiments von Winterfeldt (2. Oberschlesisches) Nr. 23* (Berlin: Wilhelm Kolk, 1929), p. 117.
7. Koch, Arthur, *Die Flieger-Abteilung (A) 221: Nach den Kriegstagebüchern und Flugmeldungen der Abteilung bearbeitet* (Oldenburg: Gerhard Stalling, 1925), p. 24.
8. *ibid.*, p. 25.
9. *ibid.*, p. 21.
10. Falkenhayn, Erich von, *General Headquarters 1914–1916 and its Critical Decisions* (London: Hutchinson, 1919), p. 262.
11. *SS553: Experience of the German 1st Army in the Somme Battle, 24 June to 26 November 1916, First Army H.Q.*

(30 January 1917, translated 3 May 1917), p. 3; Lossberg, Friedrich, *Meine Tätigkeit im Weltkriege* (Berlin: Mittler & Sohn, 1939), pp. 215–17; *Weltkrieg*, p. 341.
12. Sheldon, Jack, *The German Army on the Somme 1914–1916* (Barnsley: Pen & Sword, 2005), pp. 115–16.
13. Soden, Franz von, *Die 26. (Württembergische) Reserve-Division im Weltkrieg 1914–1918* (Stuttgart, Bergers Literarisches Büro, 1939), p. 97.
14. Sheldon, *Somme*, pp. 115–16.
15. *ibid.*
16. *ibid.*; Edmonds, p. 316.
17. Sheldon, *Somme*, p. 116; *Weltkrieg*, p. 342.
18. Falkenhayn, p. 247; Neame, Edward, *German Strategy in the Great War* (London: Edward Arnold, 1923), p. 89.
19. *ibid.*, p. 250.
20. Falkenhayn, p. 263.
21. *Weltkrieg*, pp. 344–5; Stosch, pp. 249–56.
22. Falkenhayn, pp. 262–3.
23. Sheffield, Gary, *The Somme* (London: Cassell, 2003), pp. 26–7.
24. Falkenhayn, p. 250.
25. Falkenhayn, pp. 262–3.
26. *Weltkrieg*, p. 343.
27. Edmonds, p 318.
28. *ibid.*, p. 316.
29. *ibid.*, pp. 317–18; *Weltkrieg*, p. 343.
30. *Weltkrieg*, p. 343.
31. Edmonds, p. 316.
32. *SS553*, p. 3; Lossberg, pp. 215–17.
33. Strohn, Matthias, *World War I Companion* (Oxford: Osprey, 2013), p. 109.
34. *ibid.*, p. 109; there is some evidence to suggest Falkenhayn's doctrine was circulated before October 1915, and specifically in Below's Second Army.
35. *SS471: Essential Principles for the Defence of Positions as Laid Down in Instructions Issued by G.H.Q., German Second Army H.Q.* (1 August 1915, translated 1916).
36. Strohn, p. 109; Neame, p. 89.
37. *ibid.*, p. 109.
38. Stosch, Albrecht von, *Somme-Nord, I Teil: Die Brennpunkte der Schlacht im Juli 1916* (Berlin: Gerhard Stalling, 1927), pp. 249–54; Stein, Hermann von, *A War Minister and His Work: Reminiscences of 1914–1918* (London: Skeffington & Son, Ltd, 1920), p. 118; order of battle is that given for 30 June 1916, following the late-May reshuffle. Stein (p. 118) states that his corps' strength 'before the summer offensive' was 'somewhere

about seventy thousand.' At this time his command was c.75,500 officers and men of 26th Reserve (c.18,000), 28th Reserve (c.15,000), 12th Infantry (c.15,000), 52nd Infantry (c.15,000) and 10th Bavarian Infantry Divisions (c.12,500), but not 2nd Guards Reserve Division (c.18,000). The arrival of 2nd Guards Reserve Division boosted Stein's corps to c.93,500. This number included divisional artillery, infantry, machine-gun and ancillary units. If corps' troops were included, XIV Reserve Corps' nominal strength comfortably reached 95,000, maybe even 100,000. The 26th Reserve and 2nd Guards Reserve Divisions each had four regiments, whereas Stein's other divisions comprised three apiece.

39. Stein, p. 103.
40. Stosch, p. 39.
41. Gerster, Matthaus, *Die Schwaben and der Ancre* (Heilbronn: Eugen Salzer, 1918), p. 117.
42. Sheldon, Jack, *The Germans at Thiepval* (Barnsley: Pen & Sword Military, 2006), p. 130.
43. Stosch, p. 83.
44. Sheldon, *Somme*, p. 141.
45. Schwarz, Dr Richard, 'Truppen-Sanitatsdienst wahrend der Sommeschlacht,' in *Treffen der 26.R.D. am 5. Juli 1936*, ed. Matthaus Gerster (Stuttgart: unknown publisher, 1936), p. 35.
46. Holtz, Georg von, *Das Württembg. Res. Inft. Regt. No. 121 im Weltkrieg 1914–1918* (Stuttgart: Chr. Belsersche Verlagsbuchhandlung, 1921), p. 34.
47. Soden, p. 109.
48. *ibid.*, pp. 102–3; Holtz, p. 34.
49. Fiedel, p. 104.
50. *SS490: The Principles of Trench Warfare as Laid Down in the XIV Reserve Corps* (19 May 1916, translated 13 October 1916).
51. Sheldon, *Somme*, p. 80.
52. Soden, p. 85.
53. *ibid.*, p. 98.
54. Sheldon, *Somme*, p. 80.
55. Sheldon, *The Germans at Beaumont Hamel*, (Barnsley: Pen & Sword, 2006), p. 63.
56. Soden, p. 81.
57. Sheldon, *Beaumont Hamel*, p. 63.
58. Soden, p. 97.
59. *SS490*, p. 5.
60. *SS490*, p. 5.
61. *ibid.*, p. 4.
62. *ibid.*, p. 5.

63. Greiner, Lt. d. R. and Vulpius, Lt. d. R., *Reserve-Infanterie-Regiment Nr. 110 im Weltkrieg 1914–1918* (Karlsruhe: Macklotsche, 1934), pp. 117–18.
64. Stein, p. 98.
65. 'Bericht des Kommandierenden Generals XIV. Reserve-Korps, Generalleutnant v. Stein,' by Hermann von Stein, in *Der 180er: Festnummer: zum Treffen der 26. Reserve-Division vom 4. Bis 6. Juli 1936 in Stuttgart*, 4 July 1936.
66. Soden, p. 98.
67. *ibid.*
68. *ibid.*
69. Sheldon, *Somme*, pp. 67–8.
70. Lais, Otto, *Erlebnisse Badischer Frontsoldaten: Maschinengewehr im Eisernen Regiment (8. Badisches Infanterie-Regiment Nr. 169)* (Karlsruhe: G. Braun, 1935), unpaginated translation dated 1998 by Andrew Jackson.
71. *ibid.*
72. 'Der Maulwurfskrieg,' by Albert Fickendey, in *Der 180er*, 1 February 1936.
73. Frisch, p. 98.
74. *ibid.*, p. 94.
75. 'Bericht des Kommandierenden,' *op. cit.*
76. *SS490*, p. 3.
77. Stein, pp. 98–9.
78. Lais, *op. cit.*
79. *ibid.*
80. 'General v. Soden und seine eiserne 26. Reserve-Division,' by Eugen Rueff, in *Der 180er: Festnummer: zum Treffen der 26. Reserve-Division vom 4. Bis 6. Juli 1936 in Stuttgart*, 4 July 1936.
81. Reymann, H., *Das 3. Oberschlesische Infanterie-Regiment Nr. 62 im Kriege 1914–1918* (Zeulenroda: Sporn, 1930), pp. 77–144; Fiedel, pp. 119–45; neither refers to Châles de Beaulieu inspecting his regimental positions.
82. Fiedel, p. 104.
83. Fiedel, pp. 105–20; Reymann, pp. 77–87; —, *Das K.B. 1. Infanterie-Regiment König* (München: Lindauersche Universitäts, 1922), pp. 23–7; Stosch, pp. 60–75; Bachelin, Eduard, *Das Reserve-Infanterie-Regiment Nr. 111 im Weltkrieg 1914 bis 1918* (Karlsruhe: Südwestdeut., 1937).
84. *ibid.*
85. *ibid.*
86. Reymann, p. 79, p. 87; in 26th Reserve Division it was also a case of maintaining positions during the autumn and winter, but that division had done more development work in the spring and summer of 1915.

87. Vischer, Alfred, *Das 10. Württ. Infanterie-Regiment Nr. 180 in der Somme-Schlacht 1916* (Stuttgart: Uhland'schen, 1917), p. 6; Whitehead, Ralph, *The Other Side of the Wire, Vol. 1: The Battle of the Somme. With the German XIV Reserve Corps, September 1914–June 1916* (Solihull: Helion, 2010), p. 343.

88. Reymann, p. 71; Fiedel, pp. 104–5; Frisch, p. 122.

89. Whitehead, *Vol. 1*, pp. 428–9.

90. Reymann, p. 71; Fiedel, pp. 104–5.

91. Reymann, pp. 71–87; Fiedel, pp. 105–118.

92. Stosch, pp. 249–55; Klaus, Max, *Das Württembergische Reserve-Feldartillerie-Regiment Nr. 26 im Weltkrieg 1914–1918* (Stuttgart: Christian Belser, 1929), pp. 52–3; *Weltkrieg*, pp. 348–9.

93. *ibid.*; Soden, p. 96.

94. *ibid*

95. Rudolph, M, *Geschichte des Bayrischen Fussartillerie Bataillons Nr. 10* (Zeulenroda: Sporn, 1936), p. 34.

96. Traumüller, Willi, letter, 29 January 1916.

97. *Weltkrieg*, Anlage 1. The table reveals that of the 844 barrels on Second Army's strength at 30 June, 628 (74.4%) were quick-firing weapons with recoil mechanisms, meaning 216 (25.6%) were not and needed to be re-aimed after each shot. Moreover, 278 (32.9%) were steep-trajectory guns that lacked the range of the 566 (67.1%) generally light-calibre, flat-trajectory weapons. Captured weapons totalled 118 (14%), for which ammunition and spare parts were scarce.

98. Whitehead, *Vol. 1*, p. 393.

99. This was broadly true of Second Army, too.

100. *SS490*, pp. 6–7; the shells to be stored in the event of an enemy attack were as follows: field-gun battery 2000 shells; light field howitzer battery 1500; 10 cm gun battery 1500; heavy field howitzer battery 1000; 21 cm mortar 100; German 12 cm, 15 cm ring cannon and Russian 15 cm gun batteries 800; each Belgian 8.7 cm gun 80; and each 9 cm gun 130.

101. Soden, *skizze* 23.

102. *SS490*, p. 6.

103. *ibid.*, p. 7.

104. *ibid*.

105. *ibid.*, p. 8.

106. *ibid*.

107. Renz, Irina, Krumeich, Gerd, and Hirschfeld, Gerhard, *Scorched Earth: the Germans on the Somme 1914–1918* (Barnsley: Pen & Sword, 2009), p. 36.

108. XIV Reserve Corps deployed its artillery in groups of batteries, each with a tactical level commander and collectively responsible to a divisional artillery commander.

109. *SS490*, p. 7.

110. Witkop, Philipp (2013-03-16). German Students' War Letters (Pine Street Books; Kindle Edition — Locations 4410–4417).

111. Koch, p. 143; it flew a further 104 practice flights over and around its airfield.

112. *ibid.*; the other nine were for photo (3), barrier (3) and night (3) flights.

113. Sheldon, *Somme*, p. 66.

114. Büsing, Georg, *Das Reserve-Feldartillerie-Regiment Nr. 20 im Weltkrieg 1914–18* (Hannover: Göhmann, 1932), unpaginated translation dated 2014 supplied by Bill MacCormick.

115. Sheldon, *Somme*, pp. 66–7.

116. Renz, Krumeich and Hirschfeld, p. 83.

117. Bielefeld, August, ULLC/WW1/GE29.

118. Moos, Ernst, *Das Württembergische Reserve.-Feld-Artillerie-Regiment Nr. 27 im Weltkrieg 1916–1918* (Stuttgart, Belser: 1925), p. 1

119. *ibid.*, pp. 1–3.

120. *ibid*.

121. Dellmensingen and Feeser, p. 300.

122. Büsing, *op. cit.*

123. *ibid*.

124. Rudolph, p. 35.

125. *ibid*.

126. Hermann, Heinrich, ULLC/WW1/ GE/29; Whitehead, Ralph, *The Other Side of the Wire: The Battle of the Somme. With the German XIV Reserve Corps, 1 July 1916, Volume 2* (Solihull: Helion, 2013), p. 412.

127. Büsing, *op. cit.*

128. *ibid*.

129. Dellmensingen and Feeser, p. 300.

130. *ibid*.

131. Renz, Krumeich and Hirschfeld, p. 82.

132. Eberle, Christian, postcard, 19 February 1916.

133. Renz, Krumeich and Hirschfeld, *ibid*.

134. Langford, William, *Somme Intelligence: Fourth Army HQ 1916* (Barnsley: Pen & Sword, 2013), p. 23.

135. Stein, p. 108.

136. Soden, p. 98.

137. *ibid.*, p. 97.

138. Sheldon, *Somme*, p. 77; this folk song was popularised by Elvis Presley's 'Wooden Heart.'

139. *ibid.*, p. 72.

140. *ibid.*
141. 'Vor Zwanzig Jahren,' by Rudolf Greisinger, in *Der 180er*, 1 August 1938.
142. 'Vor Zwanzig Jahren,' *Reservist* Wirth, in *Der 180er*, 10 January 1937.
143. Renz, Krumeich and Hirschfeld, p. 73.
144. *SS490*, p. 3.
145. *ibid.*
146. Renz, Krumeich and Hirschfeld, p. 31.
147. Whitehead, *Vol. 1*, p. 335; Hahn's sector at this time did not include Mametz as the XIV Reserve Corps-wide reorganisation had yet to take place, meaning all three of his regiments were holding well-constructed positions.
148. Sheldon, *Somme*, p. 119.
149. Whitehead, Ralph, *Vol. 2*, p. 413.
150. Renz, Krumeich and Hirschfeld, p. 35.
151. Greiner and Vulpius, pp. 73–4.
152. *ibid.*
153. *SS460* German Mining Officer's Diary, captured at Fricourt, July 1916.
154. *ibid.*
155. Sheldon, *Somme*, p. 99.
156. *ibid.*, p. 76.
157. *SS490*, p. 4.
158. *ibid.*
159. *ibid.*
160. *ibid.*
161. *ibid.*, p. 5.
162. *ibid.*
163. Renz, Krumeich and Hirschfeld, p. 35.
164. Sheldon, *Somme*, p. 59.
165. Collet, *op. cit.*
166. Sheldon, *Somme*, p. 101.
167. *ibid.*, pp. 101–6.
168. Lademann, Ulrich, *Das 3. Magdeburgische Infanterie-Regiment Nr. 66* (Oldenburg: Gerhard Stalling, 1922), p. 31; IR66 noted 160 men participated in the raid on 15–16 May 1916 and that 29 British soldiers were captured.
169. Reymann, p. 81.
170. 'Tapfere Schwaben,' by Hermann Klotz, in *Der 180er*, 1 July 1937.
171. Reymann, p. 82.
172. 'Eine kleine Begegnung mit dem Tommy,' by Walter Bönsel, in *Der 180er*, 1 March 1938.
173. Whitehead, *Vol. 1*, pp. 318–20.
174. *ibid.*
175. *ibid.*
176. Greiner and Vulpius, pp. 91–3.
177. Fiedel, pp. 111–20; Reymann, pp. 77–92; Lademann, pp. 30–2; Frisch, pp. 81–122; Greiner and Vulpius, pp. 96–118; Gerster, *Schwaben*, pp. 87–96; Stosch, pp. 11–21; Vischer, pp. 26–32; Holtz, pp. 20–32; Gerster, Matthäus, *Das Württembergische Reserve-Infanterie-Regiment Nr. 119 im Weltkrieg 1914–1918* (Stuttgart: Chr. Belsersche, 1920), pp. 43–9; Whitehead, *Vol. 1*, pp. 339–432; this is the minimum number of PoWs taken by the stated regiments. It does not include data for IR169, IR170, RIR55, RIR91 and RIR15.
178. Middlebrook, Martin, *The First Day on the Somme* (London: Penguin Books, 1984), p. 155.
179. Soden, p. 90.
180. Hart, Peter, *The Somme* (London: Weidenfeld & Nicholson, 2005), p. 75.
181. Frisch, p. 119.
182. Renz, Krumeich and Hirschfeld, p. 31.
183. *ibid.*, pp. 73–4.
184. *ibid.*; Langford, p. 18; Soden, p. 99.
185. Whitehead, *Vol. 1*, p. 314.
186. Schuler, Karl, letter, 29 May 1916.
187. 'An der Somme,' by Friedrich Conzelmann, in *Der 180er*, 1 November 1936.
188. Sheldon, *Somme*, p. 68.
189. 'Zapfenstreich,' by Albrecht Munz, in *Der 180er*, 1 March 1938.
190. *ibid.*
191. Lademann, p. 29.
192. Fiedel, p. 107.
193. Fickendey, *op. cit.*
194. 'Bericht des Kommandierenden,' *op. cit.*
195. Gerster, *RIR119*, p. 40.
196. Greiner and Vulpius, p. 91.
197. Reymann, p. 75.
198. Gerster, *RIR119*, p. 40.
199. Whitehead, *Vol. 1*, p. 347.
200. *ibid.*
201. Reymann, p. 74.
202. Klinkerfüss, Otto, postcard, 9 November 1915.
203. 'Bericht des Kommandierenden,' *op. cit.*
204. Keller, Wilhelm, postcard, 9 November 1915.
205. 'Eine Erinnerung an Courcelette,' by Johann Heyberger, in *Der 180er*, 1 October 1936.
206. Kaisser, Eugen, letter, 20 May 1916.
207. Bauer, Fritz, postcard, 21 March 1916.
208. 'Eine Erinnerung an Courcelette,' *op. cit.*
209. Bauer, *op. cit.*
210. Opielka, August, postcard, 17 May 1916.
211. *ibid.*, 17 January 1916.
212. Bauer, Fritz, postcard, 28 April 1916.
213. Harr, Gotthilf, postcard, 30 May 1916.
214. Hartung, Heinrich, postcard, 17 June 1916.
215. Stegmaier, August, postcard, 2 February 1916.
216. Keller, 17 February 1916.
217. Öschle, Gustav, postcard, 6 August 1915.

218. Opielka, 27 May 1916.
219. Müller, Fabeck and Riesel, p. 97.

Chapter 4: Ballad of the Blind Gunners

1. Klaus, Max, *Das Württembergische Reserve-Feldartillerie-Regiment Nr. 26 im Weltkrieg 1914–1918* (Stuttgart: Christian Belser, 1929), p. 46.
2. Liveing, Edward, *Attack on the Somme: An Infantry Subaltern's Impressions of July 1st, 1916* (Stevenage: Spa Books, 1986), p. 22.
3. Renz, Irina, Krumeich, Gerd, and Hirschfeld, Gerhard, *Scorched Earth: the Germans on the Somme 1914–1918* (Barnsley: Pen & Sword, 2009), p. 83.
4. Lushington, Franklin, *The Gambardier: Giving Some Account of the Heavy and Siege Artillery in France, 1914–1918* (London: Ernest Benn, 1930), p. 100.
5. Edmonds, Sir James, *Military Operations France and Belgium, 1916, Vol. 1* (London: Imperial War Museum, 1992), p. 299.
6. *ibid.*, pp. 299–300.
7. Hart, Peter, *The Somme* (London: Weidenfeld & Nicholson, 2005), pp. 94–5.
8. Edmonds, p. 301.
9. *ibid.*, pp. 300–1.
10. *ibid.*, pp. 300, 460.
11. *ibid.*
12. Capper, Derick, ULLC/WW1/GS/0267; Willmer, Edgar, ULLC/WW1/GS/1753.
13. Edmonds, pp. 301–2; daily totals were U day 138,118 shells, V day 188,881 shells, W day 211,886 shells, X day 235,887 shells, Y day 168,363 shells, Y1 day 189,757 shells, and Y2 day 375,760 shells.
14. Edmonds, p. 302.
15. Rawlinson, Henry, diary, 30 June 1916, Rawlinson Papers 1/5, Churchill Archive.
16. 'Ammunition Summary,' 4 July 1916, Rawlinson Papers 1/6, Churchill Archive; this figure is only for part of 1 July and therefore is at odds with the 1.73 million shells that Edmonds states Fourth Army fired 24 June–1 July.
17. 'Ammunition Dump Summary,' 19 June 1916, Rawlinson Papers 1/6, Churchill Archive.
18. Goodwin, William, diary, 19 March 1916, ULLC/WW1/GS/0644.
19. Fraser-Tytler, Neil, *Field Guns in France: With a Howitzer Battery in the Battles of the Somme, Arras, Messines and Passchendaele 1915–1918* (Brighton: Tom Donovan, 1995), p. 80.
20. *ibid.*, p. 78.
21. Capper, *op. cit.*
22. Lushington, p. 100.
23. Jack, James, *General Jack's Diary* (London: Eyre & Spottiswoode, 1964), pp. 142–3.
24. Ashurst, George, *My Bit: A Lancashire Fusilier at War 1914–1918* (Ramsbury: The Crowood Press, 1987), p. 97.
25. Heath, Philip, ULLC/WW1/WF01/H/18.
26. Price, Leonard, ULLC/WW1/MID01.
27. Fraser-Tytler, p. 78.
28. Hart, Peter, *Somme Success: The Royal Flying Corps and the Battle of the Somme, 1916* (London: Leo Cooper, 2001), p. 77.
29. Liveing, pp. 20–1.
30. Fraser-Tytler, p. 78.
31. *ibid.*, p. 79.
32. Lushington, p. 100.
33. Morland, Thomas, letter, 27 June 1916, Morland Papers, Imperial War Museum.
34. Congreve, Walter, diary, 27 June 1916, Congreve Papers, Hampshire Records Office.
35. Ashurst, p. 97.
36. Kelly, David, *39 Months: With the 'Tigers,' 1915–1918* (London: Ernest Benn, 1930), p. 25.
37. Ashurst, p. 97.
38. Smith, Aubrey, *Four Years on the Western Front* (London: Long Acre, 1922), p. 143.
39. Lewis, Cecil, *Sagittarius Rising* (London: Greenhill Books, 1998), p. 67.
40. Kelly, Robert, *A Subaltern's Odyssey* (London: William Kimber, 1980), p. 91.
41. Langford, William, *Somme Intelligence: Fourth Army HQ 1916* (Barnsley: Pen & Sword, 2013), p. 29.
42. Kircher, Felix, ULLC/WW1/MID01.
43. Büsing, Georg, *Das Reserve-Feldartillerie-Regiment Nr. 20 im Weltkrieg 1914–18* (Hannover: Göhmann, 1932), unpaginated translation dated 2014 supplied by Bill MacCormick.
44. Heinrich, Hermann, ULLC/WW1/MID01.
45. Vischer, Alfred, *Das Württ. Infanterie-Regiment Nr. 180* (Stuttgart: Christian Belsers, 1921), p. 33.
46. Sheldon, Jack, *The German Army on the Somme 1914–1916* (Barnsley: Pen & Sword, 2005), p. 121.
47. Renz, Krumeich and Hirschfeld, p. 83.
48. *ibid.*, p. 75.
49. Fiedel, Paul, *Geschichte des Infanterie-Regiments von Winterfeldt (2. Oberschlesisches) Nr. 23* (Berlin: Wilhelm Kolk, 1929), p. 121.

50. Gerster, Matthäus, *Das Württembergische Reserve-Infanterie-Regiment Nr. 119 im Weltkrieg 1914–1918* (Stuttgart: Chr. Belsersche, 1920), p. 51.
51. Maze, Paul, *A Frenchman in Khaki* (London: Heinemann, 1934), p. 134.
52. Renz, Krumeich and Hirschfeld, p. 83.
53. Sheldon, *Somme*, p. 123.
54. *ibid.*
55. *ibid.*, p. 122.
56. III Corps CRA, war diary, 25 June 1916, NAUK, WO/95/689; X Corps GS, war diary, 24 June 1916, NAUK, WO/95/851; XV Corps GS, war diary, 24–5 June 1916, NAUK, WO/95/921; VIII Corps CRA, war diary, 26 June 1916, NAUK, WO/95/824; the wind blew chlorine gas back into VIII Corps' positions and some of the gas technicians became casualties of their own weapon.
57. Senescall, William, ULLC/WW1/WF02/S/7.
58. Hunter-Weston, Aylmer, letter, 26 June 1916, Hunter-Weston Papers, BL.
59. III Corps GS, war diary, 27 June 1916, NAUK, WO/95/672.
60. Fiedel, p. 121.
61. Baumgartner, Richard, *This Carnival of Hell: German Combat Experience on the Somme*, (Huntington: Blue Acorn Press, 2010), p. 63; Thomas, Friedrich, ULLC/WW1/MID01; III Corps CRA, war diary, 25 June 1916, *op. cit.*
62. Müller-Loebnitz, Wilhelm, *Die Badener im Weltkrieg 1914/1918, Band I* (Karlsruhe: G. Braun Verlag, 1935), p. 214.
63. *SS460 German Mining Officer's Diary*, captured at Fricourt, July 1916.
64. Müller-Loebnitz, p. 215.
65. Edmonds, p. 361.
66. Sheldon, *Somme*, p. 128.
67. Falls, Cyril, *The History of the 36th (Ulster) Division* (London: M'Caw, Stevenson & Orr, 1922), p. 49.
68. 'Berichtet über den Gegestoss am Heidenkopf,' by Emil Geiger, in *Der 180er*, 1 July 1938.
69. 'Vor Zwanzig Jahren,' by Rudolf Greisinger, in *Der 180er*, 1 August 1938.
70. Westman, Stephan, *Surgeon with the Kaiser's Army* (London: William Kimber, 1968), p. 94. Westmann changed his name to Stephan Westman after he moved to the UK.
71. Renz, Krumeich and Hirschfeld, p. 84.
72. Kuster, Peter, ULLC/WW1/MID01.
73. Baumgartner, p. 65.
74. Sheldon, *Somme*, p. 133; Gerster, *RIR119*, p. 51.

75. Westman, p. 94, Baumgartner, p. 63.
76. Langford, p. 29.
77. Gerster, *RIR119*, p. 50; Gerster, Matthaus, *Die Schwaben and der Ancre* (Heilbronn: Eugen Salzer, 1918), pp. 100–1; not to be confused with delayed-detonation shells.
78. Bachelin, Eduard, *Das Reserve-Infanterie-Regiment Nr. 111 im Weltkrieg 1914 bis 1918* (Karlsruhe: Südwest-deutsche Druck- und Verlag, 1937), pp. 287–8.
79. Gerster, *Schwaben*, p. 100.
80. Whitehead, Ralph, *The Other Side of the Wire: The Battle of the Somme. With the German XIV Reserve Corps, 1 July 1916, Vol. 2*, (Solihull: Helion, 2013), p. 252: *Verlustlisten* disc; Vischer (1921), pp. 32–5; Gerster, *RIR119*, p. 51; Holtz, p. 34; Reymann, H., *Das 3. Oberschlesische Infanterie-Regiment Nr. 62 im Kriege 1914–1918* (Zeulenroda: Sporn, 1930), pp. 89–92; Bachelin, Eduard, *Das Reserve-Infanterie-Regiment Nr. 111 im Weltkrieg 1914 bis 1918* (Karlsruhe: Südwestdeut, 1937), pp. 95–6; 'Report on the Defence of Gommecourt on July the 1st, 1916,' *Royal United Services Institution Journal*, Vol. 62, Issue 447, 1917, p. 552; Sheldon, *Somme*, p. 157; Frisch, George, *Das Reserve-Infanterie-Regiment Nr. 109 im Weltkrieg 1914 bis 1918* (Karlsruhe: F. Thiergarten, 1931), pp. 122–9; Greiner, Lt. d. R., and Vulpius, Lt. d. R., *Reserve-Infanterie-Regiment Nr. 110 im Weltkrieg 1914–1918* (Karlsruhe: Macklotsche, 1934), pp. 118–28, 305.
81. Sheldon, *Somme*, p. 128.
82. *ibid.*
83. Askew, Alfred, ULLC/WW1/MID01.
84. Conyers, Frederick, ULLC/WW1/MID01.
85. Wide, Howard, ULLC/WW1/MID01.
86. Ward, Arthur, ULLC/WW1/WF02/W/4.
87. Heath, *op. cit.*
88. Goodwin, *op. cit.*
89. Williams, Herbert, ULLC/WW1/GS/1745.
90. England, Arthur, ULLC/WW1/WF01/E/7.
91. Collis-Browne, John, letter 12 November 1929, NAUK, CAB/45/132.
92. Bales, P.G., *The History of the 1/4th Battalion Duke of Wellington's (West Riding) Regiment, 1914–1919* (Halifax: Edward Mortimer, 1920), p. 70.
93. Laporte, Archibald, ULLC/WW1/GS/0920.

94. Gibbs, Alfred, letter, 22 May 1930, NAUK, CAB/45/134.

95. Croft, Henry, *Twenty-Two Months Under Fire* (London: John Murray, 1917), p. 200.

96. Jenour, Arthur, letter, 9 March 1930, NAUK, CAB/45/135.

97. Moore, Aubrey, ULLC/WW1/WF01/M/24.

98. Ashurst, p. 97.

99. Brown, Malcolm, *The Imperial War Museum Book of the Somme* (London: Pan Books, 2002), p. 45.

100. Barber, Henry, ULLC/WW1/MID01.

101. Fraser-Tytler, p. 80.

102. Jack, p. 143.

103. *ibid.,* p. 143.

104. Capper, *op. cit.*

105. Askew, *op. cit.*

106. Levine, Joshua, *Forgotten Voices of the Somme* (London: Ebury Publishing, 2009), p. 102.

107. Collis-Browne, *op. cit.*

108. Lewis, *Sagittarius*, p. 70.

109. Goodwin, *op. cit.*

110. Lushington, p. 100.

111. Smith, *Four Years*, p. 143.

112. *ibid.,* pp. 143–4.

113. Turner, P.W., and Haigh, R.H., *Not for Glory* (London: Robert Maxwell, 1969), p. 38.

114. Hunter-Weston, Aylmer, letter, 26 June 1916, Hunter-Weston Papers, BL.

115. England, *op. cit.*; Ashurst, p. 97; Willmer, *op. cit.*

116. Langford, p. 24.

117. Hart, *Somme*, p. 93; Baumgartner, p. 62.

118. Kuster, *op. cit.*

119. Langford, pp. 26–7.

120. *ibid.,* p. 29.

121. Vogler, Heinrich, ULLC/WW1/MID01.

122. Langford, p. 29.

123. Sheldon, *Somme*, p. 127.

124. *ibid.,* pp. 133–4.

125. Langford, p. 25.

126. Sheldon, *Somme*, p. 134; see also Gerster, *Die Schwaben*, p. 107.

127. Renz, Krumeich and Hirschfeld, pp. 84–5.

128. Langford, p. 23.

129. Bielefeld, August, ULLC/WW1/MID01.

130. Westman, p. 94.

131. Müller, Paul, Fabeck, Hans von, and Riesel, Richard, *Geschichte des Reserve-Infanterie-Regiments Nr. 99* (Zeulenroda: Sporn, 1936), p. 107.

132. Hart, *Somme*, p. 93.

133. *ibid.,* pp. 107–8.

134. Renz, Krumeich and Hirschfeld, p. 74.

135. Middlebrook, Martin, *The First Day on the Somme* (London: Penguin Books, 1984), p. 80.

136. Soden, Franz von, *Die 26. (Württembergische) Reserve-Division im Weltkrieg 1914–1918* (Stuttgart: Bergers Literarisches Büro, 1939), p. 106.

137. Hart, *Somme*, p. 93.

138. Langford, p. 23.

139. Holtz, Georg von, *Das Württembg. Res. Inft. Regt. No. 121 im Weltkrieg 1914–1918* (Stuttgart: Chr. Belsersche Verlagsbuchhandlung, 1921), p. 32.

140. Sheldon, *Somme*, pp. 123–4.

141. Vischer, Alfred, *Das 10. Württ. Infanterie-Regiment Nr. 180 in der Somme-Schlacht 1916* (Stuttgart: Uhland'schen, 1917), p. 12; see Reymann, p. 92, for a similarly upbeat sentiment.

142. Sheldon, *Somme*, p. 134.

143. 'Das RIR. 121 am Heidenkopf in der Sommeschlacht,' by Friedrich Stutz in *Der 180er*, 1 July 1938.

144. Müller, Fabeck and Riesel, p. 107.

145. Scheytt, Paul, ULLC/WW1/MID01.

146. Hart, *Somme*, pp. 94–5.

147. Büsing, *op. cit.*

148. Middlebrook, p. 204.

149. This figure is for British heavy artillery alone, excluding any French guns.

150. III Corps CRA, war diary, 30 June 1916, *op. cit.*; VIII Corps CRA, war diary, 26–29 June 1916, *op. cit.*; XIII Corps CRA, war diary, 27–29 June 1916, NAUK, WO/95/901; X Corps CHA, war diary, 24–30 June 1916, NAUK, WO/95/866; Records for VII and XV Corps are inconsistent, meaning the actual total could be more than 29.

151. Edmonds, p. 301.

152. Heath, *op. cit.*

153. III Corps CRA, war diary, 24–30 June 1916, *op. cit.*; VIII Corps CRA, war diary, 24–30 June 1916, *op. cit.*; 'Report on Preparations and Action of 32nd Divisional Artillery During Operations of July 1916,' 32nd Division, war diary, June 1916, NAUK, WO/95/2368/1; data for the other corps is either incomplete or not stated.

154. Sutterby, Robert, undated memoir, pp. 64–5; courtesy of the Gauldie Family.

155. XIII Corps CRA, war diary, 30 June 1916, *op. cit.*

156. Sutterby, p. 67.

157. *ibid.*

158. 'Report on Preparations and Action of 32nd Divisional Artillery,' *op. cit.*; III Corps CRA, war diary, 29 June 1916,

159. *op. cit.*; XIII Corps CRA, war diary, 25–28 June 1916, *op. cit.*

159. XIII Corps CRA, war diary, 26–28 June 1916, *op. cit.*; Edmonds, p. 122; see also Greig, Robert, letter, 22 April 1930, NAUK, CAB/45/134.

160. Jenour, *op. cit.*

161. XIII Corps CRA, war diary, 25 and 30 June 1916, *op. cit.*

162. III Corps CRA, war diary, 29 June 1916, *op. cit.*

163. XIII Corps CRA, war diary, 26–28 June 1916, *op. cit.*

164. Edmonds, p. 122; Greig, *op. cit.*

165. Edmonds, p. 122

166. 'Blindganger,' by an unknown author, in *Der 180er*, 1 July 1937.

167. Ware, Innes, ULLC/WW1/TR/08.

168. *ibid.*

169. Nanson, Musard, letter, undated, NAUK, CAB/45/136.

170. Unknown officer, letter, 8 July 1930, NAUK, CAB/45/132.

171. Moore, *op. cit.*

172. Fraser-Tytler, pp. 77–8.

173. XIII Corps CRA, war diary, 24 June 1916, *op. cit.*; III Corps CRA, war diary, 24 June 1916, *op. cit.*

174. Noted in most corps-level GS, CHA and CRA war diaries for 24–30 June 1916.

175. XIII Corps CRA, war diary, 26 June 1916, *op. cit.*

176. XV Corps CRA, war diary, 27 June 1916, NAUK, WO/95/925.

177. X Corps CRA, war diary, 28 June 1916, NAUK, WO/95/863.

178. VIII Corps CRA, war diary, 28 June 1916, *op. cit.*

179. III Corps CRA, war diary, 24 June 1916, *op. cit.*; VIII Corps CRA, war diary, 24–27 June 1916, *op. cit.*; X Corps CRA, war diary, 25 June 1916, *op. cit.*

180. XV Corps CRA, war diary, 24–25 June 1916, *op. cit.*; XIII Corps CRA, war diary, 27–28 June 1916, *op. cit.*

181. VIII Corps CRA, war diary, 28 June 1916, *op. cit.*

182. VII Corps CRA, war diary, 25 June 1916, NAUK, WO/95/811.

183. III Corps CRA, war diary, 28 June 1916, *op. cit.*

184. XIII Corps CRA, war diary, 30 June 1916, *op. cit.*

185. Prior, Robin, and Wilson, Trevor, *The Somme* (Sydney: University of New South Wales Press, 2005), p. 64.

186. *ibid.*

187. *ibid.*, pp. 64–5.

188. *ibid.*, p. 65.

189. *ibid.*

190. Prior, Robin, and Wilson, Trevor, *Command on the Western Front: The Military Career of Sir Henry Rawlinson 1914–1918* (Barnsley: Pen & Sword, 2004), p. 174.

191. Haig, Douglas, diary, 30 June 1916, NAUK, WO/256/10.

192. De Lisle, Beauvoir, letter, 12 November 1929, NAUK, CAB/45/133; de Lisle is in part also referring to the timing of the mine blast at Hawthorn Ridge and the artillery. He conveyed this to Rawlinson prior to battle.

193. X Corps CRA, war diary, 28 June 1916, *op. cit.*

194. *ibid.*, 30 June.

195. XIII Corps CRA, war diary, 26 June 1916, *op. cit.*

196. XIII Corps CRA, war diary, 27 June 1916, *op. cit.*

197. XV Corps CRA, war diary, 28 June 1916, *op. cit.*

198. *ibid.*, 30 June 1916.

199. VII Corps CRA, war diary, 28 June 1916, *op. cit.*

200. *ibid.*, 25 June 1916.

201. VIII Corps CRA, war diary, 29 June 1916, *op. cit.*

202. III Corps CRA, war diary, 29 June 1916, *op. cit.*

203. III Corps CRA messages dated 25, 26 and 28 June 1916, in III Corps CRA, war diary, June 1916, *op. cit.*

204. Wyrall, Everard, *The History of the 19th Division 1914–1918* (London: Edward Arnold, 1932), p. 35.

205. Holtz, p. 33; Gerster, *RIR119*, p 51; Reymann, p. 90; Vischer (1921), pp. 32–5; *SS460*, *op. cit.*

206. Sheldon, *Somme*, p. 133.

207. Soden, pp. 106–8.

208. Vischer (1917), p. 9.

209. Prior and Wilson, *Somme*, p. 66.

210. *ibid.*

211. *ibid.*

212. *ibid.*

213. *ibid.*, p. 67.

214. *ibid.*

215. Charteris, Brigadier-General John, *At G.H.Q.* (London: Cassell, 1931), p. 149.

216. *ibid.*, pp. 149–50.

217. *ibid.*, p. 149.

218. Baumgartner, p. 63; Whitehead, Ralph, *The Other Side of the Wire, Vol. 1: The Battle of the Somme. With the German XIV Reserve Corps, September 1914–June 1916* (Solihull: Helion, 2010), p. 436; Holtz, p. 33.

219. Holtz, p. 33.

220. Sheldon, *Somme*, p. 134.

221. Vischer (1921), pp. 99–100.
222. Gerster, *Die Schwaben*, pp. 102–3, 106.
223. Holtz, p. 33.
224. Gerster, *Die Schwaben*, p. 107.
225. Reymann, p. 91.
226. Whitehead, *Vol. 2*, p. 252.
227. Soden, p. 108; Gerster, *Die Schwaben*, p. 106; Stosch, Albrecht von, *Somme-Nord, I Teil: Die Brennpunkte der Schlacht im Juli 1916* (Berlin: Gerhard Stalling, 1927), p. 16; Vischer (1917), p. 12.
228. Reymann, p. 88.
229. *ibid.*, p. 91.
230. Charteris, pp. 149–50.
231. Gerster, *RIR119*, p. 50.
232. Lewis, *Sagittarius*, p. 68.
233. Prior and Wilson, *Command*, p. 172.
234. Edmonds, pp. 300–1, 460.
235. 'Ammunition expenditure,' Fourth Army, Battle of the Somme: Summary Operations 24–30 June 1916, NAUK, WO/158/327.
236. McDiarmid, J.I.A., letter, undated, NAUK, CAB/45/136.
237. *ibid.*
238. Prior and Wilson, *Command*, p. 172.
239. VIII Corps CRA, war diary, 26 June 1916, *op. cit.*; VIII Corps CHA, war diary, 30 June 1916, NAUK, WO/95/825; X CHA, reports 24–30.6; X Corps CHA, reports 26–27 June 1916, in X Corps CHA, war diary, June 1916, *op. cit.*; VII Corps CRA, war diary, 29 June 1916, *op. cit.*
240. Prior and Wilson, *Command*, p. 173.
241. *ibid.*
242. Dobbie, William, letter, 31 October 1929, NAUK, CAB/45/133.
243. Jones, H.A., *The War in the Air: Being the Story of the Part Played in the Great War by the Royal Air Force, Vol. 2* (Oxford: Clarendon Press, 1928), p. 208; see also Fourth Army, Battle of the Somme: Summary Operations 24–30 June, *op. cit.*
244. Ware, *op. cit.*
245. Fourth Army, Battle of the Somme: Summary Operations 24–30 June 1916, *op. cit.*
246. VII Corps CHA, war diary, 24–30 June 1916, NAUK, WO/95/813; VIII Corps CRA war diary, 24 and 27 June 1916, *op. cit.*; VIII Corps CHA, war diary, 29 June 1916, *op. cit.*; Hunter-Weston papers, letter, 29 June 1916, *op. cit.*; X Corps CRA, war diary, 25–28 June 1916, *op. cit.*; XIII Corps CRA, war diary, 27 June 1916, *op. cit.*
247. Jones, *War in the Air*, p. 208.
248. XV Corps CHA, war diary, 26 June 1916, NAUK, WO/95/926.
249. *ibid.*; see also Jones, J.H.H., letter, undated, NAUK, CAB/45/135; Hogg, Charles, letter, 6 November 1929, NAUK, CAB/45/134.
250. Jenour, *op. cit.*
251. III Corps CRA, war diary, 27 & 29 June 1916, *op. cit.*
252. Gerster, *RIR119*, p. 50; Gerster, *Die Schwaben*, p. 98; Stosch, p. 15; Moos, Ernst, *Das Württembergische Reserve.-Feld-Artillerie-Regiment Nr. 27 im Weltkrieg 1916–1918* (Stuttgart: Belser, 1925), pp. 1–5; Klaus, Max, *Das Württembergische Reserve-Feldartillerie-Regiment Nr. 26 im Weltkrieg 1914–1918* (Stuttgart: Christian Belser, 1929), pp. 45–52; Reymann, p. 89; Baumgartner, p. 67; Langford, p. 26; Holtz, p. 33.
253. Klaus, p. 47.
254. Moos, p. 4.
255. Stosch, p. 15.
256. Gerster, *Die Schwaben*, p. 104.
257. *ibid.*, p. 99.
258. Stosch, pp. 16–17.
259. Klaus, p. 48.
260. Gerster, *Die Schwaben*, p. 104.
261. Moos, p. 2.
262. Müller-Loebnitz, p. 214.
263. Büsing, Georg, *Das Reserve-Feldartillerie-Regiment Nr. 20 im Weltkrieg 1914–18* (Hannover: Göhmann, 1932), unpaginated translation dated 2014 supplied by Bill MacCormick.
264. Moos, p. 3; Gerster, *Die Schwaben*, p. 104.
265. See Chapter 3.
266. Stosch, p. 62; the division had 10 field batteries and 13 heavy batteries.
267. *ibid.*; see also Fiedel, p. 121.
268. Edmonds, p. 344; see also Stosch, p. 62; Langford, p. 24.
269. Klaus, pp. 51–2.
270. Sheldon, *Somme*, p. 128.
271. Haig, diary, 30 June 1916, *op. cit.*
272. *ibid.*
273. Haig, diary, 29 June 1916, *op. cit.*
274. *ibid.*, p. 194.
275. Hunter-Weston, letter, 30 June 1916, *op. cit.*
276. Haig, diary, 29 June 1916, *op. cit.*
277. Pulteney, William, letter, 17 May 1930, NAUK, CAB/45/136.
278. MacDonald, Alan, *Pro Patria Mori: 56th (1st London) Division at Gommecourt, 1st July 1916* (Cornwall: Exposure Press, 2006), p. 205

279. Haig, diary, 30 June 1916, *op. cit.*
280. *ibid.*
281. Charteris, p. 150.
282. *Douglas Haig: War Diaries and Letters 1914–1918*, ed. Gary Sheffield and John Bourne (London: Weidenfeld & Nicolson, 2005), p. 195.
283. *ibid.*
284. Rawlinson, diary, 30 June 1916, *op. cit.*
285. Falkenhayn, Erich von, *General Headquarters 1914–1916 and its Critical Decisions* (London: Hutchinson, 1919), p. 263; see also Kuhl, Hermann von, *Der Weltkrieg 1914–1918, Band I* (Berlin: Wilhelm Kolk, 1929), p. 491.
286. Sheldon, *Somme*, p. 128.
287. *ibid.*; see also Reichsarchiv, *Der Weltkrieg 1914 bis 1918: Die Operationen des Jahres 1916* (Berlin: Mittler & Sohn, 1936), p. 346.
288. *SS553: Experience of the German 1st Army in the Somme Battle, 24 June to 26 November 1916, First Army H.Q.* (30 January 1917, translated 3 May 1917); this formation was titled Second Army on 1 July, but from 19 July 1916 became First Army.
289. *ibid.*, pp. 5–14.
290. Stein, Hermann von, *A War Minister And His Work: Reminiscences of 1914–1918* (London: Skeffington & Son, Ltd, 1920), p. 108.
291. 'Bericht des Kommandierenden Generals XIV. Reserve-Korps, Generalleutnant v. Stein,' by Hermann von Stein, in *Der 180er: Festnummer: zum Treffen der 26. Reserve-Division vom 4. Bis 6. Juli 1936 in Stuttgart*, 4 July 1936.
292. Soden, p 109.
293. *ibid.*, p. 108.
294. 'Bericht des Kommandierenden,' *op. cit.*
295. Kelly, *Subaltern's Odyssey*, p. 91.
296. Crozier, Frank, *Brass Hat in No Man's Land* (London: Jonathan Cape, 1930), p. 98.
297. Heath, *op. cit.*
298. Taylor, James, *The 1st Royal Irish Rifles in the Great War* (Dublin: Four Courts Press, 2002), p. 77.
299. Liveing, p. 30.
300. Laporte, *op. cit.*

Chapter 5: Hunter Bunter's Folly

1. Hurst, Steve, *The Public Schools Battalion in the Great War* (Barnsley: Pen & Sword, 2007), p. 194.
2. Gerster, Matthaus, *Die Württembergische Reserve-Infanterie-Regiment Nr. 119 im Weltkrieg 1914–1918* (Stuttgart: Chr. Belsersche Verlagsbuchhandlung, 1920), p. 52.
3. Malins, Geoffrey, *How I Filmed the War* (London: Imperial War Museum, 1993), pp. 162–3.
4. Cook, Arthur, 'Fit Only for Devils to Live', in *The Great War: I Was There!*, ed. Sir John Hammerton, part 17 (London: Amalgamated Press, undated), p. 674.
5. Riegel, Lt. d. Res., *Maschinengewehr-Scharffschutzen im Felde 1914–1918: MG.SS.-Abt. 54* (Beuchdruckerei H. Kuhn, Schwenningen am Neckar, undated), p. 3.
6. Ryan, John, *Colonial Commerce No. 5*, Newfoundland, undated, p. 12; Shea, Edmund, *Daily Star*, Newfoundland, 25 September 1916; letter from Jim, *Evening Telegram*, Newfoundland, 11 August 1916.
7. Jones, Simon, *Underground Warfare 1914–1918* (Barnsley: Pen & Sword, 2010), p. 120.
8. *Yorkshire Evening Post*, 19 March 1940.
9. Hunter-Weston, Aylmer, letter, 30 June 1916, Hunter-Weston Papers, BL.
10. Carlyon, Les, *Gallipoli* (London: Bantam Books, 2003), p. 121.
11. Robbins, Simon, *British Generalship on the Western Front 1914–18* (Abingdon, France Cass, 2005), p. 14, 45, 74.
12. Packe, Edward, diary, 23 February 1918, gwydir.demon.co.uk/diaries/diary1918.htm; Robbins, p. 16.
13. Dixon, Norman, *On the Psychology of Military Incompetence* (London: Pimlico, 1994), pp. 256–80; Robbins, p. 45.
14. Carlyon, p. 121.
15. 'Fourth Army — Feeding Strength on 1st July 1916,' Rawlinson Papers 1/6, Churchill Archive; totals were 4th Division 23,373 (all ranks), 29th Division 22,613, 31st Division 22,613, 48th Division 17,348, VIII Corps' troops 10,261 and attached French soldiers 587. The corps' into-battle estimate is derived from the 29th's known attack strength of 8408 ('Strength of Battalions in Attack,' 29th Division, war diary, July 1916, NAUK, WO/95/2280/4), plus 22 other battalions directly involved at an average attack strength of 761 all ranks each (see Chapter 11).
16. Sheldon, Jack, *The German Army on the Somme 1914–1916* (Barnsley: Pen & Sword, 2005), p. 141.
17. Schwarz, Dr Richard, 'Truppen-Sanitatsdienst wahrend der Sommeschlacht,' in *Treffen der 26.R.D.*

am 5. Juli 1936, ed. Matthaus Gerster (Stuttgart: unknown publisher, 1936), p. 35.

18. Holtz, Georg von, *Das Württembg. Res. Inft. Regt. No. 121 im Weltkrieg 1914–1918* (Stuttgart: Chr. Belsersche Verlagsbuchhandlung, 1921), p. 34.

19. Soden, Franz von, *Die 26. (Württembergische) Reserve-Division im Weltkreg 1914–1918* (Stuttgart: Bergers Literarisches Buro und Verlagsanstalt, 1939), p. 109.

20. *ibid.*, pp. 102–3, 109; Holtz, p. 34; Burrows, John, *The Essex Regiment: 2nd Battalion* (Southend-on-Sea: John H. Burrows & Sons, 1928), p. 143.

21. Burrows, *2nd Essex*, pp. 142–3.

22. 'An Appreciation of Probable German Defences', 4 April 1916, Hunter-Weston Papers, BL.

23. VIII Corps Heavy Artillery (CHA), war diary, 24–30 June 1916, NAUK, WO/95/825; VIII Corps Royal Artillery's (CRA) war diary for 24–30 June 1916, NAUK, WO/95/824; the figure 363,000 has been estimated as 20% of the total Fourth Army field artillery shells fired 24–30 June. See Edmonds, Sir James, *Military Operations France and Belgium, 1916, Vol. 1* (London: Imperial War Museum, 1992), p. 302.

24. VIII CHA, war diary, 1 July 1916; VIII CRA, war diary, 1 July 1916; See also Edmonds, p. 302.

25. Edmonds, p. 427; this ratio is marginally more favourable than that for the whole of Fourth Army. See Edmonds, p. 301.

26. Macdonald, Andrew, *Passchendaele: The Anatomy of a Tragedy* (Auckland: Harper Collins, 2013), p. 233.

27. Howard, Charles, letter, 6 November 1929, NAUK, CAB/45/134.

28. Collis-Browne, John, letter, 12 November 1929, NAUK, CAB/45/132.

29. Charteris, Brigadier-General John, *At G.H.Q.*, (London: Cassell, 1931), p. 150.

30. *ibid.*

31. Edmonds, p. 430.

32. *ibid.*, p. 430; howitzers firing on the front line would step their fire back to the front-line reserve trench. Those firing on the front-line support trench would lift their fire to front-line reserve trench at 7.25 a.m.

33. *ibid.*, pp. 430–1.

34. *ibid.*, p. 431; no copy of these orders is known to have survived.

35. Jones, *Underground*, p. 118.

36. Edmonds, p. 429.

37. Edmonds, p. 430.

38. Jones, *Underground*, p. 118; Hunter-Weston knew full well that mine debris came to earth in a matter of seconds, rather than minutes, a fact that might have dispelled de Lisle's alleged concerns; see: Hunter-Weston, letter, 20 May 1916, *op. cit.*

39. Jones, p. 118.

40. Edmonds, p. 430; Jones, *Underground*, p. 118; the time was approved by GHQ. Numerous battle participants cited the timing of the mine blast as the reason for the disaster that befell VIII Corps, see NAUK, CAB/45/132–138.

41. Jones, *Underground*, p. 118.

42. Gibbon, John, letter, February 1930, NAUK, CAB/45/132.

43. *ibid.*

44. *ibid.*

45. Gerster, Matthaus, *Die Schwaben an der Ancre: aus den Kampfen der 26. Reserve-Division* (Heilbronn: Eugen Salzer, 1918), p. 109; Stosch, Albrecht von, *Somme-Nord, I Teil: Der Brennpunkte der Schlacht im Juli 1916* (Oldenburg: Gerhard Stalling, 1927), p. 32.

46. Beck, Adolf, 'Der Kampf am Heidenkopf,' in *Treffen der 26.R.D.*, ed. Gerster, p. 17.

47. Gerster, *Die Schwaben*, p. 109.

48. Sheen, John, *Durham Pals: 18th, 19th, & 22nd (Service) Battalions of the Durham Light Infantry* (Barnsley: Pen & Sword, 2006), p. 99.

49. Gerster, *Die Schwaben*, p. 110.

50. *ibid.*

51. *ibid.*, p. 113.

52. *ibid.*, p. 110.

53. *ibid.*

54. 31st Division Report on Operations, 1 July 1916, Fourth Army, Battle of the Somme: Summary Operations, NAUK, WO/158/327; Prior, Robin, and Wilson, Trevor, *The Somme* (Sydney: University of New South Wales Press, 2005), p. 80.

55. Soden, p. 102.

56. See Chapter 3 for more details; 52nd Infantry Division had an estimated 106 guns, of which about one-third were supporting Serre.

57. Klaus, Max, *Das Württembergische Reserve-Feldartillerie-Regiment Nr. 26 im Weltkrieg 1914–1918* (Stuttgart: Chr. Belsersche Verlagsbuchhandlung 1929), pp. 48–52; available data as to the number of surviving guns is inconclusive.

58. *ibid.*

59. Rees, Hubert, letter, 14 November 1929, NAUK, CAB/45/137.

60. Report on the Operations of the 29th Division, 29th Division, war diary, July 1916, NAUK, WO/95/2280/4.
61. *History of the Corps of Royal Engineers* (London: Institute of Royal Engineers, 1951), ed. H.L. Prichard, pp. 269–70.
62. 1/2nd Monmouths, war diary, 1 July 1916, NAUK, WO/95/2295/1.
63. 1st Lancashire Fusiliers, war diary, 1 July 1916, NAUK, WO/95/2300.
64. 2nd Royal Fusiliers, war diary, 1 July 1916, NAUK, WO/95/2301/3; O'Neill, Herbert, *The Royal Fusiliers in the Great War* (London: Heinemann, 1922), p. 110.
65. 16th Middlesex, war diary, 1 July 1916, NAUK, WO/95/2302/2; 1st Royal Dublin Fusiliers, war diary, 1 July 1916, NAUK, WO/95/2301/1.
66. 2nd South Wales Borderers, war diary, 1 July 1916, NAUK, WO/95/2304/2.
67. *ibid.*
68. 1st Borders, war diary, 1 July 1916, NAUK, WO/95/2305/1.
69. 1st Royal Inniskilling Fusiliers, war diary, 1 July 1916, NAUK, WO/95/2305/2.
70. *ibid.*; Edmonds, p. 433; the battalion war diary does not state that its men got into the German trench, but notes some reached the German wire.
71. 1st King's Own Scottish Borderers, war diary, 1 July 1916, NAUK, WO/95/2304/1; Edmonds, pp. 433–4.
72. Edmonds, p. 434.
73. Gillon, Stair, *The K.O.S.B. in the Great War* (London: Thomas Nelson & Sons, 1930), p. 180.
74. 1st Borders, war diary, *op. cit.*
75. 2nd South Wales Borderers, war diary, *op. cit.*; 1st Royal Dublin Fusiliers, war diary, *op. cit.*; 2nd Royal Fusiliers, war diary, *op. cit.*; 1st King's Own Scottish Borderers, war diary, *op. cit.*; 1st Borders, war diary, *op. cit.*; 1st Royal Inniskilling Fusiliers, war diary, *op. cit.*
76. Osborn, George, diary, 28 June 1916, South Wales Borderers (SWB) Museum.
77. *ibid.*, 1 July 1916.
78. *ibid*
79. Hurst, pp. 195–6.
80. Smith, Peter, letter, undated, ULLC/WW1/MID01.
81. *ibid.*
82. Fraser, A.T., interview, ULLC/WW1/GS/0585.
83. Gerster, *RIR119*, p. 55.
84. Packe, diary, 1 July 1916.
85. *Burnley Express*, 12 August 1916.
86. 11th Brigade Diagram of Formation for 1st Objective, 4th Division, war diary, July 1916, NAUK, WO/95/1445/1.
87. 11th Brigade Diagram of Formation for 2nd Objective, 4th Division, war diary, *op. cit.*; 10th Brigade Diagram of Formation, 4th Division, war diary, *op. cit.*; 12th Brigade Diagram of Formation, 4th Division, war diary, *op. cit.*
88. Prichard, p. 270.
89. *Burnley Express, op. cit.*
90. Somerville, D.H.S., letter, 4 April 1930, NAUK, CAB/45/137; Adams, Capt D.R., letter, 26 March 1930, NAUK, CAB/45/132.
91. 4th Division Report on Operations, 1 July 1916, Fourth Army, Battle of the Somme: Summary Operations, NAUK, WO/158/327; this document states three platoons of 1st East Lancashires entered, but the accepted number is about 40 men.
92. 1st East Lancashires, war diary, 1 July 1916, NAUK, WO/95/1498/1.
93. 1st Hampshires, war diary, 1 July 1916, NAUK, WO/95/1495/3; 4th Division Report on Operations, *op. cit.*
94. 4th Division Report on Operations, *op. cit.*
95. 1/6th Royal Warwicks, war diary, 1 July 1916, NAUK, WO/95/2755/2.
96. 1/8th Royal Warwicks, war diary, 1 July 1916, NAUK, WO/95/2756/2.
97. 4th Division Report on Operations, *op. cit.*
98. Adams, *op. cit.*
99. *ibid.*
100. 'Das RIR. 121 am Heidenkopf in der Sommeschlacht,' by Friedrich Stutz in *Der 180er*, 1 July 1938; this Russian Sap was better known as 'Cat Street.' Another sap nearby was known as 'Beet Street', but some sources wrongly label it 'Rat Street'.
101. Levine, Joshua, *Forgotten Voices of the Somme* (London: Ebury Publishing, 2009), p. 114.
102. 1st Rifle Brigade, war diary, 1 July 1916, NAUK, WO/95/1496/3.
103. Lewis, Fred, ULLC/WW1/01/L/8.
104. *ibid.*
105. Whitehead, Ralph, *The Other Side of the Wire, Vol. 2: The Battle of the Somme. With the German XIV Reserve Corps, 1 July 1916*, (Solihull: Helion, 2013), p. 71.
106. Kerr, John, Prisoner of War Statement, NAUK, WO/161/100/16.
107. Holtz, p. 34.

108. www.voicesofwarandpeace.org/
portfolio/fred-andrews/; last accessed
7 August 2015.
109. *ibid.*
110. Adams, *op. cit.*; 2nd Lancashire
Fusiliers, war diary, 1 July 1916, NAUK,
WO/95/1507/1; Edmonds, p. 441.
111. Stosch, p. 29.
112. *ibid.*
113. Sheldon, Jack, *The Germans at Beaumont
Hamel* (Barnsley: Pen & Sword, 2006),
p. 84; Sheldon, *Somme*, pp. 143–4.
114. 31st Division Report on Operations,
op. cit.
115. Narrative of the Operations Carried Out
by the 31st Division on 1 July 1916, 31st
Division, war diary, July 1916, NAUK,
WO/95/2341/3.
116. *ibid.*; Neill, R.B., letter, 6 December 1929,
NAUK, CAB/45/132; Edmonds, p. 442.
117. Prichard, p. 270; Edmonds, p. 429.
118. Edmonds, p. 452.
119. Edmonds, p. 443; 'Narrative of the
Operations Carried Out by the 31st
Division,' 31st Division, *op. cit.*; 15th
West Yorkshires, war diary, 1 July 1916,
NAUK, WO/95/2361/3.
120. Edmonds, p. 443.
121. 18th West Yorkshires, war diary, 1 July
1916, NAUK, WO/95/2362/2.
122. 11th East Lancashires, war diary, 1 July
1916, NAUK, WO/95/2366/1.
123. 12th York & Lancasters, war diary, 1 July
1916, NAUK, WO/95/2365/1.
124. *ibid.*
125. Edmonds, p. 443.
126. 13th York & Lancasters, war diary, 1 July
1916, NAUK, WO/95/2365/2.
127. 14th York & Lancasters, war diary, 1 July
1916, NAUK, WO/95/2365/3.
128. Edmonds, p. 444.
129. *ibid.*
130. 12th York & Lancasters, war diary,
op. cit.
131. 18th West Yorkshires, war diary, *op. cit.*
132. Oldfield, Paul, and Gibson, Ralph,
*Sheffield City Battalion: The 12th
(Service) Battalion York & Lancaster
Regiment* (Barnsley: Pen & Sword, 2010),
p. 164.
133. *ibid.*, p. 161.
134. *ibid.*, p. 166.
135. Howard, Alfred, ULLC/WW1/MID01.
136. *ibid.*
137. Cooksey, Jon, *Barnsley Pals: The 13th
& 14th Battalions, York & Lancaster
Regiment* (Barnsley: Pen & Sword, 2008),
p. 205.
138. Sheen, pp. 99–100.
139. *ibid.*, p. 98.
140. Cooksey, p. 223.
141. Durrant, Arthur, ULLC/WW1/
WF01/D/19.
142. Lushington, Franklin, *The Gambardier:
Giving Some Account of the Heavy and
Siege Artillery in France, 1914–1918*
(London: Ernest Benn, 1930), p. 101.
143. Sheen, p. 98.
144. Crook, Wilfred, ULLC/WW1/MID01.
145. *Evening Telegram*, Newfoundland,
22 July 1916.
146. Middlebrook, Martin, *The First Day on
the Somme* (London: Penguin Books,
1984), p. 157.
147. *ibid.*, p. 204.
148. Lushington, p. 101.
149. Hunter-Weston, letter, 1 July 1916,
op. cit.
150. 'Narrative of Operations of 1st July 1916,'
VIII Corps GS, war diary, July 1916,
NAUK, WO/95/820.
151. Gillon, p. 180.
152. Edmonds, p. 440.
153. Carden Roe, William, private
papers, Imperial War Museum,
Documents.7153.
154. 10th Brigade Diagram of Formation, 4th
Division, war diary, *op. cit.*
155. Edmonds, p. 440; 2nd Duke of
Wellington's, war diary, 1 July 1916,
NAUK, WO/95/1508/1; 12th Brigade
Diagram of Formation, 4th Division,
war diary, *op. cit.*
156. 2nd Royal Dublin Fusiliers, war diary, 1
July 1916, NAUK, WO/95/1481/4.
157. *ibid.*
158. 2nd Seaforth Highlanders, war diary,
1 July 1916, NAUK, WO/95/1483/5.
159. *ibid.*
160. 4th Division Report on Operations,
op. cit.; 2nd Essex, war diary, 1 July
1916, NAUK, WO/95/1505/1; 1st King's
Own, war diary, 1 July 1916, NAUK,
WO/95/1506/1.
161. 2nd Duke of Wellington's, war diary,
op. cit.; Edmonds, p. 440.
162. 4th Division Report on Operations,
op. cit.
163. 2nd Duke of Wellington's, war diary,
op. cit.; Edmonds, p. 446; 4th Division
Report on Operations, *op. cit.*
164. Riegel, p. 3.
165. *ibid.*
166. Hart, Peter, *The Somme* (London:
Weidenfeld & Nicholson, 2005), p. 144.
167. Killed: Lieutenant-Colonels
R.C. Pierce, 1st Royal Inniskilling
Fusiliers, D. Wood, 1st Rifle Brigade,
J.A. Thicknesse, 1st Somerset Light
Infantry, the Honourable L.C.W. Palk,

1st Hampshires, G.S. Guyon, 16th West Yorkshires, M.N. Kennard, 18th West Yorkshires, E.A. Innes, 1/8th Royal Warwick, and Major J.N. Bromilow, 1st King's Own; died of wounds: Major L.P. Walsh, 2nd Royal Dublin Fusiliers; Wounded: Lieutenant-Colonels A.V. Johnson, 2nd Royal Fusiliers, A.J. Ellis, 1st Borders, J.E. Green, 1st East Lancashires, Sir G. Stirling, 2nd Essex, A.W. Rickman, 11th East Lancashires, W. Franklin, 1/6th Royal Warwicks, Cyril Howkins, Royal Army Medical Corps, and Majors A. Plackett, 12th York & Lancaster, and R.B. Neill, 15th West Yorkshires.

168. 29th Division, war diary, 1 July 1916, NAUK, WO/95/2280/4; Burrows, John, *The Essex Regiment: 1st Battalion* (Southend-on-Sea: John H. Burrows & Sons, 1923), p. 208.

169. Spencer-Smith, Richard, letter, 17 January 1930, NAUK, CAB/45/137.

170. Day, Walter, interview, 1977, Memorial University of Newfoundland, Extension Service, L-2260.

171. Edmonds, p. 436.

172. *Evening Telegram*, Newfoundland, 11 August 1916.

173. Edmonds, p. 436 and addenda and corrigenda; Burrows, 1st Essex, p. 208; 1st Essex, war diary, 1 July 1916, NAUK, WO/95/2309/1.

174. Burrows, *1st Essex*, p. 208.

175. 29th Division, war diary, *ibid.*

176. 'Report on Operations of the VIII Corps on the 1st July, 1916,' Fourth Army, Battle of the Somme: Summary Operations, NAUK, WO/158/327; VIII Corps GS, war diary, 1 July 1916, *op. cit.*; Edmonds, p. 445; a variety of times are given for this order, but all are between 10.15 a.m. and 10.25 a.m.

177. 1st Royal Warwicks, war diary, 1 July 1916, NAUK, WO/95/1484/3; 1st Royal Irish Fusiliers, war diary, 1 July 1916, NAUK, WO/95/1482/1; Edmonds, p. 447.

178. Edmonds, p. 447.

179. *ibid.*

180. Hunter-Weston, letter, 1 July 1916, *op. cit.*

181. Edmonds, p. 448.

182. *ibid.*

183. 31st Division, war diary, 1 July, 1916, NAUK, WO/95/2341.

184. *ibid.*

185. Edmonds, p. 448.

186. *ibid.,* p. 449

187. *ibid.*

188. Holtz, pp. 33–4; Gerster, *RIR119*, pp. 51–4; Soden, p. 110; Sheldon, *Somme*, p. 145.

189. Stosch, p. 29.

190. *SS490: The Principles of Trench Warfare as Laid Down in the XIV Reserve Corps* (19 May 1916, translated 13 October 1916).

191. O'Neill, Herbert, *The Royal Fusiliers in the Great War* (London: Heinemann, 1922), p. 110.

192. Hurst, p. 187.

193. Berkeley, Reginald, *The History of the Rifle Brigade in the War of 1914–1918* (London: The Rifle Brigade Club, 1927), p. 166.

194. *ibid.*, p. 168; Burrow, *2nd Essex,* pp. 145–6.

195. Stosch, p. 29.

196. Berkeley, p. 168.

197. Holtz, p. 34.

198. Berkeley, p. 168.

199. Burrows, *2nd Essex*, p. 146; Holtz, p. 34.

200. Cook, p. 679.

201. 'Berichtet über den Gegestoss am Heidenkopf,' Emil Geiger, in *Der 180er*, 1 July 1938.

202. *ibid.*

203. 'An der Somme,' by Friedrich Conzelmann, in *Der 180er*, 1 November 1936.

204. Beck in *Treffen der 26.R.D.,* ed. Gerster, p. 19.

205. Holtz, p. 34.

206. *ibid.*, p. 35.

207. Hurst, p. 194.

208. Oldfield and Gibson, p. 168.

209. Sheldon, *Somme*, p. 142.

210. Lais, Otto, *Die Schlacht an der Somme 1916* (Karlsruhe: G. Braun, 1940), pp. 16–8.

211. *ibid.*

212. *ibid.*

213. Hurst, pp. 173–4.

214. *ibid.*, p. 174.

215. *ibid.*, p. 175.

216. *ibid.*

217. *ibid.*

218. *ibid.*, p. 196.

219. Malins, p. 164.

220. *ibid.*, p. 163.

221. Slater, William, ULLC/WW1/MID01.

222. *ibid.*

223. Beck in *Treffen der 26.R.D.*, ed. Gerster, p. 17.

224. *ibid.*, p. 18.

225. *ibid.*

226. *ibid.*

227. Lind, Francis, *The Letters of Mayo Lind: Newfoundland's Unofficial War*

Correspondent 1914–16 (St John's: Killick Press, 2001), p 147.
228. *ibid.*, pp. 147–55.
229. *ibid.*, p. 144.
230. *Twillingate Sun*, Newfoundland, 21 October 1916.
231. Hunter-Weston, '*Message to all Officers, NCOs and Men of VIII Army Corps,*' 4 July 1916, VIII Corps GS, war diary, July 1916, NAUK, WO/95/820.
232. Jones, *Underground*, p. 120; Hunter-Weston's message and other papers imply there was some diversionary quality to the attack, while de Lisle says he was 'in ignorance' that the main attack was south of the Ancre. Both are highly implausible.
233. Hunter-Weston, letter, 3 July 1916.
234. *ibid.*
235. Hunter-Weston, '*Message to all Officers,*' *op. cit.*
236. Edmonds, pp. 436–48.
237. 1/8th Royal Warwicks, war diary, July 1916 appendices, NAUK, WO/95/2756.

Chapter 6: Loitering without Intent
1. Middlebrook, Martin, *The First Day on the Somme* (London: Penguin Books, 1984), pp. 241–2.
2. Unknown correspondent, letter, 26 May 1926, Morland Papers, Imperial War Museum.
3. Morland, Thomas, letter, 8 July 1916, Morland Papers, Imperial War Museum.
4. Morland, letter, 10 July 1916.
5. Morland, Thomas, obituary, *The Times*, 25 May 1925.
6. *ibid.*
7. *ibid.*
8. Haig, Douglas, diary, 22 May 1917, NAUK, WO/256/18.
9. Girdwood, Austin, letter, 30 June 1930, NAUK, CAB/45/134.
10. Stosch, Albrecht von, *Somme-Nord, I Teil: Die Brennpunkte der Schlacht im Juli 1916* (Berlin: Gerhard Stalling, 1927), p. 39.
11. *ibid.*; Gerster, Matthaus, *Die Schwaben and der Ancre* (Heilbronn: Eugen Salzer, 1918), p. 117; Sheldon, Jack, *The Germans at Thiepval* (Barnsley: Pen & Sword, 2006), p. 130; Sheldon, Jack, *The German Army on the Somme 1914–1916* (Barnsley: Pen & Sword, 2005), p. 141; Schwarz, Dr Richard, 'Truppen-Sanitatsdienst wahrend der Sommeschlacht,' in *Treffen der 26.R.D. am 5. Juli 1936*, ed. Matthaus Gerster (Stuttgart: unknown publisher, 1936), p. 35; Holtz, Georg von, *Das*

Württembg. Res. Inft. Regt. No. 121 im Weltkrieg 1914–1918 (Stuttgart: Chr. Belsersche Verlagsbuchhandlung, 1921), p. 34; Soden, Franz von, *Die 26. (Württembergische) Reserve-Division im Weltkrieg 1914–1918* (Stuttgart: Bergers Literarisches Büro, 1939), pp. 102–3, 109.
12. Operation Order No. 27, 13 June 1916, X Corps GS, war diary, June 1916, NAUK, WO/95/850.
13. Morland, letter, 27 June 1916.
14. 'Fourth Army — Feeding Strength on 1st July 1916,' Rawlinson Papers 1/6, Churchill Archive; totals were 25th Division 21,444 (all ranks), 32nd Division 23,358, 36th Division 22,000, 49th Division 19,987, X Corps' troops 6417 and attached French soldiers 590. The corps' into-battle estimate is calculated from the combined attack strength of 3805 for five battalions (see Chapter 11 notes for details), plus 23 other battalions directly involved at an average attack strength of 761 all ranks each (see Chapter 11).
15. Edmonds, pp. 400–4.
16. Morland, letter, 4 July 1916; see also Yatman, Clement, letter, 23 May 1930, NAUK, CAB/45/132.
17. Edmonds, Sir James, *Military Operations France and Belgium, 1916*, Vol. 1 (London: Imperial War Museum, 1992), p. 398.
18. Operation Orders, No. 1, X Corps CHA, undated, war diary June 1916, NAUK, WO/95/866; X Corps' CHA and CRA war diaries do not tabulate actual daily ammunition usage. Records are fragmentary. Estimate is based on the known guns (Edmonds, p. 398.) and daily ammunition consumption allowed for by the preparatory bombardment. It may vary from the actual. Estimate excludes French guns present (Edmonds, pp. 300–1).
19. *ibid.*
20. Edmonds, p. 398.
21. Gibbs, Alfred, letter, 22 May 1930, NAUK, CAB/45/134.
22. *ibid.*
23. Hart, Peter, *The Somme* (London: Weidenfeld & Nicholson, 2005), p. 152.
24. *ibid.*
25. 32nd Division Report on Operations, 1 July 1916, Fourth Army, Battle of the Somme: Summary Operations, NAUK, WO/158/327.
26. 17th Highland Light Infantry, war diary, 1 July 1916, NAUK, WO/95/2403/3.

27. Jardine, James, letter, 13 June 1930, NAUK, CAB/45/135.
28. 17th Highland Light Infantry, war diary, *op. cit.*; 16th Highland Light Infantry, war diary, 1 July 1916, NAUK, WO/95/2403/2; *History of The Corps of Royal Engineers* (London: Institute of Royal Engineers, 1951), ed. H.L. Prichard, pp. 268–9.
29. 32nd Division Report on Operations, *op. cit.*
30. Abercrombie, Charles, letter, 23 June 1930, NAUK, CAB/45/132.
31. 32nd Division Report on Operations, *op. cit.*; Operation Order No. 37, 96th Brigade, war diary, June 1916, NAUK, WO/95/2395/2; 16th Highland Light Infantry, war diary, *op. cit.*; 2nd King's Own Yorkshire Light Infantry, war diary, 1 July 1916, NAUK, WO/95/2402/1.
32. 2nd King's Own Yorkshire Light Infantry, war diary, *op. cit.*
33. 16th Northumberland Fusiliers, war diary, 1 July 1916, NAUK, WO/95/2398/1; 16th Highland Light Infantry, war diary, *op. cit.*
34. Henderson, Stanley, ULLC/WW1/WF01/H/19.
35. 17th Highland Light Infantry, war diary, *op. cit.*
36. 1st Dorsets, war diary, 1 July 1916, NAUK, WO/95/2392/1.
37. *The Bath Chronicle*, 15 July 1916.
38. *ibid.*
39. Edmonds, p. 409.
40. Ingham, George, letter, 8 July 1916, Fraser Family Collection; Graham, James, letter, 25 June 1930, NAUK, CAB/45/134.
41. *The Cumberland News*, 25 August 1917. The poem's opening lines are: 'We little thought when he left home he would no more return; And he so soon in death would sleep and have us here to mourn.' Its final lines are: 'He left his home for ever in a foreign land to die; Ever remembered by his sorrowing wife and four children.'
42. Graham, *op. cit.*
43. 15th Highland Light Infantry, war diary, 1 July 1916, NAUK, WO/95/2393/2.
44. 32nd Division Report on Operations, *op. cit.*
45. 2nd Manchesters, war diary, 1 July 1916, NAUK, WO/95/2392/2; Shakespear, J., *A Record of the 17th and 32nd Service Battalions Northumberland Fusiliers (N.E.R.) Pioneers 1914–1919* (Newcastle-upon-Tyne: Northumberland Press, 1926), p. 34.
46. *ibid.*
47. Edmonds, p. 410.
48. 32nd Division Report on Operations, *op. cit.*
49. 16th Lancashire Fusiliers, war diary, 1 July 1916, NAUK, WO/95/2397/4.
50. 32nd Division Report on Operations, *op. cit.*
51. Crozier, Frank, *Brass Hat in No Man's Land* (London: Jonathan Cape, 1930), pp. 102–7.
52. 32nd Division Report on Operations, *op. cit.*
53. Henderson, *op. cit.*
54. Abercrombie, *op. cit.*
55. Yatman, Clement, letter, 23 May 1930, NAUK, CAB/45/132.
56. Kuster, Peter, ULLC/WW1/MID01.
57. Middlebrook, p. 157.
58. Hart, *Somme*, p. 159.
59. Brown, Malcolm, *The Imperial War Museum Book of The Somme* (London: Pan Macmillan, 2002), pp. 66–7.
60. Lange, Wilhelm, ULLC/WW1/MID01.
61. Middlebrook, p. 203.
62. Hart, *Somme*, p. 159.
63. *ibid.*, pp. 159–60.
64. Operation Order No. 1, 108th Brigade, war diary, June 1916, NAUK, WO/95/2505/1.
65. Unknown correspondent, letter, 4 May 1930, NAUK, CAB/45/132.
66. McKeever, Sam, transcript of interview with Mrs Elizabeth Wilson, undated, ULLC/WW1/MID01.
67. Whitehead, Ralph, *The Other Side of the Wire Vol. 2: The Battle of the Somme. With the German XIV Reserve Corps, 1 July 1916* (Solihull: Helion, 2013), p. 60.
68. Falls, Cyril, *The History of the 36th (Ulster) Division* (Belfast: M'Caw, Stevenson & Orr, 1922), p. 53; Blacker, Stewart, letter, 20 March 1930, NAUK, CAB/45/132.
69. Falls, p. 53.
70. *ibid.*
71. Blacker, Stewart, letter, 20 March 1930, NAUK, CAB/45/132.
72. 36th Division Report on Operations, 1 July 1916, Fourth Army, Battle of the Somme: Summary Operations, NAUK, WO/158/327.
73. Edmonds, p. 405; Operation Order No. 1, 108th Brigade, *op. cit.*
74. *ibid.*, p. 404; Operation Order No. 1, 108th Brigade, *op. cit.*; Order No. 50, 109th Brigade, war diary, June 1916, NAUK, WO/95/2507/2.
75. Whitehead, *Vol. 2*, *Verlustlisten* disc.

76. Order No. 50, 109th Brigade, war diary, *op. cit.*
77. 14th Royal Irish Rifles, war diary, 1 July 1916, NAUK, WO/95/2511/1; 11th Royal Inniskilling Fusiliers, war diary, 1 July 1916, NAUK, WO/95/2510/5.
78. 36th Division Report on Operations, *op. cit.*
79. *ibid.*
80. Mitchell, Gardiner, *Three Cheers for the Derrys!* (Derry: Yes! Publications, 1991), p. 116.
81. *ibid.*, p. 117.
82. *ibid.*
83. *ibid.*, pp. 117–18.
84. Brownlee, Edward, ULLC/WW1/MID01.
85. Operation Order No. 1, 108th Brigade, *op. cit.*
86. *Dundee Evening Telegraph*, 17 July 1916.
87. *ibid.*
88. Crozier, p. 106.
89. *ibid.*
90. 8th Royal Irish Rifles, war diary, 1 July 1916, NAUK, WO/95/2503/1; 9th Royal Irish Rifles, war diary, 1 July 1916, NAUK, WO/95/2503/2; Edmonds, p. 407.
91. Edmonds, p. 407.
92. *ibid.*
93. Kircher, Felix, ULLC/WW1/MID01.
94. Whitehead, *Vol. 2*, pp. 201–3.
95. Klaus, Max, *Das Württembergische Reserve-Feldartillerie-Regiment Nr. 26 im Weltkrieg 1914–1918* (Stuttgart: Christian Belser, 1929), p. 49.
96. Kircher, *op. cit.*
97. 9th Royal Rifles, war diary, *op. cit.*; 8th Royal Irish Rifles, war diary, *op. cit.*; Edmonds, pp. 407–8.
98. 36th Division Report on Operations, *op. cit.*
99. 9th Royal Irish Rifles, war diary, *op. cit.*
100. *ibid.*; the exact time is unclear, but Corporal Short was last reported alive at 10.40 a.m.; Falls, p. 56.
101. *ibid.*, p. 408.
102. Orr, Philip, *The Road to the Somme: Men of the Ulster Division Tell Their Story* (Belfast: Blackstaff Press, 2008), p. 205.
103. *ibid.*, p. 210.
104. Middlebrook, p. 176.
105. Orr, p. 204.
106. Sheldon, *Somme*, p. 152.
107. Orr, p. 200.
108. Middlebrook, p. 176.
109. *ibid.*, p. 176.
110. Devennie, James, ULLC/WW1/MID01.
111. Mitchell, p. 103.
112. *ibid.*, p. 102.
113. Orr, pp. 201–2.
114. Hart, *Somme*, p. 155.
115. Grange, John, ULLC/WW1/MID01.
116. Megaw, James, ULLC/WW1/MID01.
117. Crozier, p. 111; Orr, pp. 205–6.
118. Mitchell, p. 100.
119. Lloyd, George, ULLC/WW1/MID01.
120. Mitchell, p. 113.
121. *ibid.*, p. 155.
122. *ibid.*, p. 100.
123. Stosch, p. 38.
124. *ibid.*, p. 39.
125. Soden, p. 111.
126. Stosch, p. 39.
127. Moos, Ernst, *Das Württembergische Reserve.-Feld-Artillerie-Regiment Nr. 27 im Weltkrieg 1916–1918* (Stuttgart: Belser, 1925), p. 3; Gerster, *Die Schwaben*, p. 104; Büsing, Georg, *Das Reserve-Feldartillerie-Regiment Nr. 20 im Weltkrieg 1914–18* (Hannover: Göhmann, 1932), unpaginated translation dated 2014 supplied by Bill MacCormick.
128. Crozier, p. 103.
129. *ibid.*, p. 104.
130. Falls, p. 55.
131. 10th Royal Irish Rifles, war diary, 1 July, 1916, NAUK, WO/95/2503/4.
132. 16th Royal Irish Rifles, war diary, 1 July 1916, NAUK, WO/95/2498/2.
133. Edmonds, p. 417.
134. *ibid.*, p. 417.
135. 'Family's shock as Gateshead war hero found 98 years after Battle of the Somme,' accessed from www.chroniclelive.co.uk on 21 March 2015.
136. Gerster, Matthaus, unpublished manuscript about 52nd Reserve Infanterie Brigade; unpaginated translation supplied by Jack Sheldon.
137. *ibid.*
138. Sheldon, *Somme*, p. 150.
139. Edmonds, p. 408.
140. *ibid.*
141. Falls, p. 55.
142. *ibid.*
143. Edmonds, p. 408.
144. *ibid.*, p. 408.
145. *ibid.*
146. Watson, Frank, letter, undated, X Corps GS, war diary, July 1916, NAUK, WO/95/851.
147. Abercrombie, *op. cit.*
148. Cameron, Archibald, letter, 25 May 1930, NAUK, CAB/45/132.
149. Watson, *op. cit.*
150. *ibid.*
151. Allen, Herbert, ULLC/WW1/WF01/A/6.

152. Edmonds, p. 418; see also Liddle, Peter, *The 1916 Battle of the Somme* (Ware: Wordsworth Edition, 2001), p. 56.
153. Falls, p. 55; Edmonds, p. 407.
154. Girdwood, Austin, letter, 30 June 1930, NAUK, CAB/45/134.
155. Edmonds, pp. 417–18.
156. Gerster, *Die Schwaben*, p. 119.
157. Gerster, unpublished manuscript, *op. cit.*
158. Gerster, *Die Schwaben*, p. 119.
159. Edmonds, pp. 417–18.
160. Cameron, *op. cit.*
161. Gerster, *Die Schwaben*, p. 119.
162. Abercrombie, *op. cit.*
163. 32nd Division Report on Operations, *op. cit.*; times for this attack vary between sources.
164. Wyrall, Everard, *The West Yorkshire Regiment in the War 1914–1918, Vol. 1* (London: John Lane The Bodley Head, 1927), p. 220.
165. Edmonds, p. 414; Edmonds notes that Morland believed there were some 2nd Royal Inniskilling Fusiliers near a cemetery a few hundred yards north of Thiepval on the road to Grandcourt. This was highly unlikely to have been the case. See 2nd Royal Inniskilling Fusiliers, war diary, 1 July 1916, NAUK, WO/95/2397/1.
166. 36th Division Report on Operations, *op. cit.*
167. Falls, p. 57.
168. *Narrative of Events Relating to 148th Brigade, 1–8th July 1916*, 148th Brigade, war diary, July 1916, NAUK, WO/95/2803/2.
169. *ibid.*; 1/5th York & Lancasters, war diary, 1 July 1916, NAUK, WO/95/2805/2.
170. Prichard, p. 269.
171. 36th Division Report on Operations, *op. cit.*
172. Falls, p. 57.
173. Orr, p. 222.
174. 146th Brigade, war diary, 1 July 1916, NAUK, WO/95/2792/3.
175. 146th Brigade, war diary, *op. cit.*
176. *ibid.*; 1/5th West Yorkshires, war diary, 1 July 1916, NAUK, WO/95/2794/1. These unit moves should be treated with caution as they are based on frequently confused after-the-fact accounts in various official documents and books. For instance, the regimental history (Wyrall, p. 221) makes a number of significant editorial assumptions that deviate from the brigade report of the day, most notably as regards the number of 1/8th West Yorkshires' companies that moved up to Thiepval Wood versus the number that subsequently ventured across to Schwaben Redoubt.
177. Middlebrook, p. 224.
178. 1/5th West Yorkshires, war diary, *op. cit.*; 1/7th West Yorkshires, war diary, 1 July 1916, NAUK, WO/95/2795/1; 1/8th West Yorkshires, war diary, 1 July 1916, NAUK, WO/95/2795/2.
179. 146th Brigade, war diary, *op. cit.*
180. *ibid.*
181. Sheldon, *Somme*, p. 152.
182. Whitehead, *Vol. 2*, pp. 228–9.
183. *Narrative of Events Relating to 148th Brigade, op. cit.*
184. 36th Division Report on Operations, *op. cit.*
185. *ibid.*
186. *ibid.*
187. Sheldon, *Somme*, p. 155.
188. Orr, p. 225.
189. See casualty figures within chapter.
190. Killed: Lieutenant-Colonels P.W. Machell, 11th Border, and H.C. Bernard, 10th Royal Irish Rifles; wounded: Lieutenant-Colonels D. Laidlaw, 16th Highland Light Infantry, J.V. Shute, 1st Dorsets, and H.O. Wade, 1/6th West Yorkshires.
191. Wyrall, p. 222.
192. Wurmb, Herbert *Ritter* von, *Das K.B. Reserve-Infanterie-Regiment Nr. 8* (Munich: Zeulenroda, 1929), p 78.
193. Whitehead, *Vol. 2, Verlustlisten* disc; these numbers include soldiers initially reported missing but later determined to be dead or prisoner of war.
194. Müller, Paul, Fabeck, Hans von, and Riesel, Richard, *Geschichte des Reserve-Infanterie-Regiments Nr. 99* (Zeulenroda: Sporn, 1936), p. 120.
195. *ibid.*; Whitehead, *Vol. 2*, p. 252; Stosch, Albrecht von, *Somme-Nord, II Teil: Die Brennpunkte der Schlacht im Juli 1916* (Berlin: Gerhard Stalling, 1927), p. 170; RIR99 was in the line 24 June to 4 July, and then again 12–28 July (approximately). Müller, Fabeck and Riesel (p. 120) give RIR99's casualties as 2541 for the period 23 June to 31 July (394 dead, 1081 wounded, 635 missing and 431 sick, mostly gassed). From these can be deducted 472 casualties (Whitehead, *Vol. 2*, p. 252) for the period 23–30 June (97 killed, 319 wounded and 56 missing) and a further 221 unspecified casualties (Stosch, *Teil II*, p. 170) incurred in the nine days to 22 July. It is highly unlikely many of the 431 sick (mostly gassed) occurred on 1 July.

196. Renz, Irina, Krumeich, Gerd, and
     Hirschfeld, Gerhard, *Scorched Earth:
     the Germans on the Somme 1914–1918*
     (Barnsley: Pen & Sword, 2009), p. 75.
197. Klaus, p. 49.
198. Morland, letter, 4 July 1916.
199. Maultsaid, Jim, 'One Man's War: The
     Lost Generation,' in *City Week*, June
     1966, p. 31.
200. *ibid.*
201. *ibid.*
202. *ibid.*, pp. 32–3.
203. *ibid.*, p. 33.
204. Whitehead, *Vol. 2*, p. 213.
205. *ibid.*, p. 209.
206. Sheldon, *Somme*, pp. 156–7.
207. *ibid.*
208. *ibid.*
209. *ibid.*
210. *ibid.*
211. Whitehead, *Vol. 2*, p. 59.
212. Henderson, *op. cit.*
213. George Kane-Smith, via www.ulster-
     scots.com/uploads/1601126274187.PDF.
214. Gliddon, Gerald, *V.C.s of the Somme*
     (Norwich: Gliddon Books, 1991), p. 21.

Chapter 7: Ovillers, La Boisselle or Bust
1. Alexander, Jack, *McCrae's Battalion: The
    Story of the 16th Royal Scots* (Edinburgh:
    Mainstream Publishing, 2003), p. 160.
2. Hart, Peter, *Somme Success: The Royal
    Flying Corps and the Battle of the
    Somme, 1916* (London: Leo Cooper,
    2001), p. 98.
3. Lewis, Cecil, *Sagittarius Rising* (London:
    Greenhill Books, 1998), p. 72.
4. Stearn, Roger T., 'Pulteney, Sir William
    Pulteney (1861–1941)', *Oxford Dictionary
    of National Biography*, Oxford
    University Press, Oct 2008; online edn,
    Sept 2011 [www.oxforddnb.com/view/
    article/96949, accessed 3 April 2014].
5. Bourne, John, *Who's Who in World War
    I* (London: Routledge, 2001), p. 239.
6. Travers, T.H.E., *How the War Was Won:
    Command and Technology in the British
    Army on the Western Front: 1917–1918*
    (London: Routledge, 1992), p. 6.
7. Haig, Douglas, diary, 11 May 1916,
    NAUK, WO/256/10.
8. Stearn, *op. cit.*
9. *Evening Telegraph*, 16 May 1941.
10. 'Fourth Army — Feeding Strength on
    1st July 1916,' Rawlinson Papers 1/6,
    Churchill Archive; totals were 8th
    Division 25,382 (all ranks), 12th
    Division 19,572, 19th Division 17,512,
    34th Division 24,164, III Corps' troops
    7250 and attached French soldiers 580.

The estimate is calculated from the 22
battalions directly involved in the battle,
each with an average attack strength of
761 (all ranks). (See also Chapter 11.)
11. Edmonds, Sir James, *Military Operations
    France and Belgium, 1916, Vol. 1*
    (London: Imperial War Museum, 1992),
    p. 375; the three right-most columns
    each comprised three battalions
    echeloned. The fourth column, which
    attacked immediately north of the
    Albert–Bapaume road, saw the 20th
    and 23rd Northumberland Fusiliers
    attack abreast, together followed by 25th
    Northumberland Fusiliers.
12. Lochnagar was a double-core mine with
    charges of 36,000 and 24,000 pounds
    that were laid 52 feet underground.
13. Edmonds, p. 373.
14. Prior, Robin, and Wilson, Trevor, *The
    Somme* (Sydney: University of New
    South Wales Press, 2005), pp. 91–2.
15. *ibid.*, p. 91.
16. Greiner, Lt. d. R., and Vulpius, Lt. d. R.,
    *Reserve-Infanterie-Regiment Nr. 110
    im Weltkrieg 1914–1918* (Karlsruhe:
    Macklotsche, 1934), p. 132.
17. *III Corps Summary of Operations
    Carried Out During the Month of July,
    1916*, III Corps, war diary, July 1916,
    NAUK, WO/95/673; Edmonds, p. 376.
18. Shakespear, John, notes, NAUK,
    CAB/45/137.
19. Steward, Godfrey, letter, 5 September
    1930, NAUK, CAB/45/137.
20. Prior and Wilson, *Somme*, p. 93.
21. Jack, James, *General Jack's Diary*
    (London: Eyre & Spottiswoode, 1964),
    p. 151.
22. Greiner and Vulpius, pp. 116, 123.
23. *ibid.*, p. 132.
24. *ibid.*, p. 304.
25. Vischer, Alfred, *Das 10. Württ.
    Infanterie-Regiment Nr.180 in der
    Somme-Schlacht 1916*, (Stuttgart:
    Uhland'schen, 1917), p.12.
26. Vogler, Heinrich, letter, 9 May 1970,
    ULLC/WW1/MID01.
27. Edmonds, p. 392.
28. Stosch, Albrecht von, *Somme-Nord,
    I Teil: Die Brennpunkte der Schlacht
    im Juli 1916* (Berlin: Gerhard Stalling,
    1927), p. 54; Vischer, p. 14; Whitehead,
    Ralph, *The Other Side of the Wire,
    Vol. 2: The Battle of the Somme. With the
    German XIV Reserve Corps, 1 July 1916*
    (Solihull: Helion, 2013), p. 257.
29. 'Die 180er in der Somme-Schlacht,'
    by Christian Fischer, in *Der 180er*,
    10 November 1938.

30. Gerster, Matthaus, *Die Schwaben and der Ancre* (Heilbronn: Eugen Salzer, 1918), p. 109.
31. *ibid.*
32. Boraston, J.H., and Bax, Cyril, *The Eighth Division in War, 1914–1918* (London: The Medici Society Ltd, 1926), p. 78.
33. *III Corps Summary of Operations, op. cit.*
34. Savile, Henry, letter, 19 May 1930, NAUK, CAB/45/137.
35. Edmonds, p. 374; Fischer, *op. cit.*
36. Whitehead, *Vol. 2*, p. 260.
37. Stosch, pp. 62, 252–3; Rudolph, M., *Geschichte des Bayrischen Fussartillerie-Bataillons Nr. 10* (Thüringen: Bernhard Sporn, 1936), pp. 35–6; Müller-Loebnitz, Wilhelm, *Die Badener im Weltkrieg 1914/1918* (Karlsruhe: G. Braun, 1935), p. 215; no precise figures have yet been found for 28th Reserve Division's artillery complement. An estimate based on Stosch suggests about 33 batteries comprising 125 guns. About 60 appear to have been deployed between Fricourt Spur and La Boisselle, the remaining 65 between Fricourt and the ground east of Mametz. Gun losses are calculated at 30% (Stosch, p. 62).
38. 34th Division, war diary, 1 July 1916, NAUK, WO/95/2457; Somerset, Charles, letter, 21 March 1930, NAUK, CAB/45/133.
39. Stosch, pp. 251–3; Klaus, Max, *Das Württembergische Reserve-Feldartillerie-Regiment Nr. 26 im Weltkrieg 1914–1918* (Stuttgart: Christian Belser, 1929), pp. 52–3; Soden, Franz Freiherr von, *Die 26. (Württembergische) Reserve-Division im Weltkrieg 1914–1918* (Stuttgart: Bergers, 1939), p. 102; 26th Reserve Division's artillery complement totalled 154 guns across 39 batteries, by far the most of any division north of the River Somme and, respectively, 23% and 18% more than the 28th Reserve Division. This disparity in artillery allocation and deployment demonstrates that Second Army and XIV Reserve Corps saw Soden's divisional sector as the most tactically and strategically important north of the river.
40. Langford, William, *Somme Intelligence, Fourth Army HQ* (Barnsley: Pen & Sword, 2013), p. 44.
41. Turner, Archibald, ULLC/WW1/MID01.
42. Senescall, William, ULLC/WW1/WF01/S/7.
43. Sheen, John, *Tyneside Irish: 24th, 25th, 26th & 27th (Service) Battalions of Northumberland Fusiliers* (Barnsley: Pen & Sword, 1998), p. 93.
44. Corbett, William, ULLC/WW1/ MID01.
45. Somerset, *op. cit.*
46. Whitehead, *Vol. 2, Verlustlisten* disc; Schwabenhöhe area was held by 5/RIR110, which suffered 36 fatalities on 1 July. The number of fatalities due to the mine blast must be either exactly that number or more likely fewer.
47. Greiner and Vulpius, p. 132.
48. Operation Order No. 32, 102nd Brigade, war diary, June 1916, NAUK, WO/95/2459/1; Operation Order No. 34, 101st Brigade, war diary, June 1916, NAUK, WO/95/2455/2.
49. Edmonds, p. 377.
50. Stosch, p. 252; RIR110 had two machine-gun companies each of 12 weapons, plus six more guns of the attached *Maschinengewehr Scharfschützen Trupp 161*.
51. Operation Order No. 32, 102nd Brigade, *op. cit.*; Operation Order No. 34, 101st Brigade, *op. cit.*
52. Amendment to Operation Order No. 24, 103rd Brigade, war diary, June 1916, NAUK, WO/95/2464/2; see also: 25th Northumberland Fusiliers, war diary, 1 July 1916, NAUK, WO/95/2467/1; 26th Northumberland Fusiliers, war diary, 1 July 1916, NAUK, WO/95/2467/2., 27th Northumberland Fusiliers, war diary, 1 July 1916, NAUK, WO/95/2467/3.
53. Alexander, *McCrae's Battalion*, p. 159.
54. *Evening Telegraph*, 28 August 1916.
55. 15th Royal Scots, war diary, 1 July 1916, NAUK, WO/95/2457/5; 16th Royal Scots, war diary, 1 July 1916, NAUK, WO/95/2458/1; 101st Brigade, war diary, 1 July 1916, NAUK, WO/95/2455/2.
56. 15th Royal Scots, war diary, *op. cit.*; 16th Royal Scots, war diary, *op. cit.*; 101st Brigade, war diary, *op. cit.*; Shakespear, J., *The Thirty-Fourth Division 1915–1919: The Story of Its Career from Ripon to the Rhine* (London: H.F. & G. Witherby, 1921), p. 42.
57. Sheen, *ibid*, p. 103.
58. Alexander, p. 160.
59. 16th Royal Scots, war diary, *op. cit.*
60. 27th Northumberland Fusiliers, war diary, 1 July 1916, NAUK, WO/95/2467/3; 24th Northumberland Fusiliers, war diary, 1 July 1916, NAUK, WO/95/2466.4.
61. Alexander, p. 163; Sheen, p. 101; Shakespear, *Thirty-Fourth Division*, p. 44; *Falkirk Gazette*, 26 July 1916.
62. *Falkirk Gazette, op. cit.*

63. 11th Suffolks, war diary, 1 July 1916, NAUK, WO/95/2458/3; Shakespear, *Thirty-Fourth Division*, pp. 41–2.
64. 11th Suffolks, war diary, *op. cit.*; see also 10th Lincolns, war diary, 1 July 1916, NAUK, WO/95/2457/1.
65. Greiner and Vulpius, p. 302.
66. 11th Suffolks, war diary, *op. cit.*
67. 24th Northumberland Fusiliers, war diary, 1 July 1916, *op. cit.*
68. Sheldon, p. 159; Greiner and Vulpius, p. 125.
69. Somerset, *op. cit.*
70. *ibid.*; 34th Division, war diary, 1 July 1916, *op. cit.*
71. Somerset, *op. cit.*
72. *ibid.*
73. Shakespear, *Thirty-Fourth Division*, p. 42.
74. Alexander, *McCrae's Battalion*, p. 162.
75. Sheen, p. 95.
76. Corbett, *op. cit.*
77. *ibid.*
78. Senescall, *op. cit.*
79. *ibid.*
80. *ibid.*
81. *Newcastle Journal*, 13 July 1916. Dyke's rank is as stated in the article.
82. Hart, Peter, *The Somme* (London: Weidenfeld & Nicholson, 2005), p. 171.
83. *ibid.*
84. Middlebrook, Martin, *The First Day on the Somme: 1 July 1916* (London: Penguin Books, 1984), p. 219.
85. *Grantham Journal*, 5 August 1916.
86. *III Corps Summary of Operations*, *op. cit.*; the tunnel used was designated 'No. 1' and was 410 feet long and ended 180 feet shy of the German front line. The other two bores were predictably 'No. 2' and 'No. 3'. The former was 600 feet long and 9–15 feet deep and ended 40 feet from the German line. The latter was 'similar in nature to the first two.' Third Corps noted that tunnels 'No. 2' and 'No. 3' were 'made use of when the German trenches in front were taken.'
87. *ibid.* more specifically, this tunnel was 8 feet and 8 inches high, 3 feet and 6 inches wide at floor level and 3 feet and 6 inches wide at its ceiling.
88. 34th Division, war diary, 1 July 1916, *op. cit.*
89. *ibid.*
90. 34th Division, war diary, 1 July 1916, *op. cit.*
91. Easton, Thomas, ULLC/WW1/GS/0490.
92. Greiner and Vulpius, p. 304.
93. 21st Northumberland Fusiliers, war diary, 1 July 1916, NAUK, WO/95/2462/5; 22nd Northumberland Fusiliers, war diary, 1 July 1916, NAUK, WO/95/2463/1; 26th Northumberland Fusiliers, war diary, 1 July 1916, NAUK, WO/95/2467/2.
94. Fiedel, Paul, *Geschichte des Infanterie-Regiments von Winterfeldt (2. Oberschlesisches) Nr. 23* (Berlin: Wilhelm Kolk, 1929), p. 123.
95. Easton, *op. cit.*
96. *ibid.*
97. Sheen, p. 97.
98. Sheldon, Jack, *The German Army on the Somme 1914–1916* (Barnsley: Pen & Sword, 2005), p. 159; Müller-Loebnitz, p. 216.
99. Nugent, George, last will and testament, 8 January 1916, www.gov.uk, FAEJ988504.
100. The rest of the epitaph: 'But never forgotten/May he rest/In eternal peace.'
101. *Newcastle Journal*, 22 July 1916.
102. Pery-Knox-Gore, Ivan, diary, 1 July 1916, NAUK, CAB/45/136.
103. *ibid.*
104. *ibid.*
105. Hart, *Somme*, p. 173.
106. Lewis, p. 72.
107. 20th Northumberland Fusiliers, war diary, 1 July 1916, NAUK, WO/95/2462/4; 23rd Northumberland Fusiliers, war diary, 1 July 1916, NAUK, WO/95/2463/2; 25th Northumberland Fusiliers, war diary, 1 July 1916, NAUK, WO/95/2467/1.
108. Edmonds, p. 382.
109. Shakespear, letter, *op. cit.*
110. *Newcastle Journal*, 18 July 1916.
111. *ibid.*
112. 25th Northumberland Fusiliers, war diary, *op. cit.*
113. Greiner and Vulpius, pp. 295–6.
114. Gore, Robert, letter, 5 July 1916, NAUK, CAB/45/134; 10th Lincolnshires, war diary, NAUK, WO/95/2457.
115. Hart, *Somme Success*, pp. 89–90.
116. 34th Division, war diary, 1 July 1916, *op. cit.*
117. *ibid.*
118. Hart, *Somme*, p. 174.
119. Greig, *op. cit.*
120. *ibid.*
121. Killed: Lieutenant-Colonels C.C.A. Sillery, 20th Northumberland Fusiliers, F.C. Heneker, 21st Northumberland Fusiliers, A.P.A. Elphinstone, 22nd Northumberland Fusiliers, W. Lyle, 23rd Northumberland Fusiliers, and L.M. Howard, 24th Northumberland Fusiliers; wounded

Lieutenant-Colonels J.H.M. Arden, 25th Northumberland Fusiliers, and M.E. Richardson, 26th Northumberland Fusiliers.

122. Greiner and Vulpius, p. 305.
123. *ibid.*, pp. 311–50; Whitehead, *Vol. 2, Verlustlisten* disc.
124. *ibid.* At least some of these casualties were incurred against 21st Division atop Fricourt Spur, but the confused nature of fighting there makes precise attribution impossible. RIR110's casualties are thus dealt with entirely in this chapter.
125. *ibid.*
126. Fiedel, pp. 303, 308–9.
127. Stosch, p. 71.
128. *ibid.*, p. 71.
129. *ibid.*, p. 58.
130. *ibid.*, pp. 53–9, 71; 'Die 26. Reserve Division im Weltkrieg,' by General der Infanterie, *Freiherr* von Soden, in *Der 180er: Festnummer: zum Treffen der 26. Reserve-Division vom 4. Bis 6. Juli 1936 in Stuttgart*, 4 July 1936.
131. Jack, pp. 145–6.
132. Hart, *Somme Success*, p. 89.
133. Levine, Joshua, *Forgotten Voices of the Somme: The Most Devastating Battle of the Great War in the Words of Those Who Survived* (London: Edbury Press, 2009), p. 127.
134. Robbins, p. 62.
135. Edmonds, p. 385.
136. *ibid.*
137. *ibid.*, p. 386.
138. Vischer, p. 14.
139. Stosch, p. 251; IR180 had two machine-gun companies, each with 12 guns.
140. Levine, p. 127.
141. Preliminary Operation Order No. 35, 23rd Brigade, war diary, June 1916, NAUK, WO/95/1708/5.
142. 2nd Devons, war diary, 1 July 1916, NAUK, WO/95/1712/1; 2nd Middlesex, war diary, 1 July 1916, NAUK, WO/95/1713/1.
143. *ibid.*
144. Operation Order, 2nd Royal Berkshire, war diary, June 1916, NAUK, WO/95/1729/1.
145. 2nd Lincolns, war diary, 1 July 1916, NAUK, WO/95/1730/1; 2nd Royal Berkshire, war diary, 1 July 1916, *op. cit.*
146. Vogler, *op. cit.*
147. Vischer, p. 14.
148. Bastard, Reginald, letter, 19 March 1930, NAUK, CAB/45/132.
149. 2nd West Yorkshires, war diary, WO/95/1714/1; Taylor, James, *The 1st Royal Irish Rifles in the Great War*

(Dublin: Four Courts Press, 2002), p. 78.
150. *ibid.*
151. 2nd West Yorkshires, war diary, 1 July 1916, NAUK, WO/95/1714/1.
152. *ibid.*
153. Lobel, Frank, ULLC/WW1/WF01/L/11.
154. Hart, *Bloody Somme*, p. 89.
155. Brown, Malcolm, *The Imperial War Museum Book of The Somme* (London: Pan, 2002), p. 69.
156. Savile, *op. cit.*
157. *ibid.*
158. Jack, p. 148.
159. Greiner and Vulpius, pp. 132–3.
160. Perry, Fred, ULLC/WW1/MID01.
161. 'Tapfere Schwaben,' by Gottlob Trost, in *Der 180er*, 1 July 1938.
162. Bastard, *op. cit.*
163. *ibid.*
164. Operation Order No. 63, 70th Brigade, war diary, June 1916, NAUK, WO/95/2185/3.
165. 'Brief narrative of course of the action,' 70th Brigade, war diary, July 1916, NAUK, WO/95/2185/3.
166. Fischer, *op. cit.*
167. *ibid.*
168. Walz, Karl, postcard, 6 April 1916.
169. 8th King's Own Yorkshire Light Infantry, war diary, 1 July 1916, NAUK, WO/95/2187/2.
170. 8th York & Lancasters, war diary, 1 July 1916, NAUK, WO/95/2188; 'Brief narrative of course of the action,' 70th Brigade, *op. cit.*
171. 'Brief narrative of course of the action,' 70th Brigade, *op. cit.*
172. Levine, p. 123.
173. *Derby Telegraph*, 29 July 1916.
174. 'Tapfere Schwaben,' by an unidentified soldier, in *Der 180er*, 1 August 1936.
175. Fischer, *op. cit.*
176. Goodwin, Billy, ULLC/WW1/GS/0644.
177. *ibid.*
178. Fischer, *op. cit.*
179. Boraston and Bax, p. 76.
180. Edmonds, p. 389.
181. *ibid.*, pp. 389–90; III Corps, war diary, 1 July 1916, NAUK, WO/95/672.
182. *III Corps Summary of Operations, op. cit.*
183. 8th Division, war diary, Appendix K, July 1916, NAUK, WO/95/1675/1.
184. *ibid.*
185. Robbins, p. 62.
186. Edmonds, p. 390.
187. *ibid.*, p. 391.
188. Boraston and Bax, p. 77.
189. Edmonds, pp. 387–9.
190. Fischer, *op. cit.*

191. Killed: Lieutenant-Colonels B.L. Maddison, 8th York & Lancasters, and A.J.B. Addison, 9th York & Lancasters; died of wounds: Lieutenant-Colonels A.M. Holdsworth, 2nd Royal Berkshires, and C.C. Macnamara, 1st Royal Irish Rifles; wounded: Lieutenant-Colonels H.F. Watson, 11th Sherwood Foresters, E.T.F. Sandys, 2nd Middlesex, and Captain K.E. Poyser, 8th KOYLI.
192. Middlebrook, p. 261.
193. Vischer, p. 18.
194. Whitehead, *Vol. 2*, p. 280.
195. Renz, Irina, Krumeich, Gerd, and Hirschfeld, Gerhard, *Scorched Earth: The Germans on the Somme 1914–1918* (Barnsley: Pen & Sword, 2009), p. 75.
196. Soden, p. 111.
197. Pulteney, William, letter, 17 May 1930, NAUK, CAB/45/136.
198. *ibid.*
199. Edmonds, p. 391.
200. See calculations for IR23, IR180 and RIR110 earlier in this chapter.
201. Shakespear, *Thirty-Fourth Division,* p. 54.
202. Somerset, *op. cit.*
203. Shakespear, *Thirty-Fourth Division,* p. 54.
204. Soden, pp. 111–12; Stosch, pp. 36–75; Gerster, pp. 108–38; Reichsarchiv, *Der Weltkrieg 1914 bis 1918: Die Operationen des Jahres 1916* (Berlin: Mittler & Sohn, 1936), pp. 341–53.
205. Levine, p. 132; Murray gives the battalion's strength as 800, which is presumably the total number of soldiers on its books rather than battle strength. The battalion's war diary reveals 685 officers and men went into action. The latter figure is used.

Chapter 8: Fluttering for Fricourt
1. Whitehead, Ralph, *The Other Side of the Wire, Vol. 2: The Battle of the Somme. With the German XIV Reserve Corps, 1 July 1916* (Solihull: Helion, 2013), p. 363.
2. Gibbs, Philip, *The Battles of the Somme* (London: Heinemann, 1917), p. 33.
3. *ibid.*, p. 28.
4. *ibid.*
5. *ibid.*, p. 31.
6. *ibid.*, p. 33.
7. *ibid.*, p. 31.
8. *ibid.*, pp. 36–7.
9. Gibbs, Philip, letter, 26 July 1930, NAUK, CAB/45/134.
10. Sheldon, Jack, *The German Army on the Somme 1914–1916* (Barnsley: Pen & Sword, 2005), p. 160.
11. *ibid.*
12. Stosch, Albrecht von, *Somme-Nord, I Teil: Der Brennpunkte der Schlacht im Juli 1916* (Oldenburg: Gerhard Stalling, 1927), p. 62.
13. Horne, Henry, obituary, *Cheltenham Chronicle*, 17 Aug 1929, BLNC.
14. *The First World War Letters of General Lord Horne*, ed. Simon Robbins (Stroud: The Army Records Society, 2009), p. 3.
15. Robbins, *Horne*, pp. 14–18; Horne, obituary, *op. cit.*
16. Robbins, *Horne*, pp. 14–18.
17. Horne, obituary, *op. cit.*
18. Robbins, *Horne*, p. 15.
19. *ibid.*, Horne, p. 25.
20. Horne, obituary, *op. cit.*
21. Haig, Douglas, diary, 9 July 1916, NAUK, WO/256/11.
22. *ibid.*, 4 July 1916.
23. Robbins, *Horne*, p. 5.
24. Horne, obituary, *op. cit.*
25. Cook, Tim, *The Madman and the Butcher: The Sensational Wars of Sam Hughes and General Arthur Currie* (Toronto: Allen Lane, 2009), pp. 257–8.
26. *ibid.*, p. 258.
27. *ibid.*, pp. 257–8.
28. 'XV Corps Scheme of Operations,' XV Corps GS, war diary, June 1916, NAUK, WO/95/921.
29. 'Fourth Army — Feeding Strength on 1st July 1916,' Rawlinson Papers 1/6, Churchill Archive; totals were 7th Division 22,325 (all ranks), 17th Division 20,263, 21st Division 23,391, XV Corps' troops 10,074 and attached French soldiers 618. The estimate is calculated from the 24 battalions directly involved in the battle, each with an average attack strength of 761 all ranks (see Chapter 11).
30. Collins, Robert, letter, 7 February 1930, CAB/45/132.
31. *ibid.*
32. *ibid.*
33. *ibid.*
34. Edmonds, p. 346.
35. The 5000-yard corps' frontage divided by the 1 field gun per 25 yards.
36. Edmonds, p. 346.
37. Prior and Wilson, *The Somme*, p. 102.
38. *ibid.*
39. Stosch, pp. 249–55; Klaus, Max, *Das Württembergische Reserve-Feldartillerie-Regiment Nr. 26 im Weltkrieg 1914–1918* (Stuttgart: Christian Belser, 1929), pp. 52–3; see also Chapter 7. The 28th is estimated

to have had a nominal 65 guns between Fricourt and the ground east of Mametz, with about 40 of these directly supporting the salient and the remainder the ground east of Mametz.

40. Stosch, p. 62.
41. Bicknell, Henry, letter, 4 March 1930, NAUK, CAB/45/132.
42. Frisch, George, *Das Reserve-Infanterie-Regiment Nr. 109 im Weltkrieg 1914 bis 1918* (Karlsruhe: F. Thiergarten, 1931), p. 117; Greiner, Lt. d. R., and Vulpius, Lt. d. R., *Reserve-Infanterie-Regiment Nr. 110 im Weltkrieg 1914–1918* (Karlsruhe: Macklotsche, 1934), p. 111; RIR109 had a battle strength of 3159 officers and men, with RIR111's totalling 3056.
43. Bachelin, Eduard, *Das Reserve-Infanterie-Regiment Nr. 111 im Weltkrieg 1914 bis 1918* (Karlsruhe: Südwestdeut, 1937), p. 99.
44. 4th Middlesex, war diary, 1 July 1916, NAUK, WO/95/2528/2.
45. 'Rethinking 10/West Yorkshires at Fricourt,' by Dave Stowe, *Stand To! Journal of the Western Front Association, No. 83*, p. 37.
46. Stosch, p. 56; Bachelin, p. 102.
47. Bachelin, p. 99.
48. Middlebrook, p. 156.
49. *ibid*.
50. *ibid.*, pp. 156–7; see also Thomas, Friedrich, ULLC/WW1/MID01.
51. Whitehead, *Vol. 2*, p. 363.
52. Middlebrook, p. 204.
53. Bachelin, p. 99.
54. Middlebrook, pp. 156–7.
55. 2nd Gordon Highlanders, war diary, 1 July 1916, NAUK, WO/95/1656/2; 2nd Borders, war diary, 1 July 1916, WO/95/1655/1; 22nd Manchesters, war diary, 1 July 1916, NAUK, WO/95/1669/1; 9th KOYLI, war diary, 1 July 1916, NAUK, WO/95/2162/1; 8th Somerset Light Infantry, war diary, 1 July 1916, NAUK, WO/95/2158/3; 10th York & Lancasters, war diary, 1 July 1916, NAUK, WO/95/2158/4; 4th Middlesex, war diary, *op. cit.*; Operation (Attack) Orders No. 36, 9th KOYLI, war diary, June 1916, *op. cit.*; Operation Order 6, 10th KOYLI, war diary, June 1916, *op. cit.*; Operation Order No. 70, 62nd Brigade, war diary, June 1916, NAUK, WO/95/2151/3; Operation Order 7, 15th Durham Light Infantry, war diary, June 1916, NAUK, WO/95/2161; Appreciation of the Task of 91st Infantry Brigade, Appendix E, 91st Brigade, war diary, June 1916, NAUK, WO/95/1666/1;

Operation Order No. 76, 50th Brigade, war diary, June 1916, NAUK, WO/95/1998/3.
56. 'XV Corps Scheme of Operations,' *op. cit.*
57. Edmonds, pp. 350–1.
58. Bicknell, *op. cit.*
59. Symes, Maurice, interview with Jan Stovold, Imperial War Museum, 9455/1986.
60. *Machine-Gunner 1914–1918: The Personal Experiences of the Machine Gun Corps*, ed. C.E. Crutchley (Folkestone: Baley Brothers & Swinfen Ltd, 1975), p. 48.
61. Barton, Peter, *The Somme: The Unseen Panoramas* (London: Constable & Robinson, 2006), p. 156.
62. Wilkinson, George, ULLC/WW1/MID01.
63. King, Victor, ULLC/WW1/MID01.
64. Wide, Howard, ULLC/WW1/MID01.
65. Stowe, p. 37.
66. *History of the Corps of Royal Engineers*, ed. H.L. Prichard (London: Institute of Royal Engineers, 1951), pp. 267–8.
67. 10th West Yorkshires, war diary, 1 July 1916, NAUK, WO/95/2004/1; Wyrall, *The West Yorkshire Regiment in the War 1914–1918, Vol. 1* (London: John Lane The Bodley Head, 1927), pp. 201–2.
68. Gardiner, Brian, *The Big Push* (London: Consul, 1963), p. 92.
69. Edmonds, p. 357; 10th West Yorkshires, war diary, 1 July 1916, NAUK, WO/95/2004/1; for a different figure, see: Atteridge, A. Hilliard, *History of the 17th (Northern) Division* (Glasgow: Robert Maclehose & Co, 1929), pp. 109–10.
70. 'Their Glory Shall Not Be Blotted Out: the 7th (Service) Battalion, the Battle of the Somme, 1st July 1916,' by Steve Erskine, in *The Green Howard*, Issue No. 10, April 2011, p. 31.
71. *ibid*.
72. Bachelin, p. 101; the company's formation is not given in its war diary; see 7th Yorkshires, war diary, 1 July 1916, NAUK, WO/95/2004/2.
73. Sheldon, *Somme*, p. 161; this gun team may also have fired at 10th West Yorkshires. It had the effective range to reach both battalions. It is entirely possible the gunner was referring to 7th Yorkshires' attack later in the day.
74. Sheldon, *Somme*, p. 161.
75. Bachelin, p. 99; Stosch, p. 53.
76. *ibid*.
77. 9th KOYLI, war diary, 30 June and 1 July 1916, *op. cit.*

78. Grieve, Grant, and Newman, Bernard, *Tunnellers: The Story of the Tunnelling Companies, Royal Engineers, During the World War* (London: Herbert Jenkins Ltd, 1936), p. 121.
79. Bachelin, p. 99.
80. 9th KOYLI, war diary, *op. cit.*; Edmonds, p 359; Bachekin, p. 99.
81. Liddle Hart, Basil, paper titled 'Impressions of the Great British Offensive on the Somme,' NAUK, CAB/45/135.
82. 15th Durham Light Infantry, war diary, 1 July 1916, NAUK, WO/95/2161/1; 1st East Yorkshires, war diary, 1 July 1916, NAUK, WO/95/2161/2.
83. Renz, Irina, Krumeich, Gerd, and Hirschfeld, Gerhard, *Scorched Earth: the Germans on the Somme 1914–1918* (Barnsley: Pen & Sword, 2009), p. 86.
84. *ibid.*
85. *ibid.*
86. *ibid.*, p. 87.
87. 8th Somerset Light Infantry, war diary, 1 July 1916, *op. cit.*; 4th Middlesex, war diary, 1 July 1916, *op. cit.*
88. Bachelin, p. 102; Stosch, p. 56; it is not clear how big this blast was. It took place in front of 1/RIR111, probably around 7.30 a.m. Bachelin implies it was north of The Tambour area. There is no obvious reference to this event in British accounts. The mention of British infantries returning to their own trenches under heavy fire suggests the blast might be linked to 4th Middlesex. But there is no evidence to suggest the mine and 4th Middlesex's stalled advance were linked. The estimate of 80 British soldiers buried is almost certainly far too high.
89. 4th Middlesex, war diary, 1 July 1916, *op. cit.*
90. 10th York & Lancasters, war diary, 1 July 1916, *op. cit.*; *The History of the Lincolnshire Regiment 1914–1918*, ed. C.R. Simpson (London: The Medici Society, 1931), pp. 164–5.
91. Willis, Arthur, ULLC/WW1/TR/08.
92. Johnston, Robert, letter, 15 February 1930, NAUK, CAB/45/135.
93. 14th Northumberland Fusiliers, war diary, 1 July 1916, NAUK, WO/95/2146/1.
94. Nanson, Musard, letter, undated, NAUK, CAB/45/136.
95. 'Operations Carried Out by 21st Division, July 1st–July 3rd 1916,' 21st Division, war diary, July 1916, NAUK, WO/95/2130/3.
96. *ibid.*
97. Watkin, Matthew, ULLC/WW1/MID01.
98. Gliddon, Gerald, *V.C.s of the Somme* (Gliddon Books, 1991), pp. 11–12.
99. *ibid.*, p. 12.
100. Fisher, Alex, ULLC/WW1/TR/02.
101. *ibid.*
102. *ibid.*
103. Symes, Maurice, interview with Jan Stovold, Imperial War Museum, 9455/1986.
104. Barton, p. 155.
105. Money, Robin, ULLC/WW1/GS/1126.
106. Deverell, Cyril, letter, 15 February 1930, NAUK, CAB/45/133.
107. Fiedel, Paul, *Geschichte des Infanterie-Regiments von Winterfeldt (2. Oberschlesisches) Nr. 23: Das Regiment im Weltkriege* (Berlin: Verlag Tradition Wilhelm Kolt, 1929), p. 125.
108. 22nd Manchesters, war diary, *op. cit.*
109. 1st South Staffords, war diary, 1 July 1916, NAUK, WO/95/1670/2.
110. Edmonds, p. 352.
111. More-Molyneux, FC, letter, 29 April 1930, NAUK, CAB/45/136.
112. 2nd Gordon Highlanders, war diary, *op. cit.*; 9th Devons, war diary, 1 July 1916, NAUK, WO/95/1656/1.
113. 8th Devons, war diary, 1 July 1916, NAUK, WO/95/1655/2.
114. Deverell, Cyril, letter, 15 February 1930, NAUK, CAB/45/133.
115. 2nd Borders, war diary, 1 July 1916, *op. cit.*
116. *ibid.*
117. Barton, p. 157.
118. Wicks, Charles, ULLC/WW1/SEV/01.
119. Wide, *op. cit.*
120. 'The Attack,' by R.H. Tawney, *The Westminster Gazette*, August 1916.
121. *ibid.*
122. Goebelbecker, Emil, ULLC/WW1/MID01.
123. Middlebrook, p. 203.
124. *ibid.*, p. 233; this anecdote is reminiscent of a battle scene in the 1930 film of Erich Maria Remarque's *All Quiet on the Western Front*.
125. Whitehead, *Vol. 2*, p. 348.
126. *ibid.*, p. 348.
127. *ibid.*, p. 361.
128. Upcott, John, diary, 10 July 1916, ULLC/WW1/GS/1644.
129. Medomsley, Jack, *William Noel Hodgson: The Gentle Poet* (Durham: Mel Publicataions, 1989), p. 140.
130. 'The Devonshires Held This Trench — The Devonshires Hold It Still,' by

Jeremy Archer, in *Stand To!*, No. 88, April–May 2010. Article extract at westernfrontassociation.com. Last accessed 16 August 2015.

131. Stosch, p. 62.
132. *ibid.*
133. *ibid.*
134. *ibid.*
135. Bielefeld, August, ULLC/WW1/MID01.
136. Stosch, p. 58.
137. *ibid.*, pp. 62, 57–8.
138. *ibid.*, p. 62.
139. *ibid.*, pp. 57–8.
140. *ibid.*, p. 62.
141. *ibid.*
142. *ibid.*
143. Renz, Krumeich and Hirschfeld, p. 87.
144. Stosch, p. 62.
145. *ibid.*, p. 71
146. Bachelin, p. 102.
147. *ibid.*
148. Stosch, p. 71.
149. Bachelin, p. 103.
150. Stosch, p. 71.
151. Strohn, Matthias, *World War I Companion* (Oxford: Osprey, 2013), p. 109.
152. Sheldon, *Somme*, p. 179.
153. Renz, Krumeich and Hirschfeld, p. 88.
154. XV Corps GS, war diary, 1 July 1916, *op. cit.*
155. *ibid.*; a report led Horne to believe 10th West Yorkshires made good progress.
156. Edmonds, p. 352.
157. XV Corps GS, war diary, 1 July 1916, *op. cit.*
158. *ibid.*
159. Edmonds, p. 353.
160. *ibid.*, pp. 352–3.
161. *ibid.*, p. 353.
162. XV Corps GS, war diary, 1 July 1916, *op. cit.*
163. *ibid.*
164. *ibid.*
165. *ibid.*
166. Robbins, *Horne*, p. 171.
167. 'Operations Carried Out by 21st Division,' *op. cit.*; Edmonds, p. 363.
168. Edmonds, p. 364.
169. *ibid.*, p. 364; Erskine, p. 31.
170. Edmonds, p. 365.
171. Bachelin, *op. cit.*, p. 103.
172. Erskine, p. 31.
173. *ibid.*
174. Askew, Alfred, ULLC/WW1/MID01.
175. Fell, Robert, letter, undated, NAUK, CAB/45/133.
176. Barton, p. 156.
177. Stedman, Michael, *Fricourt-Mametz* (Barnsley: Pen & Sword, 2011), p. 63.
178. 20th Manchesters, war diary, 1 July 1916, NAUK, WO/95/1663/1.
179. *ibid.*
180. *Siegfried Sassoon Diaries 1915–18*, ed. Rupert Hart-Davis (London: Book Club Associates, 1983), pp. 83–4.
181. *ibid.*, p. 84.
182. *ibid.*
183. *ibid.*
184. More-Molyneux, *op. cit.*
185. *ibid.*
186. *Perthshire Advertiser*, 12 July 1916.
187. Atkinson, C.T., *The Seventh Division 1914–1918* (London: John Murrary, 1927), pp. 263–4.
188. Norman, William, letter, 28 February 1930, NAUK, CAB/45/136.
189. *ibid.*
190. Drake-Brockman, Guy, letter, 7 February 1930, NAUK, CAB/45/132.
191. *ibid.*
192. Cloudsdale, Frank, ULLC/WW1/MID01.
193. Prichard, p. 267; Edmonds, p. 366.
194. Wicks, *op. cit.*
195. Walsh, Arthur, ULLC/WW1/SEV/01.
196. *ibid.*
197. Liddle Hart, *op. cit.*
198. *ibid.*
199. 15th Durham Light Infantry, war diary, 1 July 1916, *op. cit.*
200. Spicer, Lancelot, *Letters from France 1915–1918* (London: Robert York, 1979), p. 61.
201. *ibid.*, p. 61.
202. *ibid.*, p. 62.
203. *ibid.*, p. 63.
204. Nanson, *op. cit.*
205. Prichard, *op. cit.*
206. Whitehead, *Vol. 2*, p. 364.
207. Bachelin, p. 106.
208. Goebelbecker, *op. cit.*
209. Bachelin, p. 107.
210. Knies, L., *Das Württembergische Pionier-Bataillon im Weltkrieg 1914–1918* (Stuttgart: Chr Belser, 1927), p. 77.
211. Sheldon, *Somme*, p. 162.
212. Whitehead, *Vol. 2*, p. 363.
213. *ibid.*
214. *ibid.*, p. 356.
215. *ibid.*
216. *ibid.*
217. *ibid.*, pp. 356–7.
218. *ibid.*
219. Renz, Krumeich and Hirschfeld, p. 88.
220. Thomas, *op. cit.*
221. Bachelin, p. 110.
222. Renz, Krumeich and Hirschfeld, p. 88.
223. Reeves, Brian, letter, 8 May 1930, NAUK, CAB/45/137.

224. Robbins, *Horne*, p. 171.
225. Bachelin, p. 102.
226. Greiner and Vulpius, p. 134; Frisch, p. 131.
227. Palmer-Cook, Francis, ULLC/WW1/TR/06.
228. Killed: Lieutenant-Colonels H. Lewis, 20th Manchesters, C.W.D. Lynch, 9th KOYLI, and H. Allardice, 13th Northumberland Fusiliers; died of wounds: Lieutenant-Colonels M.B. Stow, 1st East Yorkshires, and A.E. Fitzgerald, 15th Durham Light Infantry; wounded: Lieutenant-Colonels J.W. Scott, 8th Somerset Light Infantry, and H.J. King, 10th KOYLI.
229. Killed: Lieutenant-Colonel A. Dickson, 10th West Yorkshires.
230. Robbins, *Horne*, p. 171.
231. Frisch, p. 129; Whitehead, *Vol. 2*, p. 411; Frisch tabulates RIR109's 24 June to 1 July casualties as 108 dead, 267 wounded and 1773 missing, giving a combined total of 2148. Whitehead states 59 of these deaths were 23–30 June, which gives a 1 July casualty total of up to 2089.
232. Whitehead, *Vol. 2*, *Verlustlisten* disc; data is incomplete but these lists suggest approximately half the regiment's fatal casualties occurred in its First Battalion, along with three companies of its Second Battalion. German and British unit boundaries were unaligned and this, along with the confused nature of fighting immediately east of Mametz, mean greater accuracy is difficult to achieve.
233. Bachelin, *op. cit.*, pp. 95–6, 111.
234. *ibid.*, *Ehrentafel*; Edmonds, p. 368; a ballpark estimate of 650 prisoners is arrived at by deducting RIR109's 943 prisoners from XV Corps' haul of 1625.
235. Knies, p. 77.
236. Fiedel, pp. 125, 309–11.
237. Whitehead, *Vol. 2*, *Verlustlisten* disc. Many of the prisoners were wounded.
238. This is the middle stanza of a German poem titled 'Ich hatt' einen Kameraden' ('I had a comrade'), which is often played to musical accompaniment and is the equivalent of the 'Last Post' and 'Ode' combined.
239. Sheldon, Jack, *The Germans at Thiepval* (Barnsley: Pen & Sword, 2006), pp. 150–2.

Chapter 9: The Straw Man of Montauban

1. *Dundee Courier*, 11 July 1916.
2. Bidder, Harold, diary transcript 1 July 1916, NAUK, CAB/45/132.
3. Bidder, Harold, letter, undated, *op. cit.*
4. Stanley, F.C., *The History of the 89th Brigade, 1914–1918* (Liverpool: Daily Post, 1919), pp. 112–13; Heath, Philip, ULLC/WW1/WF01/H/18.
5. *Evening Telegraph*, 2 March 1927; *The First World War Letters of General Lord Horne*, ed. Simon Robbins (Stroud: The Army Records Society, 2009), p. 226.
6. *Evening Telegraph*, 2 March 1927.
7. Gough, Hubert, *Fifth Army* (London: Hodder & Stoughton, 1931), p 151.
8. Congreve, Walter, diary, 1 July 1916, Congreve Papers, Hampshire Records Office.
9. BRIR6 was drawn from corps reserve and attached to 12th Infantry Division.
10. Reymann, H., *Das 3. Oberschlesische Infanterie-Regiment Nr. 62 im Kriege 1914–1918* (Zeulenroda: Sporn, 1930), p. 90.
11. Bezzel, Oskar, *Das Königlich Bayerische Reserve-Infanterie-Regiment Nr. 6* (München: Schick, 1938), p. 93.
12. Congreve, 1 July 1916, *op. cit.*
13. Reymann, p. 90.
14. Whitehead, Ralph, *The Other Side of the Wire, Vol. 2: The Battle of the Somme. With the German XIV Reserve Corps, 1 July 1916* (Solihull: Helion, 2013), p. 420.
15. *ibid.*
16. *ibid.*, p. 421. Reymann, pp. 90–2.
17. Congreve, 2 July 1916, *op. cit.*
18. Reymann, p. 91.
19. Whitehead, *Vol. 2*, p. 421; Reymann, pp. 90–2.
20. Bezzel, p. 118.
21. *ibid.*, pp. 111–12.
22. Edmonds, Sir James, *Military Operations France and Belgium, 1916, Vol. 1* (London: Imperial War Museum, 1992), p. 324; this had a lot to do with the corps' comparatively narrow frontage.
23. Stosch, Albrecht von, *Somme-Nord, I Teil: Die Brennpunkte der Schlacht im Juli 1916* (Berlin: Gerhard Stalling, 1927), pp. 252–3; the 28th had about 33 batteries in nominal terms and the 12th about 25. By contrast 26th Reserve Division possessed 39 batteries, the most of any division in XIV Reserve Corps.
24. *ibid.*, pp. 62, 252–3; Rudolph, M., *Geschichte des Bayrischen Fussartillerie-Bataillons Nr. 10* (Thüringen, Bernhard Sporn, 1936), pp. 35–6; Müller-Loebnitz, Wilhelm, *Die Badener im Weltkrieg 1914/1918* (Karlsruhe: G. Braun, 1935), p. 215; see Chapter 3 for calculations. In both cases the ground opposite XIII

Corps represented only a small portion of both divisional sectors.

25. Edmonds, p. 344; Stosch, p. 62.
26. Stosch, p. 62.
27. 'Fourth Army — Feeding Strength on 1st July 1916,' Rawlinson Papers 1/6, Churchill Archive; totals were 9th Division 21,114 (all ranks), 18th Division 20,965, 30th Division 24,247 and XIII Corps' troops 8289. The corps' attack strength is estimated as 20 battalions directly involved at an average bayonet strength of 761 all ranks each.
28. Edmonds, p. 322.
29. Congreve, 1 July 1916, *op. cit.*
30. Maddocks, Graham, *Liverpool Pals: A History of the 17th, 18th, 19th and 20th (Service) Battalions, The King's (Liverpool Regiment) 1914–1919* (London: Leo Cooper, 1991), p. 91.
31. *ibid.*, p. 89.
32. *Liverpool Echo*, 14 July 1916.
33. *ibid.*
34. *ibid.*
35. Operation Order No. 30, Appendix A, 89th Brigade, war diary, June 1916, NAUK, WO/95/2331/3.
36. 2nd Bedfords, war diary, 1 July 1916, NAUK, WO/95/2333/1.
37. 18th King's, war diary, 1 July 1916, NAUK, WO/95/2330/1; Narrative of Operations Carried Out by the 19th Battalion Manchester Regiment, 19th Manchesters, war diary, July 1916, NAUK, WO/95/2329/4; 19th Manchesters, war diary, 1 July 1916, *op. cit.*
38. *ibid.*
39. 2nd Yorkshires, war diary, 1 July 1916, NAUK, WO/95/2329/2.
40. *ibid.*; 2nd Wiltshires, war diary, 1 July 1916, NAUK, WO/95/2329/1.
41. *Liverpool Echo*, 14 July 1916, *op. cit.*
42. 17th King's, war diary, 1 July 1916, NAUK, WO/95/2334/1.
43. 19th Manchesters, war diary, 1 July 1916, *op. cit.*
44. Willmer, Edgar, ULLC/WW1/GS/1753.
45. *ibid.*
46. *The Liverpool Echo*, 8 July 1916.
47. Maddocks, p. 89.
48. 17th King's, war diary, 1 July 1916, NAUK, WO/95/2334/1; 20th King's, war diary, 1 July 1916, NAUK, WO/95/2330/1; 20th King's, war diary, 1 July 1916, NAUK, WO/95/2335/2; 19th Manchesters, war diary, 1 July, *op. cit.*
49. 18th King's, war diary, 1 July 1916, NAUK, WO/95/2330/1.
50. *ibid.*, p. 87.

51. Reymann, p. 93.
52. Whitehead, *Vol. 2*, pp. 423–5.
53. *ibid.*, p. 425.
54. *ibid.*
55. Reymann, p. 93.
56. Whitehead, *Vol. 2*, pp. 431–2.
57. *ibid.*, p. 427.
58. *ibid.*, p. 426.
59. Heinrich, Hermann, ULLC/WW1/MID01.
60. *ibid.*
61. Healey, Charles, ULLC/WW1/WF01/H/17.
62. *ibid.*
63. Bidder, *op. cit.*
64. Frank, Thomas, ULLC/WW1/WF01/F/12.
65. *ibid.*
66. *Liverpool Daily Post*, 18 July 1916.
67. *ibid.*
68. Maddocks, p. 85.
69. *ibid.*, p. 86.
70. Willmer, *op. cit.*
71. *Liverpool Daily Post*, 18 July 1916.
72. *ibid.*
73. *ibid.*, 20 July 1916.
74. Maddocks, p. 88.
75. *ibid.*, p. 88.
76. *ibid.*, p. 89.
77. *ibid.*
78. 16th Manchesters, war diary, 1 July 1916, NAUK, WO/95/2339/1; 17th Manchesters, war diary, 1 July 1916, NAUK, WO/95/2339/2.
79. 17th Manchesters, war diary, *op. cit.*; Supplementary Order to Operation Order No. 23, 90th Brigade, war diary, July 1916, NAUK, WO/95/2337/2.
80. 2nd Royal Scots, war diary, NAUK, WO/95/2340/1; Supplementary Order to Operation Order No. 23, 90th Brigade, *op. cit.*
81. 18th Manchesters, war diary, 1 July 1916, NAUK, WO/95/2339/3.
82. 'Somme Battle, July 1, 1916,' by J. Hubert-Worthington, NAUK, CAB/45/137.
83. Sotham, Ernest, letter, 16 February 1930, NAUK, CAB/45/137.
84. *Liverpool Daily Post*, 18 July 1916.
85. Sotham, *op. cit.*; Worthington, *op. cit.*
86. Fraser-Harris, Alfred, ULLC/WW1/SEV/01.
87. Brookes, Squire, ULLC/WW1/SEV/01.
88. *ibid.*
89. Gudgeon, Frank, ULLC/WW1/MID01.
90. Bell, Allan, ULLC/WW1/MID01.
91. *ibid.*
92. *Dundee Courier*, 11 July 1916.
93. Worthington, *op. cit.*

94. *The Liverpool Echo*, 8 July 1916.
95. *ibid*.
96. *ibid*.
97. *Liverpool Daily Post*, 18 July 1916.
98. Cornes, Hugh, narrative of battle, 15 December 1929, NAUK, CAB/45/132.
99. Whitehead, *Vol. 2*, p. 436.
100. *ibid*., p 436; it is quite remarkable that this soldier knew what was afoot several miles away at Mametz.
101. *ibid*.
102. *ibid*.
103. *ibid*.
104. 'Report on Operations, 30th Division, July 1st till 10 a.m. July 5th,' 30th Division, war diary, July 1916, NAUK, WO/95/2310/5.
105. Heinrich, *op. cit*.
106. Worthington, *op. cit*.
107. Report on actions 1–2 July, 17th Manchesters, war diary, 1 July 1916, NAUK, WO/95/2339/2.
108. Worthington, *op. cit*.
109. *History of the Corps of Royal Engineers*, ed. H.L. Prichard, (London: Institute of Royal Engineers, 1951), p. 266.
110. Worthington, *op. cit*.
111. Report on actions 1–2 July, 17th Manchesters, *op. cit*.
112. Robbins, Simon, *British Generalship on the Western Front 1914–18* (Abingdon: Frank Cass, 2005), p. 58.
113. 30th Division, war diary, 1 July 1916, *op. cit*.
114. 'Report on Operations, 30th Division,' *op. cit*.
115. Edmonds, p. 341; killed: Lieutenant-Colonel H.A. Johnson, 17th Manchesters.
116. *ibid*.
117. Bezzel, p. 106.
118. Whitehead, *Vol. 2*, *Verlustlisten* disc; many of the prisoners were wounded. The three missing soldiers were later located.
119. Reymann, p. 94; this figure is averaged at 33% of the regiment's total casualties for 1 July, this based on the fact that four of IR62's 12 companies were deployed across positions attacked by XIII Corps.
120. Maddocks, p. 89; the quotes refer to the 1947 book *Off to Philadelphia in the Morning*, by Jack Jones.
121. Grindley, Ernest, ULLC/WW1/WF01/G/14.
122. Dunn, Harold, undated manuscript, Hampshire Records Office.
123. *ibid*.
124. *ibid*.
125. *The Courier*, 21 July 1916.

126. *The Courier*, 5 August 1916; Tullock was killed 20 July 1916.
127. *ibid*.
128. *ibid*.
129. Norton, Norman, ULLC/WW1/MID01.
130. Heath, *op. cit*.
131. 'My Experiences in the Great War,' by Clarrie Jarman in *Stand To! Journal of the Western Front Association*, Summer 1983, No. 8, p. 5.
132. Cousins, John, ULLC/WW1/MID01.
133. 11th Royal Fusiliers, war diary, 1 July 1916, NAUK, WO/95/2045/1; 7th Bedfords, war diary, 1 July 1916, NAUK, WO/95/2043/3; 6th Royal Berkshire, war diary, 1 July 1916, NAUK, WO/95/2037/1; 8th Norfolks, war diary, 1 July 1916, NAUK, WO/95/2040/1; 7th Queen's, war diary, 1 July 1916, NAUK, WO/95/2051/1; 8th East Surreys, war diary, 1 July 1916, NAUK, WO/95/2050/1; 7th Buffs, war diary, 1 July 1916, NAUK, WO/95/2049/1. Some battalions, such as 6th Royal Berkshires and 8th East Surreys, allocated different start times for their leading two companies due to the widening breadth of no-man's-land on their battalion frontages.
134. *ibid*.; Operation Order No. 27, Table C, 55th Brigade, war diary, July 1916, NAUK, WO/95/2046/2; Operation Order I and Appendix H, 2nd Royal Berkshires, war diary, June 1916, NAUK, WO/95/2037/1/2 and /3.
135. Operation Order No. 27, 55th Brigade, *op. cit*.; 8th Norfolks, war diary, 1 July 1916, *op. cit*.
136. 7th Buffs, war diary, 1 July 1916, *op. cit*.; Banks, T.M., and Chell, R.A., *With the 10th Essex in France* (London: Gay & Hancock, 1924), pp. 117–18; 10th Essex, war diary, 1 July 1916, NAUK, WO/95/2038/2; 6th Northamptons, war diary, 1 July 1916, NAUK, WO/95/2044/2; Operational Order No. 10, 6th Northamptons, war diary, June 1916, *op. cit*.
137. 11th Royal Fusiliers, war diary, 1 July 1916, *op. cit*.; 7th Bedfords, war diary, 1 July 1916, *op. cit*.
138. Cousins, *op. cit*.
139. Rowan, E.W.J., *The 54th Infantry Brigade 1914–1918: Some Records of Battle and Laughter in France* (Aldershot: Gale & Polden, undated), p. 36.
140. Edmonds, p. 332.
141. Cousins, *op. cit*.
142. Thomas, Friedrich, ULLC/WW1/MID01.

143. Edmonds, pp. 332–3.
144. Cousins, *op. cit.*
145. 7th Bedfords, war diary, 1 July 1916, *op. cit.*
146. Edmonds, p. 333.
147. 7th Bedfords, war diary, 1 July 1916, *op. cit.*
148. Luttgers, Gustav, ULLC/WW1/MID01; Luttgers was in Jaminwerk.
149. Middlebrook, Martin, *The First Day on the Somme* (London: Penguin Books, 1984), p. 204.
150. Cousins, *op. cit.*
151. Capper, Derick, ULLC/WW1/GS/0267.
152. Two others due to be deployed were destroyed by German shellfire.
153. Barton, Peter, *The Somme: The Unseen Panoramas* (London: Constable & Robinson, 2006), pp. 167–8.
154. *The Courier*, 5 August 1916.
155. 'The Biscuit Boys: The Somme — 6th Battalion (July–Oct 1916).' Accessed from www.purley.eu/RBR0000.html.
156. Middlebrook, p. 126.
157. Norton, *op. cit.*; 'Weekly Mine Report,' 183 Tunnelling Company, Royal Engineers, in 18th Division, war diary, July 1916, NAUK, WO/95/2015/2.
158. 'Weekly Mine Report,' *op. cit.*
159. 8th Norfolks, war diary, 1 July 1916, *op. cit.*; 6th Royal Berkshires, war diary, 1 July 1916, *op. cit.*
160. *ibid.*
161. Norton, *op. cit.*
162. *ibid.*
163. *ibid.*
164. Kind, August, postcard, 3 June 1916.
165. Jarman, *op. cit.*
166. Edmonds, p. 331.
167. 7th Queen's, war diary, 1 July 1916, *op. cit.*
168. *ibid.*, p. 330.
169. *News & Mail*, 2 January 1975.
170. Heath, *op. cit.*
171. *ibid.*
172. *ibid.*
173. Price, Leonard, ULLC/WW1/MID01.
174. 7th Royal West Kents, war diary, 1 July 1916, NAUK, WO/95/2049/2.
175. *ibid.*
176. Kenchington, Arthur, diary, 1 July 1916, NAUK, CAB/45/135; 18th Division, war diary, 1 July 1916, *op. cit.*
177. *ibid.*
178. Edmonds, p. 339.
179. 'The Biscuit Boys,' *op. cit.*
180. 7th Queen's, war diary, 1 July 1916, *op. cit.*
181. *The Courier*, 21 July 1916

182. 12th Middlesex, war diary, 1 July 1916, NAUK, WO/95/2044/1.
183. Middlebrook, pp. 156–7.
184. Scheytt, Paul, ULLC/WW1/MID01.
185. Heath, *op. cit.*; *Liverpool Daily Post*, 18 July 1916.
186. *The Courier*, 21 July 1916.
187. *ibid.*
188. Norton, *op. cit.*
189. *ibid.*
190. Prichard, p. 266.
191. Rowan, p. 38.
192. Hart, Peter, *Somme Success: The Royal Flying Corps and the Battle of the Somme, 1916* (London: Leo Cooper, 2001), p. 98.
193. Heath, *op. cit.*
194. 18th Division, war diary, 1 July 1916, NAUK, WO/95/2015/2.
195. *ibid.*
196. *ibid.*
197. Grove-White, Maurice, letter, 10 January 1931, NAUK, CAB/45/134.
198. *ibid.*
199. Nichols, G.H.F., *The 18th Division in the Great War* (London: William Blackwood & Sons, 1922), p. 46.
200. *ibid.*
201. See Chapter 8.
202. Fiedel, pp. 303, 307.
203. Prior, Robin, and Wilson, Trevor, *The Somme* (Sydney: University of New South Wales Press, 2005), p. 108.
204. Stosch, p. 71.
205. *ibid.*
206. Langford, William, *Somme Intelligence: Fourth Army HQ 1916* (Barnsley: Pen & Sword, 2013), p. 58.
207. Stosch, p. 71.
208. Reymann, p. 94.
209. Whitehead, *Vol. 2*, pp. 423, 431.
210. Stosch, pp. 65–7.
211. *ibid.*
212. *ibid.*
213. *ibid.*, p. 67.
214. *ibid.*
215. *ibid.*; most commonly by their breach blocks being removed.
216. Fiedel, Paul, *Geschichte des Infanterie-Regiments von Winterfeldt (2. Oberschlesisches) Nr. 23* (Berlin: Wilhelm Kolk, 1929), pp. 121–2, 127–8; Stosch, pp. 71–3.
217. Whitehead, *Vol. 2*, p. 438; Reymann, p. 94.
218. Stosch, p. 72.
219. Reymann, p. 94.
220. Goebelbecker, *op. cit.*
221. Stosch, p. 71.

222. *ibid.*, p. 73.
223. *ibid.*
224. Middlebrook, pp. 212–13, 285–6.
225. *ibid.*
226. Congreve, 1–2 July 1916, *op. cit.*
227. XIII Corps GS, war diary, 1 July 1916, NAUK, WO/95/895; 30th Division, war diary, 1 July 1916, NAUK, *op. cit.*; 18th Division, war diary, 1 July 1916, *op. cit.*; including all reports contained in these war diaries for the month of July.
228. Edmonds' correspondence with numerous officers present on 1 July 1916, NAUK, CAB/45/132–9; Edmonds, pp. 320–45.
229. Haig, Douglas, diary, 1 July 1916, NAUK, WO/256/11; Rawlinson, Henry, diary, 1 July 1916, Rawlinson Papers 1/5, Churchill Archive; Gough, Hubert, *Fifth Army* (London: Hodder & Stoughton, 1931), pp. 136–7.
230. Fourth Army Summary of Operations, *op. cit.*
231. *ibid.*
232. Edmonds, p. 337.
233. *Les Armées Françaises dans la Grande Guerre, Tome IV, Vol. 2*, Annexes Vol. 2, Annexe 840, page 801, 'XX Corps Account of events 7 pm, 30th June, to 7 pm, 1st July'; Edmonds, p. 343.
234. Sotham, Ernest, letter, 16 February 1930, NAUK, CAB/45/137.
235. Kiggell, Launcelot, to Edmonds, James, letter, 2 December 1937, NAUK, CAB/45/135; see also Heath, Philip, ULLC/WW1/WF01/H/18.
236. Unknown correspondent, letter, 25 January 1931, NAUK, CAB/45/135.
237. Fiedel, p. 122; Stosch, p. 71.
238. Schiedt, Major, *Das Reserve-Infanterie-Regiment Nr. 51 im Weltkriege 1914–1918* (Zeulenroda: Bernhard Sporn, 1936), pp. 154–8; Stosch, pp. 73–5; Hasselbach, Major, and Strodzki, *Hauptmann, Das Reserve Infanterie Regiment Nr. 38* (Zeulenroda: Bernhard Sporn, 1934), pp. 114–17.
239. Norton, *op. cit.*
240. Heath, *op. cit.*; see also Chell, Randolph, letter, 13 December 1929, NAUK, CAB/45/132.
241. Heath, *op. cit.*
242. Middlebrook, p. 223.
243. Bennett, Thomas, ULLC/WW1/MID01.
244. Cornes, *op. cit.*
245. Edmonds, p. 341.
246. Grove-White, *op. cit.*
247. *ibid.*
248. Congreve message, 1 July 1916, 18th Division, war diary, July 1916, *op. cit.*

Chapter 10: 'This Tragic Adventure'
1. Lockhart, Noel, ULLC/WW1/MID01.
2. Masefield, John, *The Old Front Line* (New York: Macmillan, 1917), p. 29.
3. Lettow-Vorbeck, Friedrich von, *Geschichte des Fusilier-Regiments von Gersdorff (Kurhessisches) Nr. 80* (Marburg: W Braun, 1913), p. 268.
4. 'Report on the Defence of Gommecourt on July the 1st, 1916,' *Royal United Services Institution Journal*, Vol. 62, Issue 447, 1917, p. 551.
5. *Histories of Two Hundred and Fifty-One Divisions of the German Army Which Participated in the War (1914–1918)* (Washington: Government Printing Office, 1920), p. 56.
6. 'Defence of Gommecourt,' pp. 546–51.
7. *ibid.*; Süsskind makes no critical comment on Borries' work.
8. Büsing, Georg, *Das Reserve-Feldartillerie-Regiment Nr. 20 im Weltkrieg 1914–18* (Hannover: Göhmann, 1932), unpaginated translation dated 2014 supplied by Bill MacCormick.
9. *ibid.*
10. 'Defence of Gommecourt,' p. 553; the report states 60 field guns and howitzers and 20 heavy guns and howitzers were firing 24 June–1 July. These figures do not include available enfilade firepower from 111th Infantry Division further north and 52nd Infantry Division to the south.
11. Stosch, Albrecht von, *Somme-Nord, I Teil: Die Brennpunkte der Schlacht im Juli 1916* (Berlin: Gerhard Stalling, 1927), pp. 250–1; analysis of XIV Reserve Corps' order of battle reveals 52nd Infantry Division had about 28 batteries totalling roughly 100 guns on strength. By contrast 2nd Guards Reserve Division's 80 guns were spread across about 22 batteries.
12. Edmonds, Brigadier General Sir James E., *Military Operations, France and Belgium 1916: Sir Douglas Haig's Command to the 1st July: Battle of the Somme* (London: Macmillan, 1932), p. 460.
13. Büsing, *op. cit.*
14. *The Confusion of Command: The War Memoirs of Lieutenant General Sir Thomas D'Oyly Snow, 1914–1915*, ed. Dan Snow and Mark Pottle (Barnsley: Frontline Books, 2011), p. xvi.
15. *ibid.*, pp. 6–7.
16. Robbins, Simon, *British Generalship on the Western Front 1914–18: Defeat into Victory* (Abingdon: Frank Cass, 2005), p. 65.

17. *Confusion of Command*, p. 17.
18. Robbins, p. 65.
19. *ibid.*
20. *ibid.*, pp. 30, 65.
21. *ibid.*, p. 62.
22. *ibid.*, p. 61.
23. *ibid.*
24. MacDonald, Alan, *Pro Patria Mori: the 56th (1st London) Division at Gommecourt, 1st July 1916* (Liskeard: Diggory Press, 2006), pp. 23–4.
25. MacDonald, *Pro Patria*, p. 24; Edmonds (p. 454.) hints this option would probably have been better.
26. Edmonds, p. 454.
27. Home, Brigadier-General Sir Archibald, *The Diary of a World War I Cavalry Officer* (Tunbridge Wells: DJ Costello (Publishers) Ltd, 1985), p. 113.
28. *ibid.*, p. 107.
29. *ibid.*
30. MacDonald, *Pro Patria*, p. 407.
31. *ibid.*
32. Moore, Aubrey, ULLC/WW1/WF02/M/24.
33. Southam, Lionel, letter, 1 July 1929, NAUK, CAB/45/137.
34. 'Report on Operations at Gommecourt 1st July 1916,' 56th Division, war diary, July 1916, NAUK, WO/95/2931/3.
35. Edmonds, p. 460.
36. *ibid.*
37. *ibid.*
38. *ibid.*, pp. 460–1.
39. MacDonald, Alan, *A Lack of Offensive Spirit? The 46th (North Midland) Division at Gommecourt, 1st July 1916* (London: Iona Books, 2008), p. 208; the 56th had 90,000 18-pounder shells for bombardment days U–Y, of which 27,500 were for wire-cutting. By contrast, the 46th had 79,358 shells, of which 10,790 were for wire-cutting.
40. Kümmel, Adolf, *Reserve Infanterie Regiment Nr. 91 im Weltkriege 1914–18* (Oldenburg: Gerhard Stalling, 1926), pp. 210–11; RIR91 refers to the wire being destroyed or swept away. This does not tally with British accounts. Presumably RIR91 meant formal stands of wire, rather than the tangles that remained.
41. *ibid.*, p. 210.
42. 'Defence of Gommecourt,' p. 552.
43. Kümmel, p. 209.
44. Wohlenberg, Alfred, *Das Reserve-Infanterie-Regiment Nr. 77 im Weltkrieg 1914–18* (Hildesheim: Gerstenberg, 1931), p. 172.
45. Smith, Aubrey, *Four Years on the Western Front* (London: Long Acre, 1922), p. 149.
46. *ibid.*
47. Edmonds, p. 460; see also Shipley, Charles, letter, 5 June 1929, NAUK, CAB/45/137.
48. *ibid.*, p. 459.
49. *ibid.*, p. 460.
50. MacDonald, *Pro Patria*, p. 28; Reichsarchiv, *Der Weltkrieg 1914 bis 1918: Die Operationen des Jahres 1916* (Berlin: Mittler & Sohn, 1936), p. 342.
51. Edmonds, p. 461.
52. Kümmel, p. 211.
53. Forstner, Kurt *Freiherr* von, *Das Königlich-Preussische Reserve-Infanterie-Regiment Nr. 15*, (Oldenburg: Gerhard Stalling, 1929), pp. 301–3.
54. *ibid.*
55. Liveing, Edward, *Attack on the Somme: an Infantry Subaltern's Impressions of July 1st, 1916* (Stevenage: Spa Books, 1986), pp. 60–1.
56. *ibid.*
57. MacDonald, *Pro Patria*, p. 240.
58. *ibid.*
59. Edmonds, p. 462; the Official Historian incorrectly states that this frontage was 900 yards.
60. Report of Operation of the 56th (London) Division, 56th Division, war diary, July 1916, NAUK, WO/95/2931/3.
61. Liveing, p. 66.
62. *ibid.*
63. Schuman, Arthur, ULLC/WW1/WF02/S/3.
64. Hart, Peter, *The Somme* (London: Weidenfeld & Nicholson, 2005), p. 118.
65. Carrington, Charles, *Soldier From the Wars Returning* (London: Hutchinson, 1965), p. 114.
66. Lockhart, *op. cit.*
67. Carrington, p. 115.
68. Hart, *Somme*, p. 126.
69. Schuman, *op. cit.*
70. Stosch, p. 24.
71. Barber, Henry, ULLC/WW1/WF01/B/4.
72. Stosch, p. 24.
73. Sheldon, Jack, *The German Army on the Somme 1914–1916* (Barnsley: Pen & Sword, 2005), pp. 140–1.
74. *ibid.*, p. 141.
75. *ibid.*
76. Berkefeld (Plot 3, grave 1101); Niemeyer (Plot 3, grave 1102); Schultheiss (Plot 3, grave 1042).
77. 'Defence of Gommecourt,' p. 540.

78. Hawkings, Frank, *From Ypres to Cambrai* (Morley: Elmford Press, 1974), p. 97.
79. Liveing, p. 69.
80. Schuman, *op. cit.*
81. MacDonald, *Pro Patria*, p. 269.
82. *ibid.*
83. *ibid.*, p. 239.
84. Stosch, p. 24.
85. Lademann, Ulrich, *Das 3. Magdebeurgische Infanterie-Regiment Nr. 66* (Oldenburg: Gerhard Stalling, 1922), p. 33.
86. Büsing, *op. cit.*
87. Bowles, John, letter, 1 July 1929, NAUK, CAB/45/132.
88. 'Defence of Gommecourt,' p. 553.
89. 1/5th Londons, war diary, 1 July 1916, NAUK, WO/95/2961.
90. *ibid.*
91. Harris, Percy, letter, 10 April 1974, ULLC/WW1/MID01.
92. 'Defence of Gommecourt,' pp. 540–1.
93. Hart, *Somme*, p. 120.
94. *ibid.*, p. 121.
95. *ibid.*
96. Macdonald, Lyn, *Somme* (London: Papermac, 1986), p. 68.
97. Tennant, Cecil, ULLC/WW1/MID01.
98. Hart, *Somme*, p. 124.
99. *ibid.*
100. Barber, *op. cit.*
101. MacDonald, *Pro Patria*, p. 291
102. Hart, *Somme*, p. 125.
103. *ibid.*
104. 56th (1st London) Division, war diary, 1 July 1916, NAUK, WO/95/2931/3.
105. 'Report on Operations at Gommecourt 1st July 1916,' *op. cit.*
106. 56th (1st London) Division, war diary, 1 July 1916, *op. cit.*
107. 'Defence of Gommecourt,' p. 538.
108. There is no known reference to Borries or Süsskind-Schwendi interfering in local-level responses to the incursion. Nevertheless, it seems improbable two such hands-on commanders would shy from offering crisp guidance.
109. 'Defence of Gommecourt,' p. 541.
110. Tauscher's battalion was sent to counterattack immediately south of Gommecourt. The tactical situation there prohibited a flanking counterattack and so Tauscher applied his battalion in IR170's sector, commanding them from a high point on Garde Stellung about 1000 yards east of Gommecourt. Tauscher would be captured at Beaumont Hamel later in 1916, imprisoned in Derby and Leicester and then repatriated due to illness.
111. 'Defence of Gommecourt,' p. 541.
112. *ibid.*
113. *ibid.*, p. 551.
114. Ihlenfeld, Otto von, *Das 9. Badische Infanterie-Regiment Nr. 170 im Weltkriege* (Oldenburg: Gerhard Stalling, 1926), p. 34; Stosch, pp. 22–30; 'Defence of Gommecourt,' pp. 538–43; MacDonald, *Pro Patria*, pp. 310–23.
115. *Express & Star*, 28 July 2014; www.expressandstar.com/news/great-war/2014/07/28/1916-the-somme-such-high-hopes/.
116. Williams, Herbert, ULLC/WW1/GS/1745.
117. *ibid.*
118. MacDonald, *Pro Patria*, p. 323.
119. Keegan, John, *The Face of Battle: A Study of Agincourt, Waterloo and the Somme* (London: Pimlico, 1992), p. 253.
120. Hart, *Somme*, p. 128.
121. 'Defence of Gommecourt,' p. 541.
122. Forstner, p. 305.
123. Schuman, *op. cit.*
124. MacDonald, *Pro Patria*, p. 337
125. Schuman, *op. cit.*
126. 'Defence of Gommecourt,' pp. 541–2.
127. 56th (1st London) Division, war diary, 1 July 1916, NAUK, WO/95/2931/3.
128. *ibid.*
129. *ibid.*
130. Southam, *op. cit.*
131. 'Defence of Gommecourt,' p. 552; from the regiment's total 1 July casualties of 397 are deducted those of its battalion in the northern half of the salient, which are dealt with elsewhere in this chapter.
132. Edmonds, p. 475.
133. Whitehead, *Vol. 2*, p. 132.
134. *ibid.*, *Verlustlisten* disc.
135. Forstner, p. 301.
136. *ibid.*
137. Middlebrook, Martin, *The First Day on the Somme* (London: Penguin Books, 1984), p. 235.
138. Higgins, Thomas James, *Tommy at Gommecourt* (Leek: Churnet Valley Books, 2005), p. 38.
139. *ibid.*
140. Moore, *op. cit.*
141. *ibid.*
142. Kümmel, p. 211.
143. Stosch, p. 21.
144. Kümmel, p. 212.
145. Edmonds, p. 467.
146. MacDonald, *Offensive Spirit*, p. 341.
147. *ibid.*
148. Raymer, Robert, letter, 25 June 1929, NAUK, CAB/45/137.

149. 137th Brigade, war diary, 1 July 1916, NAUK, WO/95/2683/3.
150. *Walsall Observer and South Staffordshire Chronicle*, 29 July 1916.
151. MacDonald, *Offensive Spirit*, p. 334.
152. Adams, George, letters, Imperial War Museum.
153. *ibid.*
154. *ibid.*
155. MacDonald, *Offensive Spirit*, p. 318.
156. Moore, *op. cit.*
157. Kümmel, p. 212.
158. MacDonald, *Offensive Spirit*, p. 332.
159. *ibid.*, p.331.
160. Higgins, p. 39.
161. MacDonald, *Offensive Spirit*, pp. 328–9.
162. Kümmel, p. 213.
163. Stansby, John, ULLC/WW1/MID01.
164. *ibid.*
165. Kümmel, p. 213.
166. *ibid.*
167. Stosch, p. 21.
168. Edmonds, p. 467.
169. Singleton, Joseph, ULLC/WW1/MID01.
170. *ibid.*
171. Tomlinson, Auberon, ULLC/WW1/MID01.
172. MacDonald, *Offensive Spirit*, p. 373.
173. Smith, Sidney, Prisoner of War Statement, NAUK, WO/161/100/292.
174. Kümmel, p. 212.
175. *ibid.*
176. *ibid.*
177. 'Statements of men who reached the German Front Line,' 139th Brigade, war diary, July 1916, NAUK, WO/95/2692/5.
178. *ibid.*
179. *ibid.*
180. 1/5th Notts & Derby, war diary, 1 July 1916, NAUK, WO/95/2695/1.
181. *ibid.*
182. Jones, Charles, letter, 15 August 1929, NAUK, CAB/45/135.
183. Good, Claude, ULLC/WW1.WF01/G/9.
184. MacDonald, *Offensive Spirit*, p. 504.
185. Edmonds, p. 469.
186. 46th (North Midland) Division, war diary, 1 July 1916, NAUK, WO/95/2663/3.
187. *ibid.*
188. Edmonds, p. 469.
189. Good, *op. cit.*
190. *ibid.*
191. 46th (North Midland) Division, war diary, *op. cit.*
192. Edmonds, p. 469.
193. *ibid.*, p. 470.
194. MacDonald, *Offensive Spirit*, p. 449.
195. Moore, Aubrey, *op. cit.*
196. *ibid.*
197. MacDonald, *Offensive Spirit*, p. 462.
198. Sandall, Thomas, *A History of the 5th Battalion, the Lincolnshire Regiment* (Oxford: Basil Blackwell, 1922), p. 77.
199. Ward, Arthur, ULLC/WW1/WF02/W/4.
200. Killed: Lieutenant-Colonels D.D. Wilson, 1/5th Sherwood Foresters, L.A. Hind, 1/7th Sherwood Foresters and C.E. Boote, 16th North Staffords; died of wounds: Lieutenant-Colonel W. Burnett, 1/5th North Staffords; wounded: Lieutenant-Colonel R.R. Raymer, 1/5th South Staffords.
201. MacDonald, *Offensive Spirit*, p. 312.
202. *ibid.*, p. 312; Kümmel, p. 212; 'Defence of Gommecourt,' p. 552; Whitehead, Ralph, *The Other Side of the Wire, Vol. 2: The Battle of the Somme. With the German XIV Reserve Corps, 1 July 1916* (Solihull: Helion, 2013), p. 177.
203. MacDonald, *Offensive Spirit*, p. 500.
204. Home, p. 113.
205. 'Defence of Gommecourt,' p. 546.
206. *ibid.*
207. Edmonds, p. 475.
208. Edmonds, p. 475; Whitehead, *Vol. 2*, p. 132; there are apparent contradictions between the figures given in these sources, and also 'Defence of Gommecourt,' *op. cit.*, p. 552.
209. Whitehead, *Vol. 2*, p. 177.
210. 'VII Corps Report on Operations at Gommecourt, 1st July 1916,' VII Corps GS, war diary, July 1916, NAUK, WO/95/804.
211. *ibid.*
212. *ibid.*
213. Snow, diary, 1 July 1916, Imperial War Museum.
214. Hawkings, p. 103.
215. *ibid.*
216. Wallis, Ferdinand, letter, 9 September 1929, NAUK, CAB/45/132.
217. *ibid.*
218. Read, Isaac, *Of Those We Loved* (Durham: The Pentland Press, 1994), p. 130.
219. *ibid.*

Chapter 11: The Earth Abideth
1. Barber, Henry, ULLC/WW1/MID01.
2. Farrar-Hockley, A.H., *The Somme* (London: Pan Books, 1966), p. 174.
3. Edmonds, Sir James, *Military Operations France and Belgium, 1916, Vol. 1* (London: Imperial War Museum, 1992), p. 483.
4. Rawlinson, diary, 1 July 1916, Rawlinson Papers 1/5, Churchill Archive.

5. Haig, Douglas, diary, 2 July 1916, NAUK, WO/256/11.
6. Edmonds, p. 483.
7. Haig, diary, 2 July 1916, *op. cit.*
8. Sheffield, Gary, *The Chief: Douglas Haig and the British Army* (London: Aurum Press, 2011), p. 176.
9. *ibid.*, p. 176.
10. Haig, diary, 1 July 1916, *op. cit.*
11. *ibid.*
12. II Corps, war diary, 1 July 1916, NAUK, WO/95/637.
13. Haig, diary, 1 July 1916, *op. cit.*
14. *ibid.*
15. *ibid.*
16. II Corps, war diary, 1 July 1916, *op. cit.*
17. Continuation of Fourth Army Operation Order No. 2, 22 June 1916, Fourth Army Operations Papers, NAUK, WO/158/234.
18. Sheffield, *The Chief*, p. 170.
19. *ibid.*
20. Stosch, p. 62; Fiedel, p. 121.
21. 1st Borders, war diary, 1 July 1916, NAUK, WO/95/2305/1; 1st Essex, war diary, 1 July 1916, NAUK, WO/95/2309/1; 2nd South Wales Borderers, war diary, 1 July 1916, NAUK, WO/95/2304/2; 16th Highland Light Infantry, war diary, 1 July 1916, NAUK, WO/95/2403/2; 9th Royal Irish Rifles, war diary, 1 July 1916, NAUK, WO/95/2503/2; 2nd Middlesex, war diary, 1 July 1916, NAUK, WO/95/1713/1; 8th King's Own Yorkshire Light Infantry, war diary, 1 July 1916, NAUK, WO/95/2187/2; 10th Lincolns, war diary, 1 July 1916, NAUK, WO/95/2457/1; 2nd West Yorkshires, war diary, 1 July 1916, NAUK, WO/95/1714/1; 16th Royal Scots, war diary, 1 July 1916, NAUK, WO/95/2458/1; 8th York & Lancasters, war diary, 1 July 1916, NAUK, WO/95/2188; 11th Sherwood Foresters, war diary, 1 July 1916, NAUK, WO/95/2187/3; 20th Manchesters, war diary, 1 July 1916, NAUK, WO/95/1663/1; 21st Manchesters, war diary, 1 July 1916, NAUK, WO/95/1668/1; 2nd Royal Warwick, war diary, 1 July 1916, NAUK, WO/95/1664/3; 12th Middlesex, war diary, 1 July 1916, NAUK, WO/95/2044/1; 1/2nd Monmouths, war diary, 1 July 1916, NAUK, WO/95/2295/1; 15th Highland Light Infantry, war diary, 1 July 1916, NAUK, WO/95/2393/2; 15th Lancashire Fusiliers, war diary, 1 July 1916, NAUK, WO/95/2397/3; 19th Lancashire Fusiliers, war diary, 1 July 1916, NAUK, WO/95/2394/1; 10th Royal Inniskilling Fusiliers, war diary, 1 July 1916, NAUK, WO/95/2510/4; 29th Division Unit Strengths Table, 29th Division, war diaries, March–August 1916, NAUK, WO/95/2280.
22. Excludes two platoons of 7th Buffs.
23. Buchan, John, *The Battle of the Somme: First Phase* (London: Thomas Nelson & Sons, 1916), p. 31.
24. Edmonds, p. 77.
25. Rawlinson, diary, 1 July 1916, *op. cit.*
26. *ibid.*
27. Fourth Army Summary of Operations, 1st July, 1916, Fourth Army, Battle of the Somme: Summary Operations, NAUK, WO/158/327.
28. Rawlinson, diary, 1 July 1916, *op. cit.*
29. *ibid.*
30. *ibid.*
31. *ibid.*
32. *ibid.*
33. Fourth Army Summary of Operations, *op. cit.*
34. *ibid.*; the reference to Contalmaison is taken from map references stated in the report.
35. Rawlinson, diary, 1 July 1916, *op. cit.*
36. Edmonds, p. 480.
37. Maze, Paul, *A Frenchman in Khaki* (London: Heinemann, 1934), pp. 136–7; Gough, Hubert, *Fifth Army* (London: Hodder & Stoughton, 1931), pp. 136–7.
38. Maze, *op. cit.*
39. Gough, p. 137.
40. See Chapter 1.
41. 3rd Cavalry Division, war diary, 1 July 1916, NAUK, WO/95/1141/3.
42. *ibid.*
43. Haig, diary, 27 June 1916, *op. cit.*
44. *ibid.*
45. Rawlinson, diary, 28 and 30 June 1916, *op. cit.*
46. *ibid.*, 1 July 1916.
47. *ibid.*
48. *ibid.*
49. *ibid.*
50. Fourth Army Summary of Operations, *op. cit.*; Rawlinson, diary, 1 July 1916, *op. cit.*
51. See Chapter 9.
52. Stosch, Albrecht von, *Somme-Nord, I Teil: Die Brennpunkte der Schlacht im Juli 1916* (Berlin: Gerhard Stalling, 1927), p. 83.
53. Rawlinson, diary, 1 July 1916, *op. cit.*; Haig, diary, 1 July 1916, *op. cit.*; Rawlinson makes no mention of Haig's arrival at Querrieu in his time-stamped and detailed diary up to 3.15 p.m. The

next entry thereafter, to 7.30 p.m., notes Haig had been at Querrieu, meaning he arrived between 3.15 p.m. and 7.30 p.m. Rawlinson noted in his next time-stamped diary entry, at 10 p.m., that General Foch had visited Querrieu at 9 p.m. Haig must have left Querrieu at 4.30 p.m., if not earlier, if he was to have driven the roughly 30 minutes' journey to Villers-Bocage, where he arrived at 5 p.m.

54. Haig, diary, 1 July 1916, *ibid.*; II Corps, war diary, 1 July 1916, *op. cit.*
55. *ibid.*; Rawlinson, diary, 1 July 1916, *op. cit.*
56. 1st Cavalry Division, war diary and appendices, 1 July 1916, *op. cit.*; 2nd Indian Cavalry Division, war diary and appendices, 1 July 1916, *op. cit.*; 3rd Cavalry Division, war diary and appendices, 1 July 1916, *op. cit.*; Reserve Army, war diary and appendices, 1 July 1916, *op. cit.*; II Corps war diary and appendices, 1 July 1916, *op. cit.*; Fourth Army Operations Papers, July 1916, *op. cit.*; Reserve Army Operations Papers, July 1916, NAUK, WO/95/518.
57. Edmonds, p. 481; Edmonds' comment is based on Fourth Army Operation Order No. 3, 1 July 1916 and Fourth Army Operations Papers, *op. cit.*
58. *ibid.*
59. Reserve Army, war diary, 1 July 1916, NAUK, WO/95/518; 1st Cavalry Division, war diary, 1 July 1916, NAUK, WO/95/1097/5; 2nd Indian Cavalry Division, war diary, 1 July 1916, NAUK, WO/95/1180/1; 3rd Cavalry Division, war diary, 1 July 1916, *op. cit.*
60. Haig, diary, 1 July, *op. cit.*; OAD 32, 1 July 1916, Fourth Army Operations Papers, *op. cit.*; OAD 33, 1 July 1916, Fourth Army Operations Papers, *op. cit.*; 'Decisions of C.-in-C — 5 p.m., 1-7-16,' 1 July 1916, Fourth Army Operations Papers, *op. cit.*; 23rd Division, war diary, 1 July 1916, NAUK, WO/95/2167/4; 38th (Welsh) Division, war diary, 1 July 1916, NAUK, WO/95/2539/4.
61. OAD 32, 1 July 1916, Fourth Army Operations Papers, NAUK, WO/158/234; Decisions of C-in-C at 5 p.m. on 1 July 1916, Fourth Army Operations Papers, *op. cit.*
62. Rawlinson, diary, 1 July 1916, *op. cit.*
63. Sheffield, *The Chief*, p. 172.
64. Norman, William, letter, 28 February 1930, NAUK, CAB/45/136.
65. Fourth Army Operation Order No. 3, 1 July 1916, Fourth Army Operations Papers, *op. cit.*
66. *ibid.*
67. *ibid.*
68. Charteris, Brigadier-General John, *At G.H.Q.* (London: Cassell , 1931), p. 151.
69. *ibid.*, p. 152.
70. Gough, Hubert, *Fifth Army* (London: Hodder & Stoughton, 1931), pp. 138–9.
71. Haig, diary, 2 July 1916, *op. cit.*
72. *ibid.*
73. OA136, telegram, 2 July 1916, Fourth Army Operations Papers, *op. cit.*
74. Gough, p. 139.
75. Kiggell, Launcelot, to Edmonds, James, letter, 2 December 1937, NAUK CAB/45/135; Macdonald, Andrew, *Passchendaele: The Anatomy of a Tragedy* (Auckland: HarperCollins, 2013), pp. 47–9, 63–4.
76. The French 39th Division suffered 728 total casualties, and the French 11th Division accrued at least 670 total casualties.
77. Sixty-first Division suffered 1058 dead, wounded and missing, Third Colonial Division about 2522 for the period 1–5 July, but mostly on the first day of that range. Casualty data for 2nd Colonial Division is incomplete, but it is known to have evacuated 757 wounded French soldiers in 24 hours to 8 a.m. on 2 July.
78. Edmonds, p. 343.
79. Philpott, William, *Bloody Victory: The sacrifice on the Somme* (London: Abacus, 2011), p. 197.
80. *ibid.*
81. Reichsarchiv, *Der Weltkrieg 1914 bis 1918: Die Operationen des Jahres 1916* (Berlin: Mittler & Sohn, 1936), p. 351.
82. *Weltkrieg*, p. 351.
83. *ibid.*, p. 352.
84. *ibid.*
85. *ibid.*
86. *ibid.*
87. Dellmensingen, Konrad von, and Feeser, Friedrichfranz, *Das Bayernbuch vom Weltkriege 1914–1918* (Stuttgart: Belser, 1930), p. 304.
88. German units reported casualties incurred over 10-day periods, rather than individual days. Whilst records such as war diaries and muster rolls for several German units that participated in the first day of the Somme have survived, more have not. Such records, along with post-war regimental histories, are the main source for these figures.
89. Lossberg, Friedrich, *Meine Tätigkeit im Weltkriege* (Berlin: Mittler & Sohn, 1939), p. 214. Lossberg makes it clear

Grünert's sacking was decided by 10.30 p.m. on 1 July, the time at which Lossberg was offered the job as Second Army's chief of staff.

90. *ibid.*, pp. 220–1.

91. *ibid.*, p. 220.

92. Falkenhayn, Erich von, *General Headquarters 1914–1916 and its Critical Decisions* (London: Hutchinson, 1919), pp. 264–5.

93. Lossberg, pp. 214–15.

94. *ibid.*

95. *ibid.*, p. 220.

96. Stosch, p. 83.

97. Sheldon, Jack, *The German Army on the Somme 1914–1916* (Barnsley: Pen & Sword, 2005), p. 179; for a slightly different version, see Stosch, p. 109.

98. Falkenhayn, pp. 265–6.

99. Miles, Captain Wilfrid, *Military Operations, France and Belgium 1916: 2nd July to the End of the Battles of the Somme* (London: Macmillan, 1932), pp. XV–XVI; German casualties are given as base total of 500,000, which excluded those incurred during the seven-day bombardment (estimated at 10,000) and less seriously wounded (estimated at 150,000). Miles also cites various other comparative data from German sources.

100. Sheffield, *Somme*, p. 155.

101. Hindenburg, Marshal von, *Out of My Life* (Uckfield: Naval and Military Press, undated), p. ix.

102. Sheffield, Gary, *The Somme* (London: Cassell, 2003), p. 155.

103. Hindenburg, pp. 241–2.

104. Sheffield, *Somme*, p. 156.

105. Haig, Douglas, diary, 29 March 1916, NAUK, WO/256/9.

106. GHQ, 'The Opening of the Wearing-out Battle', 23 December 1916, in Sir Douglas Haig's Despatches, ed. Lt.-Col John H. Boraston (London: JM Dent & Sons, 1919), pp. 58–9.

107. The figure for the number of casualties on the memorial is taken from the Commonwealth War Graves Commission website (www.cwgc.org). Its database links 72,403 names to the Thiepval Memorial, but 148 of these are soldiers who listed under aliases and are therefore included twice. Website last accessed 16 January 2016.

Bibliography

Alexander, Jack, *McCrae's Battalion: The Story of the 16th Royal Scots* (Edinburgh: Mainstream Publishing, 2003).

Ashurst, George, *My Bit: A Lancashire Fusilier at War 1914–1918* (Ramsbury: The Crowood Press, 1987).

Astill, Edwin, ed., *The Great War Diaries of Brigadier Alexander Johnston 1914–1917* (Barnsley: Pen & Sword, 2007).

Atkinson, C.T., *The Seventh Division 1914–1918* (London: John Murrary, 1927).

Atteridge, A. Hilliard, *History of the 17th (Northern) Division* (Glasgow: Robert Maclehose & Co, 1929).

Bachelin, Eduard, *Das Reserve-Infanterie-Regiment Nr. 111 im Weltkrieg 1914 bis 1918* (Karlsruhe: Südwestdeut, 1937).

Bales, P.G., *The History of the 1/4th Battalion Duke of Wellington's (West Riding) Regiment, 1914–1919* (Halifax: Edward Mortimer, 1920).

Balfour, Michael, *The Kaiser and his Times* (Boston: Houghton Mifflin, 1964).

Banks, T.M., and Chell, R.A., *With the 10th Essex in France* (London: Gay & Hancock, 1924).

Barton, Peter, *The Somme: The Unseen Panoramas* (London: Constable & Robinson, 2006).

Baumgartner, Richard, *This Carnival of Hell: German Combat Experience on the Somme* (Huntington: Blue Acorn Press, 2010).

Bax, Cyril, *The Eighth Division in War, 1914–1918* (London: The Medici Society, 1926).

Beach Thomas, W., *With the British on the Somme* (London: Methuen & Co., 1917).

Berkeley, Reginald, *The History of the Rifle Brigade in the War of 1914–1918* (London: The Rifle Brigade Club, 1927).

Bezzel, Oskar, *Das Königlich Bayerische Reserve-Infanterie-Regiment Nr. 6* (München: Schick, 1938).

Boraston, John H., ed., *Sir Douglas Haig's Despatches* (London: JM Dent & Sons, 1919).

Bourne, John, *Who's Who in World War I* (London: Routledge, 2001).

Brown, Ian Malcolm, *British Logistics on the Western Front 1914–1919* (Westport: Praeger, 1998).

Brown, Malcolm, *The Imperial War Museum Book of the Somme* (London: Pan Books, 2002).

Buchan, John, *The Battle of the Somme: First Phase* (London: Thomas Nelson & Sons, 1916).

Burrowes, A.R., *The 1st Battalion, The Faugh-A-Ballaghs in the Great War* (London: Gale & Polden, 1925).

Burrows, John, *The Essex Regiment, 1st Battalion (44th)* (John H. Burrows & Sons, 1927).

Burrows, John, *The Essex Regiment: 2nd Battalion (56th) (Pompadours)* (John H. Burrows & Sons, 1927).

Büsing, Georg, *Das Reserve-Feldartillerie-Regiment Nr. 20 im Weltkrieg 1914–18* (Hannover: Göhmann, 1932).

Carlyon, Les, *Gallipoli* (London: Bantam Books, 2003).

Carrington, Charles, *Soldier From the Wars Returning* (London: Hutchinson, 1965).

Cave, Joy, *What Became of Corporal Pitman?* (Portugal Cove: Breakwater Books, 1976).

Charteris, Brigadier-General John, *At G.H.Q.* (London: Cassell, 1931).

Cook, Tim, *The Madman and the Butcher: The Sensational Wars of Sam Hughes and General Arthur Currie* (Toronto: Allen Lane, 2009).

Cooksey, Jon, *Barnsley Pals: The 13th & 14th Battalions, York & Lancaster Regiment* (Barnsley: Pen & Sword, 2008).

Coppard, George, *With a Machine Gun to Cambrai: The Tale of a Young Tommy in Kitchener's Army 1914–1918* (London: HMSO, 1969).

Croft, Henry, *Twenty-Two Months Under Fire* (London: John Murray, 1917).

Crozier, Frank, *Brass Hat in No Man's Land* (London: Jonathan Cape, 1930).

Crutchley, C.E., ed., *Machine-Gunner 1914–1918: The Personal Experiences of the Machine Gun Corps* (Folkestone: Baley Brothers & Swinfen Ltd, 1975).

Das K.B. 1. Infanterie-Regiment König (München: Lindauersche Universitäts, 1922).

Das Königl. Preuss. Infanterie-Regiment Nr. 63 (4. Oberschlesisches) (Berlin: Bernard & Graefe, 1940).

de Lisle, Beauvoir, *Reminiscences of Sport and War* (London: Eyre & Spottiswoode, 1939).

Dellmensingen, Konrad von, and Feeser, Friedrichfranz, *Das Bayernbuch vom Weltkriege 1914–1918* (Stuttgart: Belser, 1930).

Dixon, Norman, *On the Psychology of Military Incompetence* (London: Pimlico, 1994).

Duffy, Christopher, *Through German Eyes: The British and the Somme 1916* (London: Weidenfeld & Nicholson, 2006).

Dunlop, John, *The Development of the British Army 1899–1914* (London: Methuen, 1938).

Edmonds, Brigadier General Sir James E., *Military Operations, France and Belgium 1916: Sir Douglas Haig's Command to the 1st July: Battle of the Somme* (London: Macmillan, 1932).

Falkenhayn, Erich von, *General Headquarters 1914–1916 and its Critical Decisions* (London: Hutchinson, 1919).

Falls, Cyril, *The History of the 36th (Ulster) Division* (London: M'Caw, Stevenson & Orr, 1922).

Farrar-Hockley, A.H., *The Somme* (London: Pan Books, 1983).

Fiedel, Paul, *Geschichte des Infanterie-Regiments von Winterfeldt (2. Oberschlesisches) Nr. 23* (Berlin: Wilhelm Kolk, 1929).

Forstner, Kurt Freiherr, *Das Königlich-Preussische Reserve-Infanterie-Regiment Nr. 15,* (Oldenburg: Gerhard Stalling, 1929).

Fraser-Tytler, Neil, *Field Guns in France: With a Howitzer Battery in the Battles of the Somme, Arras, Messines and Passchendaele 1915–1918* (Brighton: Tom Donovan, 1995).

Frisch, George, *Das Reserve-Infanterie-Regiment Nr. 109 im Weltkrieg 1914 bis 1918* (Karlsruhe: F. Thiergarten, 1931).

Gardiner, Brian, *The Big Push* (London: Consul, 1963).

Gerster, Matthaus, *Die Schwaben and der Ancre* (Heilbronn: Eugen Salzer, 1918).

Gerster, Matthäus, *Das Württembergische Reserve-Infanterie-Regiment Nr. 119 im Weltkrieg 1914–1918* (Stuttgart: Chr. Belsersche, 1920).

Gibbs, Philip, *The Battles of the Somme* (London: Heinemann, 1917).

Gibbs, Philip, *Now it Can be Told* (London: Harper & Brothers, 1920).

Gillon, Stair, *The K.O.S.B. in the Great War* (London: Thomas Nelson & Sons, 1930).

Gliddon, Gerald, *VCs of the Somme* (Gliddon Books, 1991).

Godley, Alexander, *Life of an Irish Soldier* (New York: EP Dutton, 1939).

Gough, Hubert, *Fifth Army* (London: Hodder & Stoughton, 1931).

Greenwell, Graham, *An Infant in Arms: War Letters of a Company Officer, 1914–1918* (London: Penguin, 1972).

Greiner, Lt. d. R., and Vulpius, Lt. d. R., *Reserve-Infanterie-Regiment Nr. 110 im Weltkrieg 1914–1918* (Karlsruhe: Macklotsche, 1934).

Grieve, Grant, and Newman, Bernard, *Tunnellers: The Story of the Tunnelling Companies, Royal Engineers, during the World War* (London: Herbert Jenkins Ltd, 1936).

Griffith, Paddy, *Battle Tactics of the Western Front: The British Army's Art of Attack 1916–18* (New Haven: Yale University Press, 1994).

Griffith, Paddy, ed., *British Fighting Methods in the Great War* (Portland: Frank Cass, 1998).

Harris, J.P., *Douglas Haig and the First World War* (Cambridge: Cambridge University Press, 2008).

Harris, Ruth, *Billie: the Neville Letters, 1914–1916* (London: Julia MacRae Books, 1991).

Harrison, Gerry, ed., *To Fight Alongside Friends: The First World War Diaries of Charlie May* (London: William Collins, 2014).

Hart, Peter, *Somme Success: The Royal Flying Corps and the Battle of the Somme, 1916* (London: Leo Cooper: 2001).

Hart, Peter, *The Somme* (London: Weidenfeld & Nicholson, 2005).

Hart-Davis, Rupert, ed., *Siegfried Sassoon Diaries 1915–18* (London: Book Club Associates, 1983).

Hasselbach, *Major*, and Strodzki, *Hauptmann*, *Das Reserve Infanterie Regiment Nr. 38* (Zeulenroda: Bernhard Sporn, 1934).

Hasting, Max, *Catastrophe: Europe Goes to War 1914* (London: William Collins, 2014).

Hawkings, Frank, *From Ypres to Cambrai* (Morley: Elmford Press, 1974).

Higgins, Thomas James, *Tommy at Gommecourt* (Leek: Churnet Valley Books, 2005).

Hindenburg, Marshal von, *Out of My Life* (Uckfield: Naval and Military Press, undated).

Holmes, Richard, *Tommy: The British Soldier on the Western Front, 1914–1918* (London: Harper Perennial, 2005).

Holtz, Georg von, *Das Württembg. Res. Inft. Regt. No. 121 im Weltkrieg 1914–1918* (Stuttgart: Chr. Belsersche Verlagsbuchhandlung, 1921).

Home, Brigadier-General Sir Archibald, *The Diary of a World War I Cavalry Officer* (Tunbridge Wells: D.J. Costello (Publishers) Ltd, 1985).

Hurst, Steve, *The Public Schools Battalion in the Great War* (Barnsley: Pen & Sword, 2007).

Ihlenfeld, Otto von, *Das 9. Badische Infanterie-Regiment Nr. 170 im Weltkriege* (Oldenburg: Gerhard Stalling, 1926).

Jack, James, *General Jack's Diary* (London: Eyre & Spottiswoode, 1964).

Jones, H.A., *The War in the Air: Being the Story of the Part Played in the Great War by the Royal Air Force, Vol. 2* (Oxford: Clarendon Press, 1928).

Jones, Simon, *Underground Warfare 1914–1918* (Barnsley: Pen & Sword, 2010).

Keegan, John, *The Face of Battle: A Study of Agincourt, Waterloo and the Somme* (London: Pimlico, 1992).

Kelly, David, *39 Months: With the 'Tigers' 1915–1918* (London: Ernest Benn, 1930).

Kelly, Robert, *A Subaltern's Odyssey* (London: William Kimber, 1980).

Klaus, Max, *Das Württembergische Reserve-Feldartillerie-Regiment Nr. 26 im Weltkrieg 1914–1918* (Stuttgart: Christian Belser, 1929).

Knies, L., *Das Württembergische Pionier-Bataillon im Weltkrieg 1914–1918* (Stuttgart: Chr Belser, 1927).

Koch, Arthur, *Die Flieger-Abteilung (A) 221: Nach den Kriegstagebüchern und Flugmeldungen der Abteilung bearbeitet* (Oldenburg: Gerhard Stalling, 1925).

Kuhl, Hermann von, *Der Weltkrieg 1914–1918, Band I* (Berlin: Wilhelm Kolk, 1929).

Kümmel, Adolf, *Reserve Infanterie Regiment Nr. 91 im Weltkriege 1914–18* (Oldenburg: Gerhard Stalling, 1926).

Lademann, Ulrich, *Das 3. Magdeburgische Infanterie-Regiment Nr. 66* (Oldenburg: Gerhard Stalling, 1922).

Lais, Otto, *Erlebnisse Badischer Frontsoldaten: Maschinengewehr im Eisernen Regiment (8. Badisches Infanterie-Regiment Nr. 169)* (Karlsruhe: G. Braun, 1935).

Lais, Otto, *Die Schlacht an der Somme 1916* (Karlsruhe: G. Braun, 1940).

Langford, William, *Somme Intelligence: Fourth Army HQ 1916* (Barnsley: Pen & Sword, 2013).

Lettow-Vorbeck, Friedrich von, *Geschichte des Fusilier-Regiments von Gersdorff (Kurhessisches) Nr. 80* (Marburg: W Braun, 1913).

Levine, Joshua, *Forgotten Voices of the Somme* (London: Ebury Publishing, 2009).

Lewis, Cecil, *Sagittarius Rising* (London: Greenhill Books, 1998).

Liddle, Peter, *The 1916 Battle of the Somme* (Ware: Wordsworth Edition, 2001).

Lind, Francis, *The Letters of Mayo Lind: Newfoundland's Unofficial War Correspondent 1914–16* (St John's: Killick Press, 2001).

Liveing, Edward, *Attack on the Somme: An Infantry Subaltern's Impressions of July 1st, 1916* (Stevenage: Spa Books, 1986).

Lossberg, Friedrich, *Meine Tätigkeit im Weltkriege* (Berlin: Mittler & Sohn, 1939).

Lushington, Franklin, *The Gambardier: Giving Some Account of the Heavy and Siege Artillery in France, 1914–1918* (London: Ernest Benn, 1930).

MacDonald, Alan, *Pro Patria Mori: 56th (1st London) Division at Gommecourt, 1st July 1916* (Cornwall: Exposure Press, 2006).

MacDonald, Alan, *A Lack of Offensive Spirit? The 46th (North Midland) Division at Gommecourt, 1st July 1916* (London: Iona Books, 2008).

MacDonald, Alan, *Z Day: VIII Corps at Beaumont Hamel and Serre* (London: Iona Books, 2014).

Macdonald, Andrew, *On My Way to the Somme: New Zealanders and the Bloody Offensive of 1916* (Auckland: HarperCollins, 2005).

Macdonald, Andrew, *Passchendaele: The Anatomy of a Tragedy* (Auckland: HarperCollins, 2013).

Mace, Martin, and Grehan, John, eds, *Slaughter on the Somme: 1 July 1916* (Barnsley: Pen & Sword, 2013).

Maddocks, Graham, *Liverpool Pals: A History of the 17th, 18th, 19th and 20th (Service) Battalions, The King's (Liverpool Regiment) 1914–1919* (London: Leo Cooper, 1991).

Malins, Geoffrey, *How I Filmed the War* (London: Imperial War Museum, 1993).

Masefield, John, *The Old Front Line* (New York: MacMillan Co., 1917).

Maurice, Major-General Sir Frederick, *The Life of General Lord Rawlinson of Trent* (London: Cassell, 1928).

Maze, Paul, *A Frenchman in Khaki* (London: Heinemann, 1934).

Mead, Gary, *The Good Soldier: The Biography of Douglas Haig* (London: Atlantic Books, 2008).

Medomsley, Jack, *William Noel Hodgson: The Gentle Poet* (Durham: Mel Publicataions, 1989).

Middlebrook, Martin, *The First Day on the Somme* (London: Penguin, 1984).

Miles, Captain Wilfrid, *Military Operations, France and Belgium 1916: 2nd July to the End of the Battles of the Somme* (London: Macmillan, 1932).

Mitchell, Gardiner, *Three Cheers for the Derrys! A History of the 10th Royal Inniskilling Fusiliers in the 1914–18 War* (Derry: Yes! Publications, 1991).

Moos, Ernst, *Das Württembergische Reserve.-Feld-Artillerie-Regiment Nr. 27 im Weltkrieg 1916–1918* (Stuttgart: Belser, 1925).

Müller, Paul, Fabeck, Hans von, and Riesel, Richard, *Geschichte des Reserve-Infanterie-Regiments Nr. 99* (Zeulenroda: Sporn, 1936).

Müller-Loebnitz, Wilhelm, *Die Badener im Weltkrieg 1914/1918, Band I* (Karlsruhe: G. Braun Verlag, 1935).

Neame, Edward, *German Strategy in the Great War* (London: Edward Arnold, 1923).

Nichols, G.H.F., *The 18th Division in the Great War* (London: William Blackwood & Sons, 1922).

Oldfield, Paul, and Gibson, Ralph, *Sheffield City Battalion: The 12th (Service) Battalion York & Lancaster Regiment* (Barnsley: Pen & Sword, 2010).

O'Neill, Herbert, *The Royal Fusiliers in the Great War* (London: Heinemann, 1922).

Orr, Philip, *The Road to the Somme: Men of the Ulster Division Tell Their Story* (Belfast: Blackstaff Press, 2008).

Passingham, Ian, *All the Kaiser's Men: The Life and Death of the German Soldier on the Western Front* (Stroud: The History Press, 2011).

Perry, Nicholas, ed., *Major-General Oliver Nugent and the Ulster Division, 1915–1918* (Stroud: Sutton Publishing for Army Records Society, 2007).

Philpott, William, *Bloody Victory: The Sacrifice on the Somme* (London: Abacus, 2011).

Prichard, H.L., ed., *History of the Corps of Royal Engineers* (London: Institute of Royal Engineers, 1951).

Prior, Robin, and Wilson, Trevor, *Command on the Western Front: The Military Career of Sir Henry Rawlinson 1914–1918* (Barnsley: Pen & Sword, 2004).

Prior, Robin, and Wilson, Trevor, *The Somme* (Sydney: University of New South Wales Press, 2005).

Pugsley, Christopher, *On the Fringe of Hell: New Zealanders and Military Discipline in the First World War* (Auckland: Hodder & Stoughton, 1991).

Read, Isaac, *Of Those We Loved* (Durham: The Pentland Press, 1994).

Reichsarchiv, *Der Weltkrieg 1914 bis 1918: Die Operationen des Jahres 1916* (Berlin: Mittler & Sohn, 1936).

Renz, Irina, Krumeich, Gerd, and Hirschfeld, Gerhard, *Scorched Earth: The Germans on the Somme 1914–1918* (Barnsley: Pen & Sword, 2009).

Reymann, H., *Das 3. Oberschlesische Infanterie-Regiment Nr. 62 im Kriege 1914–1918* (Zeulenroda: Sporn, 1930).

Riegel, Lt. d. Res., *Maschinengewehr-Scharffschutzen im Felde 1916–1918: MG.SS.-Abt. 54* (Beuchdruckerei H. Kuhn, Schwenningen am Neckar, undated).

Robbins, Simon, *British Generalship on the Western Front 1914–18* (Abingdon: France Cass, 2005).

Robbins, Simon, ed., *The First World War Letters of General Lord Horne* (Stroud: The Army Records Society, 2009).

Rowan, E.W.J., *The 54th Infantry Brigade 1914–1918: Some Records of Battle and Laughter in France* (Aldershot: Gale & Polden, undated).

Rudolph, M., *Geschichte des Bayrischen Fussartillerie Bataillons Nr. 10* (Zeulenroda: Sporn, 1936).

Sandall, Thomas, *A History of the 5th Battalion, the Lincolnshire Regiment* (Oxford: Basil Blackwell, 1922).

Schiedt, *Major, Das Reserve-Infanterie-Regiment Nr. 51 im Weltkriege 1914–1918* (Zeulenroda: Bernhard Sporn, 1936).

Shakespear, J., *The Thirty-Fourth Division 1915–1919: The Story of Its Career from Ripon to the Rhine* (London: H.F. & G. Witherby, 1921).

Shakespear, J., *A Record of the 17th and 32nd Service Battalions Northumberland Fusiliers (N.E.R.) Pioneers 1914–1919* (Newcastle-upon-Tyne: Northumberland Press, 1926).

Sheen, John, *Tyneside Irish: 24th, 25th, 26th & 27th (Service) Battalions of Northumberland Fusiliers* (Barnsley: Pen & Sword, 1998).

Sheen, John, *Durham Pals: 18th, 19th, & 22nd (Service) Battalions of the Durham Light Infantry* (Barnsley: Pen & Sword, 2006).

Sheffield, Gary, *Forgotten Victory, The First World War: Myths and Realities* (London: Headline Book Publishing, 2001).

Sheffield, Gary, *The Somme* (London: Cassell, 2003).

Sheffield, Gary, *The Chief: Douglas Haig and the British Army* (London: Aurum Press, 2011).

Sheffield, Gary, and Bourne, John, ed., *Douglas Haig: War Diaries and Letters 1914–1918* (London: Weidenfeld & Nicolson, 2005).

Sheffield, Gary, and Todman, Dan, ed., *Command and Control on the Western Front: The British Army's Experience, 1914–1918* (Stroud: Spellmount, 2007).

Sheldon, Jack, *The German Army on the Somme 1914–1916* (Barnsley: Pen & Sword, 2005).

Sheldon, Jack, *The Germans at Thiepval* (Barnsley: Pen & Sword, 2006).

Sheldon, Jack, *The Germans at Beaumont Hamel*, (Barnsley: Pen & Sword, 2006).

Simpson, Andy, *Directing Operations: British Corps Command on the Western Front, 1914–1918* (Stroud: Spellmount Publishing, 2006).

Smith, Aubrey, *Four Years on the Western Front* (London: Odhams Press, 1922).

Snow, Dan, and Pottle, Mark, eds, *The Confusion of Command: The War Memoirs of Lieutenant General Sir Thomas D'Oyly Snow, 1914–1915* (Barnsley: Frontline Books, 2011).

Soden, Franz von, *Die 26. (Württembergische) Reserve-Division im Weltkrieg 1914–1918* (Stuttgart: Bergers Literarisches Büro, 1939).

Spicer, Lancelot, *Letters from France 1915–1918* (London: Robert York, 1979).

Stanley, F.C., *The History of the 89th Brigade, 1914–1918* (Liverpool: Daily Post, 1919).

Statistics of the Military Effort of the British Empire During the Great War 1914–1920 (London: The War Office, 1922).

Stedman, Michael, *The Somme 1916 & Other Experiences of the Salford Pals: A History of the 15th, 16th, 19th & 20th Battalions Lancashire Fusiliers 1914–1919* (Barnsley: Pen & Sword, 1993).

Stedman, Michael, *Fricourt-Mametz* (Barnsley: Pen & Sword, 2011).

Stein, Hermann von, *A War Minister and His Work: Reminiscences of 1914–1918* (London: Skeffington & Son, Ltd, 1920).

Stosch, Albrecht von, *Somme-Nord, I Teil: Die Brennpunkte der Schlacht im Juli 1916* (Berlin: Gerhard Stalling, 1927).

Stosch, Albrecht von, *Somme-Nord, II Teil: Die Brennpunkte der Schlacht im Juli 1916* (Berlin: Gerhard Stalling, 1927).

Strohn, Matthias, *World War I Companion* (Oxford: Osprey, 2013).

Strong, Paul, and Marble, Sanders, *Artillery in the Great War* (Barnsley: Pen & Sword, 2011).

Taylor, James, *The 1st Royal Irish Rifles in the Great War* (Dublin: Four Courts Press, 2002).

Terraine, John, *Douglas Haig: The Educated Soldier* (London: Hutchinson, 1963).

Travers, T.H.E., *How the War Was Won: Command and Technology in the British Army on the Western Front: 1917–1918* (London: Routledge, 1992).

Turner, P.W., and Haigh, R.H., *Not for Glory* (London: Robert Maxwell, 1969).

Vischer, Alfred, *Das 10. Württ. Infanterie-Regiment Nr. 180 in der Somme-Schlacht 1916* (Stuttgart: Uhland'schen, 1917).

Vischer, Alfred, *Das Württ. Infanterie-Regiment Nr. 180* (Stuttgart: Christian Belsers, 1921).

Westman, Stephan, *Surgeon with the Kaiser's Army* (London: William Kimber, 1968).

Whitehead, Ralph, *The Other Side of the Wire, Vol. 1: The Battle of the Somme. With the German XIV Reserve Corps, September 1914–June 1916* (Solihull: Helion, 2010).

Whitehead, Ralph, *The Other Side of the Wire, Vol. 2: The Battle of the Somme. With the German XIV Reserve Corps, 1 July 1916.* (Solihull: Helion, 2013).

Wilmott, H.P., *The First World War* (London: Dorling Kindersley, 2003).

Witkop, Philipp, *German Students' War Letters* (Pine Street Books, Kindle Edition).

Wohlenberg, Alfred, *Das Reserve-Infanterie-Regiment Nr. 77 im Weltkrieg 1914–18* (Hildesheim: Gerstenberg, 1931).

Wurmb, Herbert *Ritter* von, *Das K.B. Reserve-Infanterie-Regiment Nr. 8* (Munich: Zeulenroda, 1929).

Wyrall, Everard, *The West Yorkshire Regiment in the War 1914–1918, Vol. 1* (London: John Lane The Bodley Head, 1927).

Wyrall, Everard, *The History of the 19th Division 1914–1918* (London: Edward Arnold, 1932).

Acknowledgments

Writing this book was always going to be a challenge that required considerable time and application. All told, it consumed two years of my life, which capped off several more filled with background research, reading, preparation and visits to battlefields, archives, libraries and museums.

Were it not for my understanding wife, Lara Schönberger, this book would surely not have been completed. She kept me organised, fed and watered throughout, and provided support and encouragement to keep this sometimes-delinquent writer on track. Not once did she complain when I had to disappear off to my study for hours on end or travel to some place in the name of research. I owe her so much more than these few lines can ever express.

Innumerable files and thousands of dusty pages were pored over — I learned to take an antihistamine before visiting National Archives in London. The British Library's stack was invaluable, so, too, the amazing collection of books at Royal Military Academy Sandhurst (RMAS). The University of Leeds' Special Collections department was of great assistance. The South Wales Borderers Museum, Hampshire Records Office, Churchill Archive and the Royal Engineers Museum were professional and obliging.

German material was sourced from a variety of places. *Württemberg Landesbibliothek* in Stuttgart and *Badische Landesbibliothek* in Karlsruhe retain collections invaluable to the military historian. Most of the

German photographs were found in private collections. Rare or obscure German regimental histories were acquired from antique bookshops, or from my friend Patrick Schallert, who has an amazing library. I have but a smattering of schoolboy German and so I retained the essential services of three skilled translators, all of whom were talented in working with old-German handwriting.

Dr Jack Sheldon, author and leading international authority on the German army in the First World War, critiqued the draft manuscript and suggested a number of changes and additions for the better. Dr Matthias Strohn, a senior lecturer at RMAS, offered advice and favourable comment on my German-specific chapters.

This book, perhaps most importantly, was in part written on the Somme battlefields, including in the stifling heat of summer and the brolly-bashing winds of autumn and winter. So it was that I trekked around Gommecourt, Serre, Beaumont Hamel, Thiepval, Ovillers, La Boisselle, Fricourt, Mametz and Montauban, and many places in between. Along the way I met people from all over the world, among them military historians, battlefield guides, the families of several soldiers, and plenty of others.

With me always were a camera and notepad, a flask of hot tea and a ham-and-cheese baguette. Top-notch battlefield guide Pete Smith, who shares my interest in First World War military history, has world-class knowledge of the Somme and the land on which 1 July was fought out. Many times we struck out to walk the old battle lines and piece together events from 1916. Sara Azzopardi must have despaired as her partner Pete and I talked shop, sometimes for hours on end. Sara and Pete's hospitality and friendship made the lot of this sometimes-exhausted Somme traveller much happier and more productive.

My good friend and colleague Dr Christopher Pugsley, not long retired as a senior lecturer at RMAS, offered sound advice throughout amid a busy publishing schedule of his own. He helped me thrash out more than a few tactical conundrums, offered encouragement from the outset, as he had done with both my previous books, and never shied from objectively criticising my work. This book is much the better for this guidance. In fact, I owe much to Chris for supporting my career as a military historian for more than 25 years.

Professor Peter Simkins, Honorary Professor of Western Front Studies at the University of Wolverhampton and President of the Western Front Association, kindly read the manuscript and offered critical comment and advice for which it is very much the better. His scholarship relating to the Somme, Kitchener's Army and, more generally, the British army on the Western Front is essential reading for all military historians, and particularly the emerging generation of which I am part.

Others who appraised the manuscript included first-day-of-the-Somme expert and author Bill MacCormick. Bill and I not only debated the Somme, but also the UK general elections and the quality rugby outfit that is the All Blacks. Fellow author and battlefield guide Martin Pegler cast a discerning and critical eye over my efforts, as did Marty Pelling, a not-long-retired regimental sergeant major of the Royal Marines. Marty and I spent numerous hours walking the ground between Ovillers and Montauban following the course of battle, deconstructing the German defensive positions and machine-gun fields of fire of that day. I would also like to thank a presently serving army officer, who did not wish to be named here, who discussed then-and-now defensive machine-gun tactics and accompanied me to the battlefields several times.

Professor Glyn Harper, Massey University, supported the project from start to finish, and offered constructive criticism on the draft. This, too, applied to Major-General Mungo Melvin, now retired from the British army, whose knowledge of German defensive doctrine and tactics in the First World War proved most useful. A nod of thanks must go also to Dave Stow, an expert on the 10th West Yorkshires at Fricourt, who kindly appraised that part of my manuscript. My good friend and former newsroom colleague Frank Prenesti cast an objective journalist's eye over the manuscript and suggested a number of 'pars' for the proverbial spike and areas of the manuscript that could otherwise be improved upon.

Several people at HarperCollins were integral in bringing this book to publication. Publishing Director Shona Martyn first spied this book's potential and set the wheels in motion for it to happen. The company's New Zealand publisher, Finlay Macdonald (no relation to the author), accompanied me on the two-year writing journey with patience, humour and sound advice. This pastoral care is essential in big, long-running writing projects and I greatly value his contribution. Senior Editor Scott

Forbes was efficient in shepherding this book through the production process, and his patient attention to fine detail is greatly appreciated. Copy editor Emma Dowden is to be commended for working through the manuscript carefully and posing several tough questions on content, all of which resulted in improvements.

Finally, I must thank veterans of 1 July, whether British, German or Newfoundland, for recording their experiences at the time and, often, years later. Without them, and the numerous people who assisted in this essential work over the decades, our understanding of the 1914–18 war would be much the worse.

Andrew Macdonald

Index of Military Units

Artillery

Brigade Machine-gun Companies

Brigade Trench Mortar Batteries

Cavalry

95, 97; in bombardment 121, 128, 130, 134, 138; on 1 July 144, 148, 194, 212, 218, 234, 243, 249, 314; assessed 363, 373, 375–76, 381; casualties 175–76, 205–206, 242

28th Reserve Division xiii, xvii; planning and preparations 75–76, 78, 80, 85, 88, 90–92, 95, 104; in bombardment 134, 137; on 1 July 212, 218, 232–33, 249, 252, 265–67, 279, 286–88, 313, 319; assessed 363, 375–76, 383; casualties 232–33, 244, 280–81, 300, 319

52nd Infantry Division xiii, xvii; planning and preparations 76, 78, 81, 85, 88, 92, 95; in bombardment 134, 137; on 1 July 144, 148, 322, 324, 355–56; assessed 363, 375–76; casualties 342, 354, 356

111th Infantry Division 324, 355

121st Infantry Division 380, 382

185th Infantry Division 76, 381

Infantry and Pioneer Units

Bavarian Infantry Regiment 16 (BIR16) 315, 317, 383

Bavarian Infantry Leib Regiment (BILR) 103

Bavarian Pioneer Regiment (BPR) 265, 281; casualties 281

Bavarian Reserve Infantry Regiment 6 (BRIR6) 87; on 1 July 286–88, 292–93, 298, 300, 319; casualties 292, 300

Bavarian Reserve Infantry Regiment 8 (BRIR8): on 1 July 189, 196, 203–204, 206, 208, 383; casualties 189, 206

Infantry Regiment 23 (IR23) 74, 87, 105; on 1 July 227–28, 232, 253, 262, 267, 277, 280, 286, 313–15; casualties 232, 280–81, 313

Infantry Regiment 62 (IR62) 87, 99, 116, 130; on 1 July 286–87, 292–93, 300, 314–15; casualties 116, 300

Infantry Regiment 66 (IR66) 74, 84, 98; on 1 July 324, 335, 342, 356; casualties 342, 356

Infantry Regiment 169 (IR169) 84; on 1 July 144, 156–57, 161, 172; casualties 157, 175–76

Infantry Regiment 170 (IR170) 333–36, 338–39, 342, 356; casualties 342, 356

Infantry Regiment 180 (IR180) vii, 93–94, 99, 103–106, 113, 115, 119, 121, 129; on 1 July 191, 196, 212, 216–18, 235, 238–40, 242–43; casualties 242

Infantry Regiment 185 (IR185) 204

Landwehr Brigade Replacement Battalion 55 (LDW55) 232, 277; casualties 232

Pioneer Battalion 13 (PB13) 277, 280; casualties 280

Reserve Infantry Regiment 15 (RIR15) 330, 338, 340, 342, 356; casualties 342, 356

Reserve Infantry Regiment 40 (RIR40) 98

Reserve Infantry Regiment 51 (RIR51) 317, 383

Reserve Infantry Regiment 55 (RIR55) 116; on 1 July 334–36, 338, 341–43, 345, 354, 356; casualties 116, 342, 354, 356

Reserve Infantry Regiment 77 (RIR77) 329, 356; casualties 356

Reserve Infantry Regiment 91 (RIR91): on 1 July 329, 343, 345, 347–49, 354, 356; casualties 354, 356

Reserve Infantry Regiment 99 (RIR99) 95, 101, 103, 109, 115–16, 120–21, 130; on 1 July 186, 189, 200, 206–207, 242; casualties 116, 130, 206

Reserve Infantry Regiment 109 (RIR109) 74, 84–85, 87, 95, 100–102, 113, 120, 122; on 1 July 252–54, 261–67, 276–80, 286, 288, 302–303, 306, 310, 313; casualties 280, 313

Reserve Infantry Regiment 110 (RIR110) 83, 94–96, 100, 102, 130; on 1 July 212, 216, 218–20, 223, 226–28, 232, 257; casualties 232

Reserve Infantry Regiment 111 (RIR111) 115, 116, 120, 121; on 1 July 246, 252–53, 256–57, 266–67, 276–81; casualties 116, 280

Reserve Infantry Regiment 119 (RIR119) 79, 86, 89, 94, 99, 100, 105, 113, 115–16, 129; on 1 July 140, 144, 147, 149, 151, 167–68, 188, 200, 208; casualties 116, 151, 175–76

Reserve Infantry Regiment 121 (RIR121) 80, 102, 115–16, 121–22, 129–30; on 1 July 144, 154–55, 167–68, 170, 174, 209, 383; casualties 116, 130, 155, 175–76

Artillery (Field and Foot)

Bavarian Field Artillery Regiment 1 (BFAR1) 93

Bavarian Field Artillery Regiment 19 (BFAR19) 74, 92

Bavarian Foot Artillery Regiment 10 (BFtAR10) 88

Field Artillery Regiment 21 (FAR21) 113, 293, 298

Foot Artillery Battery 550 (FtAB550) 88

26th Reserve Artillery Brigade 376

Reserve Field Artillery Regiment 20 (RFAR20) 90, 92, 105, 112–13, 122, 134, 335

Reserve Field Artillery Regiment 26 (RFAR26) 48, 108, 112, 133, 148, 192

Reserve Field Artillery Regiment 27 (RFAR27) 92, 133

Reserve Field Artillery Regiment 28 (RFAR28) 114, 228

Reserve Field Artillery Regiment 29 (RFAR29) 91, 108, 228, 258, 267

Reserve Foot Artillery Regiment 16 (RFtAR16) 91, 120, 266

Air Service

Artillery Air Detachment 221 (AAD221) 74–75, 90

Artillery Air Detachment 229 (AAD229) 90

Field Flying Detachment 62 (FFD62) 48

Machine-gun Units

Field Machine-gun Platoon 55 (FMGPn55) 104

Machine-gun Sharp-shooter Troop 73 (MGSST73) 334

Machine-gun Sharp-shooter Troop 198 (MGSST198) 163

Cavalry

Württemberg Reserve Dragoon Regiment 104–105

General Index

Bazentin-le-Petit 36, 278, 297, 311, 313
Beaucourt 26, 80, 144–45, 180, 190, 202, 389
Beaucourt Redoubt 144–45, 191
Beaucourt Station 188
Beaumont Hamel xvi–xvii, 20, 42–43, 61–62, 78–
    80, 96; in bombardment 113, 115–116, 127–29;
    on 1 July 140–41, 143–45, 147, 149, 152, 161,
    164–67, 180, 186, 190, 206; assessed 361–62,
    365, 367, 369–71, 389; *see also* Hawthorn Ridge
    mine, crater and redoubt
Beaumont Hamel–Auchonvillers road 141, 149,
    173
Beauquesne 361
Beck, *Leutnant-der-Reserve* Adolf 174
Bécordel-Bécourt 249, 261
Bécourt 63, 91, 223, 260
Bécourt Valley 65
Bécourt Wood 58, 219
Beetle Alley 268, 303
Belgium vii–viii, ix, 4–7, 14–15, 34, 361
Bell, Private Allan 296
Bell VC, Captain Eric 210
Bell, Private Leslie 68
Below, *General-der-Infanterie* Fritz von xi, xiii, xvii;
    planning and preparations 75–81, 87, 100–101,
    106, 180; in bombardment 112, 116–17, 135,
    137; on 1 July and assessed 363, 374–76,
    380–87
Bennett, Sergeant Thomas 43
Bergwerk 143, 145
Berkefeld, *Gefreiter* August 334
Berlin 4, 119
Bernafay Wood 288–89, 293, 297–99, 311, 314–15,
    317–18, 374–75, 383
Bernard, Lieutenant-Colonel Herbert 195
Bethmann-Hollweg, Theobald von 5
Bethune 63
Bicknell, Lieutenant-Colonel Henry 252, 255
Bidder, Lieutenant-Colonel Harold 283, 293
Biefvillers 167, 194
Bielefeld, *Leutnant-der-Reserve* August 91, 120, 266
Binstead, Private Charles 66
Birch Tree Wood 221–22
Birch, Major-General Sir Noel 31
Birmingham 155
Bismarck, Otto von 4
Blacker, Lieutenant-Colonel Stewart 188
Blakey, Sergeant David 196
Blenk, *Musketier* Karl 161
Blighty Valley Cemetery 241
Bloye, Bombardier Ben 47
Bocker, *Vizefeldwebel* Hermann 99
Bois Favière 315, 370
Bois Français 249, 263–65, 273, 277
Bönsel, *Unteroffizier* Walter 99
Booth, Corporal George 240
Borries, *Generalleutnant* Karl von xvii, 78, 80–81,
    85–86, 137; on 1 July 322, 338, 342, 356–57;
    assessed 375–76
Bosnia and Herzegovina 5
Bottom Wood 277, 378
Bowles, Major John 335

Brachat, *Unteroffizier* Gustav 226
Bram, *Oberstleutnant* Alfons Ritter von 204
Branson, Lieutenant Douglas 71
Brasenose College 3
Bray 45, 50, 63, 91
Breslau Support Trench 309
Brew, Gunner James 46
British Expeditionary Force (BEF) 4, 6, 10, 58
Brooke, Rupert 265, 271
Brookes, Private Squire 43, 51–52, 56, 61, 296
Brown, Lance-Corporal Horace 318
Brownlee, Private Edward 190
Brownlow, Captain Cecil 49
Brusilov, General Aleksei 76
Brusilov Offensive 34, 76, 361
Buckingham Palace 3
Bucquoy 330, 337–38
Bulgar Point mine and crater 262, 369
Bull, Captain Wilfred 303
Bundy, Lieutenant Alfred 233, 237
Bunny Alley 273
Burke, Private Pat 272
Burkhardt, *Generalmajor* Hermann Ritter von
    xvii, 78
Burma 15–16,
Burnett, Corporal Clarence 310
Bush, Lance-Corporal William 184
Büsing, *Leutnant-der-Reserve* Georg 90, 92, 134,
    335
Busl, *Offizierstellvertreter* Joseph 287, 293
Buxton, Lieutenant Jocelyn 118

C
Caesar, Julius 20
Calais 63
Cameron, Brigadier-General Archibald 197, 200
Cameron, Private Donald 118
Cameron, Brigadier-General Neville 232
Campbell, Major-General Sir David 251, 260
Capper, Lieutenant Derick 40–41, 57–58, 61, 111,
    118, 304
Carden Roe, Captain William 162
Carlisle 184
Carnoy 62–63, 274, 284, 289, 369
Carnoy Valley 86–87, 247, 249, 261, 262, 265, 289
Carnoy craters 301, 304, 307–308, 319
Carnoy Military Cemetery 54, 308
Carnoy–Montauban road 286, 301, 304, 306, 308
Carrington, Major Charles 332
Cartwright, Brigadier-General George 66
Casino Point mine and crater 305–306, 369
Castle, The 286
Casualties: *see entries within* Index of military
    units
Caterpillar Valley 26, 87, 284, 297–99, 304, 310–11,
    314, 317–18
Caterpillar Valley Wood 288, 297, 299, 310–11,
    315
Cather VC, Lieutenant Geoffrey 210
Cattell, Corporal Douglas 159
Cayley, Brigadier-General Douglas 164
Cemetery Trench 262

Châles de Beaulieu, *Generalleutnant* Martin xvii, 78, 81, 86–87, 92, 138; on 1 July 249, 286–87, 313–14, 316, 319; assessed 375–76, 380, 382–83, 387
Champagne 24, 81
Chantilly Conference 10–13, 361
Charteris, Brigadier-General John xvi, 1, 17, 35, 57, 129, 135–36, 146
Chateau Valvion 361, 376
Chipilly 61
Clifton College 3
Cloudsdale, Private Frank 274
Coates, Orderly Sergeant Harry 337
Codrington, Staff Captain Geoffrey 65
Cole, Sergeant William 239
Collet, *Unteroffizier* Peter 74, 98
Collins, Temporary Lieutenant-Colonel Robert 251
Collis-Browne, Captain John 117–18
Colyer, Lieutenant William 69, 71, 163
Combles 25, 26, 113, 381, 383
Compton, Brigadier-General Charles 184
Congreve VC, Lieutenant-General Sir Walter xvi, 72, 112, 135; on 1 July 284, 286–89, 314, 316–17, 319–20; assessed 366, 372, 374, 378, 380
Conn, Private Albert 265
Connaught Cemetery 186, 195–96
Contalmaison 28–29, 31, 84, 91, 108; on 1 July 211–12 222, 228, 232–33, 278, 297, 371, 373; assessed 378; *see also* Fricourt–Contalmaison road
Contay 63
Conyers, Rifleman Frederick 117
Conzelmann, *Leutnant-der-Reserve* Friedrich 102, 170
Cook, Sergeant Arthur 169
Coom, Private Colin 46, 50, 52, 59
Coppard, Corporal George 57, 71
Corbett, Private William 55, 219, 224
Cornes, Captain Hugh 318
Courcelette 104, 389
Cousins, Lance-Corporal John 43–44, 301–304
Crawley ridge 272
Croft, Brigadier-General Henry 59, 117
Crook, Private Wilfred 71, 160
Crosbie, Brigadier-General James 163
Crozier, Lieutenant-Colonel Frank 60, 67, 72, 138, 191, 195
Crucifix Trench 259–60, 275
Curlu 32, 134, 363–64, 375, 380, 382–83
Currie, Lieutenant-General Sir Arthur 250

D

Damon, Private Alfred 172, 173
Dantzig Alley (North) 262, 268, 272
Dantzig Alley (South) 273
Dantzig Alley British Cemetery 256, 302
Danzig 75
Davies, Major-General Francis 17
Day, Private Walter 164
de Lisle, Major-General Beauvoir 126, 146, 162, 164–65

Delville Wood 297
Demmel, *Leutnant-der-Reserve* Franz 103
Devennie, Private James 193
Deverell, Brigadier-General Cyril 261, 263, 265
Devonshire Cemetery 265
Dickens, Major Cedric 336–37
Dickens, Charles 337
Dickins, Lieutenant-Colonel Vernon 337
Dickinson, Lieutenant Ambrose 225
Dirr, *Unteroffizier* Matthias 100
Dixon, Lieutenant Norman 62
Dobbie, Major William 132
Dompierre 380
Donaghy, Private Jim 193–94
Doullens 63
Downman, Lieutenant Theodore 349–50
Drake-Brockman, Major Guy 274
Dublin Redoubt 284, 288
Dublin Trench 289, 291, 294, 300
Dunedin 391
Dunn, Private Harold 300
Durrant, Corporal Arthur 61, 160
Dyke, Private Edward 225

E

Easton, Private Thomas 58, 227–28
Ebbetts, Corporal Roland 336
Eberle, *Reservist* Christian 93
Edward VII, King 3–4, 339
Egeren, *Gefreiter* Hugo van 342
Egypt 7 141 212 324
Eiser, *Feldwebel* Karl 91, 93, 108, 113, 115, 120, 258, 267, 278
Ellis, Private Bert 160
Elstob VC, Captain Wilfrith 55
Ely, Captain Denis 275
Englebelmer 197–99
England, Private Arthur 46, 51, 54, 60, 62, 117, 119
Estrées 363, 380–82, 385
Euston Road Military Cemetery 171
Evans, Lieutenant Alfred 48
Evans, Lieutenant Samuel 345
Eversmann, *Infanterist* Theodor 121

F

Falfemont Farm 289
Falkenhayn, *General-der-Infanterie* Erich von xi, xvii, 14–15, 75–77, 80, 106–107, 136; on 1 July and assessed 267, 380–81, 383–87, 389
Farrer, Private John 184
Fay 380, 384
Fayolle, General Marie-Emile xviii, 18, 24, 26, 32, 39, 363, 380–81, 384
Fell, Brigadier-General Robert 270
Fellows, Corporal Harry 261
Fenton, Captain George 66
Festubert, Battle of 7
Fickendey, *Vizefeldwebel* Albert 84
Fiedel, *Leutnant* Paul 74, 103, 227
Fife, Lieutenant-Colonel Ronald 256, 270
Fischer, *Reservist* 154
Fischer, *Schütze* Christian 217, 238, 240–42

Russell, Rifleman Henry 332
Russia 4 5 6 7 11 12 14 22 26 34 38 88
Russian army 76, 361
Russian Saps 61, 149–50, 152, 154, 156, 158, 185, 226, 255, 257, 271–72, 288–89, 304
Rycroft, Major-General Sir William 199, 201

S
Sackville-West, Brigadier-General the Hon. Charles 291
St Omer 13, 15
St Pierre Divion 75, 78–79, 178, 189–90
St Pol 63
St Sever Cemetery 229
Salisbury, Salisbury Plain 16, 20
Salonika 22
Sandall, Lieutenant-Colonel Thomas 353
Sanders VC, Corporal George 205, 210
Sandringham 210
Sandys, Lieutenant-Colonel Edwin 242
Sansom, Lieutenant Wilfred 255, 271
Sarajevo 5
Sassoon, Second-Lieutenant Siegfried 272
Sausage Redoubt 212, 221–23
Sausage Valley 83, 211–12, 215, 219–24, 231, 233
Savile, Major Henry 237
Saxon, Saxons 48, 78
Scheytt, *Unteroffizier* Paul 100, 310–311
Schlieffen Plan 6
Schmid, *Unteroffizier* 93
Schoch, *General-der-Infanterie* Albert *Ritter* von 87
Schreiber, Brigadier-General Acton 63–64
Schuler, *Vizefeldwebel* Karl 102
Schultheiss, *Unteroffizier* Gustav 334
Schultz, *Unteroffizier* 98
Schumacher, *Feldwebel* 129
Schuman, Corporal Arthur 332, 334, 340
Schüsle, *Unteroffizier* Otto 277
Schwaben Redoubt xvii, 72, 79; on 1 July 161, 167, 171, 178, 180–81, 189–92, 194–204, 206–210; assessed 361, 365, 368, 370, 373–74, 381–83, 386; *see also* Thiepval *and* Thiepval Plateau
Schwabenhöhe 212, 215–16, 219, 226, 361, 383; *see also* Lochnagar mine and crater, and La Boisselle
Schwalbenneste (The Z and Little Z Redoubts) 322, 344, 347–48, 353
Schwartz, *Stabsarzt* Dr Richard 80
Scotland 391
Scots Redoubt 212, 221–22, 226, 231, 233
Scott, Private Frank 221
Seeger, *Leutnant-der-Reserve* Richard 209
Senescall, Private William 51, 69, 114, 219, 224–25
Serbia 5, 11
Serre xvi–xvii, 20, 23, 25, 29, 31, 42, 70, 78, 81, 84, 86, 88, 93, 96, 98, 106; in bombardment 127–29, 134, 138; on 1 July 140, 143–45, 147–48, 153, 156–58, 161, 166–67, 171–73, 203, 286, 324, 326, 342, 352, 355–56; assessed 361–65, 367, 370–71, 373, 376, 386, 389; *see also* Serre–Grandcourt Spur
Serre, Battle of 81

Serre–Grandcourt Spur 26, 28, 31, 80, 144–45, 165, 370
Serre Heights: *see* Serre–Grandcourt Spur
Serre Road Cemetery No. 2 153, 155, 176
Shakespear, Lieutenant-Colonel John 216, 244
Shannon, Lieutenant James 194
Shaugnessy, Private Lew 224
Shea, Major-General Sir John 289, 299–300, 316
Sheffield Memorial Park 171, 367
Shelter Trench 260
Shelter Wood 275
Shipley, Brigadier-General Charles 350–52
Short, Corporal Robert 192
Shrine, The 262–65, 273
Shuter, Brigadier-General Reginald 200
Silesia 253
Singleton, Private Joseph 347
Slater, Private William 56, 173
Smith, Rifleman Aubrey 112, 119, 329
Smith, Sergeant Henry 335
Smith, Private James 289
Smith, Private Peter 151
Smith, Private Sidney 348
Smith, Private Stephen 272
Smith, Signaller William 333
Snow, Lieutenant-General Sir Thomas xvii, 135; on 1 July 324–30, 341–42, 351–54, 356–57; assessed 365–66
Soden Redoubt 143, 145
Soden, *Generalleutnant* Franz *Freiherr* von xvii, 78, 80–81, 83, 86, 88, 93, 95, 101, 107, 121, 128, 138; on 1 July 143–45, 166–67, 171, 194–96, 199, 202–204, 206, 218, 243–44; assessed 363, 373–75
Solihull 176
Somerset, Lieutenant-Colonel Charles 219, 223, 244
Somme River viii, xvii–xviii, 13–14, 20, 22, 24–26, 32, 41–42, 48, 62, 75–78, 86, 90, 95, 97, 106, 112, 137, 180, 314–15, 356, 363, 376, 380–84, 386, 389
Sotham, Captain Ernest 295, 317
South African soldiers 391
South African War 3, 15–16, 141, 214, 250, 260–61, 284, 324
Southam, Lieutenant-Colonel Lionel 327, 342
Sparks, Captain Hubert 339
Spears, Captain Edward 318
Spencer-Smith, Major Richard 164
Spicer, Lieutenant Lancelot 276
Spur Point *see* Triangle Point
Stadelbacher, *Unteroffizier* Rudolf 277
Staff College, Camberley 1, 3, 16, 214, 324
Staff College, Prussian 322
Stanley, Brigadier-General the Hon. Ferdinand 291
Stansby, Lieutenant John 346
Starrett, Rifleman Davie 193–94
Steavenson, Brigadier-General the Hon. Charles 295
Steele, Brigadier-General Julian 271
Steele, Private Sydney 294
Stegmaier, *Ersatz-Reservist* August 106–106

Stein, *Generalleutnant* Hermann von xi, xvii;
  planning and preparations 75–89, 91–94,
  97–98, 100–101, 103, 106, 167, 180, 286–87,
  319; in bombardment 130–31, 133, 137–38; on
  1 July and assessed 196, 206, 315–17, 363–64,
  373–76, 381–84, 387
Stephenson, Private Edward 186
Stephenson, Rifleman Ernest 186
Stephenson, Private Harold 186
Steward, Lieutenant-Colonel Godfrey 216
Stewart, Private Hugh 192–93, 204
Stewart-Moore, Second-Lieutenant John 182
Stöckle, *Unteroffizier* Waldemar 281–82
Stornoway 391
Streets, Sergeant John 171–72
Strüvy, *Leutnant* 228
Stubbs, Private Cyril 253, 255
Stubley, Private Frank
Stuff Redoubt 180, 191–92, 199
Stuttgart 90 196 208
Stutz, *Leutnant-der-Reserve* Friedrich 122, 154
Sudan 3, 7, 15–16, 324 *see also* Omdurman
Sunken Lane (Beaumont Hamel) 149
Süsskind-Schwendi, *Generalleutnant* Richard
  Freiherr von xvii, 78, 81, 86, 137; on 1 July 322,
  329, 338, 342, 344, 355–57; assessed 375–76
Sutterby, Sergeant Robert 123
Suzanne 63
Swabia, Swabians 218, 253
Switzerland, Swiss vii, 6, 239, 253
Symes, Private Maurice 261

T

Talus Bois 290
Tauscher, *Major* Paul 338
Tawney, Sergeant Richard 264
Tennant, Rifleman Cecil 45, 68
Ternan, Brigadier-General Trevor 230
Tambour, The 62, 251, 256, 258, 271, 369; see
  separately German Tambour, The
Theurlein, *Reservist* Michael 292
Thiepval xvii, 20, 25, 78–80, 95, 101, 105, 107; in
  bombardment 115–17, 119, 127, 129; on 1
  July 144, 161, 171, 177–83, 185–87, 190–91,
  194–95, 197, 199–201, 206–210, 212, 240, 243,
  315, 361–62; assessed 365, 367, 370–71, 373–74
Thiepval Memorial 155, 184, 186, 192, 210, 229,
  272, 275, 281, 307, 337, 341, 345, 349, 391
Thiepval Plateau 79–80, 144, 178, 180, 188–89,
  191–92, 195, 208
Thiepval Spur 20, 42, 178, 181–82, 185, 207, 212,
  242
Thiepval Wood 190, 195, 197–98, 202–203, 205,
  210
Thiepval–Hamel road 195
Thiepval–Morval ridge 20, 25, 246–47, 284, 389
Thomas, *Unteroffizier* Friedrich 278, 302
Thuringians 78
Tivey, Corporal Reg 344
Tomlinson, Private Auberon 348
Tomlinson, Private Sam 256
Train Alley 292, 294, 307

Traumüller, *Unteroffizier* Willi 88
Treaty of London 4–5
Trenchard, Temporary Major-General Hugh 118
Triangle Point 299
Triangle Strongpoint 302
Trônes Wood 289, 293, 297, 315
Trost, *Reservist* Gottlob 238
Tullock, Second-Lieutenant William 301, 305
Tunnicliffe, Private Thomas 345
Turnbull VC, Sergeant James 209
Turnbull, Lieutenant John 225, 229
Turner, Lance-Corporal Archibald 219
Tuson, Brigadier-General Harry 241

U

Ukraine 38, 76, 361
Ulyatt, Private Herbert 348
Upcott, Captain John 40, 44, 52, 70

V

Verdun, Battle of viii, xviii, 12, 14–15, 22, 24,
  29, 31–34, 37–39, 76, 81, 106, 137, 207, 361,
  380–81, 384–85, 387
Victoria, Queen 4–5
Victoria Cross xvi, 55, 72, 112, 169, 205, 209–211,
  260–61, 284, 311, 348, 366
Villers-Bocage 362, 376–78
Vimy Ridge 29
Vischer, *Oberstleutnant* Alfred 113, 121, 235–36,
  240
Vivian, the Honourable Dorothy Maud 3
Vogler, *Oberleutnant-der-Reserve* Heinrich 119,
  216, 236
Vulpius, *Leutnant-der-Reserve* Roland 100, 103

W

Wagener, *Hauptmann* Otto 83
Waghorn, Private Roger 310
Wallis, Captain Ferdinand 357
Walsh, Second-Lieutenant Arthur 274
Walz, *Gefreiter* Karl 239
Wanless-O'Gowan, Major-General Robert 166
War Committee 11–12, 15, 38
War Office 3
Ward, Private Arthur 117, 353
Ware, Captain Innes 124, 132
Warlencourt 242
Warlincourt Halte British Cemetery 348
Warloy-Baillon Communal Cemetery Extension
  184
Warren, The 286, 307
Watkin, Private Matthew 260
Watkins, Sergeant 297
Watson, Major Frank 197–98
Watts, Major-General Herbert 268
Weickel, *Vizefeldwebel* 113, 121
Westmann, *Leutnant* Stefan 115, 120
Westphalia, Westphalians 78, 208
Weymann, *Leutnant-der-Landwehr* Karl 96
Wicks, Private Charles 263, 274
Wide, Private Howard 117, 264
Wild, CQMS Gawen 228

Wilding, Brigadier-General Charles 162
Wilhelm II, Kaiser II 4–6
Wilkinson, Private George 255
Williams, Rifleman Frederick 62
Williams, Rifleman Herbert 117, 339
Williams, Brigadier-General Hugh 350–52
Williams, Brigadier-General Weir 149
Willis, Major Arthur 259
Willmer, Lieutenant Edgar 51, 291, 294
Willow Stream and Valley 247, 249, 251, 253,
    268–69, 271, 273, 378
Wimereux Communal Cemetery 47
Wirth, *Reservist* 94
Withycombe, Brigadier-General William 200
Wohlenberg, *Oberleutnant* Alfred 329
Wonderwork 178, 180, 182, 187
Wood Alley 222
Woods, Private Francis 294
Woodward, Private Harry 155

Worthington, Captain Hubert 296, 299
Wurmb, *Hauptmann* Herbert *Ritter* von 204
Württemberg, Württembergers 78, 97, 119,
    144–45, 217, 242, 253, 286, 322

Y
Y Ravine 143, 145, 164
Y Ravine Cemetery 174
Yatman, Brigadier-General Clement 186
Ypres 14
Ypres, First Battle of 10
Ypres, Second Battle of 324
Ypres, Third Battle of ix, 15
Y-Sap mine and crater 211, 215, 230, 369

Z
Z and Little Z Redoubts, *see* Schwalbenneste
Zwisele, Rifleman Charles 391